THE IMPACT OF THE MODERN CORPORATION

The Columbia University Center for Law and Economic Studies

Columbia Studies in Business, Government, and Society
Eli Noam, General Editor

THE IMPACT OF THE
MODERN CORPORATION

Edited by
Betty Bock
Harvey J. Goldschmid
Ira M. Millstein
F. M. Scherer

Columbia University Press
New York   1984

Library of Congress Cataloging in Publication Data
Main entry under title:

The Impact of the modern corporation.

   Proceedings of a conference held Nov. 12–13, 1982,
in Princeton, N.J.
   Includes bibliographical references and index.
   1. Corporations—United States—Congresses.   2. In-
dustrial concentration—United States—Congresses.
I. Bock, Betty, 1915–
HD2783.I45   1984   338.7'4'0973   84-1915
ISBN 0-231-05930-2 (alk. paper)
ISBN 0-231-05931-0 (pbk. : alk. paper)

Columbia University Press
New York   Guildford, Surrey

Designed by Ken Venezio

Contents

Preface

WHETHER large corporations have a beneficial, pernicious, or neutral social and political impact has long been hotly contested. Since almost the beginning of the industrial revolution, fears about, and praises of, corporate size have uneasily coexisted. Without question, large corporations play a critical role in our economic, social, and political lives. They produce and deliver most of the goods we depend upon, and they are highly visible participants in our social and political processes. Economic growth, community welfare, worker satisfaction, environmental protection, consumer safety, and numerous other measures of our economic and social well-being are, in the view of many, closely intertwined with the performance of large corporations. Moreover, while large corporations have been widely recognized as the primary engines of our industrial economy, concerns about the concentration of economic, political, and social power in these entities have frequently been voiced. It is little wonder, then, that the "corporate size issue" has engendered so much disparate and passionate debate.

For a long time, the public debate over corporate size was primarily focused on economic questions. The policy dialogue centered upon competing perceptions of the impact of corporate size and concentration on prices, profits, inflation, and employment. This "economic impact issue" was the subject of a two-day conference organized by the Faculty of Law of Columbia University in 1973, which resulted in the publication of *Industrial Concentration: The New Learning*, which was the first major project of Columbia's Center for Law and Economic Studies.[1]

1. H. Goldschmid, H. Mann, and J. Weston, *Industrial Concentration: The New Learning* (Boston: Little, Brown, 1974).

The economic debate over corporate size and concentration continues, but in the mid-1970s the public policy dialogue moved toward a new terrain: concern over social and political impact. Calls for regulation and deregulation, increased controls on corporate governance, increased corporate "voluntarism," and even proposals for outright limits on corporate size have come and gone as policy makers have wrestled with the question of whether large corporations have too much or too little discretionary authority.

Although debaters on corporate size issues have argued fervently in support of their respective positions, in reality there is little hard evidence as to the social and political impact of corporate size one way or the other. Rather, in general, there has been almost a complete vacuum of serious research in this area. Both proponents and opponents have, of course, had their favorite anecdotes about "good" and "bad" corporations, but anecdotes are not an adequate substitute for objective study.

In 1978, the Steering Committee for Columbia's Center for Law and Economic Studies began to discuss the need for a broad-based research project to examine this new dimension of the corporate size issue: namely, is size an important variable in the social and political impact of the modern corporation and, if so, in what way? The process of designing the "impact project," as it came to be called, was a difficult one. Dedicated scholars and researchers from around the country struggled to formulate an appropriate methodology for studying the corporate size issue. Some were convinced that the issue simply could not be studied in a systematic way and that the debate would never get beyond the level of ideology and opinion. Others formulated comprehensive research proposals, only to conclude that the data required to examine the issue did not exist. The editors of this volume ultimately settled upon what we believed were a group of highly ambitious but credible research proposals carefully designed to shed new light on five specific aspects of the corporate size issue: worker alienation, corporate philanthropy, community impact, technological change, and political impact. In each case, leading authorities in the field were selected to do the research.

The results of this research were presented at a two-day conference at the Henry Chauncey Center in Princeton, New Jersey, on November 12 and 13, 1982. At that conference, approximately one hundred social scientists, lawyers, law professors, businessmen, economists, judges, and government policy makers took part in a vigorous dialogue on the re-search that had been conducted and the public policy issues that it raised.[2] In addition, each of the research papers presented was subject to critical review by a panel of distinguished commentators from academia, business, government, and the law.

The proceedings of the conference, including the research papers, commentary, and parts of the debate, are contained in this volume.[3] We think that it makes a valuable contribution to the continuing policy dialogue on the corporate size issue and that it demonstrates that meaning-ful research can be done in this area. Although the conference did not produce any "final answers" on the corporate size question, we hope that this volume constitutes a significant beginning in the process of studying a critical policy issue that, up until now, has too often been the subject of only emotional debate.

Betty Bock
Harvey J. Goldschmid
Ira M. Millstein
F. M. Scherer

2. A list of the researchers, commentators, chairmen, and other participants in the con-ference, along with brief biographical sketches, is contained in appendix 1.

3. In order to maximize readability and comply with limitations of space, the editors have selected, and in some cases condensed and edited (without any ellipses), excerpts from the transcript of the proceedings. In no case, however, has the substance of any person's remarks been altered.

Acknowledgments

T HE project on the impact of the modern corporation was made possible by the contributions of a group of twenty-seven corporations (see appendix 3) brought together by Robert S. Hatfield, the chief executive officer of the Continental Group. Mr. Hatfield and his successor at Continental, S. Bruce Smart, played an integral role in helping this project become a reality, not only through financial support but by helping the researchers gain access to information that, without such sponsorship, might otherwise have been more difficult, if not impossible, to obtain. All of the corporate sponsors committed their funds and help on a "no-strings" basis, asking only that the highest quality research be conducted in return. They deserve the thanks of us all.

We also wish to thank our colleague on the project's steering committee, Professor Lucia F. Dunn. Putting in double duty as both a researcher and steering committee member, she made an invaluable contribution to the project in both respects.

We are also grateful to André Giraud, the former minister of industry of the Republic of France, and C. Boyden Gray, counsel to the vice-president of the United States, who served, respectively, as the dinner and luncheon speakers at the Princeton Conference. Their insightful commentary helped inform the entire proceedings.

Additionally, we would especially like to thank the law firm of Weil, Gotshal, & Manges and, in particular, two of its associates, Jeffrey L. Kessler and Michael A. Epstein. Messrs. Kessler and Epstein served as the extraordinarily hard-working arms of the steering committee from the project's inception and contributed in every way imaginable to making the project a success. We also acknowledge the able assistance that

Messrs. Kessler and Epstein received in this regard from Matthew Heller.

Finally, we gratefully acknowledge the yeoman contribution of Ms. Simone Couture, the assistant director of the Center for Law and Economic Studies, who spent countless hours making certain that every annoying administrative detail was taken care of and who responded, with great skill and grace, each time we called for help.

THE IMPACT OF THE MODERN CORPORATION

PART I

LABOR IMPACT

EDITORS' NOTE

CONCERN over worker alienation is at least as old as capitalism itself. Recently, however, the discussion has become more pointed, even if not better founded in objective evidence. Numerous scholars have used survey instruments to measure various dimensions of worker satisfaction or dissatisfaction with their jobs. The resulting data have been related to measures of organizational size, among other things, and significant correlations have emerged—sometimes implying that job dissatisfaction or certain components increase with size, sometimes implying the contrary. What these studies mean has been far from clear, in part because of both differences and ambiguities in size and satisfaction measures.

To advance the state of knowledge on this important set of questions, it was clear that new and better controlled research was needed. Professors Lucia Dunn and Jon Shepard were commissioned to undertake an unusually careful field study explicitly designed to control for many relevant variables and illuminate more clearly the links between firm size and worker satisfaction. The two essays that follow summarize the results of their pioneering research.

3

CHAPTER 1

The Effects of Firm Size on Wages, Fringe Benefits, and Work Disutility

Lucia F. Dunn

THIS paper addresses the issue of the overall well-being of employees in firms of differing sizes. It is based upon a survey of 1,036 employees taken specifically for the Impact of the Corporation project, and it examines a broad range of monetary and nonmonetary employment aspects. The central purpose of this research is to determine whether there is a systematic variation in employee well-being with firm size and, if so, what factors account for the variation. The present paper examines the individual wage, fringe benefit, and working conditions components of employee well-being by firm size, as well as a measure of overall job disutility. A separate paper by Jon M. Shepard will investigate further aspects of job satisfaction for the same sample of employees.

The size measure we shall be using throughout this study is number of employees. Our various analyses have also been carried out using annual sales and number of plants as alternative size measures. All three measures are highly correlated in our sample, and our results are qualitatively the same, regardless of which measure is used.[1] Therefore, only those results using number of employees as the measure of size will be reported. Number of employees is probably the most relevant firm size measure for a study of employees. In addition, it provides a meaningful and comparable measure of other size variables, such as plant size, which we shall also include in our analysis.

Section 1 contains pertinent details of the survey. The following four sections present four different size-related analyses of the survey data. Section 2 examines differences in wage rates by firm size for different job classifications. In section 3 we look at firm size differences in fringe benefits such as insurance and paid time off. The monetary equivalents of these benefits will be examined in relation to size for each job classification. The total compensation package (i.e., wages plus fringe benefits) will then be examined by job classification for size effects. Section 4 investigates working conditions. This will include (1) an examination of employees' own assessments of needed improvements and (2) an examination of desired and actual number of hours worked per week. Finally, in section 5, a measure of overall job disutility will be analyzed for the sample and weighed against monetary compensation in the different-sized firms in order to investigate size-related variations in total job satisfaction.

The questionnaire which was administered to the sample is presented in appendix 1A.

1. THE SURVEY

Control Features

Although previous research has examined the link betwen establishment size (often plant size) and employee well-being, none to our knowledge has attempted to control for extraneous job influences (the so-called intervening variables) as thoroughly as the current study. Much of the previous work is based upon aggregate samples of randomly selected individuals. Thus, in looking at well-being variables by establishment size, employees from many diverse skill levels and from occupations with widely differing physical circumstances may be grouped together and compared. For example, boiler room workers in large companies may be compared with workers in light industrial jobs, such as assembly line inspection, in small firms. To overcome this problem, instead of taking the broad approach and sampling widely from many different types of firms, we chose to narrow our focus to a single industry, sampling ten technologically similar plants belonging to firms of varying sizes. This control feature was carried a step further by a careful matching of employees—job by job—in the large and small firms.

Finally, the plants surveyed were confined to the same geographical regions and drew their labor forces from the same working populations. Thus, we have also attempted to eliminate differences that might arise between large and small firms due to differences in work orientation and attitude in different localities.

Other Features

The Industry. The plastics industry was selected as the industry for study. The plants included in the study were engaged in manufacturing molded and pressed products, primarily containers.[2] We feel that the plastics industry is an appropriate choice for this study because very few production economies of scale exist in the industry, and this helps to control for plant size effects—firm rather than plant size being the focus of the study. All plants in our sample used similar equipment and technological processes. In addition, the jobs of all employees in the sample were examined first-hand at the plant sites to insure comparability between large and small firms. Finally, all firms in the study were comparable in several other important aspects: all were unionized by major national unions; none had experienced layoffs in the period prior to the survey; and all produced for the national market.

Range of Sizes. At the large end of the size spectrum, our sample includes firms in *Fortune's* top 500 list and in *Fortune's* second 500 list. The largest firm had approximately 60,000 employees, over 200 separate plants, and annual sales of several billion dollars. From here the firms ranged down in size to a single-plant organization with 50 employees and annual sales of several million dollars.

In selecting the sample, an effort was made to restrict variation in plant size as much as possible while allowing for the desired range of firm sizes. Plants in the selected sample are all in the low-medium to medium-size range, having from 50 to 485 employees. As a further control for plant size variation, we have included a plant size variable in the analysis that follows.[3]

Job Classifications. The division of the sample into matching job classifications at the different-sized firms is an important aspect of this study and was carried out with considerable care. In many cases the designation of job classifications across firms was straightforward because the jobs were identical in the different firms. In other cases, however, there were firm-specific variations within the job classifications. Thus, for example, a "packer" at one firm may perform slightly different tasks than an employee with the same "packer" job designation at another firm. In order to avoid an excessive number of job classification variables, therefore, some aggregation of classifications was necessary.

Decisions with regard to this aggregation were based on first-hand observation of all production facilities by the researchers and detailed consultation with plant managers and personnel directors at the different firms. The primary consideration in grouping jobs across firms was the physical similarity of the task performed. This, of course, is intrinsically connected with skill level, and thus skill was another important criterion in the job classification decision. The similarity of the physical environment of the jobs was also taken into account, as well as how one particular job fit in with others in a plant.[4]

Finally, since the same job will often go by different names in different firms, for simplicity we have designated the job classifications by broadly descriptive names. We will consider nine such classifications, arrived at through the considerations outlined above: (1) janitorial; (2) inspector-packer; (3) material handler; (4) shipping-receiving; (5) auxiliary production servicer; (6) unskilled operative; (7) quality control; (8) semi-skilled operative; (9) skilled maintenance. This list is arranged roughly in ascending order according to skill level. However, since there is significant skill level overlap in the lower jobs classifications, the reader is cautioned not to identify this ordering strictly with skill levels. Classifications 1–7 are all primarily unskilled, although there is some variation in task complexity within the classifications.

Location. Two geographical regions were chosen for the study, with both large and small firms being drawn from each. One region was metropolitan and one was nonmetropolitan. The metropolitan case was chosen from an industrialized area in a Northeastern state. The nonmetropolitan area was in a Midwestern state. Both regions contain numerous plastics manufacturing concerns.

Survey Administration. The survey was administered personally by the researchers at the factory sites. Participation by the employees was voluntary and anonymous in that no identifying information was solicited. The survey was administered over a period of twenty months, beginning in December 1980 and running to August 1982. In order to adjust for differences in wage rates, earnings, and other monetary variables that may have arisen during that time due to inflation and union contract-scheduled increases, all such quantities used in our comparisons will be based on company data from the same point in time. This reference date is June 30, 1980. Survey responses involving monetary evaluations and wages in current values were adjusted using the consumer price index applicable to the survey date.

2. WAGE DIFFERENCES

Wage rate differentials will be examined separately for each of our nine job classifications. Our data here are for wages in the various jobs, as determined in each company's union contract. The majority of the firms used a wage progression system whereby wages increased from their entry levels at intervals ranging from thirty days to one year. We shall therefore examine both the entry-level and top-level wage for each job classification.

Throughout this paper the firm and plant size variables are defined as

$$LOGFIRM\text{-}SIZE = \log_{10} [(\text{no. of employees in the firm})/50]$$

and

$$LOGPLANT\text{-}SIZE = \log_{10} [(\text{no. of employees in the plant})/50],$$

so that the constant term in regression equations corresponds to a plant with fifty employees and a firm with fifty employees (which are the smallest sizes in the sample). The coefficient of LOGFIRM-SIZE gives the increase in wage corresponding to a tenfold increase in firm size, and similarly for the coefficient of LOGPLANT-SIZE.[5] After removing variables that were not significant at least at the 10 percent level, the equation that was fit for each job classification is

$$WAGE_i = a_0 + a_1 LOGFIRM\text{-}SIZE + a_2 \ LOCATION, \tag{1}$$

where WAGE$_i$ is the straight-time hourly wage rate for each job classification and LOCATION is a dummy variable taking the value 1 for the metropolitan region. (Plant size proved to be statistically insignificant in all job classifications.)

We have also investigated differences in shift premiums by firm size. (Every firm in our sample paid fixed hourly premiums to second and third shift employees, with the third shift premium being higher than the second shift premium.) The equation we have fit for shift premiums is

$$\text{SHIFT PREMIUM}_i = a_0 + a_1 \text{LOGFIRM-SIZE} + a_2 \text{ LOCATION}, \tag{2}$$

where the SHIFT PREMIUM$_i$ is the second or third hourly wage premium. Here also, plant size has been omitted, since it was found to be statistically insignificant in all cases.

Table 1.1 contains the results of the fits of equation 1 for entry-level

TABLE 1.1
Firm Size and Entry-Level Wage Rates

Job Classification	LOGFIRM-SIZE Coefficient	LOCATION[a] Coefficient	Constant Term	Mean Entry Wage Rate for Classification
Janitorial	$ .61*	$ − 1.21	$4.92	$5.41
	(.30)	(.71)	(.59)	
Inspector-packer	.72*	− 1.42*	4.63	5.08
	(.31)	(.70)	(.63)	
Material handler	1.19**	− 3.00**	5.62	5.13
	(.10)	(.18)	(.14)	
Shipping-receiving	.58*	− 1.34*	5.31	5.59
	(.26)	(.59)	(.53)	
Auxiliary production servicer	1.08**	− 1.82**	4.66	5.09
	(.30)	(.62)	(.53)	
Unskilled operative	.83**	− 1.67*	4.87	5.22
	(.33)	(.78)	(.64)	
Quality control	.79**	− .87	4.27	5.20
	(.22)	(.51)	(.57)	
Semi-skilled operative	.41	− .85	5.87	6.12
	(.30)	(.72)	(.55)	
Skilled maintenance	.73	− 1.86*	6.92	7.34
	(.39)	(.89)	(.75)	

NOTE: Standard errors are presented in parentheses.
[a] LOCATION is a dummy variable taking the value 1 for metropolitan.
*$p \leq .10$.
**$p \leq .05$.

TABLE 1.2
Firm Size and Top-Level Wage Rates

Job Classification	LOGFIRM-SIZE Coefficient	LOCATION[a] Coefficient	Constant Term	Mean Top Wage Rate for Classification
Janitorial	$ .52	$ − 1.22	$5.25	$5.58
	(.29)	(.69)	(.58)	
Inspector-packer	.61*	− 1.42*	5.03	5.30
	(.29)	(.66)	(.59)	
Material handler	1.07**	− 2.73**	5.88	5.43
	(.20)	(.40)	(.30)	
Shipping-receiving	.53*	− 1.05	5.49	5.82
	(.27)	(.62)	(.56)	
Auxiliary production servicer	.96**	− 1.70**	5.02	5.35
	(.24)	(.49)	(.43)	
Unskilled operative	.78*	− 1.70*	5.16	5.42
	(.33)	(.78)	(.65)	
Quality control	.75**	− .66	4.39	5.39
	(.20)	(.47)	(.53)	
Semi-skilled operative	.16	− .05	6.67	6.91
	(.21)	(.51)	(.39)	
Skilled maintenance	.37	− .62	7.49	7.85
	(.30)	(.70)	(.59)	

NOTE: Standard errors are presented in parentheses.
[a]LOCATION is a dummy variable taking the value 1 for metropolitan.
*$p \leq .10$.
**$p. \leq .05$.

wages, and Table 1.2 contains results for top-level wages. The pattern emerging from these tables shows that larger firms in general pay significantly higher wages in the lower-skill job classifications both at the entry and the top wage levels. The exceptions to this general trend were found in both the entry and top wage levels of the two highest-skill jobs, semi-skilled operative and skilled maintenance, and in the top-level wages for janitorial jobs. No significant firm size differentials were found for these jobs. These were the jobs for which firms experienced the greatest difficulty in attracting and holding competent employees. For the two high-skilled jobs, this was simply due to the relative scarcity of those skills. For janitorial positions, it was probably due to stereotyped views of the job, which demean its status and lower its attractiveness. (Efforts to maintain adequate janitorial staff had resulted in its becoming one of the highest-paid of the unskilled jobs for the firms in our sample.) The lack of firm size effects for these labor-scarce jobs may be the result of union policies, which concentrate more effort on raising the wages of lower-paid workers. This would be consistent with the existing body of evidence, which suggests that unions on average have been more effective in raising the wages of low-skill rather than high-skill workers.[6] On the assumption that the larger firms are more profitable, these results can be interpreted as implying that unions have syphoned off some of the profits of the larger firms for the lower-paid employees and, out of equity considerations, have made less of an effort for the higher-paid employees.[7]

That there are surplus returns in the larger firms is evident from the fact that these companies have been able to survive despite higher wages, which should otherwise have put them at a competitive disadvantage. One might not expect a noticeable surplus to occur in an industry with few production economies of scale. However, the plants belonging to the large firms in our sample could enjoy scale advantages in the areas of credit, marketing, and so on, if not in the production sector. Also, it should be pointed out that the large firms in our sample were conglomerates, each producing in several other industries as well as plastics. Therefore, the surplus returns from which the large firms were paying higher wages need not have come wholly or even in part from the plastics industry.[8]

We see from table 1.3 that second shift premiums contain a significant difference in favor of larger firms, but there is not a significant difference in third shift premiums. The third shift began at either 11:00 P.M. or 12:00 midnight in our sample firms. The difficulty of attracting employees for these hours is well known. As a result, market conditions appear to have driven the third shift differential above its traditional level relative to other shifts. Union bargaining policies may be linked to traditional shift differentials, and this may have lessened the union effort to raise the third shift premiums in large firms. (A similar argument might be advanced in regard to the union wage policy for janitors.)

Overall, our wage results are broadly consistent with previous findings of a positive relationship between wage rates and firm size. A similar relationship, but involving industry concentration data rather than individual firm size data, has been found by Haworth and Reuther, Pugel, and Weiss.[9] A firm size study by Mellow has found wage differences of the same order of magnitude as those in tables 1.1 and 1.2, although his

TABLE 1.3
Firm Size and Hourly Shift Premiums

Shift	LOGFIRM-SIZE Coefficient	LOCATION[a] Coefficient	Constant Term	Mean Shift Premium
Second shift premium	$ .02*	$ − .02	$ .12	$.14
	(.01)	(.02)	(.02)	
Third shift premium	.01	.02	.19	.21
	(.01)	(.02)	(.02)	

NOTE: Standard errors are presented in parenthesis.
[a]LOCATION is a dummy variable taking the value 1 for metropolitan.
*p.≤.10.

work uses discrete firm size categories, with the largest category grouping together all firms with a thousand employees or more.[10] The greater degree of disaggregation and control of nonsize characteristics in our research design allows us to examine the relationship between firm size and wages in more detail than have previous studies. In particular, we feel that the control for specific type of job is significant, since this has allowed us to identify significant exceptions to the general wage-size trend.

Our findings differ from the results of previous research, which has shown a positive relationship between plant (or individual establishment) size and wages.[11] This may be due to the fact that we have deliberately chosen to study an industry that enjoys few plant-level economies of scale. Therefore, one would expect plant size effects to be minimal. A second possibility is that in some of the previous studies the use of a plant size variable by itself may have proxied for firm size, since in general firm size and plant size are positively correlated within an industry.[12]

3. DIFFERENCES IN FRINGE BENEFITS AND TOTAL COMPENSATION

In this section we examine the monetary value of seven fringe benefits in the different-sized firms. We shall consider the weekly fringe benefits values for a typical worker in the sample for each of the nine job classifications.[13] Three different types of results will be presented here by job classification. First, we examine each fringe benefit separately in each job classification for size effects. Next, we examine the sum of the values of fringe benefits within each job classification. Finally, we examine differences in total compensation by firm size by adding wages per period to the total fringe benefit values for the same time period within each job classification. The equations we shall fit for each job in all three instances have the form

$$\text{BENEFIT VALUE} = a_1 + a_2 \text{ LOGFIRM-SIZE} + a_3 \text{ LOGPLANT-SIZE} + a_4 \text{ LOCATION} \tag{3}$$

The benefits under consideration and their method of evaluation are as follows:[14]

(1) *Paid Holidays.* Evaluated as the annual amount of holiday pay, converted to weekly terms.[15]
(2) *Paid Lunch Break.* Evaluated at the straight-time hourly wage.
(3) *Paid Rest Breaks.* Evaluated at the straight-time hourly wage.
(4) *Paid Vacation.* Evaluated as the annual amount of vacation pay, converted to weekly terms.
(5) *Health Insurance.* Evaluated as the weekly premium that a person of the age, sex, and location of the employee in question would have to pay in order to obtain on an individual basis the coverage provided by his or her firm.[16]
(6) *Life Insurance.* Evaluated as the weekly premium that a person of the age, sex, and location of the employee in question would have to pay in order to obtain on an individual basis the coverage provided by his or her firm.
(7) *Retirement Pension.* This was evaluated on the assumption that future union contracts would continue to maintain the real value of the pension payments that are stipulated in the current union contract. The valuation is then the weekly payment required to provide the stipulated pension in real terms upon retirement, assuming that the real rate of interest in the intervening years is zero. (No account was taken of the fact that the union contract pension plans, interpreted in this way, may be underfunded.)

Results of this investigation are presented in tables 1.4 through 1.12. The overwhelming trend revealed in these tables is for fringe benefit levels to increase with increasing firm size. Wherever a significant firm size effect is found among the fringe benefits—and a significant firm size effect is found in almost 70 percent of the possible cases—its direction favors the large firms. The total value of fringe benefits is higher in large

TABLE 1.4

Firm Size and Paid Holidays: Regression Coefficients
(Firm Size Effects on Weekly Values, by Job Classification)

Job Classification	LOGFIRM-SIZE	LOGPLANT-SIZE	LOCATION[a]	Constant Term	Mean Value (Total Sample)
(1) Janitorial	$ .53	$ 6.48	$−1.95	$ 6.21	$ 8.59
	(.70)	(3.48)	(1.46)	(1.76)	
(2) Inspector-Packer	1.17	3.02	−2.90	6.88	9.04
	(.79)	(3.66)	(1.79)	(3.17)	
(3) Material handler	2.23	−.31	−5.90*	10.56	9.28
	(.89)	(4.50)	(1.92)	(2.65)	
(4) Shipping-receiving	1.03	3.38	−2.56	7.58	9.87
	(.70)	(3.23)	(1.58)	(1.92)	
(5) Auxiliary production servicer	2.29*	−.24	−2.94	7.51	8.81
	(.81)	(2.82)	(1.51)	(1.67)	
(6) Unskilled operative	1.56	3.05	−3.78	7.22	9.23
	(.99)	(6.56)	(3.14)	(3.06)	
(7) Quality control	1.66**	1.84	−1.11	5.49	9.00
	(.49)	(2.10)	(1.14)	(1.45)	
(8) Semi-skilled operative	−.30	−5.48	−.09	15.93	11.64
	(1.38)	(9.79)	(3.24)	(6.84)	
(9) Skilled maintenance	1.36	3.53	−3.04	9.97	12.99
	(.78)	(3.37)	(1.84)	(2.07)	

NOTE: Mean paid holidays (all job classifications): $9.83. Standard errors are presented in parentheses.

[a]LOCATION is a dummy variable taking the value 1 for metropolitan.

*p≤.10.

**p≤.05.

TABLE 1.5

Firm Size and Paid Lunch Breaks: Regression Coefficients
(Firm Size Effects on Weekly Values, by Job Classification)

Job Classification	LOGFIRM-SIZE	LOGPLANT-SIZE	LOCATION[a]	Constant Term	Mean Value (Total Sample)
(1) Janitorial	$ 4.55**	$ .56	$ .79	$ 1.33	$ 7.02
	(1.60)	(7.98)	(3.34)	(4.03)	
(2) Inspector-packer	4.31**	1.29	1.12	−1.39	6.88
	(1.31)	(6.08)	(2.98)	(3.61)	
(3) Material handler	2.60	−.36	5.13	1.28	5.23
	(3.97)	(20.16)	(8.61)	(11.85)	
(4) Shipping-receiving	−1.35	14.07**	−.40	2.70	2.87
	(1.15)	(5.35)	(2.62)	(3.17)	
(5) Auxiliary production servicer	3.37	2.99	1.40	−.96	6.13
	(2.78)	(9.64)	(5.18)	(5.71)	
(6) Unskilled operative	4.27**	2.89	.06	1.13	9.02
	(1.36)	(9.05)	(4.33)	(4.21)	
(7) Quality control	3.85*	2.56	.13	.17	9.11
	(1.73)	(7.38)	(4.03)	(5.10)	
(8) Semi-skilled operative	6.50	29.84	12.33	−11.38	12.22
	(3.57)	(25.31)	(8.38)	(17.68)	
(9) Skilled maintenance	−.43	20.75**	−4.40	−6.20	12.94
	(1.18)	(5.08)	(2.78)	(3.12)	

NOTE: Mean lunch break (all job classifications): $6.82. Standard errors are presented in parentheses.
[a] LOCATION is a dummy variable taking the value 1 for metropolitan.
*p≤.10.
**p≤.05.

TABLE 1.6
Firm Size and Paid Rest Breaks: Regression Coefficients
(Firm Size Effects on Weekly Values, by Job Classification)

Job Classification	LOGFIRM-SIZE	LOGPLANT-SIZE	LOCATION[a]	Constant Term	Mean Value (Total Sample)
(1) Janitorial	$1.06	$ 8.29	$ − 2.80	$4.32	$ 9.19
	(.86)	(4.28)	(1.79)	(2.16)	
(2) Inspector-packer	1.61*	5.60	− 3.56*	4.66	8.67
	(.76)	(3.52)	(1.73)	(2.09)	
(3) Material handler	1.73	− 1.46	− 1.58	7.58	7.86
	(1.27)	(6.43)	(2.75)	(3.78)	
(4) Shipping-receiving	1.44	6.10	− 3.27	5.38	9.53
	(.77)	(3.59)	(1.76)	(2.13)	
(5) Auxiliary production servicer	2.50**	3.28	− 5.83**	7.58	9.53
	(.69)	(2.39)	(1.28)	(5.36)	
(6) Unskilled operative	1.60**	− 2.80	− .89	7.65	8.17
	(.56)	(3.73)	(1.78)	(1.73)	
(7) Quality control	1.17	6.21	− 4.15*	6.29	9.54
	(.76)	(3.24)	(1.77)	(2.24)	
(8) Semi-skilled operative	1.80*	3.65	.59	3.65	10.06
	(.55)	(3.91)	(1.30)	(2.73)	
(9) Skilled maintenance	1.91	7.52	− 4.81	7.42	12.89
	(1.56)	(6.72)	(3.68)	(4.13)	

NOTE: Mean rest breaks (all job classifications): $9.49. Standard errors are presented in parentheses.
[a] LOCATION is a dummy variable taking the value 1 for metropolitan.
  *p≤.10.
  **p≤.05.

TABLE 1.7
Firm Size and Paid Vacation: Regression Coefficients
(Firm Size Effects on Weekly Values, by Job Classification)

Job Classification	LOGFIRM-SIZE	LOGPLANT-SIZE	LOCATION[a]	Constant Term	Mean Value (Total Sample)
(1) Janitorial	$1.68**	$ 2.56	$ −1.50	$ 6.70	$10.21
	(.45)	(2.27)	(.95)	(1.14)	
(2) Inspector-packer	2.12**	−.29	−2.12	7.03	9.57
	(.58)	(2.71)	(1.33)	(1.61)	
(3) Material handler	1.88	−3.93	−2.69	10.78	9.07
	(.71)	(3.62)	(1.55)	(2.13)	
(4) Shipping-receiving	2.01**	.45	−1.77	7.81	10.45
	(.46)	(2.13)	(1.04)	(1.26)	
(5) Auxiliary production servicer	2.28*	−1.21	−2.27	8.09	9.18
	(.94)	(3.25)	(1.75)	(1.93)	
(6) Unskilled operative	2.58**	−1.11	−2.27	7.84	10.00
	(.63)	(4.18)	(2.00)	(1.94)	
(7) Quality control	2.31**	−.43	−1.16	6.76	10.15
	(.53)	(2.26)	(1.23)	(1.56)	
(8) Semi-skilled operative	2.74*	4.22	−3.21	6.21	12.40
	(.88)	(6.27)	(2.08)	(4.38)	
(9) Skilled maintenance	2.84**	.04	−2.99*	10.05	13.68
	(.62)	(2.66)	(1.46)	(1.64)	

NOTE: Mean paid vacation (all job classifications): $10.52. Standard errors are presented in parentheses.

[a] LOCATION is a dummy variable taking the value 1 for metropolitan.

*$p \le .10$.

**$p \le .05$.

TABLE 1.8
Firm Size and Health Insurance: Regression Coefficients
(Firm Size Effects on Weekly Values, by Job Classification)

Job Classification	LOGFIRM-SIZE	LOGPLANT-SIZE	LOCATION[a]	Constant Term	Mean Value (Total Sample)
(1) Janitorial	$1.52**	$1.32	$ -.36	$5.49	$8.59
	(.39)	(1.95)	(.82)	(.99)	
(2) Inspector-packer	1.35**	2.35	-.12	5.21	8.67
	(.33)	(1.56)	(.76)	(.92)	
(3) Material handler	1.70	5.86	-1.19	3.25	9.15
	(.90)	(4.58)	(1.96)	(2.69)	
(4) Shipping-receiving	1.35**	2.35	-.12	5.21	8.67
	(.33)	(1.56)	(.76)	(.92)	
(5) Auxiliary production servicer	1.32	2.30	.12	4.93	8.11
	(.61)	(2.10)	(1.13)	(1.25)	
(6) Unskilled operative	1.40**	2.78	.07	5.13	8.68
	(.25)	(1.63)	(.78)	(.76)	
(7) Quality control	1.37**	2.14	-.07	5.27	9.05
	(.39)	(1.65)	(.90)	(1.14)	
(8) Semi-skilled operative	1.84	7.86	-1.96	2.25	9.59
	(.79)	(5.59)	(1.85)	(3.90)	
(9) Skilled maintenance	1.34**	2.33	-.08	5.24	8.86
	(.40)	(1.71)	(.94)	(1.05)	

NOTE: Mean health insurance (all job classifications): $8.82. Standard errors are presented in parentheses.

[a]LOCATION is a dummy variable taking the value 1 for metropolitan.

**$p \leq .05$.

TABLE 1.9
Firm Size and Life Insurance: Regression Coefficients
(Firm Size Effects on Weekly Values, by Job Classification)

Job Classification	LOGFIRM-SIZE	LOGPLANT-SIZE	LOCATION[a]	Constant Term	Mean Value (Total Sample)
(1) Janitorial	$.09**	$.17	$-.10	$.13	$.34
	(.03)	(.16)	(.07)	(.08)	
(2) Inspector-packer	.10**	.16	-.10	.14	.33
	(.02)	(.12)	(.06)	(.07)	
(3) Material handler	.17**	.24	-.24*	.09	.29
	(.04)	(.19)	(.08)	(.002)	
(4) Shipping-receiving	.11**	.13	-.10	.14	.34
	(.03)	(.12)	(.06)	(.07)	
(5) Auxiliary production servicer	.14**	.06	-.17*	.18	.31
	(.03)	(.63)	(.06)	(.07)	
(6) Unskilled operative	.11	.10	-.08	.15	.33
	(.03)	(.20)	(.10)	(.10)	
(7) Quality control	.12**	.12	-.07	.09	.35
	(.03)	(.13)	(.07)	(.09)	
(8) Semi-skilled operative	.12	.11	-.005	.07	.39
	(.06)	(.43)	(.14)	(.30)	
(9) Skilled maintenance	.11**	.08	.06	.17	.38
	(.03)	(.11)	(.06)	(.07)	

NOTE: Mean life insurance (all job classifications): $0.34. Standard errors are presented in parentheses.
[a] LOCATION is a dummy variable taking the value 1 for metropolitan.
*p≤.10.
**p≤.05.

TABLE 1.10

Firm Size and Retirement Pension: Regression Coefficients
(Firm Size Effects on Weekly Values, by Job Classification)

Job Classification	LOGFIRM-SIZE	LOGPLANT-SIZE	LOCATION[a]	Constant Term	Mean Value (Total Sample)
(1) Janitorial	$ 7.28**	$ 9.98	$ −5.18	$ 1.01	$16.23
	(1.94)	(9.68)	(4.06)	(4.89)	
(2) Inspector-packer	8.34**	3.63	−6.64	2.69	14.94
	(1.72)	(8.00)	(3.92)	(4.75)	
(3) Material handler	10.33*	−3.49	−10.95	7.26	11.04
	(2.79)	(14.18)	(6.06)	(8.34)	
(4) Shipping-receiving	8.18**	4.55	−6.43	2.45	15.07
	(1.68)	(7.78)	(3.82)	(4.62)	
(5) Auxiliary production servicer	10.49**	−1.33	−11.34**	5.87	12.83
	(1.79)	(6.19)	(3.32)	(3.67)	
(6) Unskilled operative	8.19**	−5.74	−1.20	5.56	14.27
	(1.87)	(12.44)	(5.96)	(5.79)	
(7) Quality control	8.82**	4.00	−5.07	.12	15.94
	(2.09)	(8.93)	(4.87)	(6.17)	
(8) Semi-skilled operative	9.57	6.48	−1.76	−5.18	17.74
	(4.88)	(34.61)	(11.46)	(24.18)	
(9) Skilled maintenance	8.82**	6.84	−5.80	1.24	17.87
	(2.44)	(10.49)	(5.74)	(6.45)	

NOTE: Mean retirement pension (all job classifications): $16.78. Standard errors are presented in parentheses.

[a] LOCATION is a dummy variable taking the value 1 for metropolitan.

*p≤.10.

**p≤.05.

TABLE 1.11

Firm Size and Total Fringe Benefits: Regression Coefficients
(Firm Size Effects on Weekly Values, by Job Classification)

Job Classification	LOGFIRM-SIZE	LOGPLANT-SIZE	LOCATION[a]	Constant Term	Mean Value (Total Sample)
(1) Janitorial	$16.71**	$29.37	$−11.10	$22.52	$61.20
	(3.91)	(19.55)	(8.21)	(9.87)	
(2) Inspector-packer	19.00**	16.33	−14.32	25.21	58.09
	(3.75)	(17.41)	(8.54)	(10.33)	
(3) Material handler	20.65	−3.44	−17.43	38.34	50.92
	(8.20)	(41.62)	(17.78)	(24.47)	
(4) Shipping-receiving	12.79**	31.02*	−14.66*	25.87	56.80
	(3.08)	(14.29)	(7.01)	(8.48)	
(5) Auxiliary production servicer	22.38**	5.84	−21.02	33.21	54.91
	(5.77)	(19.98)	(10.73)	(11.84)	
(6) Unskilled operative	19.71**	−.82	−8.09	34.67	59.70
	(3.94)	(26.17)	(12.53)	(12.19)	
(7) Quality control	19.30**	16.43	−11.50	24.20	63.05
	4.55	(19.45)	(10.61)	(13.44)	
(8) Semi-skilled operative	22.26	46.69	−19.17	11.55	74.04
	(10.63)	(75.43)	(24.98)	(52.69)	
(9) Skilled maintenance	15.94**	41.10	−21.18	27.89	69.64
	(5.13)	(22.05)	(12.08)	(13.56)	

NOTE: Mean total fringe benefits (all job classifications): $60.92. Standard errors are presented in parentheses.

[a]LOCATION is a dummy variable taking the value 1 for metropolitan.

*p≤.10.

**p≤.05.

TABLE 1.12
Firm Size and Total Wage–Fringe Benefit Compensation: Regression Coefficients
(Firm Size Effects on Weekly Values, by Job Classification)

Job Classification	LOGFIRM-SIZE	LOGPLANT-SIZE	LOCATION[a]	Constant Term	Mean Value (Total Sample)
(1) Janitorial	$31.04**	$116.53	$−59.65	$194.44	$281.26
	(13.94)	(69.07)	(29.23)	(35.16)	
(2) Inspector-packer	43.01**	60.53	−76.69*	200.31	265.92
	(15.14)	(70.29)	(34.48)	(41.71)	
(3) Material handler	67.57**	21.97	−137.70**	255.12	262.00
	(9.22)	(46.80)	(19.98)	(27.52)	
(4) Shipping-receiving	32.12**	83.11	−68.73*	220.38	286.05
	(12.35)	(57.34)	(28.13)	(34.03)	
(5) Auxiliary production servicer	65.56**	−12.48	−90.32**	233.62	263.64
	(15.78)	(54.68)	(29.35)	(32.41)	
(6) Unskilled operative	52.00*	33.21	−89.39	222.89	273.05
	(19.66)	130.53	(62.50)	(60.78)	
(7) Quality control	48.29**	41.38	−45.89	188.20	274.85
	(12.23)	(52.21)	(28.48)	36.09	
(8) Semi-skilled operative	24.10	11.07	−35.30	305.89	339.85
	(24.07)	(170.74)	(56.55)	(119.26)	
(9) Skilled maintenance	36.29	73.72	−75.69	302.26	373.65
	(18.56)	(79.76)	(43.68)	(49.06)	

NOTE: Mean total wage fringe–benefit compensation (all job classifications): $291.14. Standard errors are presented in parentheses.

[a]LOCATION is a dummy variable taking the value 1 for metropolitan.

*$p \leq .10$.

**$p \leq .05$.

firms in eight out of nine job classifications. When considered in conjunction with wages, the total fringe benefit–wage compensation package is significantly higher in large firms for all job classifications except the two highest-skilled ones. Again, this probably reflects less of an effort by unions to tap large firm profits for the highly compensated jobs.

Of those benefits shown to be consistently affected by firm size across job classifications, the largest firm size impact is on retirement pensions.[17] The fewest significant firm size effects are found for paid holidays, rest breaks, and lunch break. This is undoubtedly due to government regulation setting lower limits on the values of such items.

The greater valuation of health insurance in larger firms arises from the more common provision of dental and optical insurance in large firms. Otherwise, the health insurance packages were fairly uniform in all sample firms, with all providing standard major medical benefits.

In only 4 percent of all possible cases, all but one involving lunch breaks, plant size effects are significant—always with benefits improving in large plants. These plant size variations probably reflect the greater availability of manpower to fill in for workers during break time in the larger plants.

The positive relationship of size to fringe benefits in our results is consistent with earlier findings showing a positive association with firm size[18] and with plant size.[19] In cases where, unlike previous research, we find no plant size effects, we attribute this to our control for firm size as well as to the greater degree of disaggregation in our analysis.

DIFFERENCES IN WORKING CONDITIONS

Employee Assessments of Needed Improvements in Working Conditions

There are, of course, other job conditions that do not have an obvious monetary equivalent, although they do add utility or disutility for the employee. Here we investigate employees' desires for improvements in the following areas: (1) how interesting their jobs were; (2) how stressful and/or physically tiring their jobs were; and (3) how pleasant their job environment was with respect to temperature, cleanliness, noise, and so forth.

A survey technique was used to obtain numerical evaluations of these conditions. Each employee was asked to state how much he would be willing to pay per week to have (1) more interesting work, (2) less stressful and/or tiring work, and (3) more pleasant work (each taken separately).[20]

The monetary evaluations obtained in this manner have been examined for differences according to the following size variables: firm size, plant size, work group size, and department size (LOGDEPT-SIZE)—all entered as the logarithm of number of employees, with the firm and plant size variables standardized to a size of 50, as described earlier.[21] Since these subjective evaluations may vary with socioeconomic characteristics, we have included location, age, sex, race, family income, and skill level as control variables in our regressions. RACE is a dummy variable taking the value 0 for whites and 1 for all others, including Hispanic and Oriental.[22] The age, sex, family income, and skill level variables are never significant in any of the regressions and are thus not reported in the results. This is also the case for the plant size and work group size variables.

Table 1.13 presents the regression results for each of the three proposed improvements. Of the three, only one showed a significant firm size relationship. This was the desire for more interesting work,[23] which increased in larger firms and hence indicated more dissatisfaction. Since actual tasks performed have been controlled for, this result must come from more subtle psychological features of the work. Additional survey data show that large firm employees feel more strongly that they lack an understanding of how their jobs are related to the work of others in the organization.[24] This factor could presumably make a job less interesting and may give rise to the difference in evaluation here.

The evaluations indicate that stress and physical fatigue were more of a problem in larger departments and among older employees and minorities. These conditions were not related, however, to firm or plant size. The desire for a more pleasant work environment with regard to temperature, cleanliness, noise, and so on was uniform across all size variables. This probably reflects the similarities of the technologies used by the different firms in the sample—a deliberate control feature of the survey. The desire for a more pleasant work environment was the most valued of all considered improvements, and neither largeness nor small-

TABLE 1.13
Firm Size and Desire for Improvements in Working Conditions

Evaluation of Need for Improvement	LOGFIRM-SIZE	LOGDEPT-SIZE	LOCATION[a]	RACE	Constant Term	Mean Evaluation (Total Sample)
More interesting work	$.90** (.43)	$1.15 (1.05)	$-1.84** (.89)	$-.70 (1.12)	$4.09 (1.76)	$4.88
Less stressful/ tiring work	.65 (.45)	2.27** (1.10)	.43 (.94)	2.85** (.17)	.58 (1.86)	4.93
More pleasant work environment	.92 (.57)	.06 (1.41)	-2.67** (1.20)	.40 (1.49)	7.90 (2.37)	7.68

NOTE: Larger variable values indicate lower satisfaction levels. Standard errors are presented in parentheses.
[a] LOCATION and RACE are dummy variables taking the value 1 for metropolitan and nonwhites, respectively.
**$p \leq .05$.

ness appears to have given the firms any advantage in ameliorating these unpleasant aspects of the work for their employees.

Desired and Actual Number of Hours Worked per Week

The survey obtained information on both the actual number and the desired number of hours worked per week for each employee.[25] The lack of freedom to adjust the quantity of one's labor input is an important source of dissatisfaction in modern industrial jobs. There was, in fact, a discrepancy between the actual and desired number of weekly hours of work for 62.6 percent of the workers in our sample.

TABLE 1.14
Firm Size and Discrepancy Between Desired and Actual Number of Weekly Working Hours

Hours Discrepancy	LOGFIRM-SIZE	LOGPLANT-SIZE	Constant Term	Mean Discrepancy
Desired—Actual >0	$-.71$	$3.88**$	6.46	8.93 hrs.
	$(.51)$	(1.87)	(1.66)	
Desired—Actual <0	$-.81**$	$.23$	-8.59	-10.10
	$(.36)$	(1.50)	(1.41)	

NOTE: Standard errors are presented in parentheses.
$**p \leq .05.$

Our investigation of this phenomenon has been carried out separately for those employees desiring more hours than their actual number and for those desiring fewer hours than their actual number. All four size variables—representing firm, plant, department, and work group sizes—have been included in the analysis. In addition, control variables have been entered for location and other socioeconomic characteristics. Table 1.14 presents the regressions for variables found to be significant at least at the 10 percent level in at least one equation.

For those employees desiring to work longer hours per week, firm size has no significant effect on the size of the discrepancy between actual and desired number of hours. We do find, however, that the discrepancy is larger in large plants.

Turning to employees who wished to work fewer hours per week, we find that the only significant effect on the discrepancy arises from firm size, with the difference between actual and desired hours being greater

TABLE 1.15
Firm Size and Desired and Actual Number of Weekly Working Hours

	LOGFIRM-SIZE	(LOGFIRM-SIZE)²	LOGPLANT-SIZE	LOGDEPT-SIZE	LOCATION[a]	WAGE RATE	SKILLED
Desired hours	1.88	-.51	-79	.85	2.07**	-.38	2.99**
	(2.33)	(.65)	(1.99)	(.76)	(.83)	(.42)	(1.48)
Actual hours	-5.81**	2.04**	1.93**	1.05**	4.45**	1.01**	2.43**
	(1.12)	(.31)	(.96)	(.36)	(.40)	(.20)	(.70)

	SHIFT2	SHIFT3	AGE	SEX[a]	Constant Term	Mean Value
Desired hours	1.44**	.04	-.08**	3.45**	38.71	41.06 hrs.
	(.72)	(.85)	(.03)	(.78)	(2.72)	
Actual hours	-.81**	1.19**	-.02*	1.10**	33.23	42.77
	(.34)	(.40)	(.01)	(.37)	(1.31)	

NOTE: Standard errors are presented in parentheses.
[a]LOCATION and SEX are dummy variables taking the value 1 for metropolitan and males, respectively.
* $p \le .10$.
** $p \le .05$.

in large firms. To investigate this phenomenon further, we need to know whether it is due to a desire by large firm employees to work fewer hours than employees in small firms or to the fact that large firm employees are actually working longer hours. We have therefore estimated an equation relating desired number of hours to our size variables[26] and a set of socioeconomic characteristics. We have also estimated an equation relating actual hours of work to the same set of independent variables. The results of these analyses are presented in table 1.15; only variables significant at least at the 10 percent level in at least one regression have been included.[27] We see in the first regression that the desired number of hours of work does not vary significantly with firm size. Actual hours worked, however, is found in the second regression to decline with firm size initially and then to increase continuously after a size of approximately 1,300 employees is reached. We conclude therefore that the greater observed discrepancy for employees of large firms arises from the fact that they actually do work longer hours.

This result has an explanation consistent with known institutional evidence. We might expect forced overtime hours to be more common in large firms, since fringe benefit levels are higher in large firms. Under such circumstances, it is frequently cheaper for a firm to press currently employed workers into longer hours (even at overtime wage rates) than to add new workers to the rolls of costly insurance and pension plans. A small firm offering less expensive benefits would be more likely to hire additional workers to meet labor requirements rather than paying overtime wages.[28]

5. OVERALL WORK DISUTILITY AND COMPENSATING DIFFERENTIALS

In this section we use a measure of work disutility to examine differences in overall job satisfaction in the different-sized firms. Then, using individual survey responses, we examine differences in wages by firm size for the sample members. Finally, an examination of the difference between work disutility and wages will allow us to determine whether compensating wage differentials are being paid to offset differences in work disutility in the different-sized firms.

The Marginal Rate of Substitution

Scholars have approached the measurement of work disutility in a number of ways. The most frequently used measures employ either the cat-
egorial responses to job satisfaction surveys or hedonic wage equations
including as independent variables various job characteristics with which
disutility might be associated. Both types of measurement are useful for
investigating particular components of disutility or dissatisfaction under
explicit consideration. However, if not explicitly included, the other more
subtle factors affecting job satisfaction will be unaccounted for. Therefore, an overall measure of disutility from *all* work sources is necessary
for a complete analysis of employee well-being. In the present study, an
overall measure is especially important, since some nonwage job aspects are found to be better in large firms and some are not, as has generally been the case in previous research on size.[29] A single overall disutility measure allows a comparison to be made without having to assign
arbitrary weights to the different job components.

The marginal rate of substitution (MRS) of income for leisure, which
we shall use here, is such a measure of the total disutility of an hour of
work. This quantity measures the intrinsic value of a person's time according to his or her internal preferences. Put differently, it is the amount
of monetary compensation necessary to induce a person to give up an
additional hour of leisure time and to take on instead the disutility associated with another hour of work on a job.[30] It is thus a convenient
way of summarizing in a single number the totality of factors that make
the last hour of work on a job unpleasant or pleasant and hence require
more or less compensation. If, for example, we find that after controlling
for other influences the MRS is higher for employees in firms of a certain
size, this would mean that the total disutility of the last hour on the job
(from whatever source) was higher in firms of that size.

The MRS is measured in terms of dollars per hour. Therefore, used as
a measure of disutility, it has the advantage that differences in it can be
compared directly with differences in actual wages to determine whether
compensating differentials exist at different-sized firms to offset different
levels of work disutility.

A survey technique has been employed to gather data used to ascertain marginal rates of substitution for sample workers. First, the employees were asked how much money per week they would be willing to

pay to have each of various benefits on their jobs if those benefits were not provided by the employer. They were than asked to indicate how much time they would be willing to work longer each week with *no pay* to have the same benefits. Nine job benefits, each evaluated *separately* in this manner in both the money and time dimension, form the basis for determinating the MRS in our study.[31] However, one can see intuitively that if a worker says he would pay five dollars per week for health insurance, or alternatively that he would work one hour longer per week with no pay, then the internal value of his time (or MRS) is about five dollars per hour.[32]

In appendix B we also discuss how an employee's MRS—the constant term α in equation 7 of that appendix—is estimated from the monetary and time evaluation data. We now consider α to depend upon the various size and socioeconomic variables. Department and work group size were found not to be significant at the 10 percent level in any of the regressions under consideration in this section. We have therefore omitted them. In addition to our firm and plant size variables, we have included below those socioeconomic variables found to be significant at least at the 10 percent level. The equation estimated for the MRS is:

$$\text{RATIO} = 6.16 - 2.42 \text{ LOGFIRM-SIZE} + .63 \text{ (LOGFIRM-SIZE)}^2$$
$$\quad (.63) \quad (1.34) \qquad\qquad (.37)$$

$$+ 1.20 \text{ LOGPLANT-SIZE} + 1.05 \text{ RACE} - 2.05 \text{ } \Delta L + .26 \text{ } \Delta L^2, \qquad (4)$$
$$\quad (1.06) \qquad\qquad (.48) \qquad (.24) \quad (.04)$$

with standard errors in parentheses beneath the estimated coefficients. Here RATIO is the ratio of the monetary evaluation to the time evaluation by a given individual for a given job benefit.[33] ΔL is the magnitude of the time evaluation. A quadratic firm size term was found to be significant and was thus included. As before, RACE is a dummy variable taking the value 1 for nonwhites.

We see from equation 4 that firm size has a significant effect on the MRS of the sample members. The relationship is nonlinear. Disutility decreases as firm size increases up to a certain point. It then increases slightly as firm size increases beyond that point; but at very large firm sizes (i.e., 50,000 employees), it has not returned to the level observed for the very smallest firms in our sample. The minimum of disutility is reached at a firm size of about 4,000 employees. In our sample this would correspond to a firm with 22 plants and approximately $272 million in annual sales.[34]

There are undoubtedly many subtle and hard-to-measure aspects of job satisfaction that contribute to the differences in overall disutility in the different ranges of firm size.[35] The upturn in disutility for very large firms indicates that the negative features of size begin to outweigh the positive features in these size ranges. A feeling on the part of large firm employees that jobs are less interesting and less correspondence between desired and actual hours worked in large firms are two such negative features we have been able to identify. Other possible factors cited in previous size research include impaired channels of communication, impersonal atmosphere, and the subjection of numerous employees with presumably heterogeneous tastes to a uniform company policy.[36]

Overall job disutility is not found to vary significantly with plant size, whereas previous research has shown a link between plant size and various aspects of job satisfaction. This again may be due to the fact that we have surveyed an industry in which plant size effects are expected to be small. Alternatively, in previous research, plant size may have proxied for firm size to some extent. The only significant result among the socioeconomic variables shows that disutility is greater for non-whites.

We should emphasize that the purpose here is to find the *overall* effect of firm size on the level of job disutility (as measured by the MRS). At a more detailed level, one would find that job disutility is affected by many things varying with firm size and plant size. These would include not only variables describing the intrinsic "unpleasantness" of the job, such as physical characteristics of the workplace and relationships with supervisors and other workers, but also variables of a more "economic" nature, such as level of income, number of overtime hours that can be worked, and dissatisfaction with the wage rate or benefits. The MRS is a summary measure of all these effects. It is, of course, of interest to "explain" the level of job disutility in terms of these and other variables, and this will be explored elsewhere. But in order to investigate the overall effect of firm size and plant size on job disutility, it would not be appropriate to select some of these variables as "explaining" the MRS and to control for them in the regression. Instead, we estimate a "reduced form" in equation 4, controlling only for individual worker characteristics while allowing all job-specific variables (whether measured or not) to vary with firm and plant size as they do in the sample. We can then make a direct comparison with the dependence of the marginal wage rate on firm and plant size.

Work Disutility and Wage Rates

If we are to draw a conclusion concerning general employee well-being in different-sized firms, we must compare the actual wages of the sample members with their marginal rates of substitution to see whether compensating wage differentials exist at the high-disutility firm sizes. That is, we must see if the high levels of disutility for the last hour worked are being offset by correspondingly high wage rates. To determine whether or not this is the case, we have first estimated equation 5 for the marginal wage rates (i.e., wage rates for the last hour worked[37]):

$$\begin{aligned}
\text{MARGINAL} \\
\text{WAGE} = 5.29 &- .97 \text{ LOGFIRM-SIZE} + .55 \text{ (LOGFIRM-SIZE)}^2 \\
&\ \ (.24)\ \ \ (.04) \qquad\qquad\qquad (.13) \\[4pt]
&+ 2.49 \text{ LOGPLANT-SIZE} - .75 \text{ LOCATION} + 2.23 \text{ SEMI-SKILLED} \\
&\ \ \ (.38) \qquad\qquad\qquad\ \ (.12) \qquad\qquad\qquad (.18) \\[4pt]
&+ 4.03 \text{ SKILLED} + .03 \text{ SENIORITY}, \qquad\qquad\qquad\qquad (5) \\
&\ \ \ (.26) \qquad\qquad\ \ \ (.01)
\end{aligned}$$

with standard errors in parentheses beneath the estimated coefficients. Here SENIORITY is represented as the deviation from the sample mean years of seniority, which was six years. The other socioeconomic variables are as specified earlier. Socioeconomic variables that proved to be statistically insignificant were omitted.

Note that the marginal wage rate is to be compared with the level of job disutility, as measured by the MRS. Since the MRS measures job disutility from all sources, including such economic variables as hours worked and income, one should not control for variables such as number of hours worked in determining the effects of firm size and plant size on marginal wages.

We see from equation 5 that the marginal wage rate of the sample at first decreases with increasing firm size, as does the MRS. This decreasing trend reaches a minimum at a firm size of about 200 employees, with marginal wages increasing sharply with firm size thereafter. On the other hand, as we have seen, the MRS or disutility continues to decline until a firm size of about 4,000 employees is reached.

The extent to which wage differences represent compensating differentials in different-sized firms can best be seen by a regression of the difference between the marginal rate of substitution and the marginal wage rate. We have therefore estimated the following equation:[38]

$$\text{MRS} - \text{MARGINAL} = .46 - .88 \ \text{LOGFIRM-SIZE} - 1.24 \ \text{LOGPLANT-SIZE}$$
$$\phantom{\text{MRS} - \text{MARGINAL} = } (.42) \ (.10) (.40)$$

$$+ 1.05 \ \text{RACE} - .09 \ \text{SENIORITY} - 1.84 \ \text{SEMI-SKILLED}$$
$$ (.29) (.02) (.29)$$

$$- 3.53 \ \text{SKILLED} - 2.26 \ \Delta L + .30 \ \Delta L^2, (6)$$
$$ (.39) (.26) (.05)$$

A quadratic firm size variable was not included because the estimated coefficients were approximately the same in equations 4 and 5. They would therefore cancel out in equation 6, leaving only a linear dependence on the logarithm of firm size. Statistically insignificant socioeconomic variables have again been omitted.

The estimated coefficients in equation 6 indicate that, up to a firm size of approximately 150 employees, the disutility of the last hour of work is greater than the wage rate for the last hour.[39] Therefore, in very small firms, employees are not fully compensated at the margin for the disutility of the work. At a firm size of about 150 employees, the disutility of the last hour is exactly offset by the marginal wage. The significant negative coefficient of LOGFIRM-SIZE indicates that, as one moves above this size, employees are increasingly overcompensated for the disutility of work. Thus, even though work disutility increases slightly after a firm size of 4,000 is reached, employees are more than compensated.

SUMMARY AND CONCLUSIONS

This paper has examined wages, fringe benefits, working conditions, and overall work disutility for a sample of employees in firms of different sizes. The survey covered employees in a specified set of jobs in different-sized firms within the same industry. Thus, the survey was especially designed to control for as many nonsize influences on employee well-being as possible, and the data are analyzed at a higher level of disaggregation than has been done in the past.

Our results show that large firms pay higher wages and higher shift premiums than small firms, except in two no-effect cases, the two highest-paid job classifications and special situations (janitors and third shift premia) where market forces have apparently driven the wage differentials above their traditional levels. These exceptions are consistent with previous research, which has found reduced union effort for highly paid workers. We have also examined the monetary value of seven fringe benefits and again find that, in the large majority of cases, fringe benefit levels rise with increasing firm size.

With regard to working conditions, two negative features of large firms have emerged. Large firm employees feel that their jobs are intrinsically less interesting, possibly because they understand less well how their jobs fit in with the jobs of others in the organization. In addition, large firm employees are more commonly required to work more hours per week than they desire. We believe this to be connected with the higher level of fringe benefits found for large firms, since firms with expensive benefit programs frequently save money by working their existing labor force longer—even at overtime rates—than by adding the fixed costs of additional workers to their benefit payments.

Finally, we have investigated overall work disutility for employees in the different-sized firms to make an unambiguous determination of employee well-being with regard to nonmonetary conditions. The survey obtained information allowing us to estimate directly the marginal rate of substitution of wage income for leisure. This quantity was used as a dollar measure of disutility, since it indicates how much money an employee requires to be compensated for the overall disutility of an extra hour of work. Our results show that overall employee disutility decreases as firms get larger up to a size of about 4,000 employees. After this point, there is a slight upturn in disutility, although for the largest firm in our sample it does not reach the levels observed for the smallest firms.

The marginal rate of substitution was then compared with marginal wage rates in the different-sized firms to see whether compensating wage differentials existed. We have found that, for employees in firms with fewer than 150 employees, wages do not fully compensate for the disutility of the work. As firm size increases beyond that point, however, employees receive wages that increasingly overcompensate them for work disutility.

Three explanations are commonly advanced to explain the existence of higher wages in larger firms. They may be summarized as follows: (1) larger firms use more sophisticated technologies and thus require a higher degree of employee skill or discipline; (2) the wage difference represents a compensating differential needed to offset the greater disutility of work in large firms; and (3) (the so-called monopoly wage hypothesis) through its organized bargaining efforts, labor in large firms has appropriated some of the firms' higher profits.

One might expect any or all three of these linkages to contribute to the relationship between firm sizes and wages. However, since our survey selected a case in which the technology of large and small firms is similar, the first nexus cannot be the cause of the observed wage differentials. Our finding of greater work disutility in small firms shows that the second linkage is not applicable to the difference in wages between small and medium-sized firms, but the slight upturn in disutility for firms with more than about 4,000 employees indicates that it may play some role in this size range. Even in this latter case, however, we have seen that the increase in wages with firm size more than compensates for the increase in disutility. We conclude therefore that the third nexus, the appropriation by labor of large firms' higher profits, is the dominant influence on the observed wage–firm size relationship. Similar conclusions can be drawn for the greater level of fringe benefits observed in the larger firms.

APPENDIX 1A: THE SURVEY QUESTIONNAIRE

NORTHWESTERN UNIVERSITY
COLLEGE OF ARTS & SCIENCES
EVANSTON, ILLINOIS 60201

DEPARTMENT OF ECONOMICS

Dear Participant:

The purpose of this survey is to assess people's attitudes about their jobs and the organizations for which they work. The attached questionnaire asks for your views on your job and your organization, as well as for some background information which will be useful in analyzing this data.

The questionnaires are being distributed by and will be collected by university researchers. Your completed questionnaire will only be seen by the university researchers. No one from this company will ever see your answers to this questionnaire. *No names* of any participants will ever be revealed.

Please read the following instructions carefully and then complete the attached questionnaire.

1. This is *not a test*. There are no right or wrong answers to any of the questions. It is a survey to obtain information about the work people do and the feelings they have about their work.
2. We are interested in your personal thoughts and feelings. Please complete the questionnaires on your own; don't discuss your answers with others.
3. Please be sure that you answer each and every item.
4. *Please ask for help if you do not understand how to complete any part of this questionnaire.*

Thank you for your participation.

Lucia Dunn
Northwestern University

Jon Shepard
University of Kentucky

1. Sex (check one)
   ____ (1) Female
   ____ (2) Male

2. What is your current job title? _____

3. How long have you worked for this company? _____

4. What shift do you work? _____

5. Approximately how many people work in your department on your shift? _____

6. How many people do you work with in your immediate work group?
   _____

7. Have you ever worked for a company whose overall size was significantly *larger* than the one you work for now?
   ____ (1) Yes
   ____ (2) No

8. Have you ever worked for a company whose overall size was significantly *smaller* than the one you work for now?
   ____ (1) Yes
   ____ (2) No

9. In a typical week, how many hours do you put in on this job? ____

10. How many of these hours are overtime hours? _____

11. Ideally, how many hours a week would you like to work? _____

12. In what year were you born? _____

13. How many years of schooling did you complete (including college, if any)? _____

14. Check below your marital status.

_____ (1) Single
_____ (2) Married
_____ (3) Widowed, Divorced, or Separated

15. If you are married, does your spouse work for money outside the home?
_____ (1) Yes
_____ (2) No
_____ (3) Not married

16. Do you have children?
_____ (1) Yes
_____ (2) No
(16a.) If yes, how many? _____
(16b.) How many are under 18 years of age? _____

17. How many people do you contribute financial support to, including yourself? _____

18. Check below the one statement that most applies to you:
_____ (1) I am the primary income earner in my household.
_____ (2) My spouse is the primary income earner in my household.
_____ (3) My spouse and I earn equal incomes.
_____ (4) Someone other than myself or my spouse is the primary income earner in my household.

19. Check below your ethnic background:
_____ (1) White
_____ (2) Black
_____ (3) Hispanic (Spanish-speaking)
_____ (4) Oriental
_____ (5) Other (Specify) _____

20. Check below the type of place you lived most of the time when you were growing up:
_____ (1) On a farm
_____ (2) In or near a small town (under 2,500 people)
_____ (3) In or near a larger town (2,500 to 10,000 people)
_____ (4) In or near a small city (10,000 to 50,000)
_____ (5) Within a medium-size city (50,000 to 200,000)
_____ (6) In the suburbs of a medium-size city (50,000 to 250,000)
_____ (7) Within a large city (over 250,000 people)
_____ (8) In the suburbs of a large city (over 250,000)

21. Check below the type of place you currently live in:
    _____ (1) On a farm
    _____ (2) In or near a small town (under 2,500 people)
    _____ (3) In or near a larger town (2,500 to 10,000 people)
    _____ (4) In or near a small city (10,000 to 50,000)
    _____ (5) Within a medium-size city (50,000 to 200,000)
    _____ (6) In the suburbs of a medium-size city (50,000 to 250,000)
    _____ (7) Within a large city (over 250,000 people)
    _____ (8) In the suburbs of a large city (over 250,000)

22. Approximately how long (in hours and minutes) does it take you to travel to work each day? _____hours _____minutes

23. Approximately what is the usual amount of your take-home pay after taxes (and check whether this is weekly or monthly)? $_____
    Check one: weekly _____; every 2 weeks _____; monthly _____

24. Approximately what was your total *yearly* family income from all sources in 1981 before taxes? $_____

25. If you are paid by the hour, what is your hourly wage? _____per hour (If not paid by the hour, leave blank).

26. This part of the questionnaire asks you to evaluate a number of benefits and working conditions that you may or may not have on your job. Not all people value the same things equally, so we would like to know how you value these items. In order to find out how important or unimportant each item is to you, we would like to ask you to think about each item in this way:

    Assume that you currently do *not* have these items on your job. If you could get an item on your job—just as if you could buy it in a store—then how much do you think this item would be worth to you? That is, would you be willing to pay some money each week to have this item; and if so, what is the *most money in dollars and cents per week* that you would pay?

    Of course, you are not now paying for any of these items, and you will *not* be asked to do so at any time in the future. We just want to know your opinion about these items so that we can determine how much value you place on them.

    Consider each item separately. Indicate the highest dollar and cents amount per week that it alone would be worth to you *if* you did not have it on your job. If you don't feel the item would be worth paying for if you did not have it, then simply write "0" on the blank beside that item.

Please ask for assistance if you have any questions on how to complete this section.

The highest amount in DOLLARS AND CENTS PER WEEK that I would be willing to pay for this item:	Item
(1) $_____ per wk.	A seniority system to determine work schedules, lay-off, job choice, etc.
(2) $_____ per wk.	Eight paid holidays per year.
(3) $_____ per wk.	Well-established work rules and grievance procedure.
(4) $_____ per wk.	Thirty-minute lunch break.
(5) $_____ per wk.	Two ten-minute rest breaks during your scheduled work shift.
(6) $_____ per wk.	A pension plan based on your highest three years' earnings.
(7) $_____ per wk.	Paid vacation based on your seniority with the company
(8) $_____ per wk.	A health insurance plan covering three-fourths of hospital and doctor bills for an illness (with option to add dependents for additional fee).
(9) $_____ per wk.	Nurse at plant.
(10) $_____ per wk.	A work site that is within ten minutes' distance from your residence.

AND NOW, HOW MUCH WOULD YOU PAY PER WEEK FOR EACH OF THE FOLLOWING JOB CONDITIONS?

(11) $_____ per wk.	More interesting work.
(12) $_____ per wk.	Work that is less stressful and/or less physically tiring.

(13) $_____ per wk.   A more pleasant work environment with
                              regard to temperature, cleanliness, light-
                              ing, noise, ventilation, etc.

27. Again, assume that you do *not* currently have these items on your
    job. If you would like to have a particular item, then assume that
    you could buy it with your *time*. That is, you could work extra time
    each day *without pay* in order to have a particular item. If you would
    be willing to do this, how much extra time would you be willing to
    work without pay in order to have the item present on your job? If
    a specific item has no value to you and you would not be willing
    to work extra to have the item, then place a "0" on the blank be-
    side that item. Consider each item separately, and indicate the amount
    of time in hours and minutes that you would work extra for it alone.

    Of course, you will not be asked to give more time in order to have
    these items on your job. Again, this set of questions just gives us
    more information about how you value the items.

HOURS AND MINUTES   *Item*
PER DAY that I would
be willing to work extra
to have this item:

(1) _____ per day   A seniority system to determine work
                            schedules, lay-off, job choice, etc.

(2) _____ per day   Eight paid holidays per year.

(3) _____ per day   Well-established work rules and griev-
                            ance procedure.

(4) _____ per day   Thirty-minute lunch break.

(5) _____ per day   Two ten-minute rest breaks during your
                            scheduled work shift.

(6) _____ per day   A pension plan based on your highest
                            three years' earnings.

(7) _____ per day   Paid vacation based on your seniority with
                            the company.

(8) _____ per day   A health insurance plan covering three-
                            fourths of hospital and doctor bills for an
                            illness (with option to add dependents for
                            additional fee).

(9) _____ per day   Nurse at plant.

(10) _____ per day   A work site that is within ten minutes' distance from your residence.

AND NOW, HOW MUCH LONGER PER DAY WOULD YOU WORK FOR EACH OF THE FOLLOWING JOB CONDITIONS?

(11) _____ per day   More interesting work.

(12) _____ per day   Work that is less stressful and/or less physically tiring.

(13) _____ per day   A more pleasant work environment with regard to temperature, cleanliness lighting, noise, ventilation, etc.

28. Below you will find a list of *work* characteristics. Put Y beside an item if the item describes the work on your job. Put N beside the item if it does not describe your work, and "?" if you cannot decide.

    (a) WORK
    _____ Fascinating
    _____ Routine
    _____ Satisfying
    _____ Boring
    _____ Good
    _____ Creative
    _____ Respected
    _____ Hot
    _____ Pleasant
    _____ Useful
    _____ Tiresome
    _____ Healthful
    _____ Challenging
    _____ On your feet
    _____ Frustrating
    _____ Simple
    _____ Endless
          Gives sense of
    _____ accomplishment

    (b) SUPERVISION
    _____ Asks my advice
    _____ Hard to please

_____ Impolite
_____ Praises good work
_____ Tactful
_____ Influential
_____ Up-to-date
_____ Doesn't supervise enough
_____ Quick-tempered
_____ Tells me where I stand
_____ Annoying
_____ Stubborn
_____ Knows job well
_____ Bad
_____ Intelligent
_____ Leaves me on my own
_____ Lazy
_____ Around when needed

(c) PAY

_____ Income adequate for
normal expenses
_____ Satisfactory profit sharing
_____ Barely live on income
_____ Bad
_____ Income provides luxuries
_____ Insecure
_____ Less than I deserve
_____ Highly paid
_____ Underpaid

(d) PROMOTIONS

_____ Good opportunity for
advancement
_____ Opportunity somewhat limited
_____ Promotion on ability
_____ Dead-end job
_____ Good chance for promotion
_____ Unfair promotion policy
_____ Infrequent promotions
_____ Regular promotions
_____ Fairly good chance for promotion

(e) CO-WORKERS

_____ Stimulating
_____ Boring

_____ Slow
_____ Ambitious
_____ Stupid
_____ Responsible
_____ Fast
_____ Intelligent
_____ Easy to make enemies
_____ Talk too much
_____ Smart
_____ Lazy
_____ Unpleasant
_____ No privacy
_____ Active
_____ Narrow interests
_____ Loyal
_____ Hard to meet

29. Listed below are statements that describe certain job characteristics and attitudes toward jobs. Please indicate the extent to which you agree or disagree with each of these statements by checking the appropriate slot.

(1) Cutting the costs of this company is of little importance to me.
_____ (1) Strongly agree
_____ (2) Agree
_____ (3) Undecided
_____ (4) Disagree
_____ (5) Strongly disagree

(2) The reputation of this company is very important to me.
_____ (1) Strongly agree
_____ (2) Agree
_____ (3) Undecided
_____ (4) Disagree
_____ (5) Strongly disagree

(3) The quality of this company's products is very important to me.
_____ (1) Strongly agree
_____ (2) Agree
_____ (3) Undecided
_____ (4) Disagree
_____ (5) Strongly disagree

(4) The only reason the company's profits are important to me is that they affect the amount of money I make.

_____ (1) Strongly agree

_____ (2) Agree

_____ (3) Undecided

_____ (4) Disagree

_____ (5) Strongly disagree

(5) Successful competition of this company with other firms is not important to me.

_____ (1) Strongly agree

_____ (2) Agree

_____ (3) Undecided

_____ (4) Disagree

_____ (5) Strongly disagree

(6) I have a feeling of closeness with many of the people who work for this company.

_____ (1) Strongly agree

_____ (2) Agree

_____ (3) Undecided

_____ (4) Disagree

_____ (5) Strongly disagree

(7) This company is too large to take care of my needs.

_____ (1) Strongly agree

_____ (2) Agree

_____ (3) Undecided

_____ (4) Disagree

_____ (5) Strongly disagree

(8) I would be more satisfied with the kind of work I do if this company were larger.

_____ (1) Strongly agree

_____ (2) Agree

_____ (3) Undecided

_____ (4) Disagree

_____ (5) Strongly disagree

(9) Supervisors in this company could do a better job if the company were smaller.

_____ (1) Strongly agree

_____ (2) Agree

_____ (3) Undecided

_____ (4) Disagree

_____ (5) Strongly disagree

(10) I would have a better chance of being promoted if the company were larger.
_____ (1) Strongly agree
_____ (2) Agree
_____ (3) Undecided
_____ (4) Disagree
_____ (5) Strongly disagree

(11) My relationships with co-workers would be better if the company were smaller.
_____ (1) Strongly agree
_____ (2) Agree
_____ (3) Undecided
_____ (4) Disagree
_____ (5) Strongly disagree

(12) I would have more freedom and control on my job if the company were smaller.
_____ (1) Strongly agree
_____ (2) Agree
_____ (3) Undecided
_____ (4) Disagree
_____ (5) Strongly disagree

(13) This company is simply too large.
_____ (1) Strongly agree
_____ (2) Agree
_____ (3) Undecided
_____ (4) Disagree
_____ (5) Strongly disagree

(14) I would much prefer to work in a larger company.
_____ (1) Strongly agree
_____ (2) Agree
_____ (3) Undecided
_____ (4) Disagree
_____ (5) Strongly disagree

(15) The size of the organization in which I work has no bearing on how I feel about my job and company.
_____ (1) Strongly agree
_____ (2) Agree
_____ (3) Undecided

_____ (4) Disagree

_____ (5) Strongly disagree

(16) My job allows me to use my skills and abilities most of the time.

_____ (1) Strongly agree

_____ (2) Agree

_____ (3) Undecided

_____ (4) Disagree

_____ (5) Strongly disagree

(17) My job gives me a predictable, secure future.

_____ (1) Strongly agree

_____ (2) Agree

_____ (3) Undecided

_____ (4) Disagree

_____ (5) Strongly disagree

(18) My job gives me high status and prestige.

_____ (1) Strongly agree

_____ (2) Agree

_____ (3) Undecided

_____ (4) Disagree

_____ (5) Strongly disagree

(19) My job gives me a good chance for advancement.

_____ (1) Strongly agree

_____ (2) Agree

_____ (3) Undecided

_____ (4) Disagree

_____ (5) Strongly disagree

(20) My job is interesting most of the time.

_____ (1) Strongly agree

_____ (2) Agree

_____ (3) Undecided

_____ (4) Disagree

_____ (5) Strongly disagree

(21) My job gives me a chance to make friends.

_____ (1) Strongly agree

_____ (2) Agree

_____ (3) Undecided

_____ (4) Disagree
_____ (5) Strongly disagree

(22) My job is one that most people look up to and respect.
_____ (1) Strongly agree
_____ (2) Agree
_____ (3) Undecided
_____ (4) Disagree
_____ (5) Strongly disagree

(23) My job lets me see the results of what I do.
_____ (1) Strongly agree
_____ (2) Agree
_____ (3) Undecided
_____ (4) Disagree
_____ (5) Strongly disagree

(24) My job gives me a chance to earn a good amount of money.
_____ (1) Strongly agree
_____ (2) Agree
_____ (3) Undecided
_____ (4) Disagree
_____ (5) Strongly disagree

(25) My job is worthwhile to society.
_____ (1) Strongly agree
_____ (2) Agree
_____ (3) Undecided
_____ (4) Disagree
_____ (5) Strongly disagree

(26) Employees here are under a lot of pressure to perform their jobs well.
_____ (1) Strongly agree
_____ (2) Agree
_____ (3) Undecided
_____ (4) Disagree
_____ (5) Strongly disagree

(27) Employees here feel rushed.
_____ (1) Strongly agree
_____ (2) Agree
_____ (3) Undecided

_____ (4) Disagree
_____ (5) Strongly disagree

(28) This is an easygoing place to work.
_____ (1) Strongly agree
_____ (2) Agree
_____ (3) Undecided
_____ (4) Disagree
_____ (5) Strongly disagree

(29) Work assignments are added without regard to the amount of work I am already doing at the time of assignment.
_____ (1) Strongly agree
_____ (2) Agree
_____ (3) Undecided
_____ (4) Disagree
_____ (5) Strongly disagree

(30) I lack sufficient time to do the quality of job I want to do.
_____ (1) Strongly agree
_____ (2) Agree
_____ (3) Undecided
_____ (4) Disagree
_____ (5) Strongly disagree

(31) I feel tense when I think about the demands of my job.
_____ (1) Strongly agree
_____ (2) Agree
_____ (3) Undecided
_____ (4) Disagree
_____ (5) Strongly disagree

30. The questions below list several characteristics that might be connected with your present job. For each characteristic, please circle the number (1 through 7) that best indicates the extent to which it is associated with your present job.

Circle only one number for each question.

Circle a _1_ if the characteristic exists to a _MINIMUM AMOUNT._

Circle a _2_ if the characteristic exists _JUST A LITTLE._

Circle a _3_ if the characteristic exists a _BELOW AVERAGE AMOUNT._

Circle a 4 if the characteristic exists an *AVERAGE AMOUNT*.

Circle a 5 if the characteristic exists an *ABOVE AVERAGE AMOUNT*.

Circle a 6 if the characteristic exists to a *GREAT EXTENT*.

Circle a 7 if the characteristic exists to a *MAXIMUM AMOUNT*.

(1) To what extent are you free from close supervision while doing your job?

(minimum)   (maximum)

    1   2   3   4   5   6   7

(2) To what extent can you help decide on methods and procedures used in your job?

(minimum)   (maximum)

    1   2   3   4   5   6   7

(3) To what extent do you have influence over the things that happen to you at work?

(minimum)   (maximum)

    1   2   3   4   5   6   7

(4) To what extent can you increase or decrease the pace at which you work?

(minimum)   (maximum)

    1   2   3   4   5   6   7

(5) To what extent do you know how your job fits into the total work organization?

(minimum)   (maximum)

    1   2   3   4   5   6   7

(6) To what extent do you know how your work contributes to company products?

(minimum)   (maximum)

    1   2   3   4   5   6   7

(7) To what extent can you control how much work you do?

(minimum)   (maximum)

    1   2   3   4   5   6   7

(8) To what extent do you know how your job fits in with other jobs in the company?

(minimum)   (maximum)

    1   2   3   4   5   6   7

(9) To what extent do you know how your job fits into the work of other departments?

(minimum)   (maximum)
   1   2   3   4   5   6   7

(10) To what extent do you know how your work affects the jobs of others you work with?

(minimum)   (maximum)
   1   2   3   4   5   6   7

(11) To what extent are you learning a great deal about the company while doing your job?

(minimum)   (maximum)
   1   2   3   4   5   6   7

31. How much, in percentage terms, has the general level of prices changed in the *past 12 months?*

_____ %

32. How much, in percentage terms, do you expect the general level of prices to change in the *coming 12 months?*

_____ %

APPENDIX 1B: ESTIMATION OF MARGINAL RATES OF SUBSTITUTION

W E will now explain how the equivalence between the monetary and time evaluations of the job benefits leads to a worker's marginal rate of substitution of wage income for leisure.[40] The survey technique gives the quantities ΔW, the monetary evaluation, and ΔL, the time evaluation, in the indifference curve diagram below, where W_o and L_o are the worker's actual after-tax wage income and leisure time, $U(W, L, x)$ is his utility with job benefit x present, and $U(W, L, O)$ his utility in the absence of x. (Note that both indifference curves here are at the same level of total utility u_1).

We consider the nine job benefits used for this derivation as representative of a continuous range of job benefits, so that ΔW is a continuous function of ΔL. From the figure we see that $\Delta W/\Delta L$ is the slope of the line CB, which becomes the slope of the curve at C in the limit $\Delta L \rightarrow O$. In this limit the two curves appoach each other and $C \rightarrow D$ so that

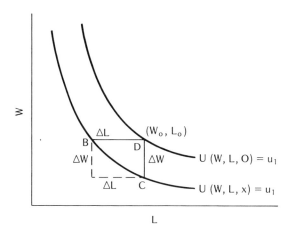

Figure 1.1 Indifference Curves With and Without x

$$\lim_{\Delta L \to O} \frac{\Delta W}{\Delta L} = MRS_o, \tag{6}$$

where MRS_o is the marginal rate of substitution of wage income for leisure at (W_o, L_o). In order to extrapolate to $\Delta L = O$, we approximate the relationship between ΔW and ΔL by the polynomial form

$$\Delta W \simeq \alpha \Delta L + \beta (\Delta L)^2 + \delta (\Delta L)^3. \tag{7}$$

We determine α β and δ by making a least squares fit of $\Delta W / \Delta L$ to the values obtained from our data.[41] Note that $\alpha = MRS_o$.

NOTES

1. The correlation coefficients between sales and employees, number of plants and employees, and number of plants and sales are all greater than 0.96 for our sample of firms. Capital assets is another possible measure of size. In general, it is also highly correlated with number of employees and with sales. See S. S. Shalit and U. Sankar, "The Measurement of Firm Size," *Review of Economics and Statistics* (August 1977), 59:290–298.

2. Although all of the firms in the study are in the plastics industry, some of the plants were also manufacturing rubber and glass products. However, only those employees in strictly comparable job categories in technologically similar steps of the manufacturing process were included in the sample.

3. In the analysis of job satisfaction variables, we have also included variables for department size and work group size. The values of these variables have been determined from questions 5 and 6 in the survey (see appendix 1A). Department and work group sizes, as reported by the participants, both ranged from 1 to 400 in number of employees. All other size-related information used in the study was obtained from industrial directories and management sources at the individual firms.

4. Where certain jobs were extremely unlike those in other firms, these subjects were omitted from the sample.

5. A logarithmic form is used for all size variables since their range is so large.

6. Frank Stafford, "Concentration and Labor Earnings: Comment," *American Economic Review* (March 1968), 58:174–181; and Orley Ashenfelter, "Discrimination and Trade Unions," in O. Ashenfelter and A. Rees, eds., *Discrimination in Labor Markets* (Princeton: Princeton University Press, 1973), pp. 88–112.

7. An alternative interpretation of the lack of firm size differentials for the higher-skill job classifications is that unions have exerted a greater effort to standardize wages at high levels across firms for the higher-skill jobs, aided of course by the relative scarcity of these jobs.

8. To determine exactly how unions have managed to syphon off some of the surplus returns in the larger firms would require an investigation of bargaining strategies beyond the scope of this paper. We should note, however, that industry sources suggest that unions negotiate more skillfully in contract talks with larger firms.

9. Charles T. Haworth and Carol Jean Reuther, "Industrial Concentration and Interindustry Wage Determination," *Review of Economics and Statistics* (February 1978), 60:85–95; Thomas A. Pugel, "Profitability, Concentration and the Interindustry Variation in Wages," *Review of Economics and Statistics* (May 1980), 62:248–253; and Leonard W. Weiss, "Concentration and Labor Earnings," *American Economic Review* (March 1966), 56:96–117.

10. Wesley Mellow, "Employer Size and Wages," BLS Working Paper No. 116 (Washington, D.C.: U.S. Department of Labor, April 1981).

11. See John E. Kwoka, Jr., "Establishment Size, Wages, and Job Satisfaction: The

Tradeoffs," in John J. Siegfried, ed., *The Economics of Firm Size, Market Structure and Social Performance,* pp. 359–379 (Washington, D.C.: Federal Trade Commission, 1980); Richard Lester, "Pay Differentials by Size of Establishment," *Industrial Relations* (October 1967), 7:57–67; Stanley H. Masters, "An Interindustry Analysis of Wages and Plant Size," *Review of Economics and Statistics* (August 1969), 51:341–345; Mellow; Edward M. Miller, "Variation of Wage Rates with Size of Establishment," Working Paper No. 14 (Houston: Jesse H. Jones Graduate School of Administration, Rice University, September 1981); Pugel; F. M. Scherer, "Industrial Structure, Scale Economics, and Worker Alienation," in Robert T. Masson and P. David Qualls, eds., *Essays on Industrial Organization in Honor of Joe S. Bain,* pp. 105–121 (Cambridge, Mass.: Ballinger, 1976).

12. In our sample, the correlation between LOGFIRM-SIZE and LOGPLANT-SIZE was only .27. See Edward M. Miller, "Size of Firm and Size of Plant," *Southern Economic Journal* (April 1978), 44:861–872.

13. Our typical worker is a thirty-six-year-old employee with six years of seniority, based on the characteristics of our sample. We further assume that this employee is a male, on the first shift, and earning the average wage in his job classification. This level of specification is necessary because the fringe benefits differ with these characteristics. Information used in this section, on the provision of fringe benefits was obtained from management and union sources at the individual firms.

14. Other fringe benefits might be examined, of course. We have omitted benefits from consideration where an element of probability is involved—for example, time off for a death in the family.

15. Note that the valuations of benefits 1 through 4 vary both with the wage rate and with the amount of time involved. No attempt was made to place a value on unpaid time off.

16. This figure was chosen rather than the amount per worker actually paid by the company since (1) the comparable cost to the individual should more accurately reflect the value to the individual and (2) the cost advantage of large-scale purchase would bias this figure downward for large firms. (None of the firms in our sample required employee contributions for insurance.) Rate schedules and area classifications used in calculating all insurance premiums for this investigation were taken from *Massachusetts Group Trust* (Springfield, Mass.: Massachusetts Mutual Life Insurance Company, 1980).

17. Firm size also had a very large effect on lunch breaks, but this was significant for fewer job classifications than retirement pension.

18. See Mellow; and Robert G. Rice, "Skill, Earnings, and the Growth of Wage Supplements," *American Economic Review* (May 1966), 56:583–593.

19. See Lester, pp. 57–67.

20. The survey's verbal instructions indicated that the employee's current job condition was to be the reference point in answering these questions. For a more detailed description of this survey technique, see question 26 in appendix 1A.

21. None of our size variables is correlated with any other at a level greater than .28.

22. See question 19 of appendix 1A. The constant term of our regression represents the evaluation of a white, nonmetropolitan employee. For analyzing the survey data, job classifications have been grouped according to skill level as (1) unskilled, (2) semi-skilled, and (3) skilled.

23. The coefficient of annual family income in this regression was $0.08 (.05) per thousand dollars of income. Thus the income effect in the evaluations is negligible.

24. See question 30, parts (9) and (10) in appendix 1A.

25. See questions 9 and 11 in appendix 1A. The survey's oral instructions indicated that

the desired number of work hours was to be considered with reference to the current wage and usual overtime pay arrangement.

26. A quadratic firm size variable was found to be significant here and was thus included.

27. The variable AGE is represented as the deviation from the mean age of the sample, thirty-six years. SEX is a dummy variable taking the value 1 for males. The constant term therefore represents the discrepancy for a thirty-six-year-old female. SHIFT 2 and SHIFT 3 are dummy variables representing the second and third shifts; WAGE RATE is the straight-time hourly wage; and SEMI-SKILLED and SKILLED are dummy variables representing the semi-skilled and skilled job levels.

28. If fringe benefits were the only factor involved, then it would be cheaper to hire new workers unless the costs of providing the fringe benefits exceeded half of the wage costs for straight-time work. In our sample, benefit costs were typically about 35 percent of wages in large firms, but there are other fixed costs associated with recruiting and training new workers (as well as other benefits not explicitly considered in the survey).

29. L. L. Cummings and C. J. Berger, "Organization Structure: How Does It Influence Attitudes and Behavior," *Organizational Dynamics* (Autumn 1976), 5:34–49.

30. Note that the MRS need not equal the actual wage rate due to institutional constraints on the number of hours worked.

31. These are benefit items 1–9 on questions 26 and 27 in appendix 1A. Items 11–13 are not used in the derivation of the MRS because these benefits would significantly improve working conditions and thus tend to reduce the MRS. Item 10 would increase the time available to the worker and thus also tend to reduce the MRS.

See appendix 1B for a more detailed explanation.

32. Although the workers' evaluations are subject to a certain amount of experimental uncertainty, we nevertheless believe that the *relative* money–time tradeoffs of different workers do accurately reflect the *relative* values of their time.

33. A generalized least squares estimation procedure employing an error components model has been used. The error term has the form u_i & v_{ij}, where i refers to the individual employee and j refers to the response for a particular job benefit. The variances of the two components were found to be approximately equal. Only observations for which both the money and time evaluations are nonzero have been included.

34. These numbers are obtained from regressions between (1) the logarithm of annual sales and the logarithm of number of employees, and (2) the logarithm of number of plants and the logarithm of number of employees.

35. Additional links between job satisfaction and firm size for the sample are discussed in the paper by Jon M. Shepard.

36. Frank Stafford, "Firm Size, Workplace Public Goods and Worker Welfare," Siegfried, ed., *The Economics of Firm Size, Market Structure and Social Performance*, pp. 326–347.

For a review of the existing literature on job satisfaction and organizational size, see Berger and Cummings, pp. 169–208; and E. E. Lawler III, and L. W. Porter, "Properties of Organizational Structure in Relation to Job Attitudes and Behavior," *Psychological Bulletin* (1965), 64:23–51.

37. The marginal wage rate takes into account overtime rates of pay for employees who worked longer than forty hours per week.

38. The generalized least square procedure described in footnote 33 has again been used.

39. This figure is based upon the characteristics of a representative employee in the

sample. We take this to be a white unskilled employee with six years of seniority in a plant of size 50. (A plant size of 50 is used here to be compatible with the range of firm size in the sample, i.e., 50–50,000.) Because of the relatively large standard error of the constant term in equation 6, we cannot make a very precise estimate for the firm size at which there is equality between marginal disutility and the marginal wage rate. The standard error of LOGFIRM-SIZE at equality is .75, which corresponds to the firm size interval of 24–748 employees.

40. For further explanation see Lucia F. Dunn, "Measurement of Internal Income–Leisure Tradeoffs," *Quarterly Journal of Economics* (August 1979), 93:373–393.

41. Including a further term in the polynomial does not statistically improve the fit.

CHAPTER 2

Organizational Size and Worker Satisfaction

Jon M. Shepard and
James G. Hougland, Jr.

IN a 1981 article entitled "Trend Toward Bigness in Business Speeds Up," *U.S. News and World Report* noted an apparent increase in corporate takeovers. The article reports merger experts as contending that the business scene will become more and more dominated by fewer and bigger firms in the decade of the 1980s.[1] Moreover, the policies of the Reagan administration were expected to add considerable fuel to the merger movement.[2]

The trend toward corporate consolidation is viewed by many as a part of what E. F. Schumacher calls the "idolatry of giantism."[3] Fears related to bigness include the reduction of competition and the stifling of innovation, the inability of small businesses to pay rising interest rates fueled in part by big lines of credit, risks encountered by large companies investing in lines of business in which they have little or no expertise, the development of conforming "organization men," worker alienation, worker sabotage, and lowered productivity.

While many fear for the myriad of negative consequences flowing from the consolidation trend, others are optimistic that larger organizations will produce positive results.[4] This lack of consensus, in part, prompted the Columbia Center for Law and Economic Studies to sponsor the larger project investigating political, social, and economic consequences of corporate bigness. The present paper will focus on organization size and worker job satisfaction.

RESEARCH ON ORGANIZATION SIZE AND ATTITUDES

As Porter and Lawler point out, research on the effects of organization structure on job attitudes and behavior did not become intensive until the 1950s.[5] This was the case despite the long-term interest in bureaucracy growing out of Max Weber's work in the 1920s and the Hawthorne Studies in the early 1930s. Classical organization theorists such as Fayol, Urwick, and Taylor failed to recognize the existence of people in organizations, while modern organization theorists such as Likert, McGregor, and Argyris spoke of people without reference to organization structure.[6] If scholars interested in organizations were slow to investigate the effects of organization structure on individual attitudes and behavior, they have since made up for it. Cummings and Berger reported that fifty research studies examining the relationship between organization structure and its members' attitudes and behavior had been conducted between 1964 and 1974.[7]

Prominent among the organization characteristics investigated has been organization size. This includes both organization subunit size (for example, work group, department) and total organization size. Since the present study deals with total organization size, we will emphasize that particular part of the body of literature on the effects of organization structure on its members. It is necessary, however, to review briefly first the research on subunit size.

Organization Subunit Size and Attitudes

Most of the research on organization size and member attitudes has focused on the subunit level within organizations. Consequently, the samples have been work groups, departments, or plants (in multiplant firms). Major reviews of this literature have all reported the same conclusion:

attitudes and behavior of workers tend to be more positive as subunit size decreases.[8] While Worthy did not offer hard evidence, his early statement on the relationship between subunit size and employee attitudes is still taken to represent reality: "Our researches demonstrate that mere size is unquestionably one of the most important factors in determining the quality of employee relationships: the smaller the unit, the higher the morale, and vice versa."[9]

To state that smaller organizations produce better employee attitudes than larger ones, however, is too broad a generalization. The most we can say from this body of literature is that employee attitudes are more positive in smaller groups. This is the case because the units involved in the above studies were primarily subunits of the same organization rather than different organizations.[10] In order to determine the effects of total organization size, we need studies comparing employee attitudes in organizations of varying sizes; however, studies of this kind are much more scarce than those of organization subunits.[11]

Total Organization Size and Employee Attitudes

Most of the research on organization size and employee attitudes has either focused on subunit size within organizations or confounded subunit size and total organization size by combining them in a single sample.[12] This mixing of subunits with total organizations makes it difficult to draw firm conclusions.

Four studies of blue collar workers profess to deal with total organization size and attitudes. Benge, using "attitude toward the boss" as an indicator, reported that morale is higher in smaller companies than in larger companies.[13] The problem with this study is that no information was provided on the number of respondents or the number of companies.

The most often quoted study of total organization size and employee attitudes is Talacchi's. Using the SRA employee inventory in ninety-three firms, Talacchi found an inverse relationship between organization size and job satisfaction.[14] This study, however, has been criticized for mixing subunit size and total organization size. Porter and Lawler point out that, at maximum, forty-five of Talacchi's ninety-three companies were actually factories belonging to only five companies: "Thus, most of the findings . . . are difficult to interpret if one is interested in the effects of total organization size, since the distinction between subunits and total organizations has been completely blurred."[15]

Studies by Gartrell and Scherer come closer to examining employee attitudes by total organization size. In a study of Canadian and U.S. workers, Gartrell reported a positive, but weak, relationship between size and alienation.[16] Scherer, in an analysis of 1972–1973 data collected by Michigan's Survey Research Center, found an inverse relationship between *company* size and job satisfaction.[17] Still, these two researchers blur the total organization-subunit size dimension by limiting size classifications to plants at which employees were located. This approach does not take into account the fact that many of the plants were doubtlessly part of a larger corporate entity and therefore were actually subunits.

Although subject to this same criticism, there have been some studies attempting to assess the influence of total organization size among white collar personnel. Using an instrument based on Maslow's need hierarchy,[18] Porter concluded, "There are no trends in any of the five need areas for small-sized companies to have either larger or smaller perceived deficiencies in need fulfillment than larger-sized companies."[19] He did, however, find an interaction effect between management level and size. Specifically, he found that lower- and lower-middle–level managers in small companies were more satisfied than large company managers at the same level. On the other hand, managers at upper-middle and vice-president levels in larger companies were more satisfied than their counterparts in smaller organizations.[20] Using a modified version of Porter's questionnaire, El Salmi and Cummings came to the opposite conclusion. In their sample, top-level managers in small-sized firms had greater need fulfillment than their peers in larger companies. On the other hand, middle- and lower-level managers in large companies were more satisfied than similar managers in smaller companies.[21] In a later paper, Cummings and El Salmi report that need fulfillment was higher in small companies than either medium-sized or large companies and that managers in medium-sized companies showed the least need fulfillment.[22] England and Lee, in a comparative study of managers in Japan, Korea, and the United States, found that managers from larger companies were more supportive of organizational goals than were managers in smaller organizations.[23] In a study of the nursing staff of three psychiatric hospitals in Adelaide, South Australia, Rump found an inverse relationship between organization size and satisfaction.[24]

As this review of the literature on total organization size and attitudes indicates, research in this area, despite some evidence that total organization size has effects similar to subunit size, is inconsistent and inconclusive, and for at least two basic reasons. First, the distinction between subunit size and total organization size has not been built into research designs. As a result, it is difficult to know whether total organization size has the same effects as subunit size. Second, subunit size has not been controlled when the impact of total organization size has been investigated. It may be, for example, that working in a large organization may not promote higher job dissatisfaction among those working in small subunits. Similarly, employees in small organizations may be highly dissatisfied if they are working in large subunits. The present study attempts to overcome these deficiencies by distinguishing among firm size, plant size, department size, and work group size.

EXPLANATIONS FOR THE EFFECTS OF ORGANIZATION SIZE

Many scholars have pointed out that organization size affects attitudes and behavior through intervening variables because its influences are indirect. Beer, for example, contends that many organization characteristics change as size increases and that these alterations are probably more directly responsible for the observed link between organization size and job satisfaction.[25] Talacchi hypothesizes that organization size affects people through an increased division of labor and greater status differentiation.[26] According to Porter and Lawler, large subunit size lowers cohesiveness, increases task specialization, and creates poor communication. These conditions lead to high job dissatisfaction, which, in turn, heightens turnover, absenteeism, and labor strife.[27] Indik traces job satisfaction, absenteeism, and turnover to the increased role specialization and decreased job complexity brought about by increased organization size.[28] Worthy offers the most comprehensive and succinct summary of organizational change associated with increased size:

In broader terms, the smaller organization represents a simpler social system than does the larger unit. There are fewer people, fewer levels in the organizational hierarchy, and a less minute subdivision of labor. It is easier for the employee to adapt himself to such a simpler system and to win a place in it. His work becomes more meaningful, both to him and to his associates, because he and they can readily see its relation and importance to other functions and to the organization as a whole. The organization operates primarily through the face-to-face relationships of its members and only secondarily through impersonal, institutionalized relationships. The closer relations between the individual employee and the top executive in such a situation are only one aspect—but an important one—of the relatively simple and better-integrated social system of the smaller organization.[29]

METHODS

Sources of data and sampling procedures are described in the first essay in this volume, by Dunn. Measures of variables are shown (with recodes when applicable) in the appendixes to the present paper. Most measures

TABLE 2.1.
Reliability and Descriptive Statistics for JDI Scales

Scale	Cronbach's Alpha	Range of Possible Responses	Mean	Standard Deviation	N
Work	.823	0–54	20.85	12.58	976
Supervision	.848	0–54	31.72	14.00	968
Pay	.755	0–27	12.09	7.37	972
Promotion	.763	0–27	8.34	7.33	964
Co-workers	.861	0–54	31.49	14.58	962

are self-explanatory, but it should be noted that aspects of satisfaction are measured by the job description index (JDI), developed by Smith, Kendall, and Hulin. The index involves indications of "yes," "no," or "?" to descriptive phrases in each of five areas of work.[30] Because of the dimensional approach underlying the index, an overall job satisfaction score is not computed.

The index's validity and reliability have been carefully established.[31] Cronbach's alphas for each scale are shown in the first column of table 2.1. For each scale, an acceptable level of reliability has been obtained. It is also advantageous that completing the JDI instrument does not require a high verbal level because complicated and vague abstractions are avoided. According to Vroom, the index "is without doubt the most

TABLE 2.2
Correlations Between Predictor Variables

	1.	2.	3.	4.	5.	6.	7.	8.	9.	10.	11	12.	13.
1. Sex	1.00												
2. Age	-.24	1.00											
3. Education	.11	-.24	1.00										
4. Racial status	-.11	-.05	-.08	1.00									
5. Marital status	.01	.21	-.06	-.03	1.00								
6. Income	.05	.06	.14	-.09	.39	1.00							
7. Size of community of origin	.07	-.07	.10	.12	-.01	-.03	1.00						
8. Size of community of residence	.07	-.03	.05	.24	-.00	.01	.31	1.00					
9. Rural–urban plant location	-.11	-.03	.02	.38	-.05	-.04	.16	.30	1.00				
10. Skill level of job	.50	-.04	.10	-.16	.11	.14	.02	.04	-.02	1.00			
11. Firm size (log)	-.11	-.01	.03	-.05	-.04	-.00	-.01	-.04	-.01	-.18	1.00		
12. Plant size (log)	-.08	-.04	-.01	-.05	.03	.12	-.02	-.04	-.12	-.18	.27	1.00	
13. Department size (log)	-.24	.05	-.06	.15	-.05	-.03	.02	.01	.07	-.23	.14	.25	1.00
14. Work group size (log)	-.13	.07	-.03	.04	-.00	-.01	-.04	-.04	.02	-.12	.03	.12	.28

carefully constructed measure of job satisfaction in existence today."[32]

Relationships of predictor variables to JDI scales are assessed through correlation and regression analyses. In the regression analyses, all predictors except those related to organization or group size were entered in a single step (p<.10). The size variables were then entered in a second step (p<.10). Through this technique, variables reflecting size could not enter the equation unless they possessed some degree of predictive power after other variables had been controlled.

Correlations between predictor variables are shown in table 2.2. As the table shows, multicollinearity did not pose a serious problem for the regression analysis. It is particularly noteworthy that correlations between aspects of size are only of moderate magnitude.

FINDINGS

Levels of Satisfaction

Mean values for the JDI scales are shown in the third column of table 2.1. Respondents tended to express more satisfaction regarding supervision and co-workers than other aspects of their jobs. Work and promotions elicited particularly low expressions of satisfaction.

Smith, Kendall, and Hulin have presented average scores for large samples of men and women pooled across twenty-one plants.[33] Levels of expressed satisfaction are lower in the sample for the present study than in the pooled twenty-one–plant sample. For example, the mean score of 20.85 regarding work in table 2.1 can be compared with means of 36.57 for men and 35.74 for women reported by Smith, Kendall, and Hulin.[34] Similar differences were found for the other scales.

Results of Correlation Analysis

Although the correlations are generally small, table 2.3 shows that a number of significant relationships exist. Attitudes toward work and pay are particularly likely to be related to the predictor variables. The zero-order correlations suggest that older, married workers with higher skill levels are relatively likely to express satisfaction with work.

Workers in rural plants and those with higher incomes are relatively

TABLE 2.3
Zero-Order Correlations = JDI Variables with Predictors

	Work	Supervision	Pay	Promotion	Co-workers
Sex (male = 1)	.11**	.01	− .00	.06*	.05
Age	.17**	.02	.01	.07*	.02
Education	− .01	− .02	.02	− .06	− .02
Racial status (white = 1)	.09**	− .01	− .09*	.14***	.02
Marital status (married = 1)	.14***	.01	.01	− .04	.03
Income	.07*	.01	.12**	− .05	− .01
Size of community of origin	− .00	− .01	− .04	.02	− .02
Size of community of residence	.03	− .04	− .06	.03	− .01
Rural−urban plant location (urban = 1)	.09**	− .02	− .23***	.08*	− .10**
Skill level of job	.21***	.01	− .07*	− .06	− .01
Firm size (log)	− .06	− .00	.13***	.11**	− .05
Plant size (log)	− .05	.03	.10**	.09**	− .06
Department size (log)	− .10**	.05	.09**	.12**	− .06
Work group size (log)	.00	.03	− .02	.01	.02

*p≤.05.
**p≤.01.
***p≤.0001.

likely to express satisfaction with pay. However, the relatively small correlation involving income, considered in combination with the small negative correlation involving skill level, suggests that the ability of income to increase satisfaction with pay is limited by a tendency for workers to compare their pay levels with other workers of similar occupational status.

Although table 2.3 contains several significant correlations, no single variable stands out as a consistently useful predictor. Every predictor that generated three or more significant correlations is shown to have inconsistencies in the directions of the relationships. It is particularly important to note that both increases and decreases in organization size can be shown to be related to specific dimensions of satisfaction. Some hints of patterns exist, however. Satisfaction with work shows some tendency to be enhanced by small organization size. On the other hand, the resources available to large organizations appear to promote some satisfaction with pay and promotion. Satisfaction with the more interpersonal aspects of the job (supervision and co-workers) is not significantly related to size.

Results of Regression Analyses

The usefulness of zero-order correlations is diminished by the fact that potentially confounding variables are not controlled. Table 2.4 therefore summarizes results of regression analyses in which all variables significantly related to a dimension of satisfaction are entered and controlled. Conclusions suggested by table 2.4 are quite consistent with those suggested by the simpler correlation coefficients. Variables in the model more

TABLE 2.4
Summary of Regression Analyses (Standardized Regression Coefficients)

	Work	Supervision	Pay	Promotion	Co-workers
Sex	.08	—	—	.15	—
Age	.21	—	—	—	—
Education	—	—	—	− .08	—
Racial status	—	—	—	.08	—
Marital status	—	—	− .09	− .08	—
Income	—	—	.17	—	—
Size of community of origin	—	—	—	—	—
Size of community of residence	—	—	—	—	—
Rural–urban plant location	.08	− .07	− .27	—	− .11
Skill level of job	.19	—	− .07	—	—
Firm size (log)	—	—	.17	.15	—
Plant size (log)	—	—	—	—	− .07
Department size (log)	− .09	—	—	.10	—
Work group size (log)	—	.06	—	—	—
R^2	.11	.01	.12	.07	.02

successfully predict satisfaction with work and pay than with the other dimensions. Focusing specifically on the size variables, small department size is shown to be related to somewhat greater satisfaction with work but to somewhat less satisfaction with promotions. Large firm size is related to somewhat greater satisfaction with pay and promotions. Plant size and work group size are associated with only one dimension of satisfaction each.

DISCUSSION

The present research represents an attempt to clarify the relationship between size and satisfaction by (1) distinguishing among firm size, plant size, department size, and work group size; (2) relating size to five specific dimensions of satisfaction; and (3) using regression analyses to control for other significant predictors when examining size–satisfaction relationships. The results indicate that satisfaction with the relatively tangible rewards involved in pay and promotion is enhanced by larger firm size and, in the case of promotion, department size. However, the more intangible rewards associated with work itself may be somewhat more enjoyable in smaller departments. Interpersonal relationships associated with supervision and co-workers are not greatly affected by size. Slight tendencies exist for satisfaction with supervision to increase with large work groups (conceivably reflecting a tendency for more capable supervisors to be assigned to larger groups or a desire among some workers to escape the close supervision found in small groups) and for satisfaction with co-workers to be associated with smaller plants.

Although directions of relationships between aspects of size and dimensions of satisfaction are suggested by these results, the small correlation and regression coefficients suggest that statements about causation must be treated with caution. Indeed, the general weakness of the relationships may constitute the most important finding of this research. Considerable controversy has existed about the possibly deleterious effects of increasing size on organizations, their participants, and the larger society. While this essay speaks only to a small subset of those concerns, it does indicate that large organizations are not associated with dramatic increases in dissatisfaction.

A possible explanation for this finding has been provided by Hall, who suggests that the effects of size are often moderated by other factors. While large organization size inevitably produces tendencies toward depersonalization and stress, these tendencies may be moderated by such structural arrangements as granting autonomy to subunits.[35] In addition, the well-established tradition of research on the informal work group suggests that interactions between co-workers buffer individuals from the effects of large organization size. Since contemporary economic and technological conditions seem conducive to large organization size, it is important to understand the potential for structural modifications and informal relationships to moderate the effects of size on the individual.

APPENDIX 2A: MEASUREMENT OF PREDICTOR VARIABLES

Sex

Are you:
1. Male
2. Female

NOTE: Female coded "0"; male coded "1."

Age

In what year were you born? _____

Income

Approximately what was your total *yearly* family income from all sources in 1981 before taxes? $_____

Education

How many years of schooling did you complete (including college, if any)? _____

Marital Status

Check below your marital status
1. Single
2. Married
3. Widowed, Divorced, or Separated

NOTE: Categories 1 and 3 were combined for regression analysis and coded "0"; category 2 was coded "1."

Racial Status

Check below your ethnic background:
1. White
2. Black
3. Hispanic (Spanish-speaking)
4. Oriental
5. Other (Specify) _____

NOTE: Categories 2–5 were combined for regression analysis and coded "1"; category 1 was coded "0."

Size of Community of Origin
 Check below the type of place you lived most of the time when
 you were growing up:
 1. On a farm
 2. In or near a small town (under 2,500 people)
 3. In or near a larger town (2,500 to 10,000 people)
 4. In or near a small city (10,000 to 50,000)
 5. Within a medium-size city (50,000 to 200,000)
 6. In the suburbs of a medium-size city (50,000 to 200,000)
 7. Within a large city (over 250,000 people)
 8. In the suburbs of a large city (over 250,000)
NOTE: Categories 5 and 6 and categories 7 and 8 are combined for
 regression analysis.

Plant Location
 1. Nonmetropolitan
 2. Metropolitan
NOTE: Nonmetropolitan coded "0"; metropolitan coded "1."

Size of Community of Residence
 Check below the type of place you currently live in:
 1. On a farm
 2. In or near a small town (under 2,500 people)
 3. In or near a larger town (2,500 to 10,000 people)
 4. In or near a small city (10,000 to 50,000)
 5. Within a medium-size city (50,000 to 200,000)
 6. In the suburbs of a medium-size city (50,000 to 200,000)
 7. Within a large city (over 250,000)
 8. In the suburbs of a large city (over 250,000)
NOTE: Categories 5 and 6 and categories 7 and 8 are combined for
 regression analysis.

Skill Level
 What is your current job title? _____
NOTE: Responses were categorized as follows:
 1. Unskilled
 2. Semi-skilled
 3. Skilled

Work Group Size
 How many people do you work with in your immediate work
 group? _____

Department Size

Approximately how many people work in your department? _____

Plant Size

Designated by company officials

Company Size

Designated by company officials

APPENDIX 2B: MEASUREMENT OF CRITERION VARIABLES

EACH of the five scales was presented on a separate page. The instructions for each scale asked the subject to put "Y" beside an item if the item described the particular aspect of his job (e.g., work, pay), "N" if the item did not describe that aspect, or "?" if he could not decide. The response shown beside each item is the one scored in the satisfied direction for each scale. These answers were each scored 3. Opposite answers were scored 0. Question marks were coded 1.

Work
Y	Fascinating
N	Routine
Y	Satisfying
N	Boring
Y	Good
Y	Creative
Y	Respected
N	Hot
Y	Pleasant
Y	Useful
N	Tiresome
Y	Healthful
Y	Challenging
N	On your feet
N	Frustrating
N	Simple
N	Endless
Y	Gives sense of accomplishment

Supervision

- _Y_ Asks my advice
- _N_ Hard to please
- _N_ Impolite
- _Y_ Praises good work
- _Y_ Tactful
- _Y_ Influential
- _Y_ Up-to-date
- _N_ Doesn't supervise enough
- _N_ Quick-tempered
- _Y_ Tells me where I stand
- _N_ Annoying
- _N_ Stubborn
- _Y_ Knows job well
- _N_ Bad
- _Y_ Intelligent
- _Y_ Leaves me on my own
- _Y_ Around when needed
- _N_ Lazy

Co-workers

- _Y_ Stimulating
- _N_ Boring
- _N_ Slow
- _Y_ Ambitious
- _N_ Stupid
- _Y_ Responsible
- _Y_ Fast
- _Y_ Intelligent
- _N_ Easy to make enemies
- _N_ Talk too much
- _Y_ Smart
- _N_ Lazy
- _N_ Unpleasant
- _N_ No privacy
- _Y_ Active
- _N_ Narrow interests

_Y_ Loyal
_N_ Hard to meet

Pay
_Y_ Income adequate for normal expenses
_Y_ Satisfactory profit sharing
_N_ Barely live on income
_N_ Bad
_Y_ Income provides luxuries
_N_ Insecure
_N_ Less than I deserve
_Y_ Highly paid
_N_ Underpaid

Promotions
_Y_ Good opportunity for advancement
_N_ Opportunity somewhat limited
_Y_ Promotion on ability
_N_ Dead-end job
_Y_ Good chance for promotion
_N_ Unfair promotion policy
_N_ Infrequent promotions
_Y_ Regular promotions
_Y_ Fairly good chance for promotion

NOTES

1. "Trend Toward Bigness in Business Speeds Up," *U.S. News and World Report,* August 24, 1981, pp. 69–70.

2. This trend is reflected in the value of shipments by the 200 largest firms in the United States, as a proportion of the nation's total shipments. In 1967, the 200 largest firms accounted for 42.6 percent of the nation's total shipments; ten years later, the 200 largest firms accounted for 45.3 percent of the nation's total shipments.

3. E. F. Schumacher, *Small Is Beautiful: A Study of Economics As If People Mattered* (London: Bland & Briggs, 1973).

4. Lyman W. Porter, "Where Is the Organization Now?" *Harvard Business Review* (November–December 1963), 41:53–61; idem, "Job Attitudes in Management: IV. Perceived Deficiencies in Need Fulfillment as a Function of Size of Company," *Journal of Applied Psychology* (December 1963), 6:386–397.

5. Lyman W. Porter and Edward E. Lawler III, "Properties of Organization Structure in Relation to Job Attitudes and Job Behavior," *Psychological Bulletin* (1965), 64:23–51.

6. See Warren G. Bennis, "Leadership Theory and Administrative Behavior: The Problem of Authority," *Administrative Science Quarterly* (March 1970), 15:1–10.

7. Larry L. Cummings and Chris J. Berger, "Organization Structure: How Does It Influence Attitudes and Performance?" *Organizational Dynamics* (Autumn 1976), pp. 34–49.

8. Bernard P. Indik, "Some Effects of Organization Size on Member Attitudes and Behavior," *Human Relations* (November 1963), 16:369–384; Lawrence R. James and Allan P. Jones, "Organizational Structure: A Review of Structural Dimensions and Their Conceptual Relationships with Individual Attitudes and Behavior," *Organizational Behavior and Human Performance* (June 1976), 16:74–113; Porter and Lawler; George Strauss and Leonard R. Sayles, *Personnel: The Human Problems of Management* (Englewood Cliffs, N.J.: Prentice-Hall, 1960); Edwin J. Thomas and Clinton F. Fink, "Effects of Group Size," *Psychological Bulletin* (July 1963), 60:371–384; and Morris S. Viteles, *Motivation and Morale in Industry* (New York: Norton, 1953).

It also appears that smaller subunits experience less absenteeism, turnover, and labor disputes. There is, however, no consistent relationship between subunit size and accident rates and productivity (Porter and Lawler, p. 39).

9. James C. Worthy, "Organizational Structure and Employee Morale," *American Sociological Review* (April 1950), 15:172–173.

10. Porter, "Job Attitudes in Management," and "Where Is the Organization Now?"

11. Porter and Lawler, p. 40.

12. There has been an almost total absence of research on total organization size and employee behavior. In a study of eight English firms in the light engineering industry, Ingham found a positive relationship between firm size and absenteeism; a similar relationship was not found for turnover. See Geoffrey K. Ingham, *Size of Industrial Organization and Worker Behavior* (Cambridge: Cambridge University Press, 1970).

13. E. J. Benge, "How To Learn What Workers Think of Job and Boss," *Factory Management and Maintenance* (May 1944), 102:101–104.

14. Sergio Talacchi, "Organization Size, Individual Attitudes and Behavior: An Empirical Study," *Administrative Science Quarterly* (December 1960), 5:398–420.

15. Porter and Lawler, p. 41.

16. John W. Gartrell, *Organization and Alienation: A Background Report,* Study No. 27 (Ottawa, Canada: Royal Commission on Corporate Concentration, Ministry of Supply and Services, 1976).

17. F. M. Scherer, "Industrial Structure, Scale Economies, and Worker Alienation," pp. 105–121, in Robert T. Masson and P. David Qualls, eds., *Essays on Industrial Organization in Honor of Joe S. Bain* (Cambridge, Mass: Ballinger, 1976).

18. Abraham Maslow, *Motivation and Personality* (New York: Harper & Row, 1954).

19. Porter, "Job Attitudes in Management," p. 389.

20. Porter, "Where Is the Organization Now?" and "Job Attitudes in Management."

21. Aly M. El Salmi and Larry L. Cummings, "Managers' Perceptions of Needs and Need Satisfactions as a Function of Interactions Among Organizational Variables," *Personnel Psychology* (1968), 21:465–477.

22. Larry L. Cummings and Aly M. El Salmi, "The Impact of Role Diversity, Job Level, and Organizational Size on Managerial Satisfaction," *Administrative Science Quarterly* (March 1970), 15:1–10.

23. George W. England and Raymond Lee, "Organization Size as an Influence on Perceived Organizational Goals: A Comparative Study Among American, Japanese, and Korean Managers," *Organizational Behavior and Human Performance* (February 1973), 9:48–58.

24. E. E. Rump, "Size of Psychiatric Hospitals and Nurses' Job Satisfaction," *Journal of Occupational Psychology* (1979), 52:255–265.

25. Michael Beer, "Organizational Size and Job Satisfaction," *Academy of Management Journal* (1964), 7:34–44.

26. Tallachi, p. 401.

27. Porter and Lawler, p. 40.

28. Indik, p. 380.

29. Worthy, p. 173.

30. Patricia C. Smith, Lorne M. Kendall, and Charles L. Hulin, *The Measurement of Satisfaction in Work and Retirement* (Chicago: Rand McNally, 1969).

31. James L. Price, *Handbook of Organizational Measurement* (Lexington, Mass.: Heath, 1972), pp. 166–167.

32. Victor H. Vroom, *Work and Motivation* (New York: Wiley, 1964), p. 100.

33. Smith, Kendall, and Hulin, chapter 5.

34. See Price, p. 166.

35. Richard H. Hall, *Organizations: Structure and Process,* 3rd ed. (Englewood Cliffs, N.J.: Prentice-Hall, 1982), pp. 58–60.

COMMENTATORS' REMARKS

ORLEY ASHENFELTER

I 'M especially pleased to be able to comment on these papers because both of them reflect a kind of research effort that's all too often missing, especially in economics. Collecting your own data for an economic study, as the authors have done here, is much to be admired, but not to be emulated. Fortunately, the authors of these papers have not taken the profession's advice.

Lucia Dunn points out that the relationship historically found between the establishment's size, or the firm's size, and the wage rates it pays can be attributed to three different factors.

The explanations have been, first, that the differences in wage rates really reflect the differences in worker qualifications. It may be, for example, that for one reason or another, large firms demand workers with greater qualifications and therefore have to pay more to get them.

The way to test this hypothesis is to collect data like those used in these papers, where workers are doing the same kinds of jobs and presumably have the same kinds of qualifications, and to determine whether the firm size–wage rate relationship continues to exist. Even with these data, however, it would be interesting to know whether workers in the various occupational groups really do have similar levels of schooling, experience, time on the job, and so forth. This would doubly insure that in the authors' constructions of the data set the workers do have the same qualifications.

Assuming the authors have done a good enough job, a relationship between firm size and wage rates found in these data presumably cannot reflect differences in qualifications associated with differences in pay. Since the relationship does persist, we can reject the differential qualifications explanation.

A second explanation for the wage–firm size relationship is that, for one reason or another, large firms have to pay higher wages to compensate workers for the unpleasant characteristics of working in large firms. This unpleasantness can come from many sources, ranging all the way from having to work longer hours than desired to having to put up with unpleasant supervisors. Both papers address whether or not the relationship of firm size to wage rates can be explained by this hypothesis. They conclude that it cannot.

I want to come back to this issue later, because it is the major alternative explanation.

The third explanation for the firm size–wage rate relationship is the so-called "monopoly rents" hypothesis. The idea here is that large firms have managed to exploit some monopoly power. Perhaps the workers in large firms have therefore managed to do likewise. This idea certainly has at least some superficial plausibility.

I have often thought, for example, that you could explain the presence of unionization in certain parts of American industry by the fact that there is a particular productive factor to be exploited. The profits available to this factor might be exploited by lower prices for consumers, higher profits for the owners of the factor, or conceivably by higher wage rates. Factors susceptible to exploitation of this sort range all the way from technologies that lead to natural monopolies, as in the newspaper industry, to natural resources such as coal or oil.

If the "monopoly rents" hypothesis for the explanation of the wage rate–firm size relationship is correct, two important issues must be raised. First, does the presence of this relationship signal an inefficiency in the allocation of resources? It seems that the source of the monopoly rents now becomes of importance. For example, if the monopoly rents arise because of a natural resource, perhaps it is irrelevant whether workers or shareholders capture the profits so generated. Coal and hydropower will still exist, after all, and perhaps they will be efficiently utilized also. On the other hand, the presence of monopoly rents may imply an inefficient allocation of resources. For example, in the trucking industry, government regulations have historically led to the rents that firms and workers have shared and are now losing.

Second, what is the distribution of these monopoly rents among workers? We would like to know, if there are rents in the system, do black workers get their fair share of them? Do women get their fair share of them? These are important issues for further research.

Finally, I would like to turn to the broader question of whether the econometric analysis in these papers is strong enough to back up the notion that there are rents in the system, that workers are capturing some of them, and that from them comes the relationship between firm size and wage rates.

It seems to me that the evidence in these two studies is consistent with this hypothesis. First of all, we find that wage rate differences are correlated with firm size. We also find that workers are not happier in small firms than in large firms with respect to working conditions. Moreover, workers in large firms are happier with respect to pay than are workers in small firms. These findings suggest that monopoly rents are being accrued by large firms and that workers are capturing some of them. Despite these findings, however, one may still want to suspend judgment on the monopoly rents explanation.

Should we believe that any rents in the economic system are likely to be correlated with firm size? That proposition is apparently taken as an article of faith in this paper, and I would have thought that, at a minimum, we deserve from the authors a demonstration that there is at least some reason to suppose such a relationship exists.

Also, there is at least one alternative explanation for the authors' findings: working conditions may, in fact, be different in large and small firms, despite the care with which the authors' data are constructed. For example, there seems to be a greater gap between the number of hours that workers would like to work and the number of hours they do work in the large than in the small firms. Perhaps this accounts for the wage difference observed.

One thing the authors could do to test this hypothesis is to include in their analyses some measure of the difference between the actual and desired hours and see whether or not the correlation between firm size and wage differences is really due to the fact that in the larger firms there is less flexibility for workers with respect to their hours. It may be that there is a compensating wage differential associated with inflexibility in worker hours and that large firms tend to have less flexibility in this dimension than do small firms. One could think of a variety of reasons for this. This seems to me to be the only serious alternative candidate for explaining the wage rate–firm size relationship found.

One other factor bears on the possibility of drawing generalizations from this study. The sample is specific to the plastics industry. One must always wonder whether the results found there could be generalized to other industries. Since there are no returns to scale in the industry, why are there rents in the large firms that do not exist in the smaller firms? It seems the authors owe us an answer to this question if we are to accept the monopoly rents hypothesis.

In conclusion, I want to say again how much I appreciate this research study. I think it's a fine effort and something that will produce more useful results in the future as well.

PETER ECKSTEIN

THIS has been a very useful effort, enabling us to get a handle on three separate dimensions of size—firm size, plant size, and department size. There's a vast wealth of data these researchers have gathered and personally exploited.

There is also a danger, however, in this kind of research. Size has many correlates. The authors have developed very good evidence that wages and hours are a direct function both of the size of plants and the size of firms. Yet, as we try to measure the impact of size, what we really want to measure is not these obvious economic characteristics of larger plants or firms but rather some *other* variables that might be more inherently attached to the larger corporation.

The real issue—for these papers and for this conference—is this: Is there a kind of inherent "nastiness" associated with a larger firm or a larger plant? If so, that nastiness may have manifestations in such features as harsh supervision or rigid working conditions. It is one thing to say that large plants work long hours and long hours create tension. It is another, more interesting thing to say that large plants create tension well beyond what can be explained by the longer hours they work. I question whether certain parts of the papers are making that distinction.

In the Dunn paper there is a lot of good work on wages, fringe benefits, and working conditions. However, let me dwell on my area of substantial disagreement, which is the analysis of the relationship of work, leisure, and wages to the marginal disutility of labor. There are two sets of equations that deal with this.

First, there is the analysis of the discrepancy between the desired hours worked and actual hours worked. Are workers happy with the number of hours they have to work? Dunn reaches the interesting conclusion that if you look at the subset of workers who wish to work more, the discrepancy that says, "I'm not getting enough work," increases with plant size. And if you look at those who wish to work less, the discrepancy increases with firm size.

What concerns me is that if you ask, "Am I happy with how long I'm working?," the next question is, "How long am I working?" Obviously, if I am working eighty-five hours a week in a plastics factory, I'm unhappy. I want to work fewer hours regardless of whether it's a great, big plastic factory or it's a little, bitty plastic factory. Eighty-five hours is too long. So I don't think we can really specify an equation that seeks to explain how happy people are with their working hours without including the basic variable of the number of hours actually worked.

Of course, we do find in the Dunn data that both in larger plants over most size ranges and in larger firms in most size ranges hours worked do go up with size. For purposes of explaining satisfaction with hours worked, I am sure that the longer work week is the dominant characteristic of these larger firms. It has yet to be shown that, if one controls for longer hours worked, there is any additional influence of size on this element of satisfaction, any inherent nastiness or disutility that can be measured.

We should turn next to the "marginal rate of substitution," which I would be more than comfortable calling the "marginal disutility of work"—how much would you have to pay me to get me to work another hour, given that it is getting a little vexatious to work more.

Dunn's major finding here is that the marginal disutility of work is also a function of firm size and plant size. It goes down and then goes again up with larger firm size.

Again, we must ask a basic question: Are we observing the inherent nastiness that attaches to large size—"You would have to pay me a whole lot more to go back into that horrible plant"—or are we observing simply a byproduct of the relationship between size and the hours worked and wages paid?

Dunn's choice is clear. She attributes this increased marginal disutility of work to "the negative features of size"—the less interesting job, the disparity in hours of work, a long list of possible nasty features of the larger plant or the larger firm.

I would begin with a very different analysis. We would have to recognize that the marginal disutility of work is not exogenous to the labor market, to the basic arrangement by which wages and hours are set. In fact, it is highly related to hours worked and wages paid, independent of such factors as working conditions, plant size, or firm size.

The actual marginal disutility we may observe is very much a function of the wage itself. The easiest case is that in which the individual worker has the ability to adjust the hours worked. All economic theory says that in this case the marginal disutility work would equal the wage rate. The worker adjusts his or her hours so as to achieve a static equilibrium in which the marginal disutility of work just equals the wage rate itself.

Obviously, this is not the typical case in large modern corporations, where hours are imposed by management. My own hypothesis, however, would be that even in this case there are accommodations—some instantaneous and some over time—that tend to equate the marginal disutility of the work and the wage rate. There is a dynamic equilibrium at work—not an exact one, as in the static model, but an approximate one.

Let me illustrate with an example of two identical twins. Assume you sent the two twins, both single men, into separate factories. In one factory, regardless of size and working conditions, the pay is five dollars an hour, and, in the other, the pay is ten dollars an hour. The poor twin might be accommodated immediately. A 40-hour week might be perfect for the poor twin, and his marginal disutility of work would equal his wage. He can only earn enough to pay for basic necessities, so he needs to work a full 2,000 hours a year.

But consider the rich twin, the one who is earning twice as much. He might be getting more money than he needs, so he is saying, "When I've got the money to buy an electric guitar I can play on four-day weekends, or to bum around in Florida for several months a year, why should I put up with this hassle of 2,000 hours a year in the factory?" He wishes that he could earn that ten dollars an hour while working a fewer number of hours. So there is an initial disequilibrium.

But there can be an accommodation to that disequilibrium. First of all, that rich worker has the option of absenteeism. We've seen some substantial accommodation in this form. Over time there's a tendency for the rich twin to accommodate in another way, by escalating his life style. Even if he can't adjust his hours, he can afford to do something his poor twin can't afford to do, and that is to get married. Maybe he can even afford to have children and take on a more expensive life style. Later on, if he's rich enough, he can even afford to get divorced. Or maybe he indulges certain other expenditures—a large house, a boat, a summer cottage.

This escalation has a tendency to accommodate the worker to the larger number of hours worked. After a while he needs all that extra money because he has locked in numerous fixed expenditures. In short, there are many reasons for expecting that the marginal disutility of work will be highly related to the number of hours worked and to the rate of wages in the firm. In the equations Dunn has presented, you will find that the relationship to firm size shown by the marginal disutility of labor is strikingly similar to the relationships shown by the marginal wage rate and the hours worked. The marginal disutility of labor has a J-shaped relationship with firm size. Likewise, the marginal wage rate and the hours worked also show a J-shaped relationship with firm size and a linear relationship with plant size.*

So I'm not convinced. This analysis of the marginal disutility of labor does not prove any clear, independent relationship to the nastiness—or the pleasurability—of working in the larger plant or the larger corporation. In fact, all we are really seeing is that the marginal disutility of labor is a function of wages and hours.†

I'd like to return to Shepard and Hougland's conclusion. They say that their most important finding is the general weakness of the relationship of size with satisfaction in the job because "the effects of size are often moderated by other factors." Perhaps this is just as well. In spite of the much-heralded power of academic thinkers to influence public policy, very few corporate mergers are going to be significantly deterred by a clear-cut sociological finding that worker satisfaction decreases with corporate size. It may be fortunate, then, that such findings continue to be blurred, at best. It may also be accurate, because the quality of life

---

*Dunn states that the bottom of the "J" is at a firm size of 3,400 for the marginal disutility of labor, 200 for the wage rate, and 1,300 for hours worked.

†The issue could have been examined more directly by first regressing disutility on marginal wages and hours and, if possible, on such other relevant factors as intramarginal income, dependents, financial commitments, assets, and wage history. The size variables—plant and firm—could then be added to the equation to see whether they added any independent explanatory power. Fortunately, the data gathered appear to be rich enough to permit this kind of analysis.

can vary tremendously across large corporations and even within the same large corporation.

Just a quick example. Recently Ford Motor Company initiated a quality-of-worklife program in some, but not all, of its parts depots. When the recent wage concessions contract came up for ratification, workers in the depots with the quality-of-worklife program ratified the contract overwhelmingly. Where the program was not in effect, workers defeated the contract.

In short, there is much room for variation in job satisfaction within the modern corporation. Sadly, it has been possible to dehumanize the large corporation. Happily, it is within our ingenuity to humanize it again.

ELI GINZBERG

I KNEW that with Peter and Orley in front of me I didn't have to do more than note: "I got the papers; I didn't fully understand them, but I like them."

But my long-time research has been in and around the arena of work, so I'm going to talk to that theme rather than to the papers.

Professor Kaden, before he left, said that I was writing a book with a collaborator, George Vojta, which we are calling "Human Resources in Large Organizations: Challenge Without Response." That's our working title. The theme, as you can see from our title, centers around large organizations and their use of people. Since we are meeting in New Jersey, let me recall what my old friend James P. Mitchell, the distinguished secretary of labor in the Eisenhower administration, had to say about frustrated or alienated workers. Prior to becoming secretary, Jim was the general manager of Bloomingdale's in New York City. At lunch one day, I asked him about his views on frustrated workers. Jim said, "Frustrated workers? What the hell are they?" I said "You know, frustrated workers." He said "I don't know. After all, if the labor market is good and workers are frustrated they can look and find another job. There are costs to changing jobs, but if the labor market is strong, a good worker can surely make a change. And if there are a lot of unemployed people around and a worker has a job, he will not be very frustrated."

I believe that Jim Mitchell's comment is worth remembering, especially these days with unemployment at such high levels. I have just returned from a visit to Germany, where they are experiencing a 300 percent increase in unemployment in two years—from 800,000 to an estimated 2.5 million by next spring. As you know, the unemployment rate in Great Britain is over 13 percent.

At a time of such high and still growing unemployment, I question the utility of placing much emphasis on "frustrated" workers. The key challenge is to see that many of the unemployed get back to work, sooner rather than later.

A few comments about the context of the papers: a manufacturing model was used. I want to remind everybody that about seven out of ten jobs in the United States at this time, and even more in the future, will lie outside of manufacturing and the other goods-producing industries. Service jobs, mostly white collar work, have come to dominate our economy.

The city I come from, New York, has six out of seven jobs outside of goods production, that is, other than manufacturing and construction. There is a tremendous difference in my view between working in a plastics plant and working in an office, be the office a bank, Columbia University, or Mount Sinai Hospital. A manufacturing plant and an office belong to two different worlds. If you don't believe it, I suggest that you look at Robert Schrank's book called *10,000 Working Days*, published by MIT Press.

Schrank, a perceptive analyst, has had tremendous experience in many different sectors of the economy. He details in his book how he felt after making the transition from the factory floor to white collar work, where people spent their time at conferences. He said, "Do you call that work?" One cannot deal with work and working unless one specifies the work environment in which people are engaged.

Second, concepts of satisfaction and dissatisfaction must be dealt with dynamically, as Peter suggested, in terms of what people expect, as well as what they have invested in getting prepared to work. Expectations and investments are the key to satisfactions.

I studied at Heidelberg in 1928–1929. I recall students who, after obtaining a doctorate, went out into the labor market, couldn't find a job, and returned to the university and obtained a second degree. Once again they couldn't get a job, and at that point they joined the Nazi party. In my view, Hitler's success was closely tied to the growing dissatisfaction of large numbers of educated persons who couldn't find a place in the labor market.

In exploring the question of work dissatisfaction it is necessary to inquire into how much effort, investment, and involvement, people have devoted to preparing themselves for work.

Admittedly, other people may also experience dissatisfactions at work. I never thought that an assembly line job was a fulfilling activity, but nevertheless, many assembly workers in autos, rubber tires, etc. received above-par wages, which took care of some, if not all, of their frustrations.

I believe that a modern society must be most concerned about whether large numbers of people are unable to find work. In this view I can call on the authority of Pope John Paul II, who has stressed in recent communications the horrendous societal costs of large-scale unemployment and the need to address the issue and develop solutions.

I have no doctrinal objections to exploring the theme of "the quality of working life." But one can talk meaningfully about the quality of working life only if people have a working life. The fundamental danger at the present time is that many people these days are cut off from any type of working life.

The last point I want to explore relates to the dissatisfactions of many people who work in large organizations. And in that connection, I want to focus on middle management, who comprise the largest number of dissatisfied persons.

Ordinary workers don't expect too much from their jobs. They look forward to decent earnings. They expect to be in a position where their supervisors can't stomp on them. They want to be able to fool around a bit at work and not lose their jobs if they come in drunk once or twice. They want the boss to treat them more or less equitably. Years ago, Ivar Berg and I wrote a book on *Democratic Values and the Rights of Management,* which drew attention to these basics that could be subsumed in the theme "due process in the work place."

But it is middle management that is caught up in the bureaucratic excrescences of large organizations. My friend John Gardner commented that "middle management is like the Van Allen belt: nothing can get through in either direction." That's a pretty frustrating environment if messages don't come down and information doesn't get up.

The amazing thing is not that large organizations are in trouble—and they will be in considerably more trouble in my opinion—but that they have been able to make crucial decisions and earn considerable profits over many years. Of course, if one looks at International Harvester and several other large organizations, it is far from clear whether the past will continue to be prologue.

A second point worth noting is that every large organization is a political entity, which means that people get rewarded largely on the basis of their political skills, not in terms of their professional competence and performance. The larger the organization and the more complex it is, the more the payoff is for political skill. It's who you know and how you play the game, not what you contribute.

The third point is that many large organizations are wrapped up in their own silly rules and regulations. In the former days I did a little consulting for Dupont. This cutting edge company did not permit its research staff to go into the laboratories on Saturdays and Sundays. Why? "We must keep the entire premise locked; otherwise our insurance rates will go up."

Just think about the message that is coming from the executive committee: insurance rates are more important than the commitment of the senior research staff to work to their capacity.

The next point relates to the reward system. As in all bureaucracies, the system is basically perverse. One gets rewarded for moving up through the organization. The more peaceful one is, the less one rocks the boat, the higher one goes.

If rewards are geared at best more to personality than to performance, to conformity more than to innovation, it should be no surprise that many large organizations are in trouble.

Let me conclude by reminding you that if alienation were as serious a problem as Karl Marx considered it to be, we would have had long before now a revolution. In the absence of a revolution we are justified in downgrading the alienation theme—at least somewhat.

As you will recall, Durkheim tied alienation to suicide. Well, we have a relatively high suicide rate, but there is little if any evidence tying it to gross discontent on the job.

We need to rethink the theme in macro context. That's where the major issues are. I don't want to suggest that Professor Dunn's and Professor Shepard's hard work is unimportant. But from my perspective, it is essential to place it in a larger context.

DIALOGUE

MR. GINZBERG: I change my role to that of acting chairman. I am supposed to make sure that a discussion from the floor occurs.

MR. WHITE: I want to address two aspects of Professor Dunn's work: the comparison between the marginal wage rate and the wage rate paid, and the discussion of how long people want to work.

There is a discrepancy there that I'm surprised Orley didn't point out. The workers in the small firms at the margin are being paid less than their marginal disutility, but they don't seem to want to work less. The workers in the large firms are being paid more than their marginal disutility, but they don't seem to want to work more. There's a discrepancy there. And the second point is, assuming that people can't adjust the number of hours they can work at the margin, they must judge their jobs on the basis of that lump of 40 hours a week, or 2,000 hours a year, and what the overall utility or disutility that lump gives them.

Unfortunately, everything you have measured here is at the margin. Marginal calculations make sense for differentiating among the three hypotheses only if people can adjust at the margin. If not, then you must look at the overall summation of utility and disutility compared with the overall wage plus the package of fringe benefits, because you haven't measured that intramarginal disutility.

It may be the case that for the first couple of hours, people would just love to work in a small firm. They'd pay you to work in a small firm, and it's only at the thirty-ninth hour that the disutility gets up to around $6 an hour, whereas if you go into an auto assembly plant, the first hour and the last hour, it's all got a disutility of $4.50.

MS. DUNN: That is a good point. The discussion of disutility all refers to the last hour of work. I don't have a total measure of disutility for all hours worked.

I don't know how you would get it. If you take a sample of people where some work ten hours, some twelve hours, some twenty-five hours, etc., then you might be able to draw some inferences from that. But I do not have such a measure of total disutility. My measure is for the last hour of work. However, I should point out that economists feel that's where the action is, that's the determining hour.

MR. WHITE: Only for those hours.

MS. DUNN: Let me address your point about my finding that large firm employees want to work less and yet their marginal disutility is less than their marginal wage rate. If workers in large firms are being forced to work longer than they would like, you would expect their marginal rate of substitution or marginal disutility to be greater than their wage rate, which it is not as reported in my paper.

The resolution of this problem lies in the fact that the regressions in tables 1.14 and 1.15 are based upon a different subset of the sample than the marginal rate of substitution regression in equation 4 and the marginal wage regression in equation 5. Equations 4 and 5 are based upon the total sample of employees. When I looked at people who had a discrepancy between their desired and actual number of hours worked, I just took the group of people whose desired number of hours of work did not correspond to their actual number of hours of work, and that was about 60 percent of the sample. So you see, about 40 percent of the people were getting the number of hours they wanted. Then there is a further subdivision because only about 40 percent of the 60 percent not working their desired number of hours wanted to work less. The rest wanted to work more.

So the set of figures in table 1.14 showing large firm employees want to work less is based upon about one-quarter of the total sample. If you just look at this subset of the total sample you should find that their marginal rate of substitution is greater than their marginal wage rate. In the overall disutility investigation, in equation 4, however, I am looking at the total sample.

MR. SCHERER: One of the things that's magnificent about this study is the very high degree of control over technological characteristics that the investigators have been able to maintain. That, of course, as everyone recognizes, is also a limitation. Two specific points are relevant.

First of all, Lucia concluded that this study may cast doubt on the previous studies showing plant size correlated with positive wage differentials. However, the controls for this study tried to net out what one would expect to be the effect of plant size, taking an industry where there are no significant economies of scale at the plant level. Therefore, what's going on in other industries, where there are economies of scale at the plant level, may be different from what is happening in this industry.

Second, by process of elimination, Lucia identifies the "monopoly wage hypothesis" as the prime source of firm size–related wage differentials. My question: Do the sample firms have a companywide wage policy? If you take a small division in which there happen to be no economies of scale and impose upon it the superstructure of a large firm, in the rest of which there may be economies of scale, and if you add a companywide wage policy imposed at the company's initiative, you might get the rent effects that you're finding.

Ms. DUNN: Yes.

MR. SCHERER: Is that what's going on?

Ms. DUNN: I think that's what's going on. That's a very good point. I want to address this with regard to some comments of Professor Ashenfelter also.

The very largest firms in the sample were in the plastics industry, but they were in many other industries also. While it's true that there may be no production economies of scale in their molded plastics plants, there may be some economies of scale in their other operations.

In the largest firms, many of the contract negotiations were carried on on a companywide basis with a particular union. There were some variations among the plants; not every plant at the same firm, unionized by the same union, got the exact same contract. But I'm sure it was a force bringing a certain uniformity to the contracts.

So the workers in these plastics plants may have been benefiting from the fact that the other divisions of the company had rents that they could draw on.

So yes, indeed, you are right.

Ms. DiTomaso: The issue was raised that the correlates of plant size are candidates for explaining what these findings seem to show. In the sociology of organizations, we had a lively debate for a while about size as an indicator and measure of other aspects of organizational structure. In this study, it is laudatory that you had controls to isolate size as an indicator. But perhaps this situation is unique, since it is not usually the case that as the size of an organization increases, technology, job type, and work rules stay the same. In larger firms, perhaps one can't choose one's hours of work as well as in smaller firms. It is also possible, and probably the case, that workers are not the same in large firms as in small firms, even if they have the same observed characteristics. There are things you can't measure. It seems to me that larger firms tend to have different production methods, different profitability, different work rules (particularly if they are unionized), and so on, and they cannot be strictly separated from size. Thus, size does correlate with things that can't be separated.

Finally, I did some work looking at manufacturing and nonmanufacturing industries, service and otherwise. In preliminary analyses, I found that satisfaction tended to be mostly explained by whether or not the job was a job the worker felt that he or she did best. If it was a job they thought they could do best, it was the job they would be much more satisfied with. These are better indicators for job satisfaction.

Ms. Tepper-Martin: One of my questions is, did you make any attempt to hold seniority constant? Is it possible that there is a significant difference in the seniority of workers at the larger firms than at the smaller?

The second concerns the differential between top management and worker compensation. I doubt that anybody would be surprised to find that top management in the large firms earns more than top management in small firms. What happens to the differential between the lower- and the higher-paid people among companies?

Mr. Kramer: You have been discussing worker alienation and the modern corporation. Have you concluded that workers, that is, the employed workers in the modern corporation, are alienated, or are they not?

Mr. Ginzberg: I'll take one more question.

Mr. Markowitz: Without knowing the sample of companies, I'd like to add to the points Mike Scherer made. I'm pretty confident that plastic divisions are units of much larger conglomerates. One way to see whether their wages reflect an overall company wage, or the specific plastics wage, is to look at each of the other divisions, testing whether they are above or below their particular industries as well, and try to standardize and see if that's the reason for the higher wages of large companies.

Ms. Dunn: Yes, that would be interesting to do. Addressing Professor DiTomaso's comments, there are, of course, many things that affect job satisfaction. And one reason I went to the marginal rate of substitution measure is that, presumably, it captures any element that impinges on disutility at work—the things that we wouldn't even think about that may be important for workers, like how the supervisor smiles at them when they walk in in the morning. So that's why I used this measure, hoping that I could capture the things that were not specifically addressed.

And the other point, yes, seniority was put in the regressions, either seniority or age. You couldn't put both in because they are so highly correlated with each other that you can't get significant coefficients on both of them at once. If you will look at the different tables, you will see that seniority and/or age is significant in many of these results.

PART II

PHILANTHROPIC IMPACT

EDITORS' NOTE

IN recent years in particular, governmental policy makers have attempted to encourage corporations to increase their support for the so-called third sector, or nonprofit sector, of the economy. For the past several decades, corporations have given approximately 1 percent of pretax profits to nonprofit institutions, and this has constituted about 6 percent of total private giving.

As the commentators' remarks and dialogue in this chapter indicate, there is evidence that corporations—spurred in part by governmental initiatives and by a sense of social responsibility—have begun to give more. But why would the substitution of corporate giving for government grants be desirable? The conceptual answer, at least for many, has been to focus on words like "diversity," "creativity," and private sector "efficiency."

There has, however, been relatively little empirical evidence available about how—and how well—corporations spend their philanthropic dollars. There has been almost no focus on the quantitative and qualitative differences, if any, between the philanthropic giving of large, medium, and small corporations and the likely consequences if either merger activity (e.g., the creation of a large corporation out of two medium-size companies) or corporate giving dramatically increase.

The main paper in this chapter, by Katherine Maddox McElroy and John J. Siegfried, goes far towards filling some important empirical gaps. For example, using old and new data bases, McElroy and Siegfried demonstrate that large corporations make proportionately lower contributions of their profits than do medium-size corporations, but large corporations make proportionately higher contributions than do small firms. Similarly, the merger of a large corporation with a medium-size corporation is likely to result in philanthropic "winners" and "losers." In such a merger, large corporations, with national markets, are likely to shift the pattern of giving from local health and welfare organizations and religious organizations to educational institutions and national organizations.

The McElroy–Siegfried paper and the commentators' remarks and dialogue that follow address almost every important issue in the philanthropic contributions area. This chapter should provide a rich resource for all future discussions—on either an empirical or a policy level—of the impact of corporate giving.

CHAPTER 3

The Effect of Firm Size and Mergers on Corporate Philanthropy

Katherine Maddox McElroy and John J. Siegfried

C ORPORATIONS can enhance community welfare and influence the distribution of income through their contributions to charitable organizations. Corporate contributions, which totaled about $3 billion in 1982 and represent 6 percent of total private donations, are generally made as large, discrete gifts. Because they serve as a substitute for government funding, policy makers have attempted to encourage corporations to increase their support of the not-for-profit sector.

A goal of proposed Senate bill S. 600, the Small and Independent Business Protection Act of 1979,[1] sponsored by Senator Edward Kennedy, was to encourage corporate support of surrounding communities by preventing conglomerate mergers by firms over a certain size. Testimony on the bill revealed that a basic tenet was that larger companies, many of which are created by mergers, do not value social goals, such as community welfare, as much as do smaller firms. This reflects a populist belief that big firms are "bad."[2] One implication is that larger firms make proportionately lower contributions than smaller firms and therefore corporate contributions will be higher if mergers are discouraged.

Whether larger corporations contribute proportionately less than smaller corporations is an empirical question, which we address in this paper. The general question elicits several more probing questions. Why would firm size influence contributions, and as firm size increases, do contributions increase at the same rate? Is the important issue the magnitude of contributions or their allocation among various types of recipients? Also, where do corporations direct their contributions, to the community housing the headquarters office or to operating locations? Does this distribution between headquarters and plant cities vary according to the size of the firm? This leads to a final question: Does the amount of giving (and its allocation) by a firm that has been acquired through merger increase or decrease?

First we examine the ratio of contributions to profits over time and by size of corporation using a simple tabular analysis. Then we explore why firms make contributions, based on personal interviews with corporate giving officers. Our conclusions from these interviews are the basis of a model that predicts the expected effect of firm size and other economic factors on contributions. In the third section we review earlier empirical studies of corporate contributions. The remainder of the paper contains results of our statistical analysis using two data sets. The first analysis updates and improves the statistical studies of IRS corporate income tax statistics on contributions, which have been the basis of most previous empirical studies. The second analysis uses data collected during our interviews with corporate giving officers. A concluding section summarizes policy implications.

THE CONTRIBUTION–PROFITS RATIO

As the corporate income tax rate has risen over the past fifty years, aggregate corporate contributions as a percentage of net income before taxes have increased from approximately 0.4 percent in 1936, the first year the Internal Revenue Code permitted giving as a deductible item, to approximately 1.0 percent in 1960, a level that has remained relatively constant through 1980.[3] Periodic increases in the giving to net income ratio correspond to the three periods of temporarily higher tax rates: World War II and the Korean War, during which an excess profits tax was imposed, and 1969, the year of the tax surcharge on corporations. In the recession years of 1938, 1949, and 1958, the ratio rose, even though the dollar volume of giving fell, because of the greater relative decline in profits.[4]

The average percent of corporate profits contributed by firms does not distinguish which firms make the contributions and how much is given by those that do contribute. A special analysis of corporate income tax returns performed by the Treasury Department reveals that only 20 percent of 1.7 million companies filing returns in 1970 declared some contributions as a deduction, and only 6 percent donated more than $500. Table 3.1 reports 1970 contribution statistics for corporations with positive net income according to asset size class. For these corporations, 37 percent contributed, and 20 percent contributed more than $1,000.

The frequency of giving varies across asset size classes. Eighty or more percent of firms with assets exceeding $5 million made contributions. For firms with fewer assets, the proportion giving declined, falling to 16 percent for firms with assets valued at less than $25,000.[5] That these larger asset firms earned almost 76 percent of corporate net income implies that firms with larger assets and higher profits are more likely to contribute. These statistics, however, exaggerate the philanthropic role of larger companies because smaller companies with less formal accounting methods are more likely to classify contributions into other budget categories, thereby understating their contributions.

The contribution to profits ratio is often used to compare the relative levels of giving between small and large firms. As shown in table 3.1, the ratio declines from 1.2 to 0.8 percent as assets increase from $5 million to the highest asset size class, and it also decreases as assets fall to zero. Thus it appears that medium-size firms contribute a greater proportion of their profits than do either larger or smaller firms. This inverted V-pattern across asset size classes is also evident in IRS data for the years 1945, 1946–1949, 1953, 1954–1961, 1957, and 1969.[6]

Because the magnitude of profits for larger asset firms is so high, the dollar value of their average contribution is substantially higher than the average contribution for smaller asset firms. In the 1970 IRS tables, the average contribution per firm is $100,000 to $800,000 for the largest asset size classes, compared with $5,000 to $25,000 for contributing corporations with assets between $5 million and $100 million. Therefore, although giving as a proportion of profits declines, the absolute amount of contributions increases dramatically with firm size. The changes

TABLE 3.1
Corporate Contributions Reported on Corporate Income Tax Returns, 1970

Asset Size (000)	Percent of Total Firms	Contributing Firms as Percent of Firms in Asset Size Class	Percent Distribution of Net Income	Average Contribution by Contributing Firms (000)	Contributions as Percent of Total Pretax Net Income of Size Class
$0	1.0	15.5	0.8	$ 1.2	0.5
1–25	6.2	16.0	0.6	—[a]	0.1
25–50	7.4	23.8	0.8	0.1	0.2
50–100	13.0	29.7	1.8	0.1	0.3
100–500	42.4	43.5	8.8	0.1	0.6
500–1,000	11.9	58.1	4.4	1.0	1.0
1–5 million	11.5	67.9	9.5	2.5	1.1
5–10 million	2.4	79.0	3.9	5.3	1.2
10–25 million	2.2	83.5	4.8	7.1	1.2
25–50 million	0.9	85.4	4.1	14.1	1.2
50–100 million	0.5	83.3	4.4	25.1	1.0
100–500 million	0.4	84.4	14.2	101.8	1.2
500–1,000 million	0.1	86.7	9.9	265.2	0.8
1,000 million and over	0.1	75.4	31.9	854.3	0.8
Total	100.0	36.5	100.0	$ 2.5	0.9

SOURCE: Thomas Vasquez, "Corporate Giving Measures," in John H. Filer, chairman, *Foundations, Private Giving and Public Policy: Report and Recommendations of the Commission on Foundations and Private Philanthropy,* 5 vols. (Chicago: University of Chicago Press, 1979), 3: 1839–1851.

NOTE: These are 1970 corporate income tax return data of corporations with positive net income, collected by the Internal Revenue Service and analyzed by the Office of Tax Analysis, Office of the Secretary of the Treasury.

[a] Less than $50.

in the average contributions across size classes reported in the table do not clearly reveal the rate of change in giving with respect to size. It is this response of giving to changes in size as measured by pretax net income that is the focus of the theoretical and statistical analysis in this paper. We undertake a more sophisticated analysis of the rate of giving by relatively large corporations. An important discovery of our study is that contributions do not decline as rapidly with respect to increasing firm size as an inspection of table 3.1 would suggest.

A MODEL OF CORPORATE GIVING

In order to understand why corporations make contributions, we conducted personal interviews with corporate giving officers of 229 large corporations headquartered in fourteen metropolitan areas. Interviewees responded to questions about policy, rationale, process, magnitude, and allocation of contributions and about various influences on the contribution decision.[7] A model of the firm that incorporates the role of contributions was developed based on these responses. The influence of various factors on contributions is derived from the model and tested statistically.

From the comments made by executives and the formal policy statements issued by the corporations, it seems that corporate executives are motivated to make corporate contributions when they perceive resulting benefits to the firm. In our model, there are two general types of benefits from contributions: long-term profit maximization, and enhancement of the company's public image in the community.

First, executives recognize that their companies benefit from the surrounding community and its social institutions. Because a socially healthy environment is propitious for long-run profits, firms support the not-for-profit organizations that provide the community with critical services.

Second, executives who make the contribution decision for their firms are aware of the public image of the firm in the community. They are more willing to fulfill a responsibility to the community when they perceive that this support serves to enhance the firm's good will in the community.

Several factors that potentially influence the contributions decision are introduced into the model to represent the role of these two categories of benefits. Predictions of the effect of these factors on contributions are derived from the model and expressed in two equations. One equation explains total contributions, and the other contributions in the headquarters city.

Total contributions depend on the ability to earn economic profits and city-specific variables for the operating locations of the firm. The total, once decided, influences the allocation of giving between the head-quarters area and other operating locations. Headquarters contributions are also influenced by the city-specific characteristics for the headquarters city. These city-specific variables include contributions by other firms, government funding of social services, the size of the community, the implicit tax-price of contributions, and the extent of philanthropic resources (capital) owned by the local not-for-profit organizations.

The remainder of this section explains the model according to the two major types of benefits—long-run profit maximization, and enhancement of the company's public image.

Profit Maximization

Contributions to the philanthropic sector enable charitable organizations to provide services, which in the long run may lower the operating costs of companies and consequently increase long-run profits. Health care organizations, such as hospitals and clinics, and social service agencies providing services such as day care and counseling to lower income citizens, improve the health and welfare of the entire community. Universities provide the community with educational offerings and the business sector with educated graduates. Cultural institutions, such as symphony orchestras, museums, and dance and acting companies, enhance the cultural environment of a city, and civic programs, which train and find employment for disadvantaged youth, minorities, and unskilled workers, may serve to reduce crime.

Because employees who are residents of the community value these environmental amenities, they may be willing to work for lower wages in cities that offer more of them. For companies that depend on highly trained professionals, an attractive community living environment is conducive to persuading potential employees to move to the headquarters city. When employees take advantage of the medical facilities, cultural activities, and educational opportunities, then companies do not have to provide the services internally.

Frequently, interviewees cited examples of how their firms supported local hospitals in plant communities instead of operating an emergency medical unit on the plant premises. Many firms actively recruit at the educational institutions they support, and several mentioned support of vocational schools, which provide them with trained workers (e.g., machinists, welders). Several executives also cited the effect of a reduced crime rate and subsequent diminution of vandalism and theft in lowering the costs of repairs and replacement to operating facilities.

In a formal profit-maximizing model of corporate giving, these community-enhancing services provided by charities serve to lower the firm's total costs. The production of services from the not-for-profit sector is a function of financial support from corporations, individuals, government, and fees and from the accumulated stock of physical and human resources owned by the not-for-profit sector. Each of these variables is explained separately below.

Contributions by Other Firms and Government Funding. Although payment for services by direct users provides one source of funds, these fees are usually insufficient to cover expenses for charitable services. This is because some charitable services cannot be provided adequately on a fee-for-service basis. There may be externalities (suppliers and/or users do not pay all costs or receive all benefits from the transaction) or public goods problems (nonpayers cannot be excluded cheaply from enjoying the benefits, and/or the marginal cost of providing the services is trivial). Consequently, their efficient provision relies on nonmarket sources of funding, which may not be sufficient because of the free-rider problem inherent in the provision of public goods. Free riders are individuals who cannot be excluded from receiving benefits and therefore refuse to pay, hoping to take a "free ride" on the services paid for and provided by others.

In order to illuminate the potential effect of the incentive to be a free rider, we have separated contributions made by the firm from those made by other firms and from government support. Any firm can reap the benefits of dollars contributed by other firms and the government because it is difficult to exclude that firm from the services provided by the charities. A firm would nevertheless elect to contribute as long as additional benefits from its contribution dollars exceeded the effective incremental cost of those contributions. However, charitable services are likely to reduce costs to the firm at a diminishing rate (e.g., the *first* hospital, college, and arts center have a greater added value to a community than the second hospital, college, and arts center), and the additional dollars contributed by the firm produce these services at a diminishing rate (the principle of diminishing marginal returns to added variable inputs).

As the returns from additional contribution dollars diminish when *others* provide funds, profit-maximizing firms have an increased incentive not to contribute at all (to be a free rider) or not to increase their contributions (to be a cheap rider). Thus, a company that makes contributions based on the profit-maximizing motive is more likely to give less when other firms or the government are providing more support to the not-for-profit sector.

Stock of Not-for-Profit Resources. The flow of philanthropic services also depends on the quality and physical stock of resources owned by the not-for-profit sector. For example, a medical facility is able to provide more patients with better medical care if it has more beds and diagnostic equipment, and a university can better educate students if it has better qualified faculty. Although additional private or public dollars provide diminishing incremental levels of philanthropic services, when these dollars are directed to institutions with greater physical and human resources, the added flow of services will be greater. The greater added benefits to the company provide a stronger incentive for corporate contributions. Thus, firms are more likely to make contributions when philanthropic organizations have a greater stock of physical and human assets.

Implicit Tax-Price. Contribution expenditures are a direct cost to the firm and a drain on profits, as well as a potential source of benefits. As a deductible expense, they have no greater tax advantage than other types of expenditures. Their implicit price is lowered, however, by state tax credit provisions (in two states in our sample), which apply solely to corporate contributions to the community. The corporate costs of donation dollars are lowered as a result of the provisions. Thus, we would expect greater levels of contributions to communities where the tax credit is in effect.

Profits. Although contributions potentially enhance long-run profits, most firms determine the dollar amount of contributions according to profits in the current year. According to the interviewed executives, contributions seem to be very responsive to changes in short-run profits. Executives adjust contributions as soon as they recognize a deviation in current profits from the forecast level.

Executives also indicated that contributions are budgeted incrementally, depending on the previous year's contributions. The firm's commitment to make contributions to an organization often reflects an "implicit contract" to provide continual support. Respondents considered a large share of their contributions to be "obligatory," meaning that at least a minimum level of funding for some organizations receiving their support would be maintained even in the face of several years of disappointing earnings. This implies that contributions may adjust more slowly than profits.

The direction of causality between contributions and profits is theoretically ambiguous. Contributions respond to short-run economic profits but also enhance long-run profits by increasing demand or reducing costs. Because the focus of this study is on contributions, however, a profits equation that includes contributions as an independent variable was not specified. Our primary interest is the rate of response of contributions to short-run profits. Sorting out the simultaneity between profits and contributions remains for subsequent research.

A company's profit level is also a measure of its size. The model employs profits rather than assets, revenues, or other size measures, because executives considered profits rather than other size measures in determining contributions.

Public Image Enhancement

Corporate contributions also serve to relieve executives of a perceived community support responsibility imposed by other local executives and fund raisers. As long as the obligation is unmet, then the firm's self-perceived public image is diminished. Therefore, donations to local charities are a means of enhancing the firm's image in the community. Company executives clearly recognize the benefits of contributions in improving corporate name recognition, but most do not view it as a substitute for advertising to the consumer or as a means of increasing sales. The effect of contributions on community good will, rather than market image, dominated the qualitative remarks in our interviews.

The relationships among corporate executives in a community frequently constitute an informal social network through which community activities are initiated. Executives shoulder community responsibility by participating in fund-raising drives and serving on the boards of directors for philanthropic agencies, government–business task forces, local chambers of commerce, and school boards. Such involvement has costs, since executive time spent on these activities could be redirected toward the operations of the company. The benefits to the firm, as perceived by executives, are the higher esteem for the company and its executives held by the community and the lower costs of supporting philanthropic organizations when the costs are shared by many companies.

Contributions by Other Firms. Through the social network of corporate officers within cities, executives raise corporate funds for charities. Efforts to persuade other local executives to contribute are more effective if the fund raiser's own company reciprocates when appeals are made to it. Since the contributions by a firm represent its expectations that other firms will also give, contributions by other firms increase the perceived social obligations to a firm. These social costs are mitigated when a firm increases its contributions relative to those of other companies.

Therefore, based on the image enhancement motivation for making contributions, a firm would be likely to increase its giving when other firms increase their giving. If a firm considers both the profit-maximizing and image enhancement motives, the effect of giving by other local firms is indeterminate. The additional benefit of meeting social obligations for firms whose executives value highly the public image of the firm in the community offsets, but does not necessarily eliminate, the incentive for the firm to behave as a free rider.

Size of City. Fund raising, either by corporate officers or recipient agencies, is more effectively directed toward more visible firms, which are usually large relative to the size of the city. Within a city, firms with greater revenues often induce greater expectations for giving. Conversely, officers in firms with the same level of revenues perceive fewer obligations when located in a larger city. Therefore, we would expect similar sized firms to give more in smaller cities than in larger cities.

REVIEW OF EARLIER STUDIES

Three major empirical studies have examined the relationship between contributions and profits. They were performed by Robert Schwartz, Ralph

Nelson, and Paul Whitehead.[8] All used corporate income tax data. There are also two other studies by Orace Johnson and Ferdinand Levy and Gloria Shatto.[9]

Corporate tax return data are compiled in the annual *Source Book of Statistics of Income: Corporation Income Tax Returns.* The data are reported by IRS minor industry, by major industrial groups, and in the aggregate, permitting both time-series and cross-section analysis. Schwartz, Nelson, and Whitehead primarily employed multiple regression analysis, as did Levy and Shatto, for testing the effect of various explanatory variables on corporate contributions. Nelson and Whitehead supplemented the regressions with a tabular presentation of cross-sectional data. Johnson relied on graphical analysis exclusively for examination of the 1936–1961 *Source Book* data.

The empirical results of both the time-series and cross-section studies are summarized in table 3.2. Because regressions with the fewest explanatory variables in addition to pretax net income are most similar to the regressions of this study, those estimates are the only ones reported in the table.

Time-series studies of the aggregate data were conducted by Schwartz for the years 1936–1961, by Nelson for 1936–1963, and by Levy and Shatto for 1946–1972. Schwartz also ran a separate time-series regression for each of nine major industry groups for 1936–1961 to compare the relationship of contributions with various explanatory factors across industries. The cross-section regressions vary by the number and definitional level of industries chosen for the observations. Schwartz used 60 IRS major manufacturing industries for 1960; Nelson, 121 IRS minor manufacturing industries for 1954–1957; Whitehead, 76 IRS minor manufacturing industries for 1968–1970; and Levy and Shatto, 56 Standard Industrial Classification (SIC) major industries for 1971.

The most relevant variables employed by these authors, which seem to be truly exogenous to the firm's decision to contribute and not directly under the control of the firm, are pretax net income, price (i.e., 1-tax rate), time trend, government welfare payments, and the number of firms per industry. These variables correspond to variables normally employed for specifying a demand function. Other variables frequently included in the regressions are other expenses that are determined in conjunction with the contribution decision: employment, advertising, dividends, and officers' compensation. The cross-section studies conducted for different periods by Schwartz, Nelson, and Whitehead pri-

TABLE 3.2

Selected Elasticities from Corporate Contribution Regressions of Earlier
Studies

Description of Study	Pretax Net Income Elasticity	Price Elasticity	R^2	Other Variables in the Regression
Time-Series				
Nelson: 1936–1963 aggregate	1.05	−1.03	.93	trend
Schwartz: 1936–1961 aggregate	.63	−2.00	.77	—
Nine major industry groups 1936–1961	.25 to .64	−1.12 to −2.73	—	—
Cross-Section				
Nelson: 1954–1957 121 manufacturing industries	.68	—	.64	number of firms
Schwartz: 1960 60 manufacturing industries	.44	—	.82	advertising
Whitehead: 1968–1970 76 manufacturing industries	.58	—	.90	number of firms, officers' compensation, advertising/sales, employment, dividends

SOURCES: Ralph L. Nelson, *Economic Factors in the Growth of Corporate Giving* (New York: National Bureau of Economic Research, 1970); Robert Schwartz, "Private Philanthropic Contributions: An Economic Analysis" (Ph.D. diss., Columbia University, 1966); and Paul James Whitehead, "Some Economic Aspects of Corporate Giving" (Ph.D. diss., Virginia Polytechnic University, 1976).

NOTE: Only estimates from double logarithmic form regressions with the fewest explanatory variables are reported. All coefficients are statistically significantly different from zero at the 5 percent level. Price is defined as 1 minus the marginal income tax rate.

marily included income, number of employees, advertising, officers' compensation, dividends, and number of firms as exogenous variables.

The estimated income elasticity ranges from 0.25 to 1.05 for the time-series regressions and from 0.44 to 0.68 for the cross-section regressions. Except for one aggregate time-series estimate of unity, the remaining time-series and all cross-section income elasticities average approximately 0.6. Such an inelastic response implies that contributions increase by less than two-thirds of the percentage increase in pretax net income.

EMPIRICAL ANALYSIS OF IRS DATA

The effect of a firm's ability to earn economic profits on the size of its total contributions budget can be evaluated with corporate income tax return data published by the IRS. Because headquarters contributions and the location of the headquarters offices are not reported in the data, we could not examine separately the determinants of giving to the headquarters community or the effect of city-specific variables. As explained earlier, the short-run determination of most firms' contributions budget is based on the current level of profits, although contributions in the long run may serve to lower costs and enhance profits.

The response of contributions to pretax profits is estimated for cross-sectional data for the years 1972 and 1976 and can be compared with previous studies, which used similar data for earlier years. An important advantage of our analysis, however, is the use of less aggregated data.

Data Description

Contributions as a tax-deductible expense and pretax net income of firms are available as averages for groups of firms in the *Source Book of Statistics of Income: Corporation Income Tax Returns.* The IRS classifies firms into 169 minor industry categories according to the firm's principal business activity, that is, the product that constitutes the largest percentage of total company sales. This classification method means that the data do not represent economically meaningful markets. For our purposes, however, this is not a problem, since our unit of analysis is the firm and not an economic market.

Data for each minor industry are divided into twelve asset size classes, whose less aggregated averages are the observation units for our empirical analysis. Although the use of asset size class averages is an improvement over the minor industry totals used in previous studies, the remaining aggregation of the data continues to cause estimation problems. The average contribution per asset size class is a misleading indicator of typical individual firm contributions for firms in the size class, because the majority of firms that make no charitable contributions cannot be separated from the minority that do contribute. Therefore, regression estimates of the relationship between contributions and profits do not capture the variation within each asset size class, only the variation among the averages. This problem and our correction for it are discussed in detail in the section on empirical analysis.

Contributions are only those gifts that are classified into the contribution category of the federal corporate income tax return. Since contributions are a tax-deductible expense like any other business expense, there is no incentive to classify them in a separate budget. Therefore, donations may appear in budgets such as advertising or payroll because of the accounting cost of separating the expenses or, in unusual cases, to avoid the 5 percent maximum allowable deduction for contributions.[10] This is more likely to bias reported contributions downward for smaller firms with less sophisticated and less formal accounting systems.

Pretax income, defined as taxable income (total receipts minus total expenses), excludes contributions and includes extraordinary items and taxes. The varying magnitude of profits across asset size classes reflects the varying ability of firms to earn economic profits.

The contributions and profits data reported to the IRS contain distortions from the actual amounts. Reported contributions may differ from actual charitable contributions because firms use corporate foundations as a conduit for their giving or because they carry forward deductions limited to 5 percent of pretax net income in earlier years. Profits may be in disequilibrium or underreported. These sources of measurement error are discussed below.

IRS data include only contributions made by the corporation, not those distributed by corporate foundations. Since corporate foundations are usually established to smooth the flow of contributions over time, there is likely to be a discrepancy between a corporation's annual deductible contribution expense and the actual dollars contributed to charities from the corporation and its (captive) foundation. Also, in 1980 the five-year carry-forward provision (section 170[d][2] of the Internal Revenue Code) allowed a company to carry forward for up to five years any contributions exceeding the 5 percent of taxable income limit. If a firm were taking advantage of this provision, then in the year that the 5 percent limit was exceeded, contributions would be understated, and in subsequent years contributions would be overstated.

When there are disequilibrium market conditions, profits diverge from their long-run level. Contributions to charities may change only incrementally, however, because they are often based on a "normal" or "permanent" level of profits rather than on profits resulting from transitory changes in market conditions.[11] Abnormally high (low) profits tend to understate (overstate) the long-run rate of contributions to profits.

The measurement error in contributions will not bias the estimated response of contributions to profits because the contributions figure is the dependent variable of the regression. Random errors in the dependent variable merge with the stochastic error term of the regression, which is additive and therefore does not alter the estimated coefficient. The measurement errors created by the smoothing of contributions via the use of foundations and the leveling of deductions by the 5 percent limitation will offset each other over time and can be reasonably assumed to be random.

However, the measurement error in profits, the explanatory variable, causes a downward bias in the estimated relationship. Because the measured explanatory variable, which includes an error component, is not distributed independently of the disturbance term in the linear regression, the variance of the error component will cause the estimated coefficient to understate the true relationship.[12] The use of data averaged over several years would avoid the problem of disequilibrium profits. Such averages, unfortunately, cannot be meaningfully computed with the available IRS data because diversified firms may be classified into different industries from year to year if the primary product of the firm shifts over time.

Interpretation of the estimated relationship between contributions and profits must take into account the downward bias caused by the measurement error of profits, the explanatory variable. The estimated elasticity of contributions with respect to profits is likely to be biased downward relative to the true long-run relationship and thus provide a lower bound to the true elasticity.

Empirical Analysis

Theory does not predict a specific functional relationship between contributions and pretax profits. Therefore, we tested the relationship with two functional forms: the linear form and the double logarithmic form, which was employed in the prior studies on corporate philanthropy.[13] Each functional form was estimated with the entire set of 169 IRS minor industries and also on only the subset of 76 manufacturing industries for both 1972 and 1976.

The manufacturing industries are estimated separately because they exhibit a more homogeneous production process across firms and also for comparison with the results of earlier studies, which had used only manufacturing data. Tables 3.3 and 3.4 report the results using these four data subsets. Of major concern in testing the profits–contributions relationship is the sign and magnitude of the coefficient on profits and, in particular, the magnitude of the elasticity of contributions with respect to profits. For the linear form, elasticities were computed from the estimated coefficients at the means of contributions and profits. All coefficients are significantly different from zero at the 1 percent level.

Linear Form. Estimation of the contributions–profits regression with ordinary least squares and IRS data is unreliable because of two estimation problems. One is heteroscedasticity (unequal variance of the error term), and the other is caused by the large number of firms that make no contributions. Below is a discussion of each problem and how we corrected for it. Our regression results reflect corrected estimation procedures.

TABLE 3.3
Linear Form (Weighted Least Squares) Regressions for Corporations with Assets Exceeding $10 Million, 1972 and 1976
(dollar amounts in thousands)

	All Industries		Manufacturing Industries	
	1972	1976	1972	1976
Dependent variable: contributions				
Constant	1.0833	1.6656	5.879	7.5748
Pretax net income	.0085*	.0065*	.0093*	.0079*
	(31.59)	(29.41)	(30.06)	(26.33)
Elasticity at means	.96	.90	.96	.87
R²	.70	.60	.83	.78
F	582	481	483	526
Number of observations	501	652	236	301
Univariate statistics				
Pretax net income: mean	$10,178	$20,825	$14,546	$25,351
Standard deviation	26,142	88,375	32,022	60,467
Contributions: mean	91	149	141	231
Standard deviation	204	371	262	480

*Coefficient significantly different from zero at 1 percent level; t-statistics are in parentheses.

TABLE 3.4

Double Logarithmic Regressions for Corporations with Assets
Exceeding $10 Million, 1972 and 1976

	All Industries		Manufacturing Industries	
	1972	1976	1972	1976
Dependent variable: contributions				
Constant	−3.095	−3.078	−4.303	−4.260
Pretax net income	.7695*	.7685*	.9689*	.9475*
(elasticity)	(28.62)	(39.19)	(40.32)	(40.35)
R^2	.82	.88	.99	.98
F	1133	2381	8083	8647

*Coefficient significantly different from zero at 1 percent level; t-statistics are in parentheses.

There are two sources of heteroscedasticity. One source arises from the nature of the contributions–profits relationship.[14] The second arises from the data, which are aggregations of the individual observations in each asset size class.[15] The heteroscedasticity caused by both sources can be corrected by employing a weighted least squares estimation procedure.[16]

The second estimation problem—many zero contributors—cannot be corrected because the data are aggregated; it can, however, be mitigated. Conceptually, an analysis of corporate contributions consists of two questions: which firms are the givers, and how much is donated by these contributing firms. Empirically, the two questions cannot be separated using data that are averages of both positive and zero givers. An estimation process that takes into account both the probability that a firm will contribute at all and the elasticity of contributions with respect to profits can only be applied to individual firm data.[17]

Since ordinary least squares estimation of averaged data does not capture both effects, it yields unreliable estimates. The estimates represent an expected average response of contributions by all firms to an increase in pretax profits, without regard to the noncontributors and the probability that firms will make a contribution at all.[18]

The variation in the fraction of firms that contribute across asset size classes, as reported in table 3.1 for 1970, implies a corresponding variation in the probability that a firm will contribute. The percentage of firms that contribute exceeds 80 percent for firms with assets of $10 million or more (with the exception of the highest asset size class). Therefore, in order to minimize the bias caused by the nonlinear influence of zero givers, the variability in probabilities of giving is reduced by applying ordinary least squares estimation to only those firms with assets of $10 million or more.

The linear form results are reported in table 3.3. For all subsets of data, the elasticities at the mean are similar, ranging from .87 for manufacturing industries in 1976 to .96 for all industries in 1972. The marginal contributions rate appears to be between 0.5 percent and 1 percent of pretax net income. The coefficients imply that a $10,000 increase in pretax net income results in an increase in contributions of $65 to $93.

Double Logarithmic Form. The double logarithmic form is useful for deriving direct estimates of elasticities. Estimates are unreliable, however, because of the heteroscedasticity associated with averaging individual observations in the IRS data. Therefore, weighted least squares estimation is employed to correct for the problem.[19]

The double logarithmic form results are reported in table 3.4. The elasticities are close to the elasticities computed from the linear estimates for manufacturing industries, .97 and .95, for 1972 and 1976, respectively, whereas those for all industries are smaller for both years. The higher coefficient of determination for the manufacturing regression relative to the all-industry regression indicates a better fit, suggesting that the higher elasticity estimates of the manufacturing regression are more reliable.

Summary and Comparison with Earlier Studies

The functional form does not seem to influence the magnitude of the elasticity estimates, which in almost every case are close to unity.[20] The regressions were run for asset size classes of $10 million or more in order to mitigate the problem of zero givers by holding constant the probability that a firm will make a contribution. Nevertheless, the highest confidence can be placed on estimates for only the middle range of contribution values. Our estimates probably understate the elasticity of contributions with respect to profits because of the downward bias caused by disequilibrium profits and greater incentives of small firms to understate profits.

All of these results differ markedly from those of the three earlier cross-sectional studies. As shown in table 3.2, the estimated elasticities of the previous cross-section regressions range from 0.44 to 0.68 for manufacturing industries. Even the lowest elasticity obtained in our study, the double logarithmic form estimate of 0.77 (for large asset firms of all industries in both 1972 and 1976), is higher than 0.68, Nelson's 1954–1957 estimate.[21]

The most obvious explanation for these differences is failure of the earlier studies to disaggregate the data by asset size class and to correct for heteroscedasticity. The range of profit and contribution levels is considerably narrower for averages of only 60 to 121 industrywide observations. Also, although the number of firms included in each industry observation was added as a separate variable in the Nelson regression, the number was not used in any of the earlier studies to correct for the heteroscedastic error variances that the aggregation causes. The difference between earlier results and ours is not a result of the downward bias caused by underreported and disequilibrium profits, however; this bias affects the earlier studies as well as ours.

EMPIRICAL ANALYSIS OF INTERVIEW DATA

Financial data collected during the interviews with corporate giving officers are the basis of our second empirical investigation. First we describe the interview data. Then we report the results of the regression used to predict total contributions, compare them with the regression results based on IRS data, and discuss the implications of both. Later we shall examine the allocation of giving geographically and across categories of charities and report the results of our regression used to predict contributions to the headquarters community.

Data Description

Most of the firms we interviewed were large, averaging about 14,000 employees, $91 million in annual pretax net income, and 105 operating locations. Fifty-one of the 135 industrial firms in the sample were on the 1980 *Fortune* 500 list. They also were large contributors, typically making an average of 220 separate gifts per year (United Way classified as one gift) for a total annual value of about $770,000.

The sample firms contributed 0.84 percent of their pretax net income to charities. This is a slightly greater fraction of PTNI than has been reported in other surveys. For example, the Conference Board's 1979 survey of about 500 large firms found a contributions to pretax net income ratio of 0.7 percent for firms with average annual pretax net income of $122 million.[22] The ratio of contributions to PTNI for all corporations with assets greater than or equal to $10 million in the *1976 Statistics of Income, Corporation Income Tax Returns* is also 0.7 percent, although these firms are much smaller on average than our sample members. It appears that the firms in our sample are more generous than the firms in other, more comprehensive large firm data sets.

Of the 229 firms that we interviewed, 162 provided financial information on their contributions and profits. Most of the data pertain to fiscal year 1980, although for some firms only 1981 data were available.

Contributions. Contributions include dollars donated to tax-exempt, charitable organizations or to umbrella organizations that raise money for these agencies, such as United Way. Excluded are political contributions and community improvement investments that are not classified as a tax-deductible contribution. Also, in most cases, funding of research grants in higher education institutions is counted in the research and development budget rather than in the contributions budget. Other forms of corporate support for the community, such as donated services, are not reflected in the contributions figure.

The definition of contributions differs from that reported to the IRS. Instead of representing only those dollars contributed by the corporation, contributions in the individual firm data include all dollars that flow out of the corporation and its affiliated foundation *into* the not-for-profit sector. This concept fully captures corporate monetary support received by charities. For firms with corporate foundations, the IRS figure only includes dollar outflows from the corporate budget and does not distinguish whether these dollars are directed immediately to charitable organizations or to the foundation.

Forty-two percent of the interviewed firms had corporate foundations through which they administered at least some of their annual corporate contributions. Sixty-eight percent of that subset used their foundations as a conduit for contributions, with the express purpose of stabilizing the flow of dollars to philanthropic organizations in an environment of fluctuating earnings. Most of the foundations held assets sufficient to carry contributions at a reasonably steady level for one to three years. Only a few firms had foundations with considerable assets, the earnings from which constituted almost the entire contributions budget of the firm.

The figures we collected in the interview process are the sum of monies flowing directly to charities from the corporate budget plus those flowing out of the corporate foundation. In years when the foundation's principal is increased, more funds are added to the foundation than flow out of it. Although funds accruing to the foundation may be based upon profits for that year, the dollars flowing out of the foundation may not be governed by current profits. Therefore, profits may not be as good a predictor of the magnitude of annual corporate giving *to charities* as of the annual outflow from the corporation, which is measured by the IRS data. In other words, although profits may be lower than normal, the demand from fund-raisers continues to evoke contributions, and the foundation's principal provides a supply (although perhaps temporary) of donations.

We measure both total contributions and contributions to charities located in the headquarters community of the firm.

Pretax Net Income. The pretax net income, or profit, of the firm is the published dollar figure for net income before taxes but excluding contributions. Contributions are excluded from the profit definition for simplicity because executives employ this definition in determining total contributions and because profits net of all expenses except contributions most accurately represents the maximum ability of firms to make contributions.

Empirical Analysis

We estimated the total contributions regression using two functional forms: linear and double logarithmic. As with the regressions employing IRS data, the linear form estimates are unreliable because of nonconstant variances. The five-percentage-point range of giving to pretax net income becomes a much larger absolute dollar value for firms with higher net income than firms with lower net income. The resulting unequal variance in the error term is corrected (again) with a weighted least squares estimating technique. The multiplier applied to each variable is the square root of the reciprocal of pretax net income.

Table 3.5 presents the regression results. For the linear weighted least squares regressions, the coefficient of pretax net income is 0.0082, which is in the same range (0.0065–0.0093) as the coefficients estimated from the IRS large firm data (table 3.3). As with the IRS data estimates, the type of functional form does not seem to make a difference in the estimated magnitude of the elasticity of contributions with respect to profits.

The elasticity of total giving with respect to profits for the linear form (computed at the means) and for the double logarithmic form is 0.72.[23] This is smaller than the elasticities estimated using the IRS data, which

TABLE 3.5
Total Monetary Contributions Regressions
(dollar amounts and population in thousands)

Variable Definition	Expected Sign	Linear	Logarithmic
Constant		− 3.5678	.4891
Pretax net income	+	0.0082* (10.98)	.7208* (18.01)
Elasticity at means		.72	.72
Other firm contributions in headquarters city[a,b]	?	0.0523 (1.6963)	1.113* (2.474)
Government funding[a,b]	?	− 0.0000 (− 0.0180)	.2554 (.4963)
Population of headquarters city[b]	—	− 0.1108 (− 1.3718)	− 1.819* (− 3.264)
State tax credit dummy[b]	+	− 11.4453 (− 0.1114)	.4395 (0.9538)
Philanthropic resources[b]	+	− 17.9977 (− 0.4770)	− 0.0432 (− 0.2488)
R[2]		.0706	.7216
F		3.161	70.56
N		162	162

NOTE: T-statstics are in parentheses.
[a]These variables are tested for significance with a two-tailed t-test. All others have unambiguous expected signs, so are tested with a one-tailed test.
[b]See text and footnote 24 for a brief explanation of these city-specific variables.
*Significantly different from zero at 1 percent level.

range from 0.90 to 0.96 for the linear form and from 0.82 to 0.99 for the double logarithmic form. The elasticity estimates are probably biased downward because of measurement error in the profits variable. Yet they are noticeably higher than earlier elasticity estimates from cross-sectional studies reported in table 3.2, which range from 0.44 to 0.68.

Table 3.5 regression equations, unlike the IRS data estimates, include city-specific variables. The motivation for these variables has already been explained under the theoretical model of corporate giving. These variables, unavailable for the IRS analysis, have some explanatory power that may have been captured by the pretax net income variable in the IRS data estimation. The table 3.5 logarithmic form estimates in particular imply that a firm's contributions increase when other firms in the cities where the firm operates increase their contributions and when the firm is located in smaller cities.[24]

Implications

Coefficients of the aggregate IRS and individual firm regressions must be interpreted differently because of their differential treatment of noncontributors. The coefficient in the aggregate IRS data regressions estimates the average responsiveness of giving by *all* firms to increase in profits. In the individual firm regressions, the coefficient represents the responsiveness of giving by firms *that make contributions* with respect to increases in their profits.

All the firms in the interview sample made at least some contributions, whereas firms with both positive and zero contributions are included in the asset size class averages of the IRS data. In the IRS data, zero contributions are averaged with positive contributions (see figure 3.1). According to table 3.1, firms with lower assets contribute a higher percentage of pretax net income, but a greater percentage of low asset firms make no contributions. Since profit and asset levels are highly correlated, firms with lower incomes, although contributing a higher percentage of pretax profits, are more likely to make no contributions than are firms with higher incomes. Thus, the regression line for the IRS data is likely to be biased in its attempt to account for noncontributors. The intercept is likely to be understated and the coefficient with respect to profits overstated as the regression line rotates counterclockwise from an individual firm regression, including only positive givers. Therefore, be-

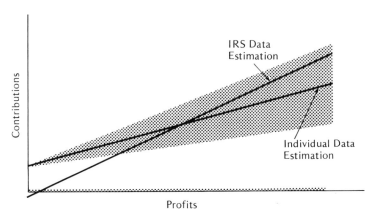

Figure 3.1 Comparison of the Estimation Using Individual and IRS Data.

cause of the exclusion of noncontributing firms, the elasticity of contributions with respect to profits is smaller for the interview data than for the IRS data.

The IRS elasticity of nearly unity includes both the response of increasing contributions to profits by firms with giving programs and the response of beginning a giving program in reaction to increased profits by firms that formerly made no contributions. The elasticity of 0.72 for the individual firm (interview) data does not include the propensity of some nongivers to begin making contributions as profits increase. The elasticity—much smaller than unity—indicates that, for large firms with giving programs, contributions increase less than proportionally with increases in pretax net income.[25]

Although the linear regression results of both data sets are similar, they are also subject to different interpretations. The IRS data coefficient implies that when corporations increase profits by an average of $1 million, contributions will increase by from $6,500 to $9,500. The individual company sample coefficient implies that when a contributing firm increases profits by $1 million, contributions are likely to rise an average by from $7,000 to $9,500.

The implications of these findings for predicting the impact of mergers on corporate contributions vary according to whether the acquiring and acquired firms have giving programs. A detailed analysis of the impact is presented in the final section of this paper on concluding implications.

THE DISTRIBUTION OF CONTRIBUTIONS

The distribution of contributions both geographically and across types of philanthropic endeavors may affect the environment of individual communities as much as the total amount of contributions. Using data gathered through our interview sample, we consider the distribution of giving between the headquarters city and the communities housing operating units along with the pattern of giving among types of charities. In this section, we first examine simple ratios reflecting the contribution pattern and the responses of interviewees to questions about the impact of mergers on giving in headquarters versus nonheadquarters cities. Then we report the results of our statistical analysis of contributions to the headquarters city, explaining the impact of city-specific factors.

The Contribution Pattern

Table 3.6 reports the average percentage of total contributions in our sample that were directed to each of five types of charities. The bulk of the contributions (45 percent) is given to health and welfare organizations, most of which are United Way gifts. Education receives almost one-fourth, and both arts and culture and civic organizations receive most of the remainder.

Our interviews suggested that mergers would alter this pattern. Since mergers create larger firms, we can estimate the impact of mergers by examining the effect of firm size on the pattern of giving. By grouping the firms into five size classes (based on employment) in table 3.6, we observe how the pattern varies according to firm size.

As firms increase in size, contributions to the health and welfare area diminish. This is probably because United Way gifts, which constitute most of the health and welfare contributions, are regarded by many firms as a fixed obligation, which does not increase proportionately with the size of the firm. Larger employers, which generally hire greater numbers of highly educated managers and researchers and skilled workers, also tend to give more to educational institutions. The interviews indicated that larger firms are more likely than smaller firms to have a corporate policy prohibiting giving to certain types of philanthropic organizations, particularly religious organizations. In addition, larger firms, which have

TABLE 3.6
Percentage Contributed to Charity Types, by Firm Size

		Employment Size Class					
Charity Type	Total	less than 1,500	1,501– 2,500	2,501– 5,000	5,001– 10,000	10,001– 35,000	More than 35,000
Health and welfare	45.3	49.0	45.5	48.5	40.1	48.2	37.9
Education	24.3	20.7	20.0	25.6	29.1	25.0	31.6
Arts and culture	12.7	10.8	13.9	12.1	10.8	10.8	13.2
Civic	12.0	13.9	16.2	9.8	13.1	10.9	12.0
Other	5.7	5.5	4.4	4.0	6.7	5.2	5.3
National causes	9.2	6.1	8.8	7.7	10.7	10.0	17.4
Medium number of employees	4,000	800	2,000	3,700	7,100	18,300	72,000
Sample size	195	38	31	31	32	28	24

national markets, were more likely to contribute to national organizations than were small firms.

Thus, it seems that giving patterns are likely to change when a firm becomes larger as a result of merger. National organizations and educational institutions are the likely beneficiaries of the redistribution, whereas religious organizations may be the losers.

The Distribution Between Headquarters and Operating Locations

The firms in our sample donated about 70 percent of their contributions to charities in their headquarters city. However, executives at the headquarters office controlled almost 90 percent of the contributions budget. This implies that such executives direct part of their budget to charities located outside their city of residence, presumably taking into account benefits accruing to the firm at its various operating locations.

As explained earlier, contributions are hypothesized to lower average (per employee) labor costs. For example, community hospitals may benefit some employees and community arts programs other employees. One could assume that contributions to such programs lower per employee labor costs uniformly for every operating location including the headquarters city. Under this assumption, for a profit-maximizing firm, one would expect the giving to labor ratio to be the same for each operating location.

However, executives at headquarters may value the quality of life in the headquarters city more than workers in plant communities value their living environment. They may be more willing than workers at plant locations to accept lower incomes when compensated by a better living environment. This would imply that average labor costs are lowered to a greater degree in the headquarters city than in the plant locations. Under this assumption for a profit-maximizing firm, the contributions to labor ratio would be greater in the headquarters city.

In our economic model, contributions also enhance the firm's public image in all of the operating communities. Fund-raisers or other local executives tend to impose greater social obligations on executives at the headquarters level, so that the benefits of contributions in mitigating these social costs of doing business are greater at headquarters. This assumption, inferred from comments made by executives, also leads to the hypothesis that the giving to output ratio is higher in the headquarters city.

The mean ratio of giving per employee was found to be statistically significantly higher in the headquarters cities ($214) than in the plant locations ($43). This provides support for the assumptions that executives at headquarters receive greater benefits from contributions than do workers at operating locations. Benefits take the form of perceived nonmonetary compensation and the ability to diminish social pressure.

The implication is not necessarily that firms headquartered in a city contribute the greatest amount to the not-for-profit sector of the city, however. Although companies tend to contribute more per employee in the headquarters city than in plant locations, if fewer employees are working in the headquarters area, then fewer dollars may be directed to the philanthropies at the headquarters. Corporations that operate a plant in a city outside their headquarters city may make more contributions to that plant city than a company headquartered in the city with plants elsewhere because their lower donations per employee are multiplied by a greater number of employees.

Effect of Headquarters Move and Merger

Of the 229 interviewed firms, 14 had recently made intercity headquarters moves, and 130 had either made an acquisition or been acquired in recent years. We asked these affected firms to evaluate the impact of the change on the distribution of their contributions.

The executives reported that, when the firm's headquarters moved, in four cases contributions decreased in the vacated area and increased in the new headquarters area. Six cases of headquarters moves were thought to have no impact on the distribution of contributions, and four firms could not evaluate the effect. Thus, 40 percent of those who could evaluate the impact of a headquarters relocation thought it reduced giving in the old headquarters city and increased it in the new headquarters city, the remainder attributing no effect of the move on contributions in the original headquarters area.

We also asked about the impact of acquisitions on contributions in the headquarters city of the acquired firm and received an evaluation for 115 of the 130 merger cases. Forty-one percent were reported to have increased contributions in the previous headquarters city, 21 percent were thought to have reduced contributions, and 38 percent reported no impact of the acquisition on contributions. Somewhat surprisingly, acquisitions were reported to *increase* contributions in a metropolitan area losing a corporate headquarters at a two-to-one rate. The reason is that most mergers involve a large firm with a substantial, systematic contributions program that acquires a smaller firm with a small, unstructured contributions history. The extension of the larger firm's more generous policy frequently benefits the local community of the acquired firm. Although a larger firm may have a smaller contributions to profit ratio than the smaller acquired firm, this fraction times a much larger total contributions budget than the smaller firm's may generate a larger absolute amount of contributions for the former headquarters city.

Empirical Analysis of Headquarters Contributions

As explained in the review of earlier studies, after the total contribution amount has been determined based on profits and indirectly influenced by city-specific factors, the allocation between headquarters and other operating locations is determined. We discuss the response of headquarters contributions to the total and to each city-specific factor. The empirical results are reported in table 3.7.

Total Contributions. The expected large positive response of headquarters contributions to total contributions is empirically supported. The

TABLE 3.7
Headquarters Monetary Contributions Regressions
(dollar amounts and population in thousands)

Variable Definition	Expected Sign	Linear	Linear: Per Capita	Logarithmic
Constant		833.05	1,039.30	−0.1996
Total		.3849*	.3777*	0.9356*
contributions	+	(21.30)	(20.17)	(19.15)
Elasticity at				
means		.80	.78	.94
Other firm		−0.1259*	−95.78**	−0.1993
contributions[a]	?	(−2.795)	(−1.502)	(−0.4864)
Government		0.0002	0.0480	−0.0857
funding[a]	?	(0.6493)	(0.0993)	(−0.2182)
Population of		−0.0857	−0.3679**	−0.2587
city	−	(−0.8170)	(−2.505)	(−0.5400)
State tax credit		−350.7	−74.24	−0.2125
dummy	+	(−2.936)	(−0.7725)	(−0.8481)
Philanthropic		301.1*	253,007**	0.0463
resources	+	(3.576)	(2.485)	(0.2684)
R^2		.7502	.7407	.7162
F		81.58	77.67	68.73
Number of				
observations		162	162	162

NOTE: T-statistics are in parentheses.
[a] These variables are tested for significance with a two-tailed t-test. All others have unambiguous expected signs, so are tested with a one-tailed test.
*Significantly different from zero at 1 percent level.
**Significantly different from zero at 10 percent level.

linear estimate predicts that an increase of $1,000 in total giving leads to an increase in headquarters giving of about $400, which implies that giving in the plant locations increases by a greater amount, $600.

The estimated elasticities of 0.78 to 0.94, however, indicate that the percentage increase in headquarters giving does not match the percentage increase in total giving.[26] Contributions to the headquarters city rise by a rate of only 78 to 94 percent of the growth rate in total contributions. Thus, when firms make more contributions at higher profit levels, firms tend to direct an increasingly larger proportion to the plant locations.

City-Specific Variables. Five city-specific variables were also entered as independent variables in the headquarters contribution regression.

Although none of these city-specific variables is significant in the logarithmic form regression, three are significant in at least one of the linear forms. The government funding and the state tax credit dummy variables are not significant in any of the regressions.[27] The three variables with significant coefficients are contributions by other firms in the home city, population of the home city, and local philanthropic resources.

Contributions by other local businesses is measured by corporate funds contributed to United Way, which does not encompass all other business giving to the city. The significantly negative coefficient in the linear form suggests that firms decrease their giving by $95 to $125 when corporate donations to United Way increase by $1,000. This result supports the hypothesis that firms act as cheap riders with respect to other firms. The insignificance of the logarithmic form estimate implies either that there may be no effect or that the follow-the-leader effect counterbalances the incentive to be a cheap rider. Thus, the empirical results do not provide clear guidance toward resolving this issue.

Fund-raising efforts aimed at more visible firms, which have larger revenues relative to the community, suggest that firms may contribute more when located in smaller cities. The contributions response to city size is significantly negative only in the per capita regression, in which all city-specific variables except population and the state tax credit dummy are expressed as per capita rather than absolute values. Expressing these city-specific variables relative to the city population allows the population variable to show significance, since all the other city-specific variables (except the tax dummy) tend to have a positive relationship with population. These estimates apply to the population range of the fourteen metropolitan areas in the sample, which is 770,000 to 2.4 million. The implication is that a firm would give $400 less to its headquarters city if it were located in a city that is 1,000 people larger.

One variable represents the joint effect of the capital and human resources in health and welfare, education, and culture and arts. The response of contributions to the joint presence of these resources is positive and significant in both linear forms. This implies that firms contribute more in headquarters cities that have a greater collective social service capacity, a more professional symphony, a larger private medical complex, a large, high quality private university, and more accredited museums.

Although philanthropic resources seem to be highly correlated with city size, each of these two variables has the opposite effect on contributions in the headquarters city. According to the results, a firm tends to give more in a smaller city, where it is more visible, but less if there are fewer resources (and accompanying fund-raisers) in the not-for-profit sector.

Implications

Our analysis of the distribution of contributions reveals that national organizations and educational institutions may expect more from larger companies. Also, philanthropies in cities with plants operated by larger corporations may expect an increasing proportion of the corporation's giving budget as its profits rise.

Whether or not a city would gain or lose after a merger depends on the size and giving level of the acquiring and acquired firms. A city benefits from the giving by firms whose headquarters offices are in the city, since a disproportionately high fraction of total contributions is directed to the headquarters city. However, if the firm were acquired by a much larger firm that directs an increasingly higher fraction to operating locations, the absolute level of giving directed to that city may rise.

Philanthropies can expect more contributions from relatively larger firms in a city and can expect firms to give more to those cities with accumulated philanthropic resources. There is evidence, however, that firms tend to behave as cheap riders and reduce their giving when other firms incur the contributions expense.

CONCLUDING IMPLICATIONS

This study addresses the question of whether larger firms, whose size is enhanced by conglomerate merger, support the not-for-profit sector as much as do smaller corporations. First we develop a theoretical economic model that encompassed factors motivating corporations to make philanthropic contributions. The design of this model was based on personal interviews with corporate giving officers in over 200 firms. We paid particular attention to the effect of firm size, which we measured as profits, on the magnitude and distribution of contributions. We tested the expected relationships empirically with two data sets: IRS corporate income tax returns data for 1972 and 1976, and the individual firm data that we collected during the interview process.

Merger Impact Based on Estimated Elasticities

Most of our estimates of the elasticity of contributions with respect to profits using the IRS data range from 0.9 to 1.0. The elasticity estimated from the individual firm data regressions is 0.72.

These estimates differ in that the IRS data include both large firms that give and those that do not, while the individual firm (interview) data include only firms that do make contributions. Therefore, the elasticity based upon IRS data represents the response by nongivers who begin making contributions when profits increase, as well as the response of giving firms to profit increases. For giving and nongiving firms combined, average contributions will increase at about the same rate (0.9 to 1.0) as the increase in profits. The smaller elasticity for individual firm data implies that larger firms with an existing contributions budget will increase their contributions less than proportionally with profits.

The impact of mergers on contributions can be evaluated from these results. The elasticity estimated from the individual firm data can be applied to specific merger situations in which the acquiring firms are large and make contributions. The elasticity from the IRS data can be used to predict the effect of mergers involving giving and nongiving acquiring firms with assets greater than $10 million.

We consider various combinations of acquiring and acquired firms— ones where the acquiring firm is an above average contributor and the acquired firm is a below average giver, and vice versa. If the distribution of the contributions to profits ratio is random across acquiring and acquired firms, then the impact of mergers in the aggregate on corporate contributions depends on the elasticity of giving with respect to profits and the relative size of acquiring and acquired firms. If, on the other hand, acquiring firms were generally higher contributors than acquired firms (or vice versa), the aggregate impact of mergers on contributions depends on the elasticity, relative size, and deviation of the giving–profits ratio for each of the merger partners (where it is assumed that the acquiring firm's policies will control the joint behavior after the merger occurs). We attempt to examine this latter possibility.

First, we interpret the individual firm elasticity, which applies to giving firms making acquisitions. Second, we interpret the IRS elasticity, which applies to giving and nongiving firms making acquisitions. Our interpretations are made under the assumption that conglomerate mergers do not per se increase efficiency and, hence, profits.

Giving Firms Making Acquisitions. The interpretation of the individual firm elasticity will be clearer if we first assume an elasticity of unity. When a large giving firm acquires a nongiving firm, contributions are expected to rise by a rate equal to (for elasticity of unity) the rate of increase in profits of the acquiring firm realized from the merger. When a giving firm acquires another giving firm, the net effect on contributions

TABLE 3.8
Impact of Mergers Between Contributing and Noncontributing Firms on Contributions

Relationship of Contribution–Profits Ratio of Acquiring Firm to Acquired Firm	IRS Elasticity of Contributions to Profits	Impact on Contributions
=	1	0
<	1	−
>	1	+
=	<1	−
=	>1	+

depends on the relative size of the contribution to profits ratio for each firm. If each firm had the same ratio prior to the merger, then, for a unitary elasticity, net contributions will not change. The increase in contributions by the acquiring and surviving firm will exactly replace the former contributions of the acquired and disappearing firm. This is because the increase in contributions of the acquiring firm is equal to its contribution–profits ratio times the increase in profits, which is equal to the former profit level of the acquired firm. The contribution formerly made by the acquired firm is also equal to the same contribution–profits ratio times its former profit level.

When the acquiring firm's contribution–profits ratio exceeds that of the acquired firm, then, for a unitary elasticity, the increase in the acquiring firm's contributions exceeds the contributions formerly made by the acquired firm. In this case, the higher contribution–profits ratio of the acquiring firm multiplied by the former profits of the acquired firm is greater than the lower ratio of the acquired firm multiplied by its former profits.

The implications are altered slightly when we consider the estimated elasticity of 0.72, which is less than unity.[28] The acquiring firm will increase contributions by only about three-fourths rather than the whole percentage increase in profits. This means that contributions increase by three-fourths of the product of the contribution–profits ratio and the increase in profits, which is the former profit level of the acquired firm. If the acquiring and acquired firms have the same contribution–profits ratio, then the acquiring firm's increased contribution is three-fourths the former contributions level of the acquired firm, and net contributions fall. Net contributions will not change if three-fourths (the elasticity) times the contribution–profits ratio of the acquiring firm is equal to the contribution–profits ratio of the acquired firm. Net contributions will increase if three-fourths the contribution–profits ratio of the acquiring firm exceeds the contribution–profits ratio of the acquired firm.

Giving and Nongiving Firms Making Acquisitions. The impact of mergers on contributions can be estimated with the IRS elasticity and estimates of the average contribution–profits ratio for the acquiring and acquired firms. Net contributions will increase if the product of elasticity and the ratio for the acquiring firms exceeds the ratio for the acquired firms. The IRS elasticity is based on data that average information for both giving and nongiving firms. Therefore, the elasticity represents the weighted average response of contributions for giving and nongiving firms whose profits change through mergers with other giving and nongiving firms.

The analysis is similar to that described for giving firms. Table 3.8 summarizes the effect of the IRS elasticity and the contribution–profit ratios of acquiring and acquired firms on contributions. For an elasticity of unity, contributions will remain unchanged when the average contribution–profit ratio for acquiring firms is equal to the contribution–profits ratio for acquired firms. For an elasticity of less than unity, when the average contribution–profits ratio is the same for acquiring and acquired firms, the net effect of mergers is to reduce contributions by the product of contributions formerly made by the acquired firm and one minus the elasticity.

We can predict the impact of a set of mergers using both the IRS elasticity estimates of 0.9 to 1.0 and the relative average contribution–profits ratios of the acquiring and acquired firms. If we know the average asset size of the firms involved in the mergers, we can obtain estimates of the average contribution–profits ratios by asset size classes from table 3.1. If most mergers were between firms of the same asset size class, then, according to table 3.1, the average contribution–profits ratio for the acquiring and acquired firms would be the same. Based on the estimated elasticity of 0.9 to 1.0, the net effect of mergers on contributions would be a slight drop or no change.

If most mergers were expected to involve the acquisition of medium-size firms by larger firms, the average estimated contribution–profits ratio would be 0.8 for the larger acquiring firms and 1.2 for the medium-size acquired firms. The predicted impact of mergers in this case would be a definite decline in contributions. Not only would there be a tendency for a decline caused by the slightly less than unitary elasticity (0.9 to 1.0) but also a decline because the contribution–profits ratio is lower for the acquiring firms than the acquired firms.

If medium-size firms were expected in general to acquire smaller firms, table 3.1 indicates that the contribution–profits ratio of the acquiring firms (1.2) would generally exceed that for the smaller acquired firms (approximately 0.2). The higher relative ratio of the acquiring firms would tend to cause net contributions to rise after the merger. However, the elasticity of slightly less than unity will exert downward pressure on the increase in contributions. We can estimate the effect more decisively by comparing the product of the elasticity and the contribution–profits ratio of the acquiring firms to the ratio of the acquired firms. A conservative computation using an elasticity of 0.9 rather than 1.0 yields the higher product of elasticity and acquiring firm ratio (1.08) than the acquired firm ratio (0.2). In this case, contributions would rise.

The Impact of Mergers on the Distribution of Contributions

Although the fraction of total contributions that remains in the headquarters city is disproportionately high (70 percent), as firms become larger and make more contributions, they direct an increasing fraction toward operating locations. Therefore, operating locations are likely to receive a larger share of a firm's increased contributions when the firm acquires another firm.

Whether the operating location that was formerly the headquarters city of the acquired firm will receive a net increase in contributions after the merger is ambiguous and depends on the premerger level of giving by the acquiring and acquired firms. Contributions tend to rise when the acquiring firm directs a larger proportion of the higher contributions to operating locations. However, contributions tend to fall because of the large proportion of total contributions directed to the headquarters city of the acquiring firm rather than to the operating locations. The former headquarters city will gain contributions from the merger if the portion of the acquiring firm's larger contributions budget directed to the city exceeds the level of contributions to the city formerly made by the acquired firm.

The results of patterns of giving by employment size of firm can be directly applied to mergers. Firms that become larger through merging are likely to allocate a larger portion of contributions to national organizations and educational institutions and a smaller fraction to religious causes.

NOTES

1. U.S. Congress, Senate Committee on the Judiciary, Subcommittee on Antitrust, Monopoly, and Business Rights, *The Small and Independent Business Protection Act, Part 2: Hearing on S. 600*, 96th Cong., 1st sess., 1979.

2. Ralph Nader, quoted in "Government May Abandon Fight To Stem Conglomerate Takeovers," *Wall Street Journal*, November 24, 1980, p. 18.

3. American Association of Fund-Raising Counsel, Inc., *Giving USA* (New York: American Association of Fund-Raising Counsel, 1981), p. 19.

4. Ralph L. Nelson, *Economic Factors in the Growth of Corporation Giving* (New York: National Bureau of Economic Research, 1970), pp. 4–7.

5. A more recent Treasury Department analysis of 1977 corporate income tax returns reveals the same pattern of the incidence of firms making contributions across asset size class. See Thomas Rosen, "1977 Statistics of Income, Charitable Deduction Tabulations," mimeographed (Washington, D.C.: Office of the Secretary of the Treasury, Office of Tax Analysis, October 19, 1981), table 2.

6. For 1945, 1946–1949, 1953, and 1954–1961, see Orace E. Johnson, "Corporate Philanthropy: An Analysis of Corporate Contributions," *Journal of Business* (October 1966), 39:496–501. For 1957, see Nelson, p. 62. For 1969, see Paul James Whitehead, "Some Economic Aspects of Corporate Giving" (Ph.D. diss., Virginia Polytechnic University, 1976), p. 69.

7. For details of the interview process and statistics of the interviewed firms, see Katherine E. Maddox, "Corporate Philanthropy," Ph.D. diss., Vanderbilt University, 1981; and John J. Siegfried and Katherine M. McElroy, "Corporate Philanthropy in the U.S.: 1980," Working Paper No. 81-W26 (Nashville: Vanderbilt University, Department of Economics and Business Administration, 1981).

8. Robert Schwartz, "Private Philanthropic Contributions: An Economic Analysis," Ph.D. diss., Columbia University, 1966; Schwartz, "Corporate Philanthropic Contributions," *Journal of Finance* (June 1968), 23:479–497; Nelson, *Economic Factors*, and Whitehead "Some Economic Aspects."

9. Orace E. Johnson, "Business Corporations and Philanthropy: A Study of Why Corporations Give," Ph.D. diss., University of Chicago, 1966; and Ferdinand K. Levy and Gloria M. Shatto, "The Evaluation of Corporate Contributions," *Public Choice* (March 1978), 33:19–28.

Other relevant articles include a critique of Schwartz by Orace E. Johnson and Walter L. Johnson, "The Income Elasticity of Corporate Philanthropy: Comment," *Journal of Finance* (March 1970), 25:149–152; the reply by Schwartz, "Reply," in *Journal of Finance* (March 1970), 25:153–157; two critiques of Levy and Shatto, one by Gerald D. Keim, Roger E. Meiners, and Louis W. Frey, "On the Evaluation of Corporate Contributions," *Public Choice* (June 1980), 35:129–136, and the other by James T. Bennett and Manuel H. Johnson, "Corporate Contributions: Some Additional Considerations," in *Public Choice*

(June 1980), 35:137–143; and the reply by Levy and Shatto, "The Evaluation of Corporate Contributions: A Reply," in *Public Choice* (June 1980), 35:145–149.

10. Prior to 1982 the Internal Revenue Code limited deductions for charitable contributions to 5 percent of pretax net income. In 1982 the limit was increased to 10 percent.

11. This source of measurement error is similar to Friedman's permanent (versus transitory) income as a determinant of consumption.

12. For a proof of the bias, see Michael D. Intrilligator, *Econometric Models, Techniques, and Applications* (Englewood Cliffs, N.J.: Prentice-Hall, 1978), pp. 190–193.

13. In addition, to check for consistent estimates, we estimated a quadratic and generalized nonlinear form. The quadratic form is a variation of the linear form with the profit term squared as an additional variable. The general nonlinear form is derived from an iterative technique based on a power transformation. This technique determines which type of functional form yields the best fitting relationship. A complete explanation can be found in Maddox, pp. 124–125.

14. The five-percentage-point range of giving to profits, from zero to the 5 percent limit, is a much larger absolute dollar value for higher profit than for lower profit firms. Consequently, the higher profit observations with larger error variances are weighed more heavily than those smaller profit observations with smaller error variances.

15. The variance of the error term varies systematically with the number per asset size class.

16. Each variable in the equation is transformed by a multiplier that forces the variance of the constant term to remain fixed. In this case the multiplier is equal to the square root of the ratio of the number of observations to the average profit level per asset size class.

17. The Tobit estimation procedure, appropriate for this problem, combines maximum likelihood estimates of the probability that firms will contribute (probit estimation) and regression analysis that disregards the zero givers.

For an explanation of the Tobit model, see James Tobin, "Estimation of Relationships for Limited Dependent Variables," *Econometrica* (January 1958), 26:24–36. For an explanation of the probit model, see Robert S. Pindyck and Daniel L. Rubinfield, *Econometric Models and Economic Forecasts*, 2d ed. (New York: McGraw-Hill, 1981), pp. 280–287.

18. Because the limit cases of firms with zero contributions have no negative deviations from the estimate, the assumption of normally distributed deviations around the expected value of the dependent variable is violated. For the central range of contributions values, the ordinary least squares regression line will be close, but because of its relative flatness it tends to diverge at the extremes. It will not produce good predictions of the response of contributions to a change in profits.

19. Since the error variance varies according to the number of firms per asset size class, the transforming multiplier is the square root of the number of observations.

20. The quadratic and nonlinear form elasticity estimates of the same subsets of firms are also close to unity. The elasticities estimated from the quadratic form range from 1.07 to 1.19, and from the power transformed nonlinear function, 0.90 to 0.97. See Maddox, pp. 125–131, for a complete presentation.

21. Nelson.

22. Kathryn Troy, *Annual Survey of Corporate Contributions* (New York: Conference Board, 1981), p. 20.

23. The elasticity of total giving with respect to profits estimated from the power transformed nonlinear function is 1.11.

24. City-specific variables are discussed in the section on the distribution of contributions, which reports the results of the headquarters contribution regression. A complete explanation of the measurement of these variables can be found in Maddox.

25. Because the individual firm data do not include nongiving firms, we could not test the likelihood that nongiving firms would respond to an increase in profits by making contributions. A probit analysis would reveal the probability that firms make a contribution at all as income rises. See Pindyck and Rubenfield, pp. 280–287.

26. The elasticity of headquarters giving with respect to total giving, estimated from the power transformed nonlinear function, is 0.91.

27. With respect to the state tax credit dummy, corporations may not be influenced by the existence of a state tax credit since state taxes are such a small percent of total taxes paid by firms.

28. In order to derive conditions for determining whether there is a net increase or decrease in contributions as a result of a merger, let us *assume* that the increase in contributions by the acquiring firm is equal to the contributions formerly made by the acquired firm. Thus:

$$\Delta X_o = X_1 \tag{1}$$

where X_i = premerger contributions and subscript $i = 0, 1$ where o = acquiring firm and 1 = acquired firm. When this equality holds, then the net effect of a merger is no change in contributions. The acquiring firm's additional contributions after the merger exactly replace the contributions formerly made by the acquired firm.

This assumed equality can be expressed by first restating ΔX_o:

$$\Delta X_o = \frac{\Delta X_o}{X_o} X_o \tag{2}$$

The change in contributions of the acquiring firm is equal to the percentage change in contributions times the initial level of contributions. The percentage change in contributions may also be restated by multiplying by ratios of unity:

$$\frac{\Delta X_o}{X_o} = \frac{\Delta X_o}{X_o} \frac{\pi_o}{\pi_o} \frac{\pi_1}{\pi_1} \tag{3}$$

and

$$\frac{\Delta X_o}{X_o} = \frac{\Delta X_o}{X_o} \frac{\pi_o}{\pi_1} \frac{\pi_1}{\pi_o} \tag{4}$$

where π_i = premerger profits and subscripts are defined as above. Knowing that in the merger case, the increase in profits of the acquiring firm is equal to the profits of the acquired firm, i.e., $\Delta \pi_o = \pi_1$,

$$\frac{\Delta X_o}{X_o} = \frac{\Delta X_o}{X_o} \frac{\pi_o}{\Delta \pi_o} \frac{\pi_1}{\pi_o} \tag{5}$$

The product of the first two ratios forms the elasticity of contributions with respect to profits, denoted by η. Thus:

$$\frac{\Delta X_o}{X_o} = \eta \frac{\pi_1}{\pi_o} \tag{6}$$

The percentage change in contributions is equal to the responsiveness of contributions to profits (η) times the percentage change in profits.

Combining (2) and (6),

$$\Delta X_o = \eta \left(\frac{\pi_1}{\pi_o} \right) X_o \tag{7}$$

Now, using (7), our assumed equality (2) can be restated:

$$\eta\left(\frac{\pi_1}{\pi_0}\right)X_0 = X_1 \tag{8}$$

The acquiring firm's increase in contributions (X_1) is equal to the elasticity (η) times the percentage increase in profits (π_1/π_0) times the former level of contributions (X_0).

Equation 8 can be rewritten as

$$\eta\left(\frac{X_0}{\pi_0}\right)\pi_1 = X_1 \tag{9}$$

The simple algebraic adjustment of the lefthand side reveals a different interpretation of the increase in the acquiring firm's contributions. It is equal to the elasticity (η) times the contribution–profits ratio (π_1/π_0) times the increase in profits (π_1).

Finally, the equation can be rewritten to yield the conditions for no change in contributions as a result of mergers:

$$\eta\left(\frac{X_0}{\pi_0}\right) = \frac{X_1}{\pi_1} \tag{10}$$

Net contributions will not change when the elasticity times the contribution–profits ratio of the acquiring firm is equal to the contribution–profits ratio of the acquired firm.

COMMENTATORS' REMARKS

STEPHEN STAMAS

I BELIEVE the McElroy–Siegfried paper provides a useful framework for looking at a number of issues relating to contributions, and as a practitioner, I particularly welcome the research and interest in a subject that is no longer peripheral in large corporations.

I would agree generally with the conclusions in the paper about large corporations. They are more likely to have an established contributions policy, to involve their executives in the not-for-profit sector, to have professional staff and as a result a more programmatic thrust in their activities.

I believe that the effort to think programmatically is part of the reason that the large corporations give more at the national level and more to education and the arts—along, of course, with having national markets and recruiting employees nationally.

I find it difficult to conclude much about the impact of a merger on the level of contributions. As has been already pointed out, to the extent that larger companies have higher pretax ratio contributions targets, this plus the resulting efficiencies of any merger should lead to higher and not lower contributions when a merger occurs.

The paper has identified an inversion where the largest companies appear to be giving lower percentages of their pretax income than the middle-size companies. I have no reason to doubt the historical data, but my perception of what is going on now is that it is the largest companies that are moving to higher targets, in some cases to 2 percent or more. I also suspect that the largest companies contribute more in the form of

139

executive time and other volunteer involvement and in equipment. This makes me wonder whether there is not too much emphasis in the analysis on the differences between middle-size and the largest companies.

Judging from my experience, the paper probably exaggerates the impact of tax rates on corporate contributions levels. While I do not want to discount the after-tax cost, because all of us carry that around implicitly as businessmen, I have never heard one discussion in Exxon of the after-tax cost. Contributions have grown as marginal tax rates have if anything declined. While one can argue that contributions would have grown more if the after-tax cost had been lower, I am skeptical that this factor weighs heavily in most corporations.

In my view, perception by management of what is expected of them in contributing to community and national concerns is probably the key to the increase in corporate contributions in the last ten years. These corporate perceptions develop as part of the "cake of custom" in our society and are a pragmatic response to widely held expectations of opinion leaders and the general public. Of course this expectations argument merges with the "direct business benefits" or interest rationale for contributions. But experience tells me that companies that have increased their ratio of contributions to earnings did not do so by adding up the potential corporate benefits of a contribution (such as image, employee recruiting, and morale). They decided to go to 2 percent or 5 percent over a period of time in response to expectations and looked for the best mix of grants to accomplish this.

There is of course a point of view that corporations should not accept a broader role beyond their economic mission or, failing that, that the noneconomic activities should be minimized. This is the other end of the spectrum from the views of some theorists that the modern corporation is much more than an economic entity.

I find myself in the middle on this issue. I don't think that corporations can be expected to substitute for government and others in dealing with many social or political problems. Some of the rhetoric coming out of Washington today is similar to the 1960s pressures to use the corporation and its resources to accomplish social and political change. I do believe, however, that there is a reasonable band of activity for corporations that has broad acceptance, and within that a corporation can make knowledgeable decisions and contributions to problem solving. This includes not only giving but also public service loan and volunteer programs through which the human expertise and commitment of corporations are made available and applied to the not-for-profit or the nongovernment sector.

I have one minor quibble about the report's conclusion that corporate contributions are very responsive to short-term changes in earnings. Over time contributions have to relate to earnings. We all live in the real world, and in the longer term the contributions activity cannot be going one way while the earnings of the corporation are going the other way. Many companies, however, cushion their contributions against short-term earnings changes. We at Exxon, for example, use a rolling average of the prior three years' earnings to determine the current year's level of contributions.

I am not surprised that there have been some cuts by individual companies in contribution activity in this depressed economic climate. In fact, I am surprised that contributions have not fallen in the aggregate despite the recession. Over time, of course, the best thing that can happen to stimulate corporate contributions is resumption of corporate earnings growth.

One final comment about the subject of who decides on the recipients of corporate grants. We are conscious in Exxon of accountability to shareholders and the public. We try to obtain professional judgment before making grants and to involve as many people as possible in the process. One device that helps is a matching gifts program for higher education, which puts the decision in the hands of our employees and annuitants, most of whom are also shareholders. We have $8 million going to higher education this year through the matching grants program.

We have looked at Mr. Sproul's plan and the Berkshire Hathway plan. You have to strike a balance between participation and efficiency. You do have to worry about the complexity and the diffuseness of these approaches, especially for a large company, for example, the administrative nightmare of deciding who qualifies as an Exxon shareholder if you were to go to some of the schemes that have been mentioned.

LAWRENCE A. WIEN

THE McElroy–Siegfried paper is very well done. Of course, it addresses only one phase of corporate philanthropy, which is the effect of mergers on corporate giving. The paper does, however, contain a lot of interesting material somewhat removed from the specific issue described in its title.

I think it is a bit unfortunate that the paper was prepared at this time because it is predicated to a large extent on figures that I think are obsolete. In 1981 and 1982 there was a dramatic increase in philanthropic contributions as a result of efforts made by quite a few to get corporations to increase their giving.

I bought stock in over 400 corporations and have communicated with executives in all of them. In 150 or more corporations, I filed proxy proposals, where the corporations did not adopt a program for increased giving. However, it was not necessary for me to speak at more than twenty-five annual meetings, because most of the corporations in which proxy proposals were filed did wind up adopting a program for philanthropic increases. So that, while the information in the paper is helpful and accurate, I think that the picture would be considerably different if the years involved were 1981 and 1982. When we talk of the percentage of pretax earnings in relation to corporate gifts, it should also be remembered that 1982 will show a dramatic increase in the percentage of pretax earnings, because of a colossal reduction in earnings. If some corporations gave only on the basis of earnings, a lot of habitual donors would disappear from the picture altogether because they simply made no profit in 1982.

I would like to digress a bit from the particular subject in the paper to give you a little of the picture of the entire problem of corporate philanthropy and how I feel about it.

I believe that corporations have a distinct social responsibility. Corporations are not individuals protected by our Constitution. The corporation is a fictitious legal entity, created by legislative enactment—an imaginary person. Corporations were created to allow people to enter into a venture with a certain amount of money and to risk losing that amount only. Under the common law, there was no such limit on liability, and everything one owned would be subject to the claims of the creditors of a business. In authorizing corporations, legislatures, usually state legislatures, imposed certain obligations, such as income taxes, franchise taxes, and other requirements. Corporations are required to pay for the privilege of existing as corporations.

The question is whether we go further and require corporations, because we feel that they have a social responsibility, to contribute to the social needs of the communities in which they operate, and even perhaps to contribute on a national scale.

First, let us look at the social benefits a corporation enjoys. I might say that I believe every corporation should allocate its grants first to the agencies that are most meaningful to it. Thus, I think that corporations should make contributions to local hospitals in the many communities in which they are involved. I was on the board of Borden for thirteen years, and it had fifty-five profit centers, which means fifty-five different businesses. In every one of them was a local hospital, some of which were not geared to provide good medical care to the employees of the corporation who used those hospitals. I think it incumbent upon a corporation to help to improve medical care for its employees. Healthier individuals made better and more efficient employees.

Many corporations employ a host of engineers. Without engineering schools, they would not have trained engineers. It is certainly sensible for the corporation to give to engineering schools. The same is true for other areas. For example, even trade schools are deserving of support from corporations because their graduates may ultimately become corporate employees.

In New York City, we once had a lot of corporations moving to nonurban areas. However, there was one thing that kept many corporations from moving. In New York City you have the greatest center of cultural exposure in the world. Lincoln Center, with which I happen to be involved, caused many officers to say that they did not want to go out of the city because they and their families felt that the exposure to the many cultural activities in the city was something they wanted to continue.

I think you might also mention that many corporations have a better corporate image, particularly corporations dealing with consumer products, when it is known that they support various socially beneficial agencies and programs from which all of us benefit. When I buy gas today, I usually go to either Exxon or Mobil because I think they do the best job of contributing to socially beneficial programs.

I must say that it was most interesting to get the reaction of chief executive officers in the corporations with which I dealt. I did find some executives who followed the reported thinking of Milton Friedman. In my opinion, however, this great Nobel laureate did not know what he was talking about when he said that the corporations should not contribute to any philanthropic agencies because their job was to make money.

A few executive officers, particularly those who might some day look for a better job in another corporation and want the best possible bottom line record, expressed agreement with Mr. Friedman's thinking. We used to describe such individuals as "having their impulse to generosity under complete control." Many of them spoke as though they were giving away their own money. I was surprised by the thinking of these few, because the vast majority of corporate executive officers were completely in agreement with the need for and the propriety of corporate giving.

Most corporate executive officers serve as trustees of universities or of hospitals, or on the boards of various philanthropic agencies. They know the problems of the agencies and the urgent need for support if the worthwhile agencies are to survive. I had an interesting experience with the American Cyanamid Corporation. I am a lawyer and my firm has done some legal work for that corporation. Before starting my program of stock acquisition and proxy proposals, I had invited a group of prominent individuals to a luncheon, at which I described my intentions. I created a committee from this group, which included individuals such as John Connor, Douglas Dillon, John L. Loeb, William May, and many others of considerable stature in the corporate world. They were not asked to do anything, but the stationery had their names on it. When I wrote to a corporation and asked information about its charitable giving, the names of the committee members made a great difference.

One of the men I invited to that lunch was the chief executive officer of American Cyanamid Corporation. He called me and said that he did not believe that corporations should give anything to charity and that he approved the thinking of Milton Friedman. Obviously, he did not become a member of the committee. Being a stubborn individual, I purchased stock in American Cyanamid Corporation anyway, and I asked for a record of what they gave. Shortly after, the chief executive officer called me and said that I knew how he felt about this program. However, he went on to say that he had brought up my letter at a meeting of the board of directors and the directors were unanimous in disagreeing with him. As a result, he had appointed a corporate contributions committee, and as a matter of fact, I later received a lovely letter from him, thanking me for encouraging them to look at themselves and what they were doing in the field of corporate social responsibility. I have a number of such letters from corporations, and they are very gratifying.

The vast majority of executive officers were sympathetic to what we were trying to do with respect to corporate philanthropic giving. Corporations like to do what other corporations are doing, particularly those in the same area, and so a pattern is something that is significant to most corporate officers. When, not long ago, the Business Roundtable, which is a very significant organization in corporate circles, recommended that all corporations should increase their charitable giving to 2 percent of pretax earnings, it had a definite effect on corporate officers. I think that corporate pretax earnings should normally be used to measure corporate philanthropic giving. Many corporations do create foundations that help to stabilize corporate giving during unfavorable years. Basically, however, I believe that there should be a relationship between the profits earned and the grants made as a fulfillment of the corporation's social responsibility.

There are only three other things that I want to mention briefly. First, very few people actually realize how little it costs to increase philanthropic giving substantially. I remember that with Georgia Pacific Corporation I suggested an increase of about $2 million. They gave a little more than $1 million. I showed that it would cost the stockholders after the saving in income taxes less than one penny a share. Increased corporate giving costs very little, would rarely, if ever, affect dividends materially, and would help to enable many threatened important social agencies to avoid extinction.

Remember that corporations can give about twice as much as the shareholder can give from his dividends. I do not approve of the suggestion that shareholders should designate the agencies to which the corporation should give the shareholders' portion of dividends. Some agencies might well be adverse to the interests of the corporation, and also corporations would be deprived of the opportunity to select the agencies that are most important and beneficial to the corporation.

Two final things. First, I usually end my speech when I speak at an annual meeting by telling the story of the two families, like the McCoys and the Hatfields, who had a terrible fight. The dispute got to court and the whole proceeding was extremely unpleasant. Finally, the judge charged the jury and it withdrew. After a while, the jury returned, and the judge said to the foreman, "Has the jury reached a decision?" The foreman said, "Yes, Your Honor." "What is the decision of the jury?" The foreman replied, "The jury has decided not to get involved in this case."

Second, I suggested something perhaps a bit radical when I spoke recently in Chicago at a luncheon of the Donors Forum. I urged that we ought to think about what we can do with respect to the corporations that give very little or nothing at all. How can we change that picture? We all believe in voluntarism, but if corporate support of social agencies is a responsibility and inadequate, voluntarism is apparently not enough.

It seems to me that there may well be a couple of other methods of getting corporate involvement in social responsibility. One suggestion I made was that the federal government might state that it is the considered policy of the government to encourage corporations to give at least 2 percent of their pretax earnings to socially beneficial programs. Incidentally, the giving does include things other than money—such as gifts in kind and loaned executives. Many corporate executives take jobs with the United Way for a period of time, and their salaries are paid by the corporation. This is really the equivalent of a corporation making a gift of money that the agency would use to employ others.

I might also mention that corporate charitable giving is a misnomer for me. It is not charity. Such giving is part of the fulfillment of a corporation's social responsibility.

To revert to my suggestion, suppose the government said that a minimum of 2 percent of pretax earnings is our policy, and the difference between a corporation's actual gifts, if less than 2 percent, and 2 percent of pretax earnings, would be taxed by the government at 100 percent. It is a very interesting idea. It was welcomed by practically no one. I had one of my friends, a member of Congress, write to certain people, asking their reaction. It was quite uniformly opposed as unwise.

Suppose, as an alternative, the government were to give some extra tax benefit to corporations that go beyond a certain suggested figure. Thus, suppose that gifts above 2 percent of pretax earnings would be given a deduction of 150 percent for income tax purposes. After all, corporations are authorized to give up to 10 percent of pretax earnings for charitable gifts, and 2 percent is very modest. In any event, we do have to find a way of getting the laggards to assume their share of social responsibility so that some day these two very bright young people who wrote today's paper can prepare another report that speaks of the tremendous gain in the acceptance of social responsibility by American corporations.

ARTHUR H. WHITE

I AM prepared to do two things here: first, to comment on the McElroy–Siegfried paper, and second, to add some things that Yankelovich, Skelly, and White have learned particularly from a very comprehensive study we did last year for the Council on Foundations among 219 companies from the *Fortune* 1300 down to companies with $25 million in sales.

To us, one of the interesting things is that we received more cooperation from CEOs while making this study than we have ever received in our history. CEOs wanted to talk about philanthropic giving because there is a problem and they are uncertain about many aspects of it.

I want to make four points with respect to the McElroy–Siegfried paper. First, our work shows that the larger the company, the more likely it is to be a corporate giver. For example, 100 percent of the *Fortune* 1300 companies we studied were givers, and 96 percent of those between $50 million and $100 million were givers, but only 22 percent of those between $25 million and $50 million were givers. There is a direct correlation by size.

Second, as to the motivation for giving, we found that enlightened self-interest—and the word *enlightened* is the word to emphasize—is the dominant factor. It was interesting to talk to the CEOs on this subject and to hear them say that they justify giving by convincing themselves that it does help to recruit employees and does help to make employees' lives better. It does help a consumer products company with its image, and so forth.

Third, on the allocation between headquarters and other locations, our work does substantiate the fact that headquarters tends to get a disproportionate share.

Fourth, allocations to health and welfare go down as the size of the company increases; conversely, the larger the company, the more it gives to education.

Now let me go on and try to add to what was highlighted in your study. First, the broad question: Will it help a company to give?

I would like to say that it is not easy in a a few brief words to summarize all that we have learned on this subject in more than a thousand studies of corporate image. But on the basic "gut" question—Does giving generally improve a company's image—my answer is yes. It helps a company in a number of different ways, but a lot depends on the company's particular circumstances. For example, it is harder for Exxon to get the benefit of corporate giving than it is for a company that is not the object of as much criticism as the oil companies have been.

It also depends on the history of the company. We have done much publicized work for ITT in the period that it has been in deep trouble. And we have tried to help it to improve its image. It makes a lot of difference if you have that kind of burden to overcome or if you are coming in with a relatively untarnished image. It depends on how well a company publicizes what it does. It depends finally on the amounts that it gives and how and to whom it gives money.

There are a lot of different effects from giving. I do not remember doing a study of a corporation that has a significant corporate giving program that concluded anything but that the program had had a positive effect among its customers, whether they were consumers or industrial users. It also helps among a company's employees or potential employees, meaning those whom managers would like to recruit to work for the company.

In the work we did, another major factor was the role of the CEO. This was just fascinating to us. CEOs wanted to talk to us and wanted to participate. But this study was distinguished from others in that when CEOs talked to us they often talked to us one on one. Normally, when we talk to CEOs about marketing, finance, production, employee relations, you name it, they would not think of having that kind of discussion without having some of their staff people with them.

In this study, many of the interviews were held with the CEO alone because he or she is number one. CEOs did say that potentially the board can and does influence decisions, but organizations outside of the company really have much less influence than we would have thought when we started the study.

Having made the point of CEO centrality in the giving process, we went on to establish the relationship between CEO commitment to giving and size of company and found this interesting picture; among companies with a high CEO commitment, the following percentages apply to their giving: 1.1 percent of profit is given by the biggest companies; 1.5 percent by the medium-size companies; and 2.0 percent for the small companies. And the companies with a CEO with a low level of commitment report about 0.4 percent for the largest, 0.7 percent for the medium, and 1.3 percent for the smallest. It is clear that the CEO and his commitment is what makes the difference.

Another point, is the extraordinary lack of self-confidence and knowledge that CEOs exhibit in this area. Many of you know CEOs well. They do not get to that role in companies by saying, "I don't know," or "We don't feel that we are doing a particularly good job." Yet that is what so many said about corporate giving.

When we asked them whether they were going to give more, we expected a lot of them to point to the economic conditions—the recession—and say, "Leave us alone. We'll be lucky to be able to give what we have in the past." But two out of three of them said that they expected that their corporations will give more in the future than in the past, the reason being that they support the president's effort, believe in reducing the role of government, and recognize that business will have to do more if they are to escape the charge of being hypocrites.

I wish to make a final point. I believe that American business is in trouble, and I can tell you a lot of reasons why. But a principal reason is because the country is in trouble and business is being turned to as a source of help, remedy, and support.

A type of major new effort business might advantageously make in this era would be to pitch in and help the country to upgrade the secondary school system. American business has supported higher education well. The same kind of effort is needed for secondary education. I am not saying that business has to put in the money, but it has to help in a lot of ways. Unless business does, I think that it will suffer along with the rest of us.

BEVIS LONGSTRETH

I AM not going to comment directly on the good paper by Katherine McElroy and John Siegfried. After hearing the comments made and reading the paper I am, however, tempted to say one thing about the effect of firm size and mergers on corporate philanthropy. It reminds me of the story about the professor who spent a long time writing a book on the snakes of Ireland. The unveiling of the study was a celebrated event. Many had long awaited its arrival and a chance to peek at its contents. On looking inside the cover, the reader found but a single sentence, stating: "There are no snakes in Ireland." In a way this captures the essence of the relationship between mergers and corporate giving.

What I would like to talk about is the premise on which the study is based. That premise is that, since corporate gifts are a substitute for government funding, policy makers are today attempting to encourage corporations to increase the amounts they give to charities. Thus, for example, President Reagan's advisory panel on charity recently gave the president a variety of proposals designed to double the nation's corporate giving. But should not policy makers be asking why does one want to increase corporate giving as a surrogate for government funding? Is that really a good thing for society, and if it is a good thing, at what level of giving might it turn into something else?

I don't think that you can answer these questions without answering some others.

First, does it make a difference how a corporation goes about the business of giving away its net pretax profits?

There are various ways of doing this. The directors can make the decisions. The CEO can make the decisions, which we have heard is the dominant way in which gifts are made. The employees can make the decisions under a matching program, which today is in widespread use and perhaps will increase in the future. Finally, shareholders can be permitted to decide whether and when to give, which is the approach now being implemented by Warren Buffett at Berkshire Hathaway. It is not a model that many people are following, but it is a model that I think corporations ought to look at closely.

There is a bill in Congress, introduced by Senator Moynihan and Representative Conable, to make generally available the favorable tax ruling that Berkshire Hathaway obtained to protect individual shareholders from adverse tax consequences.

Another question that should be answered before one can reach a conclusion as to whether we should try to increase corporate giving is this: How should we define or redefine the corporate purpose?

What is the purpose of the corporation? In raising this question, of course, I recognize that it is posed year in and year out. But I want to call to your attention the approach to defining the corporate purpose being taken in the draft Restatement and Recommendations on Principles of Corporate Governance and Structure, currently being considered by the American Law Institute.

This is a document with which many of you, I think, have had much to do. It is an important document now undergoing wide debate. It defines the objective and conduct of business corporations, and in one respect that definition is different from the laws that now exist. Generally, it says that the corporate objective is to conduct business activities with a view to corporate profit and shareholder gain. There are exceptions, however. One exception provides that, even if corporate profit and shareholder gain are not thereby enhanced, the corporation "may devote resources, within reasonable limits, to public welfare, humanitarian, educational, and philanthropic purposes." This exception would work a change in the law. Virtually all states now have in place statutory provisions empowering corporations to make contributions for the public welfare and for charitable, educational, and scientific purposes. These powers, however, have been widely interpreted to permit their use *only* in the interests of the corporation. In short, the economic purpose test applies.

I think that one should seriously question—and I do seriously question—the need or desirability for this kind of change. I think that this change would invite the corporation to enter charitable fields beyond its area of expertise. It would encourage charitable activities outside of those closely identified with the economic purposes of the corporation.

One must ask whether it is wise for the government to delegate its public functions to corporations through the device of tax deductions for charitable giving wholly disconnected from corporate profit and shareholder gain. It is essentially a governmental function to decide what public interest goals we, as a society, ought to be pursuing and then to fund the pursuit with government dollars. If we do not like the policies that the government has set for us, we should change the government rather than try to get the corporate structure retooled to perform what is essentially a governmental function.

Moreover, one should ask whether there is a demand for this change. I am aware of no evidence suggesting that the present powers have proved inadequate to support the philanthropic impulses of our business leaders. Some would argue that the change is necessary to leave elbow room for the "decent instincts" that corporate managers are unwilling to—or cannot—rationalize under the profitability test. But there is no solid evidence of this need. And my instinct leads me to believe that the present rule serves the important purpose of making top management think twice (or more) before making gifts of corporate assets to express what may be decent instincts but what also are essentially the personal interests of those managers, where those personal interests are not obviously congruent with corporate interests.

I now want to share with you some recent thinking on matters of corporate purpose. It may provoke discussion later. Professor Robert Clark of Harvard Law School, in a recent paper delivered to the Academy of Arts and Sciences, looked at the proper role for the corporation in its relationship to governmental tasks from five possible perspectives. They present an interesting way of thinking about the corporate purpose.

The first is what he called *realism*, which is strict profit maximization. It presupposes a just distribution of wealth and acceptable institutional arrangements in government.

The second is *monism*, which he defined as the long-run identity between public and private interests. In other words, it is in the long-run private interest of the corporation to carry out public interests. This theory Clark sees as uncritically conventional and merely palliative.

A third theory he called *modest idealism*, which is simply voluntary compliance with law. If you scan the corporate horizon with care, this goal may be more difficult to achieve than it sounds. Total compliance with law by corporations is unusual. Some corporate managers feel that if it is cost effective not to comply and to accept the consequences of noncompliance, then they will follow that policy as long as it works. Clark sees modest idealism as not likely to be widely practiced.

A fourth model would be what Clark called *high idealism*, which is interest group accommodation, with the public interest as a residual goal. The normal residual goal under a realistic model of the corporation is the shareholder, who is entitled to all that remains of earnings and assets, after the other specific obligations of the corporation are met. The *high idealism* model would substitute for the shareholder, as the residual goal of the corporation, the public interest, to be expressed through agreement among the different constituencies represented on the board of the corporation.

In effect, the corporation would be governed by constituencies that represented not just the shareholders but the many other elements of society affected by the corporation. Clark saw this model as destroying the chief virtue of the business corporation (a critical focus on profits) and as spreading to the business corporation the failure of government in being unable to define its goals.

Finally, Clark offered *pragmatism,* which he defined as the contracting by corporations with government to carry out public goals. This model would be consistent with the *realism* model we started out with.

I think that the ideas expressed in this paper, although unfortunately not leading to any ringing conclusion as to what the optimum corporate purpose would be, are well worth the attention of this group.

In considering the questions that I have raised, it is important to take into account some of the numbers that help to place our subject in proper perspective. As you know, since World War II, the average giving level has been about 1 percent of taxable income. This level has remained remarkably steady. I do not have as current data as Mr. Wien, however, and it is possible that very recently the level has tended toward 2 percent, particularly among the larger corporations.

Of course, it has long been government policy to encourage corporate giving up to 5 percent of taxable income. This encouragement is found in the Internal Revenue Code, which affords a corporate tax deduction for gifts to charity up to 5 percent of a corporation's taxable income. Now, this policy was changed overnight—and I mean that literally—from 5 to 10 percent, when during the summer of 1981, Senator Kennedy introduced an amendment to increase the ceiling.

Thus, without any debate in Congress, the government doubled the amount that corporations are officially—by favorable tax treatment—encouraged to give to charities out of taxable income.

I find it profoundly disturbing that something like that could be done without debate. Isn't it worth some inquiry as to the wisdom of delegating in such magnitude an essentially governmental function to business corporations? Let me just give you an idea of what it would mean for AT&T to give the full 10 percent. With a taxable income of some $100 billion, this policy encourages AT&T to give $1 billion a year to charitable causes of its own selection and at taxpayers' expense. That is ten times the annual giving level of the Ford Foundation.

I submit that it is difficult to give away, effectively, $1 billion to the public and still tend to one's main business, which is to earn profits through the delivery of goods or services.

I am not standing up here opposed to any charitable giving by corporations. Far from it. I am saying only that there is room for debate as to what is in the best interests of the country.

A couple of other numbers. The Rockefeller Foundation gives away $48 million with a staff of 200; Exxon gives away $52 million with a staff of 22. They ought to get together and compare notes. Obviously, assuming no feather bedding, these organizations are engaged in very different kinds of charitable activity.

What I submit is going on, and why I urged the American Law Institute not to change the standard, is that these two organizations give to very different kinds of charities. The Rockefeller Foundation, and I am just using it as a surrogate for all effective foundations, is, or at least should be, at the cutting edge of philanthropy. It should be putting risk capital where neither business nor government will put funds, in order to reach a goal—to meet an important societal need.

I do not think that corporations should do that sort of thing because it would take a big and highly trained staff to do it well and because it is not their main business. By definition, it would not meet the economic purpose test. Thus, a corporation would not consider making such a gift if the powers it has to give money away are limited to what is close to its economic self-interest.

One final observation. I read Edwin Epstein's excellent paper (see part V), and I am struck by some parallels between corporate philanthropy and corporate political action committees.

In each case one could assert that the corporation becomes an agent with discretion for principals, empowered to spend the principals' money as the agent sees fit. In the case of charitable giving, the principals are the shareholders of the corporation.

In the case of the PACs, the principals are the employees. In each case it is important to note that the benefits derived from this use of money are bestowed upon the agent and to some extent its officers rather than on those who provide the money.

Now, in small sums with small corporations, maybe none of this is very important. However, given the growing concentration of our industries in the hands of fewer and fewer corporations, what do these developments—projected forward in time—portend? Should we be concerned about the power to affect public policy given to top corporate managers who may, by means of these two similarly delegated functions, dispense other people's money as they see fit?

I ask these questions not because I think that top corporate managers do not have as good judgment or perhaps even better judgment than anyone else but because there is an accountability in our governmental system that is very important and that calls the makers of public policy to account through the electoral process. No comparable system of accountability exists among corporations.

DIALOGUE

Ms. TROY: I am from the Conference Board. First, I want to make some comments on the overall level of corporate giving.

With reference to Mr. Wien's comments as to whether philanthropy is going up, it is indeed up again for 1981 and we collected data for 1982. We studied eight hundred large corporations, and they are expecting the budget in 1982 to be up to about 2.82 percent of pretax profits.

With respect to the effect of mergers, in evaluating headquarters versus plant location, one other element that you have to look at is how decentralized the company is. If it is a decentralized company, the contributions come out of the profits and the plant manager is under pressure to make profits, and the last thing he is worried about is making contributions.

MR. BATES: I think this was a good paper. I am concerned about the use of this paper, at least if it stands alone, if it purports to represent what corporations are doing about corporate philanthropy. We are dealing with the social and political impact of large corporations, and this certainly is good and useful material that has been assembled, but it is pretty far short of representing what corporations are really doing as far as corporate philanthropy is concerned.

Three of our speakers have addressed the subject of what corporations are doing in kind; what they are doing in providing leadership. For example, in most communities they are providing the leadership for all sorts of activities, be it hospitals, Little Leagues, colleges, or universities. That is the sort of leadership that they are providing, and Mr. Wien, I believe it was, mentioned that they loan people who are devoting full time for a certain period to these activities. I think that the cash giving of corporations is really probably less than half, although I do not know of any measures on it, of the total of what they give. Certainly so far as the influence of corporations on their communities is concerned, cash giving is far less than half.

MR. HANSON: I want to take note of the fact that this corporate giving discussion implicitly suggests a pressure model for the largest corporation. I would hope that some of the research would get at that. It could be a chance for the large corporation to demonstrate that there is an accountability system in place. The best anecdote is that in the late 1960s, when there was a lot of activism against banks in California, Wells Fargo would schedule its banking meetings at the same time as those of the Bank of America.

MS. MADDOX: I wanted to respond to the noncash gifts discussion. We looked at that. It is very hard to quantify, and we did the best we could. I think we have about 83 percent of total gifts, cash and nonmonetary, for our sample.

MR. GOLDSCHMID: We will soon discuss "community impact," and many of the noncash giving issues will be expanded upon there.

MR. WHITE: The concern of many of us here is will corporations be responsible if they give more? Is there not a negative side to this increased giving? That is a possibility.

MR. WIEN: I would like to have somebody do a paper on the corporations who give little or nothing and how we can, in effect, pressure them, if necessary, to recognize their responsibilities.

MR. STAMAS: On the question of the limit of corporate power and what kind of accountability we should have. I take a relatively narrow view of how far a corporation should go to begin with. We at Exxon insist on reporting everything we do. We put it out into the open. There is diversity in our giving. We are not at the point where size and accountability is the problem.

I must say that if you believe that corporations give to create a kind of soft umbrella for their image, you are making a bad guess. There is evidence showing that Mobil and others have absolutely no impact on what is done on television. If that is the reason for giving, the people are being very misguided.

PART III

COMMUNITY IMPACT

D URING much of the first part of this century economic freedom was seen as the corporate counterpart of political democracy, but then social critics began with increasing vigor to see many aspects of the enterprise system as a danger to public welfare, as when large enterprises were perceived to be monopolizing or sharing the monpolization of markets. At the same time, bigness as such, or diversification over a range of markets, was perceived as excess economic and social power. Thus, high individual market shares, high market concentration, and high aggregate concentration were all seen as dangerous not only to the economy as a whole but to its citizens as individuals.

The high tide of this structural view of the enterprise system was reached in the late 1960s, but in the 1970s new commentators noted that persistent bigness is not necessarily antithetical to competition and that it may equate with efficiency rather than with the possession of undue economic power. The economic dialogue continued into the late 1970s and early 1980s, but during this period a new "antibigness" rationale came into prominence, based on the premise that, regardless of economic justifications, high market shares or great corporate size are bad for social reasons—because, for example, "dominance" or size lead to worker alienation, unresponsive absentee ownership, and the alienation of mobile plant management to the concerns of the communities in which the facilities they manage are located. Despite widespread concern that large conglomerate absentee parents are bad for the communities in which their plants are located, there had by the late 1970s been little research to show how responsive or unresponsive such managements were to the needs of communities, as compared with smaller companies or owner-managements who had always lived in the communities in which their facilities were located. In order to begin to fill any gap between social beliefs and the facts, three research professionals were asked to undertake empirical examinations of these issues.

Professor Jon Shepard of the University of Kentucky undertook to examine management mobility and the degree to which geographically and hierarchically mobile managers reporting to absentee superiors take part in organizations that focus on community concerns; Professor Roger Schmenner of Duke University examined the rationale for, and the effects of, plant openings, closings, extensions, and contractions; and Professor Ivar Berg of the University of Pennsylvania carried out an in-depth study of workers' responses to union activity and to unemployment in two small communities in western Michigan.

Professor Shepard found that mobile managers participate in community activities as fully, if not more fully, than do their less mobile counterparts; indeed, of greater significance in predicting community participation of managers than the size or diversification of a parent company, or the geographic distance of top management, is the parent's attitude toward management participation and the degree to which a manager's friends in the community engage in such work. Professor Berg, however, found that "local owners and their managers are far more often involved in community-related and community-serving activities than are their peers among absentee-owned firms."

Professor Schmenner found that plant openings and closings are more closely related to overall economic considerations and to plant design requirements than to corporate size; he did not find any tendency to favor headquarters' locales at the expense of more distant sites in planning for plant closings.

Finally, Professor Berg found that, although local union leaders originally feared ownership of local firms by absentee parents, they have (at least to some degree) come to benefit from outside union and management expertise. He also found that, in the small western Michigan communities he studied, unemployment led to less severe human problems than earlier research studies have indicated. He suggests, on the basis of his data, that where wage earners are, on average, young, are members of multi-wage earner families, and have health, education, and income-preserving organizations available to support them, plant closings and the resulting unemployment are not necessarily as grim a condition as other researchers have found.

In summary, the work on the community impact of the major corporation suggests that there are no black and white effects of bigness or absentee ownership as such. The evidence suggests that the impact of size and remote ownership differs with corporate policy—and the specific structure and organization of community services.

CHAPTER 4

Organization Size, Managerial Mobility, and Corporate Policy: A Study of the Community Participation of Managers

Jon M. Shepard and
James G. Hougland, Jr.

T HE influence of business and industry on community life has long
been of interest to social scientists.[1] Proponents of the power elite
perspective have consistently contended that decisions are dominated
by business and industrial leaders, to the advantage of corporate interests.[2] Although pluralists have not denied that business and industrial
leaders are among the important actors in community affairs, they do
not see them as dominating all community decisions.[3]

It is widely acknowledged that corporations have some influence over
community affairs, but the effects of that influence are by no means certain. Such uncertainty partly reflects conflicting findings of previous researchers, but it also stems from changes in the role of business and industry in community affairs. These changes include increasing firm size,
managerial mobility, and corporate policy regarding community involvement.

The business scene is increasingly being dominated by fewer and larger firms. This trend toward bigness in business has in recent years drawn expressions of both optimism and pessimism.[4] Most analysts would agree that extensive social and political activity is largely a "big business" phenomenon,[5] but such conclusions tend to be based on examination of national rather than local activities. The social science literature on the community effects of company size has focused less on size per se than on absentee ownership. The assumption, of course, has been that increased absentee ownership is a major consequence of corporate growth.

A major trend throughout the twentieth century has involved a replacement of local ownership by absentee ownership. Social scientists have been concerned with the effects of absentee ownership on community well-being.[6] Stern and Aldrich also expressed that concern:

The creation of absentee owned corporations created a calculus of corporate welfare separate from that of community welfare. Though the corporation still required the cooperation of local governments and labor forces, the community simply became a geographic location in which to operate as long as relative cost advantages were maintained. Commitment to the community itself and knowledge of the local social structure declined because professional managers sent to run these branch plants were more concerned with their careers in the larger corporation than with the quality of community life.[7]

In his study of Ypsilanti, Michigan, Schulze predicted that the increasing trend toward absentee ownership would have the following effects:

As the activities of these units became increasingly directed toward—and by—populations and groups other than the local ones, the relevance of local community organizations and the impact of local political influences on the major economic units would accordingly diminish. As this occurred, the local power structure would in effect bifurcate—with those who exercised primary direction over its sociopolitical system no longer being essentially the same set of persons who exercised primary control over its economic system.[8]

Schulze's prediction is quite compatible with what he reported finding in Ypsilanti, suggesting that economic units with absentee ownership may avoid day-to-day involvement in local affairs because of their limited dependence on the local community for economic success. Results from other studies suggest that Schulze may have underestimated the amount of corporate involvement in local affairs.[9] However, the theme developed by Schulze has become a dominant one in the literature.[10]

The focus of a manager's concerns is based in part on his daily experience. "When a business centralizes its offices in the community, its major owners or executives come to reside there and their concern for the community is heightened. . . . Decentralization has the opposite effect."[11] Absentee-owned corporations, then, may fail to encourage local managerial involvement because local problems are not part of the action framework of corporate decision makers.

The above analysis implies that organization size alone determines corporate policy regarding managerial participation in local community affairs. This could be misleading. Any apparent effects of size may stem in part from the tendency for large organizations to transfer their managers from one location to another. We therefore turn to a consideration of the geographic mobility of managers.

MANAGERIAL MOBILITY

Like organization size (and its concomitant, absentee ownership), managerial mobility has become increasingly important in the American economy. Managers, mobile and immobile, are likely to possess demographic and social characteristics ordinarily associated with high levels of participation in community affairs. For reasons similar to those discussed in the case of absentee ownership, however, managerial mobility may have the effect of decreasing involvement on the local level. Despite some exceptions,[12] many studies (not confined to managers) show that a recent move is associated with relatively low managerial participation in such settings as voluntary organizations.[13]

A prevalent theme in such popular writings as Vance Packard's *A Nation of Strangers* and Alvin Toffler's *Future Shock* has been that, with increased mobility, Americans feel that they have little "stake" in the cities or neighborhoods where they presently live. Rather than working with others to solve common problems, they are likely to anticipate the time when they will move elsewhere. In fact, the "cosmopolitan" nature of mobile individuals will direct much of their interest away from the local community. Thus, mobile managers are likely to experience low levels of dependence on their present communities.

Length of residence is important partly because it affects one's degree of involvement in informal networks through which strategic friendships are formed and ideas are shared. The existence of organizations expediting such contacts has been documented on the local level by Domhoff.[14] Chambers of commerce, service clubs, and prestigious social clubs appear to serve this function on the community level.[15] Such organizations may be joined, of course, for purely social reasons. The contacts they provide, however, can involve their members in community decision making to an important degree. Thus, Perrucci and Pilisuk contend that effective local power requires involvement in a local interorganizational network and that interorganizational leaders have a history of community participation.[16] A consequence of corporate policies transferring managers frequently may therefore be the reduced involvement of managers in local community affairs.

Such consequences may be overcome, however, by formal and informal pressures on mobile managers. Company policy encouraging community participation may be a particularly important influence.

CORPORATE POLICY TOWARD COMMUNITY PARTICIPATION

Many corporations encourage managers to participate in the affairs of the communities in which their facilities are located. In fact, community service has long been seen as one way of satisfying public demands for corporate social responsibility.[17] In addition, community participation is frequently seen as a viable method of improving the local "business climate" to the corporation's advantage. Thus, General Electric advises its managers to participate in a variety of local organizations:

What is needed is *direct action at the local level* to identify and eliminate deterrents to profitable operation and growth at the community level. Only when we have sufficient activity at the grass roots level . . . can we expect to achieve a ground swell which will make itself felt statewide and even nationally.[18]

On the other hand, executives of many corporations appear to find dangers in local involvement. Executives of the Jones & Laughlin Steel Corporation, for example, have indicated in interviews that their goals include minimizing corporate visibility on the local level: "The desired impression was that the steel mill was in the community but not of it.

Management believed this impression would serve to limit demands (often financial) the community would place on J&L."[19]

Corporate policy toward community participation, then, varies, and these variations may lead to differing effects on managers' behavior. Consequently, it will receive explicit attention in our research.

AN OVERVIEW OF THE RESEARCH

Our study focuses on the relationship between organization size and the community participation of managers. Specifically, we will examine the links between plant and company size, managerial mobility (past transfer experience and expected transfer), corporate policy toward community participation, and managers' reports of their actual participation in community affairs.

Although the above variables are of primary theoretical importance, others must be examined to insure that reported relationships are not spurious. The literature suggests that characteristics of individual actors and the communities in which participation will occur must be taken into account.[20] For this reason, we also consider the effects of individual background characteristics, community characteristics, and the professional position and experience of managers on their participation in local community affairs.

The stepwise regression analysis we use is designed on the assumption that, although participation is initially influenced by an individual's background characteristics, other variables take on increasing importance through time. Smith, Smith and Reddy, and Hougland and Wood have attempted to specify combinations of variables for predicting participation.[21] The participation of corporate managers, however, is particularly likely to be influenced by professional experiences and company characteristics and policies. Such factors are expected to influence both the manager's own predisposition to participate and the tendency for others to encourage such participation.

In the specific case of corporate managers, it is proposed that (1) individual background characteristics within (2) a particular community context lead to a general predisposition toward participation. (3) The manager's professional position and experience influence the likelihood of participation because of their effects on participation-related skills and the manager's general prestige and visibility in the community. (4) Experiences and expectations about transfers to other locations may modify or reinforce the effects of the above factors by influencing perceptions (of both the manager and other community actors) of the manager's stake, future availability, and general standing in the community.

The influences of the individual and community characteristics identified above are in turn likely to be modified or reinforced by characteristics of the organization employing the manager. (5) Company and plant size influence the visibility and perceived importance of managers to the community. (6) Company policy toward community participation influences the manager's perception of the legitimacy and career implications of participation. For the purposes of this paper, it is particularly important to assess the extent to which organizational factors add to the variation in participation explained after individual and community characteristics have been allowed to explain as much variation as possible.

METHODS

Source of Data

A nationwide sample of production managers was compiled in fall 1981 from mailing lists. The sample was stratified by number of employees in local plant. Since industries are likely to vary regarding ease of access to names of personnel, the sample is not perfectly representative of all industries in the United States. Table 4.1, however, shows that respondents represent a number of major industries.

Of 1,427 questionnaires mailed, 191 (13 percent) were returned as undeliverable. A combination of four mailings (including the original mailing of the questionnaire, a postcard reminder, a second mailing of the questionnaire, and a third mailing of the questionnaire using certified mail) led to the return of usable questionnaires by 810 respondents. This represents 56.8 percent of the original sample. When the 191 "undeliverables" are removed from the sample, the revised response rate is 65.5 percent. As table 4.2 shows, higher response rates were obtained from managers in larger plants.

TABLE 4.1
Respondents' Industrial Categories

Category	Frequency	Percent
Primary metals	90	11.1
Fabricated metal products	128	15.8
Machinery, except electric	184	22.7
Electrical and electronic machinery, equipment, and supplies	133	16.4
Transportation equipment	128	15.8
Instruments and related products	54	6.7
Other industries	69	8.5
Unknown	24	3.0
Total sample	810	100.0

TABLE 4.2
Response Rates by Size of Plant

Plant Size (number of employees)	Questionnaires Mailed	Returned Undeliverable	Questionnaires Completed	Adjusted Response Rate
100–249	203	26	104	.588
250–499	329	42	183	.638
500–999	342	47	191	.647
1,000–4,999	431	63	240	.652
5,000 or more	122	13	76	.697
Size Unknown	—	—	16	—
Total sample	1427	191	810	.655

Statistical Technique

For the regression analysis, each predictor variable was included in one of the six categories of variables discussed above. For each set, variables were added to the regression equation as long as the F-ratio associated with each variable's addition to the equation was significant at the .05 level. (In some cases, no variables within a set satisfied this criterion.) Table 4.3 shows the variables that were treated as eligible for inclusion in each set. Appendix 4A shows the wording of items used to measure the variables. An examination of correlations among the predictor variables indicated that multicollinearity did not pose a serious problem in

TABLE 4.3
Variables Within Sets of Predictors

(1) Individual background characteristics
    Time in community
    Time at current address
    Size of community of origin
    Number of children
    Age
    Gender
    Racial status
    Income
    Marital status
    Education
(2) Community characteristics
    Community size
    Home, work place in different communities
    Commuting time required
(3) Professional position and experience
    Years as manager
    Job title
(4) Experiences and expectations about transfers
    Imminence of transfer (expected)
    Number of transfers (with present employer)
    Total transfers (with all employers)
(5) Organization size
    Company size
    Plant size
    Comparative size of company
(6) Policy toward participation
    Company expectation

the regression analyses. (Correlations between predictor variables of central theoretical importance are shown in table 4.5.)

FINDINGS

A Profile of Respondents

Before considering the results of the correlation and regression analyses, it is useful to be aware of some of the respondents' characteristics. Respondents are likely to live either in a small town (29 percent) or the suburbs of a large city (24 percent). A majority (60 percent) have lived in their present community for more than ten years, but a substantial proportion (24 percent) have lived in their present community for five years or less. About half (49 percent) of them have been transferred from one to four times. One manager reported sixteen transfers, but 40 percent said they had never been transferred.

Demographic and socioeconomic characteristics indicate considerable privilege. Sixty-three percent reported 1980 incomes of $50,000 or more, and 62 percent were college graduates. Most respondents were married white males (95 percent or more for each variable), and only about one-fourth of their spouses worked.

Many respondents appeared to be involved and influential in community affairs. Ninety percent of them voted in the last local election, 75 percent have contacted elected officials about problems, and 24 percent have been appointed to an advisory board, such as a zoning board or a planning board. However, their attachment to the community is not without qualifications. Only 30 percent agreed that they would refuse to move from their present community if they thought the refusal would harm their career. A question reading, "At this time, would you say that you are more satisfied with your community or your job?" elicited a number of written protests that such a choice is unrealistic.[22] Interestingly, however, 75 percent of those answering indicated greater satisfaction with their job.

One item, asking managers to choose the single statement that most closely reflected their view of community participation, shows tendencies to favor participation within carefully defined limits. Their responses, which are summarized in table 4.4, indicate that, while virtually no one endorses the avoidance of community involvement, most managers believe that involvement should be limited to a few carefully chosen activities and that the welfare of the company must not be overlooked.

Results of Correlation Analysis

The predictor variables of most concern in the present study are organization size, company policy toward participation, and experiences and expectations about transfers. Table 4.5 indicates that these variables are positively and significantly interrelated (with the sole exception of com-

TABLE 4.4

Respondents' Views of Appropriate Community Participation

Response	Frequency	Percent
Managers should be closely involved in community affairs.	85	11
Managers should be involved in community affairs, but they should limit their efforts to a few carefully chosen activities.	344	44
Although managers should sometimes become involved in community affairs, they should remember that their first professional responsibility is to their company.	348	45
It is important to participate in community affairs only if it makes the company look good.	2	0
Managers should avoid community involvement whenever possible.	3	0
No response	18	—
Total sample	810	100.0

TABLE 4.5

Correlations Between Variables Reflecting Policy Toward Participation, Organization Size, and Experiences and Expectations About Transfers

	1	2	3	4	5	6
1. Company expectation						
2. Company size	.09*					
3. Plant size	.20***	.29***				
4. Imminence of transfer	.06	.23***	.10*			
5. Number of transfers	.13***	.34***	.27***	.38***		
6. Total transfers	.14*	.13*	.14***	.25***	.51*	

*p≤.05.
***p≤.001.

pany expectation regarding participation and imminence of transfer). Thus, we can tentatively conclude that company encouragement of managerial participation in local community affairs appears to increase as company, and especially plant, size increases. This is true despite the fact that transfers tend to be more prevalent in larger companies and plants and that transfers are positively related to company encouragement of participation.[23]

Table 4.6 reveals an inconsistent pattern of relationships between the three transfer indicators and the measures of participation. On the other hand, there is a consistent and positive relationship between company and plant size and each of the indicators of participation. That is, as company and plant size increase, so does managerial participation in community affairs. Company expectation toward participation was also consistently and positively associated with participation. In fact, company expectation showed a stronger relationship with each of the indicators of participation than did company or plant size. It appears, therefore, that transfer experience and expectation are not as important in community participation as are organization size and company policy toward participation. However, the importance of size and policy cannot fully be understood until we examine the results of regression analyses taking all variables into account simultaneously.

TABLE 4.6
Zero-Order Correlations Between Policy Toward Participation, Organization Size, Experiences and Expectations About Transfers and Community Participation

	Friendship with Major Community Actors	Number of Memberships in Local Voluntary Organizations	Number of Local Voluntary Organizations in Which Respondent Is an Active Participant	Active Participation in "Higher Status" Voluntary Organizations
Company expectation	.34***	.33***	.37***	.31***
Company size	.04	.09*	.14***	.19***
Plant size	.12*	.18***	.21***	.27***
Imminence of transfer	.00	.05	.08*	.13***
Number of transfers	.04	.06*	.10*	.10*
Total transfers	−.01	.04	.07*	.10*

*p≤.05.
***p≤.001.

Results of Regression Analyses

Since community involvement reflects a variety of factors, we turn to an examination of regression models predicting several aspects of involvement. It should be noted that, because organizational characteristics (size and company policy toward community participation) are entered last, the models provide a conservative test of their predictive usefulness.

Friendship with Major Community Actors. Since community influence is often based on informal channels, we asked about respondents' friendships with "elected officials," "presidents or owners of banks or major retail businesses," "managers or owners of major manufacturing or service businesses," and "any other people who, in your opinion, have an important influence on community affairs." Table 4.7 summarizes the results of a regression analysis for predicting scores on the resulting scale (the reliability of which is indicated by a Cronbach's alpha of .71).

Correlations (r) and standardized regression coefficients (beta) show that such friendships are encouraged by having lived for a relatively long time in a small community from which one does not have to commute. High levels of education and income, a comparatively long time in a managerial position, and being married are positively associated with the existence of such friendships. The best single predictor, however, is company expectation toward community participation.[24] Table 4.7 shows that, even after all other variables have been allowed to explain as much variance as possible, company policy explains an additional 6.8 percent. When the change in R^2 is used as a criterion, community characteristics and company policy toward participation are shown to be the most useful predictors.

Membership and Participation in Local Voluntary Organizations. Respondents were asked to indicate whether they were (1) not a member, (2) a member in name only, or (3) an active member of each of thirteen categories of organizations.[25] They were asked to confine their responses to organizations that offered activities in their community.[26] Respondents who indicated membership in name only or active membership were asked to indicate the number of organizations to which they belonged or in which they were active. Their responses allowed analyses to be based on the total number of memberships, whether ac-

TABLE 4.7

Summary of Stepwise Multiple Regression for Predicting Friendship
with Major Community Actors

Variable Set	Cumulative R²	Change in R²	Variables in Set	r	beta
(1) Individual background characteristics	.057	—	Time in community	.165	.186
			Income	.120	.056
			Marital status	.095	.050
			Size of community of origin	−.062	.002
			Education	.061	.107
			Age	.103	−.083
(2) Community characteristics	.146	.089	Community size	−.191	−.174
			Home, work place in different communities	−.217	−.092
			Commuting time required	−.184	−.090
(3) Professional position and experience	.155	.009	Years as Manager	.165	.128
(4) Experiences and expectations about transfers	.160	.005	Imminence of transfer	.006	.063
(5) Organization size	.163	.003	Plant size	.101	.012
(6) Policy toward participation	.231	.068	Company expectation	.355	.278

NOTE: N = 640; r is the simple correlation; beta is the standardized regression coefficient.

tive or passive (table 4.8), the number of active memberships (table 4.9), and participation in "higher status" categories of organizations (table 4.10).

Table 4.8 shows that company policy toward participation, individual background characteristics, and to a lesser extent, community characteristics are useful for predicting membership. Although active participation involves a greater degree of commitment than membership, table 4.9 leads to similar conclusions. Note, however, that organizational pol-

TABLE 4.8
Summary of Stepwise Multiple Regression for Predicting Number of Memberships in Local Voluntary Organizations (Total Number)

Variable Set	Cumulative R^2	Change in R^2	Variables in Set	r	beta
(1) Individual background characteristics	.064	—	Income	.144	.018
			Age	.123	.025
			Education	.131	.145
			Time at current address	.106	.114
			Marital status	.091	.061
			Number of children	.092	.058
			Racial status	.085	.070
(2) Community characteristics	.090	.026	Home, work place in different communities	−.153	−.101
(3) Professional position and experience	—	—	—	—	—
(4) Experiences and expectations about transfers	.094	.004	Imminence of transfer	.025	.038
(5) Organization size	.103	.009	Plant size	.162	.062
(6) Policy toward participation	.172	.070	Company expectation	.331	.278

NOTE: N = 718; r is the simple correlation; beta is the standardized regression coefficient.

icy and size increase the variance explained for active participation to a greater extent than nominal membership.

Some organizations, of course, are relatively likely to attract higher status members. They may be particularly attractive to managerial personnel, and they may provide an effective setting in which active members exert influence. Factor analysis revealed that active participation in four categories of organizations—civic, cultural, professional, and health—tended to cluster together.[27] Table 4.10, which summarizes the regres-

TABLE 4.9

Summary of Stepwise Multiple Regression for Predicting Number of Local Voluntary Organizations in Which Respondent Is an Active Participant

Variable Set	Cumulative R^2	Change in R^2	Variables in Set	r	beta
(1) Individual background characteristics	.053	—	Race	.071	.060
			Income	.144	.028
			Time at current address	.112	.149
			Education	.116	.102
			Marital status	.084	.040
			Gender	.055	.043
(2) Community characteristics	.070	.017	Home, work place in different communities	−.108	−.030
			Commuting time required	−.078	−.034
(3) Professional position and experience	—	—	—	—	—
(4) Experiences and expectations about transfers	.083	.014	Number of transfers	.100	−.002
			Imminence of transfer	.072	.062
(5) Organization size	.104	.021	Plant size	.201	.071
			Company size	.152	.086
(6) Policy toward participation	.198	.094	Company expectation	.367	.322

NOTE: $N = 711$; r is the simple correlation; beta is the standardized regression coefficient.

sion analysis for predicting participation in these categories of organizations, reveals (as did table 4.9) the predictive usefulness of organizational policy and size. It should be noted in both tables that, while the influence of size is only of moderate magnitude, community participa-

TABLE 4.10

Summary of Stepwise Multiple Regression for Predicting Active Participation in "Higher Status" Local Voluntary Organizations

Variable Sets	Cumulative R^2	Change in R^2	Variables in Set	r	beta
(1) Individual background characteristics	.059	—	Income	.183	.082
			Gender	.128	.126
			Education	.102	.047
			Time at current address	.050	.097
			Marital status	.047	.018
(2) Community characteristics	.077	.018	Home, work place in different communities	−.116	−.069
(3) Professional position and experience	.086	.009	Job title	.035	.016
(4) Experiences and expectations about transfers	.098	.012	Imminence of transfer	.110	.066
			Total transfers	.107	.026
(5) Organization size	.132	.034	Plant size	.257	.111
			Company size	.201	.108
(6) Policy toward participation	.190	.058	Company expectation	.314	.253

NOTE: $N = 676$; r is the simple correlation; beta is the standardized regression coefficient.

tion is significantly associated with employment in larger plants and larger companies.

Size and Absentee Control: Results of Analyses of Variance

While plant size and, to a lesser extent, company size have been shown to predict participation, the effects of absentee control must still be isolated. This question is particularly important, since our review of the literature revealed that absentee ownership is often associated with size.

We used the proportion of local plant employees to total company employees to estimate the extent to which local or absentee control exists. Companies with at least half of their employees in the local plant were assumed to have a local orientation. Companies with fewer than half of their employees in the local plant were assumed to have a weaker local orientation and, therefore, to have a nonlocal locus of control. This categorization led to approximately 38 percent of the managers being classified as subjected to strong local control and 62 percent being classified as subjected to absentee control. Since extent of absentee control was treated as a dichotomous variable, company and plant size were also categorized. Analyses of variance were used to assess the predictive strength of main effects and interactions. The results are shown in table 4.11.

The table shows that the effects of absentee control do not weaken the impact of size. Multiple classification analyses (not shown) revealed slight tendencies for absentee control to reduce the likelihood of community participation when the effects of size are controlled. With one exception, however, the effects of absentee control are not significant. Moreover, only one of eight possible interaction effects was found to be significant. The regression analyses showed that the effects of company and plant size were rather modest but that they do not appear to be confounded by the effects of absentee control.

DISCUSSION

This project has attempted to understand how company and plant size, the geographic mobility of managers, and company policy affect managers' participation in community affairs. These three major sets of predictor variables were shown in table 4.5 to be related. Large plants and companies are likely to transfer their managers, and large plants (and to a lesser extent, large companies) are likely to encourage participation in community affairs. It is possibly because encouragement increases with organizational size that large organizations are shown in table 4.6 to be associated with relatively high degrees of community participation.

In regression analyses (tables 4.7–10), individual and community

TABLE 4.11
Two-Way Analyses of Variance for the Prediction of Community Involvement

Source	Friendship with Major Community Actors				Number of Memberships in Local Voluntary Organizations			
	Sum of Squares	Degrees of Freedom	Mean Square	F	Sum of Squares	Degrees of Freedom	Mean Square	F
Main effects								
Absentee control (A)	0.261	1	0.261	0.140	83.939	1	83.939	5.490*
Company size (C)	4.804	3	1.601	0.862	233.905	3	77.968	5.099**
Interaction								
A×C	17.566	2	8.783	4.727**	68.327	2	34.163	2.234
Explained	22.553	6	3.759	2.023	302.707	6	50.451	3.300**
Main effects								
Absentee control (A)	0.195	1	0.195	0.105	10.447	1	10.447	0.692
Plant size (P)	17.286	3	5.762	3.100*	366.852	3	122.284	8.100***
Interaction								
A×P	6.791	3	2.264	1.218	83.158	3	27.719	1.836
Explained	24.260	7	3.466	1.865	450.484	7	64.355	4.263***

	Active Participation in Local Voluntary Organizations				Active Participation in "Higher Status" Voluntary Organizations			
Source	Sum of Squares	Degrees of Freedom	Mean Square	F	Sum of Squares	Degrees of Freedom	Mean Square	F
Main effects								
Absentee control (A)	20.577	1	20.577	2.346	10.363	1	10.363	3.229
Company size (C)	77.695	3	25.898	2.953*	60.778	3	20.259	6.312***
Interaction								
A×C	7.498	2	3.749	0.427	3.204	2	1.602	0.499
Explained	89.324	6	14.887	1.697	71.629	6	11.938	3.719***
Main effects								
Absentee control (A)	1.222	1	1.222	0.143	0.337	1	0.337	0.107
Plant size (P)	228.693	3	76.231	8.892***	106.201	3	35.400	11.237***
Interaction								
A×P	0.802	3	0.267	0.031	1.564	3	0.521	0.166
Explained	233.629	7	33.376	3.893***	115.413	7	16.488	5.234***

NOTE: *$p \leq .05$; **$p \leq .01$; ***$p \leq .001$.

characteristics and managers' professional position and experience were considered in combination with the three predictor variable sets discussed above to explain community participation. The variable sets found to be comparatively powerful as predictors were individual background characteristics, community characteristics, organization size, and most especially, company policy. Analyses of variance (table 4.11) showed that relationships involving organization size cannot be attributed to absentee control.

The predictive power of managers' professional position and experience and their history and expectations about transfers was generally not impressive. However, there is some tendency for people who have been transferred, or who expect to be transferred, to be involved in community affairs to a comparatively great extent. Such results, while weak, are somewhat surprising, because individuals who are frequently transferred might be expected to be relatively unlikely to become attached to their local communities. However, the influence of other actors should not be overlooked. Many companies appear to transfer executives who are viewed as relatively capable and promising, so that they will receive a variety of experiences and opportunities for promotion. Because they are perceived as capable, frequently transferred managers may be encouraged (by community or corporate actors) to become involved in community affairs. Sills suggests that relatively busy people are particularly likely to contribute to organizational affairs.[28] These findings may represent a modest instance of the same phenomenon.

Findings regarding organization size were somewhat stronger. Large companies and—more especially—large plants are likely to have managers who are active in community affairs. Contrary to popular opinion, greater organization size does not lead to a lack of involvement. The predictive power of plant size suggests that other local actors are exerting an influence here, as well as in the case of transfers. Because of their relatively high visibility within the community, plants with many employees are likely to be approached by many interested outsiders with suggestions, requests, and demands.[29] Participation by managers is a technique through which such demands can be met with minimal effects on company resources.

Company policy toward participation was the best single predictor of community participation. While managers' participation decisions are influenced by many factors, the expectations of their superordinates in the company hierarchy are certainly not ignored. This finding suggests that research systematically examining the relationship of community participation to incentives within work organizations would be quite useful. The correlations in table 4.5 provide one useful lead by showing that pressure to participate is particularly likely to occur in large organizations. Finally, it must be recognized that the analyses explain only a modest amount of variation in most aspects of community participation. This stems in part from the fact that some potentially important predictor variables—for example, attitudes toward the specific types of participation[30]—were not included in the models. It also reflects the fact that a sample of production managers is unusually homogeneous in terms of many individual background characteristics. However, the generally low explanatory power also reflects the probability that participation involves important elements of voluntarism that cannot be predicted entirely on the basis of generalized environmental characteristics. Future work might be improved by using additional predictors, including individual attitudes, organizational characteristics in addition to size, and other aspects of company policy and the incentives attached to it.

Considerable concern has been expressed about the effects of increasing organization size on the communities in which organizations are located. In fact, the present analysis has shown that greater size is associated with enhanced participation in community affairs. This is true despite the fact that managers in large organizations are relatively mobile. Whether voluntarily or in response to external pressure, large organizations appear to develop policies that overcome the potentially deleterious effects of size and mobility. During their community participation, of course, managers are unlikely to overlook the interests of their corporate employers. The extent to which their participation contributes to the welfare of other community members cannot be determined by the present research.

APPENDIX 4A: MEASUREMENT OF PREDICTORS

Time in community
How long have you lived in this community?
1. Less than a year.
2. One to five years.
3. Six to ten years.
4. More than ten years.

Time at current address
How long have you lived at your present address?
1. Less than a year.
2. One to five years.
3. Six to ten years.
4. More than ten years.

Size of community of origin
During most of the time when you were growing up, did you live:
1. In a rural area, not near a town or city.
2. In or near a small town (under 2,500 people).
3. In or near a larger town (2,500 to 10,000 people).
4. In or near a small city (10,000 to 50,000).
5. Within a medium-size city (50,000 to 200,000).
6. In the suburbs of a medium-size city (50,000 to 200,000).
7. Within a large city (over 200,000 people).
8. In the suburbs of a large city (over 200,000 people).
NOTE: Categories 5 and 6 and categories 7 and 8 were combined for regression analysis.

Number of children
How many children are living in your household? _____

Age
What is your present age? _____ years.

Gender

Are you:
1. Male.
2. Female.

Racial status

Are you:
1. Black.
2. White.
3. Other (Please specify: _____)

NOTE: Categories 1 and 3 were combined for the regression analysis.

Income

Which income group (below) includes your total family income before taxes in 1980? Please consider all sources such as salary, rents, profits, and interest.

NOTE: Eleven categories were listed. Midpoints were used for regression analysis.

Martial status

What is your current marital status?
1. Single.
2. Widowed.
3. Divorced.
4. Separated.
5. Married.

NOTE: Categories 1 through 4 were combined for regression analysis.

Education

How many years of school did you complete?
1. 0–8 years.
2. 9–11 years.
3. 12 (high school graduate).
4. 12 + business or technical school after high school.
5. 13–15 (some college).
6. 16 (college graduate).
7. 17 or more (graduate work after college degree).

NOTE: Midpoints were used for regression analysis.

Community size

Where do you presently live?
1. In a rural area, not near a town or city.
2. In or near a small town (under 2,500 people).

3. In or near a larger town (2,500 to 10,000 people).
4. In or near a small city (10,000 to 50,000).
5. Within a medium-size city (50,000 to 200,000).
6. In the suburbs of a medium-size city (50,000 to 200,000).
7. Within a large city (over 200,000 people).
8. In the suburbs of a large city (over 200,000 people).

NOTE: Categories 5 and 6 and categories 7 and 8 were combined for regression analysis.

Home, work place in different communities

Are your home and the plant where you work located in the same community?
1. Yes.
2. No.

Commuting time required

On an average day, about how long does it take you to travel (one-way) between your home and your work?
1. Less than 10 minutes.
2. 10–20 minutes.
3. 20–30 minutes.
4. 30–45 minutes.
5. 45–60 minutes.
6. More than an hour.

Years as manager

For how many years of your entire working life have you been a manager (including positions at the first-line supervisory level or above)? _____years.

Job title

What is your current job title? _____

NOTE: Responses were categorized as follows:
1. President.
2. Vice-president.
3. Plant manager or equivalent.
4. Lower-level manager.

Imminence of transfer

If you stay with your present employer, do you expect to be transferred to another community?
1. No.
2. Yes, but not for several years.

3. Yes, probably in the next few years.
4. Yes, probably in the next few months.

Number of transfers
   How many times has the company employing you transferred you from one community to another? _____times.

Total transfers
   Consider all the companies for which you have been a manager, how many times have you moved from one community to another because of a change in managerial position? _____times.

Company size
   About how many people are employed by the entire company for which you work, including plants and offices in other locations?

   _____

Plant size
   About how many people are employed at the local plant where you work?_____

Comparative size of company
   Compared with other companies in the same industry or general field, would you say that the company employing you is:
   1. One of the largest.
   2. Larger than average.
   3. About average in size.
   4. Smaller than average.
   5. One of the smallest.

Company expectation
   My company expects me to participate in community affairs.
   1. Strongly disagree.
   2. Disagree.
   3. Don't know.
   4. Agree.
   5. Strongly agree.
NOTE: Codes for all dichotomous variables entered in regression analysis were 0 and 1.

NOTES

1. William H. Form and Delbert C. Miller, *Industry, Labor and Community* (New York: Harper & Row, 1960).

2. See, for example, Floyd Hunter, *Community Power Structure: A Study of Decision Makers* (Chapel Hill: University of North Carolina Press, 1953); Edward C. Hayes, *Power, Structure, and Urban Policy: Who Rules in Oakland?* (New York: McGraw-Hill, 1972); and G. William Domhoff, *Who Really Rules? New Haven and Community Power Reexamined* (Santa Monica, Calif.: Goodyear, 1978).

3. See Robert A. Dahl, *Who Governs? Democracy and Power in an American City* (New Haven: Yale University Press, 1961); and Roscoe C. Martin et al., *Decision in Syracuse: A Metropolitan Action Study* (Bloomington: Indiana University Press, 1961).

4. "Trend Toward Bigness in Business Speeds Up," *U.S. News and World Report*, August 24, 1981, pp. 69–70.

5. Lee E. Preston, "Corporate Power and Social Performance: Approaches to Positive Analysis," in John J. Siegfried, ed., *The Economics of Firm Size, Market Structure and Social Performance* (Washington, D.C.: Federal Trade Commission, 1980), pp. 29–42.

6. See Form and Miller.

7. Robert N. Stern and Howard Aldrich, "The Effects of Absentee Firm Control on Local Community Welfare: A Survey," pp. 162–181, in Siegfried, ed., *The Economics of Firm Size, Market Structure and Social Performance*.

8. Robert O. Schulze, "The Role of Economic Dominants in Community Power Structure," *American Sociological Review* (February 1958), 23:3–9.

9. Roland J. Pellegrin and Charles Coates, "Absentee-Owned Corporations and Community Power Structure," *American Journal of Sociology* (March 1956), 61:413–419; Paul E. Mott, "The Role of the Absentee-Owned Corporation in the Changing Community," pp. 170–179, in Michael Aiken and Paul E. Mott, eds., *The Structure of Community Power* (New York: Random House, 1970); and Lauren H. Seiler and Gene F. Summers, "Corporate Involvement in Community Affairs," *Sociological Quarterly* (Summer 1979), 20:375–86.

10. Richard E. Ratcliff, Mary Elizabeth Gallagher, and Kathryn Strother Ratcliff, "The Civic Involvement of Bankers: An Analysis of the Influence of Economic and Social Prominence in the Command of Civic Policy Positions," *Social Problems* (February 1979), 26:298–313.

11. Form and Miller, p. 512.

12. See, for example, Charles Wright and Herbert H. Hyman, "Voluntary Association Membership of Adults: Evidence from National Sample Surveys," *American Sociological Review* (June 1958), 23:284–294; and Gerald J. Hunt and Edgar W. Butler, "Migration, Participation and Alienation," *Sociology and Social Research* (July 1972), 56:440–452.

13. Basil Zimmer, "Participation of Migrants in Urban Structures," *American Sociological Review* (April 1955), 20:218–224; Howard K. Freeman, Edwin Novak, and Leo C.

Reeder, "Correlates of Membership in Voluntary Associations," *American Sociological Review* (October 1957), 22:528–533; Aida K. Tomeh, "Empirical Consideration on the Problem of Social Integration," *Sociological Inquiry* (Winter 1969), 39:65–76; and Edgar W. Butler, Ronald J. McAllister, and Edward J. Kaiser, "The Effects of Voluntary and Involuntary Residential Mobility on Females and Males," *Journal of Marriage and the Family* (May 1973), 35:219–227.

14. G. William Domhoff, *The Bohemian Grove and Other Retreats: A Study in Ruling-Class Cohesiveness* (New York: Harper & Row, 1974).

15. Peter H. Rossi, "The Organizational Structure of an American Community," in Amitai Etzioni, ed., *Complex Organizations: A Sociological Reader* (New York: Holt, Rinehart and Winston, 1961); William V. D'Antonio and William H. Form, *Influentials in Two Border Cities: A Study of Community Decision-Making* (South Bend, Ind.: University of Notre Dame Press, 1965): and Domhoff, *Who Really Rules?*

16. Robert Perrucci and Marc Pilisuk, "Leaders and Ruling Elites: The Interorganizational Bases of Community Power," *American Sociological Review* (December 1970), 35:1040–1057.

17. Sandra L. Holmes, "Corporate Social Performance: Past and Present Areas of Commitment," *Academy of Management Journal* (September 1977), 20:433–438.

18. The quote appears in Eugene Litwak, "Voluntary Associations and Neighborhood Cohesion," *American Sociological Review* (April 1961), 26:258–271.

19. Seiler and Summers, p. 377.

20. For representative analysis and reviews of the literature, see Herbert H. Hyman and Charles R. Wright, "Trends in Voluntary Association Memberships of American Adults: Replication Based on Secondary Analysis of National Sample Surveys," *American Sociological Review* (April 1971), 36:191–206; Raymond Payne, Barbara P. Payne, and Richard D. Reddy, "Social Background and Role Determinants of Individual Participation in Organized Voluntary Action," in David Horton Smith, Richard D. Reddy, and Burt R. Baldwin, eds., *Voluntary Action Research: 1972* (Lexington, Mass: Heath, 1972); Constance Smith and Anne Freedman, *Voluntary Associations: Perspective on the Literature* (Cambridge: Harvard University Press, 1972); James G. Hougland, Jr., Kyong-Dong Kim, and James A. Christenson, "The Effects of Ecological and Socioeconomic Status Variables on Membership and Participation in Voluntary Organizations," *Rural Sociology* (Spring 1979), 44:602–612; James G. Hougland, Jr., and James R. Wood, "Correlates of Participation in Local Churches," *Sociological Focus* (October 1980), 13:343–358; and David Horton Smith, Jacqueline Macaulay and Associates, *Participation in Social and Political Activities* (San Francisco: Jossey-Bass, 1980).

21. David Horton Smith, "A Psychological Model of Individual Participation in Formal Voluntary Organizations: Applications to Some Chilean Data," *American Journal of Sociology* (November 1966), 72:249–266; David Horton Smith and Richard D. Reddy, "An Overview of the Determinants of Individual Participation in Organized Voluntary Action," pp. 321–339, in Smith, Reddy, and Baldwin, eds., *Voluntary Action Research: 1972;* and Hougland and Wood.

22. This may well be. Compare William B. Lacy, James G. Hougland, Jr., and Jon M. Shepard, "Relationship Between Work and Nonwork Satisfaction: Is It Changing and Does Occupational Prestige Make a Difference?" *Sociological Spectrum* (April–June 1982), 2:157–171.

23. Size was measured on the basis of information provided by respondents regarding number of employees. We did not follow the common practice of converting size to a logarithmic function. While logarithmic transformations are useful for reducing variance

in the distribution of size, they assume curvilinear relationships between size and other variables. The literature suggests that such an assumption is warranted when size is being related to other aspects of organization structure: e.g., John Child, "Predicting and Understanding Organizational Structure," *Administrative Science Quarterly* (June 1973), 18:168–185. However, the relationship between size and managers' community involvement is not sufficiently understood to assume the existence of curvilinear relationships without evidence. In fact, a comparison of zero-order correlations between (1) raw measures and logarithmic transformations of plant and company size and (2) the four dependent variables used in the regression equations showed that logarithmic transformations did not substantially affect the predictive importance of size. The largest change involved a reduction in the correlation between plant size and active participation in "higher status" organizations from .275 to .257.

24. Company expectation toward participation is based on respondents' perceptions, as measured by an item shown in appendix 4A. The item was placed in a section of the questionnaire removed from the items measuring participation.

25. The categories were veterans; lodges, fraternal societies, and mutual benefit associations; service and civic; political; nationality groups; cultural or educational; business or professional; local church; church-affiliated groups; health-related organizations; country club; other social or recreational organizations; and any other organizations. Examples were offered to aid recall.

26. The instructions were as follows:

Listed below are several types of organizations. Please indicate your membership or participation in each type of organization, but confine your response to organizations which offer activities *in your community*. If, for example, you belong to a national professional society which has no activities in the community where you live, do not count it among your memberships.

27. The examples provided for "health-related organizations" were hospital board, Red Cross, and March of Dimes. These examples suggested opportunities for the administration of charitable and health-related service activities. Mutual benefit associations, which traditionally carry low prestige, were referred to in another category.

28. David L. Sills, *The Volunteers: Means and Ends in a National Organization* (Glencoe, Ill.: Free Press, 1957).

29. J. Victor Baldridge and Robert A. Burnham, "Organizational and Environmental Impacts," *Administrative Science Quarterly* (June 1975), 35:165–176.

30. Hougland and Wood.

CHAPTER 5

Aspects of Industrial Plant Openings and Closings

Roger W. Schmenner

A CORPORATION is seldom more visible to the communities of America than when it opens or closes an industrial plant in or near them. The impact either one of these capacity adjustments has on an area can be profound. This essay examines aspects of the incidence and character of plant openings and closings in an effort to supply some hard evidence for an issue that too often is the subject of anecdotes.

This paper first investigates the incidence of all kinds of plant capacity changes, including openings and closings, using data from the Cincinnati metropolitan area and from a selection of the largest industrial corporations in the United States. Large companies are contrasted to smaller ones and the implications for community growth, or decline, are noted. Building on this concern for community growth, the paper than investigates the relationship between plant capacity change and headquarters location. This leads to an exploration of the character of plant openings and closings. The paper concludes with an examination of the location decisions of conglomerates.

THE INCIDENCE OF PLANT EMPLOYMENT CHANGE

In the United States, there are no federal statistics on plant openings and closings. All the Census of Manufactures reports is the net increases in plants and employment by various industries and/or geographic areas. Thus, we cannot know whether an area's employment increase, for example, is the result of more plant openings than closings, expansion of plants already sited in the area, or more relocations into the area than out. To ascertain such things, researchers must resort to privately available data. Such privately provided "plant census" data, checked with the companies involved, are the source for the table 5.1 and 5.2 results for the Cincinnati metropolitan area during the years 1971–1975–76 and for a selection of 410 of the largest U.S. manufacturers, almost all of which are drawn from the *Fortune* 500 list, between 1970 and 1979.

A few words are in order about the categories of employment change depicted in tables 5.1 and 5.2:

—A "stay-put" plant is one that was in existence at the start of the period (e.g., 1970 for the 410 major manufacturers) and that continued to operate at the same site throughout all of the period. The plant may have expanded on site with new "bricks and mortar" construction and increased employment, or it may have contracted on site through employment drops or the sale or lease of space it once occupied.

—A plant opening refers to the start-up of a new operation for the company, be it in a newly constructed plant or in an already existing building.

—A plant closing, on the other hand, refers to the cessation of company operations at a site. The company may have absorbed the operations into another facility, or it may have abandoned the plant's product line entirely.

—A relocation is a combination of a plant closing and a plant opening. A relocation involves the near simultaneous closing of one facility and the opening of another to perform essentially the same tasks. Managers, workers, and equipment may well make the transfer from the closed facility to the newly opened one.

—An acquisition involves the purchase during the period of another company's already existing plant, a plant that may subsequently be expanded or contracted.

—A divestiture involves the sale during the period of a company's existing plant to another company.

TABLE 5.1
Plant Employment Change

	Stay-Puts	Openings	Closings	Acquisitions	Divestitures	Relocations	Other	Total
Panel A. Earlier Year Employment								
Cincinnati metropolitan area,								
1971–1975/76	142,297	N.A.	8,692	N.A.	N.A.	3,847	N.A.	154,836
410 major U.S. manufacturers,								
nationally, 1970–1979								
Largest 50 (by employment)	2,865,529	N.A.	73,414	N.A.	53,541	23,684	11,452	3,027,620
Next largest 50	949,144	N.A.	38,738	N.A.	47,302	14,279	7,546	1,057,009
Next 160	1,435,472	N.A.	54,483	N.A.	73,860	24,690	12,702	1,600,207
Smallest 150	563,010	N.A.	45,664	N.A.	40,571	11,121	6,982	667,348
All 410 companies	5,813,155	N.A.	212,299	N.A.	214,274	73,774	38,682	6,352,184
Panel B. Later Year Employment								
Cincinnati metropolitan area,								
1971–75/76	142,787	3,690	N.A.	N.A.	N.A.	4,737	N.A.	151,214
410 major U.S. manufacturers,								
nationally, 1970–1979								
Largest 50 (by employment)	2,994,620	122,992	N.A.	192,362	N.A.	30,410	150	3,340,534
Next Largest 50	1,005,053	70,973	N.A.	157,363	N.A.	18,598	275	1,252,262
Next 160	1,510,816	140,626	N.A.	275,636	N.A.	34,181	839	1,962,098
Smallest 150	608,421	52,954	N.A.	123,845	N.A.	13,694	230	799,144
All 410 companies	6,118,910	387,545	N.A.	749,206	N.A.	96,883	1,494	7,354,038

TABLE 5.1 (continued)

	Change in Employment at Stay-Put Plants		Openings less Closing	Acquisitions less Divestitures	Relocations	Other	Totals	As % of earlier employment	As % of earlier employment excluding acquisitions, divestitures, other
	Totals	% of earlier employment							
Panel C. Change in Employment Over Time (later year relative to earlier year)									
Cincinnati Metropolitan Area									
1971–1975/76	+490	0.3%	−5002	N.A.	+890	N.A.	−3622	−2.3%	N.A.
410 major U.S. manufacturers nationally, 1970–1979									
Largest 50 (by employment)	129,091	4.5	49,578	138,821	6726	−11,302	312,914	10.3	6.3
Next largest 50	55,909	5.9	32,235	110,061	4319	−7271	195,253	18.5	9.2
Next 160	75,344	5.2	86,143	201,776	9491	−11,863	361,891	22.6	11.3
Smallest 150	45,411	8.1	7290	83,274	2573	−6752	121,796	18.0	8.9
All 410 companies	305,755	5.3	175,246	534,932	23,109	−37,188	1,001,854	15.8	8.3

SOURCES: Schmenner 1978 and 1980 data bases.

NOTES: Technically, the Cincinnati data refer only to plant "births" and "deaths." A plant birth can include relocations into the Cincinnati area from elsewhere as well as the opening of a new facility. Similarly, a plant death can include relocations out of the Cincinnati area as well as plant closings or bankruptcies. However, such long-range relocations, as we know from other data, are rare events, and thus the statistics shown for Cincinnati probably do not overstate the incidence of openings or closings by very much. "Other" includes plants that were opened or acquired and then closed or divested within the time period and plants that were closed but then reopened during the period.

TABLE 5.2
Incidence of Plant Openings and Closings

	Plant Openings			Plant Closings			
	As a Percent of All Company Plants	As a Percent of Later Year Total Employment	Average Plant Employment	As a Percent of All Plants	As a Percent of Earlier Year Total Employment	Average Plant Employment	Average Plant Employment for Stay-Put Plants
Cincinnati metropolitan area, 1971–1975/76	17.3	2.4	10.5	17.0	5.6	25.1	97
410 major U.S. manufacturers, Nationally, 1970–1979							
Largest 50 (by employment)	10.3	3.7	307	7.2	2.4	300	1121
Next largest 50	9.8	5.7	256	8.4	3.7	193	560
Next 160	11.5	7.2	232	7.6	3.4	159	461
Smallest 150	11.1	6.6	163	9.2	6.8	197	347
All 410 companies	10.8	5.3	241	8.0	3.3	208	644

—The "other" category includes plants that were (1) either opened or acquired during the period but then subsequently closed or divested prior to the end of the period or (2) closed during the period but subsequently reopened, as occurred to some plants as a result of the 1974–75 recession.

These categories defined, tables 5.1 and 5.2 offer several insights about the composition of plant employment change for industry in general and for major manufacturers in particular.

First of all, the major manufacturing companies are vastly more important to our national economy than are smaller companies. Manufacturing employment in this country is substantially skewed toward the largest companies. We can see this in table 5.1, where, according to later year figures, 45 percent of the employment of the 410 major manufacturers studied rested with only the largest 50 companies.[1] Indeed, the employment of the 410 sample companies represents over 37 percent of the nation's total manufacturing employment of 19,590,100, according to the 1977 Census of Manufactures, up from about 33 percent a decade earlier.

These national statistics are evident as well in the microcosm that is the Cincinnati metropolitan area. There, the largest 25 plants account for fully 36 percent of the area's manufacturing employment, and the largest 50 plants, a scant 2.4 percent of the area's total number of plants, account for 46 percent.

Although major manufacturers operate many plants (an average of over 36 domestic plants for the 410 companies studied), major company employment is positively correlated with individual plant size. Nationally, according to the Census of Manufactures, 67 percent of all plants employ less than 20 people, and the average plant size is a mere 54.4. The Cincinnati area's average plant employment in table 5.2 mirrors these national statistics. The country's major manufacturers, on the other hand, have plants whose average sizes are substantially above the national averages for plant categories like stay-puts, openings, and closings. It is even true that the larger the major manufacturer, the larger, in general, are its plants, as table 5.2 attests.

Secondly, small companies are not the engine of growth in manufacturing employment; large companies are. It has been alleged by MIT's David Birch that 66 percent of the growth in private sector employment over the past decade was due to small companies (under twenty employees) rather than large ones.[2] While Birch's work relates to more than simply manufacturing, his results are certainly unfounded for the manufacturing sector.[3] For example, Cincinnati's results suggest that small manufacturers, who dominate change in openings and closings for that area, did not fare so well during the early 1970s. Plant closings there swamped the employment advances made by net on-site expansions, plant openings, and relocations.

More inclusive, however, are the national statistics. During the ten-year period from 1967 to 1977, total manufacturing employment in the United States, as measured by the Census of Manufactures, rose from 19,323,200 to 19,558,700, an increase of 265,500, or 1.4 percent. Over an overlapping, although not identical span of time, 1970–1979, the 410 major companies increased their employment due to net expansions on-site, openings less closings, and relocations by 504,110, or 8.3 percent. This figure is larger than the gain for all manufacturing from 1967 to 1977, suggesting that employment in smaller companies actually *shrank* on balance during the past decade, while the employment of major company plants grew.

The growth in net jobs generated, as a percent of initial period employment, is somewhat greater for the tier of companies just below the largest fifty, indicating that job generation is not uniform across all the major manufacturers studied. Nevertheless, the comparatively rapid growth in jobs for all segments of this major company sample is robust.

Thirdly, the character of growth or decline can vary dramatically across companies and across geography. It is helpful to translate some of table 5.1's results into more comparable form (see table 5.3). Some differences presumably associated with company size are evident.

First, on-site expansions net of contractions are much more prevalent for large companies than for small. On the other hand, relocations are more prevalent for small companies. These two findings, I think, are related. Other data, not reported here,[4] show that small companies are much more likely to lease their space and thus can only expand operations significantly by relocating to larger facilities. Even when they do own their own facilities, small companies are often restricted in how much, if any, on-site "bricks and mortar" expansion they can engage in. Large companies, on the other hand, have the means and farsightedness to purchase enough land on which to expand their operations.

Second, the largest companies are less likely both to expand on site

TABLE 5.3

Employment Change Relative to Early Year Stay-Put Employment

	Percentage Employment Ratios				
	Net On-Site Expansions	Plant Openings	Plant Closings	Relocations	Acquisitions less Divestitures
Cincinnati metropolitan area, 1971–1975/76	0.3	2.6	6.1	2.7	N.A.
410 major U.S. manufacturers, nationally 1970–1979					
Largest 50 by employment	4.5	4.3	2.6	0.8	4.8
Next largest 50	5.9	7.5	4.1	1.5	11.6
Next 160	5.2	9.8	3.8	1.7	14.1
Smallest 150	8.1	9.4	8.1	2.0	14.8
All 410 companies	5.3	6.7	3.7	1.3	9.2

and to relocate. This finding, I think, is related to plant size. The larger the company, as was noted in table 5.2, the larger the average plant employment. The ease with which a plant can relocate is understandably associated with its size, so that it is thoroughly reasonable to expect the incidence of relocating employment to decline with increasing plant— and company—size. It is also reasonable to expect that the largest companies—with the largest plants—would be less likely to expand on site, apart from any differences in companywide rates of employment growth. Most major companies have rules of thumb, explicit or implicit, that place ceilings on the employment at individual plants.[5] Large plants can readily become chaotic; most companies are sensitive to this phenomenon and take steps to avoid it. Thus, it is natural to see the incidence of on-site expansion in employment decline with increasing company and plant size.

Third, plant openings are more prevalent in large companies than in small but are less prevalent in the very largest companies. That major companies evidence a greater fraction of their employment in newly opened plants is consistent with the finding that large companies, not small, are the engine of manufacturing employment growth in the United States. Major companies outside the fifty largest do seem to be growing somewhat more rapidly than the fifty largest companies themselves, and this is demonstrated by their plant openings results in particular.

Fourth, plant closings, on the other hand, appear to be more prevalent in smaller companies than in large ones. And among major companies, the likelihood of plant closure appears to decline with increases in company size. Plant closings and small companies constitute an unfortunate but understandable association; the small companies that populate a metropolitan area like Cincinnati are simply more vulnerable to bankruptcy and cyclical fluctuations in the economy than are larger, more well-established companies. That the very largest companies threaten proportionately fewer workers with plant closings may reflect the facts that their businesses are inherently more stable than many others and that they can contract employment substantially in many cases without having to close a facility completely.

Fifth, it is also evident that acquisition employment net of divestitures declines with increases in company size, the decline being particularly steep for the largest fifty companies. While this trend may reflect different corporate strategies, it no doubt does reflect the hesitancy of larger companies to acquire or merge with other companies because of antitrust considerations. Such constraints are less stifling for the still major companies that are somewhat smaller.

In sum, major companies are a tremendously important segment of the nation's manufacturing life and are getting more so. They are the chief engine of growth for manufacturing employment, driven in large measure by plant expansions, acquisitions, and new plant openings. The growth of the largest fifty companies is somewhat more sedate than other major manufacturers', but it still outstrips that of smaller companies.

GEOGRAPHIC DIFFERENCES

As one might expect, the geographic impact of this employment change has not been evenly dispersed throughout the country. Differences are pronounced among cities, suburbs, and rural areas and among regions.

The results for Cincinnati suggest that, at least for the more traditional industrial centers, there is a significant amount of locational "churning."

The levels of plant closings, relocations, and openings—measured in terms of plant *numbers* (see table 5.2)—are high around metropolitan areas like Cincinnati, and significantly higher than those for major manufacturers. The failure of small companies to generate the same kind of job growth that prevailed at large companies during the 1970s had a particularly negative impact on selected central cities in the United States.

Indeed, even the modest incidence of major company plant closings hurt central city employment more than suburban or rural employment. As the data in table 5.4 demonstrate, what has hurt the central city most is the more frequent closing of plants there. Plant openings and expan-

TABLE 5.4
Employment Changes at 410 Major Industrial Companies in Central Cities, Suburbs, and Rural Areas, by Region, for Selected Classes of Plants, 1970–1979

Region	Change at Stay-Put Plants	Openings	Closings	Total Change, All Sources[a]	Total Change as a Percent of Early Year Employment
Central cities					
New England	1,714	2,231	− 7,239	− 3,444	− 2.7
Mid-Atlantic	− 21,635	2,394	− 17,407	− 19,728	− 5.1
South Atlantic	9,380	12,032	− 10,284	21,279	7.5
East North Central	− 18,019	8,046	− 30,250	− 9,092	− 1.0
East South Central	15,654	5,930	− 6,126	27,856	17.8
West North Central	20,401	8,528	− 5,614	39,688	16.3
West South Central	39,382	31,089	− 5,099	93,710	48.6
Mountain	8,897	7,245	− 639	29,252	46.8
Pacific	6,251	7,767	− 9,635	16,032	7.5
Totals	62,025	85,262	− 92,293	195,553	7.5
Suburbs					
New England	19,459	13,631	− 5,424	42,263	19.4
Mid-Atlantic	− 5,701	17,185	− 24,025	47,392	9.1
South Atlantic	14,117	31,857	− 4,224	60,113	24.8
East North Central	24,177	33,493	− 15,565	88,870	11.7

Region	Change at Stay-Put Plants	Openings	Closings	Total Change, All Sources[a]	Total Change as a Percent of Early Year Employment
East South Central	7,197	16,558	−1,012	30,225	32.9
West North Central	7,353	1,939	−1,316	19,059	26.5
West South Central	8,051	17,849	−492	41,133	41.6
Mountain	6,965	3,317	−770	20,301	56.8
Pacific	70,232	22,763	−19,455	124,420	35.4
Totals	151,850	158,092	−72,233	473,776	19.8
Rural areas					
New England	3,693	5,489	−3,601	24,793	31.2
Mid-Atlantic	4,308	5,764	−4,259	16,148	9.4
South Atlantic	8,758	43,744	−10,595	73,683	22.5
East North Central	22,027	17,835	−11,129	68,623	21.0
East South Central	14,891	27,427	−2,478	61,980	46.6
West North Central	17,512	15,035	−2,336	46,810	45.6
West South Central	12,953	16,304	−1,544	37,420	41.5
Mountain	3,883	8,701	−169	15,570	41.1
Pacific	2,749	3,834	−2,526	16,001	27.6
Totals	90,720	144,133	−38,537	361,037	27.2

NOTE: [a] "Total Change, All Sources" includes acquisitions net of divestitures as well as change at stay-put plants, openings, and closings.

sions in the more traditional manufacturing cities of the Northeast and Midwest have been neither numerous enough nor large enough to offset the losses incurred when plants there have been shut down. Even in regions like the Pacific and the East South Central, major manufacturers have been closing more plants in central cities than they have been opening, which presents itself as an ominous sign for the future, as on-site expansions there could be expected to taper off. Recent research for all manufacturing—not simply the major national manufacturers—in cities such as Cincinnati, Cleveland, Boston, Minneapolis–St. Paul, and New York has pointed out the significant extent of plant "deaths" in central cities and their dominance over plant "births" there.[6] Only in such rapidly growing cities as Phoenix have births led deaths for all sizes of manufacturing companies.[7]

Deaths in excess of births have had a more powerful impact on the central city than the often heralded flight of companies to the suburbs. Relocations from city to suburb for all manufacturing companies in Cincinnati during the early 1970s, for example, accounted for less than a third of the city's total drop in manufacturing employment. Deaths in excess of births accounted for over two-thirds of the drop, with employment increases and decreases at plants remaining in place during the period essentially canceling one another out.[8] Most relocations entail very short distances, often just a few miles. The extent of city–suburb–rural relocations among major manufacturers nationwide is documented in table 5.5, which shows that, while industrial relocation has been decentralizing on balance, most movement is within cities, suburbs, and rural areas themselves, with some movement even centralizing.

What seems clear from the data is that many, if not all, central cities have lost some of their power as incubators of new companies. Companies today are no longer tied to central cities by reason of labor supply, space availability, transportation nodes (e.g., railroad marshaling yards), or supplier—service—customer contacts. Labor of all types is now available at suburban locations, transportation and communication advances have freed companies to move at distances from one another, and space is both cheap and available. New companies sacrifice nothing now by starting life in the suburbs and can often grow more easily there than in frequently more confining urban quarters.

CAPACITY CHANGE AROUND HEADQUARTERS LOCATIONS

One outgrowth of this concern for the geographic impact of plant openings and closings is some hypothesizing about the relative strength of areas rich in corporate headquarters. Is a corporation, for example, more likely to open a new plant close to its corporate headquarters or to one of its division headquarters? Is it less likely to close a plant situated near one of those headquarters locations? Are communities or states with an abundance of headquarters operations doubly blessed in this sense or not?

TABLE 5.5
Urban, Suburban, and Rural Plant Relocations for 410 Major
Industrial Companies, 1970–1979

Panel A. Number of Plants, Nationally, Moving from One Type Area to Another

	To			
From	City	Suburb	Rural Area	Totals
City	114	75	14	203
Suburb	26	126	16	168
Rural area	7	13	54	74
Totals	147	214	84	445

Panel B. Post-Move Employment Nationally, Moving from One Type Area to Another

	To			
From	City	Suburb	Rural Area	Totals
City	25,413	12,335	1,775	39,523
Suburb	9,199	25,936	3,510	38,645
Rural area	1,856	2,914	13,352	18,122
Totals	36,468	41,185	18,637	96,290

Panel C. Pre-Move Employment, Nationally, Moving from One Type Area to Another

	To			
From	City	Suburb	Rural Area	Totals
City	21,316	10,807	1,374	33,497
Suburb	6,722	17,105	3,573	27,400
Rural area	1,596	1,369	9,342	12,307
Totals	29,634	29,281	14,289	73,204

These hypotheses can be tested with the plant census data. From company documents and discussions, the headquarters—corporate or divisional—to which each plant directly reports was ascertained. Codes were developed for each plant indicating whether the plant was located in the same state or metropolitan area of both the corporate headquarters and any divisional headquarters. Also known was whether the plant was classed as a plant that stayed put during the 1970s or whether it had opened or was closed, and whether it had expanded or contracted on site. Some of the results testing the impact of headquarters location are shown in table 5.6.

In evaluating these results we can, as a basis for comparison, look to the frequency with which stay-put plants and their employment fall within the same state or metropolitan area as a company's various headquarters operations. For example, are plant openings relatively more numerous around headquarters locations than company plants already in place? Or are they less numerous? The hypotheses in question are tested by making this comparison. It is clear from the results that more plants and employment of all types are found around division as opposed to corporate headquarters. More than that, the plants located near headquarters are larger, on balance, than plants located at a distance. This is not surprising, of course, since many large plants double as division headquarters anyway.

Table 5.6's findings are intriguing, since neither plant openings nor closings occur near a headquarters operation with the same frequency as the incidence of stay-put plants. Moreover, plant openings are no more probable near headquarters than are plant closings; their values are very close together and in fact are not significantly different statistically. Judging from employment figures, plant closings of substantial size are more likely near headquarters locations than are plant openings. This result runs counter to the conventional intuition, which would have relatively more openings close to headquarters. The trend is not strong, but it does appear that, relative to plants already in place, both openings and closings are more likely to occur at a distance from headquarters.

What is relatively more likely to occur near a corporate or division headquarters is the physical "bricks and mortar" expansion or contraction of stay-put plants. More on-site expansions and more, especially smaller, on-site contractions occur in the vicinity of headquarters locations than would be expected merely from the distribution of stay-put plants and employment.

While plant openings occur at less than the expected frequency in the same area or state, plant relocations are as likely, if not more so, to take place near a headquarters, as the existing distribution of plants would have us believe. In part this is due to the independent character of re-

TABLE 5.6
Percent of Plants Locating in Same Area as Headquarters

Location of Plant	All Stay-Put Plants	On-Site Expansions	On-Site Contractions	Plant Openings	Plant Closings	Relocations
Same state as corporate headquarters						
Plants	15.4	17.1	18.7	12.0	12.0	13.8
Employment	27.3	28.9	26.2	15.0	23.6	19.2
Same metropolitan area as corporate headquarters						
Plants	10.2	12.0	14.2	8.4	9.6	11.6
Employment	21.8	24.6	20.1	10.2	22.3	15.5
Same state as division headquarters to which it reports						
Plants	27.6	30.3	32.4	19.8	19.3	28.0
Employment	40.5	43.5	36.4	23.4	32.6	40.4
Same metropolitan area as division headquarters to which it reports						
Plants	21.5	24.2	28.9	15.3	15.2	25.3
Employment	34.8	38.3	30.2	18.1	26.7	38.4

Plant Category

TABLE 5.7

Distance to Division Headquarters for 410 Major Industrial Companies, by Class of Plant

| | Distance from Division Headquarters to Plant, in Miles | | | | Number of Observations |
| | Mean | Standard Deviation | Median | Average Deviation | |
Class of Plant					
On-site expansion	638	57	380	558	182
Plant opening	691	56	600	520	162
Plant relocation	808	153	600	660	37

locations, many of which, although smaller than many plants, are reasonably autonomous, frequently being their own division headquarters.

In sum, these data do not support the hypothesis that a corporation is more likely to increase capacity close to a headquarters operation and, similarly, less likely to decrease capacity near a headquarters. While there is reason to believe that on-site expansions are more likely than could be expected to be close to a headquarters, it appears that plant openings are in fact relatively less likely to occur near a headquarters. And although plant closings are relatively more probable at a distance from a headquarters operation, on-site contractions are more probable in the vicinity of a headquarters. Instead of supporting the hypothesis that a corporation cares better for the communities around its home base, the data suggest that more radical location changes (openings and closings) occur more often than anticipated at a distance from headquarters but that more evolutionary location changes (on-site expansion or contraction) are accomplished nearby.

These findings are reinforced by some other survey-based results depicted in table 5.7. There it is seen that plant openings and, to an even greater extent, plant relocations locate at a greater distance from division headquarters than do on-site expansions. This supports the view that radical capacity changes are more likely to take place at a considerable distance from any headquarters location.

The results presented in table 5.6 refer to all of the 410 major U.S. manufacturers studied. A more subtle variation of the hypothesis that headquarters location influences the siting of plant openings and closings states that larger companies may be somewhat less influenced by headquarters location than smaller companies. The largest companies may be forced to look on a more national plane for plant sites anyway, or they may have "saturated" certain home cities or states with employment.

Table 5.8 examines this hypothesis using both plant count and employment measures. This table concentrates on plant locations in the same *states* as their division headquarters and uses company rankings based on sales and assets as well as employment. As can be seen, how the companies are ranked matters little; the rankings are highly correlated with one another. Table 5.8 can be analyzed much as table 5.6 was; the reference point is all stay-put plants, and the incidence of plant expansions, contractions, openings, closings, or relocations should be compared with the existing pattern of plant locations.

Making such a comparison, we can see that table 5.6's results are, in general, sustained. Openings and closings are less likely to occur in a company's division headquarters state than are the company's stay-put plants. Plant expansions on site, on the other hand, are often as likely, or even more likely, to occur in the company's division headquarters state than the company's stay-put plants. Plant contractions on site and relocations roughly parallel the pattern of stay-put plants, although there is apparently considerable variance.

The results are also interesting because they reveal that, in the main, the larger the company is, the less likely are its plants in the same states as its divisions' headquarters. The largest companies' facilities appear to be more thoroughly dispersed across the United States than those of the smaller, although still major, companies of the 410 studied. This is true not only for stay-put plants but for categories including on-site expansions, contractions, openings, and relocations. Significantly, this is not so true for plant closings, especially when companies are ranked by employment or when employment rather than plant counts is used. This may be because the smaller companies operate fewer plants than the larger companies and, since a company would only close a division headquarters plant as a last resort, a smaller company may be forced to close one of its relatively few far-flung plants in order to protect its division headquarters facility. This would imply a lower value to the smaller company entries in table 5.8 than one might expect.

Thus, apart from plant closings, the larger the company, the less likely are its plant locations to be near its division headquarters. However, no matter what the size the company is, it does not appear to be the case

TABLE 5.8
Percent of Plants and Employment Locating in Same State as Division Headquarters, by Size of Company

	All Stay-Put Plants	Expansions On-Site	Contractions On-Site	Openings	Closings	Relocations	Number of Plants; Later Year
Panel A. Percent of Plants							
Size categories by sales							
Largest 50 companies	18.3	17.0	13.8	10.4	10.8	13.0	3,275
Next largest 50 companies	19.8	28.0	24.1	15.7	18.7	16.5	3,163
Next 160 companies	30.5	32.3	36.3	19.9	19.1	33.5	5,525
Smallest 150 companies	44.4	45.9	69.7	31.8	27.7	41.0	2,966
Size categories by assets							
Largest 50 companies	19.7	21.0	16.9	12.1	12.4	10.0	2,868
Next largest 50 companies	14.9	17.8	15.2	11.6	11.4	13.2	3,254
Next 160 companies	33.3	36.9	39.7	21.6	23.4	36.4	5,575
Smallest 150 companies	40.5	41.4	57.4	30.4	23.5	38.3	3,232
Size categories by employment							
Largest 50 companies	22.4	22.4	20.0	14.7	19.6	18.6	3,905
Next largest 50 companies	26.2	33.1	32.6	17.0	20.4	29.9	2,813
Next 160 companies	27.5	31.3	31.0	21.1	19.0	29.3	5,277
Smallest 150 companies	37.3	37.7	53.5	26.2	18.5	46.3	2,934

Panel B. Percent of Employment

							Average Employment Per Plant; Later Year
Size categories by sales							
Largest 50 companies	32.3	31.3	27.0	15.2	32.0	32.7	870
Next largest 50 companies	42.8	49.8	29.9	20.8	30.0	32.6	458
Next 160 companies	42.4	48.2	39.1	22.1	33.3	40.4	377
Smallest 150 companies	61.6	63.9	85.5	41.5	34.5	54.7	328
Size categories by assets							
Largest 50 companies	31.3	35.3	20.1	16.8	36.3	28.6	963
Next largest 50 companies	35.9	31.7	39.4	19.7	21.2	20.6	409
Next 160 companies	49.0	53.5	41.1	22.6	37.3	46.9	410
Smallest 150 companies	58.1	61.9	74.1	38.9	28.9	50.3	302
Size categories by employment							
Largest 50 companies	36.5	37.2	31.0	20.2	34.9	36.0	806
Next largest 50 companies	43.0	51.6	28.0	23.8	41.0	36.0	445
Next 160 companies	41.1	45.0	38.5	24.9	23.0	36.8	372
Smallest 150 companies	54.6	56.9	79.0	26.1	33.6	65.3	272

that capacity increases are more probable near a headquarters site and that capacity decreases are less probable near a headquarters site. The evidence remains mixed. Plant openings and closings are more likely away from headquarters, while on-site capacity expansions or contractions are more likely near headquarters. This appears true for most major manufacturers, although the closings data for the very largest companies (by the employment measure) make it somewhat less true for those giant corporations.

A BRIEF COMPARISON OF PLANT CLOSINGS AND OPENINGS

The apparent differences between plant closings and the other categories investigated highlights the need to explore the characteristics of particular capacity changes, especially plant closings as against plant openings.

How do plant openings and closings compare? Some insight into their similarities and differences can be gained by referring to table 5.9, which documents characteristics for 171 closings and 164 openings involving the 410 major manufacturing companies. Several important themes spring from these data.

First, the plant closing often involves a newer facility than one might imagine. The median age of the closings surveyed was fifteen years, and, even more striking, 33 percent of the plants were six years old or younger when they were closed. In contrast, the median age of the on-site expansions also surveyed was twenty years. Of course, many closed facilities were creaky rattletraps, but that stereotype does not prevail as often as commonly believed. That many closings involve recently opened facilities highlights the dependence, and vulnerability, of most young plants. When adversity strikes, it is these plants that often have to be closed because, from other data not reported here, we know that young plants are not typically home to the support functions of the operation. In many cases, they "just make the product," and so, for managerial reasons, they are the first candidates for closing.

Second, the plant that is closed seems clearly out of step with most modern notions of effective plant design. The closed facility, in contrast to the newly opened one, has more free-standing buildings on site, more product lines to manage, more multistory space, and more space that was not built by the company for this particular use.

TABLE 5.9
Characteristics of Plant Closings and Openings for 410 Major Industrial Companies

Item	171 Plant Closings		164 Plant Openings	
	Average	Median	Average	Median
Age at closing (years)	19.3	15	—	—
Employment				
Typical before closing	245	120	374	150
At closing	149	91		
Acreage on site	37	10	75	25
Square feet of plant	296,181	100,000	213,936	112,500
Buildings on site	2.3	1	1.5	1
Product lines manufactured	11.5	1	5.2	2

Structural item	Percentage	Percentage
Multistory	35	12
Sole occupant	93	89
Built by company	24	65
Acquired by company merger/purchase of business	47	2
Existing buildings purchased	13	13
Leased	16	23
Labor items		
Predominantly skilled labor	17	17
Predominantly unskilled labor	18	17
Unionized	67	21
Union attitude:		
Constructive, responsible	30	48
Tolerable	54	42
Militant, uncompromising	14	9
History of work stoppages	5	0
Plant charters		
Product plant strategy	31	52
Market area plant strategy	47	34
Process plant strategy	14	11
General purpose plant strategy	3	3

Third, plant closings are significantly more unionized than plant openings, and more unionized than the sample taken as a whole, which was about half union. Nevertheless, relatively few of the plant closings involved unions that were characterized as "militant, uncompromising" or that had a history of work stoppages.

Fourth, plant closings are more likely to involve plants whose "charters" define their roles as serving a particular geographic area with the division's product line. In contrast, plant openings are more likely to involve plants making a specific product to be shipped to the division's entire domestic market area, a product plant strategy as opposed to a market area plant strategy.

MORE ON THE CHARACTER OF PLANT CLOSINGS

Talk to any company's management and you will likely walk away convinced that the plant closing decision is one not embarked upon lightly and that it is as objective an economic decision as a corporation makes. Plant closings are, naturally, of serious concern to small companies, but as the survey results of tables 5.10 and 5.11 document, plant closings are of deep concern to large companies as well. About a quarter of the closings surveyed can be accounted for by business decisions to cease manufacturing altogether the product(s) formerly made there. In the majority of closings, however, the company maintains the product involved

TABLE 5.10
Disposition of Plants' Former Operations

Disposition	Percentage Affected
Operations absorbed by one or more existing company plants.	61
Company got out of the business.	24
Operations subcontracted.	2
Operations transferred out of the United States.	0
Government contract completed.	1

TABLE 5.11
Reasons Behind Plant Closings

Reason	Percentage Acknowledging
Competitive pressure	
From foreign operations:	
Price competition	10
Competition on performance and features	5
From other American operations:	
Price competition due to better production technology	22
Price competition due to lower cost labor, etc.	17
Competition on performance and features	16
Plant economics	
Inefficient/outdated production technology, layout, materials handling	46
High labor rates	21
Crippling union work rules	10
Compliance with environmental, OSHA regulations too expensive	7
Transportation costs made competition too expensive	13
Raw materials shortage, price, transportation	5
Space too small, economies of scale with consolidation	3
Maintenance, energy costs	2
High taxes, utility rates	1
Inconsistent with corporate strategy	1
Miscellaneous (poor neighborhood, high labor turnover, not near enough to other company plants, government contract completed, management change, product specification too variable)	<1 each
Product economics	
Fall off in sales, lack of sales volume	27
Product obsolete	2
Sales too cyclical	5

but shuts down the particular plant, absorbing its operation into another existing facility. That this practice is common is reinforced by another statistic, which reveals that 23 percent of the plants in the full survey sample absorbed operations from other plants, which were then closed or divested.

The reasons why plants are closed are numerous, as is plain from table 5.11. The economics of the industry, reflected in the figures on competitive pressure and product economics, are certainly major factors, especially when we observe that only 30 percent of the sample fails to list one of them. Even more impressive, however, is the importance of plant-specific considerations in driving up costs (only 22 percent of the sample fails to list one of these reasons). The dominant influence on plant economics is not labor, materials, or transportation costs but rather an inefficient and outmoded production technology, exacerbated no doubt in many instances by a poor factory layout and faulty, costly materials handling. It has already been noted that a greater than average percentage of plant closings are multistory, and a sizable fraction of the multistory factories were closed, at least in part, because of an inefficient production technology (55 percent). Older plants seem to suffer relatively more from multiple afflictions (high wages, union work rules, sales drops), but none more prevalent than inefficient production technology. About half of the plants over the median age cited inefficient/outmoded production technology, as opposed to only a third of those below the median. Still, even for the younger plants, the single most important reason for a plant closing was an inefficient, outdated production technology and layout.

A definite minority of plant closings are attributable, even in part, to labor situations that got out of hand. It is true that an above average fraction of the plant closings surveyed were unionized (67 percent versus 52 percent of the stay-put plants and 20 percent of the newly opened plants) and that union plants were disproportionately affected by price and performance competition from other American producers, poor production technology and layout, high wages, and environmental regulations. Nevertheless, union–management relations were in general very good at these plants. Thirty percent of the plants closed characterized their unions as "constructive, responsible," while only 19 percent termed their unions "militant, uncompromising" or noted a history of work stoppages. And, as table 5.11 shows, only 10 percent of the plant closings checked off "crippling union work rules" as a contributing reason for closing the plant. Of course, high labor rates are a contributing factor in 21 percent of the survey plant closings, and of the closings influenced by high labor rates, 83 percent were union, a figure somewhat higher than the corresponding 67 percent figure for the sample as a whole. Nevertheless, these data suggest that poor labor relations is a relatively minor, although observable, reason for plant closings. While a considerable number of new plants are located with union avoidance in mind, plants are only infrequently closed because of sour union relationships and the excessive costs those relationships have placed on the plant's economics.

THE CAPACITY CHANGE BEHAVIOR OF CONGLOMERATES

Conglomerates are criticized for many things, among them greater ruthlessness in closing plants than typical of companies closer to a single-product orientation. Conglomerates allegedly do not care as much for communities as do other companies. How true is this? The plant census data provide us with the opportunity to test this assertion, since conglomerate companies can be isolated from the others. Table 5.12 lists thirty companies most observers would classify as conglomerates, since each operates several very diverse product divisions. These thirty companies are contrasted in table 5.13 to the remaining 380 in the plant census data base. That table breaks out by class the plants and employment of both the conglomerate and nonconglomerate groups.

What is most striking about table 5.13's results is that conglomerates

TABLE 5.12
Companies Considered Conglomerates for the
Purposes of the Analysis

American Standard	Northwest Industries
Bangor Punta	Norton Simon
Chromalloy	NVF
Consolidated Foods	Olin
Dart Industries	Pepsico
Esmark	Phillip Morris
General Mills	Rockwell International
Greyhound	SCM
Gulf and Western	Talley Industries
Indian Head	Teledyne
ITT	Tenneco
Walter Kidde	Textron
Litton	TRW
LTV	United Technologies
Martin-Marietta	Whittaker

TABLE 5.13
Capacity Change Behavior of Conglomerates and Nonconglomerates

	Conglomerates				Nonconglomerates			
	Plants		Employment		Plants		Employment	
Class of Plant	Number	As % of Stay-Puts	Number	As % of Stay-Puts	Number	As % of Stay-Puts	Number	As % of Stay-Puts
Stay-puts	1,399	100	658,398	100	8,100	100	5,460,512	100
Opening	187	13	51,005	8	1,424	18	336,542	6
Closing	195	14	33,274	5	826	10	169,889	3
Acquisition	651	47	179,144	27	2,708	33	570,062	10
Divestiture	247	18	40,171	6	859	11	180,125	3
Relocation	87	6	18,932	3	363	4	77,951	1
Open/close within decade	157	11	23,392	4	545	7	55,828	1
Close/open within decade	2	1	315	1	9	1	1,179	1

are simply more active than other companies in changing their capacity. Most salient, naturally, is the high level of acquisitions by conglomerates. Indeed, not only are the acquisitions relatively more numerous, but they involve larger plants (more established businesses?). Divestitures are less numerous, but conglomerates divest companies at about twice the rate of nonconglomerates.

As for plant closings, it is true that conglomerates are involved in relatively more plant closings than other companies, although these closings tend to be smaller in size. The difference is not all that large, however, and is balanced somewhat by evidence that the new plant openings of conglomerates also cover a larger fraction of their base employment than is true of nonconglomerates. Conglomerates are also involved in a greater relative share of relocations and of plants opened or acquired in the 1970s and then closed or divested later in the decade.

In sum, it seems reasonable to observe that conglomerates are simply more active in their capacity decisions and that this activity implies a relatively higher rate of plant closings. However, conglomerates do not appear especially "ruthless" in their actions, taking into account their high level of activity in all phases of capacity change.

NOTES

1. The results in tables 5.1–3 are not materially altered when the companies are ranked by sales or by assets instead of by employment. For these tables, a ranking by employment merely seems to make good sense.

2. David L. Birch, "The Job Generation Process" (Cambridge: Massachusetts Institute of Technology Program on Neighborhood and Regional Change, 1979).

3. Birch's results stem from an analysis of Dun and Bradstreet's Market Identifiers file. My data for Cincinnati and for the 410 major manufacturers also originate from that source. Thus I am well acquainted with the deficiencies of the Dun and Bradstreet data for research purposes: significant omissions, double counting of plants, employment errors, industry misclassification, and so on. Because of this, I required one worker-year of effort in checking the Cincinnati data and 4.5 worker-years in checking the major manufacturer data. Birch's work does not evidence such care, and this may explain the divergence in our results. For a more thorough explanation of the Dun and Bradstreet data and its inaccuracies, see Roger W. Schmenner, *Making Business Locations Decisions* (Englewood Cliffs, N.J.: Prentice-Hall, 1982).

4. See Schmenner.

5. *Ibid.*

6. See Raymond J. Struyk and Franklin J. James, *Intrametropolitan Industrial Location: The Pattern and Process of Change* (Lexington, Mass.: Heath, 1975); Robert A. Leone, "The Location of Manufacturing Activity in the New York Metropolitan Area" (Ph.D. diss., Yale University, 1971); and Roger W. Schmenner, "The Manufacturing Location Decision" (Washington, D.C.: U.S. Department of Commerce, Economic Development Administration, March 1978).

7. Struyk and James.

8. Schmenner, "Manufacturing Location Decision."

CHAPTER 6

Corporations, Human Resources, and the Grass Roots: Community Profiles

Ivar Berg and
Janice Shack-Marquez

If you cry "Forward!" you must without fail make plain in what direction to go. Don't you see that if, without doing so, you call out the word to both a monk and a revolutionary, they will go in directions precisely opposite?

PASCAL

W HILE community studies add only a little evidence in support or contradiction of either theoretical or ideological positions regarding social relationships, they can be helpful in efforts to clarify some issues, to elaborate further on issues that have been joined but that remain unresolved or require respecification, and in efforts to identify neglected questions. We may note in this connection that economists are beginning to recognize the utility of studies, "in the field," designed to augment those based on mounds of computer printout.[1] In this essay we present a very preliminary report on such an investigation, the research not yet having been concluded,[2] in which our aims have been to:

1. compare and contrast the collective bargaining patterns in locally and absentee-owned firms in one relatively small but heavily industrialized city of nearly 20,000 people in western Michigan;
2. compare and contrast selected personnel practices of the resident managers in these two types of firms, in eight western Michigan counties;
3. tentatively explore the implications of the impact of layoffs and plant shutdowns on workers' (from different types of firms) and their families' health in two Michigan cities; and
4. gain some sense of the differences, if any, between the ways in which local and absentee firms' leaders and their organizations serve economic development, charities, voluntary activities, and related community interests.

Aside from our interests in the correlates of ownership per se, these four topics reflect our interests in labor relations and human resources problems and in looking beyond topics like "competition" and "economic performance" that are commonly the subject of economists' investigations of industry structures.[3]

We may anticipate some of our basic conclusions as follows:

First, differences between labor relations practices of absentee-owned firms and locally owned firms are temporal in character: absentee firms, conglomerate and otherwise, often take leads in staking out new directions in their labor relations; many of their initiatives are subsequently followed by local owners. "Absentees" are far quicker to shut down plants, meanwhile, than more risk-averse (and thus less financially overextended) owners of smaller, local firms, when the economy slips sideways or downward.[4] "Locals" are somewhat less willing to take strikes because their owners are obliged to live with the results. Absentee-owned establishments, otherwise, differ among themselves as much as they differ, collectively, from local firms; their intrasectoral differences appear to reflect differences among the industries in which they do business and differences in the preferred modes of operations among successive leaders who lead their corporate parents. Finally, unlike local union leaders and members, national and international union leaders who were very critical of absentees, until about 1979–1980, have recently come to see benefits as well as costs attaching to the collective bargaining practices of absentees; local and regional union leaders continue to see only disadvantages in the newer practices.

Second, ownership differences in selected personnel practices, collective bargaining aside, show up somewhat more clearly, but they tend to differ more by industry than by size or by ownership.

Third, to the limited extent that one can document the fact, it would *appear* that the most severe consequences to workers' health of economic reverses occur among those whose health was problematic "before the fact." Given the fact that those who seek help select themselves for treatment, there are great difficulties in pinpointing cause and effect in matters of etiology. There are also difficulties in adequately differentiating nonoccupationally related somatic from psychosomatic, psychological, and stress-related disorders.

Fourth, local owners and their managers are far more often involved in community-related and community-serving activities than are their peers among absentee-owned firms. Old hands at community studies will not be surprised, meantime, to learn that the noblesse oblige of either locals or absentees is less than fully appreciated by a small minority of persons in a community who are given to the view that corporate donations of money and time, especially by local owners, are homegrown elites' means to dark ends.

Fifth, larger developments in the economy, both secular and cyclical, have more dispositive effects in all four of the subject areas we have explored than do the actions of individual firms, whatever their ownership; employers would add that many of the personnel practices they undertake are responsive to what *they* regard as the initiatives of others, especially those of local unions. To put it crisply, employers generally see themselves not as initiators but as reactors to economic circumstances, public policies, market conditions, and unions' initiatives.

Finally, we suggest that when large absentee corporations in the industrial sector do have an impact upon communities, they do so as organizations and leaders whose positions are favored in the balance between the few and the many who "control" manufacturing resources—the problem of "aggregated concentration" of industrial wealth. Our own essentially ambiguous results, however, can afford lawmakers relatively little guidance regarding that larger question. Our research does suggest that the communities under study suffer, when they do so, from business decisions that are responsive, ultimately, to general economic conditions and from laws, especially tax laws, that favor the restructuring of firms—industrial conglomeration, for example—without demonstrable gains to the economy overall. Decisions to conglomerate clearly do less to create new jobs locally, for instance, than decisions to "make" rather than "buy," though it is admittedly difficult to trace the employment effects of the increased liquidity of the former owners of an acquired firm, some of whom may invest in stocks and bonds of other corporations. These investments may in turn add to the capital and thus the job-creating capacities of these other corporations. The effects of stagflation on the communities under study, finally, are more readily palpable than the specific effects of the decisions of managers either in local or absentee firms.

METHODS AND DATA

One of us paid brief annual visits to a cluster of small cities ("Lake Cities") in Michigan from 1951 to 1976 and, more intensively, spent summer periods from 1977 to 1982 reading relevant documents and newspaper files, conducting interviews with business leaders and with local, regional, and national labor leaders, community and county officials, leaders of voluntary agencies, citizens, workers, health officials, State Employment Office managers, and labor lawyer consultants to both employers and unions in Lake Cities and in two larger cities nearby. Many hours have been given to discussions with James Mackraz, the highly respected commissioner of the Regional Federal Mediation and Conciliation Service in Grand Rapids. The emphases, during the more recent and more formal periods of research, have been on conducting what are called semistructured interviews (and reinterviews) with these respondents, specifically in Lake Cities.

In a more quantitative phase, we are currently conducting our own secondary analyses of responses to surveys from employers, regarding selected aspects of their personnel policies, in eight western Michigan counties. The surveys were conducted by the Departments of Employment and Training in each of three west Michigan counties and by the Grand Rapids Area Employment and Training Council in Kent County and its four contiguous counties. The surveys' sample sizes (exclusive of the five in Kent not yet analyzed) are 151 and 361 firms, respectively.

The third section, on collective bargaining developments, is based on a preliminary analysis of field notes from intensive, semistructured interviews. The fourth section, on personnel practices, is based on preliminary analyses of data from three of the eight county survey data sets mounted on a computer at the University of Pennsylvania. The fifth section, dealing with mental health, is based on interviews with health and social services officials and the leaders of a voluntary alcoholic treatment organization in one county; on a survey in Lake Cities, by county health officials; and on interviews about their clinical experiences with these county officers. This section is also based on data describing hospital admissions and diagnostic records, prepared by a Michigan third party insuror, on the employees of corporations or corporate subsidiaries belonging to a large Lake Cities employers' association to which nearly all of the employing corporations belong.

In the sixth and final section, we consider some of the overall effects of corporations on the so-called quality of community life.

Our confidence about the validity of our preliminary reading of our qualitative data is enhanced by the fact that we have been able to double- and even triple-check our findings with many different respondents over many years and that we have had literally unimpeded access both to respondents and, when relevant, to their files. Our respondents have always been aware that we have interviewed persons who can be readily identified with one or another of all the sides to innumerable controversies. Indeed, most of our respondents have encouraged us to consider the views of what are sometimes their antagonists even about events and issues that have been highly charged emotionally.

LABOR RELATIONS IN THE LAKE CITIES

The Lake Cities' committee for economic development obtained responses to a survey in 1981 of employers whose work forces accounted for 4,379 of the 6,181 persons employed in industry in the Lake Cities. The Allied Industrial Workers of America (AIW), an international union headquartered in Milwaukee, Wisconsin, which was originally organized in auto and auto parts plants, has thirty locals in the Lake Cities setting with 1,635 members;[5] the AIW thus represents over one-third of all employed persons in the companies responding to the survey. Among these AIW members, 494 are employed in four of the five local plants belonging to a conglomerate firm managed by a holding company owned by three local families. Other Lake Cities unions include the Teamsters, Patternmakers, Carpenters and Joiners, Machinists, Operating Engineers, Draftsmen, Sheetmetal Workers, and Boilermakers. The six largest firms in this community vary in size from 160 to 380 employees. The employment numbers in the survey do not include those of a subsidiary of a non-Michigan conglomerate that was shut down in April 1981, with a loss to the community of 279 jobs, including those of members of one of the AIW locals. The survey did, however, include a plant belonging to another non-Michigan conglomerate that is currently relocating 25 percent of its 192 employees (including executives) to locations in Kentucky and South Carolina. The data also include those descriptive of a third plant belonging to still another absentee conglomerate that was about to be closed in 1982–1983 when the conglomerate's one-time board chairman and three local Lake Cities executives successfully consummated financial arrangements, including proceeds from a sizable federal loan (in August 1982) enabling them to purchase the plant from the corporate parent. In addition to the 279 jobs lost in April 1981, twelve smaller, locally owned establishments, employing 237 persons, were shut down during that year.

The employees in the companies included in the employers' association survey sample have been classified according to their establishments' ownership and their union membership in table 6.1.

Lake Cities, along with most of the nation's local economies, has been hard hit by the current recession and by the stagflation before that. Shutdowns of conglomerates' subsidiaries have occurred because absentee owners have allegedly found themselves with excess capacity and with consequent needs to realize operating economies by consolidating their properties. According to the testimony of local company leaders, after shutdowns in Lake Cities, the consolidated operations are located where the owners can either avoid collective bargaining obligations entirely or where they feel they can bargain with more sanguine unions and where, otherwise, wage levels are lower.

Lake Cities has long been known in industrial relations circles for its explosive labor–management relations; protracted difficulties have stemmed in part from the fact that only a very few of the agreements (and none involving AIW locals) between parties to collective bargain-

TABLE 6.1
Plant Ownership and Union Membership, Lake Cities, 1981

	1 Single plants; locally owned	2 Multiple plants; locally owned	3 Locally owned conglomerate	4 Absentee-owned Michigan companies (integrated)	5 Absentee-owned non-Michigan companies (integrated)	6 Absentee-owned non-Michigan companies (conglomerated)
Number of union members	353	329	494	253	373	693
Percent unionized	27	59	95	68	100	76

NOTE: Columns 1 and 2 together account for 36 firms; column 3 includes 5 plants; columns 4, 5, and 6 together include 17 firms and account for 38 percent of all workers employed by the firms in the survey.

ing contained arbitration/no-strike clauses until the late 1960s. Neither local owners nor local or regional labor leaders wanted such clauses because of anxieties about "outsiders dictating solutions." National union leaders, however, were sympathetic to these clauses beginning in the mid-1950s. There is now only one agreement in Lake Cities without such a clause, and there is no doubt that the rapid, recent proliferation of these clauses was sparked by pressures brought by large absentee-owned firms, including conglomerates, on their local unions up and down the length of the western half of Michigan in the 1970s and, as we just noted, by pressures from national and international union leaders. The managers of large absentee firms were as successful as they were in their drives to win arbitration/no-strike clauses in part, as local union leaders see it, because they were in sound enough economic condition, aided by subsidies from their integrated or conglomerate parent companies, to be able to "take" long strikes and because unions' bargaining powers had been reduced by the protracted economic slump.

It would be a mistake, however, whatever one's sympathies, to see these initiatives by large and absentee-owned companies automatically as "uncaused causes": as employers view the matter, their actions were provoked by union locals that have historically been among the *most* democratic and the *least* influenced (i.e., least tempered) by their international, national, and regional leaders, in the entire nation. Many of the local firms simply capitalized, as they have noted in interviews, on the capacities of absentee owners to engage in the same type of "whipsaw tactics" long used by the multiple locals of unions that bargain, as in the auto industry, with one parent employer at a time. It is also the case that the locally owned establishments have been just as responsive to opportunities presented by loose labor markets, in our successive recessions, to "stiffen their spines" in collective bargaining encounters. Every regional and national labor leader with whom we have spoken, meanwhile, has complained: (1) about the short shrift accorded them (and their advice) by their own union locals; (2) about the shortcomings of employers, whatever the ownership arrangements governing them, who "waited so many years to hold the line" against rising labor costs and against the "inefficient work rules" that employers have recently listed among the primary reasons for shutting down their plants; (3) about "excesses of democracy" in local unions' governance in the Lake Cities; and (4) about the longtime and "pigheaded resistance among local unionists against the negotiation of arbitration/no-strike clauses." One sophisticated employer, on learning of the unionists' assessments, pointed out that they do not understand the finances of manufacturing firms. He noted that a company's capital investment practices are a "tip-off" to unions about eventual plans to shut down local plants—sometimes ten years in advance of such shutdowns.

One must emphasize, meanwhile, that the use of the strike weapon in grievance cases by the local unions has been blunted at least as much by our economy's sideways and downward movements as by the sequence of absentee and then of locally owned firms "stiffening their backs" in collective bargaining rounds. A number of relevant developments may be outlined:

First, the numbers involved have not been uncommonly large; there has been steady acquisition of locally owned firms by either integrated or conglomerated absentee firms since the early 1950s. Several of the properties, including two that were always absentee-owned, have been resold by acquirers to still other absentee integrated or conglomerated corporations.

Second, five locally owned plants were merged into a locally owned, multifamily holding company/conglomerate in 1970.

Third, there have been chronic collective bargaining problems between almost all employers and union locals in larger plants since 1950, with regular threats by and rumors, both before and after labor settlements, about "absentees" shutting down subsidiaries, starting in 1950. The locally owned five-plant conglomerate has experienced relatively few strikes during this period.

Fourth, collective bargaining problems have resulted from a number of developments since 1950 in addition to those having to do with union democracy and arbitration/no-strike clauses: grievances in Lake Cities plants are generally submitted to rank-and-file membership votes, a procedure that generates great insecurity among union leaders, highly factionalized union locals, and, in the past, numerous strikes; local managers of absentee-owned plants are quite regularly obliged to call their distant corporate headquarters about all grievances and work rules (with consequent frustration for both local and regional union leaders and their management peers who cannot bargain with each other day by day); and growing use of labor lawyers, first by absentee owners and, very soon thereafter, by nearly all employers, in reaching agreements in labor management negotiations over new contracts; (later) employment by many union locals of a lawyer from a nearby city in contract negotiations with company lawyers.

Fifth, prior to the proliferation of arbitration and no-strike clauses, local owners were generally better able to settle grievance and work rule–related issues during the life of an agreement without strikes than the managers of absentee-owned plants because local owners could speak more quickly and pointedly for themselves (often with the advice of lawyer consultants).[6] Local owners need not clear their decisions with officers of a distant corporate parent, a circumstance that facilitates much faster and more peaceful resolutions of labor–management problems. *Some* absentee-owned plants' managers *sometimes* have considerable authority delegated to them in their relations with unions, to be sure, while others *sometimes* do not. The words *some* and *sometimes* are used advisedly, however: the degree of authority delegated to an absentees' local managers varies both with changes in policies accompanying transfers of local plant ownership among the absentee acquirers and with periodic swings in the policies of parent companies as their headquarters' corporate reins change hands and, for example, as they embark, alternately, on centralizing and decentralizing plans.[7]

Sixth, lawyers retained by corporations have, quite understandably, and very systematically, converted labor agreements—as they are sometimes still called—into contracts, in the most literal, "legal" sense of the term. Unsympathetic to their corporate clients' "old-fashioned" disposition to leave the matter of the residual rights of the parties rather vague and to work rules sanctified only vaguely by "past practices" and tradition, and mindful of the difficulties of resolving perfectly honest differences over interpretations to be applied to imprecise contract language, company lawyers have literally schooled their employer-clients, owners as well as managers, local as well as absentee, in their highly legalistic views about management methods. Lawyers would also note that NLRB rulings have obliged the parties to seek to reduce ambiguities in the language of their agreements. The impacts of growing legalism at the level of the establishment would shock many old-line students of the labor scene.

Labor–management agreements have become longer and longer documents in which lawyers avoid traditionally vague managements' rights clauses in favor of very carefully enumerated management prerogatives. Emile Durkheim's wonderful term, "the noncontractual elements of contract" is progressively (or regressively?) descriptive of less and less of the content of plant-level labor–management relations. Settlements were redefined in the early days of lawyers' involvements, in the 1970s, as contracts that tie down the details at the *end* of formal negotiations over a new contract. In other times, these settlements were regularly conceived as basic, not detailed agreements that laid the ground for the *beginning* of a bargaining relationship that would commence anew after the parties had reached an accord. By reducing more and more of the details of these settlements to detailed prescriptions and proscriptions, they assure us, the lawyers have contained the grievance process by circumscriptions that reduce, very substantially, the types and numbers of "grievable" and arbitrable issues.

During the 1970s, many of the union lawyers and national union leaders with whom we spoke deplored these developments, but by 1981–1982 lawyers on both sides of the table, in company with leaders at the national and international (but not local) union levels, began to claim that the bargaining process was becoming "more rational." Their reasoning: law firms have dramatically increased the value of their advice to client firms (and their capacities to deal effectively with their union lawyer peers) by hiring more and better labor law specialists, that is, specialists with growing industrial relations "savvy." Absentee managers, meanwhile, often discourage their local plant managers from settling grievances in the initial steps of the grievance process in favor of arbitration in which corporate lawyers can (and very often do) overwhelm their local union adversaries. Until the arbitration hearings actually convene, unionists are repeatedly said "to dig their own graves" by acting without the advice either of their national union leaders or of an able and respected local labor lawyer "until it's too late." At this writing, the company lawyers report that they are beginning to learn that they and their clients have to live with the unions' lawyers after settlement. The results, the lawyers (on both sides) claim, are salutary if not salubrious.

The losses to conglomerates' local company supervisors, local middle managers, and some plant managers of useful margins for daily and weekly manager–worker accommodations, in what we have historically known as "implicit bargaining" and "bargaining in the grievance process," may be offset by the alleged gains from the bureaucratization or "rationalization" of collective bargaining.

Seventh, among the costs of applying the new look in labor relations:

(1) *cases,* in the narrowest sense, are settled, but the underlying *problems* that gave rise to sticky issues in negotiations and, especially, in grievances are most often not solved at all;[8] (2) local union leaders and local union bargaining committees are blamed for the frequent settlements favoring employers by rank-and-file members, with the result that union leaders turn over, leaving lower-level company supervisors bereft of the flexibility and predictability needed in negotiations, day by day, that they gain when they work regularly with stable (i.e., organizationally secure) union leaders; and (3) local managers, in the words of several regional union "reps," often become glorified messengers, representing their absentee corporate chiefs essentially as intermediaries. In consequence, they learn less and less about management, more about "sticks" than "carrots," and a great deal more about giving orders, maintaining discipline, and consulting lawyers than about leading their industrial work forces. Should unions ever recover from the soft labor market conditions that have apparently served employers so well, these subsidiaries' managers and their successors will encounter a much less brave world than the one familiar to them in the period 1975–1983!

Eight, it is worth noting that the Industrial Union Department of the AFL-CIO has been unsuccessful in persuading their affiliated local unions that they can and should engage in "coordinated bargaining," thereby neutralizing the whipsaw tactics sometimes employed by corporate parents. At the very least, such coordinated bargaining would involve common contract expiration dates (which was ultimately the strategy adopted by the IU and the IUE after General Electric had long played these unions off, one against the other). The response of locals in Lake Cities and their leaders across the nation has been the pluralistic-democratic one encountered by the AFL-CIO's Industrial Union Department: "We can't let some other locals, even of our own parent union, have a significant voice in shaping circumstances in our local; our successful local settlements might be stalled, for example, because greedy and impetuous people in some other local (or other union) dealing with our company might go on strike." There is little reason at the moment for believing that the Federation's Industrial Union Department will be successful in its "restructuring drive." Indeed, workers in three of the five plants in the locally owned conglomerate belonged to one local union prior to when the conglomerate was formed; these are now separate locals.

Finally, in a fashion almost perversely parallel, the local managers of absentee firms are regularly obliged by their corporate chiefs to deal with their local unions in accord with their *company's* strategy of coordinated bargaining! We have attached, in appendix 6A, a fairly complete list of conglomerate corporations that have dealings with two or more locals (in the same or different unions) belonging to the Industrial Union Department; the reader can see the opportunities for business to use the "whipsaw tactics" invented and used so effectively by labor unions in other times.

One of the most significant local-tactical implications of the firms' strategy is that some local managers are driven to be intractably tough-minded or "stiff-spined" in their bargaining stances, even when their own interests in productivity gains, as they view them locally, or their managerial instincts, otherwise, would dictate that they be more accommodating in a given grievance or bargaining round. At the same time, and as we noted earlier, Lake Cities unions are situated at the democratic extreme of the range of ideals about democratic union governance endorsed by enthusiastic supporters of the Taft-Hartley and Landrum-Griffin acts. Thus, in Lake Cities, both locally owned conglomerate firms and the absentee-owned firms are highly structured—"bureaucratic" and "rational" in the most Weberian sense of the term—but they are obliged to deal with unstructured unions that are organized around "town meeting" principles. Under these conditions, the locally owned conglomerate firms' labor relations, in accord with a typology familiar to students of industrial relations, fall in the middle between the "arms length" or "conflict relations" typical in the absentee firms, on one side, and the "working accommodation" model of bargaining in some smaller, locally owned firms, on the other. The locally owned conglomerates, with less management turnover and a longer history in Lake Cities, follow the "outsiders' " leads in general, but they adapt the absentees' strategies and tactics to their own circumstances by smoothing down some of the abrasive edges, their intent being to minimize the slowdowns, tests of strength, and unnecessarily rigid rule applications that absentees are better prepared, in economic terms, to risk.

The following points also deserve mention:

First, enthusiastic American observers of Japan's worker participation programs in the United States, especially at the Harvard Business School, can cite little evidence from Lake Cities' labor relations in support of their claims that American employers really are beginning to see significant virtues in a new genuinely "participative" managerial philosophy. Indeed, preachments about "work reform" are offered by consultant-advocates to their managerial clients in terms that preclude the consideration of collective bargaining as a valid form of worker participation. Trendy new work reforms (like "work restructuring") are regularly viewed as valuable tools in larger efforts to take collective bargaining apart, agreement by agreement, and to redefine rather than to elaborate on the nature and practice of the more traditional forms of worker participation we have known in collective bargaining.[9]

Also the state of the general economy's health—the business cycle— is a significant factor in shaping locally owned firms' behavior. All things being equal, and precisely as one would expect, locally owned firms benefit in their labor relations, at least in the short haul, from loose labor markets.

In addition, the developments and patterns characteristic of individual industries have more significant effects on Lake Cities firms belonging to these industries than do developments in other industries in which a conglomerate parent has representatives: as firms and establishments in an industry share essentially common technologies, industry-specific market conditions and dealings with unions organized fairly generally along jurisdictional lines (though the AIW is not), their labor relations behavior, including that of conglomerates' subsidiaries, is a good deal more like that of their industry peers than that of peers of similar size or ownership structure in other industries. For one thing, as absentee firms (and many locally owned firms exclusive of the five-plant conglomerate) increasingly use more sophisticated labor lawyers, the lawyers begin to sense the subtle effects on a local union of its members' and officers' readings of trends in the rest of a given industry. Their conversations with headquarters executives in preparation for bargaining, meantime, afford corporations' lawyers opportunities to prepare their conglomerate clients for the acceptance of terms and elements in their several contracts that will differ across the company's plants. Unions' lawyers, in turn, will help a company labor lawyer sell contracts to corporate headquarters by offering the company lawyer industry-related logics in support of one or more particulars in a new settlement. Company lawyers, as they gain labor relations experience, increasingly recognize that they must come out of negotiations with an agreement that their union counterparts will buy, thus to serve themselves in future negotiations. In this process, labor lawyers who serve firms appear to be displacing the traditional company industrial relations officers; their increasing savvy serves, as a consequence, to reassure union leaders and their lawyers that unions are still able to bargain and that they will not just be bowled over by legalese. By attending these reassurances, the companies serve themselves and their corporate clients.

Furthermore, as the corporate lawyers, especially those serving conglomerates, become more "industrial relations–oriented," they help compensate somewhat for what local and national union people regard as the hopelessly "nonproduction" attitudes of local managers who serve far more as links in a reporting chain than as responsible leaders. The sentiment, expressed with pity—which is to say contempt—is an interesting one, for it is most certainly not part of the conventional wisdom that unions care very much about productivity. We will return to this matter below.

As higher-level union leaders see it, the grievance process is a mechanism for letting off steam generated by inevitable tensions in the work place; workers are better able to work effectively after the pressure valve has done its work than if pressures simply keep building. It is also the case, as union leaders see it, that "justice delayed" leads to a widespread sense of helplessness and victimization that further reduces flagging interests in work.

Finally, abler, and more industrial relations-oriented company lawyers can convey information to company headquarters about tension sources at the grass roots that are linked to budgetary constraints imposed on local managers by conglomerate headquarters. In one plant, for example, a succession of local managers has refused to urge their absentee parents to provide for the purchase of relatively inexpensive mechanical devices in replacement of those that regularly break down. The plant managers report to us, quite without embarrassment, that repairs are more readily explicable than new equipment purchases, that the urge to purchase replacements would make them "look like spenders" to company headquarters, and that their successors, not they, would be the beneficiaries of the efficiencies realized after the new equipment has been amortized. The plant's workers, all highly skilled, deplore this attitude, which they characterize as the "nonproduction" attitude of managers.

We may note, for example, that the union workers in a Lake Cities piano manufacturing subsidiary of a conglomerate belong to an international union that sponsors competitions among its locals in which music professionals judge the quality of the tones of the instruments they make. The workers in this plant so deplore the subcontracting of mill work on the instruments, and the consequent decline in the quality of the product they make, that they have lost all sense of craft pride. They also become very querulous when employers seek to institute production changes supported by the argument that they "have to be more competitive in the industry." Managers, like Wilde's cynics, are charged with knowing the price of everything but the value of nothing and with sacrificing long-term ends by the application of expedient means. We could offer countless other such cases.

The ultimate question of whether the leadership roles and economic staying power of absentee owners, either integrated or conglomerated in their structures, are pluses or minuses in general socioeconomic terms is hard to answer unequivocally. Readers who are unsettled by the near eclipse of unions as significant balancing elements in our system of industrial democracy or in what some admiringly call our pluralistic society, will chalk up another score for management exploiters of the protracted softness in the demand for labor; readers who have long worried about unions' alleged immunities from competition and from antitrust regulation and the "impunity" with which they have "extorted" wage gains and fringe benefits from their corporate victims will be enthused, and they will be gratified by the initiatives that large integrated and conglomerate firms' leaders have taken in efforts to roll back many of the gains of the so-called labor movement.

An alternative assessment, one that even many thoughtful proponents of corporations in our most conservative ranks might endorse, will be informed by their estimates about whether or not a grudging work force (faced with "rationalized" bargaining arrangements and with grievances that are settled with politically unstable union leaders in legal but not in institutionally or organizationally meaningful terms) will ever contribute positively to the margin of differences between falling and rising output per man-hour.

The view we have derived of the process from our field experiences is that collective bargaining is evolving in the not very desirable direction of plant-level bargaining in the United Kingdom. To put it another way, we observe collective bargaining to be settling into a position between "arms length" and "armed conflict," following a typology developed in the early post–World War II era, and away from the "cooperative relationships" that were characteristic in strike-free and peaceful U.S. industries, that is, in the majority of cases, in the period 1960–1979. During that period, according to the Bureau of Labor Statistics, the United States lost an average of .18 percent of estimated working time due to strikes (or lockouts) involving six or more workers and lasting at least one full shift.

Considerably less equivocal are the effects of the newest version of collective bargaining on the Lake Cities economy: threats of plant shutdowns by absentee corporations' owners and managers may not "tame" union democrats, but the greater ability of these companies to take long strikes does affect third parties in the community—creditors, merchants, voluntary associations, and so on—whether justice in a particular labor conflict lies with a striking local or with the managers and owners of a plant. And when a large absentee corporation actually shuts down a Lake Cities plant, an action the larger, locally owned companies can take less readily, the effects are even more serious, given the consequent job losses.

Once again, however, it must be recognized that the options of large absentee owners are exercised, in the first instance, in response to their assessment of business conditions and of the "containment" of workers in different locations. If one of the absentee companies sells its Lake Cities plant, in early 1983, to a local syndicate, a Florida plant will lose sales of its product in favor of sheetmetal workers and carpenters in Lake Cities. And when an auto supply operation in Lake Cities was shut down in 1981, an Ohio city became the host to a plant that is now more fully utilizing its capacity. In these events, the two absentee corporations will be cheered, or jeered, in Florida, Ohio, and Michigan, as the circumstances suggest. In these events, the decisions are either damnable or admirable exercises of businessmen's judgments about the firms' markets, their judgments about unions, and their judgments about business conditions. As Hollywood's Samuel Goldwyn once remarked, "Where you stand depends on where you sit." Problems in the area of labor relations, to put it succinctly, are secondarily, not primarily, the byproducts of actions taken by the immediate parties to collective bargaining agreements.

SELECTED PERSONNEL PRACTICES IN THREE COUNTIES

The vast literature on personnel practices in organizations, collective bargaining practices quite aside, would lead us to expect that smaller firms, especially locally owned ones, would have far less rationalized and routinized personnel procedures and that they would place less of a premium on "in-house" training than larger organizations. Larger and reputedly more rationally bureaucratic organizations, judging from this literature, not only can afford more elaborate selection, promotion, and training arrangements but are more likely to be run by employers whose professional training in management would reflect quite different values; smaller firms would be more inclined, in the current jargon, to "adhocracy" than bureaucracy as a guiding principle of human resources management.

In this section we present some preliminary results of an initial examination of the personnel practices of smaller and larger firms of different ownership type in three western Michigan counties. The data come from surveys on the hiring and training practices of private business firms in Muskegon, Oceania, and Ottawa counties in 1979 and 1980 (Muskegon and Oceania were surveyed together and are treated as one county). Mail and telephone surveys, by the Muskegon and Ottawa County Departments of Employment and Training, were directed to the individual most responsible for hiring and training employees in the surveyed firms. In Muskegon/Oceania Counties 199 firms responded, and in Ottawa County 360. Of these firms, 151 firms in Muskegon/Oceania and 351 in Ottawa provided sufficient responses to be included in the analysis. The questions in the survey dealt with five major issues: hiring policies for entry level, unskilled, and skilled workers; promotion policies for existing workers; training programs provided by firms; perceived labor market conditions; and characteristics of the firms. We have chosen to present the results separately for the two counties since, as we will see below, there are strikingly patterned differences between them.

First, we briefly present some descriptive statistics on firm behavior in the two counties, and second we present our preliminary analyses of how ownership, firm size, and industry are related to various personnel practices. Firms were asked what human capital characteristics they sought when selecting unskilled or entry-level workers. The responses were grouped into nine categories and are listed below with the percent of respondents/firms in Muskegon/Oceania and Ottawa counties that thought they were important:

	Muskegon/Oceania	Ottawa
Skill levels	34	18
Appearance	65	27
Past attendance record	78	32
Attitude during interview	74	59
Verbal communication skills	43	8
How application is filled out	49	5
Applicant asks right questions	43	4
Content of resume	14	6
Applicant's committment to stay	29	10

Attitudes, attendance, and appearance are the most important characteristics for unskilled and entry-level workers in both samples.

The same questions were posed to representatives of the firms with regard to their selection of skilled workers. The responses are listed below:

	Muskegon/Oceania	Ottawa
Skill levels	60	54
Appearance	54	13
Past attendance record	69	27
Attitude during interview	62	34
Verbal communication skills	51	6
How application is filled out	47	2
Applicant asks right questions	51	3
Content of resume	31	10
Applicant's committment to stay	38	12

As we would expect, skill levels play a central role, but applicants' attitudes and their attendance records are also judged to be important in hiring skilled workers.

A third set of questions was designed to determine what employee traits each firm stressed in evaluations of their existing workers for promotion or continued employment. In both Ottawa and Muskegon/Oceania, the respondents placed most emphasis on the extent to which workers follow the instructions of their supervisors and the least emphasis on compliance with company rules:

	Muskegon/Oceania	Ottawa
Follows supervisor's instructions	55	55
Development of fine skills	44	31
Good attendance record	44	53
Cooperates with other employees	28	33
Complies with company rules	18	18

Next, the respondents were asked about the training programs they provide to their employees; the responses afford an opportunity to gauge employers' differing perspectives about their needs and their own investments in filling their needs. Fifty-five percent of the responding firms in Muskegon/Oceania and 46 percent in Ottawa provide training to their new employees. On average, the training programs in Muskegon/Oceania last sixteen days, while those in Ottawa last eighteen days. In addition, 63 percent of firms in Muskegon/Oceania and 49 percent in Ottawa have training programs, on the job or in classrooms, for existing employees.

Beyond those relating to the personnel practices of the firms, the investigators collected data on the characteristics of firms and firms' perceptions of labor market conditions. Our tally shows, first, that 70 percent of the responding firms in Muskegon/Oceania and 92 percent in Ottawa are locally owned and, second, that the average firm in Muskegon/Oceania has ninety-eight full-time workers and eight part-time workers, in contrast to the average firm in Ottawa county with eighty-one full-time and seventy part-time workers. This discrepancy in average firm size between the two counties is partially an artifact of the data collection process: while the firms in Muskegon/Oceania were selected from a complete list of firms in the area, the Ottawa sample was supplemented with small firms. We accordingly see many more small firms and firms in the trade industry and fewer absentee-owned firms in Ottawa. The third characteristic relates to whether the number of employees changes during the year or whether the work force's size is stable. Employment in Muskegon/Oceania is much more volatile, with 47 percent of firms reporting changes in employment during the year in comparison with only 25 percent in Ottawa. The fourth characteristic is major industrial classification. The table below shows the number of companies in each industry.

	Muskegon/Oceania	Ottawa
Agriculture, mining	1	4
Construction	6	5
Manufacturing	61	40
Transportation	5	3
Trade	6	42
Finance	16	2
Other	5	4

Finally, two questions were asked about firms' views of the conditions of the labor market they face. Forty-four percent of firms in Muskegon/Oceania and 46 percent of firms in Ottawa report that they have difficulty filling jobs. And, as can be seen below, a substantially greater percentage of firms in Ottawa reported a shortage in the available labor supply than did firms in Muskegon/Oceania:

	Muskegon/Oceania	Ottawa
Shortage	14	38
Adequate	68	57
Surplus	18	5

With these frequency distributions in hand we used multiple regression techniques to explore the relationships among the several characteristics of the firms in the surveys and the personnel practices they employ. The dependent variables in our models are the personnel practices described above. The explanatory variables include (1) the characteristics of firms (ownership, size, seasonal employment changes, and industry) and (2) firms' perceptions of labor market conditions (whether they have difficulty filling jobs and whether the available labor supply is sufficient).

In accord with the suggestions of management and personnel specialists, we expected that absentee firms would utilize more impersonal hiring and promotion policies than local firms. On the basis of data we have ourselves analyzed and reported elsewhere, we anticipated some confirmation of others' findings because, we theorized, absentee owners are less likely to have the ready access to personal contacts and social networks so often used by firms in making hiring and promotion decisions.[10] However, the fundamental conclusion we can draw from the results of our regression analyses is that type of ownership does not explain, in any significant way, the personnel practices touched upon in the surveys: there are simply no significant differences between local and nonlocal firms either in the preferences they express regarding new workers' traits, in the way they make hiring and promotion decisions, or in their provision of training for employees.

Nor can our model's lack of explanatory power be accounted for, as one might reasonably expect, by firm size. Although size does explain the use of certain personnel policies, there is no pattern. It is surprising, given that large firms have more complicated personnel issues with which to contend, that size is not a more significant factor. The only statistically significant finding is that larger firms in Ottawa County are more likely to provide training programs to new employees. Recall, though, that the Ottawa sample has many more small retail shops than the Muskegon/Oceania sample, and these establishments are necessarily the least likely to provide anything more than on-the-job training.

As we would expect, firms indicating that they encounter difficulties in filling jobs are significantly more likely to provide training programs (and longer training programs) to both new and old employees than are firms that report no difficulty filling jobs. Personnel policies and training programs do differ significantly by industry in our models. However, they exhibit no pattern at all.

In general, we were only slightly surprised at how little of the variances in personnel policies we could explain using variables generally assigned great weight in the personnel literature. Our surprise was tempered by several considerations.

First, some of the managers in the multiplant, locally owned conglomerate in Ottawa County, together with managers in most of the locally owned and some of those in two absentee firms, have learned to have great confidence in the recommendations of one of the senior officials in a branch office of the Michigan Employment Security Commission (MESC). A long-time local resident, this official has opportunities to screen the recipients of unemployment compensation on the basis of acquaintanceships and memberships in community groups. In the process, the official's careful "match-up" of employers' needs and would-be workers' traits reduces the need of many employers (of both types of ownership and of all sizes) for compensatory personnel programs conventionally aimed at fitting workers to jobs. In most of these placements the MESC official operates almost as much as a friendly contact as a public official.[11] The inclination of employers to use the local MESC office originally derived from employers' needs to do constructive work in support of their obligations under equal opportunity regulations.

In addition, the director of the Ottawa County Department of Employment and Training and his modest staff afford many employer constituents the benefit of the same screening and matching skills and the same "informal" accesses as those afforded by the official in the MESC.

Furthermore, there is a large surplus of skilled workers in virtually every trade and vocation in the counties under study; training programs are thus serving no significant market.

At the same time that there are skill surpluses, many of the unemployed workers making up this surplus are the laid off workers of plants whose militant, democratic unions are among those against whose members the employers in the counties under study are determined to discriminate. This fact makes the respondents' claims that they have difficulty filling jobs (despite skill surpluses) comprehensible.

Data from the April 1969, 1972, 1975, and 1978 Current Population Surveys of Adult Education in the United States clearly show that company training programs are offered in (statistically) disproportionate numbers to white male college graduates thirty years of age and over—generally upper-level managers, professionals, and technicians.[12] These types of workers are essentially not those about which the respondents to the surveys reported here were queried.

EMPLOYMENT AND MENTAL HEALTH

Arguments in favor of "full employment policies," most recently in congressional debates over the Humphrey-Hawkins Bill (aimed at updating the Full Employment Act of 1946), have turned increasingly on the social costs of unemployment and related economic insecurities. Indeed, faithful fans of the "McNeil-Lehrer Report" will recall a widely cited program in the spring of 1982 on a sociological version of the Phillips curve in modern economic analysis. The sociological version, based on ecological data, holds that the rates of occurrence of a large number of stress-related mental and physical disorders go up and down, in predictably fixed proportions, to changes in unemployment rates. Harvey Brenner, author of a series of the best of these studies at Johns

Hopkins University, has given influential testimony before the Joint Economic Committee and other congressional committees that for many decades, while the magnitudes of morbidity and unemployment rates may vary from one industrial nation to another, the patterns of their covariance are virtually identical across countries, with a "lag factor" of about three years.

As we have noted, the data in these time series are ecological in character. We will be able, in our continuing study, to offer a more elaborately specified model than that applied to ecological data because we will be examining the annual employment *and* health experiences over the period 1968–1981 of each of the respondents of two large panel surveys. In the meantime, we can offer a few observations on the basis of a very preliminary analysis of ecological, individual-level, and "clinical interview" data descriptive of Ottawa County and of the employees of the firms belonging to the Lake Cities Committee for Economic Development, mentioned in the first section.

We may say, at the outset, that the patterns Brenner has documented on the basis of national health statistics are discernible, if a good bit more ambiguously so, at the grass roots.[13] Our data include empirical materials from the Ottawa County Department of Human Services, "clinical" materials from interviews with department officials; materials on institutional and professional services provided to employees of a sample of firms in Lake Cities for which reimbursements were made by a third party insuror; and materials from interviews with professionals who provide psychological counseling to "walk-in" clients as well as to clients referred to a social service agency funded by Lake Cities churches by school officials, employers, clergymen, physicians, and local courts.

We can report, overall, that 60 percent of the adult clients who came to the Lake Cities office of the Department of Human Services in the period October 1981 to March 1982 were unemployed. It is notable, however, that all but three of these unemployed persons had intermittently been clients of the agency over several years while they were employed; one of the three exceptions, who suffers from a serious chronic mental disease, had worked full time and without significant incident for nearly thirty years.

An inventory of the Ottawa County Department of Human Services' file of "active cases" on June 30, 1982, furthermore, shows that 22 percent of the 948 adult clients (including 181 part-time workers) were labor force participants but that, of these participants, fully two-thirds were employed. The fact is noteworthy because the inventory was conducted fourteen months after the community suffered a net loss of 518 jobs due to plant closings.

In separate discussions with the clinicians in this county department, we learned that they had never collected data on their clients with an eye to making specific judgments about the roles clients' economic circumstances might have played in their psychological problems. This is in large part because their long clinical experiences with clients left them with the very distinct impression that unemployment and related economic insecurities imposed large taxes only on a *minority* of victims and their dependents, a minority whose coping and psychological mechanisms otherwise were, and had long been, insufficient to help them contend with any significant kinds of stress. In only slightly different words, both clinicians stated, as did the clinical director of the counseling center sponsored by local churches, that among those in the large majority who sought no help, economic adversity actually helped some workers to redefine their occupational interests and that adversities otherwise had no consequential impacts on the mental health of the rest of the majority, both because of the "support systems" available to them (see below) and because of these victims' personal psychological resources.[14]

Our own observations, while attending a program conducted by a professional consultant for the employees of a conglomerate that is currently closing down a subsidiary, square well, at least in the short run, with those of our informants: the majority of these employees, on the eve of their permanent job separations, never appeared at any of over one dozen carefully organized programs dealing with stress, job search, occupational counseling, and other timely subjects. The twenty-five employees to whom we actually spoke mentioned one or more of the elements of the support system we describe below in discussions about their reactions to an experience that embittered but did not appear at all to devastate them.

Next we were able to obtain data for the period January 1980 to November 1981, on the charges submitted for institutional and professional care to a third party insuror on behalf of the employees of firms belonging to the Lake Cities Committee for Economic Development. The data cover employees in two plants that shut down in 1980–1981 and two that were planning shutdowns during 1982. We selected health items bearing upon the diagnoses listed in tables 6.2 and 6.3. We assume, in accord with a "worst case scenario," that rows 3, 4, 5, and 6 contain data on patients' problems that are entirely psychological, psychiatric, psychogenic, and stress-related in character.

We note that during one of the most disastrous twenty-three-month periods in Lake Cities' economy since the 1930s, there is little evidence in the data on professional services (table 6.2) of the type of reactions to "economic capital punishment" that one would expect in light of Brenner's findings.

When we turn to the data on subscribers' and their dependents' uses of institutional care (table 6.3), however, we see some evidence consistent with expectations suggested in Brenner's macro-level studies. Consider that while the number of "institutional days" and the "days per case" very nearly all decreased from the first to the second period, the incidence of stress-related disorders among both subscribers (workers) and dependents went up in nine of the ten possible categories. In the case of "symptoms and ill-defined conditions" (high in 1980 for both subscribers' and dependents' claims for professional services), subscribers' needs for these services increased by a factor of nearly twenty.[15]

TABLE 6.2
Professional Uses of Blue Shield by Committee for Economic Development Member Firms' Subscribers and Dependents

Diagnostic Category	Cases in 1980	Cases in 1981
Mental		
Subscribers	80	30
Dependents	63	34
Circulatory system		
Subscribers	471	81
Dependents	190	79
Digestive system		
Subscribers	225	63
Dependents	161	163
Skin diseases		
Subscribers	95	16
Dependents	96	19
Symptoms and ill-defined conditions		
Subscribers	541	150
Dependents	880	88

TABLE 6.3

Institutional Uses of Blue Cross by Committee for Economic
Development Member Firms' Subscribers and Dependents

Diagnostic Category	January–December 1980			December 1980–November 1981		
	Cases	Days	Days per Case	Cases	Days	Days per Case
Mental						
Subscribers	7	86	13	5	57	11
Dependents	2	12	6	12	59	5
Circulatory system						
Subscribers	14	84	6	41	81	2
Depedendents	7	29	4	11	6	.6
Digestive system						
Subscribers	23	115	5	51	104	2
Dependents	26	109	4	42	71	2
Skin diseases						
Subscribers	1	5	5	12	4	3
Dependents	4	33	8	6	0	0
Symptoms and ill-defined conditions						
Subscribers	13	54	6	115	9	.1
Dependents	7	74	8	134	37	.3

NOTE: One month overlap.

Given Brenner's findings that there is a three-year lagged effect of stress, one might expect even greater increases in stress-related disorders in data covering 1982, data that will not be available until Spring 1983. A regional third party insuror's officer reported in July to the employers' association that there has been an increase in these disorders during the current calendar year "of between 10 and 20 percent in [your] members' companies," but he does not report that these increases can be linked specifically to employees of companies that have noticeably poorer economic prospects or about which shutdown rumors have been and are rife or which indeed have shut down. Data on drug prescriptions (available only for 1980) show that reimbursable psychiatric and tranquilizing drug prescriptions accounted for less than 10 percent of all drug charges. In neither year were there any professional or institutional charges to the third party insurors for the treatment of those given to "substance abuse."

Finally, we have individual-level data on the "presenting symptoms," employment experiences, and employer identification for clients in all of Ottawa County's Human Services offices. These data will afford us an opportunity to test the third party insuror's estimates regarding a sample drawn from the same population and to introduce controls, in regression equations, for the clients' company size and ownership. These results will be available in the fall of 1983.

Before passing to the next section it is appropriate, as we noted above, to consider some of the reasons why, given Lake Cities' depressed economy, the malaise suggested in the institutional data is not even more marked. These may be listed briefly as follows:

Many of those laid off (nearly one-quarter of those terminated in plant closings) are young and single. Many of their economic needs can be met with help from friends and families. Indeed, many live with their parents or return to their parents' homes.

The Lake Cities area affords many seasonal jobs, from snow removal to berry picking and spring–fall nursery work (there are forty-one agricultural employers with seasonal needs).

Many of those eligible for retirement do in fact retire.

About half of laid off or separated workers have spouses who work full or part time.

All of those laid off or separated are eligible for unemployment insurance benefits.

Victims with children in college send them to a low-cost local community college (where the offspring receive financial aid packages because their families' incomes are modest) rather than send them to larger, distant state and private universities (nearly 25 percent of all households in Lake Cities have household incomes under $15,000). It is especially significant that, according to the Michigan Community College Association, one of every two community college students is twenty-four years old or older, one of every four is thirty years old or older, and over 40 percent of all Michigan college students are in community colleges. Clearly, school, more than ever before, is a substitute for work; school attendance may enhance skills and make unemployment legitimate, both of which effects may serve mental health.

Lake Cities has a large number of support services including many aided by the United Way. The fact of United Way's support of these programs, to which laid off and separated workers have in most instances made contributions, remove many of the stigmata attached to seeking help; the local view is that one is "earning returns on investments" in using these programs.

Almost every year, four to six new small companies start operations in Lake Cities; their absorption of some unemployed workers helps account for the fact that the average duration of unemployment falls below the fifteen-week cutoff for "long-term" unemployment.

Unions representing workers in all of the plants that have shut down over the past four years have negotiated severance payments for their members.

While employee credit unions in Lake Cities, as in most communities, charge relatively high interest rates, they do not repossess property. We also have the sense that the local banks are not quick to repossess property to which, as creditors, they could lay claims.

There has been a phenomenally large increase in yard and garage sales during 1980–1982, especially in "solid middle-class" and even upper middle-class neighborhoods. It is evident that the capacity to recycle virtually an entire household—household appliances, clothing, and other goods—has been a significant factor in families' capacities to meet consumer needs at very, indeed extremely, low cost.

There has been a boom in low cost do-it-yourself house and car repairs.

Lake Cities is endowed with two large state parks, a relatively inexpensive YMCA, a mile-long, beautifully maintained state beach, and municipal marinas (that are used intensively by fishing enthusiasts); there is, thus, much inexpensive and free recreation. And depending on the weather, there are at least fifty fishermen on the piers where one of Michigan's rivers enters Lake Michigan. Daily observations support the estimate that between 7,000 and 10,000 servings of fresh fish are caught from June until mid-October. The hard toe shoes, as well as the caps and windbreakers with union logos that they wear, inform one clearly of the fishermen's occupations. Agricultural produce from the area surrounding the developed sections of Lake Cities is plentiful and thus very cheap at farmers' markets from mid-June through September. The canning or freezing of pickles, sweet corn, tomatoes, applesauce, peaches, blueberries, green beans, and other produce is an important part of the community's household economies; the equipage for these ventures occupies large specialized sections of shelves in all supermarkets and discount stores.

COMPANIES AND THE COMMUNITY

Studies of "corporate responsibility"—having to do essentially with their gifts to worthy causes, their involvements in community activities and organizations, and their contributions to the so-called quality of community life overall—suddenly became an extensive cottage industry in leading American business schools during the late 1960s; indeed, these studies added usefully to the picture of corporations and communities sketched earlier by social scientists, whose interests focused somewhat more specifically on the roles of "business elites" in "community power structures." The more recent wave of studies was of a piece with the criticisms of the "establishment" so much in vogue on campuses from Berkeley to Columbia in the period 1965–1975. The picture, as we note in the papers prepared for this symposium by John Siegfried and his colleagues, is still replete with confused and confusing motifs: large absentee corporations and their leaders, like their peers in locally owned plants, turn up in all the cells of which one would conceive in a table in which specific community issues touched by corporations are cross-tabulated with estimates of "good" and "bad" performance.[16] And so it is in Lake Cities.

Consider, on one side, that the locally owned conglomerate's establishments regularly donate $25 per employee to the community's United Way drive, while absentees' establishments average $3.60 per employee; two of the seventeen absentees gave nearly $20 per employee, while six gave nothing in the most recent fund drive. And to complicate matters further for would-be judges of corporate ways, while the largest absentee firm donated as much per employee as the prize-winning locally owned conglomerate in 1981–1982, this donor's corporate parent shut down its Lake Cities plant in August! This absentee, moreover, turned out after a long investigation (and allegedly unbeknownst to the resident manager) to be the "mystery" owner of a residential housing tract so dilapidated that all of the dwellings were condemned by city officials. What the distant corporate lord can giveth, with one hand, in some cases, the corporate lord taketh with the other; the local owners, meanwhile, taketh less and giveth more than most of the absentees.

We can report that none of the absentee corporations have any local executives serving as members of the boards of any of five local foundations, of school and hospital boards, or of benevolent associations otherwise. Local owners, meanwhile, are generally active in community affairs and in the leadership of most of Lake Cities' foundations and voluntary associations. We may note, however, that a disproportionately larger number of absentee-owned firms' managers than local owners live outside the Lake Cities limits and thus may well feel less personally obligated to participate in Lake Cities' activities. It is more evidently the case, as we noted in the discussion of collective bargaining, that the managers of absentee-owned firms have shorter occupational residencies in Lake Cities' firms than those in locally owned firms. It is thus not at all obvious that the absentees' local representatives are acting as they do—or do not—because of their firms' policies governing community membership.

There is one important exception to our basic theme throughout this essay that absentee firms' impacts on Lake Cities are rather more temporal and ambiguous in character than suggested by their critics in the social science literature, and, we suggest, it is an important one. The fact is that all but two of the absentee-owned establishments in Lake Cities were once locally owned by entrepreneurs who were heavily dependent for many years upon the confidence and business acumen afforded them by the commercial loan officers in three locally owned banks. Once these firms became successful enough to be attractive to "foreign" acquirers, these firms' accounts (other than payrolls) were transferred to larger distant banks serving the corporate parent. Local banks are consequently left with the far riskier new ventures and, inevitably, the car and home loans of Lake Cities' residents, including those employed by absentee-owned firms. These workers, as we have noted, are more vulnerable to plant closings than those employed by local owners. Local banks, in consequence, have been pressed to join other banks from nearby communities in forming bank holding companies, which themselves, in turn, have then become attractive targets for acquirers. It is also the case that the local banks, in quest of earnings, "buy into" the loans granted by large banks in Chicago, Detroit, and elsewhere to borrowers all over the world. Typically, the bankers in the nation's smaller cities have little personal knowledge about the quality of these loans. While none of the Lake Cities banks have apparently been stung by highly problematic banker's judgments like those recently described in connection with the 1982 Penn Square scandal, it is not the least bit unreasonable to expect that continuing excursions of local banks beyond their old precincts will bring them increasingly into arrangements that are much less under their professional control than those obtaining between them and the local firms to whom they very evidently gave much (self-reassuring) management as well as financial assistance. The evolving pattern is, of course, not unique to Lake Cities. And no estimates, as far as we know, have been made of how many small city "loan sharer" banks should be added to the now celebrated "watch list" of 300 problematic banks recorded by the comptroller of the currency and other regulators.

CODA

The materials we have presented do not lend themselves to the construction of unambiguous conclusions about the direct impact of absentee corporations and the direct effects of conglomeration on the communities under study. It is, of course, true that we here present only a progress report, not the results of a thorough analysis of the data that are still under review, as our field work ends. It is our best sense, however, that we will not discover clearer patterns than the ragged-edged ones we have limned to date.

It is clear, nevertheless, that the communities under study, like many others, perhaps even in the once-booming Sunbelt, are affected by the problematic state of general economic conditions. Only to the extent that the business community, writ large, can or should be blamed for problematic economic conditions when the economy is ailing does Lake Cities suffer from this community's malfeasance; indeed, Lake Cities is one of the hardest hit of "impacted areas" among smaller cities. The Lake Cities area, in this event, would be the beneficiary of whatever policies have constructive effects on business decision making overall. To the extent, otherwise, that our economy suffers for reasons that lie beyond the business community's ways and means, Lake Cities would benefit from other initiatives by other agents and agencies.

APPENDIX 6A: CORPORATIONS WITH WHOM THE INDUSTRIAL UNION DEPARTMENT/AFL-CIO HAVE TWO OR MORE LOCAL UNION CONTRACTS

Allis Chalmers
Allied Chemical
AMF
American Cyanamid
American Home Products
American Standard
Anaconda Wire & Cable
Armstrong Cork
Arvin Industries
ATO
Borden
Brunswick
Carborundum
Celanese
Ciba-Geigy
Colt Industries
Combustions Engineering
Crane
Dayton-Walther
Diamond International
Dow Chemical
Eaton/Cutler-Hammer
Envirotech
Equitable
Essex
FMC
GAF
Gas Service
General Signal
Gerber Products

GK Technologies
Glidden Durkee
Globe Union
Gould
Hercules
Hooker
Johns-Manville
Koehring
3-M
Magnavox
McGraw-Edison
Merck
Monsanto
Morton-Norwich
National Gypsum
NL Industries
Okonite
Olin
Parker-Hamilton
Pennwalt
Phelps Dodge
Pirelli Cable
Questor
Refractories Industry
Revere Copper & Brass
Robertshaw Controls
Rockwell International
Rockwell International
   Electronics Division
Salt Industry

Stauffer Chemical
Tecumseh
Union Carbide
Wagner Electric

Whirlpool
Whitaker
White Consolidated
White Consolidated
Appliance Group

NOTES

1. See, for example, Barbara R. Bergmann, "Economic Affairs: The Failures of a Chair Bound Science," *New York Times*, December 12, 1982, p. F3.

2. We are pleased to acknowledge the support of the Columbia University Law School's Center for Law and Economic Studies and from the Center for Studies of Work and Mental Health, PHS/NIMH grant number MH-34245-02. We are also indebted to Messrs. James Mackraz and F. Martin Johnson for reading and commenting on this paper; while we have incorporated their suggestions, we are responsible for the paper's contents.

3. For a brief review of these studies, see Ivar Berg and Mayer Zald, "Business and Society," *Annual Review of Sociology* (1978), 4:115–143.

4. For a regional (New England) study of the subject, see Bennett Harrison and Barry Bluestone, "The Incidence and Regulation of Plant Closings," pp. 131–167, in Bennett Harrison and Barry Bluestone, eds., *Public Policies for Distressed Areas* (Lexington, Mass.: Lexington, 1981). For analyses of differential risk aversion of "locals" and "absentees," see M. Stoner, "Monopoly Power, Ownership Control, and Corporate Performance," *Bell Journal of Economics* (1976), 7:672–679; and Yakov Amihud and Baruch Lev, "Risk Reduction as a Managerial Motive for Conglomerate Mergers," *Bell Journal of Economics* (1981), 12:605–617.

5. For a fine historical overview, see Bob Repas, "Grievance Procedures Without Arbitration," *Industrial and Labor Relations Review* (April 1967), 20:381–390.

6. We noted earlier that some national union leaders *now* argue that employers did not adequately resist local union efforts in the service of restrictive work rules in the 1960s. Employers could argue that local unions, taking their lead from the United Steelworkers in the "great steel strike" of 1959, did not so easily yield to employers' efforts in that period to contain these work rules!

7. According to Arch Patton of the McKinsey Company (consultants), annual turnover rates by 1976 among 135,000 truly policy-level "executives, exclusive of retirement, has risen from close to 0 prewar to an estimated 20,000 plus . . . and appears to be increasing at a rate of 20,000 annually" "Ideas and Trends: The Boom in Executive Self-Interest," *Business Week*, May 24, 1976, p. 16.

8. The old look was of course not always a better one! Indeed, one locally owned firm had tumultuous labor–management relations until the employer retained an out-of-town lawyer. And the parties' circumstances improved further when the firm, on the lawyer's advice, hired an able director of labor relations.

9. For a discussion, see Ivar Berg, Michael Freeman, and Marsha Freedman, *Managers and Work Reform: A Limited Engagement* (New York: Free Press, 1978).

10. For a recent empirical analysis, see a report from our larger study by Janice Shack-Marquez, "Inside Information and the Employer–Employee Matching Process," Fels Institute Discussion Paper No. 159 (Philadelphia: University of Pennsylvania, September 1982); and Mary Corcoran, Lyle Datcher, and Gregory Duncan, "Information and Influence Net-

works in Labor Markets," in Gregory Duncan and James Morgan, eds., *5000 American Families*, vol. 3 (Ann Arbor, Mich.: Institute for Social Research, 1980).

11. For an empirical analysis of the roles of third party intermediaries in the employment process, see Shack-Marquez.

12. See Michael Tierney, "Trends in Company Training Programs in National Perspective," mimeographed (Philadelphia: University of Pennsylvania Graduate School of Education, 1982). Employers told us, in a series of twenty case studies during 1982–1983, that the proportions reflect the different needs for training of the white collar and blue collar occupations.

13. For a discussion, see Ivar Berg, "Economic Circumstances and the Entangling Web of Pathologies," and M. Harvey Brenner, "Health and the National Economy," both in Louis Ferman and Jeanne P. Gordus, eds., *Mental Health and the Economy* (Kalamazoo, Mich.: W. E. Upjohn Foundation, 1979).

14. Professor Louis Ferman (University of Michigan at Ann Arbor) informs us—in a conversation about a forthcoming book in which he reports on the consequences and correlates of plant closings—that he has observed the same patterns described by our clinician-informants.

15. We are aware, of course, that those who seek help, from whatever agency, may be a select group of persons who are more willing than others to seek professional/institutional help. We can only make comparisons within the help-seeking group.

16. For a brief review of "community power studies," see Ivar Berg, *Industrial Sociology* (Englewood Cliffs, N.J.: Prentice-Hall, 1980), pp. 95–97.

COMMENTATORS' REMARKS

ALLEN C. HOLMES

I HAVE been asked to comment upon the three papers prepared in connection with that portion of our conference relating to the community impact of the modern corporation. I very much enjoyed the three papers prepared by professors John M. Shepard and James G. Hougland, Jr., Roger W. Schmenner, and Ivar Berg and Janice Shack-Marquez, for they all constitute worthwhile empirical research of the type of which there has been very little, notwithstanding the importance of this subject. However, I must conclude that none of these papers indicates any significant conclusions with respect to the subject that Mr. Millstein proposed in his opening remarks. He defined that issue to be whether or not the increasing size of large modern corporations has had any significant adverse impact upon the communities in which they are head-quartered or in which they have plants or other facilities. As I read these papers they generally make the point that, except for labor relations, the increased size and even remoteness of large corporations from local communities have not been significant factors in shaping the relationship between such firms and such communities.

The conclusions of these papers are entirely consistent with my own, obviously anecdotal, observations. The involvement of senior management living in a given community of companies either headquartered in that community or elsewhere is to a major degree the result of the ethos of that community. A somewhat unusual demonstration of this fact is to be observed in the situation in my own community, Cleveland, Ohio.

Cleveland in many respects is typical of the Northeast-Midwest section of the country. It is a community that is not growing in size. Its economic base is made up of traditional manufacturing companies engaged primarily in heavy industry, steel making, machine tools, and auto parts.

On the other hand, Cleveland does have a relatively unique social and cultural structure, particularly for a community of its size. Cleveland has one of the five leading orchestras of the United States. It is the smallest of the communities enjoying such a resource. It has one of the renowned art museums of the United States and of the world, with the third or fourth largest endowment of any museum.

Cleveland has pioneered in the social service area. It is the home of the original Community Fund, and today its United Way Campaign raises more money per capita than any other major community in the country. It likewise has extensive educational resources, including an outstanding university, major art and music institutes, and world-renowned teaching and research health care facilities. This large social and cultural infrastructure reflects much about the past—a wealthy community and widely shared and intense involvement by the business community in social and cultural affairs.

As is the case in many other communities, the number of companies headquartered in the Cleveland area has steadily declined. However, the involvement of the principal local executives of the companies headquartered elsewhere has not been substantially different from the participation of executives of companies headquartered in Cleveland. In other words, neither the character nor the quantity of such participation appears to be in any way related to so-called absentee ownership of the businesses of Cleveland.

Of course, we all recognize, as the paper of Professor Shepard points out, that the most significant determinate of corporate managerial activity is the view of the most senior executives of the company concerning such involvement. If the chief executive sees the involvement as desirable and worthwhile, then it is very probable that the principal executives of local operations of such a company will see community participation as a desirable and worthwhile activity.

Professor Schmenner's paper also treats the subject of employment. His thesis is that job creation, that is, the increase in the number of jobs, will come in the future as it has in the past through the activities of the very large corporations as opposed to the smaller ones. Nationally that may be the case. But certainly in our area of the country job creation has not come about through the activities of the large corporations but rather through the growth in the number and size of smaller businesses. To a substantial degree the large corporations in the Great Lakes section of the country are primarily engaged in the mature segments of our economy, as I have noted—steel, chemicals, automotive parts, and machine tools. Smaller companies located here tend to be in the service industries or in areas of new technology in which growth has been very substantial in recent years.

In the final paper, Professor Berg again suggests no significant adverse effect on smaller communities as a result of the large size of modern corporations or the remoteness from areas in which they have substantial manufacturing operations. The regrettable decline in the rapport between management and labor in connection with the operation of the businesses in the communities studied by Professor Berg is stated to be related to the taking away of discretion of local managers and the development of rigid, hard-line management approaches by the central management of these companies. However, what seems to be the true situation really does not have much to do with absentee ownership at all. Rather, the cause of the problems of the local plants is that they have become inefficient, high-cost operations that, when confronted with competition from the world producers, have not been able to retain their competitiveness.

In sum, the problems of unemployment, changes in the quality of life, and other undesirable phenomena cannot in any reasonable way be related to the increase in size of a limited number of corporations in the United States or to the geographic remoteness of headquarters from the manufacturing or other facilities of such corporations.

JOHN D. ONG

I AM in no position to add anything by way of knowledge to the papers we are considering this afternoon, nor am I in a position to score any scholarly points on our three authors. I thought instead I might make some observations that were suggested to me by reading these papers and hearing their authors. Most of my comments are suggestions for further exploration that I hope will prove helpful to the authors as they continue their work.

I very much second Allen Holmes with regard to the matter of smaller companies versus larger companies in terms of providing additional employment, particularly in the manufacturing sphere. I live in the suburbs of Cleveland, but the headquarters of my company is in Akron, Ohio, certainly a typical Midwestern industrial city of relatively small size. Akron had 168,000 jobs in the metropolitan area in 1970, and in 1982 we have 210,000. So we actually are gaining employment even in a part of the country and in a community that's generally associated in the national consciousness with decay and all that's wrong with smokestack America. In 1970, half of those jobs were in the service sector of the economy. In 1982 services account for 144,000 out of 210,000 of those jobs, while manufacturing only accounts for 66,000.

It is even more significant, however, that only 23,000 of the 66,000 jobs are in the traditional rubber and plastics industries that were responsible for the major growth of Akron in the twentieth century, and only a little over half of those 23,000 jobs were created by the four major *Fortune* 500 companies that are headquartered in Akron—Goodrich, Goodyear, Firestone, and General Tire.

My point here is that Akron has been losing jobs in great chunks from the major companies in the past ten or fifteen years, and for each job we have lost we have gained a job in a 25-, 35-, 50- or 60-employee plant that has moved in, many in industries other than the traditional industries in that part of the country. I think you could find similar examples in other areas.

I believe that the impact on local employment of smaller companies versus larger companies is pretty much a product of where you're doing your research, that is to say, where your particular location falls in terms of the economic growth curve.

If instead of Cincinnati you were to study Greenville, Mississippi, or Anderson, South Carolina, I think you would find larger firms are accounting for a lot of growth because they are transferring production from the Midwest. If you look at Akron or anywhere in Pennsylvania, I suspect you will find a different situation.

I think Dr. Ferman was right in observing that there is a cycle in employment patterns and where your research location stands in that cycle has a great deal to do with what you're going to find. We are in a state of employment transition throughout the country, and depending on what part of the country you're in, transition is in a different phase.

I would suggest that as we look at the phenomena of employment shifts and plant relocations, we avoid constructing an oversimplified taxonomy. It's true that many companies are relocating plants because of union problems, but I do not think this is the major reason for such transfers. Even in union-inspired relocations, the motivation is more often made to escape onerous work rules than inflated wages. I also would suggest that surveys of the kind that were used to conduct much of this research may not in this particular area be well suited to determining real motivation: oftentimes the thinking behind relocations is hidden and not easily detectable in such a survey.

There are also, as one of the papers observed, intrinsic employment size limitations in plants, which has much to do with where plants are located and how much they grow.

Obviously there are many other factors that could be mentioned as well. I think the conclusion that should be drawn is that you can't make observations and generalize from them on the basis of geographically limited data without taking into account national and regional employment trends.

One of the commentators this morning mentioned that perhaps there was too much time spent by our authors on postulation and not enough time gathering data. I certainly would agree with that comment. It seems to me we should not do a lot of analysis on available random data. That's necessary in paleontology, but I suggest it is not a good idea when trying to make some sense out of the current employment scene.

The absentee owner idea was featured prominently in some of the papers this morning. I think it is a red herring. It betrays a lack of appreciation of what's really happened to the ownership of American enterprise over the last fifty years. I suggest that whether or not a plant or a company is absentee-owned (however that's defined) is not very important. I think more attention should be given in the research to differences in management attitudes because most of the companies you're studying are managed by professionals of one stripe or another. The views of those managers have a great effect upon the activities of their companies in the places where they have plants—and their views can differ widely.

There are cosmopolitan managements and provincial managements, and they can't necessarily be segregated by geography. You can have a cosmopolitan management in Iowa and parochial managers in New York City. There are great attitudinal differences between managers in these two categories, and I think examination of these differences will help to explain the differing community involvement of various companies.

Scale differences are also something that need to be looked at. They are at least mentioned in passing in several of the papers. I believe the difference between a metropolis like New York and a small but important headquarters city like Cleveland, or perhaps a city whose destiny is in the hands of two major employers, can give you very different results in data on community involvement, and those need to be considered and rationalized in some way.

Finally, I would suggest that a lot more attention be given to current data because I think that during the past five to ten years we have seen the beginning of a much more sophisticated, risk-oriented involvement on the part of corporate managers in the core problems of the communities in which they are headquartered and in which their plants are located. If you were to go to Akron, to Dayton, to Chicago, to Cleveland, or to any number of other places and investigate what private sector leadership is doing, very often in cooperation with public sector leadership, to address key problems, you would find a great deal of exciting new material for further study.

ROBERT S. COLODZIN

I WOULD like to begin by telling you two brief stories that will be pertinent to my later comments.

I was driving along a country road in Pennsylvania some years ago eating an apple. I threw the apple out the window, but the window was not open. This experience jarred me—it made me rethink my frame of reference. That is one of the things I am going to ask you to do—to rethink your frame of reference.

My other story takes us back a few years. I was trained as a teacher by one of the great teachers of teachers of that time. Before we students went out to take over our first class as student-teachers, this professor would interview each of us. When he interviewed me, he asked: "What is the first thing you ought to be thinking about when you walk into a class as a teacher for the first time?" I said: "The lesson; what do I want to tell them." "No," he said, "that is the second thing. The first thing is what language do they speak?"

I tell you that story because the language that the corporate world speaks is very, very important for you to understand. We must find a common language. All of us have certain priorities with which we have to deal. But there is one universal priority that applies in the corporate world as it does in the worlds of labor, of government, and of academia. That priority is survival. Today we live in a world where preoccupation with survival makes many formerly important subjects seem relatively peripheral.

There are some very dramatic changes developing in the thinking of corporate managers these days. There is a shift from the old concept that the responsibility of the corporation is only to its shareholders to a new idea of corporate responsibility to stakeholders. A stakeholder is defined as anyone who has a stake in the corporation: the people who work for the company, the communities where they live, and the whole range of people who are directly impacted by the activity of the corporation.

This leads directly to the central subject of these papers, the community impact of the modern corporation. I'd like to explain why these things are happening from a corporate management perspective, what's really happening to the corporation in its involvement with the community.

The Business Roundtable, which is made up of the CEOs of 200 of America's most important corporations, published a statement on corporate responsibility. Note that it was not a statement of corporate *social* responsibility but a statement of corporate responsibility. It opened with this statement: "The Business Roundtable issues this statement out of a strong conviction that the future of this nation depends upon the existence of strong and responsive business enterprises and that, in turn, the long-term viability of the business sector is linked to its responsibility to the society of which it is a part." It closed with this: "A corporation's responsibilities include how the whole business is conducted every day. It must be a thoughtful institution which rises above the bottom line to consider the impact of its actions on all, from shareholders to the society at large. Its business activities must make social sense just as its social activities must make business sense."

Let me take a moment to recap a process that has been happening in my company. I think it is somewhat unusual, but it is not unique. It's beginning to happen in other companies, too.

Almost all corporations have a business strategy. This is a long-term plan to deal with the allocation of human and financial resources to achieve a business goal. Very rarely does a corporation have an integral component of that strategy which says that over the same strategic time frame as the business plan there must also be a public affairs plan that deals with the position the corporation would like to achieve with external constituencies.

Businessmen read business documents, and in our company the document to which senior managers pay the closest attention is the strategic business plan document, which determines how they are supposed to perform and what they are expected to achieve. Until there is incorporated in that business document a section that outlines a responsibility to the community and to the companies' external constituencies as *part* of the business, companies are not dealing centrally with their impact on their communities.

In order to do that you have to look at how managers' performance in this area is being measured in these communities. Managers have to be measured and rewarded for improving the position of the company in the community as well as improving the manufacturing efficiency of a particular plant. This item becomes part of the businessman's business and reflects the stakeholder's concept, which is directly related to the changing approach of major corporations in their dealings with external constituencies.

Let me refer to the section in Professor Berg's paper on the professionalization of labor relations. He points out that labor negotiations are now primarily carried out by corporate labor lawyers, who now deal with local laywers who are also specialized in labor law.

This arm's length dealing through specialists developed out of an adversarial relationship. The parties each said, essentially, "You don't trust us and we don't trust you. Therefore everything must be spelled out to the umpteenth degree by our lawyers."

It is the story of the sinking rowboat, where one person asks the other to bail out the water and the other says the hole is not in my end of the boat.

We have planned economically as if we existed as a nation alone in the world. But we live in a world market. The transition is beginning to come, and we as companies must explain to the people living in Michigan or Montana that what happens in South Korea or somewhere else in the world may affect their ability to exist economically.

I will read you one sentence from Professor Berg's paper. It is illustrative of an attitude that I think needs to be changed: "Our research does suggest, however, very clearly that the communities under study suffer ultimately from business decision making that is responsive to general economic conditions rather than to laws."

Why do they only suffer? Perhaps they also benefit. This orientation underscores an adversarial relationship between academia and business that we can ill afford under present circumstances. The economic situation in which this country finds itself now is of immediate concern to all of us. For many years our highest priority was given to dealing with problems of a more equitable distribution of the country's wealth. We had that ability because it was based on the assumption that the wealth-creating process in this country was perpetual and automatic. We now understand that it is not.

Each of us has our own "wish list," a long list of important things for which resources need to be allocated. Our "common language" must be an understanding of our mutual dependence on the wealth-creating process. If it is damaged, we will all suffer.

DIALOGUE

MR. KRAMER: Largely because of lack of data most of the papers ignored the 32 or so largest privately held companies. I believe that if information on these companies had been included, results might have been changed because I believe some of these companies—all of whom are among the largest 500 corporations (industrial) or largest 50 (nonindustrial)—follow different practices in many of the areas with which the studies were concerned. I therefore suggest that the center consider a preliminary inquiry on the role of the largest privately held companies, or at least see whether data can be obtained from them.

MR. SCHMENNER: I did not try to go after any of the largest privately held companies. The *Fortune* 500 seemed to be a big enough task to take on myself, but, of course, more data is always better than less.

MR. KESSLER: In listening to the panelists' descriptions of the corporations' responsibility moving from shareholders to communities, to regions, to employees, and to suppliers, the question that I started to think about is what guidance we have for the corporate directors who are trying to choose between all of these competing interests? For example, one community may believe that it is great to open a plant, but another community will argue that it creates pollution someplace else. How are corporate board members to balance these different concerns?

MR. GELLHORN: Why is that different from what all of us have to do within the context of our lives in charting a pretty perilous course?

MR. HOLMES: The touchstone still is your obligation to the shareholders because the legal rules under which the board operates has not gotten to the point, and I am glad that it hasn't, where the board doesn't have to consider the interests of shareholders as their primary focus and concern.

MR. JONES: The issue on community impact is to what extent do we get different responses from business leaders in smaller organizations than we do in larger organizations and, in particular, larger organizations that are perhaps highly dispersed and perhaps highly diversified. As I read the papers by Professor Schmenner and Professor Berg, the impression I get is that the larger organizations, particularly the conglomerates, appear to be more active and adapt more rapidly to changing circumstances, so that they are opening and closing plants more often and relocating plants more often. Professor Berg suggests that they tend to be more aggressive in labor relations in taking the lead for the managerial perspective.

If my perception is correct, and this is the kind of difference that does exist, I wonder if that is a bad thing. Is it against the national interest to have an environment in the business community that seeks to adapt as rapidly as possible to the circumstances, or is it more desirable to have a business community that seeks to avoid dislocation and seeks to be protective of the status quo?

Mr. GINSBERG: I believe that larger organizations, with their more difficult decision-making processes and the greater time they take to respond may be less responsive to changing circumstances.

Mr. WHITE: I have a question on Professor Schmenner's finding that the 410 companies in his sample accounted for so much of total manufacturing employment growth. If you choose your sample of 410 at the end of the decade rather than the beginning, you will find that the sample companies have grown at about average rates. That's why they end up among the largest 500. Which way did you choose the sample?

Mr. SCHMENNER: The firms in my sample were chosen on the basis of being on the *Fortune* 500 list at the end of the 1970s.

PART IV

TECHNOLOGICAL IMPACT

EDITORS' NOTE

THE interrelations of corporate size and research and development have long attracted the attention of those concerned with the dynamics of the enterprise system. But these relations have come under increasing scrutiny in the past decade along with doubts concerning the future of many American industries. And although some earlier research seemed to show that the largest corporations have been the most effective innovators, other research seemed to show the reverse.

To begin to try to provide more definitive ways of looking at these questions, Professor F. M. Scherer of Swarthmore College was asked to undertake an examination of some new bodies of data that permitted him to ask whether America's relative decline as a technological leader was significantly influenced by the changes of the last decade in corporate size and management. Scherer concludes that the "Schumpeterian hypothesis"—that large corporations have been uniquely powerful engines of technological advance—fares badly. If size, as such, has any strong significance, it is probably most important to a corporation's ability to enter the R&D game. He also concludes that in more industries than not this phenomenon continues up to the scale of the largest sellers. But in most industries size appears neither to stimulate nor to retard innovation or patenting. He finds that large corporations as a whole accounted for a greater share of patents than their share of sales or employment, but they contributed fewer significant patents per million dollars of R&D than did smaller enterprises.

Facts such as these suggest, says Scherer, that encouragement of corporate growth in order to stimulate innovation would not be well advised. We should, however, be concerned not to impair the flow of venture capital to smaller technologically oriented enterprises, since they appear to have a clear edge in technological dynamism.

CHAPTER 7

Technological Change and the Modern Corporation

F. M. Scherer

T HE past decade has been marked by extraordinary self-doubt over American industry's prowess as a technological innovator. The growth of research and development spending has slackened, productivity growth has plummeted, and foreign firms have challenged the United States for superiority in many leading-edge technologies. Numerous possible explanations have been advanced. This essay addresses a set of hypotheses implicating the orientation of management in large corporations and the very structure of modern corporations, that is, as manifested in their size, diversity, and organization for decision making.

The signs of trouble became highly visible in the early 1970s. Real (i.e., deflated) expenditures on company-financed research and development, which had been growing at a 6.3 percent annual rate during the 1960s, peaked in 1969, fell absolutely for the first time in post–World War II history, and then (until a recent upsurge) resumed growth at a much slower rate. Had the 1960s real growth rate been sustained during

I am indebted to David Greene for research assistance and Joe Cholka for computer systems help. This paper uses data from the Federal Trade Commission's Line of Business program. A review by FTC staff has determined that individual company data are not disclosed. All conclusions are the author's and not necessarily those of the FTC.

the 1970s, U.S. corporations would have supported approximately 40 percent more real R&D in 1980 than they actually did. This slowdown in R&D growth has almost surely had an appreciable adverse impact on productivity, whose growth rate dropped by roughly half between 1968 and 1977 and then fell to essentially zero for the period 1977–1981. My own recent research indicates that a 40 percent shortfall in the amount of company-financed R&D absorbed by an average industry leads to a drop of roughly 0.25 percentage points in the industry's annual productivity growth rate.[1]

Why the support of R&D and its related productivity growth performance have been so disappointing is a key question. One simple explanation suggested through work done by David Ravenscraft and myself is that the profits from R&D dropped sharply.[2] We found for a sample of businesses covered by the PIMS data base that the average profitability of R&D in many years of the early 1970s was close to zero. For later years of the decade, the profitability of R&D then rose sharply. A plausible rationalization is that low profits induced a pruning of marginal projects during the early 1970s, and the ensuing profit rise stimulated the resurgence of R&D observed during the past few years.

Although depressed profitability is a likely explanation, it is not sufficient. Why did the profits from R&D drop? One hypothesis prompted by casual observation, unleavened by systematic evidence, is that we had moved into a period of depleted opportunities in many (though certainly not all) fields of technology.[3] I am not yet persuaded that the hypothesis is false. However, there are at least two contradictory strands of evidence. First, statistical analyses by both Zvi Griliches and myself provide no support for the hypothesis that the ability of industrial R&D to generate productivity growth fell during the 1970s.[4] Also, it is clear that others around the world have found it possible to make significant technological advances in fields where U.S. firms seemed to have run into diminishing returns, for example, in motor vehicle technology, steel making, the miniaturization of copying machines, textile machinery, and the production of advanced but reliable land warfare equipment.

Some scholars observing America's relative decline as a technological leader have pointed to changes in the corporation and its management as an important contributor to the problem. Criticism has come inter alia from the Harvard Business School—scarcely a bastion of radical thought. As Hayes and Abernathy put it in a 1980 article:

The conclusion is painful but must be faced. Responsibility for this competitive listlessness belongs not just to a set of external conditions but also to the attitudes, preoccupations, and practices of American managers. By their preference for servicing existing markets rather than creating new ones and by their devotion to short-term returns and "management by the numbers," many of them have effectively forsworn long-term technological superiority as a competitive weapon. In consequence, they have abdicated their strategic responsibilities.[5]

Among other things, Hayes and Abernathy allege, many U.S. company managers have let their energies be diverted from the important job of technological development to merger making and a wasteful quest for diversification.[6] Similar concern was expressed in the National Science Foundation's 1981 report on the outlook in science and technology:

It also has been argued that investment in long-term technological development demands a certain basic understanding of the technical base of the industry and that American recruitment and selection practices for high-level managers in some industries often are counterproductive for long-term innovation and investments. Managers in those industries are selected for their managerial or business skills and may have little appreciation of the technical base of the company. Therefore, they are less likely to appreciate the need for long-range research and development programs.[7]

Whether changes in the nature of the corporation and its management are indeed partially responsible for lagging technological innovation is what I seek to illuminate in this paper. In particular, I explore four questions: (1) whether the managerial structure of large corporations is biased away from the types of talent best suited to understand what technological innovation entails; (2) what academic knowledge the "new breed" of managers bring to their jobs; (3) what relative role the largest corporations play in supporting research and development and generating technical innovations; and (4) how corporate diversification affects the support and productivity of R&D.

THE TECHNICAL BACKGROUND OF TOP MANAGERS

One problem, it is alleged, is that U.S. corporate managers are inadequately trained in science and technology. Hayes and Abernathy cite evidence (compiled by a management consulting firm) of a decline over time in the fraction of corporate presidents with a technical background, accompanied by a sharp increase in the proportion with finance and legal backgrounds.[8] I cannot claim to know what fraction of top executives with technical training is "right." I have also been unable to assemble sufficiently consistent historical data to ascertain whether there has actually been a move away from technically trained managers. I can, however, offer a modest contribution to the debate. Using *Poor's Register*,[9] the names of the top two executives—usually the chairman and president—of *Fortune's* leading 100 industrial corporations for 1980 were identified. Each individual's biography was searched in *Who's Who in Finance and Industry* to determine what his (yes, his!) college and university specialties had been.[10] For 51 persons, no information on educational background could be found. Three others reported to their biographers that they had not received a degree or attended college. For the 146 executives on whom undergraduate degree information was available, the distribution of degrees was as follows:

	Number	Percent
B.S. in science or engineering	35	24
B.S. in unspecified field	44	30
A.B.	45	31
Bus. ad. bachelor's or similar degree	20	14
Other	2	1

The implications are ambiguous for two reasons. For one, an A.B. may have been awarded in physical science but not described as such, thereby understating the fraction of executives with technical backgrounds. But alternatively, some of the B.S. degrees were almost surely in commerce but not identified as such, so one cannot view the combined B.S. count as a minimum estimate of the fraction (i.e., 54 percent) with technical undergraduate backgrounds. The net effect of these offsetting biases is unknown, but it seems unlikely to be strongly on the side of understating technical backgrounds. To this writer, at least, the extent to which *Fortune* 100 top executives were initially trained in engineering or science appeared surprisingly high. Less surprising were the companies in which such training materialized most often—notably, those whose principal industry base was petroleum, chemicals, metals, paper, and electronic and electrical equipment.

Seventy-two of the 200 covered executives reported having graduate degrees. Counting joint degrees as one-half, the distribution was as follows:

Business administration	25
Science or engineering	22.5
Law (including LLB)	21.5
Other	3

Technical degrees continue to hold a respectable share, and it cannot be claimed with accuracy that the corporate summit is dominated by lawyers.

M.B.A. PROGRAMS AND TECHNOLOGICAL INNOVATION

The prominent role of the M.B.A. or equivalent as a (sometimes fast) track to the top is already apparent in the 1980 statistics. It may be even more the wave of the future, for the supply of M.B.A.s has grown much more rapidly than the supply of lawyers (with, however, an almost certain degradation of average M.B.A. quality). In 1955, some 3,336 masters degrees in business administration were granted, along with 8,226 LL.B.s or J.D.s. The number of degrees in the two fields reached parity during the late 1960s, and by 1980 U.S. schools conferred 55,325 M.B.A. (or equivalent) degrees and 34,104 entry-level law degrees.[11] Thus, in a quarter-century, M.B.A.-type degrees increased sixteenfold while law degrees quadrupled.

An inchoate recognition that some such trend was in motion, the Hayes–Abernathy thesis, and my own experience as an M.B.A. student (class of 1958) combined to make me ask, What do modern M.B.A. candidates learn systematically about the management of research, development, and technological innovation? In my Harvard M.B.A. days, the most popular single second-year course was Georges F. Doriot's "Manufacturing." General Doriot had already founded the premier venture capital firm American Research and Development Corporation. The leitmotif of his course was the enormous benefit, private and public, that could be reaped through the aggressive development by American business of new technological opportunities. Doriot, most of his students would agree, was inimitable. However, it piqued my curiosity to know whether something similar had gained prominence in M.B.A. curricula to mitigate the emphasis on "management by the numbers." To find out, I undertook a systematic survey of the curricula at twelve top graduate schools of business administration. Published course descriptions were analyzed, and faculty members at eleven of the twelve institutions responded to a request for further details on course enrollments and content.

Because course titles and even course descriptions often fail to reveal what is actually taught (much less learned), such a survey poses difficult characterization problems. Passing mention of R&D and technological innovation undoubtedly occurs in some standard first-year courses and in second-year options. No attempt was made to identify such fragments. Instead, M.B.A. program offerings were sifted to identify two main groups: courses directly and primarily concerned with the nature and management of technological innovation; and courses with a significant overlap into questions of managing R&D or innovation, even though the main emphasis was elsewhere. Because the second group is harder to delineate than the first, comprehensive enrollment counts could not be compiled. Identifying and getting enrollment data for courses in the first group was easier, but even then, there were gray-area cases, in two of which the best solution appeared to be dividing enrollments equally between the first and second groups. Table 7.1 summarizes the results.

Most M.B.A. programs have some kind of course on managing technological innovation, as well as various courses on the periphery. Few are box office hits. MIT's Sloan School offers by far the most comprehensive program. A simple division of total group I enrollments by total master's degree awards in 1981–82 implies that most Sloan students had some intensive exposure to questions of innovation management, but this is misleading, since "Management of Technology" program concentrators take several courses in the field, the program's course listings include non-Sloan offerings, and the enrollment counts include students from other MIT schools. Counting 617 group I course enrollments in total at the twelve surveyed schools alongside the 5,400 business administration master's degrees conferred, and assuming no double counting, we conclude that, at the maximum, 11.5 percent of the M.B.A. students acquired a systematic full-term exposure to the mainstream questions of technological innovation management. If MIT is excluded, the fraction falls to 9.3 percent. It is unclear to what extent this paucity of exposures

TABLE 7.1

Technological Innovation Management Course Survey

School	1981–82 M.B.A.s	Group 1: *Primary Emphasis on Management of Technological Innovation*		Group 2: *Related Courses*	
		Course Title	Enrollment	Course Title	Enrollment
California (Berkeley)	c. 300	Environment, Technology, Organization	26	Entrepreneurship and Business Development	32
UCLA	420	Research and Development Policy	8	Entrepreneurship and Venture Initiation	64
		Project Management	15	Socio-Technical Systems	3
Carnegie-Mellon	105	Technological Processes	11	Design and Marketing of New Products	42
				Design and Entrepreneurship	38
				Social Impact of Robotics	19
Chicago	c. 375	None listed in catalog		Laboratory in New Product Development (Marketing)	N.R.
Columbia	614	Managing Innovation	100	Marketing the New Technologies	50
		Manufacturing and Service Productivity (1/3)	8	Product Management	150
				Managing New Ventures	120
				Productivity-based Economics and Financial Decision Making	5
Harvard	780	Management of Technological Innovation	148	Managing Project Teams	N.R.
		Seminar on Management of Technology	27	Management of Small Enterprises: New Ventures	N.R.

University	Enrollment	Technology-management course	No.	Entrepreneurship / marketing course	No.
MIT	131	Research and Development Management	50	Strategic Marketing Management	N.R.
		Manufacturing/Technology Interface	16	Managing Professionals	16
		Seminar: Managing R&D and Engineering Technology Planning	23	Marketing/Technology Interface	42
		Government and the Management of Technology	14	Technical Problem Solving and Communication	12
		Cases and Problems in Engineering Management	16	New Technical Ventures	N.R.
			8		
Michigan	c. 400	Management of Product Development (Marketing) (1/2)	48	Seminar in Small Business Formation	100
				Seminar in Creative Marketing Strategy	N.R.
New York University	980	Management of Technology	8	High Technology Investing	80
				New Product Development (Marketing)	90
				Corporate Entrepreneurship	88
				Product Strategy	135
Northwestern	445	Organization and Management of Scientific and Technological Innovation	22	Introduction of New Products and Services (Marketing)	55
				Venture Capital (seminar)	N.R.
				Entrepreneurship and New Business Formation	56
				Management of Organizational Change	59
Pennsylvania (Wharton)	550	Management of Technological Innovation (seminar)	10	Entrepreneurship and New Business Formation	N.R.
		Management of Technology	30	Product Policy (Marketing)	N.R.
		Technological Venture Development (1/2) (mostly finance and marketing)	29		
Stanford	c. 300	Managing Corporate Technology and Innovation	28	Entrepreneurship: New Venture Formation	50
				Entrepreneurship: Small Business Management	50
Totals	5,400		645		

NOTE: N.R. indicates no information received.

is compensated by less intensive exposure in peripheral group II courses (e.g., emphasizing the identification of new product opportunities through market research, the formation of new businesses oriented in only a minority of cases around technically new products, and venture capital raising). Enrollments in these peripheral group II courses were clearly much greater than in the mainstream group I courses. Nevertheless, from the results of the survey, one fears that America's leading business schools may indeed be dispatching to our large corporations a generation of managers with little or no indoctrination in the Doriot vision of technological dynamism, graduates who, in the words of Hayes and Abernathy, are preoccupied with "a false and shallow concept of the professional manager . . . an individual having no special expertise in any particular industry or technology who nevertheless can step into an unfamiliar company and run it successfully through strict application of financial controls, portfolio concepts, and a market-driven strategy."[12]

CORPORATE SIZE, DIVERSIFICATION, AND INNOVATIVE ACTIVITY

Approximately 98 percent of the nation's industrial R&D is performed by industrial (i.e., manufacturing and mining) corporations. Along with changes in managerial orientation, there have been palpable changes in the structure of the largest industrial corporations. They have become larger, they have become more diversified, and although the phenomenon is more difficult to measure, their managerial structures have almost surely become more complex. Because of productivity increases, the most modest size growth occurred on the employment dimension. The number of employees in the company ranked one hundredth (by employment) on the *Fortune* 500 list for 1955 was 19,548; its 1980 counterpart had 43,799 employees. Between 1953 and 1978, production workers dropped from 81 percent to 74 percent of total manufacturing employees. Between 1954 and 1972, the number of employees occupied in the central offices, auxiliary units, and sales branches of manufacturing enterprises rose from 6.3 to 9.2 percent.[13] In 1950, 38 of the 200 largest manufacturing corporations were diversified enough to operate in more than twenty different four-digit industries. By 1968—the last year for which comparable statistics have been published—76 of the top 200 satisfied that threshold criterion.[14]

Changes in the size and managerial complexity of the largest corporations lead us to reexamine what has come to be called the Schumpeterian hypothesis. In an influential 1942 book, economist Joseph A. Schumpeter argued that large corporations possessing monopoly power were ideal vehicles for advancing industrial technology—for example, as later interpreters clarified, because of their superior access to capital, ability to pool risks, and economies of scale in the maintenance of research and development laboratories.[15] Critics of the Schumpeterian view have argued to the contrary that greater size stultifies technological dynamism because of more bureaucratic decision making (a phenomenon Schumpeter also feared) and longer chains of command between the person with the good idea and the manager able to provide the definitive go-ahead. A fierce debate, theoretical and empirical, has raged over the relative validity of these contending theses.

Diversification has also found a role in the debate. The early view, advanced by Richard R. Nelson, was that diversification was unambiguously favorable, especially to basic industrial research, because the more diversified a company was, the better poised it was to derive commercial advantage from possibly serendipitous technical advances.[16] However, diversification might also have negative effects if it means more complex decision-making channels. And in the Hayes–Abernathy view, a managerial preoccupation with diversification, especially through merger, diverts attention from the painstaking work required to take full advantage of new technological opportunities in one's home-base industries. It is at least intriguing, even though quite possibly coincidental, that the sharp slowdown in U.S. industrial R&D growth began only a year after the peak of the conglomerate merger wave of the 1960s.

These issues have since the early 1960s been thoroughly researched, surveyed, debated, and resurveyed. To add still another survey here would be the height of redundance.[17] Instead, I shall try to advance the state of knowledge by analyzing some new data, including one data set of unprecedented scope and richness.

The Gelman Research Associates Results

Having promised no survey, I immediately renege. A recent study by the Gelman Research Associates firm has been cited repeatedly in the debate over big versus small and the vigor of technological innovation, and yet, as nearly as I can tell, the study itself has not been widely available, reposing in the aloof reaches of National Technical Information Service microfiche.[18] My curiosity was aroused, so I invested four dollars and a case of eyestrain in the microfiche original.

The results actually reported turned out to be consistent with the interpretations given them in public citations. Out of a larger initial cross-section, 500 technological innovations first introduced into the market between 1953 and 1973 were selected for analysis as most important in terms of technological, social, economic, and political criteria. These were traced to their innovating (not always synonymous with inventing) organizations, in all cases business enterprises, and the companies were classified according to size at the time when the innovations were first marketed. For the 319 sample innovations contributed by U.S. enterprises, the shares originated by firms in diverse employment size classes were as follows:[19]

Company Employment	Percent of All U.S. Innovations
Less than 100	23.5
100–1,000	23.8
1,001–5,000	13.2
5,001–10,000	5.0
Greater than 10,000	34.5

Companies with fewer than 1,000 employees originated 47.3 percent of the important innovations—a fraction higher than their 41.2 percent share of all manufacturing and mining company employment in 1963, the midpoint and median year of the innovation sample. Conversely, companies with more than 10,000 employees accounted for 34.5 percent of the innovations but 36 percent of 1963 employment.[20] The implication seems clear: smaller firms are disproportionately prolific contributors to the generation of important technological innovations. Large corporations barely pull their own weight.

The validity of this conclusion depends upon the representativeness of the innovation sample analyzed by the Gelman Research group. On this point it is difficult to reach an informed judgment, since details of the innovations, including the names of the companies credited with introducing them, were kept confidential. The most that can be said is that the list of innovations, identified individually in brief qualitative terms, is impressive in its coverage; and the expert panel procedure used to winnow out the 500 most important innovations from a broader initial list of 1,310 (augmented with 150 contributions suggested by panelists) shows no obvious signs of bias toward small as opposed to large organizations. In the absence of contrary evidence, one is inclined to impute credence to the findings from an unusually ambitious data-gathering job.

One further conclusion deserves mention. The disproportionate contribution of smaller enterprises was especially marked for innovations first entering the market in the United States. Smaller businesses did less well abroad and particularly in Japan, as the following innovation shares for firms with dollar-equivalent sales less than $50 million shows:[21]

Nation	Percent of That Nation's Innovations Credited to Companies with Sales of Less than $50 Million
United States	50
France	57
West Germany	37
United Kingdom	33
Japan	20

This finding is consistent with work by scholars at Britain's Science Policy Research Unit at Sussex University, who discovered from a compilation of 2,293 significant innovations introduced into the United Kingdom between 1945 and 1980 that only 25 percent originated in companies with fewer than 1,000 employees and that, contrary to U.S. patterns, the most prolific innovators per thousand employees were companies with 10,000 or more employees.[22] It is also readily reconciled with what we know about the Japanese economy: that the universities' best and brightest graduates go preponderantly to large corporations and that the small business sector is the refuge of less educated workers and those who have received a "golden handshake" from their employers at age fifty-five. Evidently, the smaller company sector in the United States is nearly unique. This almost surely has something to do with the ease with which new technology-oriented firms can obtain venture capital here. Less certainly, it may also support the assertion by Hayes and Abernathy that large European corporations are run by executives with more intimate knowledge of their home industry's technology and a longer decision-making horizon than their U.S. counterparts, and hence with greater receptiveness to innovation proposals from their technical staffs.[23]

A New Survey: The IR Competition Winners

Since 1963, the magazine *Industrial Research & Development* (previously *Industrial Research*) has conducted an annual competition to name the hundred most significant technical advances of the year. The annual lists, published in the journal's October issue, have long seemed to me an interesting untapped resource for examining the relative roles of small and large enterprises. Preparing this paper provided an opportunity to exploit the resource.

Further probing dampened my enthusiasm. The annual "sample" of winners is decidedly nonrandom. Entrants are self-nominated and must pay an entry fee ($40 for 1981). The entries are judged by a distinguished and reasonably well-balanced panel of large corporation research directors and academicians, but the roster of winners is visibly skewed toward instrumentation and laboratory gadgets—the sort of thing with a special appeal to research directors. Conspicuously absent or underrepresented on the lists were pharmaceutical entities, weapon systems, space systems, and communications systems, where there has been much technical progress, and consumer products (only a dozen clear cases among 498). There are also company anomalies. For example, Union Carbide's Oak Ridge government contract laboratories had 20.5 winners in five years (the half shared with another organization), while other more extensive parts of Union Carbide's R&D operation had none. IBM was also absent from the list over the five years (1976–1980) for which an analysis was carried out. Since the data had to be assembled before most of these problems became evident, the analysis was completed and is reported for whatever worth it may have.

Of the 498 technical advances tallied, 357, or 72 percent, came from U.S. profit-seeking corporations. The remainder were attributed to U.S. government laboratories (12.9 percent), foreign corporations (10.7), academic institutions (2.4), and other not-for-profit entities (2.3). To determine the role of large versus small companies in the domestic profit-seeking subset, a simple dichotomy was imposed. "Large" corporations were defined as those included in the Federal Trade Commission's 1974 Line of Business (LB) survey,[24] which included the 250 largest manufacturing corporations ranked by domestic sales and other companies of almost uniformly substantial size. "Small" corporations were those not included, which, with at most 22 IR list-entering exceptions, were indeed small by any standard. Other research to be described shortly revealed that the "large" LB corporations accounted in 1974 for 73 percent of both company-financed and contract (typically federal contract) U.S. industrial R&D expenditures, as determined from a parallel National Science Foundation survey, along with roughly 55 to 60 percent of manufacturing sector sales and value added.[25] They originated 197.5, or 55 percent, of the 357 IR award-winning technical advances credited to U.S. corporations. Thus, the large corporations' share of award-winning technical advances was roughly commensurate with, or perhaps slightly less than, their share of industrial corporation sales and value added and substantially less than their share of total U.S. industrial R&D expenditures. In view of possible selection biases, the most that can be said is that this result provides no support for the Schumpeterian hypothesis that large corporations are disproportionately fecund sources of significant technological advances.

Size and Inventive Output in the FTC's LB Sample

A new data source provides the opportunity for a much richer analysis without the possible sampling biases of the Gelman Research and *Industrial Research & Development* data. It begins with data collected from 443 characteristically large manufacturing corporations by the Federal Trade Commission for the year 1974.[26] Among the variables reported was company-financed expenditure on R&D in 1974. As noted earlier, the LB sample companies together conducted 73 percent of all such domestic U.S. research and development in that year—much more than their 55 to 60 percent share of manufacturing sales and value added. Clearly, corporate size appears conducive to the conduct of R&D. Two important questions remain. First, is the advantage of size continuous, so that the few very largest entities are even more intensive supporters of R&D than their more numerous medium-sized counterparts, or do the advantages of size peter out at some intermediate scale, or does size make little difference once a certain threshold has been attained? Second, can further light be shed on the technical productivity of large enterprises' R&D programs? In particular, do large firms generate more, fewer, or roughly the same number of inventions per million dollars of R&D outlays as smaller companies?

The variable used here to illuminate this second question is a count of invention patents. Such a count has advantages and limitations. Its main advantage is comprehensiveness. The count exhausts all issued patents and is not governed by a panel susceptible to possible sample biases. The main limitation is that bias may creep in more subtly at an earlier stage, for example, in intercompany or interindustry differences in the propensity to seek patent protection on inventions of given quality. The limitation is an important one, but it can be controlled for and subjected to a variety of tests.[27] I shall therefore assume provisionally, subject to qualifications at appropriate points, that a count of issued patents provides an acceptably homogeneous index of inventive output.

On the average, various studies indicate, nine months elapse between the conception of a patentable invention (e.g., through research or development) and application for a patent. In the mid-1970s, the lag between application and issuance was nineteen months. The sample of patents linked to LB sample company 1974 R&D expenditures therefore covered the ten-month period June 1976–March 1977, centered on mid-1974 with a twenty-eight-month lag. Each patent obtained by each of 443 LB sample companies was individually inspected by a team of technically trained Northwestern University students to screen out inventions of overseas origin and to link the patents not only to the responsible companies but to the specific lines of business within those companies giving rise to the inventions. This was done because the FTC survey, unlike any previously conducted, required companies to report their R&D broken down into some 276 standardized industry categories (later reduced for purposes of my analysis to 249 categories). On average, a sample company reported its activities in 9.65 categories, so there were 4,274 individual line of business reports altogether. Again, the patents were traced to the individual LBs in which they originated, with allowance being made for multiple LBs of origin in the case of joint (e.g., central research laboratory) inventions.

Altogether, the LB sample companies obtained 15,112 U.S. invention patents in the period covered. This was approximately 61 percent of patents issued during the same period to all U.S. industrial corporations. Thus, the characteristically large LB sample companies originated a slightly higher share of patented inventions than their 55 to 60 percent share of manufacturing corporation sales and value added. In this sense, the largest corporations' performance comes off more favorably than with the Gelman Research tally of significant innovations. The difference between the LB companies' patent share (61 percent) and their share of *Industrial Research & Development* competition winners (55 percent) is in the same direction, but not large.

From another perspective, the LB companies' performance is less favorable. They accounted for 73 percent of U.S. industrial R&D expenditures but generated only 61 percent of the patented inventions. Evidently, their yield of inventions per million dollars of R&D was lower than that of the much smaller companies excluded from the LB sample. There are several possible expanations for, and clarifications of, this differential.

For one, both sampled and nonsampled companies make patentable inventions not only in the context of formal R&D programs but also through the activity of operating unit engineers and others.[28] Of the 1,271 LBs reporting no R&D outlays for 1974, 12.6 percent received patents. It is reasonable to suppose that small companies are particularly likely to sustain activity leading to patentable inventions but not formally organized as, or reported to federal statistical agencies as, research and development.

Second, it is possible that the propensity to patent inventions of given quality varies systematically with corporate size. The relationship here could go either way. On one hand, my earlier research showed a decline over time in the propensity to patent for the characteristically large corporations subjected during the 1940s and 1950s to antitrust compulsory patent licensing decrees.[29] However, the level from which their patenting declined could have been a high one. Surveys in both the United States and West Germany reveal that the largest corporations commercially utilize an appreciably smaller fraction of their patented inventions than do relatively small companies.[30] This implies either a lower propensity to patent in smaller corporations, or higher average inventive quality, or both. Either interpretation would be consistent with the observed differences in the Gelman and patent sample size relationships.

But third, there is evidence of at least one relationship between size and "quality" favoring the larger corporations. The patents of larger units (i.e., lines of business) tend more frequently to cover complex systems and subsystems entailing high R&D outlays per invention. The relationship is a weak one. Holding field of technology constant, an increase in LB sales from $100 million to $1 billion was found to raise the fraction of systems and subsystems inventions by 5 to 6 percent—for example, in mechanical fields of technology, from 51.0 to 53.8 percent.[31]

Leaving a final interpretation to the concluding section, we move on to the question of how size affects R&D support and patented invention output once a corporation has become large enough to be graced by inclusion in the FTC's Line of Business sample. In other words, once some substantial size threshold has been reached, do *further* scale increases lead to more or less proportional increases in innovative effort and output?

The method used to address this question is nonlinear regression analysis. The dependent variable is the count of patents received by a line of business or the amount of company-financed R&D (in millions of dollars) performed by a line of business. The size of an LB—the independent variable—is measured by its 1974 sales (in millions of dollars). To take into account the fact that some industries enjoy richer opportunities to perform R&D and make patentable inventions than others, each industry category (of 249) with five or more nonzero observations on the dependent variable was allowed to have its own best-fitting regression equation. With R&D as the dependent variable, 196 of the 249 industry categories satisfied this five-or-more criterion; with patents, 124 industries did. Observations for the industries that failed to satisfy the criterion were consigned to a common pool for which a single regression was computed.

Our basic concern is with the existence and nature of nonlinearities in the relationship between size (i.e., LB sales) and innovative activity (R&D or patents). There is a substantial literature on the theory and measurement of such relationships.[32] The theoretical literature has paid little attention to problems of measurement, so a brief expository integration may be helpful both to economists and the uninitiated. The newest theoretical works focus on the question of elasticity (denoted as E): Does innovative activity or output increase exactly proportionately with size ($E = 1$), more than proportionately with size ($E > 1$), or less than proportionately with size ($E < 1$)? These may with only slight imprecision be referred to as the constant returns, increasing returns, and diminishing returns cases, respectively. To the extent that size offers compelling

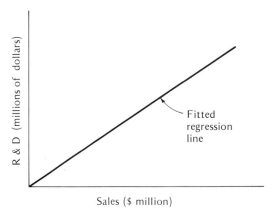

Figure 7.1 E = 1: Constant Returns

advantages, one might expect the increasing returns case (E>1) to predominate.

For compelling measurement reasons discussed elsewhere,[33] we proceed here by computing quadratic regression equations—those in which the independent (size) variable enters in squared as well as unsquared (linear) form. The translation from quadratic coefficient values to elasticity values is often, but not always, simple. If the quadratic (i.e., squared) variable's coefficient is insignificantly different from zero and if in addition the regression equation's vertical axis intercept is zero, as illustrated in figure 7.1, constant returns prevail and E = 1. Large units (LBs) are no more or less innovative relative to their size than small units, all else equal. If the intercept coefficient is zero and the quadratic coefficient is significantly positive, as, in figure 7.2, the increasing returns case holds unambiguously. As one can see, the support of R&D rises more than proportionately with size. If the intercept coefficient is zero and the quadratic coefficient is significantly negative, the relationship will be like that shown in 7.2, and diminishing returns prevail unambiguously.

Matters become more complex when the fitted regression line does not intersect the vertical and horizontal axes where they in turn intersect, that is, when the intercept coefficient is significantly different from zero. If it is negative and the fitted line is linear, as in figure 7.3, E >1 continuously despite the lack of a significantly positive quadratic coefficient. In effect, this says that there are increasing returns because a cer-

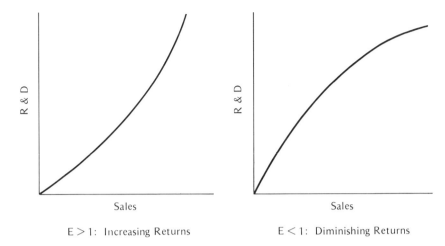

E > 1: Increasing Returns	E < 1: Diminishing Returns

Figure 7.2

tain size threshold must be reached before any R&D takes place. With a positive intercept, as in figure 7.3, E <1 continuously. Under certain conditions, elasticity transitions can occur. When the intercept is negative and the quadratic coefficient is significantly negative, too, the relationship is elastic at low sales levels but, at sufficiently high sales values, turns inelastic. With positive intercepts and quadratic terms, the relationship goes from inelastic to elastic.

Our null hypothesis—that is, the hypothesis to be contradicted—is that the relationship is linear with zero intercept, as in figure 7.1. If either the Schumpeterians or the anti-Schumpeterians are right, they should have to bear the burden of proving departures from linearity or (almost equivalent) constant returns. Because we do not want to infer departures from constant returns when they do not truly exist but occur only by chance, we impose a conventional 95 percent statistical confidence criterion on our tests for nonzero values of the estimated quadratic coefficients and intercept values. It is also useful to know the "goodness of fit" of the fitted regression line. The statistic used for this purpose is R^2, or the square of the correlation coefficient. It measures the fraction of the dependent variable's variation from its mean "explained" by the fitted regression line. An R^2 value of 1.0 reveals that all of the individual line of business observations lie exactly on the fitted regression line; there are no departures. An R^2 value of 0 means that the actual observations lie in random disarray, conforming to no systematic curve or line. R^2s for most real-world cross-sectional relationships lie somewhere in between.

We proceed now to the results, considering first LB sample companies' incentive to conduct R&D as a function of the size of the lines. The linear regression of R&D on LB sales, with each of 196 industries having its own best-fitting parameter values, has an R^2 value of 0.959. This is a remarkably high degree of explanatory power. With nearly 96 percent of the variation in R&D spending depending linearly upon LB sales and industry characteristics, there is not much left to be explained by other variables. Adding 196 quadratic sales coefficients to test for nonlinearities raises R^2 by 0.0098 to 0.969. The increment is small but statistically significant at the 99 percent confidence level. Of the fitted quadratic coefficients, 104 were positive (suggesting but not proving increasing returns), and 92 were negative. Of the smaller number that passed a 95 percent statistical significance test, 40 were positive and 16 were negative. Thus, the tests for nonlinearity provide mild support for a Schumpeterian increasing returns hypothesis in the performance of R&D.

This conclusion must be checked for possible complications from nonzero intercept coefficients. In fact, the intercept problem was minor. Only eleven regression intercept coefficients were significantly different from zero—slightly more than twice as many as one would expect to

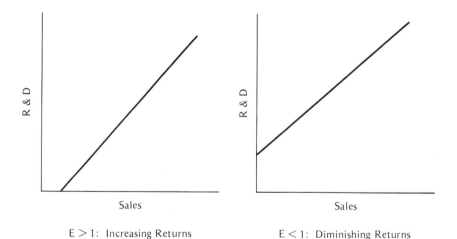

E > 1: Increasing Returns   E < 1: Diminishing Returns

Figure 7.3

appear significant purely by chance. All eleven were positive, and all eleven coincided with significantly positive quadratic coefficients. Thus, a possible transition from an inelastic relationship at low sales levels to an elastic relationship at high sales levels could occur. The transition took place at a sales level 40 percent or less than the sales of the leading LB in all but three cases, and in those three the transition had occurred at two-thirds the largest seller's sales. We therefore summarize our R&D–sales findings for the 196 industries as follows:

	Number of Industries	Percent
No significant departure from constant returns	140	71.4
Increasing returns $(E>1)$		
Throughout	29	20.4
At higher sales levels	11	
Diminishing returns $(E<1)$ throughout	16	8.2

Again, these results tilt on the side of supporting the Schumpeterian hypothesis that size is conducive to the vigorous conduct of R&D.

We turn now to our measure of inventive output, the patent counts. There were 124 industries in which 5 or more LBs had nonzero patenting. When the linear regression of patenting on sales for these 124 industries individually plus a residual pooled group is computed, the R^2 value is 0.841. Introducing 124 quadratic coefficients raises R^2 by 0.026 to 0.867—an increment statistically significant at the 99 percent confidence level. The overall nonlinear effect, although still quite small compared with the linear effect, is somewhat larger than in the R&D–sales analysis. However, the pattern of nonlinearities is different. Altogether, there were seventy negative quadratic coefficients (suggesting diminishing returns) and fifty-four positive ones. Of those that passed a 95 percent significance test, seventeen were negative and fourteen positive.

Intercept complications must also be checked. Only eight intercept coefficients were significantly different from zero, seven of them positive and one negative. One significantly negative coefficient coincided with a significantly negative quadratic term, but the transition from elastic to inelastic occurred at 22 percent of the largest LB's sales. There were five significant positive intercept, positive quadratic term cases, all with a transition at 55 percent or less of the largest LB's sales. Moving the two positive intercept, insignificant quadratic term cases into the E<1 category, we recapitulate as follows:

	Number of Industries	Percent
No significant departure from constant returns	91	73.4
Increasing returns (E>1)		
Throughout	9	11.3
At higher sales levels	5	
Diminishing returns (E<1)		
Throughout	18	15.3
At higher sales levels	1	

There is again a clear preponderance of constant returns cases. Among the exceptions, the evidence leans weakly against the Schumpeterian conjecture that the largest sellers are especially fecund sources of patented inventions.

The weak disparity between the R&D–sales and patenting–sales results is easily reconciled. When patents are regressed linearly on R&D (i.e., in an analysis of input–output relationships), there is a bias toward diminishing returns, as we see from the summary:[34]

	Number of Industries	Percent
No significant departure from constant returns	74	59.7
Increasing returns (E>1)		
Throughout	16	15.3
At higher R&D levels	3	
Diminishing returns (E<1)		
Throughout	30	25.0
At higher R&D levels	1	

Thus, the tendency toward increasing returns in the R&D–size relationship is counteracted by a tendency toward diminishing returns in the patents–R&D relationship to yield in the net a slight tendency toward diminishing returns in the patented invention output–size relationship.

Diversification, R&D, and Inventive Output

To readers who may have overlooked the point, the preceding analysis is absolutely unique. Never before have scholars been able to test the Schumpeterian innovation–size hypotheses at the level of individual lines of business. The analysis was made possible by the Federal Trade Commission's Line of Business program. Still there are other dimensions of size that might also affect innovative activity. In particular, business enterprises may be large not only by virtue of substantial sales in specific lines of business but by operating in numerous lines of business; that is, by being more diversified. The LB data also permit a test of that hypothesis.

The index of diversification used here is the inverse Herfindahl numbers equivalent, defined as $1/\sum_{i=1}^{N} S_i^2$, where S_i is the share of total company unregulated domestic sales contributed by the ith line of business (among N lines of business in total). If the company operates in only one line, the index has a value of 1.0. The index rises with an increase in the number of lines, but less so when the sizes of the various lines are highly unequal. Its value can be interpreted as indicating the equivalent number of lines in which the company operates, assuming (contrary to normal fact) each to be of equal size. For the 443 sample companies, the computed values ranged from 1.0 to an average of 19.8 for the five most diversified companies. The median value was approximately 3.0.

To ascertain the role of diversification, the residual error values from the linear regressions of R&D on sales and patents on sales, industry by industry, were correlated with our index of diversification.[35] If, say, lines of business from diversified companies were more vigorous R&D performers than their sales in an industry category and industry conditions alone dictated, their residuals would tend to be positive, and those of undiversified companies would be negative, so a positive correlation between the residuals and the diversification index would emerge. In fact, the resulting (unsquared) correlations were minute and statistically insignificant: -0.023 for residuals of the R&D on sales regressions; and $+0.018$ for residuals of the patents on sales regressions. There was, however, a weak but statistically significant correlation of $+0.040$ between diversification and residuals from the patents on R&D regression. More diversified corporations tended to receive more patents per million dollars of R&D than did their less diversified counterparts, all else equal, perhaps because they were better able to commercialize, and hence chose to patent, inventions meshing imperfectly with their main lines of endeavor. The observed effect was quite small; it indicates that a unit increase in the numbers equivalent diversification index is accompanied in the average line of business by an increase of 0.056 patents per million dollars of R&D outlay, or 3.2 percent of the mean number of patents (1.70) per million R&D dollars for all sample lines. This implies an elasticity of patenting with respect to diversification of 0.1.

CONCLUSION

Three new and in many respects unusually rich sets of data have been analyzed here to reassess the Schumpeterian hypothesis that large corporations are uniquely powerful engines of technological advance. On the whole, the hypothesis fares badly. Its best innings have to do with merely entering the R&D game. As we have long known, the largest industrial corporations conduct a share of formally organized R&D considerably larger than their share of sales, value added, or employment. The Line of Business data add the new insight that, in more industries than not, this phenomenon of size continues up to the scale of the largest seller, although in *most* industries, size appears to be neither stimulating nor retarding. What the largest corporations accomplish with their R&D dollars is less impressive. By every measure used, the group of large corporations as a whole contributed fewer significant innovations, contest-winning technical advances, and invention patents per million dollars of R&D than smaller enterprises. Only by the count of patents do the largest corporations contribute a share of inventive output greater than their share of sales or employment. Their advantage on this dimension is at best modest and, in view of possible size group-related differences in the propensity to patent, uncertain. Within the population of large corporations, it is clear that greater size does not in general contribute to a disproportionately greater output of patented inventions. Nor does greater diversification help appreciably.

From this new evidence, one is certainly not well advised to rush out and urge, as was once the wont of Schumpeter's disciples, "We must encourage the growth of giant corporations because they are our best hope for technological leadership." Rather, the evidence points in a different direction, with at least three sets of possible implications.

One concerns what should be done to stimulate the formation and growth of smaller technology-oriented enterprises, which appear to have a clear edge in technological dynamism. At the very least, actions that would impair the flow of venture capital to such companies should be strenuously resisted. Whether there is currently a capital supply problem or there are other problems hampering smaller enterprises' innovative contributions is a question beyond the scope of my paper.[36]

Given the apparently inferior technical performance of the largest corporations, at least on broad statistical average, it must be asked whether anything should be done to *curb* their growth. My reading of the evidence finds little or no support for significant changes in that direction. The best-accepted policy instrument is merger law, but until recently, most of the corporate growth through merger has been of the conglomerate variety, and my statistical analysis shows diversification to be neither harmful nor helpful in terms of R&D support and inventive output. And above the threshold that allows a company to be admitted into the community of large businesses, constant returns in R&D support and inventive output, or conditions close to constant returns, appear most commonly to prevail. Thus, changing company sizes *within* industries is likely on average to have little effect. As one who was soundly thrashed in an attempt to change the size distribution of the breakfast cereals industry, I retain no zest for a hard battle that brings little gain. To be sure, I limit my observations here to the links between size and technological innovation, intending no implications one way or the other for structural actions that might have other objectives.

Recognizing then, as Teddy Roosevelt did eight decades ago, that big business is here to stay, the most important question is what one might do to improve large corporations' innovative performance. I can claim no magic solutions. I view the problem as Engine Charlie Wilson once viewed reforming the Pentagon: like kicking a one-hundred-foot sponge. One line of approach would be to remove artificial stimuli that reward corporations who bring to the top "wheeler and dealer" types rather than executives with a thorough knowledge of, and appreciation for, their industries' technology. Sensible deregulation can help here, but the main problem probably lies in the financial community and shortsighted institutional investors, and I do not know what one might do to improve matters there. I am forced to the academician's first and last resort: education. My brief M.B.A. curriculum survey plus unsystematic observation persuade me that there is a problem. The business schools must come to recognize what is important to our nation's long-run industrial (*read:* technological) strength. They must learn how to convey the message to their students, who will be our future industrial leaders, *and* to the vanguard of the financial community. They must mobilize a hundred George Doriots. That, I recognize, is impossible. But they must come as close to the objective as they can.

NOTES

1. F. M. Scherer, "Inter-Industry Technology Flows and Productivity Growth," *Review of Economics and Statistics* (November 1982), 64:627–634.

2. David Ravenscraft and F. M. Scherer, "The Lag Structure of Returns to Research and Development," *Applied Economics* (December 1982), 14:603–620.

3. F. M. Scherer, "Technological Maturity and Waning Economic Growth," *Arts and Sciences* (Fall 1978), I:7–11.

4. Scherer, "Inter-Industry Technology Flows"; and Zvi Griliches and Frank Lichtenberg, "Productivity and R&D at the Industry Level: Is There Still a Relationship?" Working Paper No. 850 (Cambridge, Mass.: National Bureau of Economic Research, 1981).

5. Robert H. Hayes and William J. Abernathy, "Managing Our Way to Economic Decline," *Harvard Business Review* (July–August 1980), 58:70.

6. *Ibid.,* pp. 75–76.

7. National Science Foundation, *The 5-Year Outlook on Science and Technology: 1981* (Washington, D.C.: Government Printing Office, 1982), p. 15.

8. Hayes and Abernathy, p. 75, citing a 1978 study by Golightly & Co. International.

9. Standard & Poor's, *Poor's Register of Corporations, Directors and Executives: 1982* (New York: Standard & Poor's, 1982).

10. *Who's Who in Finance and Industry:1951–1982,* 22nd ed. (Chicago: Marquis Who's Who, 1981).

11. Department of Commerce, Bureau of the Census, *Statistical Abstract of the United States: 1980–81* (Washington, D.C.: Government Printing Office, 1981), tables 284, 285.

12. Hayes and Abernathy, p. 74.

13. Department of Commerce, Bureau of the Census, *Enterprise Statistics: 1958* and *Enterprise Statistics: 1972* (Washington, D.C.: Government Printing Office, 1963, 1975).

14. F. M. Scherer, *Industrial Market Structure and Economic Performance,* 2d ed. (Chicago: Rand McNally College, 1980), p. 76, citing two Federal Trade Commission studies.

15. Joseph A. Schumpeter, *Capitalism, Socialism and Democracy,* 3d ed. (New York: Harper & Row, 1942).

16. Richard R. Nelson, "The Simple Economics of Basic Scientific Research," *Journal of Political Economy* (June 1959), 67:297–306.

17. See, for example, Morton I. Kamien and Nancy L. Schwartz, "Market Structure and Innovation: A Survey," *Journal of Economic Literature* (March 1975), 13:1–37. The article is updated and expanded in their book, *Market Structure and Innovation* (Cambridge: Cambridge University Press, 1982).

18. Stephen Feinman and William Fuentevilla, *Indicators of International Trends in Technological Innovation,* Final Report to the National Science Foundation, NTIS Document PB-263-738 (Jenkintown, Pa.: Gelman Research Associates, April 1976).

19. *Ibid.,* tables 3–8. There is a possible ambiguity in the size classifications, since Feinman and Fuentevilla did not always consolidate self-standing and/or partly owned subsidiaries of large corporations. It is known from studies of aggregate concentration that

the employment data to which I make a comparison are also not fully consolidated. Although the size of the bias is probably small, its direction is unclear.

20. Department of Commerce, Bureau of the Census, "General Report on Industrial Organization" in *Enterprise Statistics: 1963*, pt. 1 (Washington, D.C.: Government Printing Office, 1968), table 8. Not surprisingly, the employment share of corporations with 10,000 or more employees was rising during the sample period. It was 32.7 percent (less than the share of innovations) in 1958, and 44.7 percent in 1972. Data for 1954 are not available.

21. Feinman and Fuentevilla, tables 3–32. These figures are for a 352-innovation subset of the 500-innovation sample, with possible nonresponse biases. The number of sampled innovations for nations other than the United States is also small, running from 16 for France to 34 for the United Kingdom.

22. Keith Pavitt, "Some Characteristics of Innovative Activities in British Industry," draft (Sussex, Eng.: University of Sussex, January 1982). See also C. Freeman, *The Role of Small Firms in Innovation in the United Kingdom Since 1945*, Committee of Inquiry on Small Firms Research Report No. 6 (London: Her Majesty's Stationery Office, 1971).

23. Hayes and Abernathy, pp. 73, 76.

24. Federal Trade Commission, Bureau of Economics, *Statistical Report: Annual Line of Business Report: 1974* (Washington, D.C.: Federal Trade Commission, 1981).

25. On the difficulties in making an exact sales or value added comparison, see the Federal Trade Commission's *Statistical Report: Annual Line of Business Report, 1976* (Washington, D.C.: Federal Trade Commission, May 1982), pp. 52–75.

26. FTC, *Line of Business Report: 1974*.

27. See F. M. Scherer, "The Propensity to Patent," *International Journal of Industrial Organization* (February 1983), 1:107–128.

28. Indeed, one invention in our sample was made by Harold Geneen, chairman of ITT.

29. F. M. Scherer et al., *Patents and the Corporation*, 2d ed. (Boston: Privately published, 1959), pp. 137–146.

30. For an evaluation of the U.S. evidence, see Jacob Schmookler, *Invention and Economic Growth* (Cambridge: Harvard University Press, 1966), pp. 47–55. On Germany, see Klaus Grefermann et al., *Patentwesen und Technischer Fortschritt* (Goettingen, Germany: Schwartz, 1974), appendix, table 57. The differences in utilization rates between the largest and smallest size classes tabulated in both nations are on the order of twenty percentage points.

31. Scherer, "Propensity to Patent."

32. On the theory, see Franklin M. Fisher and Peter Temin, "Return to Scale in Research and Development: What Does the Schumpeterian Hypothesis Imply?" *Journal of Political Economy* (January–February 1973), 81:56–70; and Meir Kohn and John T. Scott, "Scale Economics in Research and Development: The Schumpeterian Hypothesis," *Journal of Industrial Economics* (March 1982), 30:239–250.

33. See, for example, Scherer, "Propensity to Patent"; and idem, "Size of Firm, Oligopoly, and Research: A Comment," *Canadian Journal of Economics and Political Science* (May 1965), 31:256–266.

34. Details are added in Scherer, "Propensity to Patent."

35. This is equivalent to computing the partial correlation of the dependent variable with diversification, given sales and industry effects.

36. But see National Science Foundaton, *Problems of Small High-Technology Firms*, Special Report NSF 81-305 (Washington, D.C.: Government Printing Office, December 1981).

COMMENTATORS' REMARKS

JESSE W. MARKHAM

ONE cannot properly appreciate the magnitude of Scherer's contribution to the issue of how the modern corporation affects technological progress without at least passing reference to the "state of the art" as he found it. I should point out that he started with an existing "state of the art" in somewhat better condition than it otherwise would have been because of his own previous contributions.

The principal defects of the previous quantiative studies, and hence the inconclusiveness of the results, derived from problems of inadequate data. With the exception of the PIMS (Profits Impact of Marketing Strategies) data, which covered a limited portion of the U.S. economy and was not available to most researchers, available R&D data were for firms on the one hand and for relatively broad industry groupings on the other. Since any measurement of size, such as total sales or total assets, pertained to highly heterogeneous business activity (Exxon and General Motors rank as the largest and second largest industrial firms, but their assets are devoted to quite different businesses), computed regression coefficients relating size to innovational effort could not be unambiguously interpreted.

The attendant ambiguity could not be eliminated through intraindustry analyses: While DuPont may be predominantly a chemical company, all of its sales and R&D did not relate to chemicals. Moreover, its chemical and nonchemical product mixes were different from those of Dow Chemical, American Cyanamid, and Allied Chemical and Dye. Hence, even within broad industry groups, both the size variable and the R&D variable were characterized by qualitative as well as quantitative differences. To be sure, a few studies, such as those by Edwin Mansfield, or certain industry-specific studies such as Comanor's study of the drug industry, went a long way toward overcoming these data difficulties, but their coverage was far too limited to support generalizations on the central issue of corporate size and progressiveness.

Scherer's unique contribution lies in his having vastly reduced these ambiguities and inadequacies through the skillful use of the Federal Trade Commission's line of business data base. We are, of course, indebted to him for more than the new knowledge he has created, to which I shall soon turn. As director of the Federal Trade Commission's Bureau of Economics, he was a prime mover in the creation of the line of business reporting program itself.

I shall direct most of my comments to Scherer's results and their economic implications, but I have a few comments on the data and his methodology. In the Gelman Research results, Scherer notes that corporations in the 10,000-and-over employee class accounted for 36.0 percent of total *employment* but only 34.5 percent of all U.S. "noteworthy" innovations. In the later analysis, he observes that the 443 LB large corporations accounted for from 55 to 60 percent of *sales and value added,* but for only 55 percent of *Industrial Research & Development Magazine*'s award-winning technical advances, 61 percent of the patents issued, and 73 percent of the R&D expenditures. Scherer properly draws no firm conclusions directly from these facts, but they seem to be what he has in mind when he concludes that, on the basis of three new and rich sets of data, the Schumpetarian thesis fares badly, and later he refers to the large corporations' inferior technical performance. But this follows in part from the cited studies having used different data bases. Large corporations typically account for a lower percentage of total employment than of total sales. For the largest 100 or 200 manufacturing corporations on *Fortune's* list, the ratio of employment percent to sales percent is approximately 70 to 100. For example, in 1972, the 200 largest manufacturing corporations accounted for 43 percent of domestic sales, but for only 31 percent of total employment. Had the studies Scherer cites used employment consistently throughout, his conclusions would have been significantly tempered: his "large" LB corporations would have accounted for disproportionately large shares of R&D outlays, award-winning technical advances, and patents issued. The recalculated shares would have been as follows:

	Percent of Employment	Percent of R&D	Percent of Patents and Innovations
Gelman study (10,000 and over)	36.0		34.5
Award-winning advances	38.5–42.0	73	55.0
FTC LB large corporations	38.5–42.0	73	61.0

On the other hand, had Scherer's studies used sales consistently as a base, his case against the large corporation group in the Gelman study would have been much stronger: his 10,000-and-over employment group would have accounted for nearly 50 percent of total sales, but only 34.5 percent of the innovations. There is no compelling reason for using one of these data bases in preference to the other. In some of Scherer's earlier work, he used the ratio of scientists and engineers to total employment as a measurement of innovational effort; elsewhere, he and others have used the ratio of R&D dollars to sales dollars. A good case can be made for using both. However, as I shall argue later, for purposes of testing the Schumpeterian hypothesis, that the ratio of R&D to some index of market power, or R&D to profits, would be superior to either.

It is in Scherer's nonlinear regression analysis, however, where he makes his greatest scholarly and most revealing conclusion. By employing a nonlinear quadratic specification of the model, he neatly separates out the linear from the nonlinear components (his earlier 1965 logarithmic specification did not permit this). His results confirm beyond reasonable doubt, and convincingly, that once a corporation has entered the upper size group in a reasonably definable line of business, additional size in by far the majority of businesses will bring with it no more than a proportionate increase in innovational activity. This general conclusion can be stated somewhat less confidently when R&D expenditures are used as a measure of innovational effort, where increasing returns to size outweigh decreasing returns in the ratio of 2.5 to 1, than when patents are used, where increasing and decreasing returns are a virtual washout. The significant findings, however, are that in 70 percent or better of the lines of business analyzed, whether patents or R&D expenditures are used, the relationship is essentially linear.

My only major disagreement with Scherer (two minor ones will follow) is with his single concluding statement, that on the basis of his results, "on the whole, the [Schumpeterian] hypothesis fares badly." I have urged on at least three occasions, evidently without noticeable success, that there is nothing in the Schumpeterian hypothesis suggesting that innovational effort should be expected to increase proportionately, disproportionately, or in any systematically quantitative fashion with mere size, particularly after large size has already been attained. Schumpeter essentially argued that successful innovational effort, based on his analysis of the interwar period 1918–1940, had resulted in most of the measurable increases in the living standards of the Western industrialized countries, citing especially the household appliances, chemical, automobile, and synthetic fiber industries. He noted correctly that these industries were essentially oligopolistic in structure, departing in fundamental respects from the circular flow, static, equilibrated economy of perfect competition, the classical economic model on which Schumpeter earlier had written his authoritative book. In this system, he contended, since *economic* profits were zero, the firm had no funds to commit to the risky activity of research and development. One did not play roulette with the rent money. From this he contended that supracompetitive profits were both the wherewithal and the incentive for innovation. He noted in passing that, as an empirical matter, corporations possessing the requisite market power (but only temporarily) to have earned supracompetitive profits, and to seek such prospective rewards in the future through innovation, were frequently the large corporations generally viewed by antitrust authorities as inimical to the public welfare. But Schumpeter would never have expected to find a giant textile company with $500 million sales outspending Edwin H. Land's newly formed Polaroid Company with $5 million sales in the ratio of 100 to 1. To properly test the Schumpeterian hypothesis, one must not only relate innovational effort to profits and market power but must carefully and tediously analyze the origin of both. Moreover, Schumpeter defined innovation in much broader terms than narrow technological progress.

My remaining comment goes to a rather trivial point, but it deserves brief mention. Early in his paper, Scherer suggests that U.S. corporations have begun to lose the technological race to Western European and Japanese companies, citing the Abernathy and Hayes analysis as offering a possible explanation. I believe this position has been overstated and in any case can be partially explained by factors exogenous to the large U.S. corporation. Given the rapid growth of multinational corporations and the ease of international technological transfer, we should surely expect the technologies of other countries, especially those of war-damaged Europe and Japan, to have closed most of the gap that separated these economies from that of the United States immediately following World War II. Judged from both economic growth and productivity data, the major economies have tended toward convergence over the past two decades. Evidently, the same has happened to corporate R&D intensity. The latest data collected by the Committee for Economic Development show that private R&D outlays are running at 1.05 percent of GNP for the U.S., 1.18 percent for West Germany, and 1.25 percent for Japan.

Abernathy and Hayes would attribute even these differences to U.S. corporate managements' preoccupation with short-run objectives. They may be right, but the ultimate cause may not necessarily lie in some systemic malady native to modern U.S. corporate managers or their training. After all, a very large percentage of contemporary European and Japanese managers received their formal business training in United States schools of business or their faculties setting up branches abroad. Further, the early slowdown in economic growth in the United States, the resulting preoccupation of public authority with monetary and fiscal policy "quick fixes," and the uncertainties over public policy resulting from conflicting signals sent out by the White House and Capitol Hill since midway through President Johnson's administration, have scarcely been conducive to orderly long-range corporate planning. But this is incidental to the principal issue Scherer has so carefully and competently analysed, bringing forth such fruitful results.

ROBERT B. REICH

THE most provocative part of Mike Scherer's paper had to do with the relationship between corporate organizations and corporate culture on the one hand and research and development on the other.

It is somewhat unbecoming, at a conference sponsored by Columbia here at Princeton, but I want to use some survey data of Harvard graduates. Of Harvard Business School graduates last year, 3 percent took jobs in production, including management and technology, and 18.6 percent took jobs in sales and marketing; but 21.6 percent took jobs in finance. Of last year's Harvard freshmen, 28 percent said that they planned a career in law, and 8 percent in science or engineering.

Another interesting statistic. My own study of leadership of *Fortune* 500 companies—chief executives and chief operating officers—indicated that 38 percent were trained in law or finance and rose to their present position from legal or financial staffs. The interesting comparison is to 1956, when we find that only 13 percent were trained in those fields.

Between 1940 and 1960, only 1 out of 600 Americans was trained in law. Over the last decade there has been a 68 percent increase in lawyers. Now, 1 of every 400 Americans has legal training. Meanwhile, in the last decade there has been only a 15 percent increase in engineers.

Two questions immediately arise. One, is it true that the private returns on investment in legal or financial training are significantly larger than the social returns? Two, if it is true that the private return is greater than the social return, how do we explain this? Similarly, if the private returns on investment in science and engineering training are less than the social returns, why is this now the case when it was not twenty-five or thirty years ago?

In the limited time that I have, let me suggest to you some hypotheses that might explain these phenomena. The industrial base of the United States began seriously to change in the late 1960s, not only in transportation and communication—containered shipping and satellites—but also in capital markets. A world capital market began emerging in the late 1960s. Reductions in barriers to trade and engineering services enabled entire plants to be set up around the world.

As a result of these changes, the American industrial base began to become relatively uncompetitive in the world. But American managers were not able to invest in the radical changes in products and processes necessary to move to higher-valued production. When institutional investors demanded quarterly financial papers, many managers started investing in paper entrepreneurship—reducing or postponing taxes, launching unfriendly takeovers, engaging in creative accounting and litigation. None of these activities directly increased American productivity. Instead, they merely maintained profitability in the short term, because that was what was demanded. Long-term investment strategies could not be afforded.

A 1981 survey of chief executive officers of *Fortune* 500 companies showed that 49 percent thought their companies vulnerable to a takeover; the remainder had plans aimed at thwarting takeovers. The problem here is one of human capital: the time and energy of corporate managers and other very talented citizens that went into paper entrepreneurism.

Meanwhile, in the 1970s, the financial risk of becoming an engineer or scientist was much greater than that of becoming a lawyer because the federal government—which then funded about 52 percent of national research and development—was in the process of reducing its R&D expenditures; this created a glut of engineers and scientists. Now we have a shortage of engineers and scientists, but the risk remains.

A second factor concerns appropriability of investments in innovation. With increasing world communication and transportation, new discoveries can spread out beyond the investors, and more quickly, then ever before. The Japanese, for example, have concerned themselves less with investing in new technology than with investing tin the means of rapidly commercializing new technologies developed elsewhere.

Thus, the important questions may have nothing to do with relative size. They may have more to do with the pattern of investment—whether "paper entrepreneurism" or new products and processes; whether basic R&D or commercialization.

PART V

POLITICAL IMPACT

EDITORS' NOTE

ALTHOUGH it has been a widely held belief since the Federalist Papers that business size bears a relationship to political power in the United States, the nature and limits of this relationship have been a matter of almost constant debate. On the one hand, there are those who believe that large corporations have a level of discretionary power and political influence virtually equivalent to that of a sovereign state. On the other hand, there are those who argue that the discretionary power of large corporations is significantly constrained and that their political influence is dwarfed by that of other political actors.

At least three basic policy issues arise out of this debate over the political impact of corporate size. First, is there a relationship between large firm size and political power? Second, if such a relationship exists, what is its nature? And, third, is the existing relationship, whatever it is, a good or bad thing? Depending upon the answers to these questions, one may form a basis for determining whether any modifications are needed in existing public policy toward the political power of large corporations.

In an effort to provide a scholarly basis for beginning to examine these issues, the two papers in this chapter, by Professors David Vogel and Edwin M. Epstein, examine the impact of the large, modern corporation on the political process.

Professor Vogel, in "A Case Study of Clean Air Legislation 1967–1977," analyzes "the ways in which the characteristics of a particular industry—its size, its degree of concentration and the organizational links to other industries—affect its ability to influence the direction of public policy." Professor Vogel identifies four factors critical in accounting for the relative influence of companies with respect to federal clean air legislation between 1967 and 1977 (the pattern of opposition and support from other interest groups, the degree to which the lobbying effort is well organized, the perceived merits of the position, and the geographic distribution of the production). He nevertheless finds that his study does not provide a basis for concluding that firm size mechanically translates directly into disproportionate political power. Professor Vogel's conclusion is, however, critically reviewed in the comments of Dean Ernest Gellhorn, Dean Robert Pitofsky, and Professor Charles Lindbloom. Each argues that Professor Vogel's case study—although valuable—has left basic questions about corporate political power unasked and unanswered.

Professor Epstein analyzes the relationship between corporate size and influence on the political process by examining the phenomenon of corporate political action committees (PACs). After providing an overview of the increase in corporate political action committees, Professor Epstein analyzes their role and impact on the American political process, particularly at the federal level. Professor Epstein concludes that *"in their place,* properly constrained, PACs have a legitimate role to play in the modern political process, a role that can enhance rather than erode the quality of political democracy in the United States" (emphasis in original). But he recommends additional constraints that should be placed upon corporate PACs to keep their future political influence within appropriate boundaries.

CHAPTER 8

A Case Study of Clean Air Legislation 1967–1981

David Vogel

T HE purpose of this essay is to examine the relationship between corporate size and political power. Specifically, it seeks to analyze the
ways in which the characteristics of a particular industry—its size, its
degree of concentration, and its organizational links to other industries—affect its ability to influence the direction of public policy. The
particular focus of this study is federal air pollution control legislation
from the mid-1960s through the present.

There are, broadly speaking, two approaches toward measuring the
relationship between industrial structure and political influence. One
emphasizes the use of statistical methodology. Various quantitative

Interviews for this study were conducted on the understanding that no quotations would
be attributed. Quotations from interviews thus appear without citations. A list of all those
interviewed for this study appears in appendix 8A.

The author would like to thank Marcy McGaugh for typing the manuscript and acknowledge the assistance of Susan Erickson, Nancy Spencer, and Tony Daley in the preparation
of this analysis.

The research for this study was supported by a grant from the Columbia University Center
for Law and Economic Studies' project on the Impact of the Large Corporation.

measurements of corporate political participation and influence are established and then are correlated with indexes of industrial structure. If these relationships prove statistically significant, then, in the words of the best-known of such studies, "larger firm size does . . . seem to yield greater political power."[1] This research strategy does have a number of advantages: it not only makes it possible to synthesize a large amount of data, but it produces results that are capable of being both falsified and replicated. In fact, the results of several of these studies have tended to be relatively consistent. As Epstein summarizes them:

> Looking collectively at the studies discussed above in this section, their empirical analyses appear to allow for the following overarching hypothesis: the amount of political power generated by an industry is correlated at least in part to: the scope and intensity of the industry's political efforts (its "inputs"), which are in turn correlated to the politically valuable resources available to the industry (which in turn are related to the particular structural characteristics of the industry); the benefits expected by firms in the industry; and the incentives of the firms to organize for collective action.[2]

On the other hand, it is clear that these studies have by no means succeeded in resolving the problem that they address. As Epstein's review and critique of this literature concludes, they suffer from a number of important limitations. The most important is that correlativity does not by itself establish causality. Just because large firms are more active politically does not mean that firms are more politically active because they are large; the two in turn may be caused by a third factor. Moreover, there is no necessary relationship between political participation and political impact. The former simply documents a potential source of political influence; it does not necessarily mean that it has been employed effectively. A related difficulty with statistical studies of corporate participation and influence is that the selection of their data is limited by the nature of their methodology. They are confined to those manifestations of business political activity and power that lend themselves to expression in numerical terms. More fundamentally, this approach is incapable of providing us with an understanding of the actual mechanisms of corporate involvement in the policy process. As a result, much of both the drama and the substance of American politics is excluded from their purvue.

An alternative way of analyzing the basis of corporate political influence is the case study method. The efforts of a particular firm or group of firms in a particular industry to affect some public policy outcome is described in detail and an assessment is then offered of the extent to which they were successful in defining and achieving their objectives. This approach has the advantage of concreteness; it does allow us to trace and describe the actual dynamics of corporate political influence. Yet, it too has limitations. First, as Bartlett observes in his essay, "An Economic Theory of Political Power: Firm Size and Political Power," "It is not omnipotence that is at issue, but relative power."[3] Thus, the fact that a group of firms in a highly fragmented industry were able to achieve their political goals while a highly concentrated industrial sector suffered an important political defeat in itself demonstrates nothing about the political impact of corporate concentration; what may have been equally criticial was the nature of the opposition that each confronted.

A more serious objection to the case study method lies in the representativness of the issues analyzed. Clearly, specific political outcomes are contingent on a wide variety of factors, some structural and some dependent on circumstances peculiar to a particular controversy. Conclusions based on any one political outcome are thus inherently vulnerable to the criticism that the controversy analyzed or the time period in which it was resolved was somehow atypical. Unless the analyst has established some set of criteria that locates a particular conflict in the context of a broader analytical framework, the conclusions drawn from any case study, no matter how carefully documented, can be challenged.

The approach of this essay represents an attempt to synthesize elements of each of these approaches. Like the statistical analyses, it examines a fairly extensive amount of information about corporate political activity and its impact on public policy. But it does so not through the use of statistics but through a series of interrelated case studies. It is difficult to measure directly the political significance of corporate size, since relatively few important political disputes involve conflicts between individual firms. The most common units of political activity tend to be either a coalition of industries, an individual industry, or a subset of a particular industry. Although corporate size is by no means identical with corporate concentration, for the particular companies and industries examined in this study, virtually all of whom operate within national markets, the former does appear to represent a convenient surrogate for the latter: those industries that are more concentrated do tend to consist of relatively larger companies, while those industries that are highly fragmented tend to be comprised of companies that rank fairly low on a national scale. My approach compares the relative political effectiveness of a series of industries—both over time and vis-à-vis each other. Since the degree of concentration (and consequently the average size of individual firms) varies considerably from industry to industry, we can begin to distinguish the ways in which an industry's structure affects both its political strategy and political effectiveness. My conclusions make no pretensions to be definitive; they are however based on a relatively novel and reasonably sophisticated way of assessing the political impact of corporate size.

There are a number of factors that make federal clean air legislation an appropriate issue-area to examine for the purposes of evaluating the political impact of the large corporation.

First, an examination of federal air pollution legislation makes it possible to trace the evolution of public policy over a considerable time period. Between 1967 and 1977, Congress enacted three major pieces of legislation in this area: the Clean Air Act Amendments of 1967, 1970, and 1977. (The most recent revision of the Clean Air Act was originally planned to be included in this study, but its enactment has been repeatedly delayed.) The political environment within which business functioned varied enormously over this turbulent decade, ranging from diffused support to widespread mistrust. In 1967, business in America enjoyed a relatively large degree of political influence, whereas from the late 1960s through the mid-1970s large corporations in America confronted the most severe set of challenges to their power and privileges since the 1930s. The Clean Air Act Amendments of 1967 and 1970 were enacted during a period of relative prosperity, while the 1977 amendments were debated amid substantial public anxiety over the performance of the economy. An analysis that focuses on political outcomes with respect to the same set of issues during a diversity of political and economic conditions is far more likely to capture the underlying factors affecting and shaping the political influence of industry than one that addresses an issue that was resolved within a relatively few years or within a constant political and economic environment.

A second distinctive feature of federal air pollution legislation is the sheer number and diversity of interest groups that have participated in its formulation. In addition to a substantial segment of the nation's business community, including the automobile industry, the pulp and paper industry, the utility industry, the oil industry, the coal industry, the steel industry, the chemical industry, the nonferrous smelter industry, railroads, automobile suppliers and dealers, and shopping center developers, much of the trade union movement, the entire environmental movement, and organizations representing state and local governments were also heavily involved in the debate over federal clean air policy. Indeed, the Clean Air Act Amendments of 1977 probably represent the most intensively lobbied piece of federal legislation since the Taft-Hartley Act.

Equally importantly, the industries that sought to shape federal clean air policy varied considerably among themselves in terms of their industrial structures.[4] The automobile and nonferrous smelting industry are both highly concentrated, consisting of a relatively small number of relatively large companies. The four largest companies involved in the primary smelting and refining of copper produced 75 percent of the value of industry shipments in 1970 and 87 percent in 1977, while the value of industry shipments accounted for by the four largest domestic motor vehicle manufacturers was approximately 80 percent throughout the 1960s and 1970s. The chemical, iron and steel, and petroleum refining industries are moderately concentrated: in 1972 the value of industry shipments accounted for by the four largest firms in these industries was 46.1 percent, 41.7 percent, and 31.0 percent, respectively. The average size of firms in the coal and utility industries tends to be somewhat smaller: between 1974 and 1977, the value of industry shipments accounted for by the four largest coal companies ranged from 21.3 percent to 18.0 percent, while the utility industry is also relatively decentralized. In 1977, there were also a number of extremely fragmented industries that played an active role in the legislative process, including auto dealers, automobile suppliers, automobile repair shops, and a host of firms involved in the development of shopping centers—including real estate development firms, construction companies, and retail outlets of varying sizes.

The industries concerned with federal clean air politics also vary considerably in terms of their degree of diversification. At one extreme is the coal industry. As of 1976, only 8 percent of the total domestic privately controlled reserves of coal were owned by independent coal producers; 38 percent were owned by diversified energy corporations, 20 percent by railroads, 6 percent by utilities, and 4 percent by steel or smelting concerns.[5] At the other end is the automobile industry, which enjoyed no organizational overlap with any other industry discussed in this study. Other industries such as chemicals, steel, and oil fall somewhere in the middle on this continuum. Thus by the mid-1970s both the oil industry and the steel industry owned considerable coal reserves, and the latter was also engaged in the production of chemicals. (Since Congress last legislated on clean air policy, the degree of organizational overlap among the major industries concerned with federal clean air legislation has increased substantially. A significant segment of the copper smelting industry is now controlled by oil companies; steel companies have diversified into both oil and chemicals; and a merger has taken place between the nation's largest chemical company and a major energy conglomerate. The political significance of these developments is beyond the scope of this study since it is impossible to assess their political impact until Congress has once again legislated in this area. At that point, however, we will have a clear vantage point from which to examine the political significance of conglomerate mergers.)

Thirdly, by any conceivable criteria, federal air pollution control policy constitutes an extremely important dimension of public policy. Aside from tax and defense policies, probably no single area of public policy has had a more profound impact on the domestic economy over the last two decades. Between 1973 and 1982, private sector expenditures to improve air quality totaled $127.9 billion, making "the Clean Air Act . . . one of the most costly pieces of regulatory legislation in history."[6] Moreover, for a significant number of industries and individual companies it has seriously affected—and at times threatened—their economic viability. Among the most frequently voiced criticisms of studies of corporate political power is that the controversies they examine are only of secondary importance to the nation's basic structure of business power.[7] But to the extent that any political conflict in which business has been a participant over the last generation deserves to be labeled "important," clean air legislation certainly falls into that category. It has simultaneously affected the distribution of benefits among particular firms and regions, the balance of power among particular industries and between various industries and other interest groups, as well as a number of core interests of the business system as a whole. It thus falls into all three of Lowi's policy arenas: it has redistributed wealth from the business community as a whole, affected the economic position of individual industries, and redistributed resources among the nation's business firms.[8]

This essay offers neither a history nor an evaluation of federal air pollution controls. Nor is it concerned with decisions undertaken by either the executive or judicial branches, save when these affected the legislative agenda. Rather its focus is more selective: its purpose is to describe and explain the effects of business and other interest groups on clean air legislation during the last fifteen years.

Throughout the 1960s, the federal government found itself under increasing pressure to become more actively involved in controlling air pollution. In 1963, Congress enacted its first comprehensive piece of legislatgion in the area of air pollution. The 1963 Clean Air Act, which became the basic federal air pollution law, represented a compromise between those who favored a more active federal role and those who wanted to maintain the primary role of the state governments in improving air quality.

For all the intense political conflict that surrounded it, the Clean Air Act of 1963 was a rather innocuous piece of legislation.[9] While its abatement-enforcement provisions did constitute an "opening wedge" for federal intervention—one that would be dramatically widened during the next decade—the procedures for federal enforcement of abatement orders were so complex and time-consuming as to make them virtually ineffective. Four years after the legislation was passed, the federal government had still not brought one legal faction to force compliance with a pollution abatement order; the main reliance for improving air quality still rested with the voluntary cooperation of industry with officials of local governmental units. The 1963 legislation thus neither threatened the financial interests of any industry nor brought about any discernible improvement in air quality. On the other hand, the act did increase federal research expenditures and helped encourage local authorities to establish their own regulatory bodies. By 1967, more than two-thirds of the states had established agencies responsible for air pollution, as compared with only seventeen six years earlier.

Both of these developments subsequently presented the coal industry with its first political challenge in the field of air pollution. In the fall of 1965, Mayor Lindsay of New York City announced his intention of banning coal from New York City on the grounds that its sulphur emissions threatened the health and safety of the city's residents. At hearings held on the mayor's proposal in March of 1966, the coal industry strongly challenged either the prohibition of the burning of coal or the burning of only low sulphur coal; the latter could not be produced by Appalachian-based companies, which at the time produced virtually all of the nation's coal. They contended that the limited availability of both low sulphur coal and residual fuel oil made the mayor's plan impractical. In addition to hearing testimony from the National Coal Association, the United Mine Workers, and the National Coal Policy Conference, the mayor received a letter from Senator Robert Byrd of West Virginia, an important coal-producing state. It urged him to conduct more research and to weigh carefully the costs of dispensing with high sulphur coal. In addition, the city's privately owned utility, Con Edison, fully backed the stance of the coal industry. New York City's elected officials backed down, and a considerably modified air pollution control ordinance was enacted that accepted stack gas removal as an effective alternative to the burning of low sulphur fuel.

The coal industry was equally successful in meeting a similar challenge from the federal government. In 1965, the Department of Health, Education and Welfare proposed emission standards for sulphur dioxide at federal installations. Faced with "repeated strong warnings of the adverse effects of proposed HEW institutions," from the coal industry, not only were the regulations postponed but government officials assured the industry that "regulations which are finally issued will be worked out in cooperation with the coal and oil industries as well as other interested parties."[10] However, two years later, HEW, attempting to carry out the provisions of the Clean Air Act of 1963 that required it to publish a series of studies on all major air pollutants, released a report entitled "Air Quality Criteria for Sulphur Oxides." Publication of the report was "vigorously opposed" by the coal industry, coal workers, and senators from coal-producing states.[11]

As one reporter put it, "The considerable power of the coal industry, under the virtuoso direction of coal lobbyist Joe Moody, was quickly mobilized to discredit the report's findings and delay its publication."[12] W. A. Boyle, president of the National Coal Policy Conference, argued that the control regulations proposed in the report would create "real danger of an electric power and fuel shortage in the future . . . [would] bar almost all coal in existing power plants and . . . prohibit the building of new coal plants."[13] In addition, Senator Jennings Randolph of West Virginia wrote a series of letters to HEW officials urging them that any determination of the health hazards posed by sulphur oxides be delayed until "technology was developed to control sulphur emissions from smoke stacks."[14] However, HEW proved unresponsive to the arguments of the industry and its supporters. Early in 1967 HEW both formally published its report and proposed relatively strict limits on sulphur content on coal burned at new federal installations. Moody interpreted HEW's actions as an indication that it "wants such low sulphur restrictions to become a nationwide standard for all fuel-burning facilities."[15] Subsequently, HEW announced regulations designed to control sulphur oxide emissions at 154 federal installations in New York City.

The conflict over the federal regulations limiting the burning of high sulphur coal then switched to Congress. Responding to an increase in public concern over air pollution—exacerbated by an air inversion in New York City in November of 1966 that was estimated to have caused the deaths of eighty people—President Johnson decided to make improvement in air quality a part of his Great Society program. In a special message to Congress entitled "Protecting Our National Heritage," the president called for "emission control levels . . . for those industries that contribute heavily to air pollution."[16] The administration introduced a bill that authorized the HEW secretary "to establish enforceable, uniform control levels for specific pollutants in various industries."[17] While virtually all stationary sources of pollution were decidedly unenthusiastic about the proposal of additional federal regulations—particularly if they included federal emission standards—for the coal industry, "New federal legislation in 1967 did have one possible advantage: . . . it offered the possibility of Congressional action to overturn HEW's standards on sulphur oxide emissions."[18]

The conflict over the enactment of the Clean Air Act of 1967 focused largely on the issue of federal emission standards. In the spring of 1967, hearings on the administration bill were held by the Subcommittee on Air and Water Pollution, chaired by Senator Muskie. While representatives of a wide variety of industries testified before the committee—including the pulp and paper industry, the steel industry, the oil industry, the mining industry, the utility industry, and the railroad industry—it was clear that the primary concern of the business community was with federal regulations that would restrict the use of high sulphur fuel, particularly coal. Thus, more representatives from individual coal companies appeared before the hearings than from any other type of corporation; similarly, the only union official to testify was W. A. Boyle of the United

Mine Workers. The vast majority of those who were opposed to allowing the HEW secretary to set minimum national emission standards for industrial sources of pollution were either coal producers, important industrial consumers of coal, or trade associations whose members had subsidiaries that produced coal. The most important exception was the oil companies—with whom, at this point, coal producers had relatively few financial or organizational ties. However, on this issue, they had a common position: both were equally concerned about the federal government's recent effort to reduce sulphur oxide emissions since this pollutant is also produced by the burning of fuel oil.

The testimony of the "coal coalition" was both consistent and extremely well coordinated. The National Coal Policy Conference and the Edison Electric Institute, the latter representing the utility industry, played a critical role in coordinating industry testimony; individual industrial witnesses as well as Boyle of the United Mine Workers repeatedly endorsed each other's views. The legislative goals of the coal coalition—as well as the oil industry—were straightforward. They were willing to support legislation that encouraged the federal government to make additional efforts to control air pollution—including the spending of additional funds for research. However, they were opposed to national air standards and wanted the primary responsibility for enforcement to remain in the hands of the states. Most importantly, they insisted on the inclusion of three amendments offered by Senator Jennings Randolph, whose purpose was to require HEW to review its sulphur emission standards for federal installations.

In 1967, Senator Muskie's most critical contribution was to weaken significantly the bill proposed by the administration—a stance for which he was subsequently strongly criticized in the Nader task force report, *Vanishing Air*, published a few years later. Thus, while the administration favored national emission standards, Muskie instead urged the establishment of "national ambient air quality, applied as standards on a regional basis."[19] There exists some doubt as to whether Muskie accurately understood the significance of the distinction between these two approaches for dealing with air pollution; some evidence suggests that he may have viewed air quality standards as the more effective device for improving air quality. In any event, national emission standards certainly represented the more radical policy alternative—one for which significant public pressure would have been required to overcome both "industry opposition and legislative inertia."[20] In 1967, however, this pressure was simply not forthcoming. As one account of the 1967 legislation put it: "Pollution and environmental concerns, despite their recent vogue, simply do not impress most Americans as a problem of major concern to themselves or their country."[21] While six national conservationist and health groups did testify before Muskie's subcommittee, their efforts were uncoordinated and politically useless; the environmental movement had neither the manpower nor the technical capacity to participate seriously in the shaping of federal policy in such a complex area. In short, regardless of the personal preferences of Senator Muskie, emission standards were simply not politically feasible in 1967.

Shortly before the Air Quality Act was enacted into law, a spokesman for the National Coal Association summarized industry's lobbying efforts as follows:

NCA and other groups in coal and oil industries set to work to convince Congress that whatever it did about controlling air pollution must be reasonable, practical, and economically feasible. . . . As a result of these activities and others, the coal industry and allies seem to be making some progress in the face of overzealous demands for instant clean air.[22]

In fact, not only did the act satisfy the preferences of all sources of stationary source pollution by its establishment of air quality regions rather than emissions standards, but it included a special provision that ordered HEW to reevaluate its sulphur oxide criteria. As one scholar concludes:

In the view of industry and environmentalists alike, the 1967 Air Quality Act was coal's law, and *Coal Age* acknowledged the victory. As a result of "opposition" . . . mounted by coal . . . the final version . . . met most of the industry's objectives. The HEW's sulphur oxide criteria were modified and specific and detailed research . . . provided for.[23]

The coal industry began to confront federal regulation of air pollution during the very period when coal companies were increasing in size, many becoming subsidiaries of large and more diversified corporations. What effect did these developments have on the effectiveness of the coal industry through 1967? There is little evidence that these changes played a decisive role in the industry's 1967 legislative triumph. At first glance, it might appear that coal's organizational links with a number of other industries, such as oil, utility, and mining, would appear to have given it an important political advantage. Instead of just being able to influence representatives from districts or states in which there was substantial coal production, the industry now had access to the much larger number of representatives from states and districts in which companies that owned coal subsidiaries had facilities. But while it is true that the political efforts of the coal industry were certainly more sophisticated in the late 1960s than they would have been a decade or two earlier when the industry was more fragmented and independent, the political significance of this transformation is not readily apparent. In fact, the representatives from other states and regions supported the coal industry not because firms headquartered in their districts owned coal companies but because the interests of these companies and that of the coal producers coincided: neither wanted any restrictions on the burning of high sulphur coal. Thus, a particularly important ally of the coal industry was the utility industry. But like Con Edison in New York City, which did not own a coal company, utilities throughout the United States urged their representatives to back the demands of the coal industry not so much because of any organizational ties they might have had with coal companies but because they too had no desire to have their access to locally available reserves of high sulphur fuel restricted by the federal government. Such restrictions would only increase their costs.

Discussing the political significance of cross-ownership of coal reserves, an official of the National Coal Association stated:

I make every effort to have representatives of coal companies owned by chemical, steel and utility firms on committees that deal with pollution problems, not because I can necessarily expect any help from these other industries, but because their perspectives are very useful to me. They give me a sense of what other industries are thinking. To the extent that we have common interests, it makes the job of coordination a bit easier.

A lobbyist for the utility industry made a similar observation:

What matters is not so much the structure of any industry but the way in which a congressman defines his constituency. What ultimately matters is whether or not you can bring the interests of an industry down home to a congressman. Unless you can convince him that some particular policy is going to directly affect the plants located in his district, you have no particular leverage with him.

The staff member of an interindustry coordinating group noted:

If the headquarters of a diversified company are in a congressman's district, he might be persuaded to care about what happens to a particular subsidiary, even if that subsidiary doesn't employ any of his constituents. But it has to constitute a very important part of the parent company's business. Otherwise you simply can't sell it on the grass-roots level. They won't give a damn.

Nor is there much evidence that the average size of either utility or coal firms affected the political outcome in 1967. As a utility industry lobbyist noted:

Perhaps it makes my job as an industry lobbyist a little easier to the extent that a company like American Electric Power has plants in six states. This means that there are a larger number of representatives that this one company can approach. But someone still has to visit all those congressmen one at a time. Nothing beats that one-on-one relationship. So even if concentration in the utility industry was significantly greater, it would still take just as many visits.

In essence, the legislative achievements of the coal industry in 1967 were due primarily to two factors. First, the industry confronted no effective political opposition. Not only was the environmental movement not well organized, nor environmental concerns particularly salient, but equally important, Eastern coal producers confronted no opposition from other firms or industries. In principle, low sulphur coal producers, located in the West, stood to gain an increased market share if the burning of high sulphur coal by utilities was restricted. But in 1967, Western coal reserves were relatively undeveloped. They did not have a distinctive voice within the National Coal Association, nor did any other industries have a stake in their development. Moreover, both the companies that produced and burned coal had identical and clearly defined interests; the "coal coalition," and in particular its two most important components, namely utilities and coal producers, was thus completely unified. In addition, the oil industry was concerned about possible restrictions on the burning of high sulphur fuel oil and was thus an important ally.

Secondly, both the utilities and the coal industry each enjoyed considerable grass-roots political strength—though for rather different reasons. The political strength of the utilities was a function of their geographic dispersion: a significant number of congressional districts included the headquarters of a utility company. An official of the Edison Electric Institute, the trade association of the utility industry recalled:

In the mid-1960s, the utility industry was an intimate and respected part of the local community. Rates were still going down. People found it easy to relate to their local power company. We thus didn't even need to mount a national political effort during the 1960s because we enjoyed so much local grass-roots support.

This strength was particularly strong in the South, where utilities were an integral part of the local business and community power structure. And given the relative importance of Southern representatives within Congress in 1967, the industry's strength at the grass-roots level was readily translated into congressional influence. The strength of the coal industry was a function not so much of their geographic disperson as of their geographic concentration. The importance of the coal industry to the economies of the states in the Appalachian region in which it was located meant a number of representatives and senators readily identified with its welfare. Moreover, on this issue both coal operations and their employees, represented by the United Mine Workers, shared an identical interest. What made the industry's regional concentration particularly important was the pivotal position occupied by Senator Randolph of West Virginia. As chairman of the Senate Public Works Committee, of which Muskie's subcommittee was a part, he was in a uniquely favorable position to safeguard the jobs and profits of his constituents. None of the other members of the Public Works Committee, including Senator Muskie, chose to oppose his amendments, while Harley Staggers, the equally powerful chairman of the House Commerce Committee, represented a district from the coal-producing state of West Virginia. The active support of these two powerful congressmen considerably facilitated the industry's political efforts in 1967.

THE CLEAN AIR ACT AMENDMENTS OF 1970

On December 31, 1970, President Nixon signed the 1970 Clean Air Act Amendments into law. This law represents one of the toughest environmental statutes ever approved by the U.S. government or indeed any other industrialized society.[24] The 1970 legislation represented a major political defeat for one of the nation's largest and most concentrated industries, namely the automobile industry, as well as the nation's largest chemical company, DuPont. It adversely affected the financial interests of a substantial segment of the nation's industrial structure, including the coal industry, the utility industry, the chemical industry, the steel industry, the pulp and paper industry, the oil industry, and the mining industry. The only segments of the business community clearly to benefit from the legislation were the independent manufacturers of pollution control systems, particularly the Englehard Minerals and Chemicals Corporation. How had such a major decline in the political effectiveness of so many companies and industries come about in so short a time span?

A critical factor was the change in the public attitudes toward business, particularly "big business," that occurred with striking rapidity in the late 1960s. While the climate and tone of social activism and social criticism during most of the 1960s was only indirectly concerned with issues that involved or affected business, beginning in the early 1960s a steady stream of abuses on the part of specific industries and companies had begun to transform public attitudes toward the private sector. By the middle of the decade, public opinion polls had begun to report an erosion of public confidence in the people who managed large companies. In 1967, John Kenneth Galbraith published his best seller, *The New Industrial State,* which argued that big business and big government had become integral components of the same power structure, committed to the pursuit of goals inimical to those of the American public. By 1970, the issue of corporate accountability, with its explicit focus on the lack of adequate political and economic controls over the decisions of large corporations, had directly moved onto the political agenda, the subject of innumerable conferences, books, and reform proposals.[25]

This gradual and steady increase in public suspicion of big business had virtually no impact on federal clean air legislation in either 1963 or 1967. What suddenly made it politically relevant in 1970 was the sudden and dramatic increase in the public's interest in pollution control that took place between 1967 and 1970. As two students of the congressional process have noted,

The Clean Air Act of 1970 was one result of a growing interest in controlling pollution of the nation's natural resources—air, water, and land. Indeed, by the late 1960s the concern about the environment expressed for years by scientists and conservationists had spread to the general public. . . .

From the industrialized megalopolis along the Eastern seaboard from Boston to Washington, D.C., to the oil-blackened beaches of Santa Barbara, California, individual citizens were being affected and alarmed about the environmental emergency.[26]

Thus, while the *Christian Science Monitor* observed in 1967 that "national air-pollution control efforts seem caught up in a smog of political expediency thickened by public indifference," the *Monitor*'s account of the beginning of congressional deliberations in 1970 advised its readers,

"Mark the date: April 22. On that day, if the present indicators produce the expected snowballing effect, this nation will witness the largest expression of public concern in history over what is happening to the environment."[27]

The *Monitor*'s prediction proved to be an accurate one. By any standards, April 22, 1970, "Earth Day," proved to be an extraordinary political event: literally hundreds of thousands of people from throughout the United States participated in a diverse array of activities designed to express their concern about the future of the environment. As Charles Jones argues,

[Earth Day] was important not only in stimulating national public interest in the environment, but also in uncovering and publicizing the widespread activities and accomplishments in many localities. For by April 22, 1970, enough had already occurred at state and local levels to indicate to public officials, including the president, that many people were supportive of stronger legislation at all levels.[28]

Clearly, "ecology" had become a part of the political lexicon. Senator Muskie's remarks on December 18, 1970, in support of the conference report for the Clean Air Amendments that "the country was facing an air pollution crisis [with] . . . the costs of air pollution . . . counted in death, disease, and disability" reflected not so much a change in objective conditions as in the public's heightened perception of pollution as a serious problem.[29]

This change in public attitudes was reflected in the increased number and size of the environmental organizations. The membership of the Sierra Club, one of the oldest and most prominent environmental organizations, increased from 15,000 to 85,000 during the 1960s. While many environmental groups found their participation in the political process limited by the restrictions placed by the Internal Revenue Service on lobbying by groups eligible to receive tax-deductible contributions, between 1969 and 1970, two environmental organizations were established with the express purpose of influencing public policy: Friends of the Earth, formed in 1969 by the former executive director of the Sierra Club, Earl Browder, and Environmental Action, which grew out of the organization that planned Earth Day. In sharp contrast to the situation in 1963 and 1967, when environmental lobbyists played a negligible role in the congressional process, Environmental Action was active in generating support for strong antipollution legislation: "[EA] helped form a coalition favoring a tough bill, worked with several House members in sponsoring amendments to the House-passed bill, coordinated letter-writing campaigns and visits to conferees, and issued press releases."[30]

There is no necessary reason why the public's increased concern with pollution control should have developed an antibusiness focus. Indeed, many corporations welcomed Earth Day, both as a way of redirecting student energies away from antiwar radicalism and as a way of demonstrating the need for all elements of society to work together to improve the environment; some even funded Earth Day activities. Public interest in the preservation of the environment also peaked about the same time throughout Europe, and yet the environmental laws and rules adopted by various European nations did not contain the kind of adversarial stance vis-à-vis industry that underlay the legislation enacted by the U.S. Congress in 1970. The distinctiveness of the political environment with respect to pollution control issues that confronted the American business community in the 1970s lies in the superimposition of an increase in public concern with pollution on a political culture already quite suspicious of the motives, integrity, and power of the managers of large corporations. Anticipating much of the political strategy of the environmental movement, Anthony Downs wrote in 1972,

Much of the blame for pollution can be plausibly attributed to a small group of villains whose wealth and power make them excellent scapegoats. . . . Moreover, regarding air pollution, that small group actually has enough power to improve pollution seriously if it really seeks to do so. If the few leaders of the nation's top automobile manufacturing firms, power generating firms, and fuel supply firms could be persuaded to change their behavior significantly, a drastic improvement in the level of air pollution could be achieved in a relatively short time.[31]

Gladwin Hill, who covered the environment for the *New York Times* during most of the 1970s, noted a similar outlook in a piece he published in 1968. Describing the public perception of the cause of pollution, he found it dominated by the "economic giants of the steel industry, the power industry, the petroleum industry, the chemical industry, the pulp and paper industry, and many lesser enterprises."[32] Thus, while critics of the air pollution laws enacted in 1963 tended to focus on the need for a more aggressive federal stance vis-à-vis the states, the tone of public criticism of the effectiveness of the 1967 Air Quality Act was specifically directed at the intransigence of industry and its dominance of the political process.[33]

If big business in general was held to blame for pollution problems, then one industry in particular—the biggest, the most visible, and among the most concentrated—was subject to a particularly bad press: the automobile industry. Ever since GM's unsuccessful and highly embarrassing effort to intimidate Ralph Nader following the publication of his book-length exposé of auto safety efforts, the industry had been the focus of considerable "public mistrust."[34] Moreover, shortly before the debate over Clean Air Act amendments began, the automobile industry had signed a consent decree with the Department of Justice which "at least implied that the big three manufacturers had in fact illegally worked together to thwart air pollution control."[35] One scholar noted, "This incident unquestionably added to the public's impression of recalcitrance and bad faith on the part of the industry."[36] After noting that of the nation's total burden of air pollution—estimated by the U.S. Public Health Service at 133 tons—85 million tons came almost entirely from motor vehicles, Gladwin Hill concluded,

The extent to which the responsibility, if there is any such thing, for this automotive portion of the pollution laws rests upon the automobile industry, the petroleum industry, or motorists, could be argued in many ways. But in terms of political realities, rather than moral responsibility, growing public awareness of the automobile's big part in smog has tended to put the auto industry in the same uncomfortable position as if the car effluvia were coming out of the smokestacks in Detroit.[37]

During Earth Day, GM's headquarters in Manhattan were picketed by a local action group under the slogan, "GM Takes Your Breath Away," while at San Jose State College, students received considerable publicity by holding a wake for and burying a 1970 automobile. There was an additional factor at work: the state in which the public concern about air pollution was historically strongest, namely, California, was one in which the automobile industry had vritually no political influence.[38] From the perspective of the far more influential California-based utility and oil companies, having the state's pollution problems blamed on Detroit was an ideal way of deflecting public attention away from their own industrial practices. Likewise, the residents of New York City's metropolitan area, who were also particularly preoccupied about air pollution problems, had no direct stake in the economic health of the automobile industry.

Not surprisingly, the round of first hearings held to review progress under the 1967 legislation focused primarily on automobile pollution. In addition to the hearings held by the Subcommittee on Public Health and Welfare of the Interstate and Foreign Commerce Committee, Representative Leonard Farbstein of New York conducted a series of ad hoc hearings on automobile pollution in New York City. Attended by a number of members of the New York City congressional delegation, their purpose, according to Farbstein, was "to explore whether the industry is following this same course of avoiding responsibility with respect to cleaning up the dirty air we breathe, air polluted by the internal combustion engine."[39] Those testifying at the hearings included both Ralph Nader and representatives of the automobile manufacturers. The committee's report, signed by seventeen members of the New York and New Jersey Democratic delegations, concluded that the automobile was "predominantly responsible for air pollution" and recommended that strong measures be taken "to reduce and control emissions."[40]

Anxious to prevent the cause of pollution control from becoming identified with the Democratic party in general and Senator Muskie—then a front-runner for the 1972 Democratic presidential nomination—in particular, President Nixon's 1970 State of the Union message emphasized the importance of a prompt national response to the issue of environmental protection: According to the president, "Clean air, clean water, open spaces—these should once again be the birthright of every American. If we act now—they can be."[41] Reacting to substantial public criticism of the administration's record on pollution control, Nixon revealed his intention of proposing to Congress "the most comprehensive and costly program in this field in the nation's history."[42]

The president's legislative proposals, submitted to Congress on February 10, 1970, involved a substantial escalation of the federal government's role in air pollution control. They also went considerably beyond those proposed by Senator Muskie a few months earlier, thus enabling the president to emerge as the prime supporter of strong legislation. In addition to extending the 1967 Clean Air legislation for another three years, the administration's bill contained two important provisions: the first, focusing on pollution from stationary sources, gave the secretary of

HEW the power to establish national air quality standards and to supervise their administration by the states. In addition, Nixon, as had Johnson before him, proposed that the federal government be authorized to establish and enforce national emission standards for stationary sources emissions determined to "contribute substantially to endangerment of the public health or welfare."[43] With respect to mobile source pollution, the administration recommended that HEW be given the power to establish emission standards for new vehicles and engines and to regulate fuel and fuel additives as well as to set standards for fuel composition. Bills either identical to or substantially similar to the administration's were immediately introduced in the House, cosponsored by nearly 130 representatives from both parties.

In sharp contrast to the situation that prevailed in 1967, industry's political response to the 1970 Clean Air Act Amendments was neither uniform nor vigorous. There was minimal effort at interindustry coordination, and the amount of lobbying pressure brought to bear upon the bill as it worked its way through the House was rather mild. There were three reasons for the lack of intensive industry opposition to the administration's proposals. First, corporations were responding to the change in the climate of public opinion that had occurred since 1967. As an official of one large industry association told a reporter, industry is "tired of being cast in the role of the heavy."[44] An historian of the coal industry similarly noted, "In deference to the intensity of public opinion, the coal coalition did not mount a frontal assault on the proposed amendments as they had in 1967."[45] Second, many industries were finding themselves under intense political pressure at the state level; particularly with a Republican in the White House, they had a strong incentive to prefer a more active federal role. As one administrative official put it, "Industry's opposition would be less than in the past because industrial representatives had 'come around to thinking that it's cheaper and better for us to have national emission standards than to fight all these battles locally.' "[46]

Third, industrial interests, those from both stationary and mobile sources, did not view the congressional arena as particularly critical. None of the bills debated by the House of Representatives included specific standards; these would be established at some future date by executive action. However, those industrial interests that would potentially be affected by either the ambient air or emission standards felt confident that

they would enjoy substantial input into the setting of these requirements, particularly since the Nixon administration had recently established a National Industrial Pollution Control Council. The latter, formally attached to the Department of Commerce, consisted of "chief
executives of major American industries and trade associations." It
"provided a means for American industry abatement,"[47] assuring the
business community that its concerns would be carefully considered before specific regulations were promulgated.

Even the automobile industry, which President Nixon had earlier singled out as the major source of air pollution, did not actively intervene
in the deliberations of the House of Representatives. While its lobbyists
did personally visit all members of the House Interstate and Foreign
Commerce Committee, "its lobbying was not particularly intense."[48]
Testifying before the Commerce subcommittee, Paul Chenea, a GM vice-
president in charge of its research laboratories, stated, "General Motors
endorses extension of the Clean Air Act and urges that its procedures be
improved."[49] Likewise, DuPont, whose market for lead addtiives was potentially threatened by the authority over fuel composition now being
given to HEW, confined its testimony to informing the assembled Representatives that it had "developed a device called an exhaust manifold
thermal reactor," capable of "significantly reducing automotive emissions of hydrocarbons, carbon monoxide, and nitrogen, without requiring the removal of lead from gasoline."[50]

Spokesmen for the U.S. Chamber of Commerce, the major steel companies, the Manufacturing Chemists Association, and the Edison Electric
Institute all publicly indicated their support for national air quality standards, while the American Mining Congress called for an independent
study of the idea. The two trade associations that had played a particularly prominent role in the deliberations of Congress three years previously, namely the Edison Electric Institute and the National Coal Association, expressed their opposition to national air standards but indicated
they would settle for "minimal ones."[51] Only the American Petroleum
Institute, presumably reflecting the concerns of its smaller members concerned about possible restrictions on fuel additives, opposed the plan to
establish national air quality standards. With the notable exception of
DuPont, however, all industrial representatives who testified before the
House subcommittee urged Congress to deny the federal government
authority to establish emission standards.

The bill that was reported out by the House subcommittee and subsequently approved by the full House by an overwhelming margin included a provision authorizing the secretary of HEW to establish stationary source emission standards. It thus represented an important legislative defeat for a substantial segment of the American industrial community—including the steel, chemical, utilities, coal, oil refining, and mining industries—who would have preferred that the federal government confine its role to the setting of air quality standards. Nonetheless, while the bill was stronger than that favored by any interest group from the business community, most indicated that they could "live with it."

On the other hand, the House version differed from the administration bill in one important respect: over the strong opposition of the members from the New York and New Jersey congressional delegations, the committee significantly weakened the power of the secretary of HEW to control fuel standards. While Representative Farbstein of New York accused the House of "bend[ing] over backward to accommodate the auto and oil industries," in fact this provision reflected the efforts of one corporation and the congressman in whose district its headquarters were located.[52] The Ethyl Corporation, headquartered in the West Virginia district of Congressman David Satterfield, feared that any effort to regulate fuel composition would result in the banning of lead additives, a major source of earnings for the company. Because Satterfield was a member of the Subcommittee on Public Health and Welfare, he was able to exercise a significant influence over the language of the bill approved by the subcommittee. Jones writes: "What was less clear is why the committee, and subsequently the House, went along with the provision. Perhaps the principal reason was simply that this provision over others had a direct effect on a specific constituency with an aggressive spokesman."[53]

Even before the final vote by the full House, the Senate Public Works Subcommittee on Air and Water Pollution, under the chairmanship of Senator Muskie, had begun to conduct hearings. In contrast to the hearings conducted in 1967, these featured relatively little participation by industry: twenty-nine firms had testified in 1967, and only twelve either appeared or submitted statements in 1970. There was, however, substantially more representation on the part of interest groups favoring strong pollution control regulations than had been the case in 1967. Seven citizen action and professional groups, along with the AFL-CIO, testified in favor of strengthening the bill approved by the House.

It was following the formal hearings by Muskie's subcommittee, however, that the real drama of the 1970 Clean Air Act Amendments began to unfold. With the passage of the House bill, the Nixon administration had firmly established a preeminent position in the field of environmental protection. It had supported—over the objections of much of industry—a significant strengthening and broadening of the federal government's regulatory authority with respect to what was literally the most visible dimension of pollution control. At about the same time that the Nixon administration had succeeded in identifying itself with the cause of environmental protection, Senator Muskie, the Democratic party's leading presidential contender, found himself challenged from another direction. In May of 1970, Ralph Nader's Study Group Report on Air Pollution, entitled *Vanishing Air*, was released. Along with a detailed description of industry's role in effectively preventing any serious effort to address the problem of air pollution, the report included a pointed attack on Senator Muskie's role in the shaping of federal pollution control policies:

The Task Force . . . believes that Senator Muskie has failed the nation in the field of air pollution control legislation. . . . Muskie is . . . the chief architect of the disastrous Air Quality Act of 1967. That fact alone would warrant his being stripped of his title as "Mr. Pollution Control." But the senator's passivity since 1967 in the face of an ever worsening air polluton crisis compounds his earlier failure.[54]

The report added, "perhaps the senator should consider resigning his chairmanship of the subcommittee and leave the post to someone who can devote more time and energy to the task."[55] The report's criticisms of Muskie received widespread press coverage. While Muskie accused the report's authors of "distort[ing] the story of air pollution control legislation and my role in drafting it," there can be no question that it had its intended effect: Muskie was "put . . . in the position of having to do something extraordinary in order to recapture his leadership."[56]

Meeting in executive session, Muskie persuaded the other members of his subcommittee to endorse unanimously a bill significantly stronger than that approved by the House of Representatives. The subcommittee's chairman's principal innovation was to reduce substantially the amount of discretion available to the executive branch in enforcing clean air requirements. His revised bill included strict legislative deadlines for pollution abatement as well as for meeting stationary source emission standards. Its most controversial provision, however, was addressed to the problem of automotive emissions: the bill required that vehicular emissions of hydrocarbons and carbon monoxide be reduced by 90 percent by 1975, with a similar reduction in nitrogen oxide to take place a year later.

The subcommittee's report came as a total surprise to the industries affected by it. Neither the House nor the Senate hearings had given the business community any indication that such a significant escalation of the federal government's regulatory role was actually on the political agenda. An intense lobbying effort was immediately launched to weaken the bill before it was reported out by the full Senate Public Works Committee. A number of trade associations, including the National Lead Association, the American Petroleum Institute, the Manufacturing Chemists Association, the Automobile Manufacturers Association, and the Coal Policy Conference, as well as individual corporations including Standard Oil of Indiana, the Sun Oil Company, the National Steel Corporation, and the Union Carbide Corporation, either attempted to meet with members of the committee and subcommittee staffs or testified before the full committee. Not surprisingly, the four individual automobile manufacturers played the most active role. Between August 21 and September 17, General Motors, Ford, Chrysler, and American Motors launched a highly coordinated and intensive effort aimed at persuading the Senate Public Works Committee that, in the words of GM President Cole, "[We] do not have the technological capability to make 1975 production vehicles that would achieve emission levels the legislation requires."[57] The presidents of the three largest manufacturers along with the vice-president of American Motors, met with Senator Muskie on August 25, while each of the other fourteen members of the committee were "assigned" to one of the four companies in the industry. In addition, frequent strategy sessions were held among the companies' Washington representatives.

In spite of these efforts, the committee made no substantive changes in the subcommittee's stationary source requirements and only two changes in its rules affecting automotive emissions. By a ten to three vote the full committee voted to allow the Environmental Protection Agency the right to grant the auto industry a single one-year extension of the 1975 and 1976 deadlines. It also included a provision providing for judicial review of the secretary's decisions on extensions. The bill was then unanimously approved by the full committee.

Needless to say, the debate in the Senate focused primarily on the issue of the deadline for the reduction of automobile emissions. Muskie, the bill's floor manager, told his fellow senators, "Detroit has told the nation that Americans cannot live without the automobile. This legislation would tell Detroit that if this is the case, then they must make an automobile with which Americans can live."[58] Muskie publicly conceded that no hearings had been held on the issue of whether or not the automobile industry actually had the ability to meet the deadlines contained in the committee bill. He insisted that "the deadline is based not . . . on economic and technological feasibility, but on considerations of public health."[59] Senator Griffin of Detroit, after noting the importance of the automobile industry to the nation's economy, replied, "The bill holds a gun at the head of the American automobile industry in a very dangerous game of economic roulette."[60] After rejecting a number of amendments aimed at softening, though not eliminating, the 1975 deadline, the Senate approved the bill by a seventy-three to two vote.

Those interested in weakening the Senate bill then focused their attention of the House–Senate Conference Committee. The "conference was subjected to considerable pressure" on the part of industry, acting both indirectly through the administration, which strongly opposed the establishment of specific deadlines for both mobile and stationary source emissions, and directly through the various House conferees.[61] While both industry and the administration lobbied in favor of the House version, the role of the environmental movement was relatively passive: their lobbyists could only hope that Muskie would "hold the line" on behalf of the much stronger Senate version against the "heavy pressure from special interest groups."[62] After an unusually large number of extremely lengthy negotiations, agreement was finally reached on December 16. The bill finally adopted by the conference committee made relatively few concessions to either industry or the administration. With respect to automotive emissions, it agreed to grant the auto manufacturers an extra year in which to apply for an extension of the 1975 deadline and to limit automobile antipollution requirements to five years, or 50,000 miles, whichever came first, rather than the life of the car. It also agreed to some modification of the provisions governing warranties that were strongly desired by the independent manufacturers of auto parts.

The conference, however, ignored the requests of the oil industry and the manufacturers of lead additives for some modification of regulations affecting fuel composition: the government was granted the power to "control or prohibit fuels or fuel additives which harm public health or welfare or impair a device or system to control emissions."[63] It also retained a number of provisions with considerable potential for adversely affecting the interests of stationary sources of pollution. These included a requirement that the EPA promulgate national ambient air quality standards "for each air pollutant for which air quality criteria had been issued" based on "such criteria and allowing an adequate margin of safety . . . requisite to protect public health." (These became known as "primary air quality standards.")[64] The cumulative effect of various other provisions effectively established the preeminence of federal authority in air pollution control. The conference report was adopted by voice vote by both houses the day after it was formally issued and signed into law by President Nixon a few days later.

In analyzing the legislative outcome that took place in 1970, it is useful to distinguish between the defeat suffered by a large cross-section of American industry and that experienced by the automobile industry. The former was essentially a function of three factors. First, the opposition of companies to the 1970 amendments was weakened by the extent to which lobbying against a strong bill was dominated by large corporations. For their part, the automobile manufacturers made no attempt to mobilize or involve their independent dealers. Lobbying on the issue of fuel additives was led by the America Petroleum Institute. Neither the Independent Petroleum Association of America nor the National Petroleum Refiners Association, both of whose membership consisted of numerous small refiners who stood to be disproportionately hurt by restrictions on the use of leaded gasoline, played any role in the legislative deliberations. With the exception of the Ethyl Corporation, the companies who testified at both the House and Senate hearings tended to be relatively large. Thus, although the Senate committee explicitly indicated that it had determined that "existing sources of pollution either should meet the standards of the law or be closed down," it was obvious that none of the companies that represented stationary sources who testified at either set of hearings were themselves in danger of being forced out of business.[65]

The interests of those who were in such danger were, at best, represented only indirectly through the rather ineffectual lobbying efforts of the U.S. Chamber of Commerce and the National Association of Manufacturers. That Congress might conceivably have responded to the economic concerns of relatively smaller enterprises is suggested by the success of the Ethyl Corporation—in marked contrast to DuPont—in directly influencing the decision of a congressional committee. But Ethyl was unable to put together a coalition of firms with a similar stake in public policy affecting fuel composition. It counted on the influence of Congressman Satterfield, and when he failed to secure a place on the conference committee, it no longer had any meaningful political access.

Secondly, in sharp contrast to 1967, the interests of industry were divided. While the degree of interindustry conflict was considerably less than it would be in 1977—only Englehard Minerals, which stood to benefit from the production of catalytic converters, actually lobbied for strict regulations—the inability of industry to come up with a unified position certainly proved a political handicap. The most obvious division was between those companies concerned with stationary source pollution sources and those concerned with mobile emissions. Each pursued its political strategy completely independent of the others. Unlike in 1977, when the Business Roundtable was available at least to attempt to formulate a series of political positions that reflected the common interests of many larger companies, in 1970 the only interindustry organizations were the U.S. Chamber of Commerce and the National Association of Manufacturers; however, they confined their attention to the regulations affecting stationary sources. The National Industrial Pollution Control Council was in a position to represent the interests of a broad cross-section of major companies, but its status in the executive branch made it ill equipped to play a role in coordinating the lobbying efforts of business in Congress. Instead, business relied upon the lobbying activities of the administration.

What also made coordination more difficult was that differences also emerged among particular industries. Thus, while the Chamber "sponsored several meetings in its offices with representatives of companies and industry associations in an effort to develop common positions and legislative language,"[66] the industry that had spearheaded the fight against national emission standards in 1967, namely the coal industry, declined to commit its resources in opposition to the conference report. Joseph Mullan, who had directed the successful lobbying effort of the National Coal Association three years earlier, was afraid that if there was no bill in 1970 his industry might confront an even tougher one the following year. Shortly before the conference agreement, he suggested, "If we were given our druthers right this minute, we'd just as soon see a clean air bill came out."[67] He added, somewhat inaccurately, that the coal industry would not actively work with other industrial groups to maintain the House version because, "When there was hell to pay on S.O2 (in 1967) nobody came to help us." Mullan predicted, equally inaccurately, "They're big boys—they can take care of themselves."

The attempt to impose restrictions on fuel composition was also facilitated by interindustry differences, in this case between the oil and automobile industries. Early in 1970, it had become clear to those companies with a financial stake in gasoline production that a move was underway in Congress to ban lead additives. At an emergency session of the National Petroleum Refiners Association, on April 15, 1970, more than 500 members crowded into the San Antonio Convention Center to hear speakers from DuPont, Ethyl, Mobil, and Union Oil of California assert that "there are various ways of meeting the probable standards [for automobile emissions] without a prohibition on the use of organic-lead antiknock additives—a ban that could have great impact on the chemical industry."[68] A few months later the Ethyl Corporation called a press conference in New York to "tell our story in an orderly way."[69]

However, even as the major factors of lead additives and segments of the refining industry were seeking to resist being "stampeded into a costly program to produce and market nonleaded gasoline," their position was being undercut from two directions. First, in April of 1970, two major oil companies, Shell and Atlantic Richfield, announced their intention of marketing unleaded regular gasoline as a third grade, by the fall of 1970, regardless of its cost. The *National Petroleum News* wrote in 1970:

Seldom in oil industry history has such an important issue exploded so quickly. In the space of about a month, the industry found itself gearing up for a revolution that would affect every phase of its business. One by one companies stepped forward and said they were "prepared" to go unleaded—when in fact, some observers claimed, most weren't ready at all.[70]

More importantly, the automobile industry's future plans to reduce automobile emissions—unveiled even before Congress began to address itself seriously to the problem of automobile emissions—called for the use of either nonleaded or low-lead gasoline. It thus appeared that lead was likely to be banned anyway—by the marketplace if not by Congress. Peter Gammergard, the senior vice-president for environmental affairs at API, asked rhetorically: "How can we argue with Detroit? If I were running an oil company, and I got the word out of Detroit that their cars won't run on leaded gas, I'm going to make at least one grade of nonleaded gasoline."[71] Lawrence Blanchard, executive vice-president of Ethyl Corporation, was more bitter. He charged that General Motors "symbolically placed its sins in Ethyl's head."[72] A reporter for the *National Journal* summarized the whole dispute in the following terms: "With the automobile companies pointing to additives produced by the oil companies and the oil companies pointing to tailpipe emissions, each industry seemed to be trying to shift some blame to the other instead of working together against the bill."[73]

A third factor that weakened the overall influence of industry on the 1970 Clean Air Act Amendments was that the legislation that emerged from the Senate took business by surprise. The *National Journal* reported: "Senate action on the complex, one hundred-page bill was so swift that corporate interests had little opportunity to react before it was passed."[74] The director of air pollution control for the National Coal Association remarked, "The bill that came out of the Senate was not the bill that anybody had testified to."[75] When various staff members of Muskie's subcommittee met with industry representatives on August 21 to inform them of the committee's intention to report a bill requiring 90 percent reduction of various emissions by 1975, the meeting was, in the words of Leon Billings, "a little tense."[76] Industry representatives reported it was their first inkling that the 1970 amendments might contain the 90 percent provision. While environmentalists were equally surprised by the action of the Muskie subcommittee, their inability to mobilize sufficient resources to enter into the fray was not critical; all they required to triumph was for Muskie and the Senate conferees to hold firm.

Yet if one analyzes the impact of the 1970 amendments on business as a whole, it is clear that one industry suffered a far more substantial legislative defeat than all the rest. The only industry whose pollutants were actually mentioned by name in the statute and for whom percentage reductions in emission levels were specifically itemized was, of course, the automobile industry. Stationary sources of pollution had deadlines, but no numbers; the latter were left to be determined administratively.

From one perspective, the size of the automobile companies did not appear to affect their political effectiveness; after all, the industry was just as concentrated throughout the 1950s and 1960s and yet it was able to resist successfully several congressional efforts to restrict automobile emissions below a level that the industry regarded as technically feasible.[77] But as our account of the political atmosphere surrounding the 1970 amendments suggests, the industry's degree of concentration appeared to have been a political factor in 1970: it made it far more vulnerable. Given a climate of public hostility against "big business," it is not surprising that the nation's biggest industry, dominated by the nation's largest industrial corporation, became singled out for particular congressional scrutiny.

Moreover, both the modesty and ineffectiveness of the major automobile companies' lobbying appear also to have been affected by the structure of their industry. Thus, in part because of the fear of antitrust action, GM had traditionally attempted to keep a very low profile: the world's largest industrial corporation actually had no Washington office until 1969. One Michigan congressman observed in 1970:

GM probably has the worst lobby on Capitol Hill. It ranks at the bottom in terms of effectiveness. Its Washington operation is the most inept and ineffectual I've seen here.

It's not the fault of the guys in the Washington office. It's just that management has this disdain for relations in Washington. . . . GM is constantly getting hit in the back of the head because they don't pay enough attention to Washington. They get more bad surprises than any other major firm in Washington.[78]

Another added:

They send a guy up here to talk to a committee chairman or a member, thinking that is the best way to do it. It isn't. A call from the district from someone you know who will be affected by a bill is far more effective.[79]

A congressional staff member voiced a similar observation: "GM's lobbying effort in 1970 was among the most inept I have ever seen. They had no idea how to relate to Congress." Clearly, as the largest and most visible part of the automobile industry, GM's negative reputation among congressmen and congressional staff clearly weakened the overall political position of the industry.

Finally, the automobile industry, far more than any other, appeared to suffer from a significant credibility gap. The industry's arguments as to the economic and technological problems associated with rapidly reducing automobile emissions were convincing to neither the general public nor its elected representatives. One of GM's lobbyists told the *National Journal* that "the atmosphere [in the Senate] was such that offering amendments appeared hopeless." He added, "We did nothing about the bill in the full Senate. I wouldn't think of asking anybody to vote against that bill."[80] The head of GM's lobby noted, "No matter how reasonable our arguments are, we always come out looking like we are against motherhood."[81] Leon Billings typified the industry's credibility problem, when he noted, "The industry's statement before this committee as to what they are capable of doing, and their performance in California in claiming that the state standards could not be met, have made us skeptical of what they say."[82]

THE 1977 CLEAN AIR ACT AMENDMENTS

On August 7, 1977, President Carter signed into law the Clean Air Act Amendments of 1977. The most aggressively lobbied and probably among the most complex pieces of legislation approved by Congress in at least a quarter of a century, the 1977 amendments represented the culmination of more than three years of extremely intense political struggle. By the mid-1970s, the enormous stakes involved in federal regulation of air pollution had become much more apparent than they were at the beginning of the decade. For the environmentalists and their allies, the legislative struggle over the revision of the 1970 act represented their most important political challenge since the reemergence of the environment as a political issue in the late 1960s. For the companies regulated under the provisions of 1970 legislation, the 1977 amendments represented their first important opportunity to modify those particular aspects of the 1970 law, and its interpretation by EPA and the courts, that they regarded as unreasonable.

Because of the complexity of the 1977 amendments, my analysis of them is organized by issue areas rather than chronologically. The first section will discuss the conflicts over the regulation of mobile pollution sources, including that of automobile emission standards, warrantee provisions for pollution control equipment, and federal restrictions on automobile usage. The next part will analyze the disputes over the regulation of stationary sources of pollution, focusing specifically on three issues: the prevention of significant deterioration (commonly referred to as either PSD or NSD, no significant deterioration), the exemption for nonferrous smelters, and restrictions on the burning of high sulphur coal.

Mobile Pollution Sources

As in 1970, the most intense and extensive political conflict over the Clean Air Act Amendments of 1977 revolved around the issue of automobile emission standards. A series of postponements—two granted by the Environmental Protection Agency and one extended by Congress as a response to the Arab oil embargo of 1973—had given the automobile manufacturers until the 1978 model year to meet the emission standards specified by the Clean Air Act of 1970. While the cars produced by the mid-1970s emitted significantly fewer pollutants than those manufactured at the beginning of the decade, as early as 1975 the automobile manufacturers became convinced that they lacked the technology to meet the 1978 deadline—particularly its nitrogen oxide standards. As Dr. Fred Bowditch, GM's senior executive responsible for emissions control, noted, "Anything is possible in the technical community given enough time and money. What we are saying is that we don't know how to do it right now."[83] As a result, unless Congress approved legislation that either delayed or reduced the emission standards it has established in 1970, the industry would find itself unable to begin production in 1977 of its cars for the 1978 model year.

Following a lengthy series of markup sessions, on February 5, 1976, the Senate Public Works Committee granted the automobile industry an initial if modest concession. Responding to the public's heightened interest in fuel economy following the 1973 OPEC price increase, the committee voted in favor of postponing the final auto emissions standards for carbon monoxide and hydrocarbons until 1979–while relaxing the final standard for nitrogen oxides altogether. Although Senator Muskie had opposed this provision when it had previously come before his subcommittee, he nonetheless indicated his general support for the legislation, regarding it as a reasonable compromise. However, in order to encourage the industry to continue to endeavor to upgrade its technology, the bill also required the major manufacturers—excluding American Motors and some small importers—to meet all three standards on at least 10 percent of their total output. After rejecting several amendments designed either to strengthen or to weaken the auto emission standards, the bill was approved by the Senate by a vote of seventy-eight to thirteen.

Dissatisfied with this compromise, the automobile industry decided to focus its lobbying efforts on the House of Representatives. Even after the House Interstate and Foreign Commerce Committee had voted to extend the final emission standards beyond those agreed to by the Senate, the industry launched a major effort to further amend the bill when it reached the floor of the House. Congressman John Dingell of Michigan, whose district is not only a major producer of automobiles but also includes the corporate headquarters of the Ford Motor Company, and James Broyhill of North Carolina offered a floor amendment. It would not only have postponed the final emission standards until 1982 but, equally important, would have eliminated the nitrogen oxide standard from the statute entirely, leaving it to be determined by EPA. Dingell argued that his amendment would "save fuel, reduce consumer costs, promote economic recovery, and reduce unemployment in the automobile and related supplier/service industries."[84] One of his supporters, Marvin Esch, also of Michigan, contended, "[It] is designed to give predictability to the automobile industry, and quite frankly, that means jobs."[85] The Dingell–Broyhill amendment which, according to one reporter, "gave the industry virtually everything it wanted," passed the House by a vote of 224 to 169.[86] The automobile industry thus had its first important legislative victory on the issue of air pollution in nearly a decade.

The industry's victory on the House floor, however, proved short-lived. The Senate conferees refused to compromise on the issue of automobile emissions deadlines, and the bill reported out of the House–Senate conference committee more closely reflected the Senate version. Now faced with the prospect of a relatively stringent bill, the industry reversed its call for the urgent reform of clean air regulations and announced that it preferred no bill to the one approved by the conference committee. Thanks to a filibuster on an unrelated issue, Congress adjourned without approving new clean air legislation. The industry's lobbyists were pleased with the outcome. For what they had done was to raise the stakes significantly: now unless Congress acted shortly after its return to revise or delay the requirements of the 1970 act, Detroit would be forced to stop producing automobiles in the fall of 1977, an eventuality that Congress presumably would be unwilling to countenance. Muskie was understandably bitter. Pointing to a Senate gallery filled with lobbyists, he warned: "If they think they can come back in the early months of next. year and get a quick fix from the Senate to make them legal, they better take a lot of long careful thoughts about it."[87] Equally defiant, the president of General Motors declared to a wire service reporter: "They can close down the plants. They can get someone in jail—maybe me. But we're going to make [1978] cars to 1977 standards."[88]

When Congress returned in 1977, the pattern of conflict appeared to repeat itself. Once again Dingell and Broyhill offered an amendment to the bill on the floor of the House of Representatives, only now their amendment included a provision eliminating the original statutory standards for both carbon monoxide and nitrogen oxide. Following an extremely close vote in which the House defeated a compromise offered by the Carter administration, the Dingell–Broyhill amendment was adopted, 255 to 139. And again, the automobile industry was rebuffed in the Senate. While a compromise measure, approved on June 9, both gave the industry until 1980 to meet federal emission standards and somewhat reduced the original nitrogen oxide requirement, it represented a setback for the automobile manufacturers in two important respects. First, it required the industry to reduce nitrogen oxide emissions two years earlier than it would have preferred, and second, it maintained the original emission standards for carbon monoxide. After a prolonged and exhausting series of meetings between the House and Senate conferees—the final session lasted until after two in the morning—a compromise was reached. The final bill was closer to the Senate than the House version, but the Senate conferees were considerably more conciliatory than they had been in 1976. Their most important concession was to accept a smaller reduction in two out of the three major automobile pollutants for cars produced for the 1980 model year than was specified in the Senate version of the bill. The conference report was adopted by voice votes of both Houses two months later.

The automobile industry thus secured a major legislative vicotry in 1977: they won sufficient modifications in the 1970 statute to enable them to continue producing "legal" automobiles for the next five years. The extent of their impact on the 1977 amendments is particularly striking when it is contrasted to both their role in the shaping of federal air pollution legislation in 1970 as well as to the setbacks experienced by most other major industries in 1977 law. In terms of both these comparisons, the lobbying efforts of the automobile industry in 1977 must be judged extremely effective. A comparison of the success of the automobile industry with that of other major business lobbying groups in 1977 must await a discussion of the other provisions of the 1977, Clean Air Act amendments. For now it is instructive to compare the performance of the industry in 1970 and 1977. Why did it do so much better in 1977?

The explanation has little to do with the effectiveness of the lobbying efforts of the automobile companies themselves. Although it is certainly true that the automobile companies, like many large American corporations, substantially upgraded the size and budget of their Washington offices between 1970 and 1977, these changes appear to have had little political impact. The industry still faced a serious credibility problem. As Bernard Asbell wrote in 1976, "The auto lobby's biggest problem is that virtually nobody on the [Senate] Environmental Pollution Subcommittee believes them."[89] Muskie continued to view the automobile companies as "stonewalling" while his principal staff assistant, Leon Billings, characterized General Motors as "arrogant."[90] Senator James A. McClure, a conservative Republican senator from Idaho, informed one reporter in the midst of the debate over the 1977 amendments,

The thing that impressed me is that the auto company reps stationed here are so inept. The low-level staff people they send in from Detroit to work with our staff people are very competent. They're not lobbyists but technical people.

Occasionally the company hierarchies—their presidents and vice-presidents—fly in to see us, and they start reinventing the wheel. They want to tell us from the beginning what their problem is. It's a terribly wasteful exercise. They sound like they've never heard of the problem before, like they've just memorized somebody's briefing, and they assume we've never heard of it before.[91]

Nor can the changes in public policy concerning automobile emission between 1970 and 1977 be ascribed to changes in the climate of public opinion. It is true that passage of the Energy Supply and Environmental Coordination Act of 1974, which delayed the achievement of motor vehicle emission standards by two years, was a direct response to the "energy crisis" that had materialized so suddenly in the fall of 1973. But notwithstanding the rhetoric of the Carter administration, the sense of public urgency over the need to reduce energy consumption appears to have substantially diminished by the time Congress began seriously considering amendments to the 1970 Clean Air Act. To be sure, as Senator Domenici put it, the "sunny legislative atmosphere" that surrounded the passage of the 1970 legislation had, thanks to the combination of 9 percent unemployment and double-digit inflation, became "decidedly gloomier" by 1975.[92] But the fact is that, on balance, the 1977 amendments maintained relatively strict pollution control requirements for most industrial sources of pollution; the overall burdens it placed on industry as a whole were, if anything, more severe than they had been in 1970.

Rather, the key to the relative responsiveness of the Congress to the arguments of the automobile manufacturers was the alliances they were able to form with other interest groups. In a sense, the automobile industry in 1977, like the coal industry a decade earlier, was able to mobilize a broad coalition of powerful interest groups whose interests in weakening auto emission standards either were identical with or complemented their own. However, unlike in the case of the "coal coalition" of 1967, the "automobile coalition" of 1977 did not consist of businesses that were actually parts of the automobile industry itself.

The most important reason for the increased political effectiveness of the automobile industry was that in 1977, unlike in 1970, the manufacturers had the full support of the United Automobile Workers. As Billings put it, "The auto companies never got to first base in persuading Congress to relax auto emission standards until they got the support of the UAW on the issue of jobs. The UAW has got a credibility up here that the auto companies don't."[93] Another supporter of strict pollution controls asked rhetorically, "What are you going to do when you have Henry Ford and Leonard Woodcock on the same side?"[94] According to Congressional Quarterly, "Virtually all observers of the battle agreed that a union—the United Auto Workers—was the key group in the clean air lobbying fight."[95] A lobbyist from another industry recalled: "The auto companies' success in 1977 was due to one key factor: they employ so many God-damned people."

In 1970, the UAW and six major conservation groups had publicly called for the "creation of air pollution guidelines so harsh that they would banish the internal combustion engine from the automobile within five years,"[96] while the AFL-CIO had publicly opposed industry efforts to weaken the Muskie bill. However, in 1974 the UAW began to shift its position. After commissioning an independent technical study designed to sort out the conflicting contentions of Muskie and their employers, the union announced its support for a five-year pause in emission standards—provided that the industry continued to work to develop the technology that would eventually allow clean air goals to be met.

The proposal was significant for what it was saying to the American people—that the powerful UAW, in the forefront among unions on most environmental issues, felt industry deserved a break if it would only show strong good faith in moving toward the ultimate goals of the Clean Air Act.[97]

In spite of the fact that Leonard Woodcock, a strong supporter of Carter, had been nominated by the administration to be the U.S. envoy to the People's Republic of China about the same time that Congress was moving toward final passage of the 1977 amendments, Woodcock made it clear that, on this issue, he strongly dissented from the position of the administration. He told a reporter on May 25, "I sent word to the White House that if this position was a problem for them, then to forget about my being an envoy. . . . There was no question of my changing my position."[98]

In contrast to 1970, when the UAW's support for the Clean Air Act had been relatively perfunctory, their opposition to strict automobile emission standards in 1977 was extremely aggressive It was Woodcock and the UAW staff experts who originally sat down with Congressman Dingell to develop the specific provisions of the Dingell–Broyhill amendment; the automobile manufacturers, each of whom had earlier publicly advocated even weaker standards, eventually supported Dingell–Broyhill because, in the words of UAW lobbyist Howard Paster, "The companies had nowhere else to go."[99] Imitating political tactics that public interest groups had earlier employed so successfully, the UAW, working through its headquarters in Detroit, communicated its position on emission standards to forty Community Action Program councils. These councils in turn contacted every one of the union's 1.5 million members urging them either to write to or personally contact their senators and representatives. Booklets were distributed to union members with the message: "Congress must be told *quickly* that your job is at stake. . . . Tell Congress you are supporting [the Dingell—Broyhill amendments] because your future depends on protecting air quality without disrupting jobs."[100] In addition, Paster personally contacted large numbers of people on the Commerce Committee, and during the week of May 23, ten union officials from throughout the country spent two days personally lobbying on Capitol Hill.

The automobile companies also received considerable support from two groups of small businessmen whose economic interests paralleled their own. Senator Peter Domenici of New Mexico, a member of the Senate Environment and Public Works Committee, after describing the entire conflict as "a bloody two-year brawl,"[101] observed,

The toughest vote I have made in the U.S. Senate was on the issue of auto standards. For years, despite their importance to the economy, the automakers had been comparatively easy for the Congress to handle because their base of operations was in Detroit, Michigan, and Michigan has only two senators. There are 98 other ones. The mathematics was relatively easy. Since 1970, however, automakers have begun to diversify plant sites. They now are scattered throughout the country. Yet again, the math does not make them winners. . . .

But by 1975, the automakers had figured something out: Every state in the country has automobile dealers and these dealers have employees. Every state in the country has gasoline stations and they have employees. Every state in the country has automobile parts stores and they have employees. In fact, large segments of each state's economy is based on the health, care, and feeding of the automobile. Most importantly the more rural a state (and thus previously the more immune their representatives to Detroit's pleas), the more they relied on the automobile in their local economy. Accordingly, the auto industry mounted a massive grass-roots campaign.

It realized that most representatives will meet with groups of concerned constituents. And that it is very, very tough, in fact painful, for an elected representative to have to tell so many people no.[102]

Two trade associations developed a particularly close working relationship with the UAW and the automobile manufacturers. One was the National Automobile Dealers Association. One of the largest and oldest trade associations, by the mid-1970s it had 2,000 members and eight full-time Washington lobbyists. Although, like the UAW, the interests of its members and those of the auto manufacturers were frequently in conflict, on this issue they were identical: both were opposed to any public policy that threatened to reduce the volume of automobile sales. Not at all active in the deliberations over the 1970 amendments—in part because of the lack of advance warning of congressional intentions— they were well prepared when the Clean Air Act came up for renewal in 1976. In both 1976 and 1977, NADA sent separate letters to each of its 21,000 dealer members, urging them to make personal contact with their representatives in Washington. This strategy appeared to work quite effectively. As one of their lawyers put it:

Dealers are very effective lobbyists. They are important members of the local community. They serve on hospital boards, lead charity drives. Many are active in local politics and know their congressman by their first name. They tend to be outgoing, friendly. They're salesmen. So it's not surprising that they do a good job.[103]

Asbell comments:

The corridors of the House office buildings were as alive with local franchise dealers as if new models were being shown there. In a congressional district, an auto dealer is often a community leader and quite likely to be among a congressman's leading campaign contributors. A congressman from Kentucky, and who couldn't care less about the concern of the Detroit Economic Club, heeds the songs of his local Dodge Boys.[104]

Asked to account for the unexpected passage of the Dingell–Broyhill amendment during 1976, a lobbyist for the Friends of the Earth summarized his side's defeat in one word, "Dealers."[105]

The second trade association to join the ad hoc "auto coalition" was the Automobile Service Industry Association, an organization representing the 7,000 firms that manufactured and distributed automobile parts. In 1970, Congress had included in the Clean Air Act a provision requiring that automobile manufacturers guarantee the performance of pollution control systems on new cars for five years or 50,000 miles. The EPA had never implemented this part of the statute because of its failure to develop an adequate "in-use" test. But by the mid-1970s it had begun to draft regulations in anticipation of such a test. Independent part stations, repair shops, and parts dealers feared that the enforcement of this provision would seriously hurt their business, since the auto manufacturers—in order to protect themselves from legal liability—would henceforth require that the servicing and replacement of auto emissions parts be done exclusively by their dealers. Richard Turner, a lobbyist in the law firm of Courtney and McCamant, which represented ASIA, feared that the maintenance of this provision would wipe out the after-market parts industry.

While the warranty issue was regarded by many as a side issue, in 1976 ASIA, working essentially alone, waged an "intense lobbying campaign."[106] A Senate aide recalled that the service industry had "brought in gas station operations from every corner of the senator's state," while a House staff member estimated that 40 percent of the mail received by Congress on the Clean Air Act in 1976 concerned warranties.[107] On the floor of the Senate, an amendment was offered by Senator Lloyd Bentsen of Texas that would have reduced the warranty period to eighteen months or 18,000 miles. Bentsen argued that maintaining the original warranty requirement would "sharply restrict the car owner's service options; freeze tens of thousands of small, independent parts manufacturers, distributors, and service stations out of routine auto service work; and result in only a further concentration within the automobile industry."[108] Muskie opposed the amendment, contending that the longer warranty period was necessary to "make the manufacturer stick to his commitment" on pollution controls.[109] Bentsen's amendment failed by an extremely close vote: forty-five to fifty-one. However, immediately following its defeat, the Senate unanimously agreed to a compromise proposal by Senator Baker that "assured car owners that they could have maintenance and repair work done by anyone—including independent garages—without losing their warranty rights."[110] Like the car manufacturers, ASIA found the House considerably more sympathetic. Responding to fears that an extended warranty period would allow the major auto companies to monopolize the replacement parts and service business, the House voted to reduce the warranty term to eighteen months or 18,000 miles. Unlike the car manufacturers, however, ASIA emerged from the 1976 conference negotiations with its victory in the House of Representatives largely intact: the Senate conferees agreed to delay the enforcement of the original warranty until after the next three model years—unless overruled by the Congress. The legislation adopted by the conference committee also directed the FTC to undertake a study of the longer warranty's effect on competition.

Following the annulment of their 1976 legislative victory by the Senate fillibuster, ASIA decided to cooperate more closely with the automobile manufacturers in 1977. Thus, the Dingell–Broyhill amendment offered on the floor of the House in 1977 included a provision on car warranties that met the needs of both the automobile manufacturers and the after-parts dealers and suppliers. In addition to reducing the warranty period to eighteen months or 18,000 miles, it required the manufacturers to replace properly maintained, emission-related parts only if the owner could prove that they were defective at the time the car was sold. It also eliminated a provision from the bill reported by the House Commerce Committee that would have required the EPA to conduct production-line tests of new models. To demonstrate support for his amendment, Broyhill placed in the *Congressional Record* a list of more than one hundred business associations who supported his position on car warranties. A Senate committee staff member noted, "ASIA waged a very powerful big grass-roots effort. They had had a task force in every district. Overall, they were both very skillful and very effective." Both the Motor Vehicle Manufacturers Association and ASIA worked together to promote passage of the Dingell–Broyhill amendment. Turner, ASIA's lobbyist recalled, "In 1976, I fought alone. In 1977 . . . many of our interests were similar. They brought some votes to me that I wouldn't have had, and I brought some votes to them they certainly wouldn't have had."[111] As a House staff committee member closely involved in the deliberations over the 1976–1977 amendments put it, "The auto dealers and suppliers made a big difference in 1977. They helped a hell of a lot."

ASIA did less well in the Senate, where the provisions they favored were viewed as anticonsumer. The final version of the 1977 amendments to the Clean Air Act was closer to the House than to the Senate version: the automobile companies were required to guarantee that emission standards would be met for twenty-four months or 24,000 miles, with a limited performance warranty in effect thereafter. While these provisions met the industry's most vociferous objections, ASIA nonetheless was disappointed by the final legislative outcome. One congressional aide put it, "Given what they were up against, they probably did as well as they could have." On balance, they appeared to have been more successful in assisting the automobile manufacturers than in achieving their own specific legislative objectives.

What do the different political experiences of the automobile industry in 1970 and 1977 reveal about the impact of the large corporation on the political process? Most obviously, the industry's degree of concentration cannot be directly correlated with its political effectiveness: the size of the average firm in the industry did not change significantly between 1970 and 1977. Yet at the same time there is an important sense in which its domination by a relatively few, unusually large firms was politically relevant. Its concentration made it both a tempting target for those strongly committed to improving air quality in 1970 and an obstacle for those who wanted to maintain this commitment in 1977. Given a situation in which a relatively large number of individuals are employed by a relatively few companies, it becomes extremely difficult for the government to enact public policies whose effect would be to force any one of them out of business. Thus, Leon Billings noted in January 1977,

Right now the Congress has only a "nuclear" deterrent—the power to block car sales altogether—which Detroit knows we can't use. As a result we have a situation in which Detroit is challenging the credibility of the Congress as an institution. Firms like General Motors and suppliers like United States Steel are so big they think they are above Congress and can force it to change. So far, they've been right.[112]

Analyzing the problem of regulating an industry composed of only a few, relatively large companies in *The Public Interest,* Lawrence White described what he termed "the fewness problem" in somewhat more academic terms:

There are only four domestic automobile manufacturers, three of which are among the largest seven manufacturing companies in the nation. (A large truck manufacturer, International Harvester, also comes under the law due to its manufacture of large station wagons). If one meat packer out of 2,500 had to close down because it could not meet government sanitation standards, few outside a handful of workers and owners would be affected. But if one or more of the four automobile firms . . . were required to shut down, the structural consequences for the industry, and the employment consequences for the economy as a whole, would be quite serious indeed.[113]

There is considerable evidence to support White's contention. For example, several firms in the steel foundry industry, consisting of a large number of relatively small companies, were actually driven out of business by the 1970 Clean Air Act. Yet this industry secured absolutely no relief in 1977. On the other hand, precisely because the automobile industry was already dominated by a relatively few, large companies, Congress was extremely reluctant to mandate the enforcement of any regulations that would have had the effect of reducing the degree of competition still further. Thus the Senate, without any objection from Senator Muskie, overwhelmingly approved an amendment to the 1977 legislation that established a temporary delayed compliance schedule for automobile manufacturers producing less than 300,000 annually that were dependent on emission technology produced by other manufacturers. Its purpose was explicitly designed to help American Motors. In addition, a provision of the 1977 legislation specifically reduced standards on lead levels in gasoline produced by small refineries, thus enabling them to maintain their competitive position vis-à-vis the larger integrated oil companies.

On the other hand, one of the most politically successful industries in 1977 had a market structure that could not contrast more sharply to that of either the automobile or oil industry: these were the group of firms involved in the construction and operation of shopping centers. Their objective was to make certain that as great a share as possible of the burden of meeting national air quality standards took place via the reduction of automobile emissions rather than through restrictions on land use and automobile usage. Accordingly, they wanted automobile emission standards to be maintained as strictly as possible, lest the federal government mandate restrictions on automobile use. As early as 1974, when Congress began reevaluating auto emission standards in light of the sudden increase in energy prices, spokesmen for the National Realty Committee, an organization of several hundred developers, realtors, and investors told a congressional subcommittee that "delays granted the auto industry would cripple the nation's air clean-up effort."[114] Their concern was echoed by the National League of Cities, the U.S. Conference of Mayors, and the National Association of Realtors. When Congressman Paul Rogers of Florida, the floor manager of the Clean Air Act amendments in the House, presented a list of companies and trade associations that opposed the adoption of the Dingell–Broyhill amendment reducing automobile emission standards, virtually every one of them had an important financial interest in maintaining the existing pattern of urban land use, with its extensive reliance on automobile transportation. His list included the American Retail Federation, the Building Owners and Managers Association, the Independent Council of Shopping Centers, and major retailers such as J. C. Penney, Montgomery Ward, and Sears, Roebuck and Company. As a lobbyist for the International Council of Shopping Centers noted in 1975, "Clean Air is a piece of dynamite. Every time something is done to make life easier for the car manufacturers, the dynamite gets bigger."[115]

However, regardless of what decision Congress ultimately made on automobile emissions, the "shopping center coalition" had a more specific and pressing concern: to prevent the EPA from enforcing the section of the 1970 act dealing with land use and transportation controls in a way that required local governments to place restrictions on parking in urban areas. Responding to the public uproar over its effort to reduce the pollution levels in urban areas by way of transportation controls, between 1970 and 1975, Congress voted on three occasions to postpone the implementation of parking regulations by the EPA. As Congress began the long process of revising the 1970 Clean Air Act, the future authority of the EPA to restrict local development projects that created "indirect sources" of pollution emerged as a critical issue in its own right; indeed, the resentment of state and local governments at the EPA's effort to require them to enforce transporation control plans was among the earliest sources of pressure on Congress to revise the 1970 legislation.

The interests of the "shopping center coalition" in Washington were represented by a trade association, the International Council of Shopping Centers. By the mid-1970s, ICSC consisted of approximately 10,000 companies. Primarily an organization of commercial real-estate developers, its members included a variety of both large and small companies with an economic stake in the growth of shopping centers, such as construction companies, retailers, investors, and purchasers. All told, it represented a majority of the 32,000 shopping centers in the United States. ICSC not only mobilized its own members but coordinated its lobbying efforts with the building trade unions, home builders, realtors, and major retailers. Thus, most of their political constituency consisted of relatively small firms and organizations. But in the words of one of their chief lobbyists and strategists, "They are very active locally. Developers deal with local governments all the time. Retail groups also have a tradition of political involvement, as do construction trade unions."

The challenge for ICSC was to bring this tradition of local political involvement to focus on the federal government—an arena with which they had relatively little political experience or expertise. Their strategy was to form an alliance with those congressmen who favored the strict regulation of auto emissions. In return for helping "get the automobile industry," the shopping center coalition sought their support for an amendment restricting the EPA's veto power over local development projects. As their lobbyist put it,

Congressman Rogers supported our amendment in order to keep the heat on the automobile industry, while our lobbyists helped Rogers take on the automobile industry. Once we had reached an agreement with Rogers, the environmentalists were neutralized. Since they were relatively weak in the House, they could not afford to do anything that might antagonize Rogers.

The coalition also sought to capitalize on the widespread resentment against the automobile companies' relatively slow progress in reducing auto emissions. Their lobbyist continued: "The more car emission control deadlines were extended, the more EPA turned to regulate us. This created considerable sympathy. After all, our shopping centers didn't cause pollution, cars did. We were willing to do our share of reducing pollution, but no more."

How did the industry's relatively fragmented structure affect their lobbying strategy? A lawyer from the firm that spearheaded their political efforts in 1977 observed:

Our problem would have been easier if we had fewer, bigger companies, but the trade associations play some of that coordinating role. Perhaps we got a bit more sympathy because we were smaller. In my opinion the most effective trade associations are those that are democratic in structure rather than dominated by a few companies.

He added:

The biggest problem that faces an industry made up of lots of fairly small firms is in identifying its political interests. A larger company can more easily calculate the cost of regulation. But a more scattered business can't calculate as easily how much a particular regulation will cost them. It is much harder for them to figure out whether or not it pays to fight. It's harder to get smaller guys to appreciate their self-interest. But that's where a firm like mine [a Washington law firm] can play a useful role.

While the Senate strictly limited but still maintained the EPA's authority to oppose land use controls on local authorities, the House explicitly ruled out controls on parking as a transportation control strategy. The bill that emerged out of the conference committee adopted most features of the House version: strict limits were placed on the EPA's authority to require consent permits for major "indirect sources" of auto pollution—such as shopping centers, apartment complexes, sports stadiums, and airports. The Clean Air Act Amendments as finally approved satisfied virtually all of ICSC's objectives: The EPA was prohibited from requiring indirect sources review programs, except with respect to certain federally funded projects.

For relatively fragmented industries, political organization is clearly a necessary condition for effective participation in the legislative process. In contrast to both ASIA and the shopping center coalition, the steel foundry industry was able to exert no influence whatsoever on the 1977 amendments. As a lobbyist for the NAM put it, "The steel foundry industry got wiped out because it was not politically organized. It consisted of lots of small firms, who no one cared about. They never knew what hit them. They simply weren't well enough organized to cut a deal."

Yet political mobilization is not equivalent to political influence: both ASIA and shopping center developers were extremely well organized, and yet the latter proved more politically effective than the former. Moreover, both were supported by extremely broad political coalitions. Why did one do so much better than the other? One critical factor has to do with the nature of the opposition each confronted. No one actually lobbied against the shopping center coalition: the environmentalists were neutralized by Rogers, while the automobile manufacturers obviously had other priorities. By contrast, the environmental coalition strongly opposed the interests of ASIA; they regarded a reduction in the warranty provision as a way of "getting Detroit off the hook." Some of the consumer organizations opposed ASIA for a different reason: they wanted a strict warranty provision to help protect the interests of consumers. Secondly, the arguments of the shopping center developers struck many congressmen as more persuasive than those of AISIA: the interests of the former were perceived as reflecting the interests of a large number of ordinary urban motorists, while the latter was viewed as a typical trade association interested only in protecting the economic interests of its membership.

Stationary Source Pollution

The automobile industry was the major legislative "loser" in 1970, while stationary pollution sources emerged, at least from the legislative process itself, relatively unscathed. In 1977, the situation was reversed: stationary sources of pollution were, on the whole, far less successful in achieving their legislative objectives than were those companies that contributed to pollution, either directly or indirectly, from mobile sources. In 1977, it was the steel, chemical, utilities, and oil companies that achieved relatively few of their political objectives in the area of air pollution control. Indeed, if the general purpose of the 1977 amendments was to weaken or modify some of the excessively harsh standards promulgated seven years earlier, then for these industries the legislation approved in 1977 represented a significant step "backward" in several critical respects. They emerged in 1977 with stronger regulations than they had in Congress' third revision of the Clean Air Act. Summarizing the 1977 amendments, one lawyer remarked,

The new statute places Detroit on an oily pedestal, while inexorably demanding high ransom from utilities, steel mills, energy developers, and other stationary sources. I can only suggest that a lot of lobbyists for stationary sources interests should be swelling the unemployment roles after the thorough drubbing they suffered in Congress this year.[116]

The issue on which stationary pollution sources suffered a particularly important legislative setback in 1977 involved the "nonsignificant deteriorioration" of air quality. Commonly referred to either as "nondegradation" PSD or NSD, the question before the national legislature was relatively straightforward: to what extent, if any, should the federal government allow the quality of air in those areas whose level of pollution was below that mandated by the 1970 Clean Air Act to deteriorate as a result of industrial expansion? While the 1970 legislation did not include any explicit reference to "nonsignificant deterioration," the legislative history of the 1970 act did indicate the intent of Congress to prevent the deterioration of relatively clean air as well as to improve the quality of already polluted air. Thus, the Senate report accompanying the 1970 legislation stated, "The Secretary [HEW] should not approve any implementation plan which does not provide . . . for the continued maintenance of . . . areas where current air pollution levels are already equal to, or better than the air quality goals." Moreover, the act did include in section 101 the phrase "protect and enhance," lifted verbatim from the 1967 legislation.[117]

While stationary sources of air pollution were far from pleased with the 1970 legislation, they did not regard any of its provisions as particularly threatening. The actual text of the law did not hint at any change in the letter or spirit of federal policy toward industrial development in clean air areas. Equally importantly, unlike with respect to mobile pollution sources, Congress did not specify any actual numbers with respect to either primary, secondary, or new source performance standards; it delegated that task to the EPA. This meant that industry, acting in part through the National Industrial Pollution Control Council, would be able to influence the federal government's interpretation and enforcement of those regulations and rules that were critical to it. In fact, business' confidence was not misplaced: when in June 1971 the EPA sought to issue guidelines for the implementation of state air quality standards that included a nonsignificant deterioration provision, the Department of Commerce, responding to substantial pressures from the NIPCC, convinced the Office of Management and Budget to force the EPA to "drastically weaken" them.[118]

What the business community had not anticipated was the critical role that the courts would play in the interpretation of the 1970 legislation. Following the EPA's decision, the agency was promptly sued by the Sierra Club. The latter won, and in 1973 the Supreme Court affirmed a lower court ruling that enjoined William Ruckelshaus from approving state control programs that did not provide controls for the maintenance of clean air. The following year, the EPA officially promulgated regulations implementing PSD: the nation's areas were divided into three classes, according to how much deterioration would be considered "significant." Thus, regions falling into class I would be allowed virtually no deterioration of air quality; while regions falling within the other two classes would be allowed progressively more. Both the decision of the Court and the EPA's effort to enforce it created an uproar within the nation's industrial community. The National Coal Association claimed that PSD "will stop the construction of any new fossil fuel power plants in most of the United States [and] . . . wash out any prospect of producing synthetic natural gas or petroleum."[119] The American Petroleum Institute, acting on behalf of nine of its largest members, filed suit to stop the EPA from implementing NSD. It argued, "EPA's significant deterioration regulations could virtually destroy this country's goal of energy self-sufficiency, aggravate the already overcrowded and polluted conditions of our urban centers, and deprive our rural and economically depressed regions of any opportunity for economic growth."[120]

The most bitter opponent of PSD was the electric utility industry, whose members' plans to construct large-scale coal-fired plants at or near coal mines in the West would be effectively disrupted. The Electric Utility Industry Clean Air Act Coordinating Committee calculated that PSD might add as much as $15 billion to their already considerable capital requirements, estimated at $54 billion, for complying with other clean air regulations.[121] At congressional hearings held shortly after the EPA issued its guidelines, representatives of coal, electric utilities, paper, steel, chemicals, and oil all strongly urged Congress to review the Clean Air Act of 1970. As one observer put it, "By 1974, the NSD concept had become the most controversial aspect of public environmental policy."[122]

As Congress began the long process of rewriting the 1970 Clean Air Act in 1975, it was clear that preventing the EPA from implementing its PSD regulations would be the major legislative priority of much of the nation's industrial community. Attempting to coordinate industry's effort was a loose coalition, the "Washington Coordinating Committee." It included individual firms, a wide array of industrial trade associations, the U.S. Chamber of Commerce, the National Association of Manufacturers, and the Business Roundtable. Following a strategy similar to that employed by the auto manufacturers, the committee strongly encouraged local businessmen to communicate their views to their representatives. Stan Hulett, the chairman of the committee and an official of the American Paper Institute, told *Congressional Quarterly*, "We don't plan any mass marches on Washington, but we are trying to mobilize support."[123] The U.S. Chamber of Commerce, in addition to waging an aggressive lobbying campaign—it sent each member of the House and Senate committees considering the legislation a map showing areas that could be cut off from development—also organized a grass-roots effort. Seeking to refute the accusation by environmentalists that the Chamber's effort was oriented to the interests of the large oil and utility companies, Gary Knight, associate director of the Chamber's energy and environment program, affirmed that "85 percent of the organization's member-firms have less than twenty-five employees. These are *people* that are concerned, and congressmen read their mail."[124]

The focus of business' lobbying effort was to secure support for an amendment by Senator Moss of Utah that would have postponed the EPA's new policy on nondeterioration by one year, pending a study of its economic and energy impacts. While the Moss amendment went nowhere near as far as the utility industry would have wanted, its lobbyists supported it as "a practical matter." Moss' motivation was straightforward: because of the national parks that existed within its borders, much of Utah fell into class I—the most stringent classification. PSD thus threatened to interfere with the state's effort to encourage energy development, thus depriving its citizens of prospective employment opportunities and additional tax revenues. However, his amendment was defeated in the Senate by a more than two to one margin; in fact, the bill approved by the Senate contained PSD regulations that were actually more stringent than the EPA's existing rules. The regulations approved by the House were only marginally less severe than those approved by the Senate. Carl Bagge, president of the National Coal Association, stated in a trade association publication:

Congress has turned a deaf ear on all of the administration's pleas. What is more, both the Senate and House subcommittees have added insult to injury by writing a hazy environmental slogan into their bills. It's called nonsignificant deterioration, and it has already caused the coal and electric utility industries more harm than any other single interpretation of the Clean Air Act.[125]

The bill approved by the conference committee meeting in 1976 accepted the Senate version of PSD as part of a compromise by which the Senate agreed to the House's request for an extension of automobile emissions. While the automobile industry, at least initially, was willing to accept the conference committee bill, the two senators from Utah were alarmed by a map published by the American Petroleum Institute that showed huge sections of their state closed to energy development. They successfully fillibustered against the bill when it came up near the end of the congressional session. Senator Gary Hart of Colorado, a strong supporter of strict air pollution control standards, was bitter. He told his colleagues in the Senate, "What this [the killing of the Clean Air Act] suggests to me is that a few companies in a handful of industries still can control the Senate of the United States. It's as simple as that."[126] Senator Jake Garn of Utah replied: "I must say to my colleague from Colorado, our neighboring state, I resent the continuing implications that somehow big business lobbies are running this Senate. Nobody has talked to me from industry. I am trying to protect my state."[127]

In 1977, those seeking to restrict the implementation of PSD focused their attention on the House of Representatives. An amendment was offered on the floor of the House by Representative John Breaux of Louisiana that would have permitted the state governor to let the allowable increases for emissions of sulphur dioxide and particulates in class I and II areas to be exceeded 5 percent of the time, or eighteen days a year. Strongly opposed by the environmentalists and House Committee Chairman Rogers, the amendment was nevertheless adopted by a vote of 237 to 172. As in the case of auto emissions, the Senate proved less responsive to the arguments of industry. An amendment offered by Senator Stevens of Alaska, roughly similar to the Breaux amendment adopted by the House, was defeated by a vote of 61 to 33. Other efforts on the part of Western senators to modify PSD requirements on the Senate floor were equally unsuccessful. The PSD provisions in the bill reported out of the conference committee proved far closer to the Senate version. In a limited concession to the House, the conferees approved language that allowed the twenty-four-hour maximum standard for sulphur dioxide emissions to be violated up to eighteen days a year, but only in class I areas and only after public hearings. No exemption was provided for particulates. This variance would allow construction of the Intermountain Power Project in southeastern Utah (the Breaux amendment)—only nine miles from the Capital Reef National Monument—but did nothing to facilitate industrial development in class II or III areas. William Megonnell, environmental advisor for the National Association of Electric Companies, told *Industry Week*, "We got half a loaf." The more general industry reaction was, "It could have been worse."[128] On the other hand, the National Clean Air Coalition and the EPA were both extremely pleased with the final outcome.

Why was such a broad cross-section of the nation's industrial business community so unsuccessful in changing the direction of a public policy that was so important to it? The most obvious factor altering the balance of power between stationary sources of pollution and environmentalists between 1967 and 1970, on the one hand, and 1977, on the other, was the significant increase in political importance of the latter. The setbacks experienced by the automobile industry in 1970 reflected not so much the political strength of the environmental movement—which had yet to emerge as an organized political force—as the eagerness of various politicians to capitalize on the sudden increase in public enthusiasm for environmental protection. For a variety of reasons that have already been explored, the automobile industry had the misfortune of getting caught up in the rivalry between Muskie and Nixon to outdo each other in dramatizing the extent of their commitment to pollution control. By 1977, however, the environmental movement was important enough to assert its own priorities and powerful enough to exert considerable influence on the legislative process. Because of its historic concern with the preservation of wilderness areas, PSD emerged as one of its most important political priorities: it represented a way of limiting the ability of industry to expand in the one region of the country that had yet to experience the pollution associated with industrial development and with whose pristine state its members most closely identified, namely, the West.

As early as 1973, environmentalists had begun to organize a coordinated lobbying effort to resist industry efforts to weaken the 1970 amendments. By November 1973, a Clean Air Coalition had been formally organized. Operating out of the offices of the Urban Environment Conference Center, the coalition eventually included two major trade unions, the United Steelworkers and the Oil, Chemical and Atomic Workers, all the major environmental organizations, including the Sierra Club, the Friends of the Earth, Environmental Action, and the National Audubon Society, as well as the American Public Health Association, the League of Women Voters, and Common Cause. The total membership of these groups was in excess of one million people. Although the coalition operated on a rather low budget—roughly between $20,000 and $30,000 per year—it was also able to draw upon the resources of its constituent organizations, many of which included substantial numbers of people who strongly supported its legislative objectives. In addition to working through already well-established organizations, the coalition developed a field organization consisting of several hundred environmental activists who could be counted upon to contact their representatives on relatively short notice. Rafe Pomerance, a member of the staff at Friends of the Earth who organized and directed the coalition, noted,

Lobbying is a reflection of organized power, not unorganized power, and that's the weakness of it. Those with the greatest economic resources can win. . . . But there are [215] million people who breathe auto emissions and are concerned about air. . . . We must bring the issue before the American people and make them aware of what's going on and what we think about it.[129]

Yet the relative increase in political sophistication and organization of the environmental movement and its supporters between 1970 and 1977 is only part of the explanation for the inability of industry to persuade Congress to modify PSD requirements substantially. After all, the National Clean Air Coalition was only marginally less concerned about the issue of automobile emissions, yet the automobile industry was able to reduce the severity of the regulations that affected it. How can we account for this contrast in the political influence of mobile and stationary sources of air pollution in 1977?

Clearly, the relative concentration levels of these industries was not decisive: the relationship between industrial structure of the oil, chemical, steel, and utility industries and that of the automobile industry did not change between 1970 and 1977. Instead, what was most decisive was their respective ability to broaden their political base of support. In this context, the role of organized labor was particularly critical. While the automobile manufacturers had the wholehearted support of the United Automobile Workers in 1977, the other two unions that represented large numbers of employees of stationary sources of pollution, namely the Oil, Chemical and Atomic Workers Union and the United Steelworkers, sided with the environmentalists in 1977. A historian of environmental politics noted:

Especially valuable to the defense of the 1970 Act was the support of groups which, although not integral parts of the Clean Air Coalition, worked in cooperation with it. While the Oil, Chemical and Atomic Workers Union was a coalition member, having formed close ties with environmentalists on the common ground of protecting workers from pollutants in industry, other unions were not. Yet during the debate over the Clean Air Act, organized labor threw its weight in defense of the act and against weakening it, save for the major exception of postponing the automobile standards . . . they . . . refused to judge on the basic principles of the Clean Air Act.

Samuel Hays added: "Even more surprising was the degree to which labor supported the principle of prevention of significant deterioration, not itself a work place issue."[130]

Moreover, even if these unions had been persuaded that strict air pollution controls threatened the employment of their members, there is no reason to believe that they would have supported challenges in the statute that would have benefited stationary pollution sources as a whole any more than the UAW put any effort into opposing PSD. What each most likely would have done would have been to seek to secure an exemption for the particular industry or industries in which their members were employed. Thus, only those industries whose employers were heavily unionized would have been in a position to benefit from the potential support of organized labor even if it had been forthcoming. In reality, this meant only one industry: steel. The others—utilities, chemicals, oil—

were handicapped not only in that they employed relatively few people, but also in that only a relatively small proportion of their employees were unionized. As one oil company lobbyist put it: "You know what killed us in 1977? Too damn few of our employees belong to trade unions. When it comes to fighting pollution controls, you got to really envy the auto companies, the way they can get the UAW to go to bat for them." Another added, "The problem with the political effort of the petroleum industry in 1977 was a simple one. Unlike the auto companies, we couldn't get a coalition of smaller businesses and unions together."

There was also another set of factors at work. Steel, utilities, chemicals, and oil each suffered from a particular handicap in making a case for more flexible air pollution controls. In the case of steel, the industry suffered, in the words of one of its lobbyists, from a "negative image." To a large extent the reputation of each industry in Congress is shaped by the conduct or attitude of its largest member firm. In the case of the steel industry, U.S. Steel was regarded by many in Congress as among the most obstinate corporations when it came to complying with pollution controls. Indeed, the industry as a whole appeared to have made remarkably little progress in complying with the 1970 amendments. Hays writes,

A critical aspect of the give-and-take of political struggle in the evolution of the 1977 amendments was the role of the steel industry. This was one of the major industrial groups which remained to comply with the 1970 act. Its slow progress was emphasized by a rather dramatic session which took place at hearings conducted on revision of the 1970 act by the House Subcommittee on Health and the Environment, chaired by Representative Paul Rogers of Florida. At the meeting were representatives of the American Iron and Steel Institute, in the person of corporate leaders of the largest steel firms in the nation. Representative Rogers asked each one, in turn, about the progress made by his firm in meeting clean air requirements. Were any sources in compliance? Each replied that, in fact, none were. The expression of shock from Representative Rogers was repeated on later occasions; the episode was described in the Report of the House Committee and continued to play an important role in the somewhat negative attitudes toward the steel industry which persisted in Congress during enactment of the amendments.[131]

Moreover, steel plants tended to be located in heavily populated areas in which environmental groups were frequently very active. These organizations were strongly opposed to making the regulations affecting this industry more flexible.

The utility industry had suffered a considerable erosion of local support since the 1973 OPEC price hike. The steady increase in utility rates that took place throughout the country during most of the decade not only alienated the industry from the general public; equally important, they created considerable antagonism on the part of other companies. Accounting for the industry's lack of political effectiveness in 1977, a former EPA official explained, "Many industry lobbyists were privately delighted by any adversity that confronted the utilities. They reasoned that if environmental regulations prevented the utilities from building so many new power plants, the costs on which their rates were based might be lower." A Senate staff member added, "There was a decided lack of sympathy for dirty Eastern utility companies. Other companies blamed these bastards for the severity of the air pollution control legislation to begin with."

For environmentalists, utilities made an ideal target for a somewhat different reason; not only were they responsible for a major proportion of sulphur dioxide emissions, but their regulated status meant they could pass on any additional costs to their consumers. Finally, the vulnerability of the oil and chemical industries to strict air pollution control standards in 1977 was in large measure due to their relative prosperity. One official from a major chemical company recalled, "A congressional staff person kept asking me, 'What are you guys complaining about? Your make lots of money. Why not spend more of it on controlling pollution?''

As far as PSD is specifically concerned, the inability of the business community to have any substantive impact on this provision was due to another set of factors. While many industries would clearly have been better off if PSD requirements were relaxed, in fact the beneficiaries of such a modification were by no means evenly distributed either among these industries or even within them. Most obviously the auto industry, in the words of a utility lobbyist, "couldn't give a damn about PSD." In addition, the steel industry, with its production heavily concentrated in already heavily polluted (i.e., nonattainment) areas of the country (primarily the Northeast) and with little interest in expanding into pristine regions, stood to gain virtually nothing from a change in the regulations affecting PSD. Its primary preoccupation was with those portions of the Clean Air Act affecting compliance deadlines; as a consequence, its commitment to the campaign to weaken PSD was all but nonexistent.

But even companies in those industries such as chemicals, utilities, mining, and oil refining, whose corporate plans did call for substantial new investments in class I and II regions, found themselves confronted with a political handicap. For the net effect of weakening PSD requirements would be to encourage the flow of investment from relatively polluted regions, located predominantly in the Northeast, to relatively unpolluted areas, located disproportionately in the West. Such a shift in the locus of investment might well be in the economic interests of many of the companies in these industries, but it was certainly not in the interests of the residents of the communities in which their investments were already located. For them, strict PSD regulations were essential if companies were to be prevented from shifting capital and jobs from the "Frostbelt" to the "Sunbelt" in order to reduce air pollution. These industries were thus unable to appeal to the representatives in whose districts their facilities were located to support their position on PSD for the simple reason that the interests of these communities and that of the corporations themselves were quite distinct. By contrast, the environmentalists were able to form an enormous affective alliance with congressmen from industrialized regions: both had a common interest in preventing increased air pollution in regions whose air quality already exceeded national standards. For a similar reason both the U.S. Conference of Mayors and the National League of Cities endorsed strong PSD requirements. They argued:

The health of the economies of urban-industrial regions is dependent upon industrial continuation and growth. It is in the best economic interest of these regions that sources remain in them and utilize emission controls necessary. . . . The requirement of no significant deterioration prevents rural regions from allowing lenient emission controls that are so much less expensive that an industry will have a financial incentive to relocate . . . . No significant deterioration removes the possibility of economic coercion between competing regions.[132]

Thus, from one perspective, the fact that these industries were dominated by relatively large companies constituted an important political handicap: unlike in the case of the auto dealers or shopping center developers, who were closely identified with the prosperity of the particular communities from which they derived their profits, the firms in these industries had a national—if not international—orientation; the interests of each company as a whole were by no means similar to that of the communities in which it currently had facilities. On the contrary, in the case of PSD, they could be said to be diametrically opposed. Not surprisingly, congressional voting on PSD took place largely on regional lines. As one congressional staffer put it, "Frostbelt senators were more than happy to gang up on PSD to screw the Sunbelt."

There were, however, two industries that were able adequately to defend their interests with respect to the provisions in the 1977 amendments governing pollution from stationary sources. Section 119 of the Clean Air Act allows qualifying nonferrous smelters to receive nonferrous smelter orders; these orders permit smelters to meet ambient air standards through the use of either continuous or intermittent controls through January 1, 1978. This meant that copper smelters would not be required to install scrubbers to reduce their sulphur dioxide emissions; instead they had the option of employing either tall stacks or plant shutdowns during adverse weather conditions. Although the EPA has done everything possible to avoid implementing this provision—in fact, through 1981, not one bona fide NSO was actually granted—the copper smelter industry did accomplish what no other stationary pollution source was able to achieve in 1977: an explicit recognition of the financial obstacles it faced in complying with the emission requirements established by the EPA under the 1970 Clean Air Act. What accounts for its unique achievement?

There can be no doubt that the industry did have a compelling economic case for some sort of regulatory relief.[133] During the 1970s the industry's pollution control expenditures averaged nearly 18 percent of its capital expenditures—compared with 5.5 percent for all businesses; the majority of these expenditures were to control sulfur dioxide emissions. Between 1970 and 1978, the copper smelting industry spent approximately $1.1 billion on air pollution controls—more than sixteen times original government estimates. For the period 1971 through 1979, FTC data indicated that companies in the nonferrous smelting industry averaged a return on stockholders' equity of 9.6 percent compared with 13.3 percent for all manufacturing firms. Furthermore, the industry existed in an extremely competitive world market, one in which its competitive positions had been steadily eroding. Between 1972 and 1977 U.S. smelter production declined at an annual rate of 4.5 percent. As a result, the ratio of imports to domestic copper production rose from 8.8 percent in 1973 to 20.7 percent in 1977. While the industry had made substantial progress in reducing air pollution following the 1970 legislation, its emission of sulphur dioxide still remained substantially in excess of that required by the EPA. It was obvious that the likely consequence of requiring the industry to meet national ambient air standards in the manner required by the EPA under the 1970 legislation would be a substantial reduction in domestic smelting capacity—followed by an increase in imports.

Yet these facts, compelling as they might appear, cannot be themselves accountable for the inclusion of section 119 in the 1977 Clean Air Act. For as the industry's own position paper on the subject makes clear, virtually all applied with equal force to the steel industry. It too had been confronted with a low growth rate, low profits, a declining share of world output, and considerable pollution control expenditures. And yet an attempt to secure it a special exemption in the 1977 legislation was unsuccessful. Moreover, both industries are roughly equally geographically concentrated—steel in the Northeast and copper smelting in the West. Nor can the amount of workers employed in the two industries explain this variance, for the obvious reason that the steel industry employs far more people than does the smelting industry.

In this case, the difference in concentration levels between the two industries may have been a factor. The primary copper industry is heavily concentrated; in 1977 the four largest companies accounted for 87 percent of the value of industry shipments. By contrast, in 1977, the four largest companies in the steel industry account for only 45 percent of the value of industry shipments; not until the twenty largest companies are included does the steel industry account for the same value of industry shipments as the four largest primary smelters and refiners of copper.[134] As in the case of autos, the relatively small number and large size of the companies involved in the industry made their plans for regulatory relief more persuasive; the economic consequences of not addressing an industry's problems appear far more visible when it consists of a relatively few, relatively large firms. Moreover, in the case of copper smelters, Congress could provide an exemption for an entire industry and yet benefit only a handful of firms.

A second explanation has to do with the role of their respective trade unions. Although smelter workers are members of the United Steelworkers Union—which opposed any special treatment for the steel industry—the locals who represented the employees of the smelting industry broke with the position of the national union: they strongly supported the copper smelter industry's efforts to secure special treatment. (The importance of organized labor's position was underlined four years later, when Congress enacted legislation that specifically gave the steel industry additional time to meet federal air pollution standards. Critical to this shift in the industry's political fortunes with respect to federal pollution policies was a reversal of the position of the United Steelworkers Union. Concerned about increasing unemployment in the steel industry and having recently closely cooperated with management on the issue of steel imports, the USW strongly supported the steel industry's request for regulatory relief. The 1981 legislation was enacted with virtually no opposition, though lobbyists from many other industries that felt equally hardpressed by the 1977 Clean Air Act Amendments would have preferred that the steel industry work with them to secure a more general reform of clean air regulations.

Third, the environmentalists were much less concerned about emissions from smelters than they were about the air pollution produced by steel mills for the simple reason that smelters were generally located in relatively unpopulated areas. In contrast, environmental organizations drew much of their political strength from those urban residents who were most dircetly affected by emissions from steel mills. Finally, the smelters also had the good fortune to have Senator Domenici on both the Senate committee and the conference committee. Representing New Mexico, a state with an important smelting industry, Senator Domenici was able to use his considerable influence to represent this industry's interests effectively. Unlike the representatives from steel-producing districts, Domenici was not subject to any conflicting pressures from his constitutents on this issue. In fact, a deal was worked out: in exchange for Domenici's support on PSD, the environmentalists agreed not to oppose a special exemption for smelters.

The second industrial segment to secure a special provision in the 1977 Clean Air Act that safeguarded its economic interests were the producers of Eastern coal. The production of coal does not by itself create air pollution; substantial pollutants are, however, emitted by coal when it is burned by utilities. Section 111 of the 1970 Clean Air Act provided that all new plants of the same type had to meet uniform emission standards. Known as New Source Performance Standards, NSPS were to be established by the EPA so as to provide the "best system of emission reduction which (taking into account the costs of achieving such reduction) the administration determines has been adequately demonstrated."[125] The ambiguous language of the legislation left the EPA with a choice: it could allow newly constructed coal-fired utilities to reduce sulfur dioxide emissions either by installing scrubbers or by burning coal with reduced sulphur content. The latter policy was strongly favored both by utilities—who distrusted scrubbers—and by the owners of Western coal reserves, where low sulphur coal deposits were located. The adoption of this pollution control strategy, however, threatened the economic interests of Eastern coal producers, whose coal tended to be relatively high in sulphur content. Responding in part to pressures from environmentalists, who strongly favored the use of scrubbers as a means of reducing air pollution and were reluctant to antagonize the congressmen from coal-producing states, the EPA chose to require all utilities to install scrubbers. The utility industry was outraged by this decision, and the nation's largest utility, American Electric Power, waged a highly visible crusade against it. The stage was now set for Congress to address the issue.[136]

The fight over universal scrubbing was among the most intense inter-industry conflicts that Congress confronted in 1977. In favor of allowing utilities the option of reducing sulphur emissions by burning low sulphur coal was the entire utility industry as well as Western railroads and Western coal producers; the latter were owned in large measure by both oil companies and railroads. Supporting a universal scrubber requirement were, in addition to the producers of Eastern coal—most of whom were also owned by firms in other industries—a coalition of trade unions, environmentalists, and Eastern railroads. The support of the United Mine Workers, as well as the United Steelworkers and the AFL-CIO, for a mandatory scrubbing requirement was due to the fact that Eastern coal producers, including those owned by steel and utility companies, were heavily unionized. By contrast Western coal was largely produced by nonunionized workers. The environmentalists in turn opposed allowing Eastern utilities to burn low sulphur coal shipped from the West in order to prevent the Western regions of the country from being destroyed by strip mining.

The National Coal Association, faced with a strong difference of opinion among its membership, took no position. Clearly the coal coalition, notwithstanding all the extensive organizational links that had developed between coal producers and other large industries throughout the

1970s, had fallen into disarray. In fact, while the interests of Western coal subsidiaries and those of their parent companies were indentical, in the East they clearly were frequently opposed: steel and utility companies who owned Eastern coal reserves bitterly opposed mandatory scrubbing requirements, while their subsidiaries favored them.

The outcome of this legislative struggle favored Eastern coal producers or, more specifically, the producers of medium sulphur coal. The most crucial vote took place on the floor of the Senate. Senator Metzenbaum of Ohio offered an amendment, cosponsored by three senators from the coal-producing states of West Virginia, Indiana, and Pennsylvania, that would have allowed the president or the EPA to prevent utilities and other large coal users from going outside their regions to purchase coal that was locally available—provided the importation of coal from another state would produce "significant local or regional economic disruption or unemployment."[137] (According to Metzenbaum, nineteen Ohio utilities intended to comply with air quality standards by switching from Ohio coal to low sulphur Western coal). Among the organizations officially supporting Metzenbaum's proposal were the National Clean Air Coalition, the Environmental Policy Center, the Sierra Club, the United Mine Workers of America, the AFL-CIO, the United Transportation Union, the United Steelworkers of America, and the Consolidated Rail Corporation. Senator Domenici criticized the amendment as "economic Balkanization that did not belong in the Clean Air Act."[138] It was also opposed by Senator Muskie. The amendment was adopted by a forty-three to forty-two vote, with the Senate dividing largely along regional lines: Eastern and Southern senators supported Metzenbaum's amendment; Western senators opposed it. A subsequent amendment by Senator Domenici, approved by voice vote, modified the Metzenbaum amendment to require that the cost to consumers be figured in any decision to mandate the use of particular kinds of coal.

The regional distribution of coal usage was never explicitly debated on the floor of the House of Representatives. The House committee, however, did report out a bill that contained a provision whose effect was roughly similar to that of the Metzenbaum amendment. Unlike the 1970 legislation, which directed the EPA to set performance standards that reflected "the degree of emission limitation achievable through the application of the best system of emission reduction," the version of section 111 approved by the House of Representatives in 1977 required a standard that "reflects the degree of emission reduction achievable through the application of the best technological system of continuous emission reduction."[139] This phrase itself is somewhat ambiguous; however, the intention of the House staff members who drafted it was clearly to require all utilities to install stack-gas scrubbers.

Under intensive pressure to report out a bill, and faced with strong differences of opinion over PSD and auto emission standards, the House–Senate conference committee was unable to devote much attention to the coal scrubber controversy. In any event, proscrubber forces enjoyed a number of advantages. First, they had the unequivocal support of Senator Randolph of West Virginia. Senator Domenici of New Mexico, on the other hand, who opposed the mandatory scrubber requirement, cared less strongly about it: he was more preoccupied with the conflict over PSD, an issue of far greater importance to the economy of his state. Likewise, the coalition of industrial interests, who favored allowing Eastern utilities to burn Western coal, namely, the utilities, the Western railroads, and the corporations that owned substantial Western coal reserves, were unable to give the issue their undivided attention; they too were far more concerned with weakening the PSD requirement. By contrast, the Eastern coal companies, both those that were independently owned and those that were subsidiaries of firms in other industries, faced no such distractions. They were fighting for the very survival of their industry. And in this objective, they enjoyed, as they had in 1967, the strong support of the representatives of those states with significant reserves of high and medium sulphur coal.

However, what was most important in tipping the balance of influence in Congress was that Eastern coal producers enjoyed the support of two powerful nonindustry constituencies: the environmental lobby, and organized labor, particularly the United Mine Workers. It was this "clean coal/dirty air" coalition, dubbed an "unholy alliance" by one environmentalist, that ultimately triumphed in the national legislature.[140] While, as Bruce Ackerman and William Hassler point out, both the text of the 1977 act and its legislative history are somewhat muddled, the legislation can be appropriately viewed as victory for the interests of Eastern coal producers—though one that would subsequently be refought within the executive branch.

What effect did the relative size of Eastern and Western coal producers have on this outcome? It does not appear to have made any difference. In fact, the ownership of Western coal reserves is far more concentrated than is Eastern coal: there are nearly ten times as many coal companies in West Virginia as there are in Montana, Wyoming, Colorado, New Mexico, Arizona, and Utah combined.[141] Of far greater significance was the relative importance of Eastern coal production to the economies of the states in which they were located.

CONCLUSION

Four sets of factors appear to be most critical in accounting for the relative influence of various companies on federal clean air legislation between 1967 and 1977. The political impact of companies in a particular industry is affected by the pattern of opposition and support from other interest groups, how well their lobbying effort is organized, the perceived merits of their position, and the geographic distribution of their production.

Probably the most important factor influencing the ability of various companies to achieve their legislative goals was the relationship between their objectives and those of other interest groups, both business and nonbusiness. Obviously the less opposition a group of companies faces, the more likely they are to achieve their political aims. Alternately, the broader a coalition it can form to support its policy goals, the more likely it is to achieve them. The preceding pages provide numerous illustrations of this generalization. Coal producers accomplished their legislative objectives in 1967 both because of the support they received from other industries and because they faced no effective political opposition. Most industries did less well in 1970 than in 1967, in part because in 1970 they had less support from each other and faced more organized environmental opposition. The contrast in the political effectiveness of the automobile manufacturers between 1970 and 1977 is largely attributable to the fact that in 1970 they struggled alone, while in 1977 they enjoyed the support of two other trade associations as well as the United Auto Workers. The success of shopping center developers in 1977 is largely a testimony to the broad coalition they were able to put together in support of their objectives—a coalition that included not only other commercial interests but also organized labor and various organizations representing local governments. It was also abetted by the fact that it was not directly opposed by either the environmental movement or the automobile manufacturers. Similarly, in 1977, Eastern coal producers clearly benefited from the support of both the United Automobile Workers and the environmental movement. Copper smelters triumphed in 1977 both because they had an important ally—namely various locals of the United Steelworkers—and because no one, including the environmentalists, actively opposed them. The other stationary pollution sources in 1977 faced two sets of handicaps. Not only did the companies in each industry receive no support from other interest groups—indeed, these industries tended to offer relatively little assistance to each other—but they were also faced with strong opposition from both the environmental movement and organized labor. The success of the companies in the steel industry in convincing Congress to give them more time to comply with environmental standards in 1981, although beyond the scope of this study, is likewise clearly attributable to the role of other interest groups. Both the environmentalists and the United Steelworkers, who had opposed a similar extension in 1977, reversed their position four years later.

The importance of political alliances in shaping political outcomes was particularly apparent in 1977. The relative political impact of the companies in each industry in 1977 can be attributed almost completely to the role played by organized labor: whenever labor supported the companies in a particular industry, the latter attained a significant share of their objectives. On the other hand, when labor was either neutral or supported the environmentalist position, business did less well. By contrast, the environmentalists, like industry, triumphed only when organized labor did not oppose them. (This occurred only once, in the struggle over automobile emission standards; on every other legislative conflict in 1977, environmentalists and organized labor were allies.) This does not mean, of course, that in 1977 organized labor was the most politically powerful interest group in Washington: in fact, the trade union movement was notably unsuccessful in advancing its own legislative agenda. What it does suggest is the danger of generalizing about the political influence of any interest group: in the world of congressional politics, what is critical is the relative power of the coalition one is able to mobilize on any given issue. As the experience of ASIA in 1977 demonstrates, an interest group may be unable to achieve its own legislative goals, yet still constitute a critical component of a broader coalition.

To what extent does the average size of firms in a particular industry affect the nature of the coalitions they are able to organize? There does not appear to be any consistent relationship between the two. In 1977, the three most effective coalitions were organized by firms in industries with dramatically different degrees of concentration, namely, the automobile industry, Eastern coal producers, and shopping center developers. Moreover, the inability of companies in the steel industry, the oil industry, utilities, and the chemical industry to form effective alliances with other interest groups does not appear to be related to their size. Nor does diversification appear to be an important factor in affecting the ability of a given industry to enter into alliances. Neither the automobile firms nor the copper smelters were handicapped in 1977 by their emphasis on one particular product line; the producers of relatively high sulphur coal triumphed in spite of their industry's organizational links with other industrial sectors, not because of them. On the other hand, the far more closely integrated producers of Western coal were less successful.

A second set of factors affecting the political influence of a group of companies is their degree of political organization and sophistication. There is nothing automatic about business access to government; like any interest group, business must first actively communicate its positions on various issues to elected officials and their staffs. The success of both the coal coalition in 1967 and Eastern coal producers a decade later were in part a reflection of the sophistication of their lobbying efforts. One factor underlying the improvement in the political fortunes of the automobile companies between 1970 and 1977 was that they were largely caught unprepared in 1970; however, seven years later they were well organized for a major legislative struggle. The major industrial stationary sources of pollution fared relatively poorly on the PSD issue in 1977, in part because they were not prepared for the degree of political opposition to their efforts to weaken PSD requirements. (Just as the automobile industry learned from its experiences in 1970, so are the other major industries who suffered a legislative setback in 1977 seeking to benefit from their experiences: for nearly three years they have been preparing for the forthcoming congressional revision of the 1977 amendments.) The contrast in the political impact of shopping center developers and the steel foundry industry in 1977 is largely a function of their respective degrees of political organization: the former were able to establish an effective Washington presence; the latter were not. Similarly, whatever political impact was achieved by both automobile dealers and the manufacturers and servicers of automobile parts was due to the fact that they had well-established, politically experienced trade associations.

How does the size of firms in an industry affect their ability to bring their resources to bear on the policy process? Companies in concentrated industries do appear to enjoy an important advantage: firms in these industries are more readily able to perceive their political interests and can more easily communicate with each other. To the extent that firms in more concentrated industries are often relatively larger, this advantage is reinforced: larger firms are more able to monitor political developments, analyze and document the impacts of various public policies, and support a Washington office than are smaller firms. While this does not automatically translate into political power, it certainly constitutes a necessary condition for its exercise. On the other hand, while an industry comprised of large firms may find it easier to influence government, corporate concentration is by no means essential to this process. Firms in highly fragmented industries certainly can and do enjoy access and organize extremely sophisticated lobbying efforts, though the amount of effort involved is likely to be considerably greater than for firms in more concentrated industries. On occasion, organized labor can provide firms in a relatively fragmented industry with some of the advantages of larger size. Moreover, as the experience of the automobile industry in 1970 suggests, large size is not equivalent to political sophistication.

A third set of factors affecting the political influence of companies in a given industry has to do with the perceived merits of their arguments. The political climate in general and an industry's or company's reputation among legislators and the staffs of congressional committees have important political consequences. The dramatic deline in the ability of both coal and the automobile companies to shape federal air pollution policy between 1967 and 1970 cannot be understood without reference to the change in the climate of public opinion with respect to pollution control and industry's responsibility and capacity to ameliorate it. Likewise in 1977 the automobile companies benefited from the increase in public awareness of the technical and economic obstacles to reducing control emissions to the levels specified in the 1970 statute. The ability of companies in the steel industry to delay the enforcement of pollution controls in 1981 was significantly affected by a notable shift in the public's perception of its economic difficulties—a development dramatized by the closing of a major facility in Youngstown, Ohio. Similarly, the steel company's inability to secure legislative redress in 1977 was in part due to its poor reputation among environmentalists and congressional policy makers. The manufacturers and suppliers of automotive parts clearly suffered from the perception of many legislators that their legislative goals were "anticonsumer."

On the other hand, both the copper smelter companies and the shopping center developers benefited in 1977 from substantial congressional sympathy for their positions—a perception that was to some extent independent of either their political organization or the alliances they formed. Much of the conflict over coal scrubbing in 1977 took place on an ideological level: the environmentalists succeeded in part because they were able to make the installation of scrubbers into a symbol of a commitment to air pollution control. Many congressmen also appear to have been persuaded by the argument that the government's pollution control policies should not preclude the use of a significant segment of the nation's coal reserves. Alternatively, the opposition of the utility companies to scrubbers was widely perceived as demonstrating their unwillingness to reduce the amount of pollution they generated. Most dramatically, the ability of organized labor to play such an important role in the legislative outcome in 1977 was largely due to the fact that its position on environmental issues enjoyed far more credibility than that of industry: Congress was far more prepared to respond to labor's concerns about employment than it was to industry's arguments about profits.

The structure of an industry does influence the ways in which its positions are perceived by Congress, but this relationship is by no means a clear one. On one hand, it is true that, on balance, smaller firms and firms in more competitive industries enjoy more congressional sympathy than do larger firms and firms in more concentrated industries. The fact that Congress specifically exempted both smaller automobile manufacturers and smaller oil refineries from various regulations affecting their larger competitors clearly illustrates this. Similarly, the automobile dealers found Congress more responsive to their concerns about the loss of sales stemming from automotive emission standards than did the larger, more concentrated manufacturers. Moreover, the perceived identification of the companies in the automobile, steel, oil, and chemical and utility industries as "big business" weakened their influence on Congress: as large and thus presumably affluent companies, they were regarded as readily capable of absorbing any additional expenditures. As virtually the very symbol of "big business," the automobile companies undoubtedly suffered from a particular handicap in 1970.

But while there may be more sympathy in Congress for relatively small firms in relatively fragmented industries, there is also relatively more awareness in Congress of the need to maintain the prosperity of the larger more concentrated sectors of the business community. When a concentrated industry's economic viability actually appears to be threatened—as was the case with respect to the automobile industry and copper smelters in 1977 and the steel industry four years later—then Congress appears relatively likely to grant it the relief it needs to survive. In this context it is significant that few firms in relatively concentrated industries and no large companies have actually been driven out of business by federal air pollution requirements. This has not been the experience of smaller firms and firms in more fragmented industries, a disproportionate number of whom have suffered rather severe consequences as a result of air pollution regulations.

A final set of factors that appears to influence a firm's political power in Washington is the geographic distribution of its economic activity. The more a company or industry is an important factor in the economy of either a state or a congressional district, the more likely it is to find a particular congressman or senator responsive to its arguments. And if that particular representative occupies a strategic position in the congressional power structure, that company's or industry's influence is enhanced still further. We have seen how companies in the automobile industry, the copper smelter industry, and most importantly, Eastern coal producers benefited enormously from the extent to which various senators and representatives identified with their interests because of the importance of firms in these industries to their constituents. On the other hand, the very dispersion of shopping center developers and automobile dealers also worked to their political advantage: they constituted relatively influential segments of the economies of an extremely large number of legislative districts.

In a sense, geographical dispersion appears to involve a certain trade-off: the more a company is concentrated in a particular political unit, the more likely its representative in Washington will play a leadership role in defending its interests. But this also means that it will enjoy proportionately less access to other representatives in whose districts it has no facilities. Having facilities in many political units increases the number of representatives to whom one has access, but this dilution of a company's geographic concentration also decreases the likelihood that any one representative will assume a major personal responsibility for safeguarding its interests. Finally, geographical distribution appears only indirectly related to corporate size. While a large firm whose facilities are geographically concentrated is obviously likely to be of considerable importance to the economy of a particular political unit or units, a large firm whose facilities are geographically dispersed may enjoy no such advantage. On the other hand, a group of smaller companies whose operations are geographically contiguous are likely to enjoy considerable influence with their representatives.

On balance, among the most important factors underlying the relative lack of political effectiveness of business as a whole in 1977 was its lack of unity. In sharp contrast to 1967, when the business community was confronted with a relatively small number of issues that affected a relatively large number of companies, the issues involved in the 1977 legislation were both more complex and more numerous. However, in 1977 the business community did enjoy one potential political advantage that it did not have either in 1967 or 1970: the Business Roundtable, formed in 1972, now existed as a vehicle to coordinate the lobbying strategy of a significant cross-section of the nation's largest corporations. The Roundtable did take a formal position on a number of the most controversial issues that Congress confronted in 1977—including auto emission standards and PSD—but it had virtually no political impact. One can fully account for all the legislative outcomes in 1977 without any reference to its role. The explanation is a simple one: the positions of different companies in different industries were simply too disparate. No company or industry was willing to subordinate the achievement of its particular legislative goals in order to benefit other segments of the business community. As a result, the environmentalists and their congressional supporters were able to pursue a divide and conquer strategy: by giving particular industries what they wanted, they were effectively able to "neutralize" them.

A cross-industry coalition such as the Roundtable is likely to be most effective on issues whose impact is relatively sweeping and indivisible.

Thus, the very specificity of the 1977 Clean Air Act Amendments served to promote business disunity. Whether the Business Roundtable—or, for that matter, any coalition of firms in different industries—will be able to cooperate to increase the overall political effectiveness of the business community when the Clean Air Act is again revised by Congress remains, at this juncture, problematic: it is one thing for companies in different industries to agree on a common set of legislative objectives but quite another for them to resist the temptation to agree to a compromise that particularly benefits them—regardless of its impact on the economy as a whole.

There is another development that could conceivably affect the political effectiveness of particular companies when Congress again considers the fate of the Clean Air Act. Since 1977, a number of highly publicized mergers have occurred between relatively larger firms in substantially different industries. Will the influence of these larger, more diversified companies be greater than the sum of their component parts? More specifically, will they facilitate the task of interindustry coordination and cooperation? On one hand, they will certainly make the management of these companies more aware of the impact of air pollution regulations on a wider segment of industry as a whole. But at the same time, these mergers may contribute only marginally to the search for an interindustry consensus. Different industries will continue to have differing priorities, only instead of negotiations taking place between firms in different industries, they will now take place between the divisions of an individual firm. The more diversified a company, the more difficult and time-consuming will be its effort to define its corporate interest with respect to clean air legislation. It is certainly true that a diversified firm may find it easier to force each of its subsidiaries to adopt a similar position than would be the case were their divisions managed separately. But the political impact of such a strategy is unclear: a subsidiary that is forced to subordinate its interests to that of the company as a whole not only is likely to suffer a loss of credibility within its trade association but may not be in a position to use whatever political influence it possesses to benefit its parent company. Why should a representative with a copper smelter in his district care about restrictions on oil refinery construction? (Ironically, in the case of copper smelters, now owned almost wholly by energy companies, their larger size may actually work against them: they will find it more difficult to argue against strict pollution control requirements on the grounds of financial hardships.) In fact, many of the diversified companies interviewed for this study indicated that in the event of intracorporate differences, their strategy would be to turn each subsidiary "loose," letting it do its best to protect its own interests, even if they differed from that of other units within the firm. (This is what apparently occurred with respect to the conflict over the mandatory installation of coal scrubbers.) Other firms indicated their intention of enforcing a more disciplined stance.

In sum, the size of the firms has important political consequences. By itself, however, it does not directly translate into political power; there are numerous other factors involved that are equally important. While this study has focused on federal clean air legislation, there is no reason to believe that these conclusions would not also be valid for many other kinds of legislative conflicts.

APPENDIX 8A: INDIVIDUALS INTERVIEWED

John Adams, Huntin & Williams
C. B. Arrington, Jr., Atlantic Richfield
Richard Ayres, Natural Resources Defense Council
Robert Baum, Edison Electric Institute
Katherine Bennett, Crown Zellerbach, Washington Office
Bruce Beyaert, Chevron, San Francisco
Leon Billings, Former Staff, Senate Committee
David Branard, American Mining Congress
Virginia Burdick, Journalist, Government Research Corporation, *National Journal*
Frank Chapman, Atlantic Richfield
Jeffrey Conley, E. Bruce Harrison Company, Staff, NEDA-CAP
Philip Cummings, Senate Committee, Minority Staff
Jerry Dodson, Staff, Waxman House Subcommittee
Esther Foer, Environmental Industry Council
F. B. Friedman, Atlantic Richfield
Albert Fry, Business Roundtable, Air Quality Project
Peter Fury, California Council on Economics and Environmental Quality, San Francisco
Ivan Gillman, Chevron, San Francisco
Stanley Greenfield, formally at EPA
Mark Griffiths, Office of Environmental Affairs, National Association of Manufacturers
David Hawkins, Natural Resources Defense Council
John Klocko, DuPont, Washington Office
R. W. Kreitzen, Manager, Environmental Affairs, Chevron, San Francisco
Bobby Lamb, American Petroleum Institute
David Litvin, Kennicott, Washington Office
Fred Maeder, Attorney, Winston & Strawn
Earl Mallic, U.S. Steel, Washington Office
Joseph Mullan, National Coal Association
A. F. Pope, Atlantic Richfield
Carl Pope, Sierra Club, San Francisco

Charles Powers, Former Lobbyist, Cummins Engine
J. R. Radle, Atlantic Richfield
Dan Rathburn, American Petroleum Institute
Paul Rogers, Former Congressman
Jeff Schwartz, Former Majority Staff, House Committee
Philip Shabacoff, *New York Times,* Washington Office
D. M. Smith, Atlantic Richfield, Formerly at EPA
Martin Smith, Staff, Minority, House Committee
Andy Van Horn, Teknekron, San Francisco
Murray Weidenbaum, Chairman, Council of Economic Advisors
Earle Young, American Iron and Steel Institute

NOTES

1. Lester Salamon and John J. Siegfried, "Economic Power and Political Influence: The Impact of Industry Structure on Public Policy," *American Political Science Review* (1977), 71:1042.

2. Edwin M. Epstein, "Firm Size and Structure, Market Power and Business Political Influence: A Review of the Literature," in John J. Siegfried, ed., *The Economics of Firm Size, Market Structure and Social Performance* (Washington, D.C.: Federal Trade Commission, 1980), p. 252.

3. Randall Bartlett, "An Economic Theory of Political Power: Firm Size and Political Power," in Siegfried, ed., *Economics of Firm Size, Market Structure and Social Performance,* p. 298.

4. Department of Commerce, Bureau of the Census, *Census of Manufacturers* (Washington, D.C.: Government Printing Office, 1977).

5. Richard H. K. Vietor, *Environmental Politics and the Coal Coalition* (College Station: Texas A&M Press, 1980), p. 20.

6. These statistics are from the Council on Environmental Quality, quoted in Murray L. Weidenbaum, *Business, Government and the Public* (Englewood Cliffs, N.J.: Prentice-Hall, 1977), p. 78. The quotation is from Kenneth Chilton and Ronald Penoyer, "Making the Clean Air Act More Cost-Effective," Working Paper (St. Louis: Center for the Study of American Business, September 1981).

7. See, for example, Charles Lindbloom, "Commentary," in Siegfried, ed., *Economics of Firm Size, Market Structure and Social Performance,* pp. 319–324.

8. Theodore Lowi, "American Business, Public Policy, Case Studies—Political Theory," *World Politics* (July 1964), 16:667–715.

9. For an extremely comprehensive account of the political conflict surrounding the approval of this legislation, see Randall B. Ripley, "Congress and Clean Air," pp. 175–200, in David Paulsen and Robert Denhardt, eds., *Pollution and Public Policy* (New York: Dodd, Mead, 1970). See also J. Clarence Davies III and Barbara S. Davies, *The Politics of Pollution,* 2d ed. (Indianapolis: Bobbs-Merrill, 1975), pp. 44–48; and Charles D. Jones, *Clean Air: The Policies and Politics of Pollution Control* (Pittsburgh: University of Pittsburgh Press, 1975), ch. 3.

10. Vietor, p. 140.

11. "Congress Strengthens Air Pollution Control Powers," *1967 Congressional Quarterly Almanac* (Washington, D.C.: Congressional Quarterly Services, 1967), p. 878.

12. Douglas Ross and Harold Wolman, "Congress and Pollution: The Gentlemen's Agreement," *Washington Monthly* (September 1970), 2:18.

13. *1967 Congressional Quarterly Almanac,* p. 878.

14. Ross and Wolman, p. 18.

15. Vietor, p. 142.

16. Jones, p. 79.

17. *1967 Congressional Quarterly Almanac,* p. 878.

18. Vietor, p. 142.

19. *Ibid.*, p. 144.

20. *Ibid.*

21. Ross and Wolman, p. 20.

22. Vietor, p. 144.

23. Ibid., p. 149.

24. For an analysis that places the 1970 Clean Air Amendments in perspective, see Lennart Lundquist, *The Hare and the Tortoise: Clean Air Policies in the United States and Sweden* (Ann Arbor: University of Michigan Press, 1980). For more on the significance of the 1970 legislation, see Jones, pp. 175–210; and Helen Ingrams, "The Political Rationality of Innovation: The Clean Air Act Amendments of 1970," pp. 12–56, in Ann Friedlander, ed., *Approaches to Controlling Air Pollution* (Cambridge: MIT Press, 1978).

25. For an overview of these developments, see David Vogel, *Lobbying the Corporation* (New York: Basic Books, 1978).

26. Norman J. Ornstein and Shirley Elder, *Interest Groups, Lobbying and Policymaking* (Washington, D.C.: Congressional Quarterly Services, 1978), p. 160.

27. Quoted in Jones, p. 145. For more on the political impact of "Earth Days," See James Wagner, "Washington Pressures: Environmental Teach-In," *National Journal*, February 21, 1970, pp. 408–411.

28. Jones, p. 146.

29. *Ibid.*, p. 175.

30. Richard Corrigan, "Environment Report: Muskie Plays Dominant Role in Writing Tough New Air Pollution Law," *National Journal*, January 2, 1971, p. 29.

31. Anthony Downs, "Up and Down with Ecology: The Issue-Attention Cycle," *Public Interest* (Summer 1972): 27.

32. Gladwin Hill, "The Politics of Air Pollution: Public Interest and Pressure Groups," *Arizona Law Review* (Summer 1968), 10:41.

33. See, for example, John Esposito, *Vanishing Air* (New York: Grossman, 1970), esp. chaps. 4, 5.

34. Davies and Davies, p. 53.

35. *Ibid.*

36. Henry D. Jacoby and John D. Steinbruner, "The Context of Current Policy Discussions," in Henry D. Jacoby et al., eds. *Cleaning the Air* (Cambridge, Mass.: Ballinger, 1973), pp. 10–11.

37. Hill, p. 42.

38. For an overall account of the efforts of both the state of California and the federal government to regulate motor vehicle air pollution, see James H. Krier and Edmond Ursin, *Pollution and Policy: A Case Essay on California and Federal Experience with Motor Vehicle Air Pollution, 1940–1975* (Berkeley: University of California Press, 1977). See also Edwin S. Mills and Lawrence J. White, "Government Policies Toward Automotive Emissions Control," in Friedlander, ed., *Controlling Air Pollution*, pp. 348–418.

39. Jones, p. 178.

40. *Ibid.*

41. *Ibid.*, p. 179.

42. "Pollution: Will Man Succeed in Destroying Himself?" *Congressional Quarterly*, January 30, 1970, p. 279.

43. Jones, p. 180.

44. Richard Corrigan, "HEW: Air Pollution Control," *National Journal*, May 9, 1970, p. 969.

45. Vietor, pp. 157–158.

46. Jones, p. 180.

47. Henry Steck, "Why Does Industry Always Get What It Wants?," *Environmental Action*, July 24, 1971, pp. 3–11. For more on NIPC, see idem, "Private Influence on Environmental Policy: The Case of the National Industrial Pollution Council," *Environmental Law* (1975), 5:241–281; and Richard H. K. Vietor, "The NIRCC: The Advisory Council Approach," *Journal Of Contemporary Business* (1979), 8:57–70.

48. Frank V. Fowlkes, "Washington Pressures: GM Gets Little Mileage from Compact, Low-Powered Lobby," *National Journal*, November 14, 1970, p. 2498.

49. "Clean Air Bill Cleared with Auto Emission Deadline," *1970 Congressional Quarterly Almanac* (Washington, D.C.: Congressional Quarterly Services, 1970), p. 478.

50. *Ibid.*

51. Vietor, "Advisory Council Approach," p. 158.

52. *1970 Congressional Quarterly Almanac*, p. 478.

53. Jones, p. 188.

54. Quoted in *ibid.*, p. 192.

55. *Ibid.*

56. *Ibid.*

57. Fowlkes, p. 2511.

58. *1970 Congressional Quarterly Almanac*, p. 482.

59. Jones, p. 201.

60. *1970 Congressional Quarterly Almanac*, p. 483.

61. Jones, p. 207.

62. Corrigan, p. 30. The second quotation is from Jones, p. 196.

63. *1970 Congressional Quarterly Almanac*, p. 485.

64. *Ibid.*

65. Jones, p. 198.

66. Corrigan, p. 32.

67. *Ibid.*

68. "They're Not Giving up on Leaded 'Gas,' " *Chemical Week*, April 15, 1972, p. 58.

69. James Beizer, "Getting the Lead out Isn't Answer, Ethyl Says," *Iron Age*, August 15, 1970, p. 70.

70. "What Anti-Lead Uproar Means," *National Petroleum News* (April 1970): 47.

71. Corrigan, p. 32.

72. Beizer, p. 70.

73. Corrigan, p. 37.

74. *Ibid.*, p. 26.

75. *Ibid.*, p. 3.

76. Fowlkes, p. 2509.

77. See Krier and Ursin for a more detailed account of these conflicts, which began in the mid-1950s.

78. Fowlkes, p. 2504.

79. *Ibid.*

80. *Ibid.*, p. 2511.

81. *Ibid.*, p. 2498.

82. *Ibid.*, p. 2507.

83. Jean Briggs, "Detroit and Congress: Eyeball to Eyeball," *Forbes*, February 15, 1977, p. 34.

84. *1976 Congressional Quarterly Almanac*, p. 137.

85. *Ibid.*, p. 140.

86. Bernard Asbell, "The Outlawing of Next Year's Cars," *New York Times Magazine*, November 21, 1976, p. 86.

87. *Ibid.*, p. 83.

88. *Ibid.*

89. *Ibid.*

90. *Ibid.*

91. Bernard Asbell, *The Senate Nobody Knows* (Baltimore: Johns Hopkins University Press, 1978), p. 197.

92. Pete Domenici, "Clean Air Act Amendments of 1977," *Natural Resources Journal* (July 1979), 19:476, 477.

93. Ornstein and Elder, p. 172.

94. Mercer Cross and Barry Hager, "Auto Workers, Manufacturers and Dealers Unite To Dilute Car Pollution Standards on Clean Air Bill," *Congressional Quarterly*, May 28, 1977, p. 1024.

95. *1977 Congressional Quarterly Almanac*, p. 636.

96. Jerry Hultin, "Unions, the Environment and Corporate Social Responsibility," *Yale Review of Law and Social Action* (Fall 1972), 3:51.

97. Ornstein and Elder, p. 172.

98. *Ibid.*, p. 173.

99. *Ibid.*, p. 181.

100. *Ibid.*, p. 182.

101. Domenici, p. 478.

102. *Ibid.*

103. Ornstein and Elder, pp. 170–171.

104. Asbell, p. 86.

105. *Ibid.*

106. Al Gordon, "Environmentalists, Auto Makers, UAW Lobby . . . on Auto Emissions, Warranty Requirements," *Congressional Quarterly*, May 1, 1976, p. 1037.

107. *Ibid.*

108. *1977 Congressional Quarterly Almanac*, p. 131.

109. *Ibid.*, p. 134.

110. *Ibid.*

111. Ornstein and Elder, p. 171.

112. J. Dicken Kirschten, "It's Washington Taking on Detroit in the Auto Pollution Game," *National Journal*, January 1, 1977.

113. Lawrence White, "The Auto Pollution Muddle," *Public Interest* (Summer 1973), 32:103.

114. *1976 Congressional Quarterly Almanac*, p. 140.

115. Arthur Mageda, "Environment Report: New Clean Air Provisions Respond to Local Complaints," *National Journal*, November 22, 1975, p. 1590. See also, "The EPA's New Rules Hit City Planners," *Business Week*, December 7, 1974, p. 112.

116. Frank B. Friedman, "Oil and Air Do Not Mix: The Clean Air Act Amendments of 1977," *Institute on Oil and Gas Laws and Taxation* (1978), 29:333.

117. Richard H. K. Vietor, "The Evolution of Public Environmental Policy: The Case of No Significant Deterioration," *Environmental Review* (Winter 1979), 4:8.

118. *Ibid.*, p. 11.

119. *Ibid.*, p. 10.

120. Richard Vietor, "PSD: The Politics of Air Pollution" (Case distributed by the Intercollegiate Case Clearing House, 9-380-095 Rev., February 1980), p. 9.

121. *Ibid.*, p. 10.

122. Vietor, "Evolution of Public Environmental Policy," p. 13.

123. Gordon, p. 1035.

124. *Ibid.*

125. Vietor, "PSD: The Politics of Air Pollution," p. 13.

126. Asbell, p. 446.

127. *Ibid.*

128. John Sheridan, "Clean Air Compromise," *Industry Week*, August 15, 1977, p. 17.

129. Ornstein and Elder, pp. 166, 167, 168.

130. Samuel Hays, "Clean Air: From the 1970 Act to the 1977 Amendments," *Duquesne Law Review* (1978–1979): 17:62.

131. *Ibid.*, p. 63.

132. Vietor, "PSD: The Politics of Air Pollution," p. 11.

133. The statistics in this paragraph are from American Mining Congress, "Clean Air Act Issue Paper: Facts Relevant to the Copper Industry," Working Paper, March 2, 1981.

134. Department of Commerce, Bureau of the Census, *Census of Manufacturers* (Washington, D.C.: Government Printing Office, 1977).

135. Bruce A. Ackerman and William T. Hassler, *Clean Coal, Dirty Air* (New Haven: Yale University Press, 1981), p. 11.

136. See "Donald Cook Takes on the Environmentalists," *Business Week*, October 26, 1974, pp. 66–67.

137. Dick Kirschten, "Coal War in the East: Putting a Wall Around Ohio," *National Journal*, January 13, 1979, p. 50.

138. *1977 Congressional Quarterly Almanac*, p. 63.

139. Ackerman and Hassler, p. 29.

140. Kirschten, p. 51.

141. Department of Commerce, Bureau of the Census, *Census of Mineral Industries* (Washington, D.C.: Government Printing Office, 1977).

COMMENTATORS' REMARKS

ERNEST GELLHORN

D AVID VOGEL has given us an interesting paper that suggests many possible interpretations of the political power in fact exercised by large corporations. After examining the drafting and enactment of clean air legislation at the federal level during the 1970s, he concludes that substantial size and corporate resources are not necessarily an advantage. Indeed, the paper goes even further and suggests that large corporations are political eunuchs when it comes to environmental legislation except where they manage to forge alliances with labor unions, consumer groups, or environmentalists.

Fascinating as Vogel's analysis is—and the story of environmental legislation in the 1970s often has a novellike character—I want to offer a somewhat different analysis of the very same data. In particular, I will suggest that corporate size is not irrelevant, that size may in fact result in political power, and that corporate size is not necessarily disabling in the political marketplace. This is not to say that small firms are always disadvantaged in the political arena or that they cannot also assure that their wishes are fulfilled. Recent successes by the used car and funeral dealers in stopping unwanted Federal Trade Commission rules and the history of farm legislation support this additional view. On the other hand, I am not persuaded from the data presented in the Vogel paper that size is as debilitating as his analysis seems to suggest. Indeed, I will contend that the really important questions were not asked and thus remain unanswered.

Before doing so, however, I want to call attention to the need to separate independent from dependent variables. The paper, for example, argues that political organization and sophistication are important elements in determining political power, indeed, often more significant than size. Here particular emphasis is given to the insensitivity and ineffectiveness of both the automobile and steel industries in regard to non-market forces such as the Congress or executive agencies. By contrast, smaller industries and firms often achieved what they wanted from Congress—the latest and possibly most prominent examples being the used car dealers and funeral directors who obtained legislative override of Federal Trade Commission regulations.

The problem is that size may not be the most important or even particularly relevant factor. Indeed, I think it probably was not. Prior to the 1960s, government regulation had not played a significant role in either the auto or steel industries; thus, their leadership, focus, or training was directed at competing in the private marketplace. That was not true of the funeral industry, which has long been closely regulated at the state level. Similarly, used car dealers have been subject to public attack, and the FTC's rule-making process was both well advertised and lengthy. In each instance, then, the affected industry was either used to operating in the political arena or had time to gear up for a political contest. They were familiar with the need for operating through trade associations, which had become among the most effective lobbyists in Washington, D.C.

Without belaboring the point, I think similar comments can be offered on much of the remaining analysis in the Vogel paper. For an institutionalist approach, I find the paper surprisingly limited in analysis of historical and institutional factors that might have been relied upon to predict the legislative outcomes in the amendment of the Clean Air Act in the 1970s.

But to my view the more important limitation in David Vogel's study is that his paper only indirectly addresses the issue of whether or not corporate size makes a difference in the political marketplace. For years economists and others have debated whether size is significant in predicting economic outcomes. In doing so, they have focused on whether size has a *disproportionate* effect and therefore deserves closer control.

Without regard to whether their answers are persuasive—and the recent evidence suggests that size probably reflects some kind of efficiency rather than disproportionate power—it seems to me that the very same questions should have been asked in evaluating the political power of corporate size. That is to say, the issue, first, is whether large corporations can exercise or apply massive corporate power in a political contest, and, second, whether that power is disproportionate to their smaller competitors.

On the first question of whether large corporations exercise political power, Vogel's paper seems to suggest that the answer is no, at least in the environmental contests of the 1970s. He reaches this conclusion because big steel and auto companies (and I am admittedly simplifying his more complicated analysis) generally were successful only when joined with labor interests or environmental pressure groups. But does Vogel's story really support this conclusion? Would big steel and big auto have been better off if they were smaller enterprises? I wonder. It may be that size is not ultimately decisive when it comes to visible legislative contests. But surely it is important, and I suspect critical, when seeking access or acquiring the tools of persuasion. The paper seeks to answer this question indirectly by reviewing the actions of smaller firms also involved in these environmental contests. Again, however, I question whether the right questions were being asked. Unless there is some theory of critical mass or absolute size where corporate dollars make a difference, the comparisons are unlikely to lead to useful insights. This truly is a comparison of apples and oranges.

This leads to my second point, namely, that the important societal issue is whether relative size makes a difference—and whether large firms should be subject to special legal constraints (e.g., limiting campaign contributions). This is where the precedent in the economic literature is so voluminous yet ultimately futile. In order to find out whether relative size is important in the political market, it would be instructive to know whether larger auto or steel firms fared better than smaller ones, whether asset size could be correlated to political success, and so forth. Or even anecdotally, is there evidence that larger or smaller firms shared advantages when it came to buying access to the media, obtaining more effective spokesmen, marshaling their case, and otherwise rallying supporters to persuade legislators of the merits of their position?

Finally, I would urge that future studies of corporate political power concentrate on whether there are breakpoints at which the power of size becomes geometrically more impressive—or ineffective. But even this cannot be the final question, for to me the more interesting and ultimately more important issue is what is it in the electoral system that allows rewards to corporate (or other) private interest pleaders. What Vogel and others (e.g., Peter Navarro, Ackerman and Hassler) have documented is a distressing record of legislative creation of private (in contrast to public) goods. That leads me to my current concern, namely, a reconsideration of the doctrines by which legislatures are allowed to create such private goods. These are the rules permitting broad delegations of legislative power without review for public "regardingness." Recognizing that such questions are really for another conference, I will conclude my remarks here.

CHARLES LINDBLOM

WHETHER business has a disproportionate political impact is the question on which our chairman, Mr. Millstein, says we need some evidence. Many people have subscribed to the allegation of disproportion: Adam Smith, John Stuart Mill, James Madison, Mark Hanna, Woodrow Wilson, FDR, and LBJ. We do not help an examination of it by referring to it as a radical thesis. If you believe that there is anything radical about the thesis, you are out of touch with a long line of conservative people who have believed it. Some of them have rejoiced in it. Wilson did not; but Mark Hanna, James Madison, and Alexander Hamilton did. They approved of a disproportionate business influence on politics, although many today do not.

I do not think that David Vogel's paper can grapple with the question of disproportionate business influence in politics, for two reasons. First, he escapes from that question to another question: whether political effect is greater for large businesses than for small. That is a different question, and an answer to it will not answer our original question. Analogy: How serious is the problem of tobacco smoking as a menace to our health? We cannot find an answer by asking whether one kind or size of cigarette is worse than another.

Second, Vogel focuses on one particular kind of political phenomenon and ignores dozens of others of equal importance. In fact, his neglect of all but one kind of political situation means that he cannot even generalize about the effect of firm size on political power.

In order to try to show you the dimensions of what he has left out, I need to display a table to show the missing dimensions (table 8.1).

In the first row are political issues that do not command any great public attention and are settled within relatively small political circles. These are the ordinary business of politics. They include, for example, the politics of the FTC decisions on funeral homes and used cars.

TABLE 8.1
Business Influence on Politics

	Business Aims At								
	Government officials			Interest Groups			Everyone		
	immediate substantive issues	political resources	standing attitudes	immediate substantive issues	political resources	standing attitudes	immediate substantive issues	political resources	standing attitudes
Political issues not commanding public attention and settled within small circles	1	2	3	4	5	6	7	8	9
Political issues commanding public attention	10	11	12	13	14	15	16	17	18
Potential political issues not coming onto the political agenda	19	20	21	22	23	24	25	26	27

In the second row are those issues that become so conspicuous as to mobilize a number of public interest groups. This is the category of issues that Vogel's paper discusses.

The third row contains potential issues that somehow do not get on the political agenda at all. They are kept off or fall off somehow. They are issues about the basic structure of economy and politics, such as issues about corporate prerogatives or the constitutional structure of government. Basic institutions are not questioned on the political agenda because they are sacred cows. Or for some other reason politicians do not dare take them up.

Thus we have three different kinds of issues; I am suggesting that Vogel's paper takes up the second and only the second.

As for the columns, the first represents political activity of business aimed at government officials. The second represents activities of business aimed at leaders of various interest groups, who might join businessmen as allies. The third column represents the activities of business to influence all of us—the public. Within each of those three columns, we make a threefold subdivision.

The first subdivision in each column refers to business political activity directed to "the issue" at hand—air pollution, emission control, taxes, import controls, public housing—any political activity directed immediately at a substantive issue in policy.

In the second subdivision of each column is business political activity designed to influence policy indirectly by dealing with the resources and capacities that various participants employ to influence policy, for example, attempts to change the financial resources that trade unions can put into politics or influencing the development of institutions for government–business consultation. These are activities not directed at a substantive issue but designed to influence the structure of power or influence through which substantive issues are attacked.

The third subdivision of each column refers to business political activity to affect the standing attitudes, preferences, and beliefs. It is political activity not designed to win anything today but to create a disposition to act and believe in ways sympathetic to business. This can be done by inviting government officials to a hunting lodge or by providing reading materials extolling free enterprise to school children.

Now, that gives us twenty-seven squares, twenty-seven kinds of studies to make if we want to track business in politics. Of course, I would suggest that the upper lefthand corner and the lower righthand corner are perhaps going to be the most rewarding studies. The former represents the efforts of business to deal directly with substantive issues at hand that do not alert the public, an area for a somewhat private business influence not much subject to scrutiny. The latter represents efforts of business to educate, propagandize, indoctrinate—whatever you want to call it—to keep some issues off the political agenda, accomplished, among other ways, through an enormous investment in teaching materials in the public schools and in institutional TV advertising.

If you try to locate Vogel's study in the table, you will find that his is only in column one, row two, with a little spillover into row three. His paper takes a very restricted view of what politics is about, what the issues are about.

Is it fruitful to bite off so small a bite as his? As my final argument, I want to suggest that it is not until the relation of the small piece to the rest of the picture is analyzed, which Vogel does not do, that any meaningful conclusions can be drawn. One more analogy: Suppose on a canal, upstream is a group of controllers who control the flow of water that eventually arrives downstream. They know from time to time that downstream some troublesome people are going to try to divert some water in order to lower the water in the canal. In anticipation of the troublesome activists the upstream group stands ready to go down at any time and fight them off. When a fight occurs, sometimes they win but very often they lose. When they lose the level of water goes down a bit. When they win it stays up. Usually they maintain a level upstream high enough to offset downstream diversions in case they lose.

Who, then, actually controls the water level? Those who try to lower it and who are conspicuous in so doing? Not at all. The level is largely controlled upstream. Similarly the conspicuous struggles that Vogel describes may have little to do with what fundamentally determines policies. He has not looked upstream or in any of the other squares.

ROBERT PITOFSKY

LET me start by saying that I very much admire Professor Vogel's paper. I thought his methodology was sound and his analysis a valuable contribution in an area where there is too little reliable research. Until he summarized his paper this morning, I also thought I agreed with his conclusions. Now I'm not so sure. But, infinitely flexible, I'm prepared to attack the paper or support it, depending on its proper interpretation.

Let me introduce my remarks with two preliminary points, triggered by the comments of the two preceding commentators.

Professor Lindblom makes a useful point in reminding us that there are two separate questions that need to be addressed. One involves an examination of the possibly disproportionate influence of the business community on national policy. The second involves the question of whether corporate size increases the ability of companies to achieve their economic goals through political means. Professor Vogel set out only to examine the second question, and I believe that is a useful and important subject of research. Nevertheless, I agree with Professor Lindblom that it is wise to remember that there are two questions, and they are interconnected.

But whether one agrees or disagrees with Professor Lindblom about the influence of the business community on national policy, we still must address the question of what to do specifically about corporate size. For example, one important policy question that remains with us relates to the kind of rules that should be developed to prevent companies from growing "too big." Professor Vogel's analysis is relevant to that question.

Both commentators also mentioned that the Vogel study is based on a narrow sample. Of course, Professor Vogel recognized and acknowledged that point in his paper. His comments call to mind the academic theorum that, when a researcher is stuck with a sample of one, he is best advised to call it a "case study." To some extent that is what we have here.

On the other hand, I don't see how this important question can be determined other than through careful case studies. Of course, it's important to keep in mind the special characteristics of the subject of the study. I think Professor Lindblom is right that there is something special about episodes involving efforts to influence EPA legislation. That was a national policy debate with an unusually high level of visibility. After Earth Day, the press covered the legislative debate, and it was often a front page story. Also the stakes for the parties in the dispute were very high. That's only one kind of situation—and by no means the most common—in which corporate interest pressures are exercised.

I would be more concerned about the interplay of political pressures with respect to the resolution of more humdrum issues, decided in the bowels of the bureaucracy. In those kinds of matters there is a piece of legislation that has been interpreted by rule, and then the rule reinterpreted by another rule, and then there's a bureaucrat charged with determining how that twice-removed interpretation will be applied. Corporate influence (or indeed any special interest influence) in those situations could have a very different quality than in the EPA debate. Again, we must recall that Professor Vogel recognized and acknowledged the presence of these special characteristics.

Turning now to the Vogel study itself, I took two points as conclusions of his study. First he concluded that, if corporate size is relevant in any way to the ability of companies to achieve their economic goals through political means, it's just one of many factors; moreover, I took him to say that, if he were making a list of factors in order of priority, corporate size would be rather low on that list. It would never be decisive.

Other factors, such as the ability to form a coalition, and, thank goodness, the merits of the controversy are always going to be more important. Nevertheless, I thought he concluded that corporate size is on the list somewhere, though its impact is modest.

Second, I thought Professor Vogel's study indicated a distinction between two kinds of issues where corporate power is involved. One is the kind of situation where corporate power is more or less parallel to market power, that is, with respect to a policy question that affects a particular industry and even a particular market. The question is whether corporate size in concentrated markets—or, more accurately, relative size within the market—contributes to the ability of corporations to be effective in the political arena.

Another different question relates to the relative capacity of large companies and groups of small companies to influence outcomes in economywide types of issues.

I thought the Vogel study concluded—if it did not, I'm going to argue in favor of the proposition—that on the first type of question, where political power is parallel to market power, the relative size of companies does make a difference.

Why should that be the case? In recent years, small businesses in extremely deconcentrated markets have shown that they can organize themselves into effective political coalitions. For example, funeral directors and used car dealers, in their efforts to nullify Federal Trade Commission regulations, have shown considerable political sophistication. They certainly have demonstrated the will and commitment to seek political goals, and they have had experienced and able leadership. Also, as Ernie Gellhorn pointed out, small size did not seem to prevent them from working out alliances. Finally, despite their small size, these businessmen had remarkable access to their legislators. There is nothing quite like a funeral director in Washington for a national convention who wants to see his congressman for a few minutes. My impression is that every one of them seemed to get an appointment and an opportunity to make his case.

Nevertheless, the Vogel study did indicate that, where there are only a few companies in a concentrated market, their ability to communicate with each other and their ability to coordinate policy initiatives is enhanced.

I think that's exactly right. Take two industries as examples. In one, three companies dominate; in the other, there are some twenty companies that must be taken into account. In which industry is it more likely that the participants will effectuate their goals through political means? Suppose the national policy issue relates to protectionism. For example, the industry might be threatened by European and Japanese imports, and the issue is whether the members of the industry approach the government to ask for some kind of protection, and what kind of protection they seek.

On the basis of what we already know about cartel behavior, it seems to me that the three relatively large companies in a concentrated market are going to be able to achieve their goals more effectively. I don't mean they'll be successful every time or that the efforts of companies in the deconcentrated market will always flounder. I'm referring only to tendencies. But if you were a political coordinator trying to piece together a strategy, the deconcentrated industry would present often insurmountable problems. Some of the members of the industry will be more efficient than others, and therefore they won't care as much about imports. Some will be at high capacity, some low, and therefore will have different views about how great a problem the imports are creating. And, of course, some will themselves be exporters and some will not, and therefore they will be unequally concerned about whether the U.S. legislation will trigger retaliatory moves in other countries.

In a concentrated market where there are only three corporations that need to negotiate, it's almost always going to be easier to work out a political strategy—in much the same way that it's almost always easier to work out a price strategy among a few companies in a concentrated market.

In addition, there may be some free rider problems in the unconcentrated market. Any individual company may be unwilling to put substantial time, effort, and money into a political campaign for fear that others will not do the same.

Supposing all or any of this is accurate, where does it lead as far as public policy is concerned? With respect to the specific question of horizontal mergers, it seems to me that relative corporate size does make a difference. I therefore would argue that Congress was right in 1950, in what I take it was an express legislative directive to slow down the trend of horizontal mergers, partly *because* of concern about political clout. The political dimension was not a major theme—economic concerns were certainly predominant—but it was a factor. As a result, I believe one would draw the line in a slightly different place in defining which horizontal mergers are legal and which are not if you take political considerations into account.

As an aside, it seems to me that the FTC, therefore, is far more realistic in its recent guidelines in acknowledging that political concerns should play a role in merger enforcement and that the current Department of Justice guidelines are wrong when they state that political concerns will not and should not influence merger policy.

Turning now to the broader question, what about the argument that corporate size across the economy is dangerous? If that were the case, there might be more reason to support restrictive merger rules with respect to conglomerates. As I read Professor Vogel's paper, his conclusion is that there is simply nothing to support that view. He notes that corporations and corporate interests are too diverse and that many conglomerates are not even going to be able to work out policies within their own corporate structure. We do have today a more powerful Business Roundtable and a reinvigorated Chamber of Commerce. I gather his conclusion nevertheless is that these coordinating groups are not going to be able to put an economywide coalition together any more effectively than a coalition of small business trade associations.

The paper also notes that there are disadvantages to size, especially in terms of the perceived merits of the positions of very large corporations, and that would more than counterbalance any modest ability on the part of large companies to coordinate policy.

I agree that the evidence from this case study supports that view and that there is no reason to allow concern about the political influence of large corporations to dictate policy. There may be areas where corporations of large size have an undue influence on national policy—for example, with regard to PAC contributions—but those are probably better handled by dealing directly with the corporate contribution rules rather than indirectly by regulating corporate size.

CHAPTER 9

PACs and the Modern Political Process

Edwin M. Epstein

AMERICA is a society born of revolution—a rebellion against a mercantilist and imperialistic monarchical state. Our revolutionary origins have left us with a profound mistrust of concentrated power, whether in public or private hands, that permeates both our most deeply rooted political credos and our basic political institutions. Intuitively Americans have understood that the Maoist injunction to let "a hundred flowers blossom and a hundred schools of thought contend" [1] offers the best prophylactic against a hegemonic state that can monopolize social decision making and tyrannize its citizens. Concepts of separation of powers, checks and balances, representative democracy, pluralism, citizen participation, leadership legitimacy, and accountability are all

This paper was prepared under a grant from the Center for Law and Economic Studies, Columbia University School of Law. The financial and logistical support of the Russell Sage Foundation and of the Institute of Governmental Studies and the Institute of Industrial Relations, both of the University of California, Berkeley, are gratefully acknowledged. The views expressed here are my own and not necessarily those of any of any of the four above-named institutions. I acknowledge gratefully the excellent assistance, above and beyond the call of duty, of Pamela Goldschmidt and Sandra Rowland. Vicki Podberesky was of great help at an earlier stage of the project, and Alison Dundes made contributions to the manuscript. None of them, however, is responsible for errors of omission or commission in this paper.

premised on the philosophical and pragmatic virtue of diffusing social power.[2] Indeed, analysts as philosophically polar as E. E. Schattschneider and Milton Friedman agree that the essential component of the "Great American Experiment" in political economy has been the effort to split economic power and political power—to create thereby, two separate power centers that would compete with and "countervail" one another, thus establishing the social conditions most conducive for nurturing a free and independent citizenry.[3]

Such concerns about power are not merely matters of historical interest. Rather they underlie the current debate within this country regarding the appropriate roles of business and the state in the formulation and implementation of public policy about such matters as reindustrialization and industrial policy, the "New Federalism," the distribution and redistribution of income, wealth and risk, entitlements of particular classes of citizens to public resources, and the promotion, protection, and regulation of key sectors of our economy.[4]

Although initially it was the state that spawned American fears of concentrated power, within a century of our country's founding, powerful new private institutions, particularly the emerging modern large corporation, began to impress and alarm contemporaries with its potential for influencing virtually every aspect of national life.

Indeed, concern with the subject of this conference, "The Impact of the Modern Corporation," is hardly new. It dates back nearly a century, from a time when the nascent "trusts" of the day were beginning to consolidate small, regional enterprises into large national firms and to concentrate economic activity in such basic industries as railroads, petroleum, steel, tobacco, meatpacking, aluminum, copper, and sugar. The very advances in our burgeoning industrial development made possible in large measure by the imaginative use of the newly liberalized legal device of general incorporation—concentration of capital, delegation of authority to a hierarchy of professional managers, utilization of distinct operating units, substantially eased transferability of ownership, perpetual existence as a discrete legal identity and status, and limited liability—gave rise to a fear among contemporaries that these new industrial behemoths somehow jeopardized the democratic essence of American society.[5] As the late Richard Hofstadter observed in his classic analysis of the social and political consequences of the industrialization and urbanization of the United States during the late nineteenth and early twentieth centuries, *The Age of Reform*, the distrust of authority, which is a well-established trait in the American national character, has been turned on occasion primarily against the business community or some portion thereof: "In the Progressive Era the entire structure of business became the object of a widespread hostility, which stemmed from the feeling that business had become a closed system of authoritative action."[6]

Accordingly, as I have suggested elsewhere,[7] concern with corporate power, its legitimacy and accountability, is hardly a new phenomenon. Rather it has been a leitmotif in the historical drama surrounding our metamorphosis into an advanced industrial nation, a theme as generic to the operations of our political economy as the large corporations that are the basic structural components of that political economy.

Perhaps no aspect of the modern large corporation has aroused greater concern both historically and today than its political power, both real and imagined. There has long existed within this country "a fear founded in political realities" that these great business combinations as the largest centers of nongovernmental wealth and power would be able to lord it over all other interests and thus put an end to traditional American democracy.[8] We can understand the impetus for the early antitrust legislation and the attempts to break up the trusts and otherwise to regulate corporate activity only if we appreciate that these legal efforts were motivated as much by political and social considerations as by economic objectives.

More recently, there was a brief flurry of excitement surrounding the proposed Small and Independent Business Protection Act of 1979 (also known as the Anti-Conglomerate Merger Bill), which would have prohibited mergers among corporations with assets or sales above specified thresholds ($2 billion or $350 million for different purposes).[9] Although the language of the bill (S.600) was couched strictly in standard economic terms and articulated such traditional antitrust goals as "substantially enhancing competition" and "contributing to substantial efficiencies,"[10] a reading of the legislative history of S.600 makes patent that the proposed act was not predicated primarily on such conventional considerations as enhancing market competition and efficiency. Rather, the legislative proponents stressed political and social justifications for seeking new statutory limitations of merger activity.

In introducing the bill, Senator Edward M. Kennedy remarked that S.600

was designed "to help preserve the integrity of a political and economic system committed to diversity" and reflected "far more than a narrow technical concern within a given market structure." The legislation, in Kennedy's words, represented "a far broader perspective—a social concern with the impact of corporate power not only upon the character and responsiveness of individual economic markets, but upon the very social and political fabric of a nation committed to diversity and individual freedom of choice.[11]

Governmental proponents of the bill—including the Federal Trade Commission, the Antitrust Division of the Justice Department, and members of Congress—reiterated this theme during legislative hearings. Citing the "bedrock" (Jeffersonian) political principle of dispersed power, FTC Chairman Michael Pertschuk argued for the bill on the grounds that firms with substantial market power tend to have considerable "discretionary power" (i.e., some ability to make choices not based on microeconomic considerations) and that "a firm with significant discretionary power in the economic and social spheres may also have substantial discretionary power in the political arena to support or oppose a particular candidate, to facilitate or hinder a particular bill, to challenge or accept a particular regulation."[12] Large size in economic terms—defined variously in terms of assets, revenues, and market share—was considered by the proponents of the 1979 legislation to be transformed fairly automatically into substantial political power, which, they argued, must be constrained in the interests of preserving American democracy.

Considerable disagreement exists among social scientists, business and political practitioners, and laypersons—frequently based more on their normative perspectives than evidentiary bases—concerning the nature, extent and implications of corporate *political power* in the United States.[13] There has been, however, the widespread recognition that corporate *political participation* has become a ubiquitous and important aspect of the American political process. Although they have been politically active for over a century, American business firms reached unprecedented heights of involvement during the past decade, creating vigorous new peak associations such as the Business Roundtable, revitalizing such longstanding organizations as the Chamber of Commerce of the United States, modernizing industry trade associations, creating and enlarging corporate public affairs–governmental relations departments and Washington offices, conducting extensive grass-roots and political education efforts directed at management-level employees and shareholders, undertaking more timely and sophisticated executive, administrative, and legislative lobbying activities, *and* establishing political action committees. Many firms that in the past had been either politically inactive or passive have expanded the scope and intensity of their activities in the past ten years. This increase in business political vigor is not likely to decline in the foreseeable future.

Political involvement by economic interests, including business organizations, has been an enduring and inevitable concomitant both of America's democratic tradition of dispersed societal power and of the vital importance of governmental policies and decisions to the survival and well-being of virtually every business firm in an interdependent political economy. Two compelling reasons explain business political involvement both historically and today. First, within the American political economy, business corporations—particularly the largest firms—carry on much of society's essential productive, distributive, and service functions. Other social interests that are dependent upon and affected by these business institutions strive continuously via the political process to influence business operations and to assert ever escalating standards of accountability or "responsibility," typically through regulation. A second and related factor is that, with the emergence of a complex system of advanced industrial capitalism, the policies and operating decisions of virtually every governmental unit vitally affect the interests and goals of business firms. In the United States, government at all levels interfaces with business organizations through a variety of interactive modes: sponsorship and promotion, risk taking and guarantorship, allocation of tangible and intangible property interests, formal and informal planning, stabilization, purchasing, taxation, collaboration and joint-venturing, and regulation. Business firms attempt through the political process to influence governmental decision making and behavior within each of these interactive modes.

To summarize, business firms engage in political action with the intention of furthering their underlying economic objectives by molding or adapting to a volatile and frequently hostile (at least, as perceived by management) external environment to the needs and purposes of the organization. Accordingly, corporate political activity is typically instrumental and pragmatic in character rather than ideologically motivated and intended to achieve sweeping societal goals.[14]

No area of corporate political activity, of late, has evoked greater interest and concern than the PAC phenomenon—the emergence since 1974 of company-affiliated and other business-related political action committees (PACs) as important sources of campaign funds in both candidate races and ballot measure elections.[15] PACs, as we shall see, have become in less than a decade increasingly important contributors of campaign funds for state but especially federal office seekers, assuming some of the financial tasks that historically had been undertaken by the parties. Indeed, during the S.600 debate in spring 1979, proponents of the legislation made much of the rapid growth in the numbers and levels of activity among company PACs, particularly among the largest business firms, to argue that the PAC phenomenon provided compelling evidence of the need to restrict stringently the creation of additional large-scale enterprises through mergers and acquisitions by sizable companies. The propensity among the largest firms to establish PACs was deemed to document the case that these big companies had the potential—if they were not already doing so—to dominate, or at least subvert, our electoral political process together with the public officials selected by means of that process by their ability to inject large sums of money into elections.[16] If anything, events since 1979 have undoubtedly exacerbated the worries of erstwhile supporters of S.600. With each election cycle, corporate PACs (in common with all other PACs, only more so) have proliferated and become both larger and more enterprising in their electoral endeavors as they have acquired experience in operating under the permissive legal framework established by the federal government and a number of states over the past several years. Opponents of corporate PAC activity fear that if public officials are dependent on PACs for the contribution of vital campaign funds, large companies (and other economic interest groups) can dictate, or at very least influence strongly, specific policy outcomes. Such dependency, they believe, could well undermine the integrity of government and destroy democratic pluralism in the United States.

The remainder of this essay is devoted to an examination of the role and impact of corporate political action committees on American electoral politics at the federal level. The study analyzes various aspects of corporate PAC behavior since the mid-1970s. It also provides an initial, and necessarily inconclusive, look at the effects of merger activities on company PAC operations. A partial objective of this research is to examine whether the concerns of the proponents of S.600 regarding the existence of a direct and possibly deleterious relationship between firm size and PAC activity has been justified by actual experience as revealed in the available data. More generally, this paper seeks to enhance our understanding of the PAC phenomenon of the past decade, particularly as it relates to the role of the modern large corporation in the American political process.

THE PAC PHENOMENON: AN OVERVIEW

When one examines the development of federal policy in the campaign financing area over the last decade—not to mention over the past seventy-five years—the emergence of PACs, particularly those affiliated with corporations and other business-related groups, as important sources of electoral funds seems somewhat preverse. Business has been, of course, an important factor in American electoral politics throughout the twentieth century. Indeed, the very prohibitions, which have existed since 1907, against direct corporate contributions to federal candidates from organizational funds were largely an effort to safeguard "the integrity of our electoral process"[17] by preventing well-endowed economic interests from dominating that process and the public officials selected through it by means of their substantial donations to election campaigns. This longstanding restriction against direct corporate (and since 1943, union)[18] contributions has remained a constant of federal election law. However, by enacting the Federal Election Campaign Act of 1971 and Amendments (FECA) during the 1970s,[19] Congress seemingly has abrogated its longstanding public policy of limiting corporate (and union) electoral activity and de facto, through the PAC mechanism, has made it much easier for both constituencies, but especially business, to play a major role in federal campaign financing. Via political action committees, corporations and other business-related groups (and labor unions) are permitted to do indirectly what they had been prohibited from doing directly—inject large sums of money in federal election campaigns. Indeed, it is the very prohibitions against direct corporate (and union) contributions to political campaigns that have catalyzed the prolific spawning of PACs during the 1970s and 1980s under the permissive provisions of the FECA.

It is useful to review briefly the historical bases of legal restrictions against direct corporate (and union) campaign contributions in federal (and many state) elections.[20] It must be noted at the outset of this discussion that two basic policy assumptions underlie these legislative limitations: first, as we have seen, such prohibitions are necessary to protect the integrity of the electoral process and of public officials; second, restrictions are essential to safeguard the political rights of corporate shareholders (and union members) who do not share the political views of their organizational leaders. Let us examine each of these assumptions more closely since they are important in understanding the issues raised by the growth of PACs since the mid-1970s.

The first, and arguably more important, assumption is that economic interest groups, in particular large corporations, could, through substantial campaign contributions, so influence the outcomes of elections and compromise (or even corrupt) candidates who are dependent upon such contributions to conduct their campaigns that political democracy in the United States would be greatly undermined. Money has been acknowledged—in a phrase usually attributed to longtime California political figure Jesse Unruh—to be the "mother's milk of politics," and as such essential, indeed, to the electroal process. However, some observers of the American political scene, from the Progressives onward, have viewed money as a necessary evil whose sources and uses have to be restricted, monitored, and publicized widely. Adherents to this position believe that almost as important as the *fact* of interest group domination over elections is the *appearance* of such dominance, since it erodes public confidence in the integrity of the electoral process and in the legitimacy of the governmental officials who emerge from it. A ban on corporate (and labor) campaign contributions and expenditures, argue proponents, has a related advantage. Such limitations, they claim, protect, conversely, company managers and union officials from being pressured by political fund-raisers to contribute to campaigns, such as occurred in the 1972 presidential election in which the Finance Committee to Re-Elect the President used high pressure tactics to solicit corporate funds for the incumbent, Richard M. Nixon.[21] Prohibitions against corporate (and union) campaign contributions are considered, in summary, as necessary to safeguard the integrity of our political order.[22]

A second underlying assumption has also been relevant to restrictions on direct company (and union) electoral activity. This assumption posits that corporate shareholders are investors who affiliate with their companies for predominately economic purposes, and accordingly, to utilize funds contributed by them to the organization for other (political) objectives violates the duties owed them by management. Thus, another objective of the FECA and its predecessor Federal Corrupt Practices Act has been the protection of corporate shareholders, particularly dissenting minorities, from having funds that they invested in the firm used by management to support political candidates or causes with which they do not agree. Though rarely articulated, implicit in this second policy assumption is the notion that, unless the individual associates with a group whose purpose is predominately and patently political, political participation is a personal rather than a collective activity. A perceived need to protect corporate shareholders' (and union members') First Amendment rights of free speech and association against encroachment by their organizations goes to the heart of this second rationale for banning direct corporate contributions in federal campaigns.[23]

Irrespective of the policy assumptions that underlie longstanding federal statutory prohibitions, the FECA's legislative legitimation of political action committees has enabled corporate management to institutionalize and routinize the organization's electoral activity to an extent hitherto impossible. Even more importantly, the emergence of PACs as key mechanisms for electoral involvement by corporations and other business-related groups has increased the overall political importance of these constituencies. In the past decade, particularly from the mid-1970s onward, business-affiliated PACs, associated with corporations, trade and professional organizations, cooperatives, nonstock companies, and other groups have mushroomed in numbers, scope, and vigor and have joined longstanding labor-related PACs as significant sources of financial contributions and other forms of politically valuable goods and services in election campaigns. Ironically, the PAC phenomenon flies in the face of the clearly expressed policy objectives of the reform elements that were so instrumental in sculpting the key elements of the FECA and Amendments in an effort to reduce the dependency of political candidates on what Common Cause President Fred Wertheimer has termed "money with a legislative purpose."[24]

To be sure, these corporate and other business-related PACs are discrete legal entities made up of contributors who aggregate their individually small donations into substantial pools for redistribution to candidates, parties, and other political committees on the basis of decisions made by either the individual donors or (much more frequently) an allocations committee selected by the organizational leadership. Notwithstanding their separate legal status, however, these business PACs, with a few notable exceptions, are inextricably linked with their sponsoring organizations, which use internal resources to establish and administer them and whose leadership, typically, is closely involved with the formulation and implementation of PAC policies and practices.

Edward Handler and John R. Mulkern accurately describe the relationship between PAC and corporate parent in their recent book, *Business in Politics:*

PACs are authorized by CEOs because their activity is seen to be related to furthering corporate interests. The definition of PAC purpose and its implementation in a campaign-contribution strategy cannot be matters of indifference to corporate leadership. CEOs do not, in most cases, set the overall direction of PAC giving, but they will certainly have to acquiesce in the initiatives of those who do. Changes in solicitation policy requires decisions that must ultimately be made by the CEO.[25]

If not the precise alter egos of the corporations and other business entities with which they are affiliated, these PACs are at the very least their surrogates and are so considered by their employee/shareholder members and, more importantly, by the recipients of PAC funds and the public. Their access to substantial human and financial resources, together with their electoral activities, thus raise many of the same issues generated historically by direct corporate (and labor) campaign involvements. Indeed, with regard to corporate PACs, a somewhat paradoxical aspect of the relationship between the organization and management employee contributors exists. Whereas, in days past, individual executives were typically the conduits through which corporate funds reached political beneficiaries, today the company-sponsored PAC has become the channel for collecting monies from management and professional personnel (and occasionally shareholders) and for directing these funds into the campaign mainstream—with the political credit redounding to the benefit of the corporation. While there is little question that PACs have stimulated political participation (ideally of a purely voluntary nature) among previously uninvolved corporate personnel, thereby conferring a distinct benefit upon the political process, it is equally uncontrovertible that, just as in the case of labor unions, the political rewards (if any) accrue to the organization rather than to the individual contributor.

As I have detailed elsewhere,[26] the FECA as amended is the root cause of the corporate PAC phenomenon. The legislation specifies the explicitly legal campaign-related activities in which corporations can engage by authorizing them to communicate on any subject (including partisan politics) with their shareholders and executive and administrative personnel and their families; to conduct nonpartisan registration and get-out-the-vote drives among these same constituencies; to use company funds to establish and administer a "separate segregated fund to be used for political purposes," that is, to set up political action committees, through which they can solicit contributions from shareholder and employer constituents; and to establish such PACs even if they are government contractors. The cumulative effect of the four rounds of FECA legislation during the 1970s was to remove the cloud of legal uncertainty that had hung over corporate use of the PAC mechanism since the mid-1940s, when Congress first imposed restrictions on labor unions.

While corporations and other business-related entities have been the principal beneficiaries of the FECA permissive position with regard to PACs, ironically, in 1971, 1974, and 1976, organized labor rather than the business community was the prime mover for the legislative changes that cumulatively stimulated vigorous PAC activities among corporations and other business-related groups. Although successful in achieving its pressing, short-term political objective of legislatively clarifying and insuring a strong PAC role in electoral politics (PACs have been the union movement's primary instrumentality for campaign involvement since the 1930s), after a strong challenge to that role in *Pipefitters Local Union #562* V. *United States* [407 U.S. 385]), organized labor has paid a high political price. Congressional *Realpolitik* required that the statutory mandate for PAC operations conferred upon labor by the FECA be explicitly extended to corporations and subsequently, in 1976, to other business-related entities including membership organizations, trade associations, cooperatives, and corporations without capital stock. Consequently, the categories of social interests for which the PAC mechanism was made clearly available expanded greatly in a scant few years.

With the limitations placed by the FECA on contributions by individuals and political parties and the eroded position of the political parties since the 1950s as effective campaign funding and organizing mechanisms,[27] PACs during the 1970s emerged as important alternative sources of monies, campaign services, and the like. PACs constitute an effective vehicle for candidates to have access to money collected primarily from small contributors whom it would be uneconomical and inconvenient for the candidate to solicit individually. In short, it has become easier and more efficient to solicit PACs than individuals. Although recent amendments to the FECA have improved the capacity of party committees to fund candidates,[28] it has become much easier for a candidate—particularly an attractive candidate skilled in the use of the mass media—to raise money indepenently rather than to depend upon party resources for campaign funds.[29]

In recent elections, party groups gave candidates only a minor proportion of their campaign financial needs. In 1979–1980, major party committees contributed only $6 million of the $248.8 million (less than 2.5 percent) raised by congressional candidates and spent an additional $9.2 million on their behalf. By way of contrast, PACs contributed $55.2 million (22 percent) of the monies raised by these candidates and nearly 26 percent of the receipts of candidates in the general election. (Major party committees spent an additional $8 million on behalf of presidential candidates). In the 1982 campaign, the major parties contributed $3.3 million and expended another $1 million of the nearly $175.6 million (a total of 2 percent) congressional candidates received during the first eighteen months of the 1981–1982 election cycle, whereas PACs donated $34.6 million to office seekers (20 percent).[30] The 1980 and 1982 experience follows a trend noted during the 1970s by Gary C. Jacobson, a knowledgeable commentator in the campaign finance field, common for candidates of both major parties to finance campaigns "with less party money and more PAC money."[31] Indeed, an eminent political scientist, Frank J. Sorauf, has even suggested that PACs have become the "quintessential political organization" of this time, performing some of the functions traditionally handled by the parties.[32] The growth of PACs both reflects and has contributed to the eroded state into which political parties have fallen over the past dozen years.

Although the growth of PACs, particularly of the corporate and other business-related variety, has been an uncontrovertible fact of the 1970s and 1980s, the underlying motivations, precise character, and long-term implications of this PAC explosion for the American political process have been open to substantial disagreement. Political practitioners, members of Congress, and scholars have differed greatly in their assessments of the PAC phenomenon. According to one interpretation, the growth of PACs has had unfortunate consequences for American politics. This position has been articulated best by Common Cause, the public interest group that was instrumental in crafting and securing passage of many of the reform elements of the FECA. In the words of Fred Wertheimer, president of Common Cause, "PAC money has a major and negative impact on the legislative process. Not only do PAC contributions provide access and influence for the donors, but special interest PACs have played a key role in the growing fragmentation of our political process.[33] Former Congressman Tom Railsback (R-Ill.), a coauthor of the controversial and unsuccessful Obey–Railsback bill (H.R. 4970, 96th Congress, 2d session), which would have placed limits on individual and aggregate amounts that candidates could receive from PACs, justified his position thusly:

The object of the restrictions on PAC contributions, however, is not to help or hurt the incumbents, but to place reasonable restraints on that kind of campaign money likely to influence the legislative decision making process. PAC money is interested money. Even though political action committees may not always be successful in accomplishing specific legislative goals, they do have definite agendas for public law.[34]

A second and very different perspective on PACs—that they encourage personal political participation and enhance the equality of American pluralism—has been voiced with considerable vigor. A respected PAC practitioner, Bernadette A. Budde, political education director for the Business-Industry Political Action Committee, has articulated this viewpoint effectively:

PACs are a positive force in American politics for a number of reasons. First, and most important, participation in a PAC provides an opportunity for personal involvement in politics. What once might have seemed an obscure, remote activity engaged in by candidates and a few activists is now within the reach of all citizens. Second, PAC dollars offer opportunities for candidates wirhout personal wealth to run for office. Third, PACs help to elect candidates who, while perhaps not supported by a major party, do represent the view of a large segment of the electorate. Fourth, PACs assist candidates in effectively managing their campaigns and budgets. Finally, PACs reinforce the basic concept of American politics—that all viewpoints can be heard and that public policy is best formed when created in a context of open competition between interests.[35]

Representative Carroll A. Campbell, Jr. (R-S. Carolina) expresses a concurring congressional opinion:

There is nothing wrong with political action committees, as Obey–Railsback would have us believe. To say that PACs are an immoral force is to deny the right of individuals united on any given issue to join together to make themselves heard. We have already enacted safeguards to protect members of Congress from undue influence as a result of campaign contributions. Obey–Railsback purports to solve a problem that does not exist.[36]

In evaluating PACs, like modern art, beauty is clearly in the eyes of the beholder. Normative considerations and value preferences dictate ultimately what one observes, learns, and predicts about complex political phenomena. And so it is in formulating judgments about PACs, their behavior, legitimacy, and long-term desirability. Where you sit frequently determines what you see as far as the PAC role in the electoral process is concerned.

PAC ACTIVITY: OVERARCHING FACTS AND FIGURES

Given this backdrop of legislative and political developments in federal campaign regulating during the past decade, let us turn to the heart of this paper, an examination of the political behavior of corporations in American electoral politics as reflected in the operations of their political action committees.

PAC financial operations do not constitute, of course, the totality of electoral activities for corporations, labor unions, and other organizations. Political education, voter registration, and get-out-the-vote activities, internal communications, loans of personnel, equipment, and other "in-kind" gifts and services that avail candidates of organizational resources and expertise, and candidate endorsements and partisan activities by senior organizational officials are other forms of highly valuable electoral involvements. Nonetheless, given the rigorous disclosure requirements of the FECA, which has made available reasonably reliable, readily obtainable and easily comparable data, PAC financial activity is an extremely useful gauge of the nature and extent of organizational electoral activity, both in the aggregate and for individual entities. Since, moreover, FECA data now exist for three election cycles (1975–1976, 1977–1978 and 1979–1980), and fairly comparable figures are avail-

TABLE 9.1
Nonparty Political Action Committees, 1974–1981

					Number (Percent)					
Type	December 1974	November 1975	December 1976	December 1977	December 1978	December 1979	July 1980	December 1980	December 1981	July 1982
Corporate	89(14)	139(19)	433(38)	538(40)	784(48)	949(47)	1,106(49)	1,204(47)	1,327(46)	1,415(45)
Labor	201(33)	226(31)	224(20)	216(16)	218(13)	240(12)	255(11)	297(12)	318(11)	350(11)
Other[a]	318(52)	357(49)	489(43)	601(44)	631(39)	811(41)	918(40)	1,050(41)	1,256(43)	1,384(44)
Total business-related[b]	243(41)	318(44)	678(59)	839(62)	1,100(67)	1,355(68)	1,565(69)	1,729(68)	1,953(67)	2,107(67)
Total	608	722	1,146	1,355	1,633	2,000	2,279	2,551	2,901	3,149

SOURCE: Federal Election Commission data drawn periodically from FEC "B Index"; Federal Election Commission Annual Reports, 1975–1981; and periodic press releases issued by the FEC, most recently July 1982.

NOTE: Figures in parentheses are percentages. All percentages do not add to 100 due to rounding.

[a]Composed of all PACs classified by the FEC as nonconnected, trade/membership/health, cooperatives, and corporations without capital stock.

[b]Includes figures for corporate PACs plus half of the "other" PACs, which are assumed to be business-related.

able from other sources for the 1971–1972 and 1973–1974 campaigns, useful comparisons and trend-line analyses are now possible.[37]

Preliminary to the analysis of corporate activity it is instructive to look briefly at the activity in the context of the total configuration of PAC operations. The PAC phenomenon of the 1970s surged unabated into the 1980s as all categories of political action committees registered with the Federal Election Commission (FEC) reached new levels of financial involvement during the 1980 campaign. Preliminary FEC reports for the first eighteen months of the 1982 campaign give strong indications that overall PAC activity during the 1981–1982 election cycle is likely to set new records.

As table 9.1 reveals, in the less than eight years between December 31, 1974, and July 1, 1982, PACs have quintupled, increasing from 608 to 3,149. While PAC growth has been dramatic in all categories, in none has the rise been more spectacular than for corporations. The number of company-affiliated PACs has grown from less than 100 at the end of 1974 to more than 1,400 today—an increase of nearly sixteenfold! Overall PAC growth was greatest during the five-year period 1976–1980, rising from 722 to 2,551 (some 350 percent). During this period, companies registered 1,065 new PACs, nearly 62 percent of all new PAC formations. Although yearly PAC increases since 1976 have averaged 20 percent, during 1980, growth actually increased to 28 percent, sparked in large measure by a 51 percent increase in the registration of nonconnected PACs and a 27 percent growth among corporations. The most dramatic increase was between 1974 and 1976, when PAC ranks swelled by 88 percent, led by an increase among corporate PACs of 387 percent! From the end of 1980 until mid-1982, the overall rate of PAC growth fell to less than 25 percent, a substantial decline from that of the previous eighteen-month period. This declining growth rate is attributable in large measure to a reduced level of corporate PAC formation—only slightly more than 200 new company PACs (an increase of 18 percent) registered with the FEC for the period. In this most recent eighteen-month stretch, PAC growth has been greatest among "nonconnected groups" (largely single-issue and ideologically based organizations), which increased by more than 70 percent to 644. All told, at mid-1982, of nearly 3,150 PACs, 1,415 (45 percent) were corporate-affiliated, 350 (11 percent) were labor-affiliated, and 2,107 (67 percent) can be considered "business-related," that is, connected with or constituting an entity with a business purpose.[38] While the percentage of total PACs represented by corporations and business-related committees has remained virtually unchanged since December 1978 at 40 percent and 67 percent, respectively, (the July 1980 high points were corporate, 49 percent and business-related, 69 percent), labor's decline over the years has been most precipitous. Unions, once the leading PAC category, constitute only 11 percent of all registered nonparty committees, a far cry from the mid-1970s, when they accounted for a third of all PACs. As table 9.2 indicates, a substantial majority of PACs registered with the FEC (in 1980, 2,155 of 2,785, or 77 percent) actually contribute to candidates for federal office. Participation rates among categories of PAC registrants vary considerably, with corporations (87 percent) and business-related (81 percent) committees leading the list and nonconnected organizations having the lowest percentage of active PACs (only 52 percent) in 1980. Among labor-affiliated PACs, the contribution rate has been declining steadily over the past several years. In 1980, 73 percent of labor organizations contributed money to candidates, down appreciably from the 87 percent that contributed in 1976. Although some PACs that do not directly contribute funds to candidates are electorally active through the independent expenditure route, donations to parties, or offering political education consultation or other forms of support services, PAC contributions activity provides a reasonably accurate indication of overall electoral involvement.

In addition to increasing in numbers, PACs also have increased substantially (even taking into account the progressively inflated value of the dollar) their levels of financial activity in terms of receipts, disbursements, and contributions to federal candidates with each succeeding election cycle. Table 9.3, which is adopted from a highly useful study of PAC activity by Joseph E. Cantor of the Congressional Research Service, indicates the overall dimension of the growth in PAC operations. Although the pre-1976 data frequently are either unavailable or reported in a manner inconsistent with current FEC practices, thereby precluding precise comparisons, the ever-upward trend line is clear enough. PACs' financial operations during the 1979–1980 election cycle either exceeded or virtually matched that for the two previous election cycles (1975–1976 and 1977–1978) *combined* PAC adjusted receipts for the

TABLE 9.2
Nonparty PAC Congressional Campaign Contributions, 1976–1980 ($ million)

	Number			Adjusted Receipts			Adjusted Disbursements			Contributions to Candidates		
	1976	1978	1980	1976	1978	1980	1976	1978	1980	1976	1978	1980
Corporate	450	825	1,251	6.8	17.4	33.9	5.8	15.2	31.4	4.3	9.8	19.2
	(390)	(704)	(1,101)	(13%)	(22%)	(25%)	(11%)	(20%)	(24%)	(19%)	(28%)	(35%)
Labor	303	280	331	18.6	19.6	25.7	17.5	18.6	25.1	8.2	10.3	13.2
	(265)	(215)	(240)	(34%)	(25%)	(19%)	(33%)	(24%)	(19%)	(36%)	(29%)	(24%)
Other[a]	489	844	1,203	28.6	43.0	78.2	29.6	43.6	74.6	10.0	15.1	22.8
	(n.a.)	(555)	(814)	(53%)	(54%)	(57%)	(56%)	(56%)	(57%)	(44%)	(43%)	(41%)
Total business-related[b]	695	1,247	1,853	21.1	38.9	73.0	20.6	37.0	68.7	9.3	17.4	30.6
		(982)	(1,508)	(39%)	(49%)	(53%)	(39%)	(48%)	(52%)	(41%)	(49%)	(55%)
Total	1,242	1,949	2,785	54.0	80.0	137.7	52.9	77.4	131.2	22.5	35.2	55.2
	(n.a.)	(1,474)	(2,155)	(100%)	(101%)	(101%)	(100%)	(100%)	(100%)	(99%)	(100%)	(100%)

SOURCES: FEC Press Releases: "FEC Releases Final Report on 1977–78 Financial Activity," April 24, 1980, and "FEC Releases Final PAC Report for 1979–80 Election Cycle," February 21, 1982; and Joseph E. Cantor, *Political Action Committee: Their Evolution and Growth and Their Implications for the Political System*, updated (Washington, D.C.: Congressional Research Service, Library of Congress, May 7, 1982).

NOTE: Includes all PACs that engaged in activity any time during the two-year election cycle, rather than year-end figures, as in table 9.1. The numbers in parantheses represent PACs actually making contributions to federal candidates. All percentages do not add to 100 due to rounding.

[a] All PACs classified by the FEC as nonconnected, trade/membership/health, cooperatives, and corporations without capital stock.

[b] Includes figures for corporate PACs plus the half of "other" PACs that are assumed to be business-related.

TABLE 9.3
PAC Financial Activity, Full Election Cycle, 1972–1980 ($ million)

Election Cycle	Adjusted Receipts	Adjusted Disbursements	Contributions to Congressional Candidates
1972	n.a.	19.2	8.5
1974	n.a.	25.0	12.5
1976	54.0	52.9	22.6
1978	80.0	77.4	35.2
1980	137.7	131.2	55.2

SOURCE: Joseph E. Cantor, *Political Action Committees: Their Evolution and Growth and Their Implications for the Political System*, Report No. 82-92 Gov., updated (Washington D.C., Congressional Research Service, Library of Congress, May 7, 1982), table 3, p. 67.

1980 campaign of $137.7 million, and adjusted disbursements of $131.2 million were more than 150 percent greater than the 1975–1976 figures.

Turning to the all-important contributions figures, PACs in the 1980 campaign gave $55.2 million to congressional candidates, nearly equaling the combined $57.8 million that they donated in the two earlier election cycles. In 1979–1980 PAC congressional contributions were 57 percent greater than in 1977–1978, 170 percent larger than in 1975–1976, and more than 340 percent greater than in 1973–1974. Even more significantly, as table 9.4 reveals, PAC contributions as a percentage of

TABLE 9.4
PAC Contributions as a Percentage of Congressional Candidates' Overall Receipts in General Elections, 1972–1980 ($ million)

Year	Candidate Receipts	PAC Contributions	Percent Given by PACs
1972	62.2	8.5	13.7
1974	73.9	11.6	15.7
1976	104.8	20.5	19.6
1978	158.2	31.8	20.1
1980	201.6	51.9	25.7

SOURCE: Joseph E. Cantor, *Political Action Committees: Their Evolution and Growth and Their Implications for the Political System*, Report No. 82-92 Gov., update (Washington D.C., Congressional Research Service, Library of Congress, May 7, 1982), table 5, p. 74.

candidate total receipts has risen steadily during each succeeding election cycle. In the 1980 campaign, PACs contributed nearly 26 percent of the net receipts of congressional general election candidates (primary and general election activity included), an increase from 1977–1978, when PACs gave 20 percent.

As a cohort, PACs have tended to concentrate their funds on:

*House races over Senate races
This preference is hardly surprising given the fact that in any given election year, 435 House races are at issue as opposed to 33 for the Senate. In 1979–1980 for example, PACs spent 69 percent of their funds on House races and 31 percent on Senate races. From the candidates' perspective, PAC contributions account for nearly 29 percent of the total receipts of House general election candidates and almost 21 percent of the funds collected by Senate general election candidates. PAC contributions have constituted an increasing proportion of candidates' overall receipts with each succeeding election cycle.

*Democrats over Republicans
In 1979–1980, PACs gave some $27 million (52 percent) to Democratic general election candidates and nearly $25 million (48 percent) to Republicans. Several caveats are necessary, however, in interpreting this statistic. This seeming Democratic preference is heavily skewed by labor's overwhelming support of Democrats. In the 1980 campaign, union PACs gave 94 percent of their funds to Democrats and only 6 percent to Republicans. Second, whereas in 1972, 1974, and 1976, PACs favored Democrats over Republicans by an approximately two-to-one ratio, the PAC Democratic preference fell sharply during 1978 and 1980 and is moving toward a fifty-fifty party split in giving.

*Incumbents over both challengers and candidates for open seats
Although the percentages varied somewhat with each election during the period 1972–1978, PACs favored incumbents 58 percent, over challengers 22 percent and open seat candidates 20 percent. In the 1980 general elections, this preference had increased to incumbents 63 percent, challengers 26 percent, and open seat candidates 11 percent.

It is quite likely that with the increased number of Republican incumbents now in Congress (particularly in the Senate) PACs will favor officeholders to an even greater extent. PACs, not surprisingly, concentrate their funds only on viable candidates. In 1979–1980, all but $3.6 million (less than 7 percent) of PAC contributions in congressional races went to candidates who were successful in their primaries and ran in the 1980 general election. Interestingly as Joseph E. Cantor points out in his Congressional Research Service study, for House general election candidates, PAC monies throughout the 1970s have consistently constituted a higher proportion of incumbents' overall campaign funds than of challengers.[39]

In addition to contributing to congressional office seekers in current races, PACs also give funds to candidates in the presidential primaries ($1.8 million in 1979–1980) and donate funds for other purposes such as retiring debts from prior congressional campaigns or for providing "grubstakes" for potential future presidential and congressional candidates. Of the 2,785 PACs registered with the FEC for the 1980 campaign, 2,155 (77 percent) actually made contributions to candidates. This PAC contribution rate was virtually the same as in 1977–1978. During the 1970s, PACs along with parties and individuals were not heavily involved in independent expenditures activity. In the 1980 campaign, PACs, as a cohort increased their independent expenditures substantially from earlier years, expending $14.2 million (of the total independent expenditure figure of $16.1 million, 88 percent), contrasted to an estimated $317,000 in 1977–1978 and $2 million in 1975–1976. Of the 105 PACs making independent expenditures in 1979–1980, the great majority were conservatively oriented, "nonconnected" organizations that spent in excess of $12 million on behalf of the presidential candidacy of Ronald Reagan. (In 1975–1976, PACs expended $1.6 million for or against presidential candidates.) Few corporate or labor-affiliated PACs undertook this type of activity. Unions spent approximately $87,000 on independent expenditures during the 1980 campaign, primarily on behalf of Democratic congressional candidates, while companies devoted only $20,000 for such purposes.[40] Nonparty committees were somewhat more active in directing "internal communications" to their organizational constituents. In 1979–1980, a total of sixty-two groups, including fifty-seven labor organizations, four membership groups, and one corporation, reported nearly $4 million in expenditures on such communications, of which unions spent nearly $3 million of the total, while the sole corporation, Mesa Petroleum Company, expended less than $4,000 for that purpose.[41] Communication costs can be spent by corporations, unions, and membership groups as long as the funds are utilized to convey political messages to constituencies specified in the FECA—corporate shareholders and executive/administrative personnel, union members, membership organizations constituents, and the families of each.

Except for organized labor, all categories of PACs increased dramatically their financial activities throughout the 1970s and reached new heights during the 1979–1980 election cycle. The growth in PAC activity was most pronounced, not surprisingly, among business corporations, which increased their financial performance both in absolute terms as well as relative to other types of PACs. It is necessary to recall that, as recently as 1974, less than 100 company-affiliated PAC committees existed, and 1976 was, accordingly, the first year of PAC operation for the great majority of business firms. Owing to the late passage of the 1976 amendments to the FECA, many firms either postponed creating PACs until far into the 1975–1976 election cycle or refrained from doing so completely. Corporations with new PACs had relatively little time in which to organize their fund-raising and contribution programs and functioned, accordingly, at a modest level. Many companies, moreover, were extremely inexperienced in utilizing this new (for them) political mechanism and proceeded cautiously. This hesitancy was reinforced by the FEC's failure (due to limited time) to promulgate regulations covering PAC operations. Consequently, for a substantial number of firms, 1977–1978 was the first full election cycle in which they utilized their PACs. By the 1980 campaign, these companies were able to function even more effectively. Early PAC formers were joined by over 375 new corportate committees, created during the years 1977–1980. The newer PACs had much fewer start-up problems than did older committees: the FEC "rules of the game" were largely in place; companies had the benefit of the experience of the older PACs as well as of the myriad of consultants and PAC advisory groups which had come on the scene; and managerial employees were more familiar with and arguably more accepting of PACs as a means of political participation. This PAC "learning curve" phenomenon also appears to have been relevant to other business-oriented groups that increased in numbers, size, and vigor during each succeeding election cycle.

While labor PAC operations both expanded and matured during the 1970s, the trend line was far less dramatic than on the business side. As I have indicated elsewhere,[42] PACs had been the focal point of labor's financial and nonfinancial electoral activities for nearly forty years prior to the passage of the FECA. International unions with a tradition of political activism have operated PACs for more than a generation. There have been, accordingly, far fewer opportunities for spectacular PAC expansion among unions than among corporations and other business-related groups. The result has been that, throughout the past decade, labor organizations have experienced only relatively modest increases in their PAC operations. Although the PAC activities of corporate and business-oriented committees have been growing rapidly, labor has experienced a relative decline in its financial role in electoral politics. Labor PAC contributions as a percentage of overall PAC donations to congressional candidates declined sharply during the past several elections and, as table 9.2 indicates, constituted 24 percent of the PAC total in the 1980 campaign, down from 29 percent in 1977–1978 and an estimated 36 percent in 1975–1976. In 1976, labor committees outgave corporate PACs by 91 percent and were exceeded by estimated total business-oriented PAC contributions by only 12 percent. A scant four years later, labor's eroded position was manifest: corporate PACs outgave labor committees by 45 percent, and all business-oriented PACs outcontributed labor by a whopping 232 percent in 1980. From a labor viewpoint, to be sure, the substantially increased financial vigor of union-affiliated PACs in the 1980 campaign compared with 1977–1978 is encouraging. As table 9.2 indicates, labor's adjusted receipts (up 31 percent), adjusted disbursements (up 35 percent), and contributions (up 28 percent) all increased far more substantially from 1978 to 1980 than during the period 1976–1978. For the future, however, any prospects organized labor has for increasing the financial yield of its PACs relates much more to improving the quality of its ongoing activities through payroll deductions, direct mailing, and the like, rather than by simply increasing the sheer magnitude of its operations through the formation of new committees.

Preliminary FEC data for the 1981–1982 election cycle indicates that overall PAC activity for this election may exceed the 1980 campaign figures by as much as 50 percent.[43] Table 9.5 indicates actual PAC activity for the first eighteen months of both the 1981–1982 and 1979–1980 election cycles as well as for the complete 1979–1980 cycle. By calculating the percentage of overall PAC operations that occurred in the first eighteen months of the 1980 campaign and assuming the same percentages apply for the 1982 campaign, it is possible to hazard some rough estimates of likely total PAC operations in 1981–1982. If the same percentages hold true as in 1979–1980, PACs will raise and spend in ex-

TABLE 9.5

PAC Financial Activity in Congressional Campaigns ($ million)

1979–1980 Election Cycle	1/1/79– 6/30/80 (18 months)	1/1/79– 12/31/80 (24 months)	18-Month Activity as Percentage of Total Activity
Adjusted receipts	85.3	140.2	61
Adjusted disbursements	61.4	133.5	46
Adjusted contributions to 1979–1980 candidates	21.5 [a]	55.2	39

1981–1982 Election Cycle	1/1/81– 6/30/82	Assuming 18-Month Activity in 1981–1982 Equals 1979–1980 Percentages of Total Activity	Estimated Total Activity for 1981–1982
Adjusted receipts	137.2	61	225.0
Adjusted disbursements	103.9	46	225.0
Contributions to 1981– 1982 candidates	34.6	39	88.7

SOURCES: FEC Press Releases: "FEC Releases First Full PAC Study for '82 Elections," October 3, 1982, and "FEC Releases Final PAC Report for 1979–80 Election Cycle," February 21, 1982.

[a] Average of $20–23 million FEC estimate.

cess of $225 million and, more significantly, will contribute some $89 million of the estimated $325–340 million that candidates for 1982 congressional office are expected to receive in 1981–1982. Of this $89 million, the corporate share alone is likely to reach nearly $30 million if the percentages for the 1979–1980 cycle remain constant in 1981–1982. (The eighteen-month percentages for the 1982 campaign are for every PAC category within two percentage points of the 1979–1980 final percentage figures). Labor contributions will exceed $20 million, and total business-related contributions will total some $50 million. It appears almost inevitable that PAC contributions will constitute even a higher percentage of overall candidate receipts than in the 1980 campaign and could well exceed 30 percent for general election candidates, reaching perhaps as much as 35 percent. Such a development would no doubt intensify the concerns of many observers of the electoral process that PACs have become excessively important in the financing of federal election campaigns.

There are several particularly interesting aspects of the FEC eighteen-month contributions data. This "early money" has:

* Been contributed by 61 percent of all registered committees, with corporations having the highest (75 percent) and nonconnected organizations (31 percent) and labor organizations (54 percent) the lowest contribution rates.
* Favored Democrats (58 percent) over Republicans (41 percent). Corporate PACs have given more to GOP candidates (56 percent) than to Democrats (43 percent) as have nonconnected organizations (51–49 percent). Trade/membership/health groups gave to candidates of both major parties virtually equally. The Democratic majority was provided, once again by organized labor, which favored overwhelmingly Democrats (94 percent) over Republicans (6 percent).
* Gone largely to incumbents (79 percent) in preference to challengers (10 percent) and candidates in open races (10 percent) (all PAC categories save nonconnected organizations were highly incumbent-oriented) and to House (71 percent) over Senate candidates (29 percent).

PACs were clearly husbanding their resources for the fall general elections, having nearly $55 million in cash on hand as of June 30, 1982. Apart from a few ideologically oriented "nonconnected" organizations—most notably the National Conservative Political Action Committee (NCPAC), which targets sums against Democratic "liberals"—very few Pacs (twenty-seven all told) made independent expenditures during the first fifteen months of the 1981–1982 election cycle. Ninety percent of these expenditures were of the "negative" variety, that is, against incumbents running for reelection. Two corporations and three unions made independent expenditures, all of a *de minimis* nature. In summary, PAC "early money" appears to have been spent quite conventionally and conservatively, favoring incumbents, primarily House Democrats and Senate Republicans. As in past elections, it appears that in the 1982 campaign more risk-oriented contributions favoring challengers or candidates in highly speculative, open-seat races will be made at the latter stages of the general election campaign.

CORPORATE POLITICAL ACTIVITY: GROWTH AND IMPACT

Looking specifically at corporate PAC activity during the past decade, one is struck immediately by the enormous absolute and relative growth of this activity in the brief period since 1976.[44] As we have seen, during the 1979–1980 election cycle, corporate committees led PACs in all other classifications in numbers, and more importantly, in the crucial "contributions to candidates" category, by substantially outstripping their labor-affiliated counterparts. Tables 9.1 and 9.2 present this growth pattern in graphic form. To summarize, in the 1980 campaign, corporate PACs experienced increases of approximately 100 percent in adjusted receipts, adjusted disbursements, and contributions when compared with the 1977–1978 election cycle and of fourfold or better in all categories in comparison with 1975–1976. These dramatic percentage increases reflect the underlying expansion in the numbers, size, and vigor of corporate PACs within a scant few years.

Although corporations of all sizes have formed political action committees, PAC formation has been most apparent among large companies. Indeed, among the 1,300 *Fortune*-ranked companies, the incidence of PAC creation is closely correlated with firm size. As Table 9.5 indicates, whereas all told during the 1979–1980 election cycle, 520 *Fortune*-ranked companies (40 percent) operated PACs (up from 368, 28 percent in 1977–1978), table 9.6 reveals that the percentage of PAC registrations was substantially greater among the very top firms in each *Fortune* category. Among leading *Fortune* industrials in the 1980 campaign, 82 of the top 100 (82 percent), 190 of the top 250 (76 percent), and 286 of the top 500 (57 percent) had PACs, compared with only 68 (14 percent) of the second 500 firms. Indeed, within this second cohort of industrials, 31 companies were among firms ranked 501–600. Accordingly, among the top 1,000 industrials, 90 percent of all PACs were affiliated with the leading 600 firms, while the remaining 400 accounted for only a small 10 percent. This pattern is quite similar to the 1978 campaign, when the top 600 firms accounted for 225 of the 244 PACs (92 percent) operated by *Fortune*-ranked industrials during the two-year period. Interestingly, 215 of the 354 industrial PAC spenders (61 percent) had revenues of $1 billion or more in 1980. PAC formation among the largest industrial firms grouped by industry increased in virtually every category during the 1979–1980 election cycle from the 1977–1978 levels, although the rate of increase (14 percent) was more modest than for the prior two-year period (21 percent).

The reason for the decline in growth rate is manifest. The largest companies within any given industry classification tended throughout the

TABLE 9.6

PACs of *Fortune*-Listed Corporations Active in 1978 and 1980
Campaigns

Revenue Category	1978		1980	
	Number	Percent	Number	Percent
Top 1,000 industrials				
First 50	33	66	40	80
Second 50	37	74	42	84
Third 50	31	62	37	74
Fourth 50	31	62	35	70
Fifth 50	17	34	36	72
Sixth 50	13	26	25	50
Seventh 50	11	22	25	50
Eighth 50	12	24	18	36
Ninth 50	9	18	16	32
Tenth 50	8	16	12	24
Subtotal	202	40	286	57
Second 500 industrials with PACs				
First 100	23	23	31	31
Second 100	8	8	16	16
Third 100	5	5	12	12
Fourth 100	0	0	3	3
Fifth 100	6	6	6	6
Subtotal	42	8	68	14
Total 1,000 industrials	244	24	354	35
Leading 300 nonindustrials				
(50 firms per category)				
Commercial Banking	25	50	34	68
Diversified financials	19	38	29	58
Life insurance	5	10	15	30
Retailing	15	30	19	38
Transportation	29	58	30	60
Utilities	31	62	39	78
Subtotal	124	41	166	55
Total 1,300 firms	368	28	520	40

SOURCES: *Supplement to FEC Reports on Financial Activity 1977–78,* Final Report, April 1980: *Supplement to FEC Reports on Financial Activity 1979–80* Final Report, January 1982; and *Fortune* Directories. May 7, 1979, June 18, 1979, July 16, 1979, May 4, 1981, June 15, 1981 and July 13, 1981.

NOTE: Some companies have more than one PAC. For example, American Telephone and Telegraph, the top-ranked utility, has more than twenty PACs registered in the name of its separate operating companies for 1978 and 1980.

TABLE 9.7

PAC Formation Among Firms in Selected Nonfinancial Industries, 1978 and 1980

| | PACs among Top 20 Firms | | | | |
| | 1978 | | 1980 | | Number |
Category	No.	%	No.	%	Increase
Aerospace	7	64	9	82	2
Airlines	13	87	14	93	1
Automotive	11	55	14	70	3
Beverages	9	60	9	60	0
Building materials	3	17	5	28	2
Chemicals	14	70	16	80	2
Conglomerates	11	55	15	75	4
Drugs	10	50	17	85	7
Electrical, electronics	10	50	12	60	2
Food processing	11	55	15	75	4
General machinery	6	30	11	55	5
Metals and mining	10	67	10	67	0
Miscellaneous manufacturing	10	50	11	55	1
Natural resources (fuel)	15	75	17	85	2
Office equipment, computers	3	15	5	25	2
Paper	14	70	17	85	3
Railroads	6	50	7	58	1
Steel	10	59	10	59	0
Tire and rubber	3	33	4	44	1
Tobacco	2	50	2	50	0
Totals	178	53	220	65	42

SOURCES: *Supplement to FEC Reports on Financial Activity 1977–78,* Final Report, April 1980; *Supplement to FEC Reports on Financial Activity 1979–80,* Final Report, January 1982; and *Business Week,* August 17, 1981.

NOTE: PACs are ranked on basis of sales, 336 total firms, 1980 base year. There are 18 rather than 20 firms in category for building materials, 17 for steel, 15 for airlines, beverages, and metals and mining, 12 for railroads, 11 for aerospace, 9 for tire and rubber, and 4 for tobacco.

1970s to form PACs both with greater frequency, and earlier, than did their smaller competitors. Thus, they had PACs "in place" when the 1980 campaign began, and there was less room for increase among these firms. Notwithstanding the overall trend, in several industrial classifications (conglomerates, drugs, food processing, general machinery, and paper and forest products), the percentage of PAC increase was substantial— 15 percent or better in the two-year period. Save for three industrial classifications—building materials, office equipment and computers, and tire and rubber—50 percent or more of the leading firms in the industry have PACs, while in nine industries (aerospace, airlines, automotive, chemicals, conglomerates, drugs, food processing, natural resources, and paper), 70 percent or more of the top companies had PACs registered with the FEC during 1979–1980.

Even a casual scan of the industries included in table 9.6 suggests the great importance of the relationship between the federal government as regulator, promoter, purchaser, tax collector, subsidizer, stabilizer, and resource allocator and the well-being of the firms in the industry. The role of Congress is particularly crucial in determining legislative policies, establishing the parameters of the regulatory authority of administrative agencies, maintaining an oversight role through the appointment-approval process, legislative vetos, and the omnipresent congressional power over the purse, as well as in pressuring the executive branch. The 1979–1980 data are quite consistent with a proposition that I advanced in an earlier paper concerning the 1978 campaign that, in addition to size, the incidence of PAC formation within the business community "appears to depend on the extent to which federal decisions bear on the operations of any given industry or firm."[45] By way of example, it is hardly surprising that FEC regulation among large, conglomerated enterprises increased 20 percent in the 1979–1980 election cycle, during which time the Senate considered S.600 (the Small and Independent Business Protection Act), which would have prohibited mergers among many of the nation's biggest firms. Similarly, food processors have been affected in substantial ways by federal decisions. The issues ranged from the issuance of export licenses to grain shipments to Soviet bloc countries, federal land and water policies, various forms of agricultural price supports and food-related regulation by the Food and Drug Administration and the Federal Trade Commission (e.g., the celebrated Kid-Vid controversy between cereal manufacturers and former FTC Chairman Michael Pertschuk). Of the fifty leading American exporting firms in 1980,[46] all of which have a strong vested interest in U.S. trade policy, fully 88 percent had PACs in 1979–1980. Finally 55 percent of the 100 leading national advertisers (and 70 percent of the top fifty),[47] all of which are subject to rigorous monitoring by the Federal Trade Commission, operated political committees in 1979–1980.

Not surprisingly, government contractors are very conspicuous in the ranks of corporations with political action committees. Sixty percent of the top 100 Department of Defense contractors for 1978–1979 operated PACs during the 1980 campaign, including 19 of the leading 20 (95 percent) and 38 of the top 50 (76 percent) DOD-related companies.[48] Half of the top 10 corporate PACs, in terms of contributions to candidates during the 1979–1980 election cycle, were on the DOD list. Among 44 firms for which DOD contracts constituted 9 percent or greater of their total sales for 1978–1979, 32 (73 percent) had PACs. Indeed, of all corporate funds contributed to congressional candidates during the 1979–1980 election cycle, $19.2 million, the 100 leading DOD contractors accounted for $4.7 million (24 percent) (see table 9.8). It well behooves corporations that are reliant upon federal contracts for sales dollars to seek to insure a "favorable climate" for defense expenditures by assisting present or potential members of Congress who will be voting upon all-important defense authorization and appropriations acts.[49]

When we examine the PAC-formation behavior of *Fortune's* leading 300 non-industrial firms in table 9.9, we find a rate of PAC formation in

TABLE 9.8
PAC Behavior Among Top 100 Department of Defense Contractors in 1978 and 1980 Campaigns ($ thousand)

	1978			
	Top 20	*Top 50*	*Second 50*	*Total 100*
Number of PACs	17	31	19	50
Percentage	85	62	38	50
Receipts	1,884	2,851	1,023	3,873
Disbursements	1,666	2,572	857	3,429
Total contributions	980	1,450	651	2,101
Democratic contributions	425 (43%)	617 (43%)	174 (27%)	791 (38%)
Republican contributions	55 (57%)	833 (57%)	477 (73%)	1,310 (62%)
Congressional contributions				
Total contributions	978	1,449	651	2,100[a]
Total Democratic	423 (43%)	616 (43%)	174 (27%)	789 (38%)
Total Republican	555 (57%)	833 (57%)	477 (73%)	1,310 (62%)
Senate: Democratic	111 (11%)	152 (10%)	36 (6%)	188 (9%)
Senate: Republican	239 (24%)	344 (24%)	201 (31%)	546 (26%)
House: Democratic	312 (32%)	464 (32%)	138 (21%)	601 (29%)
House: Republican	316 (32%)	489 (34%)	276 (42%)	764 (36%)
Incumbents	N.A.	N.A.	N.A.	N.A.
Challenger-other	N.A.	N.A.	N.A.	N.A.
Open seat	N.A.	N.A.	N.A.	N.A.

| | 1980 | | | |
	Top 20	Top 50	Second 50	Total 100
Number of PACs	19	38	22	60
Percentage	95	76	44	60
Receipts	3,849	5,592	1,874	7,465
Disbursements	3,692	5,330	1,867	7,196
Total contributions	2,457	3,480	1,437	4,917
Democratic contributions	1,056 (43%)	1,503 (43%)	418 (29%)	1,921 (39%)
Republican contributions	1,396 (57%)	1,970 (57%)	1,018 (71%)	2,987 (61%)
Congressional contributions				
Total contributions	2,326	3,310	1,384	4,694[b]
Total Democratic	1,010 (43%)	1,449 (44%)	405 (29%)	1,854 (39%)
Total Republican	1,315 (57%)	1,863 (56%)	979 (71%)	2,840 (61%)
Senate: Democratic	318 (14%)	448 (14%)	133 (10%)	581 (12%)
Senate: Republican	466 (20%)	642 (19%)	416 (30%)	1,057 (23%)
House: Democratic	692 (30%)	1,000 (30%)	272 (20%)	1,273 (27%)
House: Republican	849 (37%)	1,220 (37%)	563 (41%)	1,783 (38%)
Incumbents	1,606 (69%)	2,339 (71%)	748 (54%)	3,087 (66%)
Challenger-other	478 (21%)	648 (20%)	463 (33%)	1,111 (24%)
Open seat	243 (10%)	324 (10%)	174 (13%)	498 (11%)

SOURCES: Council on Economic Priorities Newsletter, "The Defense Department's Top 100," November 1980; *Supplement to FEC Reports on Financial Activity 1977–78*, Final Report, April 1980; Data tapes of *FEC Reports on Financial Activity 1977–78*, Final Report, April 1980; *Supplement to FEC Reports on Financial Activity 1979–80*, Final Report, January 1982; Data tapes of *FEC Reports on Financial Activity 1979–80*, Final Report, January 1982.

NOTE: Information for incumbents, challenger-other, and open-seat race contributions was not reported by the FEC for the 1977–1978 election cycle. Percentages may not add to 100 due to rounding.

[a] The amount $2,099,767 for contributions to congressional candidates only represents 21.4 percent of the total 1977–1978 corporate PAC congressional contributions.

[b] The amount $4,694,439 for contributions to congressional candidates represents nearly 24.5 percent of the total 1979–1980 corporate PAC congressional contributions.

1979–1980 virtually identical with that of the leading 500 industrial companies. Nonindustrial PACs increased from 124 (41 percent) in 1977–1978 to 166 (55 percent) in 1979–1980. Once again, among nonindustrials, size of firms and the incidence of PAC formation are closely correlated. As table 9.9 indicates, both in aggregate and within each nonindustrial category, the incidence of PAC formation is higher for the leading 20 firms in each nonindistrial category (120 firms in all) than for the leading 300 nonindustrials as a whole. Indeed, these very largest firms account for nearly half of all the PACs formed by the leading nonindustrials. Eighty-two firms within this group (68 percent) had PACs in the 1980 campaign, up from 63 (53 percent) two years earlier. Interestingly,

TABLE 9.9
PAC Behavior of 300 *Fortune*-Listed Nonindustrials, 1980

Category	Number of PACs	Percent with PACs	Receipts		Disbursements		Contributions	
			$000	Top 20 as % Top 50	$000	Top 20 as % Top 50	$000	Top 20 as % Top 50
Commercial banking								
Top 20	18	90	704	58	648	60	289	70
Top 50	34	68	1,218		1,083		412	63
Diversified financial								
Top 20	15	75	571	59	514	60	357	
Top 50	29	58	974		859		568	63
Life insurance								
Top 20	8	40	97	37	73	34	56	
Top 50	15	30	264		217		169	33
Retail								
Top 20	10	50	783	63	637	60	567	
Top 50	19	38	1,239		1,067		927	61
Transportation								
Top 20	14	70	867	44	867	45	646	
Top 50	30	60	1,952		1,935		987	65
Utilities								
Top 20	17	85	2,248	77	2,068	76	1,234	
Top 50	39	78	2,938		2,717		1,648	75
Totals								
Top 120	82	68	5,270	61	4,807	61	3,149	
Top 300	166	55	8,585		7,878		4,711	67

SOURCES: *Supplement to FEC Reports on Financial Activity 1979–80*, Final Report, January 1982; *Final Report on Financial Activity 1979–80*, Final Report, January 1982; Data tapes of *FEC Reports on Financial Activity 1979–80*, Final Report, January 1982; and *Fortune*, July 13, 1981.

all firms in this cohort of 120 firms were $1 billion-plus entities in terms of assets or revenues.

Within each of the six *Fortune* nonindustrial categories, the top twenty firms displayed a higher incidence of PAC formation than the group as a whole. The differential rates of PAC creation were most striking among commercial banks and diversified financials, all of which had at least a 15 percent differential rate of increase between the top twenty and the group as a whole. The leading industries in terms of PAC formation in 1979–1980 were utilities (78 percent), commercial banks (68 percent), and transportation (60 percent), all of which are subject to stringent industry-specific regulation. Life insurance companies (30 percent), which are primarily state-regulated, and retailers (38 percent), which, relative to the other *Fortune* nonindustrials, are not closely regulated by the federal government, were the least inclined to establish PACs. It is noteworthy that life insurance firms demonstrated the largest rate of increase in PAC formation of any industry group. Among the top twenty life insurance carriers, PACs increased from one (5 percent) in 1977–1978 to eight (40 percent) two years later; within the industry as a whole, PACs increased from five (10 percent) in 1977–1978 to sixteen (30 percent) in 1979–1980. Diversified financial corporations also demonstrated impressive rates of PAC growth during the two-year interval: 75 percent of the top 20 firms and 58 percent for the industry group as a whole now have PACs. Savings and loans (unranked by *Fortune*) increased their numbers of PACs from 4 among the top 20 (20 percent) in 1977–1978 to 6 in 1979—1980 (30 percent), and from 7 (14 percent) to 11 (22 percent) for the top 50 savings and loans.[50] Quite possibly, the rapidly changing character of regulation (and deregulation) of financial markets, which has greatly intensified competition among various forms of financial service industries and companies, has heightened a perceived need for electoral involvement among firms in those industries.

The incidence of PAC formation among the 120 top nonindustrials (68 percent) is almost the same as among the 301 largest industrials (all with revenues of $1 million or more) ranked in table 9.6 (71 percent). Not surprisingly, it is the very largest firms in an industry that are most likely to have both the necessary financial and other institutional resources and perceive an organizational need to be politically active. As is the case with industrial firms, the greater the impact of federal decisions on a particular industrial classification, the greater appears to be the propensity of firms within that industry to establish PACs. If we aggregate the PAC contributions for the 100 leading DOD contractors (the overwhelming majority of which are industrial firms) and the leading *Fortune* nonindustrials categories that are subject to federal regulation (commercial banking, diversified financials, transportation, and utilities), we find that these companies accounted for $7.7 million of the overall PAC contributions of $19.2 million (over 40 percent) during the 1980 campaign.

In summary, the data pertaining to corporate PAC creation among *Fortune*-ranked firms through the decade 1972–1982 provides compelling evidence that firm size and the extent of industry-specific interaction with the federal government are the key variables in determining the existence and intensity of company PAC activity, and within a given industrial classification, size is the key factor.

Providing further substantiation of this position is a recent Conference Board report, which indicates that the frequency with which firms establish government relations units is in direct proportion to the size of the company and documents that "the most heavily federally regulated industries, utilities and communications companies, have the highest incidence of government relations units—94 percent—whereas life insurance companies, traditionally regulated at the state level, reported only 54 percent—the lowest showing.[51] The report also suggests that the critical size threshold regarding the corporate propensity to be involved seriously in politics, including the formation of a PAC, is $1 billion in sales. In the Conference Board's sample of 285 companies (all with sales of $10 million or greater) only 30 percent of the companies below the $1 billion level had PACs in 1979, compared with 62 percent of organizations above that amount.[52] With regard to PAC formation, as table 9.6 indicates, the sharp break in the tendency among *Fortune's* top industrials to establish political action committees occurs at a somewhat higher threshold than for the Conference Board sample. Whereas 193 of the 265 firms (73 percent) with sales of $1.3 billion or more had established PACs by 1980, only 21 of the remaining 35 $1 billion firms (60 percent) had done so. All told, 215 (71 percent) of 1980 *Fortune* industrials with sales of $1 billion or more (301 firms in all) and 151 of the 272 $1 billion non-industrials (56 percent) created PACs. Among nonindustrial firms, with the exception of transportation companies, companies with sales, operating revenues, or assets in excess of $1 billion formed PACs with greater frequency than those under $1 billion. Among commercial banks, of 142 institutions with deposits of $1 billion or greater during 1979, 48 (34 percent) had PACs, while only 10 of the remaining 158 banks did. Among the 200 largest savings and loans of which 97 had assets of $1 billion or more, 22 percent of the latter cohort had established PACs for the 1979–1980 election cycle as opposed to 7 percent of the remaining 103 (less than 15 percent for the full 200).[53] Among transportation companies, however, there was in the 1980 campaign no difference in incidence of PAC formation among firms whose operating revenues exceeded $1 billion from among those whose operating revenues were below that amount; 15 in each category established committees. Finally, a survey of PAC formation among Houston's 50 leading publicly traded nonfinancial companies provides additional evidence for the significance of the $1 billion threshold. Whereas 14 of the 19 firms (74 percent) with 1981 sales or operating revenues of $1 billion or greater operated PACs, only 12 of the remaining 31 (39 percent) had committees.[54]

Before I conclude this examination of the relationship between firm size and the rate of PAC formation, several points warrant mention. All told, of the 1,251 corporations that registered PACs during the 1979–1980 election cycle, Fortune-ranked firms (a total of 1,300) accounted for only 520, 40 percent of the total. The question remains, therefore, concerning the identities and characteristics of the remaining 780 companies (60 percent) that formed PACs. Although the non-Fortune cohort has not been subjected to exhaustive analysis, several observations about this group are possible. First, there is a substantial number of sizable companies (industrials with sales of $125 million or greater, and non-industrials with assets in excess of $1 billion) that do not appear on the Fortune lists either because the industry itself is not ranked by Fortune or, in the case of nonindustrial companies, because the inclusion of only the "top fifty firms" in an industry characterized by large units excludes, by definition, very substantial enterprises that rank fifty-first or lower but have revenues or asset levels that make them likely PAC-formers. Fortune does not rank companies in several nonindustrial categories that, nonetheless, are very substantial enterprises: firms in the savings and loan, real estate development, engineering and construction, and professional services (accounting, law, public relations, and advertising) industries. To illustrate, since Fortune does not rank savings and loan firms (except for a few of the very largest savings and loans, which appear on the diversified financial list), *Fortune* data for 1980 did not pick up the overwhelming majority of the twenty-two PACs created by the nation's largest savings and loans and the fact that all but one of the committees was formed by a $1 billion-plus institution. Until 1982, *Fortune* did not rank diversified service companies (a mélange of firms ranging from CBS and RCA to Dillingham and Turner Construction).[55] This omission undercounted the number of PACs created by $1 billion-plus corporations in 1979–1980 by sixteen (two of the eighteen companies had been $1 billion firms) ranked in other *Fortune* classifications in prior years. Although the *Fortune* top 1,000 industrials include all firms with sales of $125 million or more, the *Fortune* 50 nonindustrial listings, by way of comparison, omit all commercial banks with assets below $4.5 billion, life insurance companies with assets below $1.3 billion, diversified financial corporations with assets of less than $1.86 billion, retailers with sales of less than $1 billion, transportation companies with operating revenues of under $295 million, and utilities with assets under $2.4 billion. Since several of these industries are subject to extensive industry-specific regulations, it is not unreasonable to assume a substantial incidence of PAC formation among even the "smaller" (i.e., less than top 50) firms—many of which are actually quite large. To illustrate: in addition to the thirty-four PACs formed by the 50 *Fortune* commercial banks (68 percent), PACs were established by an additional 24 of the leading 300 banks, all with deposits in excess of $453 million.[56] Among brokerage houses, 12 of the top 20 firms had PACs in 1980. Industry leader Merrill Lynch and Co. had capital exceeding $1 billion in 1981, while the eleven other PAC-formers were bracketed between $470 million and $95 million in capital.[57]

Also omitted by the *Fortune* categories are large privately held companies. *Forbes* magazine in mid-1979 compiled a listing of the 50 largest private companies in the United States.[58] All 50 firms had 1979 estimated revenues of $600 million or more, and the revenues of 28 exceeded $1 billion. The list included 4 firms that would have ranked among the top 50 industrials (Cargill, Mocatta Metals, Continental Grain, and the Bechtel Group), and all 50 of the private companies would have ranked within *Fortune*'s 500 largest industrials. Not surprisingly, this group of companies had its fair share of PAC-formers, with 16 of the 50 concerns (32 percent) registering PACs for the 1979–1980 election cycle.

Supplementing the *Forbes* listing of private firms, a recent *Fortune* study ranked the 50 largest American private industrial companies.[59] Of this group, all of which had sales exceeding $400 million (sufficient to place them within the regular *Fortune* ranking of the leading 550 industrials) 17 were in the $1 billion or larger range (11 of the companies did not appear on the *Forbes* list.)

In summary, this examination of PAC formation among non-*Fortune*-ranked firms demonstrates that a sizable number of these corporations are large economic units in their own right. Indeed, these companies were large enough to have merited inclusion on the *Fortune* lists had they been in an industry classified by *Fortune*, had *Fortune* listed more than the top fifty firms in each nonfinancial category, or had they been publicly owned. PAC-formers among large nonindustrial companies—particularly financial service institutions—are undoubtedly under-counted by the *Fortune* classification scheme. Although it is not possible to establish an accurate count of such companies without examining the specific characteristics of each firm registering a PAC with the FEC, it appears reasonable to assume that between a quarter (183) and a third (244) of the 731 non-*Fortune*-ranked companies that registered PACs during the 1979–1980 election cycle may be considered to be a "large" business enterprise (i.e., firms with revenues or assets exceeding $125 million). When these companies are added to the 520 *Fortune*-ranked enterprises, the cohort of "big business" entities increases to between 703 and 764 firms (between 56 and 61 percent of all company PACs). The remaining 40 percent may then be considered "smaller" business entities, that is, industrials with sales of less than $125 million and non-industrials with assets or operating revenues of less than that figure. Such companies may, however, be sizable companies in their own right in terms of assets, revenues, and employees, and it is unlikely that many PAC-formers consist of truly small businesses, that is, firms in the $10 million-or-less category.

This review of data pertaining to firm size, industrial grouping, and corporate PAC formation since the mid-1970s leads to the strong conclusion that the incidence with which companies form PACs correlated closely with both the size of the firm and the extent of interaction between the firm and its industry and the federal government. All things being equal, for both industrial and nonindustrial companies, the larger the firm and the greater the industry-specific impact of federal government decision making on the company, the more likely the company is to have a political action committee.

As I shall examine more closely in the next section, there tends also to be a strong correlation between firm size and the level of PAC activities engaged in (in terms of receipts, disbursements, and contributions) by companies in all industry categories. Although the very largest companies do not invariably have the most active PACs, FEC data demonstrate that the size of a PAC tends to be related largely to the size of the enterprise. Large companies tend to have larger PACs, and smaller firms smaller PACs (see table 9.15). As was the case during the 1977–1978 election cycle, in the 1980 campaign, of the 14 corporations listed by the FEC as having the top 10 PACs in terms of adjusted receipts, adjusted disbursements, or contributions to candidates, 13 appear on the *Fortune* lists.[60] Eight were in the top 100 industrials (General Motors, Standard Oil of Indiana, General Electric, Tenneco, International Paper, Dart and Kraft, Litton Industries, and General Dynamics); 2 (Grumann Corporation and Harris Corporation) were in the 200–300 group; 1 was the twelfth-ranked retailer (Winn-Dixie Stores); 1 the twenty-eighth-rank transportation firm (Chicago and Northwestern Transportation Co.), all during 1980; and 1 (Fluor) is ranked third in the new (1982) *Fortune* category of diversified service companies. Almost all of the ranking companies for 1979–1980 (12 out of 14) had revenues, sales, or assets of $1.3 billion during 1980. Only American Family Corporation, an insurance and financial services company, did not appear on any *Fortune* list. Ten of the firms that appear at the top of the FEC's reports on PAC activity in 1979–1980 were also ranked among the most active corporate PACs during 1977–1978 (although there were changes among their order of ranking). In virtually all instances their levels of financial activity increased in the two-year period. Actually, the single largest corporate PAC in 1979–1980 was run under the auspices of American Telephone and Telegraph (AT&T), the nation's largest public utility, which raised nearly $1 million, disbursed almost $902,000, and contributed $659,000 to candidates. Since the PAC activites of each of AT&T's operating subsidiaries was listed separately by the FEC, AT&T does not appear, somewhat curiously, on the FEC listings for 1979–1980 as the largest PAC.

Although as a general proposition, larger firms tend to have bigger PACs than small competitors, when one examines the very largest firms within a given industry classification, the level of activity among companies varies considerably and appears unrelated to size.[61] For example, while the PAC affiliated with Citicorp, the nation's largest commercial bank in 1980, led all bank PACs in contributions during the 1979–1980 election cycle, the next five most active contributors were PACs connected with banks ranked eleventh, twelfth, twentieth, eighteenth, and twenty-third on the *Fortune* list, and the fiftieth largest bank was eighth in contributions among the thirty-four *Fortune*-50 banks with PACs. Among diversified financial companies in the 1980 campaign, the leading PAC in terms of contributions was affiliated with the twenty-third largest firm (E. F. Hutton Group), while the political action committee linked with the largest company sponsoring a PAC (fourth-ranked American Express) was seventh in contributions. The disparity between firm size and PAC vigor was most pronounced among life insurance companies, where the largest PAC was associated with the forty-seventh ranked firm (Liberty National) which contributed more than the next five largest insurance PACs combined (these committees were connected with the first, second, eleventh, thirtieth, and fortieth among life insurance carriers). Industry size leaders Prudential and Metropolitan operated respectively the fourth and second largest PACs. Winn-Dixie Stores, a Southern-based food chain that ranked twelfth in size among retailing firms, made contributions that were more than double those of the leading retailer, Sears Roebuck, which operated the second largest PAC. Among transportation firms, the largest PAC was run by the twenty-eighth company on the *Fortune*-50 list (Chicago and Northwestern Transportation Company) while the leading transportation enterprise, United Air Lines, placed fourth, preceded by the twenty-third and fifteenth biggest entities. Top-ranked American Telephone and Telegraph's PAC was far and away the largest among utilities and made contributions of $659.000, a sum greater than the next ten utility PACs combined. It will be recalled that the AT&T figure lumps together all PAC activities conducted by the company's operating subsidiaries. The next largest PAC belonged to second-ranked General Telephone and Electronics, followed by PACs affiliated with the eleventh and forty-seventh companies on the *Fortune* list.

Although, as table 9.9 demonstrates, the twenty largest firms within an industry classification tend collectively to operate PACs with both greater frequency and higher levels of activity than the thirty remaining *Fortune*-ranked, nonindustrial rivals, there is considerable diversity in the

PAC behavior among the firms within each category. Among large companies (firms with sales, assets, or operating revenues of $1 billion or more) another key determinant of the size and vigor of a firm's PAC is top management's philosophy on company political involvement. Corporations with the most vigorous PACs tend to be those where there exists a strong commitment on the part of the CEO or executives immediately below that level to have a committee with substantial resources.[62] A final, and much more amorphous factor in determining PAC operations is the unique configuration of a firm's political environment and needs.

Several final caveats are necessary before we leave the subject of the relationship between firm size, industry classification, and the importance of governmental decisions to the company and incidence of PAC formation among corporations. First, as table 9.1 indicates, although in absolute terms the number of corporate PACs established has been increasing steadily since 1974, not surprisingly, the rate of increase has declined with each succeeding election cycle. Absent major changes in the law or the political climate, this trend will likely continue indefinitely. Those firms most interested in being actively involved in electoral politics have, to a large degree, already set up their committees. New entrants into the PAC marketplace are likely to come from firms having a "change of heart" regarding a prior policy of PAC noninvolvement. Such firms typically either perceive that their political efficacy has been reduced through the absence of a PAC, or, perhaps, succumb to pressures from industry peers, general business groups, the company's governmental relations or Washington-based staff, the parties, or candidates themselves to establish a committee.

Although, as we have seen, many of the most likely PAC-formers— particularly among the very largest corporations—have already established their committees, thereby leaving the tip of the PAC iceberg somewhat more exposed than in either the 1978 or 1980 campaigns, the data clearly demonstrate that there remains nonetheless considerable potential for PAC formations within the corporate community. Recall that, even among the 1,300 *Fortune*-ranked firms, 780 (60 percent) did not have PACs in 1979–1980, including nearly 45 percent of both the top 500 industrials and the leading 300 nonindustrials. Focusing exclusively upon 1980 *Fortune*-ranked companies with sales, assets, or operating revenues of $1 billion or more—the dollar threshold for vigorous corporate political activity suggested by the Conference Board study—we find that, of the 573 firms (310 industrials and 272 nonindustrials) fitting into that category, 366 (215 industrials and 151 nonindustrials) (64 percent) had PACs, while 207 firms (36 percent) did not have committees in the 1980 campaign. As indicated earlier, moreover, this figure underestimates the PAC potential among $1 billion-plus companies since it excludes firms in industries not ranked by *Fortune* (e.g., in 1980 there were ninety-seven savings and loan associations with assets of $1 billion or more) or that fall below the top fifty in their industry (e.g., 132 commercial banks with assets of $1 billion fit into that category in 1980) and private companies (forty-two $1 billion-plus private firms appeared on the combined *Forbes* and *Fortune* lists). It is likely that there are another several hundred $1 billion-plus companies (at least double the 207 *Fortune*-rated firms in that category) that did not have PACs in 1979–1980. Thus, even among the highest levels of American business, there remains substantial opportunity for PAC creation. If you include an even larger pool of corporations—the 3,755 U.S. firms reporting assets of $100 million or more (1974)—you see that the 1,496 companies with FEC-registered PACs as of June 30, 1982, constituted only 40 percent of these large companies (assuming for the moment all PAC-formers fell into the $100 million-or-more asset category). Accordingly, there remain over 2,000 companies that are plausible prospects for PAC formation, not to mention another 20,000 additional corporations with assets of $10 million or greater. If only 20 percent of the $100 million or more group were to create PACs over the next half-decade— hardly an extreme assumption—the number of company PACs could reach the 1,900 mark by 1990. Absent major changes in the legislation governing PACs or an abandonment of political activity by the business community, it is not unrealistic to anticipate this number of corporate-affiliated political action committees within the next several years.

LEVELS OF CORPORATE PAC ELECTORAL ACTIVITY

Although individually corporate committees have operated on a much smaller scale than PACs that fall into the other FEC classifications, as table 9.2 documents, company-affiliated committees have become the largest source of PAC contributions to candidates. This development is based on two factors. First, as table 9.1 indicates, the number of corporate PACs is far greater than that in any other PAC category. As of July 1, 1982, the 1,415 corporate PACs constituted 45 percent of all committees registered with the FEC and were four times more numerous than the 350 labor-affiliated committees and exceeded the combined registration figures for the four remaining PAC categories (nonconnected organizations, trade/membership/health, cooperatives, and corporations without capital stock). Accordingly, while the individual company PAC may be rather small when measured in terms of receipts, disbursements, and contributions compared with PACs in the other categories, the number of company PACs is so much greater than for any other classification that, collectively, their financial activity has come to dominate the statistics. Table 9.10, which presents aggregate and average PAC activity for 1979–1980, demonstrates this point.

During 1979–1980, the "average" corporate committee had a lower level of financial operations (in terms of receipts, disbursements, and contributions) than PACs in all other PAC categories save one (corporations without stock) and for PACs as a cohort.[63] This point is illustrated well by the all-important contributions to candidates data. The average corporate PAC gave $17,400 to congressional candidates in 1979–1980, less than a third of the amount contributed by the average labor PAC, and approximately one-third less than the average contributions level of all PACs.[64] Corporate committees, however, were more likely than PACs in the other major FEC categories to make contributions once they were registered: 88 percent of company PACs actually made some contributions to candidates in the 1980 campaign, as opposed to 77 percent for trade/membership/health groups, 73 percent for labor unions, and only 52 percent for nonconnected organzations (this 52 percent figure does not take into account nonconnected organizations making independent expenditures). Accordingly, as a group, corporate PACs led the contributions category as a consequence of the volume of aggregate PAC operations as opposed to a high level of activity among individual committees. As data in the Cantor study reveal, no corporate PAC ranked among the top twenty committees in terms of financial activity (receipts, disbursements, and contributions) during the elections held between 1972 and 1980.[65] The "top twenty" lists are populated by PACs affiliated with trade groups, professional organizations, labor unions, and nonconnected membership groups. In 1979–1980, the top-rated company PACs

TABLE 9.10
Aggregate and Average Individual PAC Activity, 1979–1980

Committee Type	Number of PACs Registered	Number of PACs Contributing	Percent PACs Registered Contributing	Aggregate ($ million)			Average Individual ($ thousand)			Percent of Receipts Contributed	
				Adjusted receipts	Adjusted disburs.	Contri-butions[a]	Adjusted receipts	Adjusted disburs.	Contri-butions	Aggr.	Avg. Ind.
Corporate	1,251	1,101	88	33.9	31.4	19.2	27.1	25.2	17.4	57	64
Labor	331	240	73	25.7	25.1	13.2	82.2	75.8	55.0	51	67
Nonconnected	471	243	52	40.1	38.6	4.9	81.1	82.0	20.4	12	25
Trade/membership/ health	635	490	77	33.9	32.0	15.9	53.4	50.5	32.4	47	61
Cooperative	36	31	86	2.8	2.7	1.4	77.6	75.3	44.3	50	57
Corporation with- out stock	61	50	82	1.4	1.3	0.6	22.6	20.7	12.6	43	56
Total	2,785	2,155	77	137.7	131.2	55.2	49.5	49.1	25.6	40	52

SOURCE: FEC Press Release, "FEC Releases Final PAC Report for 1979–80 Election Cycle" February 21, 1982.
NOTE: Aggregate statistics represent the summation of all activity for each committee type. Average Individual statistics represent the average for individual PACs within each committee type based on the aggregate activity divided by the number of PACs actually active.
[a] House and Senate.

had half or less the receipts, disbursements (Chicago and Northwestern Transportation led in both categories), and contributions (Winn-Dixie Stores) of the PACs listed by the FEC as tenth in each category for the top ten political committees (all FEC classifications combined). Only AT&T would have ranked among the top ten 1980 PAC contributions leaders if it had been credited with the activity of all of the PACs affiliated with its operating subsidiaries.

A second point is also pertinent to explain the financial leadership role that corporate committees as a cohort have come to play in PAC contributions to candidates. Collectively, corporations contribute to candidates a higher percentage of their adjusted receipts than any other category of PAC. Whereas in 1979–1980 union PACs donated 51 percent of their adjusted receipts to candidates and trade/membership/health groups donated 47 percent of the money they raised, corporations actually donated 57 percent of their adjusted receipts. As a group, PACs gave only 40 percent of their adjusted receipts, and nonconnected organizations allocated a meager 12 percent to this purpose. Presumably corporations are both more efficient in their fund-raising efforts and do not have the very expensive fund-raising and administrative costs associated with direct mail operations (the mainstay of many nonconnected organizations' fund raising). Moreover, company committees have not indulged in the extensive independent expenditures activities that have drawn off substantial sums of money that otherwise could have been utilized for contributions. Indeed, if the $13.1 million that nonconnected committees spent on independent expenditures in the 1980 campaign (particularly of the negative variety) is added to the $4.9 million donated to candidates, a total of $18 million, the percentage of adjusted receipts going into the campaign, 45 percent, is much more respectable. The pertinent point with regard to corporations, however, is that a greater percentage of corporate PAC revenues actually get to candidates than do monies from other categories of PACs.

Let us now turn to specific characteristics of corporate PAC behavior. The focus will be primarily at the macro level and will concentrate on the electoral behavior of either the entire corporate cohort or the activities of particular categories of firms. As we have already seen, corporate PACs as a class have increased dramatically since the mid-1970s in numbers and scale of activity. An examination of data for the past three election cycles together with preliminary 1981–1982 figures is particularly instructive (see table 9.11). However measured, corporate PAC contributions have become increasingly important sources of campaign funds with each succeeding election cycle, both in absolute terms and relative to other types of political action committees. Whereas company PAC contributions totaled only $4.3 million in 1975–1976, they were more than four times larger in 1980–1981 and appear likely to approach $35 million in 1981–1982, an increase of over 700 percent in six years. Viewed in relative terms, in 1975–1976, corporate committees gave an estimated 21 percent of all PAC funds and constituted an estimated 4 percent of all campaign receipts by congressional candidates. By 1979–1980, these percentages had risen, respectively, to 35

TABLE 9.11
Indexes of Corporate PAC Behavior, 1976–1982 ($ million)

	Election Cycle				
	1975–76	1977–78	1979–80	January 1981– June 1982	1981–82[a]
Number of corporate PACs	450	825	1,250	1,496	1,496
Adjusted receipts corporate PACs only	6.8	17.4	33.9	32.6	53.4
Adjusted disbursements corporate PACs only	5.8	15.2	31.4	22.3	48.8
Corporate contributions	4.3	9.8	19.2	12.5	34.8
All PACs combined contributions	22.5	35.2	55.2	34.6	88.7
Corporate contributions as percent of all contributions	19	28	35	36	39
Total receipts of candidates	104.7	199.4	248.4	175.6	344.3
All PACs contributions as percent of candidates' receipts	19	18	22	20	26
Corporate contributions as percent of candidates' receipts	4	5	8	7	10
Contribution amount of average corporate PAC	$11,026	$13,920	$17,534	$11,091	$27,062

TABLE 9.11 (continued)

Indexes of Corporate PAC Behavior, 1976–1982 ($ million)

	Election Cycle				
	1975–76	1977–78	1979–80	January 1981–June 1982	1981–82
Combined contributions of top 10 corporate committees	.6	1.2	1.9	1.4	3.5–3.8
Average contribution of top 10 corporate committees	$68,000	$120,000	$190,000	$140,000	$350,000
Top 10 corporate committees contributions as percent of all corporate PAC contributions	3%	12%	10%	11%	10–11%

SOURCES: FEC Press Releases: "FEC Releases Final Report on 1977–78 Financial Activity," April 24, 1980, and "FEC Releases Final PAC Report for 1979–80 Election Cycle," February 21, 1982; Common Cause, *1976 Federal Campaign Finance*, vol. 1, *Interest Group and Political Party Contributions to Congressional Candidates* (Washington, D.C.: Common Cause, 1977); and Joseph E. Cantor, *Political Action Committees: Their Evolution and Growth and Their Implications for the Political System*, updated (Washington, D.C.: Congressional Research Service, Library of Congress, May 7, 1982).

NOTE: Amounts are reported in the millions of dollars, except for contribution amount of average corporate PAC and average contribution of top 10 corporate committees, which are reported in thousands of dollars. Only the top nine PACs' contributions were reported for the 1975–1976 election cycle.

ᵃFull cycle, estimated.

percent and 8 percent and appear likely to increase even more in the 1982 campaign to 39 percent and 10 percent, respectively. While the aggregate figures for corporate PACs have been increasing, the level of contributions for the "average" individual company committee actually functioning during the election cycle has also gone up significantly, from $11,026 in 1975–1976 to $17,534 in 1979–1980. During the current election cycle, the average functioning committee will give an estimated $27,060 to candidates. The contributions activities of the largest corporate committees has increased dramatically with each election cycle. The top ten company PACs contributed a total of $612,000 in 1975–1976, $1.2 million in 1977–1978, and $1.9 million in 1979–1980.[66] Thus far in 1981–1982, they have given candidates $1.4 million and for the complete election cycle are likely to contribute upwards of $3.5 million. Over the past several election cycles, the ten largest committees have given an average of 11 percent of all funds donated by all corporations. Thus, in less than eight years, the leading corporate committees have increased their average level of giving by more than two-fold. Even taking into account the rate of inflation during the period since 1975–1976, the level of corporate PAC operations has grown dramatically. Moreover, there is no reason to anticipate any diminution in these operations.

If past experience is any gauge of probable future PAC activity, it is reasonable to expect the level of corporate activity to increase (in real terms) with each succeeding election as companies make their PAC operations ever more comprehensive and efficient and management and professional personnel (and in some companies, shareholders) become accustomed increasingly to contributing to the company PAC and increase their levels of giving. Table 9.12 demonstrates dramatically the substantial increase in financial activities of five leading corporate PACs over the past three elections. A perusal of the list of the fifty leading DOD contractors for 1979 reveals that, of the thirty-one companies that had PACs in *both* 1978–1979 and 1979–1980, in all but three cases, the

TABLE 9.12
PAC Behavior Among Large Corporations, 1976–1980
($ thousand)

Corporation	Receipts			Disbursements			Contributions		
	1976	1978	1980	1976	1978	1980	1976	1978	1980
Standard Oil of Indiana	60	266	387	32	266	376	34	155	194
American Family	98	254	334	77	253	324	66	106	187
International Paper	80	225	248	63	240	235	42	173	164
Winn-Dixie Stores	21	232	401	7	124	268	—	113	251
LTV/Vought	105	284	492	87	256	447	47	123	229
Totals	364	1,261	1,862	266	1,139	1,650	189	670	1,025

SOURCES: Figures for Standard Oil, American Family, and International Paper for 1976 are drawn from Common Cause, *1976 Federal Campaign Finances*, vol. 50 (Washington, D.C.: Common Cause, 1977); all other data are derived from *Supplement to FEC Reports on Financial Activity 1979–80*, Final Report, January 1982; Data tapes of *FEC Reports on Financial Activity 1979–80*, Final Report, January 1982; *Supplement to FEC Reports on Financial Activity 1977–78*, Final Report, April 1980; Data tapes of *FEC Reports on Financial Activity 1977–78*, Final Report, April 1980; and Walter W. Guzzardi, Jr., "Business Is Learning How To Win in Washington," *Fortune*, March 27, 1978, pp. 52–58.

contribution level for the 1980 campaign was higher than for the previous election cycle (see table 9.8). In nine instances, the level of increase in PAC contributions to candidates rose by a multiple of two to four, and in four instances by a factor of five to nine! As a group, these fifty firms more than doubled their contributions during the two-year period, from $1.45 million in 1977–1978 to $3.48 million in 1979–1980. This phenomenon of PAC maturation is evident among PACs of all industrial classifications and supports the view that, although some of the increases may not continue to be as dramatic as between 1977–1978 and 1979–1980, company PACs typically increase their levels of financial activity with each succeeding election cycle.

The results of a survey of corporate political action committees conducted in mid-1981 by four leading business groups provides valuable insights into the future potential for financial growth by company committees.[67] The study, which elicited responses from over 275 company PACs, revealed the following information:

Over 80 percent of the responding PACs gave less than $50,000 to federal candidates in the 1979–1980 election cycle.

The more than 100,000 individuals who contributed to these PACs gave an average of $161 each over the 1979–1980 election cycle ($80.50 per year). Over 84 percent of the responding firms had an employee donation average of less than $250 for the two-year period, while half of the firms averaged less than $100 per employee.

These firms solicited an average of 63 percent of their managerial and executive personnel, and 33 percent of the solicited personnel actually made contributions to the PAC. The average number of donors per company PAC was slightly less than 400.

Only 18 percent of the PACs solicited company shareholders, and in a majority of cases, companies reported that 10 percent or less of the shareholders solicited actually contributed to the PAC.

The survey report notes correctly that there remains a great potential for corporate PAC operations: "Corporations have an extensive area in which to develop their political activities. There is evident room for expansion in shareholder solicitation, in-kind contributions, independent expenditures, and internal communications."

PATTERNS OF CORPORATE PAC CONTRIBUTIONS

Thus far, I have concentrated on the sources of corporate PAC funds. Let us turn now to the uses to which these monies are put. A table constructed by Joseph E. Cantor of the Congressional Research Service is particularly useful in exploring the overall pattern of PAC contributions to candidates (see table 9.13). Cantor's data confirm what the reader might have already anticipated. As a cohort, company PACs have tended since 1976 to support Republicans over Democrats by a margin of nearly two to one; incumbents over challengers and candidates for open seats by margins of approximately 64 percent to 24 percent to 14 percent, but the percentage of incumbent support has been declining steadily with each succeeding election cycle; and House candidates to Senate office seekers by a nearly two-to-one ratio. Corporate PACs tend to concentrate their funds on the general election races rather than on primary or run-off elections. In 1977–1978, company-affiliated PACs contributed less than 30 percent of their funds in the first eighteen months of the election cycle, saving their resources for late primaries but particularly the gen-

TABLE 9.13
Corporate PAC Contributions to Congressional Candidates in General Elections, by Party and Status of Candidate, 1972–1980
($ million)

Year	Amount Given	Party		Status			Senate	House
		Dem.	Rep.	Incum.	Chall.	Open		
1972	1.7	0.5	1.2	1.1	0.2	0.4	—	—
		(29)	(71)	(65)	(12)	(24)		
1974	2.4	0.9	1.4	1.9	0.2	0.3	—	—
		(38)	(58)	(79)	(8)	(13)		
1976	6.7	2.9	3.8	4.8	1.2	0.8	—	—
		(43)	(57)	(72)	(18)	(12)		
1978	9.1	3.1	6.0	5.4	2.0	1.7	3.6	6.1
		(34)	(66)	(59)	(22)	(19)	(37)	(63)
1980	18.1	6.3	11.8	10.5	5.6	2.0	6.9	12.3
		(35)	(65)	(58)	(31)	(11)	(36)	(64)

Sources: Joseph E. Cantor, *Political Action Committees: Their Evolution and Growth and Their Implications in the Political System,* updated (Washington D.C.: Congressional Research Service, Library of Congress, May 7, 1982), p. 121. Senate and House data taken from FEC press releases on PAC activity, April 24, 1980, and February 21, 1982.
Note: Figures in parentheses are percentages.

eral election races. In 1979–1980, company-affiliated committees contributed a somewhat larger share of funds, $9.6 million, during this eighteen-month period (44 percent) but saved the bulk of contributions for the crucial four months of the campaign and for the immediate aftermath of the election, when "bandwagoning" (and attendant bankrolling) takes place. If anything, in 1981–1982, company PACs appear to have accelerated their early contributions activity in an effort to have more impact at an earlier stage of the election cycle. As of June 30, 1982, corporate committees had donated $12.5 million to candidates seeking office in 1981–1982 congressional races, more than one-third of all PAC funds going to congressional candidates during the eighteen-month period. The 1982 campaign figure was greater than the combined amount company PACs gave to congressional candidates during a comparable stage in the 1978 and 1980 campaigns. This early money had been concentrated overwhelmingly on incumbents, particularly Republicans in the Senate and Democrats in the House. If contribution patterns of the 1980 campaign repeat themselves, it is quite likely that the money spent after September 1 went to a very substantial degree to Republican incumbents in the Senate and House and Republican challengers and open-seat candidates in both houses of Congress, with Democratic challengers and open-seat candidates receiving virtually no funds and Democratic incumbents obtaining relatively small amounts of contributions. Companies were also well positioned for an active role in the final stages of the 1981–1982 election cycle, with over $16.7 million in cash on hand after eighteen months of campaigning remaining to be spent in the final days of the election.

In earlier studies, I have suggested that corporate PACs (together with labor PACs) have tended to be risk averters rather than risk takers, contributing overwhelmingly to incumbents rather than to challengers or candidates in open races.[68] While this risk adverse behavior was particularly prevalent throughout the 1976 elections, during the 1978 and 1980 election cycles, as table 9.13 indicates, the percentages of incumbency support decreased substantially. A possible explanation for this shift in contributions is that during the second half of the 1970s many long-term congressional incumbents (a large number of whom were Democrats, particularly in the House) left congressional office through retirement, death, or defeat. Somewhat over half of the members of the Ninety-Seventh Congress did not occupy their seats in 1975. The number of well-entrenched incumbents, with substantial seniority, who hold critical committee positions is far less than it was a decade ago. Corporate PAC managers have accordingly been in a better position to support candidates whose political philosophies are closer to their own rather than blanketly supporting incumbent office holders because of their likelihood for reelection. This has meant in practice that company PAC managers have looked with greater favor at Republican challengers and open-seat candidates. It is no coincidence, as table 9.13 shows, that while corporate PACs have given greater sums to challengers and open-seat candidates they have increasingly shifted to support Republican candidates. Despite their willingness to support Democratic incumbents if they have little practical alternative, the great majority of corporate PACs would prefer, if at all possible, to support Republicans over Democrats, and conservatively oriented candidates (irrespective of party) to those more liberally inclined.

A recent study of PAC behavior by Edward Handler and John R. Mulkern, *Business in Politics,* reinforces this conclusion. Handler and Mulkern found in their study of seventy-one PACs affiliated with major American corporations that "corporate PACs are not behaving in a uniform way, nor are they pursuing similar goals and seeking identical results." Rather, they found there are two major directions of PAC giving—corporate PACs tend to be either "predominantly ideological or pragmatic in orientation."[69] The ideological PAC typically is oriented toward effecting significant political change and seeks to elect conservative (usually Republican) candidates to move Congress in a more pro-business direction. Such PACs are interested, secondarily, in access. They judge candidates primarily on the basis of their stands on a spectrum of issues that indicate their degree of advocacy for the free enterprise system. On the other hand, the pragmatic PAC accommodates and adapts to the existing balance of political forces, seeks primarily to enhance access, and judges candidates on their stances on specific company-related issues. In their sample of seventy-one firms, Handler and Mulkern found that approximately 55 percent pursued ideologically oriented contributions strategies in the 1978 and 1980 campaigns; 37 percent were pragmatically oriented; and 8 percent were indeterminant. Although these divergent orientations toward political participation within the corporate community indicate a degree of diversity much greater than among labor unions, which consistently contribute on predominately ideological grounds, giving over 90 percent of their funds to Democrats, Handler and Mulkern found that "in a political sense" it is appropriate to speak of a business community.

Cohesion appears in the wide prevalence among PACs of free enterprise sentiments, as expressed in their solicitation literature and statements of purpose. Shared political preferences among pragmatic and ideological PACs appear also in their decision to support challengers. Although pragmatic PACs focus heavily on incumbents, their behavior is similar to the ideological PACs when they do elect to support challengers. They are, then, as little likely as the ideological PACs to support other than conservatives, Republicans or Sunbelt Democrats. Pragmatic PACs may back liberal Democratic incumbents for access purposes, but rarely will they support a liberl Democratic challenger.[70]

Given the philosophical preferences and behavioral propensities revealed in the Handler–Mulkern study and present political circumstances, it is highly likely that, when absolutely necessary, corporate PACs will continue to support Democratic incumbents. However, given the increasing number of Republicans in both the House and Senate (where already they are a majority) and the declining number of long-term congressional Democrats whose seemingly invulnerable positions commanded in past years substantial corporate support, PACs should have an increasing opportunity to indulge their GOP-oriented proclivities. In short, pragmatism and ideological commitment will be able to go hand in hand for company political action committees as greater numbers of Republicans are elected to Congress. It will become, consequently, far more difficult to distinguish corporate PAC contributions patterns that are pragmatically risk-adverse—incumbent-oriented—from those that favor incumbents as a result of ideological commitment.

LEVELS OF CORPORATE PAC ACTIVITY BY INDUSTRY GROUPING

It is instructive to consider the patterns of contributions among various categories of corporate PACs segregated on the basis of industry or affinity groupings.

Defense Contractors

Among the 100 leading Department of Defense contractors,[71] as table 9.8 reveals, the overall level of PAC activity more than doubled between the 1977–1978 and 1979–1980 election cycles. Whereas these committees contributed $2.1 million to candidates in the 1978 campaign, two years later they donated $4.9 million. Indeed, in 1979–1980, contributions by PACs affiliated with the top 20 DOD contractors ($2.5 million) alone exceeded the 1977–1978 donations of all of the top 100 committees ($2.1 million) by 17 percent, making the average contribution per committee in 1979–1980 $82,000, up from $42,000 in 1977–1978. Among the top 20 contractors average PAC contributions more than doubled (to $129,000 from $58,000) in the two-year period. Looking at the activities of individual firms, the largest DOD-related PACs in the 1980 campaign, rated on the basis of contributions, were operated by American Telephone and Telegraph, $659,000 (the activities of all operating companies are lumped together), LTV corporation, $229,000, and Tenneco, $204,000. In 1977–1978 these PACs donated to federal candidates $129,000, $104,000, and $38,000 respectively. The single largest PAC run by a DOD contractor in 1977–1978 was Standard Oil of Indiana's, which contributed a total of $155,000.

Fortune-ranked Nonindustrials

A comparison of the contributions activity of the 300 *Fortune*-ranked nonindustrial firms reveals a similar rate of growth. In the 1980 campaign, this group gave $4.7 million to congressional races, nearly two and a half times more than the $1.9 million they gave in the 1978 campaign.[72] During the 1979–1980 election cycle, the 120 leading nonindustrials more than doubled their contributions level of two years earlier and exceeded the 1978–1980 donations of all 300 nonindustrial firms by 63 percent (see table 9.14). In every industry but one (transportation), the amount of contributions more than doubled in the two-year period, while for firms in three categories (commercial banking, life insurance, and utilities) there was a threefold or greater growth in contributions. Average PAC size (in terms of contributions) of the 300 leading nonindustrials nearly doubled (from $15,000 to $29,000), while among the top 120 firms, average PAC size rose from $21,000 to $39,000 in the two-year period. The *Fortune* nonindustrials operating PACs with the largest average size in 1979–1980 included retailers ($49,000), utilities ($42,000), and transportation companies ($33,000), while life insurance companies ($11,000), commercial banks ($12,000), and diversified financial institutions ($20,000) were considerably smaller. Among the top

TABLE 9.14
Detailed PAC Behavior Among *Fortune*-Ranked Nonindustrials in 1980 Congressional Elections ($ thousand)

Category	Total Receipts	Total Disburse.	Total Contrib.	Total Dem.	Total Rep.	Senate Dem.	Senate Rep.	House Dem.	House Rep.	Candidate Status Incum.	Candidate Status Chall.	Candidate Status Open
Commercial banks	1,218	1,083	382	179 (47)	203 (53)	49 (13)	77 (20)	130 (34)	126 (33)	254 (67)	85 (22)	43 (11)
Diversified financial	974	859	551	234 (42)	317 (58)	101 (18)	151 (27)	133 (24)	166 (30)	357 (65)	129 (23)	65 (12)
Life insurance	264	217	163	66 (40)	97 (60)	23 (14)	46 (28)	43 (26)	51 (31)	97 (59)	48 (29)	19 (12)
Retailing	1,239	1,067	913	360 (39)	553 (61)	122 (13)	187 (20)	238 (26)	366 (40)	586 (64)	220 (24)	107 (12)
Transportation	1,952	1,935	868	537 (62)	331 (38)	181 (21)	133 (15)	356 (41)	198 (23)	741 (85)	78 (9)	49 (6)
Utilities	2,938	2,717	1,573	782 (50)	791 (50)	168 (11)	216 (14)	614 (39)	575 (36)	1,126 (71)	308 (20)	137 (9)
Totals	8,585	7,878	4,450	2,158 (48)	2,292 (52)	644 (14)	810 (18)	1,514 (34)	1,482 (33)	3,161 (71)	868 (20)	420 (9)

SOURCES: *Supplement to FEC Reports on Financial Activity 1979–80*, Final Report, January 1982; Data tapes of *FEC Reports on Financial Activity 1979–80*, Final Report, January 1982; and *Fortune* July 13, 1981.

NOTE: Number in parentheses are percentages. Percentages may not add to 100 due to rounding.

20 firms in each non-industrial category, PACs run by utilities ($73,000), retailers ($57,000), and transportation companies ($46,000) towered over committees affiliated with the other nonindustrial classifications. Save for transportation and life insurance companies, average PAC size among the 300 nonindustrials more than doubled between 1977–1978 and 1979–1980. Only four of the *Fortune*-ranked nonindustrials made contributions exceeding $100,000 in the 1980 campaign—Sears Roebuck and Winn-Dixie Stores (retailers) and AT&T and General Telephone and Telegraph (utilities). In the case of both the DOD contractors and the nonindustrial companies, the 20 leading firms in each category increased their levels of contributions at a rate that was slightly higher than for the group as a whole.

Fortune-Ranked Industrials

For the *Fortune* leading 1,000 industrials, when grouped on the basis of firm size rather than according to industrial classification or affinity (reliance on governmental contracts), the increase in level of PAC operations is substantially less dramatic than for either *Fortune* nonindustrial firms or DOD contractors. As table 9.15 indicates, the PACs operated by the 10 largest industrials sponsoring political action committees made contributions of $876,000 in 1979–1980, an average donation per committee of $88,000. A comparable group in 1977–1978 donated $701,000, an average of $70,000 per PAC. The largest company PAC in this cohort (Standard Oil of Indiana) gave $194,000 to candidates in the 1980 campaign, while the smallest committee (Ford Motor) contributed only $39,000. Within each cohort, contributions in 1979–1980 were more than 60 percent greater than in the previous election cycle. Among PACs affiliated with firms in the fifth or lowest cohort, the average level of contributions was quite minimal, $3,000. Interestingly, firms in the third cohort (*Fortune*-ranked 254–274 in 1980) increased their contribution level threefold over 1977–1978 and, indeed, surpassed the second cohort in PAC activity. This anomaly is explained by the presence in this group of Harris Corporation and Wheelabrator-Frye, two of the dozen largest company PACs in 1979–1980 ranked on the basis of contributions. Both made contributions of more than $160,000, whereas the two largest contributors in the second group, FMC and American Cyanamid, gave $95,000 and $59,00, respectively. It is noteworthy that both Harris

TABLE 9.15
PAC Behavior Among *Fortune*-Ranked Industrials in 1980 Elections
($ thousand)

	Fortune *Ranking*				
	1–12	*101–111*	*254–274*	*455–496*	*785–981*
Receipts	1,480	362	679	134	38
Disbursements	1,440	352	611	122	34
Total contributions	876	326	497	100	31
Democratic contributions	256 (29)	130 (40)	185 (37)	30(30)	1 (3)
Republican contributions	619 (71)	195 (60)	310 (62)	70 (70)	30 (97)
Congressional contributions					
Total contributions	857	317	459	92	29
Total Democratic	253 (30)	129 (41)	178 (39)	24 (26)	1 (3)
Total Republican	604 (70)	188 (59)	281 (61)	68 (74)	28 (97)
Senate: Democratic	78 (9)	51 (16)	59 (13)	7 (8)	0 (0)
Senate: Republican	220 (26)	61 (19)	134 (29)	36 (39)	12 (41)
House: Democratic	175 (20)	78 (25)	119 (26)	17 (18)	1 (3)
House: Republican	384 (45)	127 (40)	147 (32)	32 (35)	16 (55)
Incumbents	519 (60)	207 (65)	297 (65)	35 (38)	10 (33)
Challenger-other	234 (27)	80 (25)	129 (28)	44 (48)	17 (57)
Open seat	105 (12)	31 (10)	32 (7)	13 (14)	3 (10)

SOURCES: *Supplement to FEC Reports on Financial Activity 1979–80,* Final Report, January 1982; Data tapes of *FEC Reports on Financial Activity 1979–80,* Final Report, January 1982; and *Fortune* May 4, 1981.

NOTE: Figures are totals for ten companies in each category. Totals for incumbents, challenger-other, and open-seat may not equal congressional contribution totals due to rounding. Numbers in parentheses are percentages.

Corporation and Wheelabrator-Frye had sales of $1.3 billion or greater and were, accordingly, well beyond the critical $1 billion threshold that appears to separate politically active from politically inactive firms. Harris Corporation, moreover, is a leading DOD contractor. Except for this special situation, as far as cohorts of companies are concerned, firm size and level of PAC activity were closely related among industrials.

CORPORATE PAC CONTRIBUTIONS BEHAVIOR BY INDUSTRY OR AFFINITY GROUPING

Let us now turn to see to whom various categories of corporate PACs contribute their monies.

DOD Contractors

The 100 leading DOD contributors in 1979–1980 split their $4.9 million in contributions, 61 percent for Republicans to 39 percent for Democrats. The 20 largest DOD firms were slightly more bipartisan in their giving practices, contributing 57 percent for Republicans to 43 percent for Democrats, the firms in the bottom 50 being decidedly more Republican in their orientation, favoring the GOP over the Democrats 71 percent to 29 percent. Not surprisingly, the bulk of contributions went to incumbents (66 percent), with challengers (23 percent) and open-seat candidates (11 percent) splitting the remainder. The 20 largest DOD firms were most incumbent-oriented with their contributions (69 percent), while challengers (28 percent) and open-seat candidates (10 percent) shared the remainder. Once again the lower-ranked DOD firms tended to deviate somewhat from the behavior of the larger group, giving challengers (33 percent) and candidates in open-seat races (13 percent) a somewhat larger share of the funds—incumbents received 54 percent.

A virtually identical pattern of giving existed in the 1978 campaign. House Republicans were the group most favored by DOD contractors, receiving 36 percent of the proceeds, while Democratic candidates for the Senate were given only 12 percent of the proceeds. All told, in 1977–1978 65 percent of the funds went to House candidates and 35 percent to Senate candidates. Republicans received 62 percent of the monies, and Democrats, 38 percent. Once again, PACs associated with the bottom fifty DOD-related firms tended to be somewhat more Republican in orientation than the group as a whole, favoring the GOP by 73 percent to 27 percent for the Democrats. The data regarding the contributions behavior of leading DOD contractors suggest that, whereas the group as a whole was oriented in the 1980 campaign to Republicans and incumbent candidates, the firms receiving smaller amounts of DOD dollars tended to be both more partisan in favor of the GOP and more willing to support Republican challengers and open-seat candidates than the larger firms. To use Handler and Mulkern's terminology, they tended in 1979–1980 to be somewhat more "ideologically" oriented than their typically larger, more "pragmatic" brethren.

Fortune-ranked Nonindustrials

Among the *Fortune* 300 leading nonindustrial corporations in 1979–1980 (as table 9.14 documents), a pattern of contributions similar to that demonstrated by DOD contractors emerges, but with one significant difference. While as a group the nonindustrials preferred Republicans to Democrats, their degree of preference (52 percent to 48 percent) was much less pronounced than for DOD contractors. Their strong preference for incumbents (67 percent) over challengers and open-seat candidates is virtually identical with that of the one hundred leading defense firms' PACs. As did defense contractors, the *Fortune* companies concentrated their monies on House races (64 percent) but unlike the DOD firms, they divided their contributions almost evenly between the parties. Senate races received 31 percent of the funds, with Republicans shading Democrats in contributions by 8 percent to 14 percent.

The contributions patterns among the various categories of *Fortune* nonindustrials provide some interesting comparisons. Commercial banks, diversified financial companies, life insurance firms, and retailers manifested largely consistent contributions behavior. The firms in each category favored Republicans (55–60 percent) over Democrats (40–45 percent) by ten or more percentage points; incumbents (57–63 percent) over challengers (21–28 percent) and open-seat candidates (11–12 percent) by substantial margins; and House candidates (52–63 percent) over Senate candidates (30–41 percent). Even within this group, however, there were some interesting differences. Although they strongly preferred Republican Senate candidates over their Democratic rivals, commercial banks treated Democrats and Republicans running for the House virtually identically. By like token, life insurance companies donated to Republican Senate candidates twice the amount they gave Democratic senatorial hopefuls but were much more evenhanded in making contributions to House candidates. Utilities, the classification making the largest amount of contributions ($1.6 million), divided their contributions to 1980 congressional candidates almost equally among Republicans (50.3 percent) and Democrats (49.7 percent), favoring, curiously, Republican senatorial hopefuls (56–44 percent) and Democratic House candidates (52–48 percent). They also gave somewhat more heavily to incumbents (72 percent) over challengers (20 percent) and open-seat candidates (8 percent) than did firms in the categories discussed previously. In the 1978 campaign, utilities also split their funds fairly evenly, although they moderately favored Republicans (53 percent) over Democrats (47 percent). Given the great importance of federal energy policy to most of the firms on the utilities list, it is plausible that these companies are decidedly pragmatic in their contributions policies, supporting well-placed incumbents on both sides of the aisle.

Unquestionably the most curious pattern of contributions was among the *Fortune*-ranked transportation firms. This group was the only one among the *Fortune* nonindustrials to demonstrate an overall and decided preference for Democratic candidates (60 percent of contributions) over Republicans (40 percent). Transportation firms concentrated their contributions in Senate races, and Democrats were favored over Republicans by a 58 to 42 percent margin. Companies in this category were also decidedly more incumbent-oriented than other *Fortune*-ranked nonindustrial classifications, favoring office holders heavily (85 percent) over challengers (9 percent) and open-seat candidates (6 percent) in 1980 congressional races. Another anomalous aspect of transportation firms' contributions in 1979–1980 is that a significant percentage of funds (12 percent) did not go into the 1980 campaign congressional races. The apparent interest of transportation companies in presidential races possibly results from the fact that since a variety of issues pertaining to transportation deregulation remained unresolved going into the 1980 campaign, presidential appointments to the regulatory commissions with jurisdiction over these matters were of critical importance to the firms in the affected industries. An examination of the data for the thirty *Fortune*-ranked transportation companies with PACs in 1979–1980 reveals no discernible differences in the behavior among various categories of transportation firms. Airlines, railroads, truckers, and freight forwarders had very similar patterns of contributions. Interestingly, although both airlines and railroad PACs favored Democrats over Republicans in 1977–1978, the extent of support was more limited than in 1979–1980: railroads divided their funds 57 percent for Democrats and 43 percent for Republicans, while airlines split their contributions, Democrats 53 percent and Republicans 47 percent. There is no obvious explanation of the "deviant" behavior of transportation PACs in either the 1980 or the 1978 campaign. A possible rationale is that, operating in heavily regulated industries—even in the wake of airline deregulation—transportation firms had built over the years particularly close relationships with ranking members of Congress on both sides of the aisle with oversight over transportation matters. Since, until the 1980 elections, Democrats had controlled both houses of Congress for two decades, Democrats chaired all of the committees and subcommittees relevant to transportation. It is arguable that firms in the various transportation fields are the supreme pragmatists, supporting senior, well-placed incumbents irrespective of partisan or ideological persuasion. As to why this should be the case more so than for other industry categories requires exploration beyond what is possible for this essay.

Fortune-Ranked Industrial Firms

Turning our attention to industrial companies, it is useful to examine the relationship of firm size to PAC behavior. To enable us to make this analysis, in table 9.15, I have stratified by size the Fortune 1,000 largest industrial firms (1980) into five groups, with 10 firms operating PACs during the 1979–1980 election cycle. Each grouping is heterogeneous in terms of industrial classification, except that in group 1, which includes the largest Fortune-ranked industrials, seven of the ten firms are petroleum companies (Exxon, Mobil, Texaco, Standard Oil of California, Standard Oil of Indiana, Atlantic Richfield, and Shell), two companies are automobile manufacturers (General Motors and Ford), and one corporation is a diversified electronics manufacturer (General Electric).

The anticipated relationship between firm size and level of PAC activity existed among the firms in the five groups except for cohorts 2 and 3. It will be recalled that the reversed position of groups 2 and 3 is due to the presence in group 3 of two of the largest corporate PACs operating during the 1979–1980 election cycle, Harris Corporation and Wheelabrator-Frye. Both firms placed in the top dozen corporate PACs (ranked on the basis of contributions) operating in the 1980 campaign, donating more than $160,000 a piece, more than all but two companies (Standard Oil of Indiana, $194,000, and General Electric, $170,000) in cohort 1. The level of activity among the other eight firms in group 3 is much more in keeping with what one would expect of firms in this size range. St. Joe Minerals, which sponsored the third largest PAC in this group, contributed $51,000 to candidates, less than a third of the amount donated by the two larger firms. Indeed, Harris and Wheelabrator-Frye together provided nearly two-thirds of the contributions emanating from that group. As table 9.15 indicates, the average size of PACs declined sharply (save for cohort 3) as we proceed down the list of cohorts, from $86,000 for committees sponsored by the top ten firms to $3,000 for PACs affiliated with firms in the bottom cohort. Indeed, if Harris Corporation and Wheelebrator-Frye are removed from the list and the activities of the eight remaining PACs is averaged, group 3 PACs would average $17,500 rather than $46,000.

Firms in all five groupings were heavily oriented toward Republican candidates over their Democratic counterparts, even more so than in either the *Fortune* nonindustrial or DOD contractor classifications—although the extent of preference for the GOP varied within cohorts. Not surprisingly, save for group 1, which favored Republicans over Democrats in congressional races by a very substantial (71 to 29 percent) margin, the Republican preference increased with each descending (in terms of size) cohort. Group 1's heavily Republican emphasis appears to be a consequence of its dominance by petroleum companies. Whereas the oil companies favored Republicans over Democrats (76 to 24 percent), the other three firms in the cohort were somewhat more evenhanded, supporting the GOP by a 60 to 40 percent margin, approximately the same margins of partisan support that firms in cohorts 2 and 3 demonstrated. The degree of Republican orientation increased with each descending (in terms of size) cohort. The preference for Republicans was highest among group 5 firms, the smallest companies, which bestowed some 95 percent of its contributions upon Republican office seekers.

Similar anomalies appear when we examine the degree of incumbency support among the different cohorts. Larger firms (save for oil companies) tended to be more incumbent-oriented than smaller ones. Firms in groups 1, 2, and 3 gave between 60 and 65 percent of their funds to incumbents and 25–28 percent to challengers and spent 7–12 percent on open races. These percentages are similar to those for both PACs affiliated with *Fortune's* 300 nonindustrials and defense firms. The smaller firms grouped in cohorts 4 and 5, however, gave the majority of their funds to challengers (48 and 57 percent, respectively) and candidates in open-seat races (14 and 10 percent, respectively), while incumbents received only 38 and 33 percent, respectively. Once again, cohort 1 raises some difficulties. Although the ten firms collectively supported incumbents (60 percent) over challengers (27 percent) and candidates for open seats (12 percent), there was a clear split in orientation between the petroleum group of seven companies and the three nonpetroleum companies. Whereas the latter cohort overwhelmingly supported incumbents (78 percent) over challengers (13 percent) and open-seat candidates (9 percent), the oil firms split their contributions in the following manner: 51 percent for incumbents, 35 percent for challengers, and 14 percent for candidates running in open-seat races. The oil group was paced, in turn, by the contributions activities of Standard Oil of Indiana (the fourth largest corporate PAC in 1979–1980 in terms of revenues), which alone donated slightly more than a third of all monies given to 1980 congressional candidates by the seven petroleum giants. Amoco's PAC gave incumbents only 40 percent of its donations, while challengers (42 percent) and open-seat candidates (18 percent) received the bulk of the money; the company committee overwhelmingly preferred Republicans (85 percent) to Democrats (15 percent). In summary, the heavily petroleum company composition of group 1 oriented it much more heavily toward Republican and nonincumbents than would have been anticipated with a group of the nation's largest corporations. While PACs affiliated with smaller firms, frequently run by the entrepreneur-owners who established them (or their descendants) might be expected to have a somewhat more ideological orientation, thereby favoring Republicans (frequently challengers and open-seat candidates) with a strong committment to free enterprise, such a predilection is less explicable among the petroleum giants, which are more used to dealing with the *Realpolitik* of the congressional arena. Perhaps the most plausible explanation of this behavior was a strong desire among firms in the industry to replace Democratic incumbents who were perceived to be "anti-oil."

Finally, as might be expected, firms in all size cohorts spent the bulk of their monies (53–65 percent) on House races. Interestingly, however, smaller firms tended to devote a somewhat larger proportion of their monies to Senate races than did larger companies.

Summation

What can we learn from the examination in this section of corporate PACs, stratified as to size, industry groups, and extent of dependency on decisions of the federal government (with regard either to industry-specific regulation or to government contracts)? As a general proposition, the larger the corporation and greater the degree of its reliance on governmental decisions, the more likely it is to have a PAC and the PAC will be more active in making contributions than smaller, less federally dependent firms. Within any given grouping of firms, the largest firms in the group will tend to have larger PACs and to contribute more money to candidates than will the smaller PACs. Among very large corporations, however, the so-called giants of industry, such as appear on the *Fortune* lists or the ranking of leading DOD contractors, firm size and level of PAC activity are not necessarily correlated (for example, Liberty National, the forty-seventh-ranked life insurance company had far and away the largest PAC in the industry in the 1979–1980 campaign). Top management's philosophy toward political action is an important factor in determining the level of a given company's PAC activity. Although there are obvious exceptions (the heavily Republican and nonincumbent orientation of the seven leading oil producers in the 1979–1980 election cycle is a case in point), the larger PACs in any grouping tend to be more pragmatically oriented than smaller PACs, that is, they are more likely to distribute their funds more evenly among candidates of the major parties and to prefer congressional incumbents strongly over challengers and open-seat candidates. Save for transportation companies (at least in the 1978 and 1980 congressional campaigns), corporations in virtually all groupings demonstrated a distinct preference for Republicans over Democrats. While the degree of preference varied substantially with each industry classification (the split was virtually 50–50 among utilities in 1979–1980), a 60 to 40 percent Republican preference was common in the 1979–1980 election cycle. Firms in highly regulated industries and companies that are leading DOD contractors tend, while still demonstrating a clear GOP preference, to be somewhat more "evenhanded" in their contributions than companies not subject to these considerations.

The above generalizations are offered hesitantly. Comprehensive and reliable data exist for only the past two election cycles (with partial data available for 1975–1976), a time during which our nation has been undergoing some rather profound political turmoil, which may have skewed the nature and direction of corporate campaign contributions. As I have suggested earlier in the context of introducing the Handler–Mulkern dichotomy of "pragmatic" versus "ideological" PACs, corporate committees may have a greater opportunity in the future than in the recent past to mix pragmatism and ideology if more and more Republicans are elected to the Senate and the House. Although I do not wish in any sense to suggest the existence of a monolithic political viewpoint among the corporate community, there is an inherent and decidedly Republican preference among corporate managers since, historically, it is the GOP that has been considered "the party of business." This preference is all the more pronounced among smaller (but still relatively large) firms in the $100 million to $1 billion range, which constitute, potentially, a ripe market for PAC formation. One final comment is necessary. Absent major changes in the federal legislation governing PACs—a rather unlikely prospect at this moment—corporate PACs will become even larger in the years ahead. Corporate contributions may well exceed $50 million by 1984 and become an even greater percentage of candidates' receipts. Additional funds would provide PACs with both an opportunity to contribute to more candidates and to enlarge the size of each contribution. It may also encourage some company PACs to move in a serious way into making independent expenditures and increasing their levels of internal communications to management personnel and shareholders. It could also encourage some PACs to increase appreciably their contributions to major party committees—a development that, undoubtedly, would benefit the GOP more than the Democrats but nonetheless would be beneficial to the revitalization of political parties and the overall health of the political process. Although these developments are, of course, speculative at this point, they are hardly unrealistic possibilities.

MERGER ACTIVITY AND PAC BEHAVIOR

During the debate surrounding S.600 (the Small and Independent Business Protection Act of 1979) in the spring of 1979, advocates of the legislation argued that new statutory constraints were necessary to prevent the very large firms (companies with sales or assets exceeding $2 billion or $350 million together with a specified market share) from merging or otherwise acquiring each other. In support of their position, proponents of the bill pointed out that "the largest corporations are more likely to have political action committees than smaller firms."[73] They contended, accordingly, that it was necessary to prevent the formation of additional giant corporations, which would be prime subjects either for PAC formation if the merging partners did not already have individual PACs or for enlarged PACs if committees had already been formed. There exists, therefore, the interesting issue of what impact, if any, merger activity has on PAC behavior.

Unfortunately, it is far easier to pose the question than it is to answer it—at least right now. The PAC phenomenon is still too new—dating from the 1976 campaign or, for the great majority of companies, the 1978 campaign—to be able to offer more than speculation concerning the impact of mergers on corporate PAC behavior. As we have seen with each succeeding election cycle since the mid-1970s, corporate PACs have been growing rapidly in number, size, and level of contributions activities as well as, to a lesser degree, in the extent to which they are prepared to be risk takers (supporting challengers and open-seat candidates over incumbents). In short, irrespective of merger activity, all aspects of corporate PAC activities have been reflected in a very steep growth curve.

To illustrate the difficulty in assessing the impact of a merger on PAC operations, consider the hypothetical case of a PAC established in early 1976 (immediately after the Sun-PAC decision) by a large ($2.5 billion plus in sales) (C1) company. In 1975–1976, the PAC contributes $50,000 to congressional candidates. In early 1977, the firm acquires a smaller ($250 million in sales) company that does not have a PAC (C2). C1's PAC grows very rapidly and doubles its contributions during each election cycle so that in the 1982 campaign it gives $400,000 to congressional candidates. What factor(s) stimulated this eightfold increase in contributions during a six-year period? It would be exceedingly difficult to attribute causation for the speedy growth to the merger rather than to normal (albeit substantial) increases in PAC activity that many firms experienced during this period. Moreover, unless each of the partners to the merger had sales of less than $1–1.3 billion prior to the merger, it is virtually impossible to establish that the merger enabled the new entity to cross a threshold that appears to be critical for PAC formation and effective operations. As we have noted previously, $1–1.3 billion in assets or sales appears to be a critical threshold in terms of the likelihood that a firm will be politically active. If either or both parties to the merger are in the $1–1.3 billion range, it is quite likely that, irrespective of merger activity, they would be operating a PAC, or if not, would be potential PAC formers.

As table 9.16 reveals, of eighteen mergers that occurred between 1975 (the year in which corporate PAC formations began in earnest) and 1980 (the last year for which the Federal Trade Commission merger and acquisition data are available) among companies where both the acquiring and acquired have operated PACs prior to this acquisition, in which the acquired company had assets of $100 million or more, all eighteen ac-

TABLE 9.16
PAC Behavior and Merger Activity

Acquiring Company	PAC in '80	'78	'76	1980 Fortune Rank	Year Acquired	Acquired Company	PAC in '80	'78	'76
The Signal Companies	*	*		85	1975	Universal Oil Products	*	*	
General Electric	*	*	*	10	1976	Utah International	*	*	
Time	*	*		135	1978	Inland Container	*	*	*
LTV	*	*	*	42	1978	Lykes	*	*	*
IC Industries	*	*		90	1978	Pet	*	*	
Standard Oil of Indiana	*	*	*	9	1979	Cyprus Mines	*	*	
R.J. Reynolds	*	*	*	35	1979	Del Monte	*	*	*
Wheelabrator-Frye	*	*		255	1979	Neptune International	*	*	
Pan American World Airways	*	*	*	T5	1980	National Airlines	*	*	*
Holiday Inns	*	*		R36	1980	Harrah's	*	*	
Marley	*			442	1980	Wylain	*	*	
American Electric Power	*	*		U5	1980	Columbus & Southern Ohio Electric	*		
Burlington Northern	*	*	*	T6	1980	St. Louis-S.F. Railway	*	*	*
Liberty National Life Insurance	*			L47	1980	Globe Life & Acc. Insurance	*	*	
Atlantic Richfield	*	*	*	11	1977	Anaconda	*	*	*
Getty Oil	*	*	*	26	1980	ERC	*	*	*
Tenneco	*	*		17	1980	Southwestern Life	*	*	
Kraft	*			31	1980	Dart Industries	*	*	

SOURCES: *FEC Disclosure Series No. 8: Corporate-Related Political Committees Receipts and Expenditures 1976 Campaign*, September 1977; *Supplement to FEC Reports on Financial Activity 1977–78*, Final Report, April 1980; *Supplement to FEC Reports on Financial Activity 1979–80*, Final Report, January 1982; *Fortune* May 4, 1981, and July 13, 1981; and Federal Trade Commission, *Statistical Report on Mergers and Acquisitions*, July 1981.

NOTE: Data are for acquisitions of companies with assets reported in public sources of $100 million or more, by year of acquisition, 1975–1980, in which both acquiring and acquired companies have PACs.

quiring corporations were *Fortune*-ranked, and seventeen of them (Marley was the lone exception) were $1 billion-plus companies. It is noteworthy that seventeen of the acquired firms continued to operate their PACs after the merger. The only instance in which the merged company discontinued its PAC was after Atlantic Richfield acquired Anaconda. In all other instances, save two, (Liberty National Life–Global Life and Accident Insurance–Kraft–Dart Industries mergers), acquired companies continued to operate PACs in their own name. PACs operated by the acquiring companies were substantially larger (both before and after acquisition) than those of the acquired firms. The critical point, however, is that a merger does not perforce eliminate the PAC identity of the acquired company. A further complication in assessing the effect of the merger activity on the behavior of the firms involved in the eighteen transactions is that only three of the mergers occurred before 1978, whereas in twelve instances the transactions occurred in 1979 or 1980, in the midst of the last election cycle for which complete company PAC data exist.

In another eighty-four acquisitions between 1975 and 1980 where the acquired firm had assets of $100 million or more and only one of the parties operated a PAC prior to the acquisition in the 1976, 1978, or 1980 election campaigns, not surprisingly, in seventy-seven instances it was the larger acquiring firm that, prior to the merger, operated a PAC, while in only seven cases was it the acquired company (to the exclusion of the acquiring firm) that had established a political action committee.[74] It is hardly coincidental that in sixty-four of the cases the acquiring company was ranked in the 1980 *Fortune* lists either of the 500 leading industrials or 300 largest nonindustrial companies and in fifty-four instances was a $1 billion-plus firm in sales or assets. Very large firms were making the acquisitions, and these substantial companies had tended to form political action committees.

As in the case of mergers where both the acquiring and the acquired firms had PACs, the postmerger period of PAC operations is too recent to permit any meaningful observations concerning the impact of the acquisition on PAC behavior. A few observations, however, may be useful. Only to the extent to which mergers result in new entities that exceed $1 billion in assets or sales is the merger likely to result in a new potential PAC-former. As we have already seen,[75] of the 573 *Fortune*-ranked industrials and nonindustrial companies that in 1980 had sales, assets, or operating revenues of $1 billion or more, 366—215 of 301 (71 percent) industrials and 151 of the 272 nonindustrials (a total of 56 percent). Accordingly, there exist already 197 *Fortune*-ranked $1 billion-plus companies that, irrespective of merger activity, are prime prospects to establish PACs. This figure does not include $1 billion-plus companies in categories that are either unranked by *Fortune,* do not qualify for "top 50" standing among the nonindustrials, or are privately owned. Ironically, therefore, mergers among smaller companies (those with assets or sales of $1 billion or less) are more likely than mergers among the $1 billion-plus companies to create firms that for the first time reach the scale to cause them to consider seriously the establishment of a political action committee. A second factor should be taken into account. Although a merger enlarges the pool of executive and administrative personnel and shareholders whom the acquiring company can solicit for contributions, thereby increasing the potential pool of funds, it has another—somewhat ironic—effect. As I pointed out with regard to S.600, although a firm may operate as many political action committees as it wishes, under the FECA,[76] all affiliated PACs are subject to a single $5,000 per candidate per election contribution limit. Accordingly, if two companies with PACs merge, they become subject to a single contribution limit, thereby halving the amount of money that, together, they could have contributed to a given race before the merger. Mergers, paradoxically, reduce the contributions limits for the merging firms, lessening rather than increasing the amount of money these firms can give to individual candidates and political parties. The effect of mergers on corporate contributions activities can, thus, cut both ways. We must wait until a later date to write authoritatively about the impact, if any, that mergers have on PAC contributions patterns.[77]

CONCLUSION

During the spring of 1982, a Herblock cartoon appeared in newspapers across the country. The cartoon was a play on the popular video game PAC-MAN, in which a wide-mouthed, incessantly moving, ghostlike figure rapidly gobbles up all of the other creatures standing in its way. Herblock was clearly suggesting—and none too subtly—that so, too, PACs were overwhelming the political process, and the individual citizen, in their insatiable prowl for electoral dominance. Like most political cartoonists, of course, Herblock was making his point by hyperbole. Although, as this essay has demonstrated, PACs have become over the past decade an increasingly important source of campaign funds, the bulk of political funds still comes from individual contributions.[78] In the 1981–1982 election cycles, PACs will account for an estimated one-third (33 percent) of the receipts of congressional candidates running in the November general elections.

The Herblock cartoon, which was but one of many articles, columns, cover stories,[79] cartoons, newsclips, and full-length television programs during the 1982 campaigns that highlighted PACs, symbolizes a growing concern, not merely within the media but within the informed public, that PACs had become too ubiquitous and threatening as principal actors on the political stage. Somewhat surprisingly, much of the coverage on PACs has come not from the so-called liberal press but from such bulwarks of business as the *Wall Street Journal* and *U.S. News and World Report* and has focused on the activities of corporate, trade association, and other business-oriented PACs. The predominant tone of the media coverage is reflected in the headlines of the first of a series of three articles on PACs that the *Wall Street Journal* ran in summer 1982: "Cash Politics: Special-Interest Money Increasingly Influences What Congress Enacts"; "Campaign Giving by PACS Soars, and Some Expect a Specific Vote in Return"; and "The Green Tide on K Street."[80]

Interest in PACs has been fueled in no small measure by the increasing efforts of public interest groups such as Common Cause and Public Citizen's Congress Watch to bring before the media, the Congress, and the public the subject of PAC influence on the electoral process. The efforts of these groups have been facilitated greatly by the public disclosure provisions of the Federal Election Campaign Act, which requires candidates, parties, and nonparty committees (PACs fall into this latter category) to report the sources and uses of their campaign funds. The literally millions of pages of submissions to the FEC that the commission then distills into data series, press releases, and reports have provided a treasure trove of information and "hard data" for conscientious investigative reporters, enterprising public interest advocates, and political partisans seeking some form of electoral advantage over the opposition. The ever-increasing costs of elections, the titillating possibilities of scandals, the burgeoning litigation under federal and state campaign laws, and the continuing financial and operational problems of the Federal Election Commission have brought the related issues of campaign reform and "dollar politics"[81] before the public during the past decade to an unprecedented extent. Since the passage of the FECA and the creation of the FEC, Congress has been living in a virtual fishbowl so far as the funding of elections campaigns is concerned. It is, to be sure, a fishbowl of its own making, albeit against the inclinations and better judgment of many of its members, who felt compelled to "do something" to assuage public unhappiness with politics and politicians in the aftermath of the Watergate revelations.

Evidence exists that the newly elected Ninety-Eighth Congress may feel itself obliged to "do something" when it convenes next January—once again as a consequence of public pressure rather than its innate wish to subject itself to further regulation. Indeed, the seeds for congressional action were sown by members of the Ninety-Seventh Congress. In June 1982, a Task Force on Elections of the Committee on House Administration held hearings on the role of political action committees in the political process. House members also introduced a spate of bills bearing upon PACs. Although none of these bills progressed far in the Ninety-Seventh Congress, several are likely to be reintroduced when the Ninety-Eighth Congress meets. One bipartisan bill, the Campaign Finance Act of 1981,[82] which has received considerable support in the House, placed a $75,000 limit on contributions a congressional candidate can receive from all PACs during an election cycle and established a formula based on the size of each state to limit (from $75,000 to $500,000) the amount that Senate candidates could accept per election cycle from political action committees. The bill also raised from $1,000 to $2,500 the amount that individuals could give to a congressional candidate and provide incentives for individual contributions to political parties. In addition to statistics concerning PAC growth, the sponsors of the bill cited a 1980 Harris poll in which a sizable majority of those polled felt that PACs increased the influence that special interest groups have on government, and 68 percent of the respondents expressed the view that Congress should limit the amount a candidate can receive from all PACs. A second bill, which was introduced by Congressman David R. Obey (D-Wisc.), also aroused considerable attention because it combines restrictions on PACs with overall limits on spending in House races and partial public financing of these races. Entitled the Clean Campaign Act of 1982,[83] the bill limited the total amount of PAC contributions that candidates can accept to $90,000 per election cycle; provided that individual contributions of up to $100 would be matched on a one-to-one basis with public financing up to a maximum of $90,000; and restricted total spending by a candidate on a campaign to $180,000 per election cycle.

The future of the successors of these and other bills in the new Congress as well as the depth and extent of public pressure that inevitably must be present if such proposals are to be successful will be determined in no small measure by public perceptions of the impact of PAC contributions and expenditures on the outcome of the just-completed midterm elections. This point is particularly germane to the focus of this paper—corporate political action committees. For while PACs affiliated with a wide range of interests (ranging from racial and ethnic minorities, children's organizations, environmental associations, and women's rights groups to right-to-life and fundamentalist religiously based constituencies) have flowered over the past several years, it is PACs affiliated with economic interests—business and labor—that, with the possible exception of a few strident ideological and single-issue committees, evoke the greatest public and congressional reaction. And among business-oriented PACs, although PACs affiliated with such trade and professional groups as the National Association of Realtors, the National Automobile Dealers Association, the American Medical Association, the American Bankers Association, and the Associated Milk Producers far outstrip corporate committees in receipts, disbursements, and contributions, it is corporate committees that figure most prominently in the media and in the public's mind. A number of factors bring corporate PACs to the fore of public attention: they outnumber all the other business-affiliated committees combined by a margin of nearly two to one; they outcontribute all the other groups—even the nonconnected organizations, which raise more money; the sheer size, number, and ubiquitousness of the companies with which they are affiliated makes them conspicuous; they offer the greatest potential for growth among PACs in terms of both numbers and activity; they are far more familiar to members of the public who associate them with specific goods and services, which either they have used or, at least, seen advertised on television and in the newspapers; and finally, for persons with a historical perspective, they conjure up memories of the "big bad trusts" that less than a century ago dominated the politics of many states. General Motors, Winn-

Dixie Stores (in the South), Standard Oil of Indiana, Boeing, Citicorp, and General Electric are household names and are also familiar to segments of the public as employers and important factors in the communities where they are located—in short, as corporate citizens. Conversely, the trade and professional groups mentioned above are largely nonentities that function anonymously as far as the general public is concerned.

In this paper, I have concentrated on what may be termed the "output" side of the role of corporate PACs in the electoral process to the virtual exclusion of any assessment of the "input" side of the equation. The paper has examined important aspects of the political behavior of company-affiliated political action committees since the mid-1970s and documented their rapid proliferation, their growth in financial size, and the ever-increasing scale of their operations. It has also revealed that firm size and the importance of governmental decisions to a company's well-being tend to be important factors in determining the existence and extent of PAC operations. We have also seen that, while virtually all categories of corporate PACs tend to be "pragmatists," strongly favoring incumbents over challengers and open-seat candidates, there does tend to be, all other considerations being equal, an "ideological" preference for Republicans over Democrats. The extent of ideological giving tends to be greater among smaller firms than among the corporate giants. There is also increasing evidence that companies are becoming more sophisticated in their PAC contributions as they become more experienced in operating political action committees. Finally, corporate PACs are giving, with each succeeding election, a greater proportion both of overall PAC contributions and of total candidates' receipts.

Let us now turn to the "input" side of the corporate PAC electoral equation. What is the impact of corporate PAC contributions upon election outcomes and the overall political process? These two questions are, frankly, far more difficult to answer, even in this era of public disclosure of campaign activities, than those relating to the sources and uses of company PAC funds in election financing.

With regard to the first question concerning the impact of campaign contributions by company-affiliated PACs on electoral outcomes, there is an initial difficulty. Despite the greater number and increasing sophistication of studies of campaign financing and its effects by political scientists such as David W. Adamany, Herbert E. Alexander, Gary C. Jacobson, John R. Owens, and W. P. Welch,[84] we are still unable to answer definitively the "bottom-line" question posed two decades ago by the dean of political finance scholars, Alexander Heard: Does money win elections? His answer is still instructive:

No neat correlation is found between campaign expenditures and campaign results. Even if superiority in expenditures and success at the polls always ran together, the flow of funds to a candidate might simply reflect his prior appeal rather than create it. Our understanding of voting behavior is not so precise that all the financial and nonfinancial factors that contribute to success can be sorted out with confidence. Yet it is clear that under some conditions the use of money can be decisive. And under others no amount of money spent by the loser could alter the outcome. The kinds of information available limit the analyses that can be made, but they do show clearly that financial outlays cannot guarantee victory in elections.[85]

Recent scholarship confirms the soundness of Heard's assessment that money (or more accurately, some undetermined amount of money) is a necessary but not sufficient condition of electoral success. Jacobson, for example, has concluded that in Senate races the three variables of money, incumbency, and party strength accounted for 70–75 percent of the total variance in the proportion of the vote a candidate receives and that, of the three, money was the single most important factor. Jacobson further indicates that, in House races, incumbency was the dominant factor and expenditures accounted for 21–34 percent of the variance when party strength was controlled and 30–35 percent when it was not, and collectively, the three variables explained from 76 to 82 percent of the House vote.[86] In his recent important book, *Money in Congressional Elections*, Jacobson adds, however, a crucial note of caution:

The actual structure of the relationship between spending and election outcomes cannot be confidently taken from estimates of these equations. The connections between spending and votes may be reciprocal. That is, votes and expenditures may vary together because more money is contributed to candidates who are expected to do well or because candidates attract money and votes for same reasons.[87]

In an earlier study of campaign spending in races for the California State Assembly and seats in the U.S. House of Representatives from California between 1966 and 1974, John R Owens and Edward C. Olson found that candidate expenditures, candidate incumbency, and candidate party strength are highly predictive of a candidate's general election success.[88] In four of five election years, 80 percent of the total variance of the vote is explained by these three variables, with expenditures ranking as the most predictive of influential variables for all State Assembly elections and for House elections. They further conclude that the marginal product of each political resource (expenditure, party strength, and incumbency tenure) varies and the magnitude of the productivity advantage changes with the election year. Although money is the best predictor of the vote, the causal interrelationship of the three determinants of the vote is more complex.

Illustrative of the difficulties of establishing a definitive answer to the question, Does money win elections? are 1980 congressional election results. Of the top ten congressional spenders in House and Senate races, exactly half won and half lost in each house.[89] Included in the list of high-spending losers were such prominent Democratic incumbents as George McGovern, Birch Bayh, John Brademas, James Corman, and Al Ullman. As an article in *Congressional Quarterly* noted, "National trends, not money, played the major role in the Republican Senate triumphs of 1980. Of the nine Democrats ousted, seven had a spending advantage."[90] The same conclusion can be applied to the Democrats' poor results in a number of key House races. In summary, in a "Republican year," neither incumbency nor campaign expenditures were enough to save the day for vulnerable Democrats.

Available scholarship suggests that "the effect of money in politics is probably more certain in determining who the candidates will be than in determining the outcome of elections."[91] Jacobson's work indicates strongly that money is far more important to challengers in congressional elections than to incumbents. Looking at congressional elections in 1972, 1974, and 1976, he finds that the outcomes were affected much more strongly by what challengers spent than by what incumbents spent. Indeed, the more incumbents spend, the worse they do, since their spending level is determined by the strength of the challenger they face— incumbents are more likely to get a lower percentage of the vote when they are spending the most in highly competitive races. Money is more important to challengers than to incumbents since the latter receive "free" publicity and have name recognition and some familiarity for the voters. Jacobson concludes that, if a challenger has sufficient resources to launch a substantial campaign and becomes as familiar to the voters as the incumbent, the outcome of the contest is decided by the quality of the candidates and the campaigns and not by the difference in the resources between them.[92]

What implications do these scholarly findings about the relationship between money and election results have in assessing the electoral impacts of PACs and corporate PACs in particular? To the extent to which PACs constitute an important source of funds for officeholders and potential challengers, they play an important role in determining both who will run and who will be able to mount an effective campaign. Given the high costs of campaigning today in an era of sophisticated technology and the necessity for expensive professional assistance, candidates must have sufficient financial resources to mount an effective election campaign before they can be considered seriously by the voters. Financial viability becomes a prerequisite to electoral viability. PACs have become an important factor in determining the degree to which a challenger (and an incumbent) will be financially viable. Once again Jacobson's work is instructive. The challengers' ability to raise money "depends on the extent to which they can convince the elites who finance campaigns that they have a chance to win."[93] Not surprisingly, economic interest groups (including corporations) typically like to support candidates who they think have a realistic chance to win—and will be in a position to be of service to them at a later day. For incumbents, the most effective way to avoid a challenge is to strive to deny campaign resources to potential challengers by assembling enough money both to avoid being perceived as vulnerable and to enable them to mount an effective campaign. As a recent *Congressional Quarterly* article suggests, "Early spending has become a central strategy for many Senate incumbents, even when they have no serious primary challenge. . . . It can prevent a challenger from developing momentum or even discourage the challenge altogether."[94] This strategy is particularly important for Democrats, who, if perceived to be weak, may encourage a serious challenge by PAC-supported GOP hopefuls.

PACs are logical places for both challengers and incumbents to look for funds. They are important not only for the resources that they provide individually but for their "networking potential." Groups such as the National Association of Manufacturers, the Chamber of Commerce of the United States, Business-Industry Political Action Committee (BI-PAC), and the National Association of Business Political Action Committees become informal clearinghouses for information about candidates, races, and electability. For the past several years the U.S. Chamber's National Chamber Alliance for Politics (NCAP) has targeted for Chamber members "opportunity races" in which the "campaign assistance and votes of Chamber members can help elect business-oriented candidates."[95] Both the Chamber and BIPAC hold briefing sessions in locations across the country where they provide members with the latest available electoral information. Although obviously they are not in a position to dictate the contributions strategy of a particular company, they have become important coordinating mechanisms within the business community. Candidates, often brought around by party officials, are interviewed by the leadership of these groups to receive their "blessings" or, at least, an assessment of their viability. The party national committees also hold briefings for PAC representatives to expose hopeful candidates to them. Ultimately, individual corporate PACs alone decide how they will spend their money. They do so, however, not in isolation but through a process that involves them with networking organizations and consultation with peers.[96]

The same activities also go on the labor side—perhaps even more systematically and effectively than among business groups—through groups such as the AFL-CIO COPE's Operating Committee. Irrespective of its source, the growth of PAC networking means that a challenger's viability or an incumbent's prospects for reelection can be affected seriously by the choices of a few key PAC decision makers. In a real sense, these PAC networks play today some of the roles that in years past belonged to political parties in bringing candidates to the fore and determining their election possibilities. The "certifying" of candidates through their contributions—rather than determining election outcomes—is possibly the most important effect of corporate (and other) PAC money on the electoral process.

PACs AND AMERICAN POLITICAL DEMOCRACY

This brings us to our second crucial issue: the implications of corporate PAC activity for the political process and American democracy. Let us recall the original goals underlying prohibitions against corporations (and subsequently labor unions) from making campaign contributions. The first and arguably most important purpose was to prevent large economic interests, through the use of their substantial wealth and other politically valuable organizational resources, from so dominating the selection of public officials and, consequently, the determination of public policy that the integrity of American political democracy was corrupted. The second object was to protect corporate shareholders (and at a later date, union members) from having monies that they invest in the firm, presumably for economic objectives, used by management for political purposes of which they do not approve. At the root of both of these motivations, as we have seen, was a twofold fear of corporate power: corporate political power and its impact on the essential character of American democratic institutions; and corporate power over the individual, both in the context of his relationship to the organization and in his role as a citizen-participant in a democratic society.

Seventy-five years after statutory limitations were first enacted into law in the Tillman Act,[97] the same issues posed originally by direct corporate political contributions are now raised by the operation of corporate political action committees, which have emerged over the past decade as the conduit for company participation in the electoral process. Company PACs act, in effect, as the legal surrogates or alter egos of their corporate sponsors, permitting the latter to do indirectly—that is, to contribute monies donated by company executive and administrative personnel and/or shareholders to candidates and political parties and, thereby, to influence the political process—what they are prohibited under federal law from doing directly. Critics of PACs contend that the electorate has been, in effect, flimflammed in a shell game wherein the PAC system has enlarged, institutionalized, and legitimated the corporate role in the electoral process to a degree hitherto unknown in twentieth-century American politics, to the detriment of the individual, both as corporate constituent and as citizen-participant. I shall conclude this examination of PACs and the modern political process by reflecting on this issue of the dual impact of corporate political action committees on the individual and on the overall political process.

The Company PAC and the Individual

The first part of the equation—the relationship between company PACs and the individual—is itself two-sided. In a political context, individuals relate to corporate PACs in two ways: first, as organizational constituents in their capacities as employees or shareholders; second, as citizen-participants in a democracy. Since the second aspect ties in closely with the larger question of PAC impact on the overall political process, let us focus our attention first on the effect of PACs on corporate constituents.

With regard to the corporate PAC's impact on shareholders, the matter is relatively straightforward. In the first place, relatively few PACs actually solicit their shareholders for PAC contributions. The survey conducted in late 1981 among 275 corporations by four business groups indicates that about 50 (more than 18 percent) of the firms solicit their shareholders and half of the companies making such solicitations report, moreover, that, of those shareholders solicited, 10 percent or less actually contributed to the PAC.[98] Shareholder contributions represent a far smaller percentage of total contributions to corporate PACs than do those of executive and administrative employees. Some companies that solicit stockholders limit their efforts to substantial equity holders. In a few companies, shareholder contributions represent a significant proportion of overall PAC funds. According to the *Wall Street Journal,* Mapco Inc., a Tulsa, Oklahoma, oil company, reports that a small percentage of its 24,000 shareholders each year donate about $30,000, or just under 50 percent of its PAC receipts. Sun Company, the nation's eighteenth largest industrial corporation, indicates that in the 1980 campaign, shareholders gave about one-third of the $124,000 Sun contributed to political candidates. Sun is one of several companies that allow shareholders to contribute to their PACs through automatic withholding of quarterly dividends. Except in the most unusual situation, solicitation of a company's nonemployee shareholders by its PAC does not carry with it the potential for coercion or abuse. Typically, the large publicly held firm has no effective sanctions—such as may exist in the case of its employees—to extract contributions from its equity holders. Indeed, management may be reluctant to solicit company shareholders for fear of arousing their opposition to the firm's overall PAC operations and may take the position of "letting sleeping dogs lie."[99]

The question of the use of corporate monies to establish and administer a PAC raises a somewhat more difficult question. Although a recent study provides evidence that a majorioty of corporate shareholders agrees that companies should make political contributions if these contributions are lawful and if management considers these contributions to be in the best interests of the company,[100] there are always shareholders who disagree with the use of corporate funds for political purposes either on philosophical grounds or on pragmatic grounds (such as that money spent on politics might be better used to market products or increase dividends). Such shareholders are in a position of having money they invest in the company used for purposes with which they disagree. As with virtually all other aspects of management decisions, disgruntled shareholders are in a position of having little effective redress against such activity. They can, to use Albert O. Hirschman's terminology,[101] "exit"—that is, sell their shares—undertake costly and typically ineffective representative or derivative actions, or seek passage of a shareholder proxy proposal prohibiting PAC operations. Such efforts, however, are from the outset largely doomed to failure under existing statute and case law.

Probably the most effective mechanism to influence corporate management with regard to PAC activities is that supported in 1980, by Georgetown University Law Center's Institute for Public Representation (IPR), in a proposed rule before the Securities and Exchange Commission to amend SEC rules. IPR requested the commission to require corporations to disclose to shareholders in their annual reports the existence, operations, and costs of political action committees established by them or their subsidiaries. The purpose of the proposed rule expressed in the IPR petition was the following:

To inform investors of the scope of the . . . (corporation's) . . . support of and involvement in political activities, to require issuers to keep track of the costs of such activities, and to assure that the administration of corporate political funds is conducted in an open and democratic fashion, in the best interests of the corporate entity as a whole rather than of any particular person or group within the company.[102]

In short, its objective was to "keep the rascals honest" and to render them more accountable to their shareholders—and the public—through public disclosure. Although ultimately the SEC did not make the requested rule change—and it is highly uncertain that adoption of the change would have altered to any substantial degree the behavior of corporations with regard to their PACs[103]—the IPR proposal and a related proxy proposal stimulated General Motors to report on the operations of its Civic Action Program/General Motors (CAP/GM) in its 1980 *General Motors Public Interest Report.*

In summary, shareholders are no worse off in challenging or controlling corporate management with regard to PAC activities than they are in influencing most other aspects of company operations. Nor is their individual freedom as shareholders any more infringed upon by the firm's leadership than it is by management's decisions in other areas of business activities.[104] And as the Court pointed out earlier this year in the *International Association of Machinists* case,[105] shareholders who were opposed to corporate operations of PACs were, ultimately, free to sell their stock and invest elsewhere—to exercise their right of exit from the offending corporation.

The situation with regard to the individual freedoms of company executives and administrative employees is far more complex. Although 441(b)(3)(A) of the FECA prohibits corporations from securing contributions from employees by actual or threatened physical force, job discrimination, and financial reprisals, it is evident that the possibility of coercive action by an unscrupulous management still exists. The incidence of such coercion is impossible to ascertain. Although anecdotal accounts surface from time to time about "arm twisting" and "hard ball" solicitation practices on the part part of the executives of certain corporations in raising PAC funds from lower-level managers, there exists no hard evidence on the subject.

In a litigation instituted in late 1979 by the *International Association of Machinists and Aerospace Workers* (IAMA) against the Federal Election Commission and eleven corporate defendants (companies operating the largest PACs during the 1977–1978 election cycle), the IAMA contended that the solicitation methods used by the companies in raising monies for their PACs from "unprotected career employees" violated the FECA since they yielded "donations which are not free and voluntary . . . because they result from the employment relationship."[106] IAMA also contended that 441(b) violates the First Amendment right of career employees to abstain from political expression by the inherently coercive circumstances surrounding corporate solicitation of executive and administrative personnel. In the language of the IAMA brief, because there is an "inherently sensitive and unequal relationship between an employer and his employees, . . . these solicitations are 'pregnant with coercion.'"[107] Both the factual and constitutional contentions were ultimately rejected by a U.S. Court of Appeals, which heard the case after the constitutional issues and a stipulated finding of facts were certified to it by the U.S. District Court following a dismissal of the IAMA's complaint by the Federal Election Commission. The Court of Appeals held that, based on the record before it and given the safeguards in the FECA with which "Congress has brigaded corporate PAC solicitation," it could not conclude that such solicitation "inevitably forces career employees to compromise their political beliefs in order to avoid jeopardizing their corporate positions."[108] In response to the IAMA's claim that data indicating that executive and administrative employees gave to their company PACs at "rates and in amounts" far beyond those that obtain when donors are not solicited to give to the institution that employs them indicates that corporate solicitation is per se coercive. The court determined "on the record before us, it suffices to say that the proof plaintiffs offer falls woefully short."[109]

Given the consideration, time, and resources spent by the Machinists in the Union /IAMA case to establish corporate wrongdoing in the solicitation of employees' contributions to company PACs, it is doubtful that, absent a major scandal triggered by "whistle blowing" on the part of a number of corporate employees of impeccable credentials, probative evidence of corporate coercion will become available. Moreover, despite the scoffing of the skeptics, it is probably true as Handler and Mulkern assert:

The life blood of the PAC is the money raised from voluntary contributions, and significant constituency influence and opportunity for participation flow from this fact. . . . The evidence suggests that corporate PACs generally take pains to avoid tactics (even some that the law plainly permits) that could be perceived as coercive. The inconvenient fact for holders of the view that voluntarism is a myth and PAC giving is, in reality, indirect corporate giving is the large percentage of executives who decline to make contributions or who drop out after having previously contributed.[110]

At their best, corporate PACs comply fully with the spirit and letter of the FECA, obtaining their funds voluntarily and providing a convenient and noncoercive mechanism for employees to participate in the electoral process by facilitating employee contributions to political candidates and political parties of their choice. At their worst, PACs are a subterfuge that enables companies to do legally what the law otherwise forbids and that infringe upon the constitutional rights of their managerial employees. The percentage of corporate PACs at each of these poles is impossible to ascertain. Indeed, the great majority likely reside in the middle ground between these two extremes. It is interesting to note, for

example, that even in Dart PAC, a PAC known for the "hard-sell" solicitation tactics of the company's CEO, Justin Dart (chairman of Dart Industries, now Dart-Kraft), the contribution rate among the 1,000 or so
eligible employees was, according to company officials, only, approximately 22 percent.[111] It will be recalled from the recent study by several
Washington-based business-related groups that only 33 percent of solicited corporate personnel actually made contributions to the company
PAC.[112] The critical question, of course, is how voluntary is "voluntary"
and what does the solicited employee perceive to be the subtle pressures or unarticulated expectations about his participation in the company PAC? Just as in the case of requests for donations to the United
Way or Community Chest, the ambitious—and wary—manager may deem
it expedient to be a loyal member of the "corporate team" and to make
a contribution to the firm's PAC although in his heart of hearts he may
prefer not to do so. Discretion becomes the better part of valor, and to
that extent his freedom both as employee and citizen is compromised.

The Corporate PAC and the American Political Process

This leads us, finally, to the second and arguably more important question: What has been the impact of PACs generally, and corporate PACs
in particular, specifically on the quality of citizen participation in the
American political process? It is impossible, of course, to answer this
question definitively. Arguably, PACs of all types have increased the level
and quality of individual political participation by giving hitherto uninvolved citizens a more personal stake in the electoral process as a result
of their campaign contributions as well as their votes. Although it is not
possible to ascertain with certainty the number of people making campaign contributions through PACs or directly to candidates and political
parties, it is probably larger than at any point in history. In a perverse
way, the PAC presence has probably encouraged campaign activity on
the part of persons who are not affiliated with any PAC and who, indeed, fear the PAC presence in the political process and have sought to
counteract it. To the degree that this is the case, the PAC phenomenon
has been a healthy development.

  Nonetheless, the PAC phenomenon has undoubtedly reinforced what
Theodore Lowi has termed "interest group liberalism"[113] and Peter
Bachrach "democratic elitism"[114]— a political process in which interest

groups and coalitions of groups determine public policy through a process of bargaining in which the power of each group or coalition and its resultant influence on the policy process is determined by the nature and magnitude of its political resources and its ability to use them. Although students of PACs differ on many points, there is general agreement that the PAC phenomenon, and the political reforms that gave rise to it, have weakened the position in the electoral process of both the individual citizen and the political parties.[115] The reliance on group politics erodes the effective capacity—the power—of the individual citizen to affect the political process and thereby undercuts the incentive for political participation. It also weakens the position of the political parties, which have lost much of their role as forces of intermediation, and of coalition formation and amelioration among diverse social interests. Such citizen participation in the political process as there is tends more and more to be channeled into narrowly focused groups, which frequently appeal to potential adherents on the basis of one or a few issues that evoke strong (and frequently extreme) responses on their part. They promote social fragmentation rather than societal consensus and frequently exploit the fears of citizens, who are made to feel that unless they contribute money to and otherwise support the positions of the group they will lack protection from those who seek to do them harm.

In the September 1982 issue of the *American Political Science Review*, Paul R. Abramson and John H. Aldrich argue convincingly that the decline in voter participation in presidential and congressional elections in the past two decades results "largely from two basic attitudinal trends: the weakening of party loyalties among the American electorate and declining beliefs about government responsiveness, that is, lowered fellings of 'external' political efficacy."[116] It is not unreasonable to suggest that the PAC phenomenon is both a symptom and a cause of the decline in historical patterns of electoral participation in the United States. PAC rather than party, parochial, outcome-specific goals rather than a bridging and more broadly based public policy agenda have increasingly occupied the attention of individual citizens and contributed to what may be termed a politics of selfishness. Unquestionably, so-called ideological or single-issue PACs are primarily responsible for this development. PACs run by "economic interests"—corporations, labor unions, trade and professional groups, and agricultural cooperatives—have also contributed to this politics of selfishness. They have encouraged their constituent "members" to make the organizational PAC, in effect, their vehicle for electoral participation in furtherance of public policy priorities, which are defined by the organizational leadership largely in terms of either its narrow economic ("pragmatic") needs or the perceived ("ideological") needs of the larger business community for a political climate congenial to free enterprise market capitalism. In the process of furthering the political goals of "these various and interfering interests," about whom James Madison warned his countrymen two centuries ago in the tenth of the *Federalist Papers*,[117] the individual citizen-participant compromises in many instances his political autonomy and the pursuit of his personal public policy agenda.

This leads us finally to a consideration of what is perhaps the most important question posed by PAC presence on the American political scene since the mid-1970s: What has been the PAC impact on the formulation and implementation of U.S. public policy? Put more simply, what, if anything do PAC contributions obtain for their organizational donors? I shall conclude this paper by examining this question in the context of corporate political action committees.

Although, as Handler and Mulkern suggest, corporate PACs differ in their degree of commitment to ideological versus pragmatic objectives, the essential purpose underlying the creation of political action committees by all corporations (and every other interest group) is to facilitate the company's accomplishment of its overall political goals, which, in turn, are determined by top management's perception of the long-range business needs of the firm. Putting aside the matter of managerial ego, from an organizational perspective PAC activity—in common with all political endeavors—is instrumental in character: a means to the accomplishment of the overall corporate objectives of profitability, growth, and in the final analysis, survival. Specific electoral outcomes are important only in so far as they keep or put into office public officials who, in the formulation of public policy, will be responsive to the needs of business generally and the firm specifically. This view was well articulated in the spring of 1982 by Richard L. Lesher, president of the U.S. Chamber of Commerce, who stated, "We want the business community to focus on these (opportunity) races as crucial to a business-oriented Congress. Only through aggressive political action can business have its most effective impact on Congress."[118] Or, in the words of the Articles of Organization of Rexnord's political action committee: "The exclusive purpose of the PAC is to influence the nomination or election of qualified candidates to public office. Particular emphasis will be given to candidates who have demonstrated that they are favorably disposed toward the private free enterprise system."[119]

Corporate PAC operations, in concert with other forms of company political activity, are intended to secure and preserve a favorable position for business in the American political economy. I am not suggesting that this goal is inappropriate for America's business leadership. Nor am I asserting that the business community is monolithic in its political and economic objectives. Firms and industries have conflicting business needs and goals and seek different outcomes from the public policy process. Nor, finally, am I implying that top corporate management and those who run company PACs are motivated solely by pragmatism or, to take an even more extreme view, by cynicism. My research over the past several years convinces me that most corporate executives (like the great majority of citizens) sincerely and fervently believe that they are pursuing the national interest at the same time they are seeking to achieve the objectives of their organizations. They honestly strive both to do well (in terms of their companies' needs) and to do good (in keeping with their concept of the public interest). The question remains, nonetheless, whether, as a consequence of their PAC operations, corporations as an identifiable constituency have an excessive impact on the political process.

Corporations (as do other economic interests) and elected officials (as well as persons who aspire to these positions) have a symbiotic relationship in the financing of election campaigns. For incumbent officeholders, as well as for those who seek to replace them, money, as we have seen, is a necessary albeit not sufficient condition to wage a successful election campaign. Corporate PACs are a visible and readily accessible source of such funds, and many candidates pursue them openly and aggressively. What has emerged over the past several years, in the words of a recent article in the *Wall Street Journal,* "are some shameless campaign solicitations, underscoring the need of politicians of both parties to rely more and more on special interest money. All this is legal, but it involves a lot of pandering, hyperbole, and even outright misrepresentations."[120] Political candidates are hardly innocent maidens striving virtuously to escape the clutches of the malevolent, mustached corporate suitors who seek to rob them of their virginity. Frequently, they play the role of alluring sirens, displaying their charms to entice their ardent admirers nearer but all the while attempting to keep their would-be lovers at arm's length, lest they be compromised by too passionate an embrace. Occasionally, politicians, or (as we saw in the case of former President Richard M. Nixon's 1972 Finance Committee to Re-elect the President) those who solicit for them, are hardened harlots who won't take no for an answer from their none-too-eager corporate clients and obtain their money by hook or crook.

For their part, corporate PACs seek to satisfy through this symbiosis a variety of needs. At a bare minimum, they want to see elected to public office individuals who share their public policy perspectives and goals. They seek, furthermore, to be counted among the "friends" of the candidates, a friend who helped in a time of need. In a real sense, they are also seeking to acquire an "insurance policy" that will assure them that, once elected or reelected to public office, the erstwhile candidate will recall at crucial times their generosity and, if he does not specifically help them, will not, at least, hurt them. They also seek to insure access, so that when they have a need to be heard on a particular issue they will have a hearing by the public official or key staffers. Finally, they may seek specific political outcomes from a friend in court: a bill introduced, a speech delivered, or a vote cast on behalf of the company. Reciprocal needs on the part of the corporation and the congressmen create, in short, *a system of mutual dependency.* In introducing H.R. 4070, Congressman Glickman summarized the matter well with regard to political action committees (irrespective of their sponsorship):

The problem of PAC giving is complicated by the fact that those moneys can be so easily targeted at particular members, and we are naive if we do not believe that they are targeted because of what individual members of the Congress, through their positions or committee assignments, are able to do for a group that has a PAC of its own. Though there are obviously no stated "quid pro quos" in all of this, study after study has shown a very high correlation between funds received and the way some key votes have been cast.[121]

Glickman's emphasis on *correlation* rather than causation is critical; so too is his point about the absence of articulated quid pro quos. Candidates do not sell their votes to a company for a contribution of $250–500 (usual figures in a House race) or $750–1,000 (typical donations in a Senate race). When, however, a congressman receives a substantial amount of money from PACs affiliated with a particular industry, it is not unreasonable to predict that, all other things being equal, such contributions either reflect or result in a representative's predisposition toward positions important to the group in question. In common with all other PACs, corporate committees do not contribute their funds randomly. They give to those persons whom they believe are (or will be) best able to assist them as a result of committee position, geographical affinity, or political philosophy. Thus, dairy cooperatives, for example, tend to concentrate their money on congressmen from milk-producing areas and the key members of House and Senate agricultural committees.

Despite frequent journalistic accounts and public interest group revelations linking PAC contributions to specific public policy outcomes,[122] it is virtually impossible to prove that a particular piece of legislation or a congressional appropriation resulted from such contributions. Too many complex factors enter into every governmental decision to permit an inference of direct and simple causality between contributions given and a decision made. The critical point is that made by Fred Wertheimer in a recent Common Cause publication: "PAC contributions are often contributions with a legislative purpose. . . . Although explicit *quid pro quos* are rarely involved, PAC dollars often provide the donating groups with a degree of access and influence with Members unavailable to the average constituent."[123] Through the PAC process, economic interests with substantial financial resources are better situated to influence public policy than are constituencies that lack this wherewithal.

Although it is not possible to demonstrate the effect of specific PAC donations on particular public policy outcomes, it is not unreasonable to assert that the PAC phenomenon has contributed at the macro level to increasing the influence of the business community in the overall public policy process during the past several years. A *Business Week*/Harris poll reported in the October 4, 1982, issue of *Business Week*[124] indicates that 75 percent of the top executives of 600 of the nation's largest corporations believe that business has greater political efficacy in Washington now than it did five years ago. More than two-thirds of the respondents considered business to be much better organized today than it was five years earlier to engage in political activity, and many attributed this increased effectiveness to their political action committees. Some 71 percent of all executives reported that their PACs had worked out well in terms of meeting the objectives set for them by the company. Al-

though lobbying activities and the maintenance of regular correspondence with political decision makers are rated by corporate political
specialists to be, respectively, the two most important forms of corporate
political activity, operating an effective PAC ranks a close third and is
considered as essential to carrying out the other two functions.[125]

Even if they do not share the self-congratulatory mood of the corporate respondents, most students of the political process would agree with
the conclusions of the *Business Week* Harris poll regarding business'
heightened political efficiency over the mid-1970s. Although not ame-
nable to quantification, by virtually every benchmark the business community appears to be more effective politically—in short, to have greater
political power—than a decade ago.[126] If anything, Charles E. Lindblom's observation about the "privileged position" of business seems more
accurate today than when he first penned those words in the mid-
1970s.[127] This does not mean, of course, that specific policy outcomes
conform necessarily to the wishes of particular business interests or that
the business community, perforce, gets its way in all, or even most, cases.
Rather it suggests that, on the whole, critical issues of public policy are
resolved in ways considered to be appropriate by mainstream business
leadership. "Appropriate resolution" has been particularly evident in the
United States since the mid-1970s, not least of all in the minds of some
governmental officials active during this period.[128] While the PAC phenomenon is surely not the sole cause of this development, it is undeni-
ably an important contributing factor.

And what of the future? To a large extent, the future viability of corporate and other business-oriented PACs as important mechanisms for
business political involvement lies within the hands of those who run
them. Although, not surprisingly, the PAC concept has failed to evoke
the enthusiastic support of the American electorate, there appears to have
emerged over the past several years an unstated, but nonetheless real,
acquiescence in the view that as long as they operate within limits—
unspecified as these limits may be—PACs can have a proper role to play
in the American electoral process. In a more personal vein, I have argued for over a decade that absent the legal right of corporations and
labor unions to contribute directly to political campaigns, the PAC
mechanism serves as a useful and appropriate vehicle for their limited
involvement in electoral politics.[129] The almost exponential increase in
PAC activity—particularly among corporate and other business-related
committees—over the past several years has raised serious doubts in my

mind as to whether PAC contributions do not already exceed their "fair share" of congressional candidates' campaign receipts. A few years ago, some observers of the political scene argued in essence that concern about corporate and other PAC contributions, if not precisely much ado about nothing, was at least too much ado about very little.[130] If the position was ever correct, it can scarcely be contended that it is so in 1982. As we have seen, during this election cycle, PACs overall will contribute some $89 million, approximately a third of all funds received by congressional general election candidates, and that corporate PACs will donate an estimated $35 million (10 percent) of that amount. That such a percentage of congressional campaign funds emanates from PAC sources is intolerable in a society that has prided itself on maintaining throughout most of its history both the appearance and the reality of political democracy, at least insofar as the political impact of large economic interests is concerned. If, as is likely, PACs reach their predicted levels of activities during the 1981–1982 election cycle, the time has come to limit the amounts that federal candidates can accept from PACs and to provide them with alternative sources of significant campaign funds through partial public financing and less stringent contributions limits on political parties and thereby lessen their dependence on "special interest" money. Although the specific limits per election cycle (of $90,000 in contributions that a House candidate can receive from PACs and of $180,000 for total candidate expenditures) are too low given the high costs of elections today, the type of funding formula offered by Congressman Obey in the proposed Clean Campaign Act of 1982 makes considerable sense.[131] Further adding to the bill's attractiveness is that it also seeks to stimulate small campaign contributions by individuals. The Obey bill should be extended to Senate candidates, with appropriate allowances for the higher costs associated with running for election to that body, particularly from the large states, and coupled with provisions for partial public financing of congressional races (preferably through the parties). This approach would restrain current and likely future excesses on the part of corporate and other political action committees and return them to more limited and, in my judgment, more appropriate levels of participation in the financing of federal elections. For, *in their place,* properly constrained, PACs have a legitimate role to play in the modern political process, a role that can enhance rather than erode the quality of political democracy in the United States.

NOTES

1. *Quotations from Chairman Mao Tse-Tung* (Peking: Foreign Languages Press, 1967), pp. 302–303.

2. These themes are explored in Carl Becker, *Freedom and Responsibility in the American Way of Life* (New York: Vintage, 1945); John Hart Ely, *Democracy and Distrust: A Theory of Judicial Review* (Cambridge: Harvard University Press, 1980); "The American Commonwealth," *Public Interest* (Fall 1975), particularly the essay by Martin Diamond, "The Declaration and the Constitution: Liberty, Democracy and the Founders," pp. 39–55; Seymour Martin Lipset, *The First New Nation: The United States in Historical and Comparative Perspective* (Garden City, N.Y.: Anchor, 1967); R. M. MacIver, *The Web of Government*, rev. ed. (New York: Free Press, 1965); and Samuel P. Huntington, "American Ideals Versus American Institutions," *Political Science Quarterly* (Spring 1982), 97:1–37.

3. E. E. Schattschneider, *The Semisovereign People* (New York: Holt, Rinehart and Winston, 1960), pp. 120–121; and Milton Friedman, *Capitalism and Freedom* (Chicago: University of Chicago Press, 1962).

4. See, for example, Yair Aharoni, *The No-Risk Society* (Chatham, N.J.: Chatham, 1981); Charles E. Lindblom, *Politics and Markets: The World's Political-Economy Systems* (New York: Basic Books, 1977); Arthur M. Okun, *Equality and Efficiency: The Big Tradeoff* (Washington, D.C.: Brookings Institution, 1975); Charles L. Schultze, *The Public Use of Private Interest* (Washington, D.C.: Brookings Institution, 1977); Michael Harrington, *Decade of Decision: The Crisis of the American System* (New York: Simon and Schuster, 1980); Lester C. Thurow, *The Zero-Sum Society: Distribution and the Possibilities for Economic Change* (New York: Basic Books, 1980); and Samuel Bowles and Herbert Gintis, "The Crisis of Liberal Democratic Capitalism: The Case of the United States," *Politics and Society* (1982), 2(15):51–93.

5. See Alfred D. Chandler, Jr., *The Visible Hand: The Managerial Revolution in American Business* (Cambridge: Harvard University Press, Belknap Press, 1977); James Willard Hurst, *The Legitimacy of the Business Corporation in the Law of the United States, 1780–1970* (Charlottesville: University Press of Virginia, 1970); and Richard M. Abrams, "The Modern Corporation," *Society* (March–April 1979), 16:44–51.

6. Richard Hofstadter, *The Age of Reform* (New York: Vintage, 1955), pp. 227–228.

7. Edwin M. Epstein, "Dimensions of Corporate Power, pt. 1," *California Management Review* (Winter 1973), 16:9–23; idem, "Dimensions of Corporate Power, pt. 2," *California Management Review* (Summer 1974, 16:32–47; idem, Societal, Managerial and Legal Perspectives on Corporate Social Responsibility—Product and Process," *Hastings Law Journal* (May 1979), 30:1287–1320; and idem, "The Historical Enigma of Corporate Legitimacy," *California Law Review* (November 1972), 60:1701–1717.

8. Hofstadter, p. 227.

9. S.600, 96th Cong., 1st sess., 1979.

10. S.600, sec. 3(a) and 3(b).

11. Opening statement of Senator Edward M. Kennedy upon introduction of the Small (and Independent) Business Protection Act, Press Release, Office of Senator Kennedy, March 8, 1979, p. 1.

12. Michael Pertschuk, Chairman, Federal Trade Commission, U.S. Congress, Senate Committee on the Judiciary, Subcommittee on Antitrust, Monopoly and Business Rights, *Small and Independent Business Protection Act of 1979: Hearing on S. 600*, pt. 1, 96th Cong., 1st sess., serial no. 96–26 (Washington, D.C.: Government Printing Office, 1979), p. 15 (hereinafter cited as *S. 600 Hearings*).

13. See Schattschneider; Friedman; and recent publications such as Edward S. Herman, *Corporate Control, Corporate Power* (Cambridge: Cambridge University Press, 1981); Ira M. Millstein and Salem M. Katsh, *The Limits of Corporate Power* (New York: Macmillan, 1981); Arthur S. Miller, *The Modern Corporate State: Private Governments and the American Constitution* (Westport, Conn: Greenwood Press, 1976); Ralph Nader, Mark Green, and Joel Seligman, *Taming the Giant Corporation* (New York: Norton, 1976); Alfred C. Neal, *Business Power and Public Policy* (New York: Praeger, 1981); Michael Pertschuk, *Revolt Against Regulation: The Rise and Cause of the Consumer Movement* (Berkeley: University of California Press, 1982); Frances W. Steckmest, *Corporate Performance: The Key to Public Trust* (New York: McGraw-Hill, 1981); Michael Useem, "Classwide Nationality in the United States and Great Britain," *Administrative Science Quarterly* (June 1982), 27:199–226; and Jeffrey Pfeffer, *Power in Organizations* (Marshfield, Mass.: Pitman, 1981).

14. These points are explored at greater length in a variety of sources. See, for example, Howard E. Aldrich, *Organizations and Environments* (Englewood Cliffs, N.J.: Prentice-Hall, 1979); Lindblom; Phyllis S. McGrath, *Managing Corporate External Relations: Changing Perspectives and Responses,* Conference Board Report No. 679 (New York: Conference Board, 1976); idem, *Redefining Corporate Relations,* Conference Board Report No. 757 (New York: Conference Board, 1979); Boston University, School of Management, Public Affairs Research Group, "Public Affairs Officers and Their Functions: Highlights of a National Survey," *Public Affairs Review* (1981), 2:88–99; Jeffrey Pfeffer and Gerald R. Salancik, *The External Control of Organizations: A Resource Dependence Perspective* (New York: Harper & Row, 1978); and Jeffrey A. Sonnenfeld, *Corporate Views of the Public Interest: Perceptions of the Forest Products Industry* (Boston: Auburn House, 1981).

15. The PAC phenomenon has stimulated a rapidly growing body of literature over the past few years. See, for example, Joseph E. Cantor, *Political Action Committees: Their Evolution and Growth and Their Implications for the Political System,* Report No. 82–92 GOV (Washington, D.C.: Congressional Research Service, Library of Congress, 1981, 1982); Edward Handler and John Mulkern, *Business in Politics* (Lexington, Mass.: Lexington, 1982); Michael J. Malbin, ed., *Parties, Interest Groups and Campaign Finance Laws* (Washington, D.C.: American Enterprise Institute for Public Policy Research, 1980); Frank J. Sorauf, "Political Action Committees in American Politics," Paper presented at the American Political Science Association meeting, Denver, Colorado, September 1982; and "Symposium: Political Action Committees and Campaign Finance," *Arizona Law Review* (October 1980), vol. 22.

16. Statement by Michael Pertschuk, *S. 600 Hearings,* pt. 1, p. 15.

17. Justice Felix Frankfurter, writing for the Majority in *United States* v. *International Union, UAW-CIO,* 352 U.S. 567 at 570 (1957).

18. Although this paper deals with corporate PACs (and, where pertinent, other business-related PACs), it is important to note that since 1943 labor organizations have been subject to the same legal restrictions as corporations: the Federal Election Campaign Act

of 1971 and Amendments prohibit direct union contributions to political parties and candidates but permit unions to establish PACs and to solicit funds for them from members and their families. Although, on occasion, I shall refer specifically to labor unions, the reader may assume, unless I indicate to the contrary, that legislative or judicial policies that apply to corporations in the campaign financing area apply equally to labor unions. Uniform statutory treatment of corporations and labor organizations has been a benchmark of congressional policy for nearly forty years.

19. The Federal Election Campaign Act of 1971 and Amendments are currently codified at 2 U.S.C. §§ 431–455 (1976 and supp. VI, 1982) (hereinafter referred to as FECA).

20. The current federal prohibitions against corporate and labor campaign contributions is found in sec. 441b of the FECA codified as 2 U.S.C. 441B (1976 and supp. VI, 1982). Its predecessor provisions were embodied in the Federal Criminal Code, 18 U.S.C. 610 (1951), which in turn encompassed the Federal Corrupt Practices Act of 1925, 2 U.S.C. 251 (1925). Histories of this legislation are found in Herbert E. Alexander, *Money in Politics* (Washington, D.C.: Public Affairs Press, 1972); Congressional Quarterly Inc., *Dollar Politics*, 3rd ed. (Washington, D.C.: Congressional Quarterly, 1982); Edwin M. Epstein, *Corporations, Contributions and Political Campaigns: Federal Regulation in Perspective* (Berkeley: Institute of Government Studies, University of California, 1968); Epstein, "Corporations and Labor Unions in Electoral Politics," *Annals of the American Academy of Political and Social Science* (May 1976), 425:33–58; and Earl R. Sikes, *State and Federal Corrupt-Practices Legislation* (Durham, N.C.: Duke University Press, 1982).

21. See Herbert E. Alexander, *Financing the 1972 Elections* (Lexington, Mass.: Heath, 1976); Congressional Quarterly Inc., *Dollar Politics*, vol. 2 (Washington, D.C.: Congressional Quarterly, 1974); Epstein, "Electoral Politics"; and Investor Responsibility Research Center, *The Corporate Watergate*, Special Report No. 1975-D (Washington, D.C.: Investor Responsibility Research Center, 1975).

22. This policy position is best articulated in such cases as *U.S.* v. *CIO*, 335 U.S. 106 (1948); *U.S.* v. *International Union UAW-CIO*, 352 U.S. 567 (1957); and *Cort, et al.* v. *Ash*, 422 U.S. 66 (1975). Compare *Buckley* v. *Valeo*, 424 U.S. 1 (1976), and *First National Bank of Boston* v. *Bellotti*, 435 U.S. 765 (1978).

23. *Pipefitters Local Union No. 562, et al.* v. *U.S.*, 407 U.S. 385 (1972). Compare *International Association of Machinists and Aerospace Workers* v. *Federal Election Commission*, F.2d (D.C. Cir., 1982). When confronted with the issues of the primacy of the two objectives, the Supreme Court has vacillated in its position. Compare *Pipefitters Local 562* v. *U.S.*, 407 U.S. 385 (1972), with *Cort et al.* v. *Ash*, 422 U.S. 66 (1975).

24. Fred Werthheimer, "Commentaries," pp. 193–196, in Malbin, ed., *Parties, Interest Groups, and Campaign Finance Laws*.

25. Handler and Mulkern, pp. 96–97.

26. See for example, Epstein, "Electoral Politics"; idem, "Labor and Federal Elections: The New Legal Framework," *Industrial Relations* (October 1975), 15:257–274; Epstein, "The Emergence of Political Action Committees," pp. 159–197, in Herbert E. Alexander, ed., *Political Finance*, Sage Electoral Studies Handbook Vol. 5 (Beverly Hills, Calif.: Sage, 1979); and "Business and Labor Under the Federal Election Campaign Act of 1971," pp. 107–151, in Malbin, ed., *Parties, Interest Groups, and Campaign Finance Laws*.

27. Frank J. Sorauf, "Political Parties and Political Action Committees: Two Life Cycles," *Arizona Law Review* (October 1980), 22:445–463.

28. Federal Election Campaign Act Amendments 1979, Pub. L. No. 96-187, 93 STAT. 1339 (current version codified at 2 U.S.C. 431–455) (1976 and supp. 1982).

29. See Xandra Kayden, "Parties and the 1980 Presidental Election," in Harvard University, John F. Kennedy School of Government, Institute of Politics, *Financing Presidential*

Campaigns: An Examination of the Ongoing Effects of The Federal Election Campaign Laws Upon Conduct of Presidential Campaigns. (Prepared for the Senate Committee on Rules and Administration, January 1982.)

30. The 1979–1980 summary data are drawn from the following Federal Election Commission (FEC) sources: FEC Press Release: "FEC Releases Final Figures on 1979–1980 Major Political Party Activity," Corrected Release, February 21, 1982; "FEC Releases Final PAC Report for 1979–80 Election Cycle," February 21, 1982; "FEC Releases Final Statistics on 1979–80 Congressional Races," Corrected Release, March 7, 1982; and "1982 Congressional Campaigns Spend Record Amount," p. 3.

31. Gary C. Jacobson, "The Pattern of Campaign Contributions to Candidates for the U.S. House of Representatives 1972–78," in Harvard University, John F. Kennedy School of Government, Institute of Politics, An Analysis of the Impact of the Federal Election Campaign Act, 1972–78. Prepared for the Committee on House Administration, October 1979.

32. Sorauf, p. 463.

33. Fred Werthheimer, "The PAC Phenomenon in American Politics," Arizona Law Review (October 1980), 22:605.

34. Tom Railsback, "Congressional Responses to Obey–Railsback," Arizona Law Review (October 1980), 22:669.

35. Bernadette A. Budde, "The Practical Role of Corporate Political PACs on the Political Process," Arizona Law Review (October 1980), 22:669.

36. Carroll A. Campbell, Jr., "Congressional Responses to Obey–Railsback," Arizona Law Review (October 1980), 22:674.

37. The data in this section are drawn from the following sources: Cantor; FEC, Annual Reports, 1975–1981; FEC Disclosure Series No. 8 (1977) and 10 (1978); FEC Press Releases: "FEC Releases Final Report on 1977–78 Financial Activity of Non-Party and Party Political Committees," April 24, 1980, "FEC Releases Final PAC Report for 1979–80 Election Cycle," February 21, 1982, "FEC Releases Final Statistics on 1979–80 Congressional Races," Corrected Release, March 7, 1982, "Federal Election Commission Releases PAC Figures," July 12, 1982; and Common Cause, Campaign Finance Monitoring Project: 1972 Federal Campaign Finances (Washington, D.C.: Common Cause, 1974); and idem, 1976 Federal Campaign Finances (Washington, D.C.: Common Cause, 1976).

38. In calculating an aggregate "business-related" figure for the 1979–1980 election cycle, I am following the convention I have utilized in earlier studies of adding the corporate figure to one-half of all PACs classified by the FEC as "Non-Connected," "Trade/Membership/Health," "Cooperatives," and "Corporations Without Stock." See, for example, Epstein, "Business and Labor," tables 1 and 2, pp. 116–117. Cantor also adopted this convention in his Congressional Research Service Report. See Cantor.

39. Cantor, table 20, p. 128.

40. Data on independent expenditures are drawn from the FEC Press Releases: "FEC Releases Information on Independent Expenditures," October 9, 1980, "FEC Study Shows Independent Expenditures Top $16 Million," November 29, 1981, "FEC Releases Final PAC Report for 1979–80 Election Cycle," February 21, 1982; and Cantor, p. 180.

41. FEC Press Release (untitled), Corrected Release, October 5, 1981.

42. See Epstein, "Emergence of Political Action Committees," pp. 161–162, and materials cited therein.

43. Data are drawn from FEC Press Releases: "FEC Releases First Full PAC Study for '82 Elections," October 3, 1982, and "FEC Releases Final PAC Report for 1979–80 Election Cycle," February 21, 1982.

44. This growth came on the heels of the FEC's advisory opinion in late 1975 in Sun-

PAC (*Federal Register,* December 3, 1973, pp. 56584–56588), easily the most momentous and controversial decision in its seven-year history. The FEC ruled that Sun Oil could: (1) use general treasury funds to establish, administer, and solicit contributions to its PAC; (2) solicit contributions to its PAC from both stockholders and employees; and (3) establish multiple PACs, each having separate contribution and expenditure limits. Although it was the FECA of 1971 and the 1974 amendments—not Sun-PAC—that established the legal authority for the creation of PACs and although significant aspects of the FEC ruling were changed by the 1976 FECA Amendments, for the corporate community, it was the Sun-PAC decision that truly provided the liberating imprimatur for the rapid development and widespread use of the PAC mechanism (see Epstein, "Emergence of Political Action Committees").

45. Epstein, "Business and Labor," p. 133.

46. "The 50 Leading Exporters," *Fortune,* August 24, 1981, p. 85.

47. "100 Leading National Advertisers," *Advertising Age,* September 10, 1981, p. 1.

48. The list of Department of Defense contractors appears in Council of Economic Priorities, "The Defense Department's Top 100," *Newsletter* (November 1980), pp. 3–4.

49. Gordon Adams, *The Iron Triangle: The Politics of Defense Contracting* (New York: Council on Economic Priorities, 1981), pp. 105–128.

50. The data on PAC formation by savings and loan associations is drawn from "The 200 Largest Savings Associations," *Savings and Loan News* (February 1981), pp. 81–85; *Supplement to FEC Reports on Financial Activity 1979–80,* Final Report, January 1982; Data tapes of *FEC Report on Financial Activity 1979–80,* Final Report, January 1982; *Supplement to FEC Reports on Financial Activity,* April 1980; and Data tapes on *FEC Reports on Financial Activity 1977–78,* Final Report, April 1980.

51. Phyllis S. McGrath, *Redefining Corporate Federal Relations,* Conference Board Report No. 757 (New York: Conference Board, 1979), p. 57.

52. *Ibid.,* p. 49.

53. "200 Largest Savings Associations."

54. "Houston's Top 100 Companies," *Houston* (June 1982), p. 24.

55. "The 50 Largest Diversified Services Companies," *Fortune,* July 12, 1982, pp. 132–133.

56. "The Three Hundred Largest Banks in the U.S.," *American Banker,* February 29, 1980, pp. 59–61.

57. "Ranking America's Biggest Brokers," *Institutional Investors* (April 1981); pp. 109–110.

58. "The 50 Largest Private Companies in the U.S.," *Forbes,* June 23, 1980, p. 110.

59. "The 50 Largest Private Industrial Companies," *Fortune* May 31, 1982, p. 109.

60. FEC Press Releases: "FEC Releases Final PAC Report for 1979–80 Election Cycle," February 21, 1982, p. 5, and "FEC Releases Final Report on 1977–78 Financial Activity of Non-Party and Party Political Committees," April 24, 1980, p. 6; and *Corporate-Related Political Committees Receipts and Expenditures, 1976 Campaign,* FEC Disclosure Series No. 8, September 1977.

61. The sources for all the data in this section are *Supplement to FEC Reports on Financial Activity 1979–80,* Final Report, January 1982; Data tapes of *FEC Reports on Financial Activity 1979–80,* Final Report, January 1982; and *Fortune,* July 13, 1981, pp. 121–126.

62. Handler and Mulkern, pp. 72–78.

63. U.S. Department of Commerce, Bureau of the Census, *Statistical Abstract of the United States* (Washington, D.C.: Government Printing Office, 1977), p. 561.

64. Since some companies have more than one registered PAC that makes contribu-

tions to candidates during the election cycle (e.g., AT&T, Mobil Oil, General Electric, General Telephone and Telegraph, and Dow Chemical), the "average" committee may understate the activities of given companies. The same situation is true in the case of labor unions, some of which have multiple PACs.

65. Cantor, pp. 94–98.

66. FEC Press Release, "FEC Releases Final PAC Report for 1979–80 Election Cycle," February 21, 1982, pp. 4–5.

67. The survey was conducted by Business-Industry Political Action Committee, National Association of Business Political Action Committees, National Association of Manufacturers, and Public Affairs Council, *Corporate Political Action Committees-Where?* (November 1981) (hereinafter cited as *Corporate Political Action Committees*).

68. *See, for example, Epstein,* "Business and Labor," pp. 122–124; and Epstein, "Emergence of Political Action Committees," pp. 175–176.

69. Handler and Mulkern, p. 14.

70. *Ibid.,* p. 33.

71. "Defense Department's Top 100," Council on Economic Priorities' *Newsletter,* pp. 3–4; *Supplement to FEC Reports on Financial Activity 1979–80,* Final Report, January 1982; Data tapes of *FEC Reports on Financial Activity 1979–80,* Final Report, January 1982; and *Supplement to FEC Reports on Financial Activity 1977–78,* Final Report, April 1980.

72. PACs, in 1979–1980, gave $2.6 million to national level party committees and another $.6 million to state and local party groups; see FEC Press Release "FEC Releases Final Figures on 1979–80 Major Political Party Activity," Corrected Release, February 21, 1982, p. 2. For the first eighteen months of the 1981–1982 election cycle, PACs have donated slightly over $3 million to major party political committees; see untitled FEC Press Release, October 7, 1982, p. 2. During both election cycles, PACs favored Republicans over Democrats by a two-to-one margin.

73. *S. 600 Hearings,* p. 15.

74. FEC Disclosure Series No. 8: *Corporate-Related Political Committees Receipts and Expenditures, 1976 Campaign,* September 1977; *Supplement to FEC Reports on Financial Activity 1977–78,* Final Report, January 1982; *Fortune,* May 4, 1981, and July 13, 1981; and Federal Trade Commission, *Statistical Report on Mergers and Acquisitions* (Washington, D.C.: Federal Trade Commission, July 1981).

75. See table 9.6.

76. 2 U.S.C. §441a(5)(B) (1976 and supp. VI, 1982).

77. Michael J. Malbin has suggested that corporations operating in a single industry tend to have a "special interest" focus and to contribute defensively to candidates who can influence policy pertinent to a particular line of business. On the other hand, corporations with more diverse economic interests tend to have a broader "general interest" orientation and to give to politicians who are simply "probusiness" in orientation rather than industry-specific in focus. Accordingly, a firm's degree of economic diversification is the critical determinant of the contribution behavior of its PAC. See Michael J. Malbin, "Campaign Financing and the 'Special Interests,' " *Public Interest* (Summer 1979), 56:34–35.

Handler and Mulkern tested the Malbin suggestion and found that, among their sample of seventy-one major companies with PACs, "the data provide some limited corroboration of the Malbin hypothesis, but do not lend support to the view that diversification is by itself a sufficient explanation of PAC variation. Although both higher incidences and higher levels of diversification appears among ideological PACs, a significant degree of diversification, although to a lesser degree, appears among pragmatic PACs" (Handler and Mulkern, p. 28).

78. In 1977–1980, more than 70 percent of candidates' receipts came from non-PAC

and nonparty sources, either contributions from individuals or monies donated by candidates and their families to their campaigns. FEC Press Release "FEC Releases Final Statistics on 1979–80 Congressional Races," Corrected Release, March 7, 1982, p. 3.

79. See, for example, "The PAC Men: Turning Cash Into Votes," *Time,* October 25, 1982.

80. Albert R. Hunt, "Cash Politics, Special-Interest Money Increasingly Influences What Congress Enacts"; "Campaign Giving by PACs Soars, and Some Expect a Specific Vote in Return"; "The Green Tide on K Street," *Wall Street Journal,* July 28, 1982, p. 1.

81. Congressional Quarterly, *Dollar Politics.*

82. U.S. Congress, House, *Campaign Finance Act of 1981,* H.R. 4070, 97th Cong., 1st sess., 1981.

83. U.S. Congress, House, *Clean Campaign Act of 1982,* H.R. 4277, 97th Cong., 2d sess., 1982.

84. David W. Adamany, *Campaign Finance in America* (North Scituate, Mass.: Duxbury Press, 1972); Herbert E. Alexander, *Financing the 1976 Elections* (Washington, D.C.: Congressional Quarterly Press, 1979); Gary C. Jacobson, *Money in Congressional Elections* (New Haven: Yale University Press, 1980); John R. Owens, *Trends in Campaign Spending in California, 1958–70* (Princeton: New Jersey Citizens Research Foundation, 1973); and W. P. Welch, "Money and Votes: A Simultaneous Equation Model," *Public Choice* (1981), 36:209–234. See, generally, Alexander, ed., *Political Finance,* particularly the articles by Gary C. Jacobson, Ronald D. McDevitt, James E. Zinser and Paul A. Dawson, and W. P. Welch; "Symposium," *Arizona Law Review* (October 1980), 22, particularly the articles by David Adamany and Frank J. Sorauf; Institute of Politics, "Impact of the Federal Election Campaign Act, 1972–78"; and David Adamany, "Review Article: Political Finance in Transition," *Polity* (Winter 1981), 15:314–331.

85. Alexander Heard, *The Costs of Democracy* (Chapel Hill: University of North Carolina Press, 1960), p. 16.

86. Gary C. Jacobson, "Practical Consequences of Campaign Finance Reform: An Incumbent Protection Act," *Public Policy* (Winter 1976), 24:6.

87. Jacobson, *Congressional Elections,* p. 136.

88. John R. Owens and Edward C. Olson, "Campaign Spending and the Election Process in California, 1966–1974," *Western Political Quarterly* (December 1977), 30:493–512.

89. Larry Light, "Will Money Preserve GOP Gains of 1980?" *Congressional Quarterly,* April 10, 1982, p. 815.

90. *Ibid.*

91. Heard, p. 35.

92. Jacobson, *Money in Elections.* See also Lawrence Shepherd, "Does Campaign Spending Really Matter?" *Public Opinion Quarterly* (Summer 1977), 41:196–205.

93. Jacobson, *Money in Elections,* p. 112.

94. Rob Gurwitt, "Getting and Spending: Senate Campaign Strategies, The Early Money Approach," *Congressional Quarterly,* August 14, 1982, pp. 1987–1988.

95. Chamber of Commerce of the United States, "U.S. Chamber's PAC Enters 92 Congressional Races, Endorsing 40 Incumbents, Rejecting 21 Other Members," News Release, April 20, 1982, p. 1. See also Alan Ehrenhalt, "PAC Politics: The Power of Information," *Congressional Quarterly,* May 1, 1982, p. 1027.

96. On PAC networking, see Ehrenhalt, p. 1027.

97. Tillman Act, 34 Stat. 864 (1907).

98. Paul A. Gigot, "Some Corporations Trying To Turn Shareholders into a Political Force," *Wall Street Journal,* January 19, 1982, p. 25.

99. *Ibid.*

100. Handler and Mulkern, pp. 38–42.

101. Albert O. Hirschman, *Exit, Voice and Loyalty: Responses to Decline in Firms, Organizations and States* (Cambridge: Harvard University Press, 1970).

102. Georgetown University Law Center, Institute for Public Representation, "Petition for an Amendment of Rule 14a-3 to Provide for Disclosure of Corporate Political Activities to Shareholders," before the Securities and Exchange Commission, July 21, 1980, p. 9.

103. General Motors' Political Action Committee, *1980 General Motors Public Interest Group,* April 7, 1980, pp. 116–117. On the efficacy of shareholder action, see David Vogel, *Lobbying the Corporation: Citizen Challenges to Business Authority* (New York: Basic Books, 1978), pp. 71–125.

104. See, for example, American Law Institute, *Principles of Corporate Governance and Structure: Restatement and Recommendations,* Tentative Draft No. 1 (Philadelphia: American Law Institute, April 1, 1982).

105. *International Association of Machinists and Aerospace Workers (IAMA)* v. *Federal Election Commission,* 678 F.2d 1092 (D.C. Cir. 1982). See also *First National Bank of Boston* v. *Bellotti,* 435 U.S. 765 (1978).

106. *IAMA,* CCH, Federal Election at pp. 51, 275.

107. The IAMA brief is quoted in *ibid.,* pp. 51, 287.

108. *Ibid.*

109. *Ibid.,* pp. 51, 288. The IAMA case is currently on appeal to the Supreme Court of the United States and will be argued during the 1982–83 term.

110. Handler and Mulkern, p. 97.

111. James Lindberg, "Dart PAC: Successful Political Involvement," in Fraser/Associates, *Political Action for Business: The PAC Handbook* (Washington, D.C.: Fraser/Associates, 1981), pp. 57–61.

112. See *Corporate Political Action Committees.*

113. Theodore J. Lowi, *The End of Liberalism* (New York: Norton, 1969), pp. 55–97.

114. Peter Bachrach, *The Theory of Democratic Elitism: A Critique* (Boston: Little, Brown, 1967).

115. See, for example, Sorauf, "Two Life Cycles"; the articles by Sorauf, Kayden, and Adamany in *An Analysis of the Impact of the Federal Election Campaign Act, 1972–78;* the papers by Kayden and Ruth S. Johnes in *Parties, Interest Groups;* Everett Carll Ladd, *Where Have All the Voters Gone?: The Fracturing of America's Political Parties,* 2d ed. (New York: Norton, 1982), pp. 17–28; Hugh L. Le Blanc, *American Political Parties* (New York: St. Martin's Press, 1982), pp. 265–271; and Joel L. Fleishman, ed., *The Future of American Political Parties: The Challenge of Governance* (Englewood Cliffs, N.J.: Prentice-Hall, 1982), particularly the article by Robert J. Huckshorn and John F. Bibby. Much of the recent literature on the political parties is critiqued in Roy B. Christman, "Party Reform Literature: A Review Essay," *Western Political Quarterly* (September 1982), 35:442–448.

116. Paul R. Abramson and John H. Aldrich, "The Decline of Electoral Participation in America," *American Political Science Review* (September 1982), 76:502–521, 502.

117. James Madison, "The Federalist, No. 10," in Alexander Hamilton, James Madison, and John Jay, *The Federalist Papers* (New York: New American Library of World Literature, 1961), p. 79.

118. Chamber of Commerce of the United States, "U.S. Chamber's PAC Enters 92 Races," p. 1.

119. Marion A. Youngers, "Rexnard's PAC," in Fraser/Associates, *Political Action for Business*, pp. 87–96, 90.

120. Albert R. Hunt, "An Inside Look at Politicians Hustling PACs," *Wall Street Journal*, October 1, 1982, p. 1.

121. *Congressional Record*, July 8, 1981 (remarks of Representative Glickman), 100th Cong., 1st sess.

122. See, for example, "Running with the PACs," *Time*, October 25, 1982, pp. 20–26; Albert R. Hunt, "The Green Tide on K Street" (three-part series), July 28, 1982, p. 1, July 29, 1982, p. 1, and August 2, 1982, p. 1; "Annual Report: PAC Inc.," *Common Cause* (August 1982), 8:18–22; Public Citizen's Congress Watch, "An Ocean of Milk, A Mountain of Cheese, and a Ton of Money: Contributions from the Dairy PACs to Members of Congress" (Washington, D.C.: Congress Watch, July 1982). Two recent articles by Henry W. Chappell, Jr., demonstrate the difficulty of measuring the effects of campaign contributions on congressional voting: "Campaign Contributions and Voting on the Cargo Preference Bill: A Comparison of Simultaneous Models," *Public Choice* (1981), 36:301–312; and "Campaign Contributions and Congressional Voting: A Simultaneous Probit-Tobit Model," *Review of Economics and Statistics* (February 1982), 65:77–83.

123. Fred Wertheimer, "Preface," in Common Cause, *A Common Cause Guide to Money, Power and Politics in the 97th Congress* (Washington, D.C.: Common Cause, 1981), p. i.

124. Business Week/Harris Poll, "How Business Is Getting Through to Washington," *Business Week*, October 4, 1982, p. 16.

125. Public Affairs Research Group, "Public Affairs Ofifcers and Their Functions: Summary of Survey Responses" (Boston: School of Management, Boston University, 1981), pp. 10–11. See also, McGrath, pp. 48–55.

126. See David Vogel, "The 'New' Social Regulation in Historical and Comparative Perspective," pp. 155–185 in Thomas K. McCraw, ed., *Regulation in Perspective* (Cambridge: Harvard University Press, 1981). Also instructive on this point is Vogel's "How Business Responds to Opposition: Corporate Political Strategies During the 1970s," Paper delivered at the annual meeting of the American Political Science Association, Washington, D.C., 1979.

127. Lindblom, *Politics and Markets*, pp. 170–188. See also Amitai Etzioni, "Making Interest Groups Work for the Public," *Public Opinion* (August–September 1982), 5:53–55.

128. Pertschuk, *Revolt Against Regulation*. Compare Millstein and Katsh, *Limits of Corporate Power*, and Steckmest, *Corporate Social Performance*.

129. See, for example, Edwin M. Epstein, *The Corporation in American Politics* (Englewood Cliffs, N.J.: Prentice-Hall, 1969), pp. 304–320; idem, "Business and Labor," pp. 149–151; and idem, "The PAC Phenomenon: An Overview," *Arizona Law Review* (October 1980), 22:371–372.

130. See, for example, Michael J. Malbin, "Of Mountains and Molehills: PACs, Campaigns and Public Policy," in Malbin, ed., *Parties, Interest Groups*, and Campaign Finance Laws, pp. 152–184; and idem, "Campaign Financing and the 'Special Interests.' "

131. H.R. 4277, 97th Cong., 2d sess., 1982. For thoughtful essays on the prospects and directions of changes in the FECA, see Herbert E. Alexander, "Political Action Committees and Their Corporate Sponsors in the 1980s," *Public Affairs Review* (1981), 2:27–38; and idem, "Parties, PACs and Political Finance Reform: How and Why Has Election Financing Reform Gone Awry? What to Do About It?" *Vital Issues* (1982), vol. 32.

COMMENTATORS' REMARKS

MICHAEL PERTSCHUK

IN this post-Victorian era, corporate power remains one of the few indelicate subjects that one can raise in the company of corporate leaders.

I once suggested to a group of corporate chief executives that they possessed inordinate power. I was struck by the cold fury with which they received this news. Finally, one could not constrain himself and jumped up and said: "Power? We haven't got any power. Why don't you go after Jane Fonda. Jone Fonda has power!" My experience suggests that everyone in this room perceives himself as powerless against his adversaries. The perception of powerlessness is one of the few emotions that we all share. Power is indeed an illusive commodity. I think David Vogel did very well in catching the shadows of power in the clean air battles, but it's very difficult to identify and measure it.

No one could read Ed Epstein's splendid and rich treatise without concluding that we have a pungent political problem on our hands, but what precisely is it? As Ed suggests, the political economies of scale facilitated by large mergers are not *the* problem, though I would note that Phillip Morris, for example, by acquiring both 7-up and Miller's, is more certain to gain the attention of senators from Wisconsin on the dangers of cigarette warning labels than it otherwise would.

Since *all* forms of PACs proliferate, he tells us, except labor, corporate PACs alone are plainly not the problem, although Epstein shows well that it's the *Fortune* 500 PACs that lead the rest in growth. The noncorporate business-affiliated PACs have amassed huge treasures, but, on the other hand, they have narrow and diverse goals. So they are obviously not *the* problem, though I might note the success of the auto dealers and medical society PACs in harnessing Congress to veto Federal Trade Commission rules.

Individual campaign contributions are obviously not *the* problem, because they've been going on for a long time. Corporate and business political grass-roots activity and involvement in campaigns, other than by contributing money, *can't* be the problem, because that means participation in the political system, and that, by definition, is a good thing.

So what's the problem? I put my cards on the table. I think Mark Green is right: that we have already experienced, even back in 1969 when Ed Epstein disagreed, a major imbalance of power, an unequal marketplace in which business enjoyed excessive political influence. *Each* of these discrete phenomena we have discussed makes its own distinct contribution to a further tipping of the balance of political influence. As Ed points out in his paper, the negative energy directed against corporate PACs, in a sense, has become a shorthand for public reaction against the broad range of business political action. He writes, "PAC financial activity is an extremely useful gauge of the index of the nature and extent of business electoral activity."

Some have argued this morning, that the diversity of players, some pragmatic, some ideological—from auto dealers to Mobile Oil—give evidence of a healthy pluralism. "Where does business get its one leg up?" Ken Feinberg asks. I think Ed Lindblom is right. The apparent business pluralism coalesces at key points around a fundamental narrow orthodoxy that views business and the market status quo as essentially benign and views government interference in existing market structures and arrangements for the purpose of achieving social goals as illegitimate. The result is not an open marketplace of ideas but an undernourished marketplace of ideas.

Ernest Gellhorn is also probably right, moving on to another point, in his assertion that the funeral directors association exerts more influence over the congressional veto than, say, Mobil would if it ran a chain of funeral parlours. I suspect that's true. On the other hand, Mobil has had more impact on congressional attitudes toward the generic legitimacy of regulation.

Theoretically the noncorporate PACs, the association of national auto dealers or the beer distributors, could utilize sophisticated propaganda in defense of an unfettered marketplace. But the large corporations tend to pursue a broader view of national policy.

Let us look finally at some of Ed's broad points and observations in light of the recent election. Perhaps we might be tempted to view benignly the election results, which brought defeat to many business PAC-supported candidates. The Chamber of Commerce did not do well in electing the challengers it backed. In the close races, the Chamber took a bath. So we might say: "Not to worry." I think it is clear that business is not a gross political monolith that controls our political system. It would be foolish to argue that. But I think it's also supportable, even looking at the last election, that business money and electoral activity, especially the PACs, helped to blunt and diffuse what would otherwise have evolved into a stronger popular repudiation of Reagan's market-dominated policies. I think it played a major role. The PACs may not have elected many challengers whom they funded and made viable in many races, but they succeeded in moving the incumbent to the right to meet the challenge of a strong ideologically market-oriented challenger.

On the other hand, there were relatively few challengers of those incumbents who were supported by business PACs who were able to reach a sufficient level of viability to challenge business-oriented incumbents effectively.

If you look at some of the individual races you could have some fun. Here's where the science of interpreting the significance of PACs becomes no science at all. But it does seem to me, for example, that it took great sums of money to make Orin Hatch lovable in Utah. By the same token, John Danforth was in a terribly tight race in Missouri; his own campaign people acknowledged that the money available to buy daily tracking polls, a very expensive technique that was not available for his opponent, probably helped him to shape the last part of his campaign and to tip the balance sufficiently in his favor.

Perhaps most important is the market phenomenon, the supply and demand that Ed talks about. In their voracious hunger for contributions to support the new structures of campaign consultants, the direct mail, TV and radio, phone banks, most candidates rationalize their soliciting of business money with a vision of the public good as business tends to view it.

LESTER SALAMON

THERE is an interesting irony that no one has yet noticed in the juxtaposition between yesterday's discussion at this conference and today's. Yesterday, you will recall, the big concern was with the apparent or feared decline in corporate involvement in the community. Today's discussion, it seems to me, has almost the opposite focus, a concern about whether corporate involvement in the community has grown too large. It seems to me that at some point in the course of this conference attention needs to be given to this underlying conflict: clearly the *absence* of active corporate involvement in community affairs, and its presence, cannot be equally bewailed.

Ed Epstein's paper tells us in far greater detail than perhaps many of us wanted to know what corporations are doing with all of that money that Professor Scherer told us last night they were not putting into research and development: they are using it to finance elections and political consultants. I found Ed's paper to be extremely helpful, rich, lucid, and generous in its detail.

I want to focus in my remarks, not on the paper per se but on a number of broader points that I think flow from it but that are not addressed by it. Before turning to these, however, there are a couple of points of methodology or data that are worth mentioning because I think they could improve the presentation.

In the first place, I found it troubling that all the numbers in the paper were in current dollars as opposed to making any adjustment for the reality that the value of this yardstick used to measure the involvement of the corporate PACs in political affairs has been declining radically and rapidly in value during the period that these numbers cover. Therefore, I wanted to know what was happening in real dollar terms and not simply what was happening in nominal dollar terms.

Second, I was a little troubled by the absence of any effort to standardize some of these corporate contributions in terms of something real about the corporation. I was groping for something like an effort index that would express how much the corporation was spending on PACs as a percentage of its total profits or how much it was averaging per employee. Computing such an index would make it far easier to get some coherent sense of the variation in the strategies of firms in investing in political activity of this particular sort. As it is, we are left only with the aggregate amounts of corporate contributions per industry and required to speculate about its determinants.

Third, I was a little troubled by the argument that the industries that have the highest involvement with the government are the ones that are most deeply involved in PAC activity. As my eye went down the list of industries, I picked up several that I expected to be high that were quite low. Steel and tobacco, which seemed to me to be extensively involved with government in a variety of ways appeared, contrary to Epstein's thesis, to have rather low levels of PAC activity.

Beyond those essentially methodological or data presentation issues, however, there are three broader issues that I thought I would put on the table very briefly.

The first has to do with the question of what we really make of all of this growth of PACs. Ed has masterfully laid out the undeniable fact that PACs have grown. In addition, he pointed out in his comment here today that if we had looked at this phenomenon ten years ago it would have been a nonissue. The unfortunate implication is that corporate involvement in political campaigns is in some sense a new phenomenon that is reflected in the growth of the PACs but that did not exist on a major scale before this.

In fact, of course, nothing of the sort is true. What is true, however, is that we lack the data to assess the earlier levels of corporate political contributions. Our interpretations are thus in danger of becoming the captives of the artifact of the reporting devices that were institutionalized with the passage of the 1974 campaign finance act, because that act not only authorized PACs, it also revolutionized the whole system for reporting campaign finance.

Had we looked ten years ago at corporate involvement in campaign finance, we would have been hard put to come up with solid numbers to reflect the amount of corporate political activity. John Siegfried and I recognized this when we set out to test the relationship between corporate economic and political power.* Unable to measure corporate political activity directly, we had to assess it in terms of its effects. Clearly, it may have been the case that corporate support for campaigns was as large in the past as it is now, at least as a percentage of total campaign dollars. If this were true, the real significance of PACs would be to increase corporate involvement in campaigns but to bring out into the open something that has long existed while providing a new vehicle for other groups—for example, environmentalists, social action groups—that have never had an effective vehicle for campaign finance. This is quite a different interpretation from the one Epstein's paper seems to convey.

*Lester M. Salamon and John J. Siegfried, "Economic Power and Political Influence: The Impact of Industry Structure on Public Policy," *American Political Science Review* (September 1977), 71(3):1026–1043.

One piece of evidence in Ed's paper that seems to support this alternative interpretation is the curious structure of the PAC network as far as corporations are concerned. In particular, the same kinds of corporations that in the past have developed their own separate public affairs offices as institutionalized parts of the organization also turn out to be the ones that have organized PACs, which suggests that PACs are not a new phenomenon but a new manifestation of an old phenomenon— mainly, the tendency of larger corporations to develop separate institutional structures to handle political action. That's point number one.

Point number two is in a sense a corollary to Professor Lindblom's point. Lindblom noted that there are several different kinds of policy issues. I would add to that the corollary that there are several different arenas in which policy issues are handled, and different types of political resources are differentially effective in various of those arenas. In particular, the arenas in which the unique corporate political resources are likely to be the *least* effective are in the campaign and legislative areas. This is so because these are the arenas that are most susceptible to broad public involvement. But they are not the arenas where most of the policy decision making takes place in this country. To an important degree, most policy making takes place in the administrative arena, where broad policy objectives laid out in legislation are ironed out into particular regulation. As one former FTC chairman put it, the legislature is involved in the "handicraft production of law," whereas the administrative agencies of the government are involved in the "mass production of law." I would argue that it is precisely in that administrative arena that the peculiar resources of the corporation are particularly effective. This is so because this arena is characterized by much more limited public scrutiny, by a high need for technical expertise, and by the capacity to follow issues over time and stay in regular touch with the relevant personnel. All of these are capacities that large-scale institutions like corporations are better equipped with than are ephemeral citizens' groups or electoral coalitions.

Against this backdrop, it is curious that the two cases chosen to test the effectiveness of corporate political involvement for this conference both involved arenas where I would expect corporations to be least effective. But there are other arenas in which I would suspect they would be more effective. Until we do some empirical work in those other arenas to test those notions, I would be a little skeptical about some of the conclusions we have heard today.

The third point I wanted to raise is in a sense a response to Mike Pertchuk's question about what is really so important about the growth of PACs. My point here would be to suggest that the real significance of PACs may not be what they do to corporate political power but what they mean for the functioning of the American political system more generally. PACs, in this view, represent the latest chapter in a very long history of political reform in this country stretching back at least to the Progressive era. The aim of that reform from the beginning has been to depoliticize government, to get politics out of government. Curious though that sounds to us today, it underlies much of the past century of political reform, from the introduction of the civil service systems to the spread of the primary system as a way to nominate candidates for political office. The overall effect of these reforms has been to reduce substantially the role and capacities of political parties and thereby open a vacuum into which first business and then increasingly single interest groups have moved.

In the process, what we have done is fragment the political system and make it far more difficult to get any kind of action out of it. PACs have simply continued this tendency, channeling money directly from contributors to candidates without the intervening, integrating mechanism of the party. The key issue about PACs, therefore, is not that they strengthen corporations but that they weaken parties. This point must be borne in mind as we consider proposals to reform the PAC system. The question in my mind is not the amount of money that can be spent in elections, or even the sources of that money. The issue is the vehicle through which the money reaches the candidate. In my mind the goal of any reform ought to be to structure the flow of funds so that it goes through institutions that are aggregators of interest, that are builders of consensus, as opposed to institutions that are producers of fragmentation. I would therefore be skeptical even of a public financing system for elections that channeled the money directly to candidates as opposed to a system that channeled funds through some intermediate institution like a political party.

The issue in my mind, in short, is not PACs. It is not the relative power of corporations versus other separate special interest groups. It is ultimately the strength of the integrating institutions in the society, like political parties, versus all of these assorted special interest institutions. To the extent that a reform of the PAC system further weakens political parties, I guess I would prefer to stay with the PAC system as it exists.

DIALOGUE

MR. EPSTEIN: First, let me respond to the methological question raised by Professor Salamon. His comment about taking into account inflated dollars is a point well taken.

Let me address several substantive points raised by Professor Salamon. The question of corporate involvement in electoral politics is not new. But I would argue that both the degree of involvement and also the institutionalization of this involvement makes it a far different issue today. Previously, it was largely individual contributions by corporate officials, directors, and executives. Recently, however, we have seen both an institutionalization and professionalization of the corporate political process in a way that had not existed before, in which the PAC aspect is a fragment of an overall mosaic.

One last point. I spent part of my paper talking about parties and essentially the erosion of parties from their critical historical role as integrative mechanisms and builders of consensus, and I think PACs—and in some senses here I am talking about the single issue and ideological PACs—are particularly to blame for contributing to the decline of party structure.

I would agree wholeheartedly that enhancing the role of the parties is absolutely critical as far as campaign reform is concerned. I see that reform as part of an overall legislation package that would include public financing.

MS. KARPATKIN: There seems to me to be a small problem in defining what we're talking about, and that is the policy question. What does disproportionate power of business mean? I think that I would have a different view of that question than others here, and unless we can define it in some way we will have difficulty in reaching conclusions as to what the data mean.

MS. TEPPER-MARLIN: I'd just like to call your attention to another arena extremely similar to the PAC phenomenon in which very much the same pattern is evident and the effect of it is much easier to determine than it is in electoral politics, and that's statewide ballot issues on which there's a plenary vote in states that allow it. The Council on Economic Priorities has been looking at that over the last few years and found that in three-quarters of the cases where business perceives its interest in the state and spends significant amounts of money business wins. And that the amount of money spent, while it's not given as much attention because it's not a federal campaign, is fully a third as much this year as the PAC contributions that we are talking about.

MR. COLLINS: Professor Epstein mentions that unions and corporations have been treated equally legislatively for about forty years. But I think the dollars are perhaps less important than the political activities for the unions, certainly the AFL-CIO. Ten years ago unions exercised significant political influence through indirect expenditures, through political education funds, not matched in any way by corporations, and this is a factor that ought to be taken into account in considering how corporate PACs came into being.

MR. GIRAUD: We have to be very careful about the type of reform of PACs that we propose. The question in my mind is not the amount of money that's spent in elections. It's not even who is spending the money. It is the vehicle through which the money reaches the candidate, and in my mind the key to reform is to structure the flow of funds so that it goes through institutions that are aggregators of interest, that are builders of the consensus as opposed to institutions that are producers of fragmentation.

MR. EPSTEIN: Let me try to draw together a few questions. Is bigness bad? I have never argued that. I think in a vast industrial society large units of all sorts are just what is inevitable and necessary.

What's disproportionality? The bottom line to me is the maintenance of a political order in which views can be expressed, in which a wide variety of participants have the ability to affect what takes place as far as public policy is concerned and as far as the selection of those who are going to be making public policy. Ultimately, that question of proportionality is a judgment or value judgment question.

MR. JONES: I think that Professor Gellhorn stated the issue correctly, that the problem before us is not, as Professor Lindblom suggests, the question of undue business influence on the political process. I think we could agree or disagree on that issue and, having assumed we agree on that issue, where we would go would be toward questions of how one regulates the flow of money in the political process and issues of campaign contributions and the like or more radical solutions, such as substituting government operations for business operations. But it seems to me that neither of those is on the agenda. To me the key question we are discussing today is whether things are made worse in terms of undue business influence on the political process by the substitution of large actors for small actors. I have reviewed many big-against-small regulatory and antitrust fights. Often the small companies have won (e.g., Robinson-Patman, resale price maintenance), and I think undeservedly so.

Mr. FEINBERG: After listening to the conversation today, I conclude that the subject this morning could easily be the political impact of any particular group. We talk about the modern corporation, but the points made today, based on my experience, would be the political impact of the Sierra Club, or NAACP, or the National Rifle Association. The two issues that I think determine success in Washington are the ability to get your idea accepted in the marketplace and the ability to build coalitions.

If you look at the last six or seven years, business has been, if anything, disproportionately disadvantaged in Washington in areas like the Superfund and clean air. The point that I would like to make is that there is no particular advantage that I have heard today that gives business one leg up in terms of the ultimate goal of achieving political success in Washington.

Mr. WHITE: I keep on asking myself a prediction question. I compare Professor Vogel's paper with my favorite paper by Professors Salamon and Siegfried, where they identify size and concentration as a basis for predicting which industry will get a desired tax break. I try to find the same in Professor Vogel's paper, and, all things being equal I cannot find the predictive factor.

Mr. VOGEL: I would say that one cannot predict, and that is exactly the point. If there were a clear relationship between concentration and market structure and political impact, either positive or negative, one could then make predictions.

The reason why you can't predict is that there is no one single set of factors that is always critical in determining political outcomes. Indeed, it is essential to my argument that you can't predict who would win.

Mr. ONG: I think the central point I got from the paper, which I think is an excellent one, is the very valid point that in the political market-place there is just that, a market, a market for ideas, and that it is impossible to predict who will prevail. As Professor Jones has indicated, size clearly is not a detriment and has not been historically. Certainly more historical studies would be useful. I think that listening to the comments, particularly those by Professor Lindblom, I was reminded of the fact that "boogy men" are always more formidable when viewed from a distance. Since I live right in the midst of the boogy man he was postulating to us, I can tell you they sometimes seem pretty flimsy. The business community has not been an especially successful participant in the political marketplace in recent years. In the mid-1970s they were very disadvantaged and probably did not have their fair share of ability to persuade in the legislative and regulatory process.

MR. HANSON: I drew two conclusions from David's data that I don't think have come out as effectively as they might. One is that we're confusing the issue of size. It's not so much the size of the industry or the size of the company; what is really becoming much more important is the size of the interest that is represented, and the distinctions that are being made in terms of what are the economic interests of various segments and subsegments of industries. The second conclusion I draw is the importance of organization and sophistication.

If, indeed, organization and sophistication are important, maybe there's a learning curve going on in terms of large corporations learning to deal in the political arena. You can argue, for example, that size of an individual company may become more important in the future once they get to organizing their own political structure more effectively and getting it to work in concert, and I suggest that perhaps the explanation of some of auto industry history in terms of the Clean Air Act is a growing sophistication over time—leading to the victory in 1977.

MR. MARKOWITZ: I agree with Professor Vogel that you cannot predict how an issue will come out no matter how many issues you look at and factor into your education. One of the beauties of our system is that it cannot be predicted ahead of time. I don't think any of us would like it any other way. The easiest way to criticize your paper would be to leave out some of the factors you left out, such as who was the committee chairman at the time? Or, what was the geographical makeup of the relevant congressional committee. More importantly, what was the makeup of the Congress at the time? Was the Congress a more probusiness Congress or a less probusiness Congress? What were the political activities and political contributions of the various interests working on the issue, which you did not discuss. But it's easy to come up with those kinds of criticisms.

The single most important fact is the grass-roots power of big corporations. As you have mergers with other kinds of companies and extend your geographical spread, I do think that has a positive impact on your influence.

I think another issue is the fact that bigger companies probably have greater access to the administration as opposed to the Congress. I think it's easier for a big company official than for a small company official to get in to see a presidential cabinet official.

We talked about the disadvantages of size. I think it's very easy for a member of Congress to look at a big corporation when it comes in with a problem and say whatever we do, you guys will survive it. Whereas with a small company, the case is presented as if its livelihood and existence depend on it and this somehow tilts the balance.

MR. GREEN: There are two separate points that are sometimes confused; one is big versus small and the second is that business is not all that influential anyway.

On the first point let me be diplomatic, not on the second. I don't know that there is such a great gap between the Salamon and Lindblom critique and the Vogel approach, which seem to be at odds. I would argue that on low visibility issues in Congress where there are not influential actors on both sides—like the example of getting tax preferences or Professor Lindblom's example of agenda setting—"big" can be terribly influential, disproportionately influential. The way you get tax preferences is not loudly but quietly. There, if the CEO of a big company is on the phone and a single bottler is on the phone in the other office, you take the call of the CEO. On an issue of high visibility with credible actors on both sides, people are intense on both sides. Big is not dispositive. Here technology helps Dave Vogel's argument, in an era of word processors and teleconferences and PACs. Small has not suffered the diseconomies of scale that they may have suffered previously, that is, the transaction costs of congregating a thousand bottlers or a thousand funeral home directors is less than in the past.

Is business per se disproportionately powerful? To those who are trying to argue it is not, the only thing I can ask is, Are you serious? In 1978

Walter Guzzardi, Jr. of *Fortune* wrote an article following the defeat of a consumer protection bill, which failed by eight to one in each house. He wrote an article saying "business has it all."*

And the analysis should be intuitively obvious, even to those who have never run for office or run a business lobby—business has money. One, they can afford to do the kind of information development that other lobbyists cannot. The Business Roundtable, when it's interested in the regulatory issues, funds Arthur Andersen to be an able aide. Congress does not hire. Two, business can afford to hire fleets of lobbyists. They may have a good or a bad case, but nonetheless, they can carry it to Congress. There are 535 actors in Congress. There the transaction costs of delivering your messages to them are very substantial. The more carriers you have the better.

*Walter Guzzardi, Jr., "Business Is Learning How to Win In Washington," *Fortune*, March 27, 1978, pp. 53–58.

Biographical Sketches of Researchers and Commentators

Orley Ashenfelter. Professor of economics at Princeton University and director of the Industrial Relations Section as a specialist in labor economics. Graduate of Claremont Men's College, California, 1964; Ph.D. Princeton, 1970.

Dr. Ashenfelter joined the university's faculty as a lecturer in 1968, becoming a full professor in 1973. He has headed the Industrial Relations Section since 1971.

In 1973, Dr. Ashenfelter coedited with Dr. Rees the volume *Discrimination in Labor Markets,* published by Princeton University Press. He has also contributed widely to such professional journals as the *International Economic Review,* the *Journal of Political Economy,* the *Reviews of Economic Studies,* and the *Industrial and Labor Relations Review.*

He is a member of the Board of Editors of the *Journal of Urban Economics,* the *Journal of Labor Research,* and the *Pakistan Development Review,* and is on the Advisory Board of the Institute of Labor and Management Relations at Rutgers University. Dr. Ashenfelter is a Fellow of the Econometric Society and belongs to the American Economics Association, the American Statistical Association, and the Industrial Relations Research Association.

He has also served as director of the Office of Evaluation, U.S. Department of Labor. With a Guggenheim Fellowship he received in 1976, he spent the academic year 1976–77 visiting the Center for Labor Economics at the London School of Economics. In 1981, Dr. Ashenfelter was the Meeker Visiting Professor at the University of Bristol, England.

Ivar Berg. Professor of sociology and Justin Potter Professor, Owen Graduate School of Management, Vanderbilt University. A.B., Colgate University, 1952, University of Oslo, 1954–55; Ph.D. in Sociology, 1959, Harvard University. Named H. Lyman Hooker Distinguished Visiting Professor, McMaster University, Hamilton, Ontario, 1982–83.

Dr. Berg has done service and consulting for American Telephone and Telegraph Co., International Business Machines Co., Department of Labor, National Institute of Mental Health, Postmaster Selection Panel, U.S. Postal Service.

His *Education and Jobs: The Great Training Robbery,* was named "one of Ten Most Important Books in the field of Industrial Relations" by the Princeton University Industrial Relations Section in 1971. Other publications include *Guidance, U.S.A., Managers and Work Reform: A Limited Engagement* and *Industrial Sociology.*

Professor Berg is currently working on "Structural Unemployment: An Empirical Search on Specification" and "Economic and Sociological Perspectives on the Economy: A Chapter in the Study of Social Control."

Betty Bock. Consultant, Antitrust Research, the Conference Board; professor of law, New York University School of Law; Director, the Bureau of National Affairs, Inc.; and Adjunct Member, American Bar Association, Section of Antitrust Law, Committee on Economics and Antitrust. B.A., 1936, M.A., 1937, and Ph.D., 1942, all from Bryn Mawr College.

She was formerly director of Antitrust Research, The Conference Board; Member, Academic Advisory Committee, Secretary of Commerce, Domestic Policy Review; Senior Economist, Federal Trade Commission; and liaison between the Federal Trade Commission and Attorney General's National Committee to Study the Antitrust laws. She is also a frequent speaker and witness on antitrust issues.

Her most recent publications include "Remarks on Antitrust and the Conglomerate Firm," in *The Conglomerate Corporation: An Antitrust Law and Economic Symposium;* "An Antitrust Blueprint for the 1980s" in the *New York University Law Review;* "Antitrust in the Competitive World of the 1980s: Exploring Options," and "Strategic Planning and the Future of Antitrust," both in the Conference Board's *Information Bulletin*.

Robert S. Colodzin. Vice-President, External Affairs, Champion International Corporation. B.A., Queens College; M.A., New School of Social Research, Certificate from the Sorbonne, Paris.

Mr. Colodzin served as a deputy commissioner in the New York State government immediately prior to joining Champion. He was a member of the original staff that organized Common Cause, the citizen's lobby, and served as assistant to its chairman, John Gardner. An anti-Vietnam War activist, he organized a major industrywide and antiwar communication effort.

He was a writer-producer for five years at the Fletcher D. Richards Agency and spent seven years as a television production supervisor at Benton & Bowles Inc. He also headed his own television production company and has served as a marketing/communications consultant. He has been active as a specialist in communications, serving as a consultant in campaigns at the House, Senate, gubernatorial, and presidential levels.

Lucia F. Dunn. Associate Professor, Department of Economics, University of Florida. B.A. Economics, 1966, M.A., 1967, Ph.D., 1974, all from the University of California, Berkeley. She has held assistant professorships in the Departments of Economics of Northwestern University and Purdue University and has been a lecturer at the University of California at Berkeley. Professor Dunn is a specialist in the fields of human resources and applied microeconomics, and teaches labor economics and macroeconomics.

Her research articles include, "Measurement of Internal Income-Leisure Tradeoffs," *Quarterly Journal of Economics;* "These Proud Americans," *Saturday Evening Post;* "Measuring the Value of Community," *Journal of Urban Economics,* and "Quantifying Non-pecuniary Returns," *Journal of Human Resources.*

She is currently working on "Measuring the Total Cost of Defective Consumer Products: The Case of Automobiles," and "Working Hours Constraints and Labor Market Equilibrium: A Comparison of Workers in Three Industries."

Peter Eckstein. Director, Michigan AFL-CIO. B.S., University of Michigan and M.S., Harvard University. He has recently held the position of research director, Michigan Community Action program.

Mr. Eckstein has taught economics at the University of Michigan and Western Michigan University. His most recent publication, *Basic Economic Concepts,* was coauthored with Werner and Sichel. Mr. Eckstein has written many other articles.

Edwin M. Epstein. Professor and chairman, Program in Business and Social Policy, Berkeley Business School, University of California. A.B., University of Pennsylvania, 1961; M.A., University of California, Berkeley, 1966.

Following graduation from law school, he clerked and practiced in Philadelphia before joining the faculty of Berkeley in 1964. From 1973 to 1977, he was associate dean of the school. Currently, he is an adjunct professor of religion and society at the Graduate Theological Union, Berkeley, and is chairman of GTU's Center for Ethics and Social Policy.

Much of his published research has been in the areas of business, politics, and the interconnection of government and business in the United States. His books include: *The Corporation in American Politics* (1969), winner of an Academy of Management Book Award; *Black Americans and White Business* (1971); and his most recent book, *Rationality, Legitimacy, Responsibility: The Search for New Directions in Business and Society* (1978). He has been on the editorial boards of the *Academy of Management Review* and the *Journal of General Management,* and is co-chairman of the Political Law Committee of the State Bar of California.

Ernest Gellhorn. Dean of the Faculty of Law and Galen J. Roush Professor of Law at Case Western Reserve University. LL.B., 1962, B.A., 1956, University of Minnesota.

His previous posts include professor of law, University of Virginia, 1970–1975, 1979–1982; Dean of Arizona State University College of Law, 1975–1978; Professor of Law, University of Washington, 1978–79.

His most recent publications include "The Administrative Process; A Theory of Legislative Delegation," *Cornell Law Review* (1982); and "Regulatory Reform and the FTC's Antitrust Jurisdiction," *Tennessee Law Review* (1982).

Eli Ginzberg. Graduate School of Business faculty at Columbia University since 1935. Hepburn Professor Emeritus of Economics and special lecturer. Director of the Conservation of Human Resources and director of the Revson Fellows for the Future of the City of New York.

He is a long-term consultant to the federal government, including the chairmanship of the National Manpower Advisory Committee and National Commission for Employment Policy, and also does extensive consultation with foundations and corporations.

He was director of the New York State hospital study, *A Pattern for Hospital Care* (1949). He is the author of more than sixty books, primarily in the fields of human resources and health economics.

Harvey J. Goldschmid. Professor of Law at Columbia University. B.A., Columbia, 1962; J.D., 1965.

After a year as law clerk to Judge Paul R. Hays (Second Circuit Court of Appeals) and four years of private practice with Debevoise & Plimpton, he joined the Columbia faculty. He has been chairman of the Section on Antitrust and Economic Regulation of the American Association of Law Schools and of the Committee on Trade Regulation of the Association of the Bar of the City of New York as well as director of the Columbia University Center for Law and Economic Studies, 1975 to 1978, and consultant to the Federal Trade Commission, 1978 to 1982.

He now serves as Deputy Chief Reporter for the American Law Institute's Corporate Governance Project and as chair of the Executive Committee of the Association of the Bar of the City of New York.

His publications include *Cases and Materials on Trade Regulation* (with Handler, Blake, and Pitofsky, 2d ed., 1983); *Business Disclosure: Government's Need To Know* (1979); *Industrial Concentration: The New Learning* (with Mann and Weston, 1974); a report to the Administrative Conference of the United States on civil money penalties; and articles on antitrust, corporate law, and legal education.

Allen C. Holmes. Managing Partner, Jones, Day, Reavis & Pogue, Cleveland, Ohio. A.M., University of Cincinnati 1941; J.D., University of Michigan, 1944.

Mr. Holmes joined Jones, Day, Reavis & Pogue in 1944 and became managing partner in 1975. He is a member of the American Bar Association, the Ohio State Bar Association, and the American Law Institute. He previously held the posts: chairman of the Antitrust Section of the

American Bar Association and chairman of the Federal Trade Commission Committee of the Antitrust Section.

Mr. Holmes sits on the Board of Directors of the Diamond Shamrock Corporation, National City Bank and National City Corporation, and the Sherwin-Williams Company. He is the author of numerous articles on antitrust law.

James Hougland. Associate professor and director of Graduate Studies in Sociology at the University of Kentucky. Masters and Ph.D., Indiana University, 1976. His research interests include organizational sociology, industrial sociology, evaluation research, and sociology of religion.

He has contributed articles to a number of journals in sociology, including "Control in Organizations and the Commitment of Members," *Social Forces;* "Discrepencies in Perceived Organizational Controls: Their Incidence and Importance in Local Churches" *Sociological Quarterly;* "Participation in Local Churches: An Exploration of Its Impact on Satisfaction, Growth, and Social Action," *Scientific Studies of Religion;* and "Religion and Politics: The Relationship of Religious Participation to Political Efficacy and Involvement," *Sociology and Social Research.*

His most recent research involved outcomes assessment of employment training programs.

Charles Lindblom. Sterling Professor of Economics and Political Science, Yale University; William Clyde Devane Professor, Yale University. B.A. Economics and Political Science, Stanford University; Ph.D. Economics, University of Chicago, 1945; member of the Yale University faculty since 1946.

He has served as director of the Institution for Social and Policy Studies; economic adviser to the American ambassador to India and to the director of the U.S. AID Mission to India; director of Social Science, Yale University; chairman, Department of Political Science, Yale University; president, Association for Comparative Economic Studies; and president, American Political Science Association.

His most recent publications include *Politics and Markets: The World's Political-Economic Systems/The Policy-Making Process; Usable Knowledge: Social Science and Social Problem Solving,* "The Science of 'Muddling Through,'" and "Still Muddling, Not Yet Through," both for *Public Administration Review.*

Bevis Longstreth. Sworn in as the 60th Commissioner of the SEC on July 29, 1981. B.S.E., Princeton, 1956; LL.B, Harvard Law School, 1961.

From 1962 until July of 1981, Mr. Longstreth practiced law with the New York law firm of Debevoise & Plimpton. He was admitted to partnership in that firm in 1970 and specialized in corporate securities and real estate finance law, bankruptcy, and business work-outs and not-for-profit law.

Mr. Longstreth has also been a lecturer at Columbia Law School, teaching a seminar on the corporation in modern society. He has lectured on various securities and corporate law topics for the Practicing Law Institute and at other seminars and has written numerous articles on business-related subjects. Mr. Longstreth has served on the boards of a number of charitable and educational organizations active in the New York area.

Jesse W. Markham. Research Professor in the Law and Economics Center, Emory University. B.A., University of Richmond, 1941; M.A., Harvard University, 1946; Ph.D., Harvard University, 1949.

Professor Markham has also taught at Vanderbilt University, Princeton University, and Harvard University. During the 1950s he served as chief economist for the Federal Trade Commission and chaired the Department of Commerce Task Force on Marketing and Competition.

His books include *Competition in the Rayon Industry; Conglomerate Enterprise and Public Policy;* and *Baseball Economics and Public Policy.* He has a forthcoming book entitled *Oligopology in Law and Economics.* Professor Markham has testified frequently as an expert on federal antitrust and antimerger laws before the Senate Subcommittee on Antitrust Laws.

Katherine Maddox McElroy. Economist with TCS Management Group, Inc., in Nashville, Tennessee.

She is currently involved in several studies of the economic and financial impacts of proposed federal environmental regulations. She also performs financial analyses of telecommunications equipment acquisitions for many of TCS' corporate clients. Her past research, in addition to her work in corporate philanthropy, includes a study of the incidence of price changes in the U.S. economy and studies of antitrust issues.

Dr. McElroy has published articles in the *Review of Economics and*

Statistics, Challenge, Anti-Trust Bulletin, and *Economics of Firm Size, Market Structure and Social Performance.* She received a Ph.D. in Economics from Vanderbilt University in 1981 and a B.A. in Economics (Phi Beta Kappa) from Southwestern at Memphis in 1977.

Ira M. Millstein. Senior partner, Weil, Gotshal & Manges. B.S., Columbia University School of Engineering, LL.B. Columbia University School of Law. In 1951 he was called on special assignment as special assistant to the Attorney General. He has served as special counsel to the Office of Price Stabilization and Antitrust Division, Department of Justice.

Mr. Millstein was appointed by President Carter as member of the Council of the Administrative Conference of the United States and chairman, Committee on Ratemaking and Economic Regulations, ACUS. He was appointed by President Nixon as chairman, National Commission on Consumer Finance. He was also designated by the New York State Assembly as member, New York State Energy Planning Board, and appointed by the Mayor of the City of New York as chairman, New York City's Special Commission of Inquiry into Energy Failures. The French government awarded him the rank of Knight of the National Order of Merit (1980). Mr. Millstein has served as a member of the Board of Directors of Columbia Law School Alumni Association and cofounder and member, Board of Advisers, Columbia Center for Law and Economic Studies.

Mr. Millstein is active as a chairman or member of various sections of the ABA, and he has taught at New York University, Yale University, and Columbia University. He is currently a member of the faculty at the John F. Kennedy School of Government of Harvard University.

His most recent publications are *The Limits of Corporate Power* and a book review of Areeda and Turner's, "Antitrust Law—An Analysis of Antitrust Principles and Their Application," *Harvard Law Review.*

John D. Ong. Chairman, chief executive officer, and president of the B. F. Goodrich Company. Graduate of Ohio State University and Harvard Law School.

He joined B. F. Goodrich in 1961 as assistant counsel for the corporation. He became administrative assistant to the president of the company's International Division in 1966 and was named vice-president of that division in 1969. Mr. Ong became president of B. F. Goodrich in 1972, and executive vice-president and a member of the Board of Directors in 1973. He was chairman from 1974 to 1975.

He is director of Cooper Industries, Inc., the Kroger Company, Ohio Bell Telephone, and Pittsburgh National Corporation and Pittsburgh National Bank; a member of the Board of Directors of the Rubber Manufacturers Association, of the Chemical Manufacturers Association, and of the National Alliance of Business; and president of the Board of Trustees of Case Western Reserve University. He is also chairman of Akron Development Corporation and Akron Priority Corporation.

Mr. Ong is a member of the Conference Board, the Business Advisory Council of the Graduate School of Industrial Administration at Carnegie-Mellon University, the Antitrust Task Force, and the Government Regulation Task Force of the Business Roundtable.

Michael Pertschuk. Chairman, Federal Trade Commission, 1977–1981. B.A., Yale College, 1954; LL.B., Yale Law School, 1959.

From 1964 until his appointment to the Federal Trade Commission, Mr. Pertschuk was consumer counsel and later chief counsel and staff director of the Senate Committee on Commerce with responsibility for the development of a series of major consumer protection measures, including the Magnuson-Moss Warranty–Federal Trade Commission Improvement Act and the National Traffic and Motor Vehicle Safety Act.

From 1962 to 1964, Mr. Pertschuk was legislative assistant in the office of Senator Maurine B.. Neuberger of Oregon. Earlier he was an associate in the law firm of Hart, Rockwood, Davis, Biggs & Strayer in Portland, Oregon, and from 1959–1960 a law clerk for U.S. District Judge Gus Solomon in Portland.

Mr. Pertschuk served on the Council of the Administrative Conference of the United States, the National Commission on Product Safety, the National Commission for the Review of Antitrust Law and Procedures, and the Board of Directors of the Consumers Union.

Mr. Pertschuk has been an adjunct professor at the Georgetown University Law Center, professorial lecturer at American University's Washington School of Law, and lecturer at Brooking Institution's Public Law Seminars and at the Sloan School of Management, Massachusetts Institute of Technology. He is a member of the National Academy of Public Administration.

Robert Pitofsky. Dean and professor of law, Georgetown University Law Center; of counsel, Arnold & Porter, Washington, D.C. B.A., New York University; LL.B., Columbia Law School.

Professor Pitofsky was a commissioner with the Federal Trade Commission from 1978 to 1980; director, Bureau of Consumer Protection, Federal Trade Commission; Professor of law, New York University; and an attorney with the Department of Justice in Washington. His other recent professional activities include: chairman of the Board of Directors, Institute for Public Interest Representation, Georgetown University Law Center; member of the Board of Governors, Society of American Law Teachers; member of the Task Force on Regulatory Reform, Senate Government Operations Committee; and, currently, member of the Board of Advisors, Columbia Center for Law and Economic Studies.

His recent publications include (coauthor), *Cases and Material on Antitrust Law; The Sylvania Case: Antitrust Analysis of Non-Price Vertical Restrictions and Beyond; Nader: Consumer Protection and the Regulation of Advertising.*

Robert B. Reich. Professor, John F. Kennedy School of Government, Harvard University. B.A., Dartmouth College; M.A., Oxford University; J.D., Yale Law School.

From 1977 to 1981 he was director of Policy Planning for the Federal Trade Commission. He was previously assistant director for Evaluation, Bureau of Consumer Protection, FTC; assistant to the Solicitor General, U.S. Department of Justice; law clerk to Frank M. Coffin, Chief Judge, United States Court of Appeals for the First Circuit; and an associate at McKinsey and Company, New York. Professor Reich's other professional activities include Democratic National Committee, Advisory Committee on Economic Growth and Opportunity; contributing editor, *The New Republic;* and consultant to corporations and government agencies on matters of regulation, economic policy, and business strategy.

His recent publications include *Minding America's Business;* "Ideologies of Survival," "Industrial Evolution," and "High Tech Warfare," all for the *New Republic.* His forthcoming book is entitled *The New American Frontier.*

Lester M. Salamon. Director, Center for Public Management and Economic Development Research, the Urban Institute. B.A., Princeton University; Ph.D., Harvard University. His previous positions include deputy associate director for Organization Studies, Office of Management and Budget, Washington, D.C.; director, Program in Urban and Regional Development Policy and associate professor of Political Science and Policy Sciences, Duke University; and assistant professor of Political Science, Vanderbilt University.

His other professional experience includes senior consultant, Presidential Management Panel, National Academy of Public Administration; Ford Foundation Associate; director, Duke-OMBE Laird Project; associate, Brookings Institution; director, Banking Committee Study, Ralph Nader Congress Project. Mr. Salamon is a member of the editorial boards of *Administration and Society* and *Law and Contemporary Problems,* the American Political Science Association, and a member of the Policy Studies Organization.

His most recent publications are *The Federal Budget and the Nonprofit Sector* and *The Illusion of Presidential Government.*

F. M. Scherer. Professor of economics, Swarthmore College. He previously held research or teaching positions at Harvard University, Princeton University, the University of Michigan, the International Institute of Management in Berlin, and Northwestern University. Between 1974 and 1976, he was director of the Federal Trade Commission's Bureau of Economics.

He has written books on the economics of weapons research and development, the patent system, industrial organization economics, and the economics of large multiplant firms. His research emphasis in the past three years has been on the links between research and development spending and productivity growth. He has recently begun a research project on the effects of conglomerate mergers and spin-offs.

Roger W. Schmenner. Associate professor at the Fuqua School of Business, Duke University. He teaches production/operation management and is the director of the M.B.A. Program. Prior to joining the Duke faculty, Schmenner taught at Harvard Business School and at Yale University.

Mr. Schmenner's research interests are focused primarily on industrial location, multiplant manufacturing management, manufacturing strategy, and productivity. His work on the industrial location decision making of the *Fortune* 500 and on industrial location decisions around Cincinnati and New England was recently published as a book, *Making*

Business Location Decisions (1982). He is also the author of the text-book *Production/Operations Management: Concepts and Situations.* His articles have appeared in journals such as the *Quarterly Journal of Economics, Harvard Business Review, Journal of Operations Management, Journal of Regional Science, Review of Economics and Statistics, Journal of Transport Economics and Policy, Journal of Urban Economics, Policy Analysis,* and *Public Policy.* He has contributed to several other books as well.

Mr. Schmenner has served as a consultant and/or instructor to a number of companies and public agencies, including Digital Equipment Corporation; G. D. Searle, Inc.; General Electric Company; Rockwell International; Booz, Allen, and Hamilton; Firestone Tire and Rubber Company; Liggett and Myers Tobacco Co.; the states of Connecticut and Pennsylvania; the Urban Institute; and various federal agencies.

Janice Shack-Marquez. Masters and Ph.D, School of Public and Urban Policy, University of Pennsylvania. B.A., Johns Hopkins University.

From 1981 to 1983 she worked with Ivar Berg on a project funded by the National Institute for Mental Health: "Employers' Requirements, Employees' Experience, and Mental Health." In 1981 she was the winner of the National Paperwriting Competition on Youth Employability sponsored by the National Center for Research in Vocational Education. Her winning paper was entitled, "Information and the Employment Success of Young Men."

She is presently with the Office of Research and Evaluation of the Bureau of Labor Statistics of the Department of Labor. Her written works include *Matching Workers and Jobs: A Microeconometric Analysis of Unemployment and Turnover Among Adult Male Workers.*

Jon Shepard. Associate dean for Development, College of Business and Economics, University of Kentucky; professor, Department of Sociology, University of Kentucky. B.A., M.A., and Ph.D., Georgetown College, Kentucky.

His previous positions have been: chairman, Department of Business Administration, University of Kentucky; professor, Department of Business Administration, University of Kentucky; assistant director, Social Welfare Research Institute, University of Kentucky. His other professional activities include memberships in the American Academy of

Management, American Sociological Association; North Central Sociological Association; and Society for the Scientific Study of Social Problems.

Professor Shepard has also served as a consultant to the National Science Foundation, the Kentucky State Department of Energy, the Human Relations Resources Organization, Norris Industries, and Bendix Corporation. His most recent books include *Sociology, Sociologia,* and *Social Problems.*

John J. Siegfried. Professor, Department of Economics, Vanderbilt University; also lecturer in Law and adjunct professor of Management, Vanderbilt University. B.S., Rensselaer Polytechnic Institute; M.A., Pennsylvania State University; and M.S. and Ph.D., University of Wisconsin.

Professor Siegfried's professional activities have included: economist, U.S. Federal Trade Commission, Bureau of Economics; senior staff economist, President's Council of Economic Advisers; and, currently, senior research associate, Vanderbilt University. Aside from his extensive consulting services he serves on the American Economic Association Committee on Economic Education; Board of Editors, *Industrial Organization Review;* Board of Directors, Industrial Organization Society; and the Research Advisory Committee, American Enterprise Institute's Center for the Study of Government Regulation. He is also journal referee for several publications. His latest articles include "The Economic Cost of Suboptional Manufacturing Capacity in the U.S.," *Journal of Business;* "The Incidence of Price Changes in the U.S. Economy," with Katherine Maddox McElroy and George H. Sweeney; and "The Economics and Business Economics Major in the U.S.," forthcoming in the *Journal of Economic Education.*

Stephen Stamas. Vice-president of Exxon Corporation, currently in charge of its public affairs activities. He has previously held positions in the financial, supply, and corporate planning areas of Exxon. B.A., Harvard; B.Ph., Oxford University; Ph.D., Harvard.

Before joining Exxon in 1960, he worked for the U.S. Bureau of the Budget and as a loan officer for the Development Loan Fund. He has also served as Deptuy Assistant Secretary for Financial Policy in the U.S. Department of Commerce.

Mr. Stamas is a trustee and director of the Asia Society, International

House; the William H. Donner Foundation; the French-American Foundation; Salzburg Seminar in American Studies; Council on Foreign Relations; National Bureau of Economic Research; American Council for the Arts; Ballet Theatre Foundation, Inc.; the Atlantic Council of the U.S.; the American Ditchley Foundation; the Teagle Foundation; New York Public Library; and the American Council on Germany.

He is a member of the Board of Overseers at Harvard and chairman of the Overseers' Committee to Visit the Center for International Affairs.

David Vogel. Associate professor, University of California, Berkeley. B.A., Queens College, 1967; Ph.D., Princeton University, 1974.

He has recently been a participant in conferences on "The American Economic Constitution," Center for the Study of Democratic Institutions, University of California, Santa Barbara; "Democratic Capitalism," Public Affairs Conference Center, Kenyon College; "Western Capitalism and the Economic Dimensions of Freedom," the Ditchley Foundation, Great Britain; and the Second Donald C. McNaughton Symposium in New York City.

Professor Vogel's publications include *Corporations and Their Critics: Issues and Answers on the Problems of Corporate Social Responsibilities; Ethics in the Education of Business Managers; Lobbying the Corporation: Citizen Challenges to Business Authority; Ethics and Profits: The Crisis of Confidence in American Business;* and a forthcoming article in the *British Journal of Political Science,* "The Power of Business in America: A Re-Appraisal". Aside from his extensive academic activities, Professor Vogel is an editorial consultant for several publishing companies.

Lawrence A. Wien. Senior partner of the New York law firm of Wien, Lane & Malkin, founded by Mr. Wien in 1929. B.A., Columbia College, 1925; B.L., Columbia University Law School, 1927. Honorary doctorates in law from Brandeis and Long Island universities, 1962; honorary degree of Doctor of Humane Letters, Canisius College, Buffalo, New York, 1970; honorary Doctor of Laws, Columbia University, 1974.

In 1981 he was awarded Columbia University's Alexander Hamilton Medal, the highest honor given by the Columbia College Alumni Association to an alumnus.

Mr. Wien has served as a director of Consolidated Edison Company of New York, Inc., and Borden, Inc. In addition, until his retirement in 1971, he served as a director on the boards of Jonathan Logan, Inc., Morse Shoe, Inc., and the United Nations Development Corporation.

Arthur H. White. Principal and vice-chairman of the Board of Yankelovich, Skelly, and White, Inc. A.B. Harvard University, 1947; M.B.A., Harvard Graduate School of Business Administration, 1951.

Mr. White is a frequent speaker in the United States and abroad on public perceptions of social, economic, and political issues. Recently, he has spoken on such topics as the current climate for business, changing expectations of corporate philanthropy, and changing attitudes toward the role of government, business, and the individual in our society.

Mr. White is an outspoken advocate for public service activity. Currently, he serves as national treasurer of the Reading Is Fundamental program of the Smithsonian Institute; vice-chairman of the Board of Directors of the National Minority Supplier Development Council; chairman of the Board of the Stamford Foundation; Chairman of the Connecticut Housing Finance Authority; and chairman of the Connecticut Housing Coordinating Council. In recognition of his many years of outstanding service to state government, the National Governor's Association accorded Mr. White its award for distinguished service in 1979.

Individuals Attending the Conference

Professor Susan Rose-Ackerman
School of Law
Columbia University

The Honorable Arlin Adams
U.S. Court of Appeals
Third Circuit

Dr. Walter Adams
Department of Economics
Michigan State University

George E. Ashley, Esq.
Associate General Counsel
American Telephone & Telegraph Company

Curtis Handley Barnette, Esq.
Vice-President and General Counsel
Bethlehem Steel Corporation

Professor W. Bruce Bassett
School of Law
Columbia University

Mr. G. Wallace Bates
President
The Business Roundtable

L. Earle Birdzell, Jr., Esq.
Newport, Rhode Island

Professor Harlan Blake
School of Law
Columbia University

Stephen W. Cannon, Esq.
Chief Antitrust Counsel
Senate Judiciary Committee

Commissioner David A. Clanton
Federal Trade Commission

Professor John Coffee, Jr.
School of Law
Columbia University

Mr. Thomas C. Collins
Director, Corporate Relations and Contributions
The Procter & Gamble Company

George W. Cook, Esq.
Vice-President and General Counsel
Western Electric Company

Professor Donald J. Dewey
Department of Economics
Columbia University

Dr. Nancy DiTomaso
Assistant Professor
Graduate School of Public Administration
New York University

Professor Franklin Edwards
Director
Center for the Study of Futures Markets
Columbia University

Michael A. Epstein, Esq.
Weil, Gotshal & Manges

Commissioner John R. Evans
Securities and Exchange Commission

Kenneth R. Feinberg, Esq.
Kaye Scholer Fierman Hays & Handler

Carl Felsenfeld, Esq.
Vice-President
Citibank, N.A.

The Honorable Leonard I. Garth
U.S. Court of Appeals
Third Circuit

Mark Green, Esq.
The Democracy Project

Warren Grimes, Esq.
Chief Counsel
Subcommittee on the Judiciary

Professor Robert Hamilton
School of Law
University of Texas

Professor Milton Handler
Kaye Scholer Fierman Hays & Handler

James F. Hogg, Esq.
Vice-President and Associate General Counsel
Control Data Corporation

Dr. James Hougland
Department of Sociology
University of Kentucky

Ms. Alice Howard
Consultant
Agribusiness Associates, Inc.

Richard Kalaher, Esq.
Associate General Counsel
Amex Center

Rhoda Karpatkin, Esq.
Executive Director
Consumers Union

William F. Kennedy, Esq.
Public Issues Counsel
General Electric Company

Jeffrey L. Kessler, Esq.
Weil, Gotshal & Manges

Miles W. Kirkpatrick, Esq.
Morgan Lewis & Bockius

Professor Victor Kramer
Washington, D.C.

Thomas B. Leary, Esq.
Assistant General Counsel
General Motors Corporation

Richard S. Lombard, Esq.
Vice-President and General Counsel
Exxon Corporation

Professor Louis Lowenstein
School of Law
Columbia University

Irving P. Margulies, Esq.
Deputy General Counsel
U.S. Department of Commerce

Mr. Robert H. Marik
Merck and Company

Mr. Steven Markowitz
General Manager–Governmental Relations
The Continental Group

Dr. Alice Tepper-Marlin
Council on Economic Priorities

Professor Janice Shack-Marquez
Department of Sociology
University of Pennsylvania

Dean Robert H. Mundheim
School of Law
University of Pennsylvania

Professor Eli Noam
Columbia University

Frederick M. Rowe, Esq.
Kirkland & Ellis

Professor Louis B. Schwartz
University of Pennsylvania

Robert Shapiro, Esq.
Vice-President and General Counsel
G. D. Searle and Company

David Sive, Esq.
Winer Nueburger & Sive

Ms. Merrie Spaeth
Federal Trade Commission

John A. Stichnoth, Esq.
Vice-President and General Counsel
Union Carbide Corporation

Mr. Austin J. Sullivan
Vice-President, Public Affairs
General Mills, Inc.

Professor Lawrence A. Sullivan
School of Law
University of California

Ms. Katherine L. Troy
The Conference Board

Professor Elliot J. Weiss
Benjamin Cardozo School of Law
Yeshiva University

Mr. Lawrence White
Director, Economic Policy Office
Antitrust Division
U.S. Department of Justice

Mr. Oliver Williamson
Department of Economics
University of Pennsylvania

Dr. John Virts
Corporate Staff Economist
Eli Lilly and Company

Sponsors

Amex Center
BankAmerica Foundation
Caterpillar Tractor Company
Chevron Oceanic Inc.
Coca-Cola Company
Continental Bank
The Continental Group
Control Data Corporation
Deloitte, Haskins & Sells
Exxon Corporation
Ford Motor Company
Johnson & Higgins
Kellogg Company
Koppers Company
Eli Lilly & Company
Melville Corporation
Merck and Company
Morgan Stanley & Company
Occidental Petroleum
The Procter and Gamble Company
Raytheon Company
Shell Companies Foundation
Stauffer Chemical Company
Union Carbide Corporation
Union Pacific Corporation
Universal Leaf Tobacco Company, Inc.
Wheelabrator-Frye, Inc.

Index

533

Divestiture(s), 192, 199, 217
Domenici, Peter, 344, 346, 367, 369, 370
Domhoff, G. William, 166
Doriot, Georges F., 274, 278, 295
Dow Chemical, 298
Downs, Anthony, 325
Draftsman's union, 224
Du Pont, 89, 298, 322, 329, 335, 336
Durkheim, Emile, 89, 228-29

E. F. Hutton Group, 437
Earth Day (1970), 324, 325, 326, 394
Economic freedom, 161
Economic growth, 302
Economies of scale, 12, 13, 82; political, 497
Economy (the): effect on firms' actions in community, 221, 224, 227, 232, 235,. 250, 263; and enactment of clean air legislation, 312; equilibrated, 301
Edison Electric Institute, 318, 321, 329
Educational institutions: as benefit to corporations, 104-5; as recipients of corporate contributions, 123-24, 128, 129, 134, 139, 143, 147, 149
Election cycles, PAC activity in, 412-14, 418, 424, 442-45, 463, 470
Election outcomes, effect of PACs on, 470-74
Elections: general, 447-48; party group/PAC contributions in, 410; see also Congressional elections; Presidential elections
Electoral politics: business in, 405; nature and extent or organizational, 412-23
Electoral process, see Political process
Electric Utility Industry Clean Air Act Coordinating Committee, 356-57
El Salmi, Aly M., 62
Emission standards, 328, 329-30, 332, 336, 337-39, 369-70; delays in, 340-41, 342, 343, 345, 350-51
Employee attitudes, organization size and, 60-63
Employee characteristics, and personnel practices, 236-37
Employee well-being, firm size and, 5-58
Employment: effect of conglomeration on, 222; effect of headquarters location on, 204; firm size and, 256-59; and mental health, 241-48; and political power, 350, 362
Employment shifts, 258-59
Employment size classes, and technological innovation, 280-81, 299-300
Energy Supply and Environmental Coordination Act of 1974, 343
England, George W., 62
Englehard Minerals and Chemicals Corporation, 323, 335
Entrepreneurism, paper, 303, 304
Environment: public interest in preserving, 323-25
Environmental Action, 324-25, 360
Environmental movement: and clean air legislation, 313, 319, 321, 333, 337, 339, 344, 354, 358-61, 363, 364, 367, 368, 370, 371, 372, 375, 377, 387, 389
Environmental organizations, 324-25
Environmental Policy Center, 369
Environmental Protection Agency (EPA), 332, 334, 339, 340, 341, 349, 351-52, 355-56, 357, 358, 359, 365, 366, 369; limits on authority of, 353; New Source Performance Standards, 367-68, 369
Epstein, Edwin M., 310
Esch, Marvin, 341
Ethyl Corporation, 330, 334, 335, 336
Exporting firms, 427
Exxon, 140, 141, 143, 148, 154, 298, 458
Externalities, 105

Farbstein, Leonard, 327, 330
Federal Corrupt Practices Act, 407
Federal Election Campaign Act of 1971 (FECA), 405, 406, 409-10, 411, 419, 468, 478, 479; contribution limits, 409-10, 466; data, 412-14; disclosure requirements, 412, 467; 1967 amendments, 405, 420
Federal Election Commission (FEC), 414, 415, 419, 421, 423, 442, 467, 468, 478, 479; data from, 436; regulations, 420, 427
Federal elections, PAC contributions, 415-17, 422
Federal Trade Commission, 387, 388, 390, 395-96, 397, 402, 427, 463, 497; Line of Business (LB) survey (R&D), 292-91, 292, 293, 299

Great Society programs, 317
Grievance issues, 227-28, 229, 230, 234
Grievance process, 233
Griliches, Zvi, 271
Grumann Corporation, 436

Hall, Richard H., 69-70
Hamilton, Alexander, 390
Handler, Edward and John R. Mulkern, *Business in Politics*, 408, 449-50, 455, 461, 479, 482, 493n77
Hanna, Mark, 390
Harris Corporation, 436, 453-54, 458-59
Harris poll(s), 468, 486
Hart, Gary, 358
Harvard Business School, 231, 271
Hassler, William, 370, 389
Hatch, Orin, 499
Haworth, Charles T., 12
Hawthorne Studies, 60
Hayes, Robert H., 271-73, 274, 278, 279, 281, 301-2
Hays, Samuel, 361, 362
Headquarters cities: and corporate philanthropy/firm size relationship, 100, 104, 111, 119, 123, 124-28, 129, 133-34, 147; plant capacity change around, 202-10; and plant closings, 162
Health, effect of unemployment on, 243-46
Health and welfare organizations, as recipients of corporate contributions, 123-24, 128, 143, 147
Health care services, as benefit to corporations, 104, 190n7
Heard, Alexander, 471
Hill, Gladwin, 325, 326
Hiring policies, 236-37, 240
Hirschman, Albert O., 477
Hofstadter, Richard, *The Age of Reform*, 400-1
Holidays, paid, 14, 15T, 24
Houghland, James G., Jr., 167
Hours worked per week: desired and actual, 27-29, 35, 83, 85
Household appliance industry, 301
Hulett, Stan, 357
Humphrey-Hawkins Bill, 241
Hydrocarbon emissions, 332, 340

IBM, 282
Ideology, in corporate political activity, 403, 449-50, 455, 462-62, 470, 482, 498
Impact of the Corporation project, 5
Income for leisure, marginal rate of substitution for, 30-34, 35-36, 53-54
Incorporation, 400
Incumbency, and electoral result, 471-72
Incumbents: business-oriented, 499; PAC contributions to, 418-19, 423, 447-50, 454-62, 463, 470, 472-73
Independent Council of Shopping Centers (ICSC), 351
Independent Petroleum Association of America, 334
Indik, Bernard P., 63
Individual (the): corporate PACs and, 475-80; political participation of, 407-8, 411, 467, 480-87
Industrial corporations, 278-79; PACs, 424-27, 431-32, 433, 434, 436, 439, 453-54, 458-60; *see also* Corporate PACs
Industrial policy, 400
Industrial Research and Development competition to name significant technical advances, 282-83, 285, 299
Industrial structure, and political influence, 312, 313, 338, 353-54, 361, 375-76
Industries: fragmentation of, and political participation, 353-54, 374, 376; lack of coalitions in, and clean air legislation, 334-39; political strategy of, 335
Industry characteristics: and labor relations, 220, 221, 232-33; and personnel practices, 240; and political power, 309-10, 311-12, 313-14, 351, 353-54, 361, 371-79
Industry classification, and PACs, 424-39, 450-62
Industry image, 374-75, 392; and clean air legislation, 362-63
Informal networks, and community participation of managers, 166, 174
"In-kind" gifts and services, 412, 446
Innovation, 59, 269; *see also* Research and development (R&D)
Insurance: and firm size, 6; health, 14, 19T, 24; life, 14, 20T
Interest groups, 392, 411, 481; in cam-

Local governments, and clean air legislation, 313, 371
Locally owned firms, 220-22, 256; and community, 248-50; labor relations, 256; personnel practices, 236-41
Lowi, Theodore, 314, 480
LTV corporation, 451
Lunch break, paid, 14, 16T, 24, 56n17

McClure, James A., 343
McGovern, George, 472
Machinists union, 224
Mackraz, James, 222
"McNeil-Lehrer Report," 241
Madison, James, 390, 482
Malbin, Michael, J., 493n77
Management: inolvement in community affairs, 255, 256; of largest corporations, 279; legalistic view of, 288-29, 233; and loss of technological leadership, 270, 271-72, 295, 302; and PACs, 420, 466, 477, 478; participative, 231-32; political philosophy of, 438, 449, 461-62; public policy goals of, 482, 483, 484
Management level, and employee attitude/firm size relationship, 62
Managerial employees: and corporate PACs, 420, 476, 478-80; contribution rates, 408, 409, 446
Managerial mobility, 162; and community participation of managers, 163-90
Managers: in absentee-owned firms, 228, 229, 230-31, 233-34; attitudes of, and corporate involvement in community, 259, 262; characteristics of, 167-68, 170-71, 179-82, 183; community participation of, 162, 163-90; education of, 272, 274-78, 295, 302-4; technical background of, 272-74, 295, 302-4; see also Corporate executives
Mansfield, Edwin, 298-99
Manufacturing Chemists Association, 329, 332
Manufacturing jobs, 87
Mapco, Inc., 476
Marginal rate of substitution (MRS), 30-34, 35-36, 83; estimation of, 53-54
Market conditions: effect on corporate philanthropy, 112-13, 116, 141; and firms'

actions in community, 221, 235; industry-specific, 232
Market power, and R&D, 301
Markets, monopolization of, 161
Marx, Karl, 89
Maslow, Abraham, 62
Massachusetts Institute of Technology, Sloan School, 275-78
M.B.A. programs, and technological innovation, 274-78, 295
Megonnell, William, 359
Mellow, Wesley, 12-13
Membership organizations, PACs, 409, 423, 440, 442
Mental health, 223; effect of unemployment on, 241-48
Merger law, 294
Mergers, 59, 227, 272, 279; effects on corporate PACs, 404-5, 462-66, 497; effects on corporate philanthropy, 99, 100, 122, 123-24, 125-26, 129, 130-34, 139, 142, 150; limits on, proposed, 401-2, 404, 427; and political influence, 378-79, 397; political significance of, for clean air legislation, 314
Merrill Lynch and Co., 434
Mesa Petroleum Co., 419
Metropolitan [life insurance co.], 437
Michigan Community College Association, 246
Michigan Employment Security Commission (MESC), 240-41
Middle management, 88-89
Mill, John Stuart, 390
Mining industry, and clean air legislation, 317, 319, 322, 330, 364
Minneapolis-St. Paul, 201
Mitchell, James P., 86-87
Mobil, 143, 336, 458, 498
Mobile source pollution, 328, 332, 333, 335, 339, 340-54, 361
Mocatta Metals, 434
Money/elections relationship, 406, 471-74, 484-85, 499
Money in Congressional Elections (Jacobson), 471
Monopoly rents hypothesis, 80-82
Monopoly wage hypothesis, 36
Montgomery Ward, 351

Moody, Joe, 316, 317
Motor Vehicle Manufacturers Association, 349
Moynihan, Daniel Patrick, 150
Mulkern, John R. and Edward Handler, *Business in Politics*, 408, 449-50, 455, 461, 479, 482, 493n77
Mullan, Joseph, 335-36
Multinational corporations, 301-2
Muskegon County Department of Employment and Training, 236
Muskie, Edmund, 317, 318-19, 322, 324, 327, 330-31, 332, 333, 337, 340, 342, 343, 345, 348, 350, 359, 369

Nader, Ralph, 326, 327, 331
Nader task force report, 318
National Association of Business Political Action Committees, 473
National Association of Manufacturers (NAM), 335, 354, 357, 473
National Association of Realtors, 351, 469
National Audubon Society, 360
National Automobile Dealers Association (NADA), 346-47, 469
National Clean Air Coalition, 359, 360-61, 369
National Coal Association, 316, 319, 320, 321, 329, 356, 368-69
National Coal Policy Conference, 316, 318
National Conservative Political Action Committee (NCPAC), 423
National Industrial Pollution Control Council, 329, 335, 356
National Journal, 337, 339
National Labor Relations Board rulings, 228
National Lead Association, 332
National League of Cities, 351, 364
National Petroleum News, 336
National Petroleum Refiners Association, 334, 336
National Realty Committee, 351
National Science Foundation, 272, 283
National Steel Corporation, 332
Nation of Strangers, A (Packard), 165
Navarro, Peter, 389
Nelson, Ralph, 108-10, 116
Nelson, Richard R., 279
"New Federalism," 400

New Industrial State, The (Galbraith), 323
New Source Performance Standards (NSPS), 367-68, 369
New York City, 201; air pollution, 326-27; control of sulphur emissions in, 315-16, 317
Nitrogen oxide emissions, 332, 340, 341, 342
Nixon, Richard, 322, 327-28, 329, 331, 334, 359, 406, 484
Nonferrous smelter industry, 372, 373, 375, 376, 378; and clean air legislation, 313; exemption for, 340, 365-67
Nonindustrial firms: PACs, 428-33, 434, 435, 436, 439, 451-53, 455-58
Nonsignificant deterioration (PSD, NSD), 340, 355-60, 361, 363, 365, 365, 367, 370, 373, 377
Not-for-profit sector: corporate involvement in, 139, 140-41, 144-45, 146, 166-67; resources of, 106
Number of employees: as measure of employee well-being, 5-6

Obey, David R., 468, 487
Obey-Railsback bill, 411, 412
Office of Management and Budget, 356
Oil, Chemical, and Atomic Workers, 360, 361
Oil industry, and clean air legislation, 313, 314, 317, 318, 319, 321, 322, 325, 330, 334, 336, 354, 357, 361-62, 363, 364, 373, 375-76; PACs, 458, 459, 460, 461
Oligopoly, 301
Olson, Edward C., 471
Open-seat candidates, PAC contributions to, 418, 423, 447-50, 454-62, 463, 470
Operating Engineers union, 224
Organization size, 3; and community participation of managers, 163-90; and employee attitudes, 60-64; and job satisfaction, 86-89; and worker satisfaction, 59-78; *see also* Firm size; Plant size
Organization subunit size, and employee attitudes, 60-61, 63, 70; *see also* Department size; Work group size
Ottawa County Department of Employment and Training, 236, 241

Ottawa County Department of Human Services, 242-43, 246
Owens, John R., 471-72

Packard, Vance, *A Nation of Strangers,* 165
PACS, *see* Political action committees
Parent company, attitude toward management participation in community, 162; *see also* Absentee ownership
Paster, Howard, 345-46
Patents, large corporation share of, and R&D, 269, 284-86, 290-91, 292-93, 299, 300
Patternmakers union, 224
Pay, attitudes toward, 66-67, 68, 69
Penn Square bank scandal, 250
Penney, J. C., 351
Perrucci, Robert, 166
Personnel practices, locally owned vs. absentee-owned firms, 220, 221, 223, 236-41
Pertschuk, Michael, 402, 427
Philanthropic resources of community, and corporate giving, 128-29
Philanthropy, *see* Corporate philanthropy
Phillips curve, sociological version of, 241-42
Pilisuk, Marc, 166
PIMS (Profits Impact of Marketing Strategies) data, 271, 298
Pipefitters Local Union #562 v. United States, 409
Pitofsky, Robert, 308
Plant age, and plant closings, 210
Plant capacity changes, 191, 210; of conglomerates, 215-17; around headquarters locations, 202-10
Plant cities: allocation of contributions to, 111, 123, 124-25, 126, 133-34, 147; and corporate philanthropy/firm size relationship, 100
Plant closings, 162; absentee-owned firms, 224, 235, 249; character of, 210-15; impact on workers' health, 220; and plant design, 210; unions and, 226-27; *see also* Plant openings and closings
Plant design, 210
Plant employment change: geographic differences in, 199-202; incidence of, 192-99
Plant expansions, contractions: firm size and, 162, 197-98; headquarters location and, 204, 206, 207
Plant openings and closings, 162, 210-15; comparison of, 210-12; effect on community, 191-218; firm size and, 198-99
Plant size, 7, 82; and employee well-being, 10, 24; and job disutility, 32; and job satisfaction, 69; and working conditions, 25-29; *see also* Firm size; Organization size
Plastics industry, 7, 13, 32, 81-82
Pluralism, 411, 498
Polaroid Company, 301
Political action committees (PACs), 154, 308, 399-510; assessments of, 411-12; concerns about influence of, 404, 467-74; contribution rates, 398, 415-19, 421-22, 423, 440, 445-46, 451-53, 462, 500; facts and figures re, 412-23; federal legislation governing, 462; independent expenditures, 415, 419-20, 423, 442, 446, 462; "learning curve" phenomenon, 420; networking potential of, 473-74; nonconnected, 414, 415, 419, 423, 440; noncorporate, 498; nonparty, 413T, 416T, 419; number of, 414; overview of, 405-12; participation rates, 415, 440; and political democracy, 474-87; size of, 436-38; *see also* Corporate PACs
Political democracy: effect of economic interest groups on, 406; PACs and, 474-87
Political education efforts of corporations, 402-3, 412, 415, 474
Political environment: of clean air legislation, 312, 325-26, 338, 374-75; corporate, 438
Political institutions, U.S., 399
Political organization and sophistication, and political influence, 373-74, 387-88, 395-96
Political participation, corporate, 402-5, 449-50; growth and impact of, 423-39; through PACs, 407-12; individual, 407-8, 411, 467, 480-87
Political parties, 404, 409-10; briefing sessions, 474; and electoral success, 471-72;

Reagan, Ronald, 59, 150, 419, 499
Reddy, Richard D., 167
Regulation, see Government regulation
Reindustrialization, 400
Religious organizations, as recipient of corporate giving, 123-24, 134
Relocation(s) (plant), 192, 202, 203T, 258-59; conglomerates, 217; firm size and, 197-98; headquarters location and, 204-6, 207
Republican candidates, PAC contributions to, 418, 423, 447-50, 454-62, 473-74
Research and development (R&D), 270-71, 272; corporate size and, 269, 278-93, 298-302; data on, 298-99; government funding of, 302, 304
Resource allocation, 80
Restatement and Recommendations on Principles of Corporate Governance and Structure, 151
Rest breaks, paid, 14, 17T, 24
Retailers, 431; PACs, 434, 451, 453, 456
Retirement pension, 14, 21T, 24
Reuther, Carol Jean, 12
Reward system, 89
Rexnord: PAC, 482-83
Rockefeller Foundation, 154
Rogers, Paul, 351, 352-53, 354, 358-59, 362
Roosevelt, Franklin D., 390
Ruckelshaus, William, 356
Rump, E. E., 63

St. Joe Minerals, 458
Sales class size, and PAC formation, 432-35, 436, 439, 465-66; and R&D, 299-300
San Jose State College, 326
Satterfield, David, 330, 335
Savings and loans, PACs, 431, 433-34, 439
Schattschneider, E. E., 400
Schrank, Robert, 10,000 Working Days, 87
Schulze, Robert O., 164-65
Schumacher, E. F., 59
Schumpeter, Joseph A., 279
Schumpeterian hypothesis (R&D), 269, 279, 283, 288, 289, 290, 292, 293-94, 299, 300-1
Schwartz, Robert, 108-10

Science Policy Research Unit, Sussex University, 281
Scrubbers, scrubbing, 365, 368-69, 370, 375
Sears, Roebuck and Co., 351, 437, 453
Securities and Exchange Commission, 477
Service clubs, 166
Service sector, 258
Shareholders, 407, 466; contribution rates, 446; protecting rights of, in corporate contributions, 406, 407, 408, 409, 475, 476-78
Shatto, Gloria, 109
Sheetmetal Workers union, 224
Shell, 336, 458
Shift premiums, 12-13, 35
Shopping center developers: and clean air legislation, 313, 351-53, 354, 364, 371-72, 373-74, 375, 376
Sierra Club, 324, 356, 360, 369
Sills, David L., 182
Skill level: firm size/employee well-being study, 8; and hiring policies, 236-37; and job satisfaction, 66, 67; and wage rate, 10-12, 35
Small and Independent Business Protection Act of 1979 (Proposed), 99, 401-2, 404, 405, 427, 462, 466
Smith, Adam, 390
Smith, David Horton, 167
Smith, Patricia C., 64, 66
Social activism, 323
Social clubs, 166
Social fragmentation, promoted by PACs, 481, 403-4
Social networks, and absentee ownership, 239
Social responsibility: community service and, 166-67; and corporate philanthropy, 97, 107, 140-41, 142-47; see also Corporate responsibility
Socioeconomic variables, in employee well-being/firm size relationship, 25, 31, 33
Sorauf, Frank J., 410
Source Book of Statistics of Income: Corporation Income Tax Returns, 109, 111
Special interests, see Interest groups
Stagflation, 222, 224
Staggers, Harley, 322